STUDIES IN CONTEMPORARY JEWRY

The publication of
Studies in Contemporary Jewry
has been made possible through the generous assistance
of the Samuel and Althea Stroum Philanthropic Fund,
Seattle, Washington

THE AVRAHAM HARMAN INSTITUTE
OF CONTEMPORARY JEWRY
THE HEBREW UNIVERSITY
OF JERUSALEM

JEWS, CATHOLICS, AND THE BURDEN OF HISTORY

STUDIES IN CONTEMPORARY JEWRY

AN ANNUAL

XXI

2005

Edited by Eli Lederhendler

Published for the Institute by
OXFORD
UNIVERSITY PRESS

OXFORD
UNIVERSITY PRESS

Oxford University Press, Inc., publishes works that further
Oxford University's objective of excellence
in research, scholarship, and education.

Oxford   New York
Auckland   Cape Town   Dar es Salaam   Hong Kong   Karachi
Kuala Lumpur   Madrid   Melbourne   Mexico City   Nairobi
New Delhi   Shanghai   Taipei   Toronto

With offices in
Argentina   Austria   Brazil   Chile   Czech Republic   France   Greece
Guatemala   Hungary   Italy   Japan   Poland   Portugal   Singapore
South Korea   Switzerland   Thailand   Turkey   Ukraine   Vietnam

Published by Oxford University Press, Inc.
198 Madison Avenue, New York, New York 10016
www.oup.com

Oxford is a registered trademark of Oxford University Press

Library of Congress Cataloging-in-Publication Data

Jews, Catholics, and the burden of history / edited by Eli Lederhendler.
p. cm—(Studies in contemporary Jewry, ISSN 0740-8625 ; 21)
Includes bibliographical references.
ISBN-13 978-0-19-530491-6
ISBN 0-19-530491-8
1. Judaism—Relations—Catholic Church.   2. Catholic Church—Relations—
Judaism.   3. Holocaust, Jewish (1939–1945)—Influence.   4. Christianity and antisemitism
I. Lederhendler, Eli.   II. Series.
DS125.S75 no. 21
[BM535]
261.2'6'09045—dc22   2005050872

2   4   6   8   9   7   5   3   1

Printed in the United States of America
on acid-free paper

STUDIES IN CONTEMPORARY JEWRY

Preface: Memory and Judgment

If there is a common leitmotif uniting most of the essays in this volume of *Studies in Contemporary Jewry*, it is the intertwining of memory and judgment. By memory, I mean the cultural construction of the past; by judgment, I have in mind not only a sense of guiding moral intelligence and the indictment of wrongdoing, but also the idea of balanced and knowledgeable discernment (as in the exercise of "sound judgment"). Certainly the essays in our symposium sections are related directly to both these themes, as I will briefly outline below.

The year 2005 has marked significant anniversaries in contemporary Jewish history: the 60th anniversary of the end of the Second World War and the 40th anniversary of the historic Vatican policy statement on Jews and Judaism, *Nostra Aetate*. (Unanticipated, of course, when the editors first discussed the contents of this volume several years ago was the death this past year of Pope John Paul II, which added to the general sense that 2005 marked an important turning point of our era, with potentially important implications for the Jews.)

These are distinct historical milestones and our intention is not to conflate them, but to relate them. Both 1945 and 1965 were significant watersheds dividing the "before" and "after" in the complex and fraught relations between the Jewish people and the Gentile world (in Europe in particular); and it is undeniably true that the one event (the end of the war against Hitler) bore major causal implications that led, whether directly or indirectly, to the second (the Jewish aspects of the Second Vatican Council). As readers will note, the shadow of the Holocaust, and the moral judgments made on that score, still largely define the background and tenor of interfaith relations, certainly with respect to developments in the Catholic Church, and the two themes of Catholic-Jewish dialogue and Holocaust memory are inextricably intertwined.

The notion of retrospectively tying the Catholic Church's historical positions on the Jews and Judaism to the development of modern antisemitism, and thus ultimately to the Holocaust, is notoriously contested in contemporary historical and philosophical debates. We add fresh material to these debates here, particularly in the essays by Michael Marrus, André Kaspi, and Manuela Consonni, all of which deal with the Vatican in the initial postwar years. These are not the only grounds on which the two subjects intersect, however. Rather, it is *since* 1945 that the task of attaining a new perspective—a judgment, if you will—on Christian-Jewish relations has received new urgency. In the aftermath of the Holocaust, and over the course of the ensuing 60 years, Jews, living in an overwhelmingly Gentile world, have not been called upon to confront and overcome Nazi racialism. Instead, they have been in the situation of finding a way *past* the Holocaust, back into a common world of discourse and humanity with other cultures and peoples—the "rest" of the world—which in any objective, historical view cannot be confused with the Nazis, their immediate precursors, and their direct collaborators.

Such a return to a viable existence within the world is a prerequisite, it would seem, to any meaningful cultural renewal. In a sense, this is an ongoing historical conversation, now two millennia old, that the Holocaust abruptly interrupted, and nearly extinguished. It has had to be deliberately renewed, taken up as a moral imperative despite (and in the light of) that catastrophic interruption. Yet that is no simple matter, given that the "rest" of the world has yet to find its way to an entirely nonjudgmental relationship with *Jewish* culture, symbols, and interests (see in particular the essays here by Joanna Michlic and Antony Polonsky, Geneviève Zubrzycki, and Joshua Zeitz). To one extent, this is a two-sided conversation involving both Christians and Jews, while to another it is an internal conversation that Christians (and Jews) have among themselves, pursued on their own ground. Thus, as we learn from the essays on the Catholic Church in Poland and Italy, for instance, Jews and Judaism are often a foil, a "catalyst" for the Church in its struggle to define the terms of its own spiritual and social renewal. (In a separate, "mini"-symposium, we take up some questions related to internal *Jewish* memory and judgment vis-à-vis Germany, Europe, the Holocaust, and spiritual renewal.)

The main symposium section also includes several essays on non-European and non-ecclesiastical aspects of Jewish-Catholic interrelations, specifically in the United States, a country where Jews and Catholics are both minorities; where the shadow cast by the Holocaust is less distinct and certainly less immediate; and where the relations between coexisting religious and ethnic groups have been determined by local, American social realities more than by the "burden of history" (see the essays by Kenneth Wald and Bruce Phillips). Though our authors indicate that there are enduring social, political, and cultural differences between American Jews and American Catholics, they also point to intriguing examples of contact and convergence, both in the past and in the present.

Elsewhere in this volume, readers will find a provocative essay by Jeffrey Mehlman that deals with Emile Zola's last novel. Mehlman fills in some of the long-term political and discursive background, dating back to the Dreyfus affair, that is relevant to the contemporary discussion on Jews and Catholics, and it considerably revises accepted notions about Zola's views on the Jews. In our book review section, readers will find an article by the late Egal Feldman that discusses a number of recent books on the Vatican and the Jews, which is directly related to the subjects addressed in the Jewish/Catholic symposium. This article, which Feldman prepared for publication just before he died, thus represents his own last contribution to the historiographical debate—a focus of much of his life's work—and we note his passing with sadness.

In our second, "mini"-symposium we present a major reconsideration of the role of literature in the formulation of Holocaust discourse and Holocaust memory, by David Roskies. Occasionally a monograph-length work of scholarship comes along (in this case, once in our 21-year publication history) that ordinarily would not fit—literally—into an academic journal. It is one of the advantages of publishing an annual like ours that we are not necessarily bound by the space limits of most quarterlies; this is clearly one case that justifies our book-length format. Roskies' extraordinary essay stands on its own merits and is bound to become a defining point of departure for the study of Holocaust literature in the future. In the context of our double-barreled volume, we might add, it also serves to buttress the overall consideration of the post-Holocaust era as one in which judgment (in the sense of discernment) holds a necessary place in the Jewish quest for renewal, within the context of memory.

This section of the volume also includes an essay detailing the prelude, during 1951–1952, to the opening of direct negotiations between Israel and Germany. The year 2005, in addition to the anniversaries already mentioned, also marks the 40th anniversary of the institution of full diplomatic relations between Germany and Israel, which culminated one phase of coping with historical memory and judgment (here, as both indictment and reasoned policy), and opened another. Pride of place in this story is often assigned to Nahum Goldmann, a larger-than-life figure in postwar world Jewish politics; but Yechiam Weitz places into new perspective the behind-the-scenes activities of the Israeli foreign minister at the time, Moshe Sharett.

In our own modest addendum, perhaps, to Roskies' magisterial survey of Holocaust literature, we also publish excerpts in translation from a clandestine Hebrew journal, *Nizoz*, which, incredibly, continued to be written almost without interruption from 1940 to 1945, first in occupied Lithuania and finally in a forced-labor camp in Germany. The excerpts published here, presented by Dov Levin, derive from the last few months of the war and are vitally engaged with issues of both judgment and renewal, as well as the uses of collective memory.

As for our section of independent essays, apart from the aforementioned piece by Jeffrey Mehlman, we are pleased to introduce a finely honed methodological analysis of Franz Boas' work on language and culture, by Amos Morris-Reich, which asks why the renowned anthropologist was so notably silent about the Jews in this aspect of his scholarly endeavor. Finally, Kimmy Caplan's essay, which seeks to discover how American haredi ("ultra"-Orthodox) writers and educators have begun to marshal and deploy historical discourse on behalf of their religious interests, rounds out the volume (which also includes, of course, our traditional book review section). Caplan's essay grapples with the value judgments made with reference to historical memory, and takes note of the extent to which this issue has lately come to the fore in the American haredi community.

The steady publication of our volumes, now beginning a third decade, owes everything to the sustained, joint effort, and forethought of our entire team. As always, my thanks go to all of my colleagues: to Jonathan Frankel, Peter Medding, and Ezra Mendelsohn for their inspiration, rigorous discussion, and seasoned judgment; and to Laurie Fialkoff and Hannah Levinsky-Koevary, without whose daily labors, meticulous and knowledgeable attentions, and editorial solutions none of this project would be feasible.

E.L.

Contents

Essays

Book Reviews
(arranged by subject)

Antisemitism, Holocaust, and Genocide

Cultural Studies

Symposium
Jews, Catholics, and the Burden of History

A Plea Unanswered: Jacques Maritain, Pope Pius XII, and the Holocaust

Michael R. Marrus
UNIVERSITY OF TORONTO

Occasionally, as every historian knows, new evidence coming from outside a seemingly unproductive historiographical debate can cast long-entrenched positions into sharp relief, pose new questions, and just possibly move our understanding forward. This is the case, I suggest, with an important letter written in the summer of 1946 by the famous Catholic philosopher Jacques Maritain, when he was serving as French ambassador to the Holy See. The subject, which could certainly stand some new perspectives: Pope Pius XII, antisemitism, and the Holocaust. Specifically, writing to his long-time friend and associate Giovanni Montini, the future Pope Paul VI and then Sostituto in the office of Secretariat of State—effectively the pope's chief of staff—Maritain formulated a plea to Pius XII for a solemn declaration denouncing the great scourge of antisemitism in the context of the Nazis' destruction of European Jewry and the widespread complicity of Catholics in those events. Maritain emerged disappointed, for reasons that have to do with the way in which these matters were understood in the Vatican at that time. In what follows, we shall hear the parties speak for themselves, following which I shall offer a few comments of my own.

A word, to begin, about Jacques Maritain and the background to his appeal. Born in 1882, Maritain was not only one of the leading Catholic thinkers of his day, a respected expert on St. Thomas Aquinas, he was also, in 1946, one of the most influential laymen in the postwar Catholic world. As French ambassador, Maritain was deeply respected because of his association with General Charles de Gaulle and the French Resistance and was then playing an important role in the evolution of Christian Democracy in France and Italy.

The Second World War, the context of this episode, brought Jacques Maritain to the center of the world's stage in Catholic thought and politics. During those years, as Raymond Aron later put it, Maritain became "one of the voices of the conscience of the French outside of France."[1] In the spring of 1940, when the ordeal of France under Nazi domination began, Maritain was in Canada—teaching at the Pontifical Institute for Medieval Studies in Toronto as he had done for seven years, and using that Canadian base for lectures at various American universities. With the collapse

3

of the French armies and the installation of the collaborationist regime of Vichy, Maritain challenged the defeatist policies of the French head of state, Marshal Philippe Pétain, despite the latter's ostentatious support for the institutions of the Catholic Church. He moved to New York and, as the University of Notre Dame authority Bernard Doering puts it, "became a kind of ambassador to France without portfolio, who enjoyed a far greater influence and prestige than the Vichy ambassador in Washington."[2] Maritain became deeply involved in rescue activities, seeking to bring persecuted and threatened academics, many of them Jews, from France to America. He was instrumental in founding the École Libre des Hautes Études, a kind of university-in-exile that was, at the same time, the center of Gaullist resistance in the United States. Although he respectfully declined to be a member of de Gaulle's French National Committee in 1942 (possibly because the United States, at the time, recognized General Henri Giraud as the French leader), he remained, from within the academy, closely associated with the Gaullist camp. And when the Free French were finally established in Paris, in the fall of 1944, he returned to France to work in the French foreign ministry under his friend, the Christian Democratic leader Georges Bidault, formerly head of the umbrella organization, the Conseil National de la Résistance.

After a few weeks, both Bidault and de Gaulle prevailed upon a reluctant Maritain to accept the post of French ambassador to the Holy See. To those who had fought against the collaborationist regime of Vichy, it was imperative to replace Léon Bérard, the Pétainist representative to the pope who had been in place since 1940. Moreover, it was particularly important for Paris to solidify French relations with the Vatican, given that the new French government intended to purge from the episcopacy many high-ranking French churchmen who had compromised themselves during the period of German occupation. From the standpoint of the new authorities in Paris, Maritain was unquestionably the right man for the job—stoutly republican and associated with de Gaulle, but prominently Catholic and highly respectful of the institution to which he would be accredited.

Linked with Jews through his resistance and rescue activities, Maritain had thought about Judaism for many years, beginning with his student days at the time of the Dreyfus affair when, as a Protestant, he was associated with Charles Péguy, Henri Bergson, and Léon Bloy, each of whom had much to say about the Jewish people.[3] Through his Jewish wife, Raïssa Oumansoff, who with him converted to Roman Catholicism in 1906, Maritain remained closely associated with a Jewish family and Jewish tradition, and he was also well acquainted with the intellectual heritage of Catholic writing about the subject in France. The author of an influential essay in 1937 titled "L'impossible antisémitisme," Maritain assailed in his writing and lectures the anti-Jewish tide that was rising at the time, and notably the tendency by fascists and those on the extreme Right to identify Jews with Communism and revolution.

Continuing into the war years, Maritain denounced the core ideas of antisemitism. From his point of view, Jews had a vital role to play in the history of the world. Fascism, he believed, had singled out Jews because they were the harbingers of Christianity: "The central fact, and doubtless the most important meaning from the point of view of the philosophy of history and of the destiny of the human race," he said in a broadcast to the Free French in 1944, "is that in our day the passion of Israel takes on more and more distinctly the form of a cross. Jews and Christians are persecuted together and by the same enemies: the Christians because they are faithful to Christ, and the Jews because they have given Christ to the world."[4] Closely linked as these ideas were with his own brand of Catholicism, Maritain's was one of the prophetic voices within the Catholic world that pointed toward the Second Vatican Council in the mid-1960s, with its radical transformation of Catholic perspectives on Jews and the Jewish people.[5]

Maritain's interlocutor in the exchange we are about to consider was his old friend Monsignor Giovanni Battista Montini, the wartime subordinate of the Cardinal Secretary of State Luigi Maglione and, particularly after the latter's death in August 1944, one of the very closest aides of Eugenio Pacelli, Pope Pius XII.[6] Some 15 years younger than Maritain, Montini considered the French philosopher his teacher and, as a famous interpreter of Thomas Aquinas, one of the key promoters of a Catholic response to the challenge of modernity. Chaplain to a Catholic student federation in the mid-1920s, Montini first encountered Maritain in Paris, when the latter was teaching at the Institut Catholique. Montini translated one of Maritain's works into Italian and introduced his Thomistic thought to his coterie of Catholic intellectuals in Mussolini's Italy.[7]

The Italian priest remained a champion of Maritain's philosophy in Italy during the 1930s, when confrontations between the Church and Fascism intensified and when, in 1937, he entered the Papal Curia as *Sostituto*. (Much later, apparently, even as Pope Paul VI, Montini referred to Maritain as "mio maestro.") The two shared important commitments—to Thomist philosophy, to which they had both been devoted for more than two decades, but also to the effort to renew the spiritual authority of the Catholic Church, which they hoped, in the postwar period, to disentangle from the apparatus of states.[8] Understood to be closely associated, both the ambassador and the papal aide were under some attack from the Catholic Right in 1946, partly because of Maritain's previous promotion of what was considered a culturally venturesome doctrine of "integral humanism," and likely because of his close association with de Gaulle's commitment to dealing severely with a defeated Germany.[9]

Maritain's letter to Montini is dated July 12, 1946, just two months after he had presented his credentials as ambassador. While the letter went to his disciple Montini, it was clearly his superior, the pope, to whom the message was directed. Maritain was writing, he told Montini, as a friend and not as an ambassador, "feeling impelled as a Catholic to present an appeal at the feet of the Holy Father, together with [his] sentiments of filial and profound devotion."[10]

For many years, the newly installed diplomat reminded Montini, Maritain had been aware of the most savage hatred directed against "Israel." Nazism had simply carried the ancient campaign to new levels of atrocity. "During the [recent] war six million Jews have been *liquidated*," he wrote, "thousands of Jewish children have been massacred, thousands of others torn from their families and stripped of their identity. . . . Nazism proclaimed the necessity of wiping the Jews off the face of the earth (the only people that it wanted to exterminate *as a people*). . . ." And, he went on, "among the many other crimes that have ravaged and debased humanity," this was a "mysterious tragedy" that expressed "a hatred of Christ," targeting as it did "the people who gave to the world Moses and the prophets and from whom Christ himself came."

Maritain then referred to "the tireless charity with which the Holy Father had tried, with all his might, to save and protect the persecuted" and to his "condemnations of racism that have won for him the gratitude of the Jews and all those who care for the human race." "However"—and this was obviously the point of the letter—"what Jews and also Christians need above all [at this juncture] is a voice—the paternal voice, the voice par excellence, that of the Vicar of Jesus Christ—to tell the truth to the world and shed light on this tragedy. This has been, permit me to say it, greatly lacking in the world today" [*Il y a eu à ce sujet, permettez-moi de vous le dire, une grande souffrance par le monde*].

Maritain accepted that during the war,

> for reasons of prudence and a higher good, and in order not to make persecution even worse, and so as not to create insurmountable obstacles in the way of the rescue that he was pursuing, the Holy Father had abstained from speaking directly to the Jews and from calling the solemn and direct attention of the whole world to the iniquitous drama that was unfolding. But now that Nazism has been defeated, and that the circumstances have changed, could it not be permitted, and that is the reason for this letter, to transmit to His Holiness the appeal of so many anguished souls, and to beg him to make his voice heard [*n'est-il pas permis, et c'est là l'objet de cette lettre, de transmettre à sa Sainteté l'appel de tant d'âmes angoissées, et de La supplier de faire entendre sa parole*]?

Maritain went on to make a respectful case to Montini that the time was indeed ripe. "It seems to me—and I hope that your Excellency will not see any presumption in what I am writing in all humility—it seems to me that this is a particularly opportune moment for such a sovereign declaration of the thought of the Church." Strikingly, one of the reasons had to do with the Jews themselves: "The conscience of Israel is particularly troubled," Maritain noted, "[and] many Jews feel deeply within them the attraction of the grace of Christ, and the word of the pope would surely awaken in them echoes of exceptional importance" [*la conscience d'Israël est profondément troublée, beaucoup de Juifs sentent intérieurement l'attrait de la grâce du Christ, et la parole du Pape éveillerait sûrement en eux des échos d'une exceptionnelle importance*]. At the same time, he observed, "the antisemitic psychosis has not vanished, on the contrary one sees that everywhere in America and in Europe antisemitism is spreading in segments of the population, as if the poisons issuing from Nazi racism continue to do their work. . . ."

Maritain's appeal was "urgent," he said. He referred to "the part that many Catholics had in the development of antisemitism," both in the more distant past, during the war, and in the present. An appeal such as he was proposing, in proclaiming "the true thought of the Church, would therefore be a work of enlightenment, striking at a cruel and evil error, as well as being a work of justice and reparation." Finally, Maritain underscored, he was making his appeal "as a Catholic and as one humbly devoted to His Holiness and as a Christian philosopher who has taken the liberty to write. . . ."

Four days after writing to Montini, on July 16, Maritain had an audience with the pope. Apparently informed of his ambassador's request, Pius chose not to act. The pope had, he told Maritain, "already spoken on this issue while receiving a Jewish delegation."[11] It would not do, apparently, to repeat what had already been said on that occasion. Maritain saw Montini on the 19th and expressed his disappointment. And there the matter rested. Maritain either took the trouble to research the pope's words to the Jewish delegation or else was given a copy by the pope—we know this because, as will be seen below, he referred the statement to some petitioners three days later. It makes sense to refer to the pope's remarks here, since Pius himself apparently considered it an appropriate response to the kinds of concerns that Maritain had articulated.

Pius delivered the address in question on November 29, 1945, to an audience of 70 Jewish refugees from German concentration camps who had asked for "the great honor of personally thanking the Holy Father for the generosity that he had shown them when they had been persecuted during the terrible period of Nazi-Fascism."[12] Framed in the highly apologetic and convoluted rhetoric of the day, Pius' speech appeared in the Vatican daily *Osservatore Romano* the following day. "Your presence, Gentlemen, seems to us an eloquent testimony to the psychological transformations that the world conflict has, in its different aspects, created in the world," he began. Pius then referred to "the abyss of discord, the hatred and the folly of persecution which, under the influence of erroneous and intolerant doctrines, in opposition to the noble human and authentic Christian spirit, have engulfed incomparable numbers of innocent victims, even among those who took no active part in the war."

The pope carefully wove into his address some discreet allusions to what separated his Jewish listeners from the Catholic faith: "The Apostolic See remains faithful to the eternal principles of the law, written by God in the heart of every man, which shines forth in the divine revelation of Sinai and which found its perfection in the Sermon on the Mount and has never, even in the most critical moments, left any doubt as to its maxims and its applicability. . . ." Pius took comfort in the delegation's appreciation of the charity of the Church. "Your presence here," he said, "is an intimate testimony of the gratitude on the part of men and women who, in an agonizing time, and often under the threat of imminent death, experienced how the Catholic Church and its true disciples know how, in the exercise of charity, to rise above the narrow and arbitrary limits created by human egoism and racial passions." The pope, however, was wary of political involvement:

> Without doubt, in a world which only little by little and in struggling against numerous obstacles must confront and resolve the multiple problems that are the unhappy heritage of the war, the Church, conscious of its religious mission, can only maintain a wise reserve in the presence of various questions, inasmuch as they have a purely political and territorial character. Nevertheless, while proclaiming the grand principles of a true humanity and fraternity, [the Church] goes on to establish the bases and sure foundation for a solution of those same problems with justice and equity.

Concluding, Pius used the occasion both to project his own understanding of what Holocaust survivors should feel, and also the role of the Catholic Church in that process:

You have experienced yourselves the injuries and the wounds of hatred; but in the midst of your agonies, you have felt the benefit and the sweetness of love, not that love that nourishes itself from terrestrial motives, but rather with a profound faith in the heavenly Father, whose light shines on all men, whatever their language and their race, and whose grace is open to all those who seek the Lord in a spirit of truth.

I will conclude this discussion with five observations on the episode, its context, and the conclusions that might be drawn from it.

First, as a matter of historiography, I hope it is obvious that the reconstruction of wartime attitudes toward the Holocaust can benefit from a look at the postwar era. Holocaust issues repeatedly framed the attitudes and decision-making of the period after 1945, and historians need to take this into account. While the material discussed in this essay does not appear in the *Actes et documents du Saint Siège relatifs à la seconde guerre mondiale*, the Vatican's official publication of its wartime record, I think it is plain that Maritain's attitudes and observations, as well as the pope's perspective, can help us understand the actions and mentalities of the earlier period. Students of the Holocaust period will certainly benefit from recent works such as those by Michael Phayer, David Alvarez, and Peter Kent, precisely because they are not bound by the chronological framework of the Second World War.[13]

Second, an examination of the material presented here highlights how attentive historians must be to language, having particularly in mind the Catholic discourse of an earlier era, the Vatican's own mode of discourse at the time, and the susceptibility of these words to a variety of understandings. Indeed, virtually none of the persons whose words are studied here speak with our own idiom; each comes from a particular convention of speech that the historian must keep in mind for analytical purposes. Maritain's call for a papal statement is plain enough, to be sure. But what are we to make of his appreciative reference to the "tireless charity with which the Holy Father has tried with all his might to save and protect the persecuted"? Was this a considered judgment, intended as an accurate summary of the pope's wartime efforts, or was it a formulaic appreciation of the overall standing and general good intentions of the Holy See? From our perspective, Pius' admonishing Holocaust survivors about the great benevolence of the Church and his claim that, in the midst of their agonies, they "have felt the benefit and sweetness of love" may seem an unpardonable presumption. Was this discourse understood at the time as the haughty, patronizing condescension it might seem to us? Or was this inseparable from the Vatican's conventional idiom—the posture (not to mention the prolix expression) adopted not only with Jewish issues but with virtually everything that the Holy See communicated?

Third, it is important to ponder Maritain's deep unhappiness with the pope's unwillingness to take up his suggestions on the Jewish issue. However susceptible to interpretation, there seems little doubt about the emotion and sincerity of Maritain's letter to Montini, and his hopes for a positive answer. There is some additional, pertinent context for this point: just as Maritain was pursuing his appeal on behalf of the Jews he was learning of new outbursts of antisemitism in Eastern Europe, culminating in the atrocious communal violence in the Polish town of Kielce on July 4, 1946. The Western press reported these events, which included the shocking loss of Jewish life, accusations of ritual murder, and the complicity of Polish bishops, immediately before Maritain's letter to Montini on July 12. *Le Monde* relayed the story on July 7 and 8, and the *New York Times* on the 11th. On July 16, the day he saw the pope, Maritain received an appeal from the Jewish Labor Committee in New York, which deplored the silence of the Catholic Church and asked him to denounce the atrocities.[14] Maritain responded sympathetically three days later, on the 19th.[15]

That day, with the dreadful events in Poland much on his mind, Maritain saw Montini and once again gave vent to his frustration, as he recorded in his diary: "Visit to Montini. I speak to him of Jews and antisemitism. The Holy Father never even *named* them. Catholic conscience is poisoned, something has to be done. Article in the O[sservatore] R[omano] of yesterday on the 'pretext of Kielce' in which the Kielce pogrom is declared to be *non racial*!!" [sic].[16]

Following this incident, Maritain continued to make his case at the Vatican on behalf of the Jews. He wrote to Montini a month after these events, focusing on what he felt was the collective responsibility of Germans for the genocidal crimes of Nazism.[17] He urged Montini to address the anti-Jewish prayer *pro perfidis Judaeis* in the Good Friday liturgy.[18] He appealed to the pope to issue a major statement on the Jews. Pius remained unreceptive, however. "He does not want to broach the issue of the "mystère d'Israël," the ambassador recorded in his diary in February 1948.[19] Perhaps in consequence, Maritain became increasingly disillusioned with his post. He longed to return to teaching, he told his disciple Yves Simon; he begged Bidault "to set me free."[20] When he finally did step down, in the spring of 1948, he confided to his friend Charles Jourdan about his "heart-rending ambivalence": a "growing affection for the person of the pope," on the one hand, but a "growing disappointment with regard to his actions," on the other.[21]

Fourth, for whatever reason, the Vatican was unwilling to respond positively to Maritain's appeal. The pope's stock reply ("we have already spoken") was utterly reminiscent of the wartime answers given when the Vatican was reluctant to speak, or to speak explicitly, as Maritain also noticed. In the postwar situation, there were no apprehensions that speaking out could prompt retaliation or provoke even worse persecution by the Germans. So why the refusal? Unfortunately, Maritain himself had no explanation, and none of the evidence available to us is able to provide a conclusive answer. There is, however, a remarkable encounter with Maritain that suggests that his experience was far from unique. In September 1945, Leon Kubowitzki, then secretary general of the World Jewish Congress, appealed to the pope himself to make a grand statement in support of the Jews, whose ordeal was finally over. Kubowitzki did not succeed, and when he met with Maritain in Paris in August 1946, the two compared notes on a similar experience of frustration. Kubowitzki recorded the exchange in his diary:

> I told [Maritain] of my interview with the pope and my ideas about an encyclical on the Jewish question. He smiled and told me that he had urged a similar proposal on the Pope and on Monsigniore Montini. Both had been very friendly though his impression was that they were afraid to carry out the idea. He reminded me how much he had been saddened by the Pope's silence during the war concerning the persecution of the Jews and by his attempts to evade any direct mention of the matter, confining

himself to roundabout statements. I asked Maritain whether the Pope would not be interested in having his name connected with such an important document, which would be of considerable historical significance. He replied, "I would not hesitate to answer in the affirmative, if we were speaking about his predecessor."[22]

Finally, it is impossible to finish these reflections without reference to the supersessionist theological context that was, at the time, inescapably associated with any Vatican-level discussion of the Jews. There is more than a hint, in Maritain's unsuccessful effort, that Pope Pius XII felt obliged to link any declaration about the Jews with an assertion of Catholic rectitude and universal spiritual hegemony. Why else would the pope, when meeting with Jewish survivors of the concentration camps, have felt obliged to insist on the Church's fidelity to "the divine revelation of Sinai . . . which found its perfection in the Sermon on the Mount"? And why, for that matter, would Jacques Maritain, whose goodwill toward the victims of the Holocaust cannot be doubted, nevertheless have told Montini, perhaps as an inducement for the pope, that "the conscience of Israel is particularly troubled, [that] many Jews feel deeply within them the attraction of the grace of Christ, and the word of the pope would surely awaken in them echoes of exceptional importance"? We are, as these words were spoken, still 20 years from the Second Vatican Council and the revolutionary transformation of Catholic-Jewish relations that was to begin in the mid-1960s. It is well to keep this in mind when seeking to understand both the correspondence described in this paper and the much more desperate wartime events that preceded it.

Notes

1. Quoted in Michel Fourcade, "Jacques Maritain et l'Europe en exil (1940–1945)," in Charles Adras et al, *Jacques Maritain en Europe: La réception de sa pensée* (Paris: 1996), 281.
2. Bernard E. Doering, *Jacques Maritain and the French Catholic Intellectuals* (Notre Dame: 1986), 193.
3. See Robert Royal (ed.), *Jacques Maritain and the Jews* (Notre Dame: 1994).
4. Quoted in Charles Molette, "Jacques Maritain et la Conférence de Seelisberg," *Nova et Vetera* 3 (1994), 196. See also Jacques Maritain, "The Pagan Empire and the Power of God," *Virginia Quarterly* 15 (Spring 1939), where he writes: "Never before in the history of the world have the Jews been persecuted in so universal a fashion; and never before has that persecution fallen, as it does today, upon Jew and Christian alike" (p. 168).
5. Speaking of Vatican II, Bernard Doering observes that the Council's declaration on Jews "reads like a *précis* of what Maritain had been writing years before the war. The position that had gained for him strong opposition and even abuse in many Catholic circles had become, by 1964, a commonplace among the growing number of Catholic liberal theologians." Doering, *Jacques Maritain and the French Catholic Intellectuals*, 165.
6. See Robert A. Graham, "G.B. Montini Substitut Secretary of State (in Tandem with Domenico Tardini)," in *Paul VI et la modernité dans l'Eglise: actes du colloque organisé par l'Ecole française de Rome* (Rome: 1984), 67–84. Montini worked closely with Maglione's other assistant, Domenico Tardini, the secretary of the Congregation for Extraordinary Ecclesiastical Affairs. Pius did not replace Maglione after his death, taking on himself the job of his former secretary of state and thereby significantly increasing Montini's own responsibilities.

7. Philippe Chenaux, *Paul VI et Maritain: Les rapports du "Montiniainisme" et du "Maritainisme"* (Rome: 1994), 30. On the Maritain-Montini relationship, see also Giorgio Campanini, "Montini e Maritain," *Studium* 80 (1984), 349–355; Bernard Hubert and Yves Floucat (eds.), *Jacques Maritain et ses contemporains* (Paris: 1991).

8. See Laurent Gothelf, "Jacques Maritain, Mgr Montini et l'internationalisation du Saint-Siège (1945–1948)," *Revue d'histoire diplomatique* 99–100 (1985), 149–155. According to Gothelf: "The shared views of Maritain and Mgr Montini reflected their intimate and indissoluble friendship" (ibid., 154).

9. Jacques Maritain, *Humanisme intégral: problèmes temporels et spirituels d'une nouvelle chrétienité* (Paris: 1936). For a useful summary of Maritain's views on this and related matters, see John M. Dunaway, *Jacques Maritain* (Boston: 1978), ch. 5. See also Graham, "G.B. Montini," 78–79; Doering, *Jacques Maritain and the French Catholic Intellectuals*, 208–209; Fourcade, "Jacques Maritain et l'Europe en exil (1940–1945)," 43–45; Michael Phayer, *The Catholic Church and the Holocaust, 1930–1965* (Bloomington: 2000), 178.

10. Maritain's letter is reproduced in full in Fondation du Cardinal Journet, *Journet Maritain Correspondence*, vol. 3, *1940–1949* (Paris: 1998), 917–920. It is also reprinted in Bruno Charmet, "Jacques Maritain et Pie XII: Quelques précisions d'ordre documentaire," *Sens* no. 2 (2000), online at http://www.chretiens-et-juifs.org/ETUDES/Sens/Maritain_Pie%20XII_Charmet.htm.

11. Chenaux, *Paul VI et Maritain*, 44.

12. *La Documentation catholique*, no. 1025 (12 Sept. 1948), 1183–1184, Charmet, "Jacques Maritain et Pie XII."

13. Phayer, *The Catholic Church and the Holocaust*; Peter C. Kent, *The Lonely Cold War of Pope Pius XII* (Montreal: 2002); David Alvarez, *Spies in the Vatican: Espionage and Intrigue from Napoleon to the Holocaust* (Lawrence, Kan.: 2002). Justus George Lawler, in a work supposedly dedicated to correcting factual distortions about the role of the Holy See during the Holocaust, mischaracterizes Maritain's appeal, presenting it as a demand, in July and August 1946, "for a [presumably papal] statement on Germany's collective responsibility for the Holocaust." See his *Popes and Politics: Reform, Resentment and the Holocaust* (New York: 2002), 55. Whatever his assessment of Germany, it is clear that Maritain was also concerned about the Vatican's own responsibility—something that is obviously relevant to Lawler's thesis, but which he ignores altogether.

14. *Journet Maritain Correspondence* 3:912; Molette, "Jacques Maritain et la Conférence de Seelisberg," 216–227.

15. Interestingly, Maritain's response referred to the pope's allocution to Jewish Holocaust survivors to which the pontiff had referred him three days before:

Profoundly moved by your telegram, I believe that any resurgence of antisemitism would be a shame for humanity. . . . I hope that you have noted the pope's declaration to Jewish refugees of November 30, 1945, in which he said that racist ideas "were unacceptable" and "should be considered the most deplorable and dishonorable aberrations of the human spirit" (*Journet Maritain Correspondence*, 3:913–914).

16. Ibid., 914.

17. Phayer, *Catholic Church and the Holocaust*, 179.

18. *Journet Maritain Correspondence*, 3:922–931.

19. Humbert and Floucat, *Jacques Maritain et ses contemporains*, 332.

20. Doering, *Jacques Maritain and the French Catholic Intellectuals*, 213.

21. *Journet Maritain Correspondence*, 3:622.

22. Aryeh L. Kubovy [Leon Kubowitzki], "The Silence of Pope Pius XII and the Beginnings of the 'Jewish Document'," *Yad Vashem Studies* 6 (1967), 24.

Jules Isaac and His Role in Jewish-Christian Relations

André Kaspi
UNIVERSITÉ DE PARIS I

On Monday, June 13, 1960, French scholar Jules Isaac had a private audience with Pope John XXIII. Their conversation took place in the papal study-library, beginning at quarter past one and ending 20 minutes later. Despite its brevity, this was an exchange that decisively influenced the ties between Judaism and Christianity. There was an instant liking between the two men. Isaac describes the man he spoke to: "A roly-poly fellow, quite thickset, with the somewhat coarse features of a country-dweller—a big nose—very agreeable, with a ready laugh and a searching, slightly devilish gaze, but with a manifest goodness that inspires confidence."[1]

The visitor briefly conveyed his message to the pope: Classical pagan antisemitism was insubstantial. It alone could hardly have presaged Nazi antisemitism, which was responsible for the horrors and tragedies of the Second World War. "Between these two, the only-form [of antisemitism] that has substance," he argued, is "a particular Christian theology [adopted] under the pressure of circumstances, [at a time when] Jewish rejection constituted the primary obstacle to Christian propaganda in the pagan world."[2] Isaac outlined the historical development in the Church of a "teaching of contempt" (*l'enseignement du mépris*) for Judaism. He went on to praise Pope John XXIII's outstanding efforts to rectify the Church's teachings on Judaism, and referred to the hopes raised by the upcoming Vatican Council, which would later become known as the Second Vatican Council.

As the meeting came to an end, Isaac asked a question: Might a change be hoped for in the teachings dispensed by the Catholic Church? The pope replied warmly: "You are entitled to more than hope," adding, however, that "while it's true that I'm the one in charge, I must also hold consultations, have experts study the questions that have been brought up—it's not an absolute monarchy." The two men shook hands. They would never meet again. Neither of them would live long enough to read the 1965 declaration that rejected the "teaching of contempt." Both of them died in 1963.

Jules Isaac was an outstanding individual. There was nothing in his background, his early life, or his professional career to indicate that he would eventually dedicate

20 years to the tireless pursuit of Jewish-Christian rapprochement. He was born to a Jewish family in 1877. The Isaacs, however, were French *Israélites*, Jews who had benefited from the emancipation that the French Revolution had bestowed upon them in two separate legislative acts of 1790 and 1791. This made them French through and through, convinced that they were part of the French people, like the Bretons or the Provençals. They enjoyed equal civil rights with the other French and did not try to escape their civic duties. On the contrary, Jules Isaac's grandfather fought in the Napoleonic Wars, beginning as a bugler with the rank of corporal and finishing up as a bandmaster (*chef de fanfare*) in a mounted artillery unit. He fought on Europe's battlefields, survived the hell of the Berezina engagement, and was awarded both the Legion of Honor and the medal of St. Helena. Of his five sons, four would serve in the army. The oldest joined Napoleon III's Imperial Guard, but soon began to express republican sentiments. Like his father before him, he fought in a war—the 1870 Franco-Prussian War. Also like his father, he was awarded the Legion of Honor. However, his republicanism harmed his career during the time of the empire, and later, when the Third Republic was established in 1870, the fact that he had served in the Imperial Guard became a handicap. In 1882, not long before he retired, he was promoted to lieutenant colonel.

Did these patriotic Frenchmen, devoted body and soul to defending their homeland, maintain Jewish sentiments? On the one hand, they did not hide their origins; on the other, they kept very little of their ancestors' faith, apart from observing certain traditions such as bar mitzvahs and Jewish weddings. In this sense, mothers and wives were the guardians of the faith. In any event, religion was a private affair, limited to the family circle. At best, one can speak of a Jewish social milieu within which matrimonial alliances were struck. All of which means that for the young Isaac, who did not deny his Jewish origins, Judaism was of little significance.

One highly significant example illustrates this "Israélite" way of thinking. In 1897, at the age of 20, Isaac struck up a friendship with Charles Péguy, a leading Dreyfusard. This acquaintance left a profound mark on the young man's mind, and even half a century later, it generated feelings of intense emotion, gratitude, and devotion. At the time of their initial meeting, Captain Alfred Dreyfus was incarcerated on Devil's Island, having been sentenced for treason two years earlier. The public campaign for a new trial was gaining momentum. On January 13, 1898, Emile Zola published in *L'Aurore* his "J'accuse"—the article that would breathe new life into the Dreyfus affair. Until then, Isaac had shown no interest in antisemitism, even though it was rampant at the time in France. A few years earlier, in 1886, Edouard Drumont had published *La France juive*, which became an amazing bestseller. (By the eve of the First World War, it was in its 200th edition, having sold approximately one million copies.) Drumont was also the publisher of *La libre parole*, which served as a platform for his antisemitic notions, among which was the claim that

> [t]he main signs by which the Jew can be recognized are: this famous hooked nose, blinking eyes, a clenched jaw, protuberant ears, square nails, flat feet, round knees, ankles that turn out to an incredible degree, a soft and flabby hand of the hypocrite and traitor; quite often one arm is shorter than the other.[3]

Yet Isaac was not very sensitive to this propaganda. Many years later, as his life drew to a close, he provided a strikingly candid explanation:

> I hadn't read Drumont's *La France juive*, I didn't read *La libre parole* . . . antisemitism seemed to me to be a rather embarrassing disease, regrettable above all for the people who suffered from it, and in this affair, in its explosive form, seemed like a distressing but short-lived epidemic. You can't blame me. I just wasn't aware.[4]

There was something else, too: as the son and grandson of servicemen, he had no choice other than to respect a military tribunal's decisions. "I was Jewish and, reacting honestly, I was very careful, being quite self-consciously determined not to indulge myself in any reflex of Jewish solidarity, determined to make up my mind carefully and only when I knew exactly what was going on."[5]

Péguy, however, convinced Isaac of Dreyfus' innocence—and, beyond that, initiated him into the religion of Truth and Justice. Isaac became involved with the Dreyfusard campaign to have the trial reopened and, later, to clear Dreyfus' name. He took part in demonstrations at Péguy's side, right in the middle of the crowd. In his memoirs, he writes: "What a wonderful way to prepare for a degree in history! I say this without the slightest note of irony. Not everything is to be learned from books."[6] Indeed, throughout his career, Isaac would underscore the vital importance of establishing all the facts, without distortion and free of prejudice. While fighting in the First World War, the propaganda that he heard made his hair stand on end. The only thing that counts, he would argue, is the truth as a historian manages to reconstruct it.[7]

Despite his early involvement in the Dreyfus affair, Isaac did not at first become an active proponent of Jewish-Christian rapprochement. He was trained at the Sorbonne as a historian. During the interwar years, he published a series of influential textbooks. In 1933, feeling strongly the need to take part in current historical debates, he published a meticulous study on the origins of the Great War. Convinced that everything must be done in order to avoid a second world war, Isaac occupied an eminent position among those who wished to rid history textbooks of all traces of chauvinism, bellicosity, or propaganda. He was a "history worker," to use the phrase of the time—at once very much a part of French society, fully aware of his civic responsibilities and, following the republican tradition, utterly devoted to defending the separation of Church and state, a champion of the secularist principle.

In 1939, a mere two decades after the "war to end all wars," fighting again overwhelmed Europe and much of the rest of the world. Isaac, the pacifist, lost his remaining illusions. Worse was to come. In 1940, France was defeated. Out of defeat emerged the "National Revolution," headed by Marshal Pétain, whose declared goal was a return to "traditional values." On October 18, 1940, the government promulgated the Law Governing the Status of the Jews. This law applied a racial definition in ascertaining who was a Jew. In Article 2, it listed the occupations prohibited to Jews, with paragraph 4 referring to "members of the teaching professions." French Jews became second-class citizens, or as Isaac observed, "lepers." They were no longer to be associated with, despite the fact that their ancestors had, in many cases, lived in France for centuries, their grandfathers and fathers defending the homeland, many of them decorated for valor or occupying high positions. Official France—Pétain's France—no longer wanted anything to do with them.

Jules Isaac was 63 years old. Apart from his position as inspector general, he had chaired the jury that administered the history *agrégation*, the highest competitive examination for teachers. His textbooks had been used to teach generations of French high school students and had contributed to the training of thousands of teachers. Like other Jewish public officials, he was now banned. He had until Christmas to resign all of his posts. He wrote to Pétain: "I am hereby excluded from the French national community, and with me—French to my backbone—how many others, from [Henri] Bergson our master to all the young people of the classes of '38 and '39, who have served France well with all their heart and all their might." Pétain did not reply. However, the minister of education issued a directive to the effect that Isaac had quit his post as of December 19, 1940 and hence was "entitled to apply for a retirement pension to be paid as of December 20, 1940."[8]

Returning to Paris was out of the question, since the occupation authorities prohibited Jews from going back to the capital. Instead, Isaac found refuge in Aix-en-Provence with a colleague. He was deeply distressed by his position, cut to the quick by "wicked iniquitous legislation" and "fanatical antisemitism," feeling abandoned by those too faint-hearted to come to his defense. "I had presumed too much of my country," he wrote. "In a savage bolt out of the blue, I discovered that in order to be classified as French, as a good Frenchman, it wasn't enough to be French—completely and utterly, as I was, as I had been all my life; in addition, I had to be acknowledged as such, not only by the all-powerful triumphant enemy, but by my own fellow citizens."

During 1941, the situation of the Jews in France deteriorated. On March 29, the General Commissariat for Jewish Questions was established. The second ordinance pertaining to the status of the Jews, which was even more restrictive than the first, was issued on June 2. The aryanization of Jewish businesses, the blocking of bank accounts, and a fine of one billion French francs (levied by the Germans) were the prelude to the merging of all Jewish organizations, other than the Central Consistory, into the General Union of the Israelites of France, under German control.

Isaac tried to understand. He compared the National Revolution with Athens at the end of the fifth century after its subjugation by the Spartans. He took part in encounters with other "statufied" victims of the anti-Jewish regulations, and attended meetings that were organized in the Vichy-governed "free zone" by the Central Consistory. Gradually he came to reflect on antisemitism. It is important, however, not to make the mistake of supposing that Isaac returned to Judaism. He knew nothing, or practically nothing, about Jewish practice and thought. He was not interested in knowing anything about them. On February 1, 1942, he wrote the following to his son, Daniel:

> Even in the present circumstances, I find the thought of becoming Jewish utterly abhorrent. If I were Jewish, I would have become a Christian. But it won't make any difference to issue ordinances that I am Jewish: I am not Jewish, in any shape or form. I would go even further than this and say: I thank God that there has been a Greek people, not that there has been a Jewish people to propagate religious passions and religious exclusiveness. . . . I prefer Socrates, a man of God.

Nevertheless, his outlook underwent a change. He began to dwell on the origins of antisemitism. He spoke to Jewish intellectuals and Catholic philosophers. He had taken a crucial step:

> If only because of the persecution I was suffering, and which constantly became more acute, my mind became preoccupied with the Jewish question, and my heart and my conscience with Jewish solidarity. I was from this hated, much maligned and despised Israel; in the face of the persecutors, I utterly and completely accepted that I was thus; and so we also had to ready ourselves to fight a new battle, pore over the grievances that they chose to heap on our heads.

Isaac started by reading the New Testament. He knew Greek and made a point of reading the original version. He considered the Old Testament to be out of his reach because he had no knowledge of Hebrew and hated translations. He made an astonishing discovery. It "made my head spin," he later recalled. The Church's traditional teachings betrayed the Gospels, he found. In his *Carnet du lépreux* (Leper's notebook), he recounts what he came to realize:

> I read the Gospels. . . . And having read them, pored over them earnestly, minutely, looking at everything relating to Israel and Jesus' position on Israel, I became convinced that the received tradition did not coincide with the text of the Gospels, that it went beyond it in all respects. And I became convinced that this received tradition, which has been taught for hundreds and hundreds of years by thousands and thousands of voices, was the primary and unwavering source of antisemitism, for hundreds of years the powerful rootstock on which all other varieties of antisemitism—even the most divergent—managed to graft themselves.

Under the influence of this insight, Isaac wrote a short paper (almost certainly in June 1942) titled "A Few Findings Based on the Reading of the Gospels." From then on, the question became an obsession. How could Christianity have been so distorted? Does this distortion explain the powerful, omnipresent prejudices that underlie antisemitism?

What was needed was an examination of the texts, not a flight of fancy or a philosophical study. Isaac set himself a goal: to write a historical analysis based on solid references—the kind of thorough historical investigation he had been doing ever since his student days at the Sorbonne. The Gospels, to be sure, were not historically accurate documents: they were written several years or even several decades after the events. Yet their purpose was to give a version—their version— of the facts. Isaac set out to provide a rigorous critique of their substance and content.

It was at this point that the most dreadful tragedy occurred. Isaac and his wife, Laure, had been forced to leave Aix-en-Provence when the Germans had invaded the "free zone." They decided to move to a hotel in Riom, using false identities in order to avoid arrest by the Gestapo or by the French police. Riom, a small town in the department of Allier, had two advantages. It was close to Clermont-Ferrand, a university city, whose library contained material that Isaac needed for his research. In addition, and more important, it was just a few kilometers from Vichy, the provisional French capital and the headquarters of the regime's high-level administration—which was infiltrated, on behalf of the Resistance, by Robert Boudeville, the Isaacs' son-in-law. Boudeville was arrested in October 1943. Soon thereafter, his wife, Juliette, was also arrested. Laure Isaac tried to get news of her daughter. Her phone calls were traced. The Gestapo picked her up while Jules was out on his morning walk. Neither Juliette nor Laure would return from Auschwitz.

The tragedy at Riom might have put an end to Isaac's research into early Christianity. He was forced to go underground—desperate—for a few days incapable of reacting. But then he received a note from the Drancy transit camp that Laure had managed to scribble in haste. One sentence encouraged him to continue: "Complete your work, which the world is waiting for." This, then, was the sacred mission he was duty-bound to accomplish. Nothing in this world could prevent the historian from completing his work: neither the uncertainty, which became increasingly unbearable as the months passed, nor the certainty, in the spring of 1945, that the two women had been murdered. "This book is my flesh and my blood as well," he admitted. "There is not a single line that I have written that is not dedicated to both of them: it is their work as much as mine."

Jésus et Israël was published in April 1948. It was a 585-page work that, instead of chapters, was divided into 21 propositions, each followed by its flawless demonstration, based on Isaac's reading of the Scriptures. The propositions are divided into four parts. The first part addresses "Jesus the Christ, a Jew in the flesh"; the second, "the Gospel in the synagogue"; the third, "Jesus and his people"; and the fourth, "the crime of deicide." Each proposition is stated succinctly; thus, for instance, "Jesus, the Jesus of the Gospels, the only Son and Incarnation of God for the Christians, was a Jew in his life on earth, a simple Jewish artisan. This is a fact that no Christian can ignore" (Proposition II). Proposition I is a more general introduction that also signals the work's primary message: "The Christian religion is the daughter of the Jewish religion. The Christian New Testament is constructed on the basis of the Jewish Old Testament. If only for this reason, Judaism must inspire respect." Proposition XXI concludes the book and states its profound significance:

> Whatever Israel's crimes, it is innocent, completely innocent of the crimes of which it is accused by the Christian tradition: it did not reject Jesus, it did not crucify him, Jesus neither rejected Israel nor cursed it: just as "the gifts and calling of God are not repented of" (Romans 11:29), so there are no exceptions to the evangelical Law of love. May the Christians finally acknowledge this, acknowledge and make amends for their heinous iniquities. At the present time, when a curse seems to oppress the whole of mankind, this is the pressing obligation that the lesson of Auschwitz imposes on them.

Isaac never claimed that Christianity was responsible for the murder of six million Jews. He emphasized the fact that Nazi antisemitism was practically as hostile to Christians as to Jews. Nonetheless,

> one must be able to make choices and to distinguish surface appearances from deeply embedded realities. I felt that the most profound such reality was this one, "the teaching of contempt" on a theological basis, which has been perpetuated in Christianity for eighteen hundred years. In this form, the old [characterization of the Jew as] demon offered a convenient foothold: it could be grasped, clutched, pierced, exorcized.

Indeed, *Jésus et Israël* bears witness to the tragic consequences of that anti-Jewish tradition. Isaac dedicated the book to "my martyred wife and daughter who were killed by the Germans, killed simply because they were called Isaac."[9]

Although the dedication might suggest that he was speaking on behalf of the Jews, or, more simply, as a Jew, Isaac's original foreword, written in 1943, disavowed any such intentions: "The author, who is of Jewish extraction, wishes to inform the reader that it is in no way his intention to undertake a vindication, let alone a defense, of the Jews and Judaism." Rather, he explained, his goal was to convince Christians of the need to undertake "a healthy reading of the Scriptures, combined with an accurate knowledge of the historical facts." In time, however, he came to feel that this explanation was inadequate. A revised foreword, written in 1946, was more passionate in tone, describing the work as "the cry of an outraged conscience . . . addressed to the conscience and heart of mankind." Nonetheless, it remained a scientific work because of "its infrastructure, the methods it uses for information and discussion purposes [and] its scrupulous integrity." In his revised foreword, Isaac deals once again with the question of his own identity: "The question may be asked as to what religion the author belongs to. The answer can be readily provided: none. But his entire book bears witness to the fervor that inspires and guides him."

When *Jésus et Israël* appeared in 1948, it was only rarely acknowledged that Jesus' life had been guided by Jewish law; that Judaism during his lifetime was not a degenerate religion; that the Pharisees did not deserve their bad reputation; and that Jesus' sermons, remarks, and prayers were taken from the Jewish Scriptures. As he proceeded to elaborate his points, Isaac was at pains to emphasize that Christian authors, Catholic and Protestant alike, had transformed Jesus' message. They had stripped it of its Jewish content and, to a great extent, had "Christianized" it.

Moreover—and here Isaac ventured into even less charted territory—the main charge leveled against the Jews, namely, that they had rejected Jesus and subsequently bore responsibility for his crucifixion, was historically inaccurate. As he developed this argument, Isaac's style became more forceful, even vehement. He tackled this theme, he wrote, "with some trepidation, and a certain amount of emotional turmoil." For this accusation is what provided the basis for the hatred of the Jews, having been skillfully exploited "from one century to the next, from one generation to the next," culminating "in Auschwitz, in the gas chambers and the crematoria of Nazi Germany."

Isaac focused in particular on the charge of deicide, beginning with a historical presentation of the period in which the accusation was first launched. Implicit in Matthew and John, the charge became explicit in the apocryphal Gospels, particularly of the fourth century. By then, Isaac explained, the Eastern Roman empire had officially adopted Christianity as a state religion. Judaism, however, was continuing to gain adherents and was a formidable competitor. Given these circumstances, the charge of deicide became a decisive weapon, being used as the basis of anti-Jewish legislation. From then on, the theme recurred constantly, entering the liturgy and reaching into the 20th century. Thus the infamous special dress imposed on the Jews by the Fourth Lateran Council, Isaac argued, was a precursor of the Nuremberg Laws. And now, following the massacre of six million innocent individuals, the same charges were being circulated once again. "They do indeed lead to Auschwitz," Isaac wrote.

Upon its publication, *Jésus et Israël* attracted both attention and lively debate. To this day, it is being translated, sold, and commented upon. Not everyone has agreed with Isaac's conclusions. Some have regretted the book's overly vehement tone or have criticized Isaac's anachronistic use of the term "antisemitism" in his discussion of the early Christian period, instead of the more proper "anti-Judaism." Others, particularly in Catholic circles, have defended Christian teachings, reiterating that the Jews got it wrong, that they did not understand that Jesus was the Messiah, that they remained disbelievers—but would one day convert and attain "their fulfillment." Isaac himself took a central role in this debate. As early as 1947, when the manuscript was finished, he took part in the Seelisberg Conference that brought together Christians and Jews, and which adopted a series of resolutions (the Ten Points of Seelisberg) that were drafted by Isaac himself.

In addition, shortly before *Jésus et Israël* appeared in the bookshops, Isaac became a co-founder of the Amitié judéo-chrétienne (Jewish-Christian Friendship Society). Among other Jewish figures in this society were Isaïe Schwartz (the chief rabbi of France) and his deputy, Rabbi Jacob Kaplan, the writer Edmond Fleg, the musicologist Léon Algazi, and the scholar, Samy Lattès. Catholics included Henri Marrou, Jacques Madaule, and Jacques Nantet; there were also a number of Protestant figures (Fadiey Lovsky and Jacques Martin) and several members of the Eastern Orthodox Church. This gathering asserted the confluence of Judeo-Christian beliefs and confirmed the participants' common desire to understand each others' religious beliefs, to be reconciled with one another, and to fight prejudice. The society's statutes forbade any proselytizing. Chapters were organized in Aix-en-Provence, Marseilles, Nîmes, Montpellier, Lyons, Lille, and Mulhouse. Isaac later established ties with sympathetic groups in Italy, Switzerland, the Federal Republic of Germany, Austria, Spain, and Great Britain.

In 1949, Isaac was granted a brief audience with Pope Pius XII and handed him a copy of the Ten Points of Seelisberg. Before he even met John XXIII, he managed to have the Good Friday liturgy changed. During the Oremus prayer, the genuflection (as a sign of respect) was reinstated when the faithful pray for the Jews, and the reference to *perfidis Judaeis* was abolished. Meanwhile, Isaac continued both to lecture and to publish books that often stirred controversy, among them *La Genèse de l'antisémitisme* (1956), *L'enseignement du mépris* (1962), and *L'antisémitisme a-t-il des racines chretiennes?* (1959).

It would be an overstatement to claim that just one man was responsible for the rapprochement between Jews and Christians that culminated in the Second Vatican Council. There is, however, no doubt that Jules Isaac was a major architect of this rapprochement.

Notes

This essay was translated by Ruth Morris.

1. *Cahiers de l'Association des amis de Jules Isaac*, vol. 2 (1974). Other quotes in this essay are also to be found in this volume. Jules Isaac's extensive archives are located in the Bibliothèque Méjanes in Aix-en-Provence.

2. André Kaspi, *Jules Isaac ou la passion de la vérité* (Paris: 2002), 231–236.

3. Quoted in Michel Winock, *Edouard Drumont et Cie: antisemitisme et fascisme en France* (Paris: 1982).

4. Jules Isaac, *Expériences de ma vie* (Paris: 1959), 124.

5. Ibid., 123.

6. Ibid., 155.

7. On Isaac during the First World War, see Marc Michel, *Jules Isaac: un historien dans la Grande Guerre, lettres et carnets 1914–1917* (Paris: 2004).

8. Jules Isaac, "Survol," in *Cahiers du Sud* 376 (1964).

9. The dedication was modified in the 1959 edition, where "killed by the Germans" became "killed by the Nazis."

The Church and the Memory of the Shoah: The Catholic Press in Italy, 1945–1947

Manuela Consonni
THE HEBREW UNIVERSITY

Relatively few studies have dealt with the manner in which the Catholic Church, in the years immediately following the Second World War, confronted, reflected upon, and established its position regarding the deportation and extermination of the Jews of Italy. By the "Church" I do not mean the Catholic laity, but rather the ecclesiastic hierarchy, with the focus on the Church as a political entity. In particular, I intend to examine the Church's public role, its social impact, and the consequences of its political choices as reflected in the official Catholic press between 1945 and 1947, and also to offer my own hypothesis concerning the causes and motives that impelled the Church to maintain its silence at that time.

One is struck by this odd postwar silence, which might suggest indifference, and which stands in contrast to how much was written about both the Jews and the thorny question of antisemitism in that same press, both before and during the war.[1] Why did silence dominate Vatican policy at war's end? Was it that the past the Church would have had to address was too burdensome and tragic? Or that an analysis of its own attitudes required a degree of detachment that seemed untenable, given that the past was indissolubly linked with persisting political conditions and mentalities?[2]

In order to understand the difficult relationship between the Church and the memory of the deportation and extermination, one must be aware of the context: the atmosphere of "spiritual antisemitism," to borrow Renato Moro's phrase—a theological-ethical racism that was combined with a fear of modernity, the latter being perceived and defined as anti-Christian. Such an atmosphere prevailed in Church discourse before, during, and after the Shoah, continuing at least until Pope John XXIII's encyclical *Pacem in terris* of 1963. The traditional conservative and fundamentally corporative political attitude,[3] with its strong anti-socialist and anti-communist hue, caused the Church to plunge into the political arena immediately after the liberation of Italy in April 1945, in the course of which it cast aside uncomfortable questions about the past.

Both the Jewish and the non-Jewish press brought the Nazi crimes to public attention in Italy at the end of the war. The anti-Jewish genocide, it was repeatedly and explicitly stated, was an event without precedent.[4] In December 1944, Carlo Alberto Viterbo, then the editor of *Israel*, printed the first article on the subject. If the facts regarding the annihilation of the Jewish people were still held in doubt at that time, by 1945 the Shoah had become a concrete subject of discourse in which the descriptions of atrocities had become an acknowledged reality.[5] As Viterbo wrote in March 1945:

> No people in history has ever grieved for five million victims, no people has confronted the murder of a third of its members, no people has ever lost (not in combat, with weapons in hand, but by the appalling slaughter of the unarmed) so many able-bodied men, together with so many innocent women, so many venerable old people, so many babies smiling at life.[6]

It was not only the press that concerned itself with the question. In the spring of 1945, the Minister for Occupied Italy, Mauro Scoccimarro, contacted the Jewish community of Rome, and through it the Union of Jewish Communities. He invited the recently liberated Jewish community—in its entirety—to collect and document reports on the crimes committed, and to transmit the materials gathered to a commission known as the Central Commission for Ascertaining the Atrocities Committed by the Germans and the Fascists against the Jews.[7]

And then there were the commemoration activities. No fewer than 28 memorial books dealing with the deportations and extermination, written by Jewish deportees, political deportees, and prisoners of war, were published in Italy between 1944 and 1947.[8] The Jesuit publication, *La Civiltà Cattolica*, generally considered the Vatican's mouthpiece in Italy, reviewed only one of them, Paolo Liggeri's *Triangolo Rosso*:

> No book, apparently, has succeeded in documenting the martyrdom inflicted on the political prisoners of the recent war. . . . In the face of the horrors recounted in these pages, readers linger . . . and ask themselves if the cynicism of the Nazi hyena has not perhaps infected the author's soul as well, so uninvolved and cold is the indifference with which he recounts the tortures, . . . the gas chambers, the shootings, the crematoria, the gas vans, the hangings, the electric fences, the vicious dogs, the experimental pills, the burning injections of nitrobenzene, the choking, the suffocation in pools, all of it inflicted with evident pleasure, even on old people . . . women in an advanced stage of pregnancy, children . . . [9]

Note that, in this review, the old men, the women, and the children have all been identified as "political prisoners." The word "Jew" is nowhere to be found.[10]

By January 1945, according to abundant evidence, the Vatican knew all about the outcome of the "Final Solution."[11] This observation is not made polemically but rather in an attempt to establish the continuity of themes and motives that had characterized the attitude of the Church before and after that date. On the day after liberation, the Church was, in fact, locked into preexisting mind-sets. These reflected a substantially reactionary attitude: tied to authoritarian political outlooks and circumstances, and still entirely political in its manifestations.[12]

As historian Giovanni Miccoli has noted, such tendencies had marked the history of the relations between the Church and Italian Fascism, a long and substantial collaboration that was neither defensive nor a mere matter of convenience. As

Miccoli argues, the Church under Fascism was recognized as part of the ruling bureaucracy, "a religion . . . [possessing] prestige and social weight that had made it a pillar of the constituted order."[13] The alliance, to be sure, was not without its collisions and tensions, as in 1938, in the government's infringement of the 1929 Concordat, when anti-Jewish racial laws were applied to partners in mixed marriages. This and other conflicts, however, did not substantially damage the underlying collaboration. In this context, it may be noted that after September 8, 1943 (the date of the Italian surrender and ouster of Mussolini), the Vatican secretary of state instructed its liaison with the government of Pietro Badoglio not to support the repeal of the racial laws, as formally requested by the Jewish community, because "according to the principles and traditions of the Church, such legislation still represented in the eyes of the Church, even after the fall of Fascism, arrangements that merit confirmation."[14]

The postwar Church had not yet freed itself from the anti-Jewish polemic that, since the last decades of the 19th century, had marked traditional Catholicism all across Europe. In this polemic, the growing Jewish influence on civil life, brought about by a revolutionary emancipation, was depicted as an essential factor in the de-Christianization that threatened contemporary society. And this attitude was itself influenced by all of the old formulas and motifs drawn from Christian theological and religious discourse about the Jews' stubbornness and blindness, their guilt for deicide, their innate immorality and corruption, and their antipathy toward Christians. A tradition survived, then, that identified the Church with the desire to staunch the processes of modernity, which it equated with de-Christianization and general secularization; and that tied all of this to "the Jews," to militant anticlericalism, and to revolutionary utopian or socialist ideas. In other words, the Jews were considered the bearers of a threat to the "political and spiritual" power of the Church.[15]

The Catholic polemics of the immediate postwar period in Italy again posited the image of the masses, perceived as being preyed upon by a new anticlericalism, easily manipulated by "the principal enemy of true democracy and of its ideal of liberty and equality."[16] This was an attitude that left no room for fine shadings and distinctions, but on the contrary bonded to the fears and preoccupations (principally, the fear of Communism's spread) that had first arisen during the course of the war. Even if they were toned down, the positions expressed in the encyclical *Divini Redemptoris* of 1937 continued to hold after the war and were invested by the Church with militant significance in its holy war against Communism—if no longer international, as during the Spanish Civil War, then at least domestic.[17]

The Church had a real difficulty in perceiving and understanding the enormity of what had happened to the Jews precisely because it was so deeply wedded to an uncompromising battle for supremacy against the secularism and anti-clericalism of the Left. Its openness and tolerance toward Fascism and Nazism were constituted by the conviction that somehow, as Moro put it, "the new inclination to spiritual values demonstrated by the totalitarian ideologies of the Right opened the road to a return of the true faith."[18]

In a certain sense, the Church's silence about the deportation and extermination of the Jews hung over the entire pontificate of Pius XII. The pope's appeal to the faithful in April 1945 was a simple call for a general "pacification of souls," defining the "cruel . . . atrocities committed" and the war itself as "the fruit and wages of sin."[19]

The tendency was to speak in terms of general crimes against humanity, without ever using the word "Jews."[20] Consider, for example, this excerpt from the pages of *L'Osservatore Romano*:

> The reports obtained from various sources provide a moving picture of the general conditions of the masses of internees, men and women of every age, children on the verge of exhaustion. Especially poignant are those who still remain without a homeland, of whom there are quite a few. . . . Many others, because of the demoralization suffered in so many years of imprisonment, find it hard to make the effort to resume the state of mind and habits of civil and Christian society.[21]

Or consider this piece from *La Civiltà Cattolica*:

> Returning from the mission on behalf of the prisoners of war and internees in Germany, Monsignor Carol offered several reports on the work of Christian charity . . . to succor so many victims of the war. . . . The Pontifical Mission cares for everyone, without distinction of nationality or religious faith . . . 8,000 Poles, including 450 priests.[22]

In addition, on June 2, 1945, the pope, in his first sermon in Saint Peter's Square after the end of the war in Europe, continued to call only for Christian charity and forgiveness, using vehement language to condemn the "anti-Christianism" of the period. In his view, the main cause of the war was the Nazi anti-Christianism that had been unloosed in all its violence, especially against the Catholic Church. The evil of the war and its terrible consequences were reduced to the simple fact of having denied God:

> Truly the fight against the Church became more and more bitter: there was the destruction of the Catholic organizations; . . . there was the forced separation of young people from the family and from the Church: . . . there was the systematic denigration of the Church, of the clergy, of the faithful, of its institutions, of its doctrine, of its history.[23]

At the focus of the persecution were unspecified "political detainees," along with "the cohorts of those, both clergy and laity, whose only crime was loyalty to Christ and to the faith of the Fathers or the courageous fulfillment of their priestly duties."[24] According to the pope, the Church was denounced by Nazism as the enemy of the German people:

> The manifest injustice of the accusation would have wounded to the quick the feelings of the German Catholics, as well as Our own, if uttered by other lips; but on those of such accusers, far from being an indictment, they were the most shining and most honorable testimony of the Church's firm and constant opposition to such noxious doctrines and methods.[25]

The need to defend the Church's policy of silence, of discretion, of cautious and circumspect deploring of German Nazism, was not born after the end of the war. Already in 1944, the Vatican Information Office edited a volume, *La Chiesa e la guerra* (The Church and the war), based on a series of articles previously published in the magazine *Ecclesia*, brought out in September 1942 to illustrate the work of

Pius XII on behalf of war victims. The charges of collaboration with Nazi Germany originated, naturally and principally, with the Soviet Union, as did the allegations, made in March 1945, that the bishops of northern Italy had supported the Fascists and Nazis—which, according to *La Civiltà Cattolica*, ignored "the ever more serious persecution that the Catholic hierarchy had had to confront in the North, precisely because it had not denied its moral support to the many Catholic patriots who had opposed the invader."[26] In 1945, another text, *The Activity of the Holy See between December 15, 1943 and December 15, 1944*, was published. After a systematic chronology "of the work accomplished by the Holy Father" and a look at particular aspects "of the wonderful sermons that the Supreme Pontiff of the Church has not deprived the world of," it illustrated in a few lines the pope's present "great work . . . in the midst of the conflict, whether with the accents of his fatherly word or with his vast program of assistance," on behalf of the victims.[27]

Numerous articles in *La Civiltà Cattolica* documented the efforts by Pius XII to keep Italy out of the war.[28] Doubts, perplexity, and the wish that things had happened otherwise brought the Vatican to underline its frequent skirmishes with Nazi Germany; religious (anti-Christian) persecution in Germany and the other territories occupied by the Reich; the earlier diplomatic protest by Pius XI against violations of the Concordat; the condemnation of doctrinal racism; the tension with the regime (arising repeatedly, yet always contained by Pius XII at the level of diplomatic notes); and the assistance rendered by the clergy and the Vatican to victims of persecution. The Church tried to grant itself a "patent of nobility," as Giovanni Miccoli put it, a testimony of active opposition to Nazism. The desired image was that of a Church that had done what was possible, given the ferocity of the Nazis. Above all, it had to be shown that any other course of action by the Church would have produced even worse results.[29]

This stance remained in place during the Nuremberg trials, which began in November 1945. *L'Osservatore Romano* and *La Civiltà Cattolica* gave scant attention to the extermination of the Jews even after horrifying revelations emerged during the trial.[30] *La Civiltà Cattolica* spoke of matters pertaining to law, of the problems raised by the issue of "victors' justice":

> It is only too true that the war was hard and undoubtedly certain cruelties ought to have been prohibited, [and] every need to justify them must be barred. . . . Here, at any rate, there is a good measure of agreement for the future; but how can punishment be imposed for the violation of a law that did not yet exist when the act was committed? Consider the example of the atom bomb: which is more than rockets, reprisals, indiscriminate bombings! Yet no one thinks about punishing the airmen, the general staff, or the American industrialists. Why? Because even if the use of these execrable means of slaughter and destruction were to be banned today, the law would apply for tomorrow, not for yesterday. The same here, then.[31]

"Modern and total war" was the key to explaining the death and destruction caused by Germany—which, even if responsible on the political plane (having been the first to apply match to powder) was still, according to *La Civiltà Cattolica*, historically constrained.[32] Judicial disquisitions, diplomatic considerations, scientific discoveries, and historical relativity were all invoked:

The world has certainly been horrified by the multiple crimes perpetrated by the Nazi armies; but also of those committed by or alleged against the other side. In the modern age, people first spoke of crimes against humanity after the massacres, the political and religious persecutions, the reduction to slave labor that took place in one of the countries [namely, the Soviet Union] that is now sitting in judgment at Nuremberg. [But] even during the war, prisoners were mistreated by all sides. Famine has raged in Russia and Algeria—and not only famine.[33]

This remained the tone of the newspaper in its coverage of the Nuremberg trials: its consistent focus was on questions of international law.[34] Not even the discovery of the atrocities committed during the war was allowed to modify the balance of such judgments.

The postwar Church was clearly interested in a policy that gave space, weight, and influence to ecclesiastical discourse and therefore knowingly chose to conduct a dialogue with those groups in Europe willing to engage in a common anti-subversive, anti-socialist, and anti-communist effort. Internalization of the "lessons" of Fascism took only one form: a vigorous struggle to organize, to "close ranks, to create a more capable resistance to the de-Christianization of modern civilization," to penetrate once again to the social grass roots of society.[35] The future was represented by the Church, the sole repository of the true Christian spirit, whose political identity posited that what was good for the Church was good for the people, and vice versa. Political identity and religious identity thus became one and the same, and they were built, as Miccoli put it, on the notions of a "full temporal realization, that is, of a regime organized according to the precepts of Christian doctrine," according to which the Church had the dual role of providing supreme guidance in life while orienting the social order.[36] There was to be no pause for reflection about the past; only current affairs seemed to interest the Church. This attitude demanded a significant commitment of organizational and cultural resources.[37]

In fact, the postwar years saw the proliferation of Catholic social associations, to which the Church assigned a constant vigilance on the political front.[38] Thus, in those years there were frequent public appeals by Pius XII, sermons delivered and published in *Civiltà Cattolica* that addressed the entire Catholic laity, referred to as "the people of Rome, from the Christian associations of the young people of Catholic Action to those of the Christian laborers of both sexes."[39] In a speech to the Christian Workers' Association, Pius XII referred to

cells of the modern Christian apostolate, . . . who, in the world of labor, maintain, cultivate, and care for the religious and moral foundations of life against the enemies of Christ who exploit all the difficulties and questions of the workingman's life in order to win the soul of the Christian worker, to mislead his conscience, and ultimately to detach and distance him from the divine Savior. . . . Without those Christian virtues, the working class would become its own worst enemy. . . . In the struggle against this peril the Christian associations . . . will be the nursery of the social virtues, of righteousness, of faithfulness, of conscientiousness and will provide other institutions with their best members.[40]

Calls for political confidence and moderation were accompanied by an appeal to organize in order to confront destructive tendencies and mass movements in the political struggle of tomorrow:

Catholics must prepare and organize themselves in legally constituted groups in order to make themselves fit to participate in national government and life, so that their place will not be on the side of the anti-national and Bolshevik or anti-Catholic parties that will never truly realize the people's good, but only the interests of the party.[41]

In another instance, *La Civiltà Cattolica* posed the problem of postwar reconstruction in Europe as a pretext for denouncing the dictatorship and armed might of the Soviet Union, which shared responsibility for the war with Nazi Germany.[42]

The anti-communist campaign exerted a preponderant influence on the political and religious discourse of the Church: no relations could be permitted between Catholic forces and the anti-clerical parties.[43] On this point, Alcide de Gasperi, the leader of the Christian Democrats, in a note dated November 12, 1946, following a meeting with a senior Vatican official identified only by the letter "M" (probably Monsignor Montini, the future Pope Paul VI), wrote that the latter had told him, "evidently on orders from above," that "any collaboration whatsoever with the anti-clerical parties, not only by the commune [city council] of Rome but also by the government, would no longer be permissible." If the Christian Democrats persisted "in such collaborations" it would be considered a hostile party and would no longer enjoy the support or sympathy of the Church.[44] A stand had to be taken against the Communist threat:

From Roman soil the first Peter, surrounded by the threats of a perverted imperial power, launched his proud cry of alarm: to resist the mighty in faith. On this very same soil we repeat today with redoubled energy the cry to you, whose native city is now the scene of incessant efforts aimed at weakening the struggle among the opposing sides: either with Christ or against Christ; either for His Church or against His Church.[45]

The themes and antitheses of a crusade—the sons of light against the sons of darkness—linked back to a discourse begun in the late 1930s. Together they buried, for the moment, all memories of the war, including all those associated with the deportation and extermination of the Jews.

Conclusion

The attitude of the Church throughout the pontificate of Pius XII was, above all, political and pragmatic rather than theological. Beginning in 1958, the papacy of John XXIII marked a new phase in the relations between the Church and the Italian state: the integralism of Pius XII was replaced by a different notion of the Church, tied more to its pastoral and spiritual role than to its anti-communist political vocation. The changes introduced by John's pontificate and Vatican II; the shattering, in the 1960s, of the unity of attitude and execution within the institutional Church; the juxtaposition of diverse conceptions and processes in the relations between the hierarchy and laity, all made it possible for older, historically entrenched ideas and practices to diminish. Even if they were not totally abandoned, they were nevertheless redefined, debated, refuted, and combated.[46]

Any assessment of the positions taken by the Church and its postwar silence about the destruction of European Jewry must take into account the doctrinal and ideological tradition built and founded, since the French Revolution, on the conflict between Church and modernity—a tradition that sought to juxtapose the ecclesiastical institution with human history, and which understood history as an arena of combat against absolute alienation from truth, the rejection of Christian values, and the triumph of the non-Christian and anti-Christian cultures.[47] At the end of the Second World War, as Miccoli points out very clearly, thinking within the Church was still dominated by the apologetic historical syntheses of the 19th century, in which the sequence leading from Enlightenment, Reform, and Freemasonry to the French Revolution, liberalism, and socialism described stages in the progressive estrangement of society from the teachings of Christ. All cultures and ideologies were classified according to the Christian versus anti-Christian or non-Christian scheme, in a vision of humanity's moving away from the paths marked out by the Church. In this conceptual system, as Miccoli argues, two ancient theologies of history, restated in politicized terms, were readily identified as mutually exclusive. Church and synagogue, city of God and city of Satan—these seemed to be the only true protagonists of a combat that had history for its theater, and in which all men were called upon to rally to one side or the other.[48] Thus, "Bolshevik Communism" became merely another item to add to the charges leveled against international Judaism.[49] Even if the Church was critical of genocidal Nazi antisemitism (perceived as anti-Christian in spirit and form), it was still prepared to maintain that the prime cause of antagonism toward Jews lay in their own behavior, in their intolerable and unjustified political, economic, and cultural domination. Moreover, the Holy See refused to view its own hostility as racist, since it objected not to Jewish "blood" but rather to the Jews' theological error.[50]

The silence of the Church did not apply specifically and exclusively to the Jews. It had a more general character and can be related to the entire problem of the violence and killing committed by the Fascists and Nazis during the war. This lack of comment (or, perhaps, comprehension) was associated, furthermore, with a conception of the world and not merely with an "intentional" devaluing of the Shoah, relativized within the great sea of calamities associated with the war. This attitude held constant in the reconstructions of memory immediately after the war and gained strength during the Cold War.

Qualifying the persecutions, deportations, and extermination of the Jews only in general and global terms, as, for instance, "vicissitudes of terrestrial conflicts, . . . political contrasts," was also a way to fathom the foreignness of the world. All the events of those years were collectively bound up with the historical sins of an anti-Christian or non-Christian humankind, for which the Church was not responsible—thereby laying aside the specific atrocities of the racial legislation, of the racial and political persecution, and of the extermination of the Jews. Assistance to the Jews during the war took place in the context of solitary acts of "individual charity" that, given the enormity of the catastrophe, were marginal, incomplete, and impotent. Such acts were never transformed into a strong and clear "political charity," into a prophetic effort in history, an unmitigated defense not of individual rights but of the rights of all human beings.[51] This, I suggest, is what lay behind the silence that persisted, as well, after the war.

Notes

1. I refer here specifically to the Jesuit publication *La Civiltà Cattolica* (hereafter: *CC*), of 1937–1939 and to *L'Osservatore Romano* of 1938–1939.

2. On the problematic relationship between the Church and European society after the war, see the following important studies: Giovanni Miccoli, *Fra mito della cristianità e secolarizzazione: sul rapporto chiesa-società nell'età contemporanea* (Casale Monferrato: 1985); idem, "Santa Sede questione ebraica e antisemitismo fra Otto e Novecento," in *Storia d'Italia*, vol. 2, *Gli ebrei in Italia*, ed. Corrado Vivanti (Turin: 1997), 1371–1574; Michael Phayer, *The Catholic Church and the Holocaust, 1930–1965* (Bloomington: 2000); Giovanni Miccoli, Guido Neppi Modona, and Paolo Pombeni (eds.), *La grande cesura: la memoria della guerra e della resistenza nella vita europea del dopoguerra* (Bologna: 2001); Renato Moro, *La Chiesa e lo sterminio degli ebrei* (Bologna: 2002); Susan Zuccotti, "L'Osservatore Romano and the Holocaust 1939–1945," *Holocaust and Genocide Studies* 17, no. 2 (2003), 249–277.

3. Corporative political postures historically valorized precapitalist, premodern social and economic values: the mutual duties and standards of equity of the (idealized) past were compared with the pernicious values of capitalist accumulation and profit-taking, on the one hand, and destructive class-conflict theories of social revolution, on the other.

4. For example, in *L'Unità*, the organ of the Italian Communist party, a detailed account of the "extermination camp near Lublin" appeared on December 8, 1945. In this article, Majdanek was referred to as "the largest slaughterhouse in the world" and a "death camp for the Jews." Many other articles appeared on this subject over the next few weeks, usually featured on the front page; see *L'Unità* for the following dates: 16–21 Jan. 1945; 23 Jan. 1945; 25–28 Jan. 1945; 1 Feb. 1945; and 3 Feb. 1945.

Articles also appeared in the organ of the Socialist party, *L'Avanti*—see, for example, the issue of 20 April 1945. A Roman daily, *Il Giornale del Mattino*, published an article on the liberation of Bergen-Belsen on April 19. See also the articles by Paolo Alatri on the camps of Ohrdruf, Buchenwald, Bergen-Belsen, and Nordhausen (*Il Messagero* [13 May 1945]).

The experiences of Leone Fiorentino, the first Roman Jew to return from the hell of Auschwitz, also received great play in the Italian press (for particulars of his life, see Liliana Picciotto Fargion, *Il libro della memoria: gli ebrei deportati dall'Italia (1943–1945)* [Milan: 1991], 273). *Israel* printed a long interview with him (31 May 1945), and both *L'Italia libera* (29 May 1945) and *L'Unità* (30 May 1945) published his testimony on the front page.

Even *Il Corriere della sera* and *La Stampa*, which had been affiliated with the Fascist regime, confronted the terrible reality of the concentration camps in the late summer of 1945. The former, which had maintained its name and typographic appearance even under Fascism, suspended publication between the end of April and the end of May 1945, and then reappeared as *Il Corriere di Informazione*. (*La Stampa* suspended publication on April 25, 1945, and resumed publication in the middle of July 1945).

All of these papers made use of the reports published by the foreign press and news agencies, especially English-language agencies such as the International News Service and United Press of London.

5. "The war declared on the Jews by Hitler and his followers, outside and inside the borders of Germany, is not in fact merely a struggle of armed men against the defenseless, . . . [but also] an enormous machine guided by a madman and intent on crushing without mercy men and women, old people and infants, to achieve the goal of total annihilation and total despoiling" (*Israel* [7 Dec. 1944], 1).

6. Carlo A. Viterbo, *Israel* (8 March 1945), 1. Two significant articles appeared that same day: the first, a list of the Jews deported from Rome; the second, a review, also signed by Viterbo, of the anonymous 16-page pamphlet, *Nove mesi di martirio: la tragedia degli ebrei sotto il terrore tedesco,* which documented the persecution of the Jews of Rome. The lead item was a piece commemorating a massacre that had taken place on August 1, 1944. On this day, the Nazis had murdered Giuseppe Pardo Roques—the deputy mayor of Pisa,

who was also a prestigious Jewish philanthropist and the president of the local Jewish community—along with 11 others, six of them Jews.

Israel also published two reports produced by the Deportee Search Committee, which
was established at the end of 1944 to document the deportation of the Jews from Italy. Its
report on the Fossoli di Carpi transit camp appeared on March 26, 1945; a description of
the Auschwitz death camp was featured in the paper on April 12, 1945. Five days later, on
April 19, the paper published the first reports on the arrival of Jews in Stockholm, survivors
of Bergen-Belsen (transcribed as "Berghen Blasen") and Birkenau ("Bircaneau"). These
appeared on p. 2 of the newspaper, the front page being devoted to an announcement placed
by the Deportee Search Committee concerning the arrival in Bucharest of other Jewish
survivors of Oświęcim (spelled "Oszviencim").

On May 1, 1945, the committee received information about other survivors provided by
the foreign ministry (via the Italian embassy in Moscow). See Dante Lattes, "Dobbiamo
ancora avere fiducia negli uomini," Israel (3 and 10 May 1945).

7. Israel (10 May 1945).

8. Eleven such books were published in 1945, 14 in 1946, and three in 1947; two essays
by Giacomo Debenedetti, titled "16 ottobre" and "Otto ebrei" (the former written and published in November, the latter in September 1945) should also be noted. See Manuela Consonni, "Memory and History: War, Resistance, and Shoah in Italy 1945–1985" (Ph.D. diss.,
The Hebrew University, 2002), ch. 1, "The Open Years: 1945–1947," 25–55; Anna Bravo
and Federico Jalla, Una misura onesta: gli scritti di memoria dell a deportazione dall'Italia
1944–1993 (Milan: 1993).

9. Paolo Liggeri, Triangolo Rosso: dalle carceri di S. Vittore ai campi di concentarmento
e di eliminazione di Fossoli, Bolzano, Mauthausen, Gusen, Dachau (Milan: 1946). The
review appeared in CC 97 (21 Sept. 1946), 429–430.

10. It is only in the review of a book by Benedetto Laddei, Gli ebrei nella realtà e fuori
della reltà: ricerca e proposta di una soluzione integrale attuale del problema dei pochi tra
i molti (Rome: 1946), that Jews are mentioned, but even here the reference is to antisemitism
rather than extermination. The review appeared in CC on October 19, 1945.

11. After the attack on Poland, both the Allies and the neutral press quickly began denouncing the atrocities committed by the Nazis, especially the persecution of the Jews and
the ever more systematic massacres that characterized it. Papal nuncios, German bishops,
and the bishops and clergy of countries occupied by Germany represented another source
of information. Though one might perhaps question the numbers and be unaware of the
details, the catastrophic result of the anti-Jewish campaign could not be ignored. Alongside
material transmitted by the Allies and international Jewish organizations, as early as Oct. 7,
1942, a report by Don Pirro Scavizzi added new and detailed information about the situation
in Poland, which supplemented his report of May:

> The elimination of the Jews, with the murder of almost the entire population, with no
> regard for children, not even nursing infants. . . . Before being deported or murdered
> they are condemned to forced heavy labor. . . . It is said that more than two million
> Jews have been killed. . . . Poles are being allowed to move into houses in the ghetto,
> which is depopulated day by day by means of the systematic massacre of Jews (Actes
> et documents du Saint Siège relatifs à la seconde guerre mondiale [11 volumes of
> archival material published by the Vatican between 1965 and 1981], 8:669; quoted in
> Miccoli, Fra mito della cristianità e secolarizzazione, 138).

12. This attitude was linked to the theoretical, doctrinal, and political apparatus that originated during the papacy of Leo XIII (1878–1903), whose traditions were simply carried on
by Pius XII. One example of this is the Christmas radio broadcast of 1945, in which Pius
XII cited Leo XIII's 1888 encyclical Libertas. After a brief reference to the horrors and
tragedies of the war, the pope proceeded to address political problems and the question of
democracy: "It is scarcely necessary to record that according to the teachings of the
Church,'it is not of itself wrong to prefer a democratic form of government, if only the

Catholic doctrine be maintained as to the origin and exercise of power' and that 'of the various forms of government, the Church does not reject any that are fitted to procure the welfare of the subject' " ("Christmas Radio Broadcast to the People of the Entire World on the Sixth Christmas of the War," *CC* 96 [6 Jan. 1945], 4 [English of passage from Leo XIII, *Libertas* (20 June 1888), §44, online at www.vatican.va/holy_father/leo_xiii/encyclicals/documents/hf_l-xiii_enc_20061888_libertas_en.html]).

13. Giovanni Miccoli, "La Chiesa e il fascismo," in idem, *Fra mito della cristianità e secolarizzazione*, 11–13; Pietro Scoppola, "La Chiesa e il fascismo durante il pontificato di Pio XI," in idem, *Coscienza religiosa e democrazia nell'Italia contemporanea* (Bologna: 1966), 300–320; idem, *La Chiesa e il fascismo: documenti e testimonianze* (Bari: 1971), 352.

14. The Church had always subscribed to the idea of special legislation regarding the Jews, considering it a step forward as compared with the legal equality of the liberal era, a stage toward the abolition of the chaos created by a false and dangerous notion of liberty and equality. Whereas in past centuries the principles and traditions of the Church had been promoted by a legal situation in which the Jews were not treated like other citizens, in the modern era, Judaism was viewed as one of the major authors of the secular, liberal, and revolutionary ideology that was responsible for society's current disasters. *Actes et documents du Saint Siège relatifs à la seconde guerre mondiale*, 9:459, quoted in Miccoli, *Fra mito della cristianità e secolarizzazione*, 330.

15. Aversion to modernity also characterized the link between the Church and Fascism. Saul Friedländer has underlined the anti-modern aspect of Fascism, noting that it was "the result of the crisis of a society that was passing from a traditional framework to that of industrialism, a rebellion designed to deliberately create an archaic utopia" (Friedländer, *Reflections of Nazism: An Essay on Kitsch and Death*, trans. from the French by Thomas Weyr [New York: 1984], 4).

16. "Christmas Radio Broadcast to the People of the Entire World on the Sixth Christmas of the War," 6.

17. In *Divini Redemptoris*, issued on March 11, 1937, Pope Pius XI reaffirmed the social and religious doctrine of the Church and restated the absolute incompatibility of the Christian worldview with the "Communist plague":

It is conceded that, if the only possible choice was between atheistic international Communism, on the one hand, and pagan National Socialism, on the other; or between Bolshevism and Fascism, as they are called, the conclusion of every reasonable man could not be in doubt. Because the lesser evil, even if it cannot be approved positively, is, notwithstanding, always to be tolerated in preference to the worse evil, being, in this respect or particular consideration, as St. Thomas says, something good: *aliquid boni* ("L'Eco alla lettera collettiva dei vescovi spagnoli," *CC* 58 [1937], 290).

It is well known that the Church had been afraid to weaken Germany in the latter's fight against Soviet Russia. See Saul Friedländer, *Pius XII and the Third Reich: A Documentation*, trans. from the French and German by Charles Fullman (New York: 1966), 163 and 166; see also the problematic study by Daniel J. Goldhagen, *A Moral Reckoning: The Role of the Catholic Church in the Holocaust and Its Unfulfilled Duty of Repair* (New York: 2002).

18. Renato Moro, "Il peso di una mentalità," in *La Chiesa e lo sterminio degli ebrei*, 196.

19. "Allocuzione al popolo di Roma," *CC* 96 (7 April 1945), 7–9.

20. Moro, "Il peso di una mentalità," in *La Chiesa e lo sterminio degli ebrei*, 200.

21. *L'Osservatore Romano* (29 June 1945).

22. "Cronaca Contemporanea: Missione caritativa pontificia in Germania," *CC* 96 (7 July 1945), 126.

23. "Allocuzione del Santo Padre al Sacro Collegio," *CC* 96 (16 June 1945), 370–371.

24. Ibid., 373. The article went on to provide a detailed list of the Polish priests imprisoned in Dachau between 1940 and 1945, including "the auxiliary bishop of Wladyslawa,"

who died there of typhus. This particular item was an error, as there is no town in Poland by the name of Wladyslawa. According to *The New Catholic Encyclopedia* (New York: 1967), 11:481–483, "13 Polish bishops were exiled or arrested and put in concentration camps. Of these the following died: Auxiliary Bishop Leon Wetmański of Płock on May 10, 1941, and Archbishop Antoni Nowowiejski of Płock on June 20, 1941, in Soldau (Działdowo); Auxiliary Bishop Michał Kozal of Włocławek on Jan. 26, 1943, in Dachau; Auxiliary Bishop Władysław Goral of Lublin at the beginning of 1945 in a hospital bunker in Berlin."

25. Ibid., 374.

26. *L'Osservatore Romano* (16 Feb. 1945); "Cronaca Contemporanea," *CC* 96 (17 Mar. 1945), 387.

27. *L'attività della S. Sede dal 15 dicembre 1943 al 15 dicembre 1945* (Rome: 1945); *CC* 96 (16 June 1945), 432. In this context, see also the soulful tribute of the grateful Romans to the Supreme Pontiff, as described in another book published in 1946: Leone Gessi, *Roma, la guerra, il Papa* (Rome: 1945).

28. See *CC* 96 for the following dates: 5 May; 2 and 16 June; 7 and 21 July; 4 Aug.; 1 and 15 Sept.; 20 Oct.; 1 and 15 Dec. 1945.

29. Miccoli, *Fra mito della cristianità e secolarizzazione*, 133.

30. *L'Osservatore Romano* (1945); *CC* 96 (1945). See also *CC* 97 for the following dates: 2 Mar. (pp. 332–342); 4 May (pp. 186–197); 15 June (pp. 404–416); 6 July (pp. 358–364); 20 July (pp. 92–106); 3 Aug. (pp. 213–214); 17 Aug. (pp. 295–296). See also Moro, "Il peso di una mentalità," 195–208.

31. S. Lener, S.J., "Del mancato giudizio del Kaiser al processo di Norimberga," *CC* 97 (2 March 1946), 335.

32. Ibid.

33. S. Lener, S.J., "Diritto e politica nel processo di Norimberga," *CC* 97 (19 Oct. 1946), 101.

34. S. Lener, S.J., "Delitti contro l'umanità," *CC* 97 (19 Jan. 1946), 186–197; "Le supreme barriere del diritto e i delitti contro l'umanità," ibid. (21 Dec. 1946), 404–416.

35. Miccoli, "La Chiesa e il fascismo," 113.

36. Giovanni Miccoli, "Cattolici e comunisti nel secondo dopoguerra: memoria storica, ideologia e lotta politica," in Miccoli et al., *La grande cesura*, 39–40; Paolo Blasina, "Resistenza, guerra, fascismo nel cattolicesimo italiano (1943–1948)," in ibid., 123–193.

37. Even the philosopher Benedetto Croce, in a letter to *The Times* published in *Il Risorgimento Liberale,* affirmed that in order to establish a durable peace it was necessary

to always keep in mind that only spiritual assets are effective and lasting, and that if so many empires and so many political hegemonies have succeeded one another in history, Christianity has not fallen and will not fall, a perpetual font of redemption and of renewal, and the modern world needs above all an enthusiastic rekindling in a moral state, of a Christian spiritual reawakening" (*Il Risorgimento Liberale* [7 April 1945]).

38. Scoppola, "La chiesa e il fascismo, durante il ponificato di Pio XI," 370.

39. "Allocuzione del S. S. Pio XII ai giovani romani di Azione Cattolica sull'incolumità dell'Urbe," *CC* 96 (7 July 1945); "Allocuzione del S. Padre alle lavoratrici cristiane," ibid. (1 Sept. 1945), 265–268; "Allocuzione di Pio XII alle associazioni cristiane dei lavoratori italiani," ibid. (7 April 1945). The speeches and the appeals continued in 1946 and throughout 1947. See *CC* 97 (1946) and 98 (1947).

40. "Allocuzione di Pio XII alle associazioni cristiane dei lavoratori italiani," 3–6. In this speech, too, Pius XII relied on ecclesiastical tradition, referring to the encyclical *Quadragesimo Anno* of Pius XI, which itself mentioned the "immortal" encyclical *Rerum Novarum* of Leo XIII.

41. Luigi Ganapini, *I cattolici nella crisi del 1943,* 50, quoted in Miccoli, *Fra mito della cristianità e secolarizzazione,* 380.

42. According to an article published in *CC*:

In the summer of 1939, the situation would have become so complex as to drive Poland into war, had Germany not concluded the celebrated friendship pact with Soviet Russia that was so highly praised by the totalitarian press. This accord gave Hitler and the German high command the necessary guarantee that it would not have to fight simultaneously on two fronts, so that, with Poland beaten in a few weeks, it could then turn to the West with its back covered by Russian neutrality (A. Messineo, "Le incognite della ricostruzione europea," *CC* 96 [7 July 1945], 6).

See also idem, "L'aspetto morale dei piani economici," ibid. (7 April 1945), 10. At the same time, as Palmiro Togliatti noted in April 1945, the Italian political scene was absolutely anti-revolutionary, being "a country that because of the fusion of more advanced elements of financial capitalism with feudal vestiges" still had "profoundly reactionary characteristics" (Togliatti, *Politica comunista: discorsi e documenti, aprile 1944–agosto 1945* [Rome: 1945], 282). See also Luigi Salvatorelli, "La Chiesa e il Fascismo," *Il Ponte* 6 (1950), 594–605.

43. On the anti-Communist campaign, see *CC* and *L'Osservatore Romano* of 1945–1947. More specifically, see "Allocuzione natalizia del S.S. Pio XII al S. Collegio sui problemi della pace," *CC* 98 (4 Jan. 1947), 3–12.

44. Pietro Scoppola, "De Gasperi e la svolta politica del May 1947," *Il Mulino* 23 (1974), 40; idem, "La crisi della collaborazione con i 'social-comunisti,' " in his *La proposta politica di De Gasperi* (Bologna: 1977), 310. See also Paul Ginzborg, *Storia del dopoguerra a oggi: Società e Politica 1943–1988* (Turin: 1989). An editorial signed by Father Lombardi, a confidant of Pius XII, expressed satisfaction with the results of the elections on June 2, according to which

Italy had retrieved "its soul," thanks to the presence of the Christian Democracy, which had protected the rights of the Church, and the Lateran Pacts [the Concordat of 1929], placing the accent on reconciliation between Fascists and anti-Fascists, on overcoming the past and partisan hatreds. This last had a clear objective: a union of all the "good" and all the "honorable" [forces in society] to confront Marxist materialism and Communism (R. Lombardi. S.J., "Il materialismo dialettico, filosofia dei comunisti," *CC* 97 [15 June 1946], 105–112).

See also: "Il materialismo storico," ibid., 261–270; "La storia dell'umanità secondo il materialismo storico," *CC* 97 (5 Jan. 1946), 24–34; "Il programma politico comunista," ibid. (16 Nov. 1946), 276–284; ibid. (2 March 1946), 347–358; "Discussione del programma comunista," ibid. (3 Aug. 1946), 162–173; "Discussione del materialismo dialettico," ibid. (19 Jan. 1946), 263–276; ibid. (21 Sept. 1946), 420–429; "L'ora presente e l'Italia," *CC* 98 (4 Jan. 1947), 13–20. Lombardi's articles and public interviews are quite important because of his close ties with Pius XII.

45. Pius XII, Christmas goodwill message delivered in St. Peter's Square, 22 Dec. 1946, recorded in *Il Popolo* (23 Dec. 1946), 1.

46. In July 1963, Pope John XXIII issued his last and most important encyclical, *Pacem in Terris*, a call for international reconciliation and the refusal to accept the frontiers erected by the Cold War. The spirit of this message was contrary to the calls by Pius XII for a holy war to defend the Christian West against the atheistic and Communist East. The encyclical was addressed to "all men of good will," not only to Catholics, and underlined the need for cooperation among persons of different religious and ideological creeds. What is more, it expressed the hope for an improvement in economic conditions and social development for the working classes, favored the entrance of women into public life, and demonstrated significant understanding of the anticolonial struggles in the Third World.

47. Moro, "Il peso di una mentalità," 205.

48. Miccoli, "La Chiesa e il fascismo," 131–137.

49. Renzo De Felice, *Storia degli ebrei italiani sotto il fascismo* (Turin: 1961), 39–41.

50. Giovanni Miccoli, "La Chiesa nella II guerra mondiale," in *Fra mito della cristianità e secolarizzazione,* 284. Miccoli describes how, in March 1928, the Holy Office dissolved

the Friends of Israel, a group of mainly Dutch and Italian Catholics (including several bishops and cardinals) that had proposed reviewing the relationship between Christians and Jews in an attempt to combat antisemitism. With this in mind, the Holy Office included in its decree of dissolution an explicit condemnation of antisemitism—the only such condemnation to be found in official documents of the Roman college before the end of the Second World War. It stated:

> The Catholic Church has always been accustomed to pray for the Jewish people, the trustee, until the coming of Jesus Christ, of the divine promise, despite its later blindness concerning this very matter. Moved by this spirit of charity, the Apostolic See protected that same people against unjust oppression and, just as it censures all hatreds and animosity among peoples, it utterly condemns hatred of a people once elected by God, the hatred that today is vulgarly given the name of "antisemitism" (decree dated 25 March 1928, in *Acta Apostolicae Sedis* [2 April 1928], 103 f.).

The Italian text of this decree appeared in *CC* 79 (1928), 2:171f. However, it did not lead to any real improvement in the image of the Jews that was held by Christians.

51. Moro, "Il peso di una mentalità," 205.

Catholicism and the Jews in Post-Communist Poland

Joanna Michlic
RICHARD STOCKTON COLLEGE OF NEW JERSEY

Antony Polonsky
BRANDEIS UNIVERSITY

Roman Catholicism has long been a central element of Polish national identity. This phenomenon is deeply rooted in the Polish historical experience and is closely linked with the country's collective identity. As a result, in Polish Catholicism, national ideals have become intertwined with Christian values and national identity has often taken precedence over universal principles. This has led to the widespread identification of Polishness with Catholicism, as summed up in the phrase *Polak katolik*. The dominant model of religiosity has been conservative, traditional, and "folkish," with relatively little stress on the spiritual and intellectual development of faith.[1] In the eyes of its leaders, Polish Catholicism was the most effective bulwark of Polishness against both the 19th-century partitioning powers and the 20th-century totalitarian forces of Nazism and Soviet Communism.

Political groups such as the National Democrats (Endecja), the principal exponents in Poland of ethno-nationalism and antisemitism, attempted from the end of the 19th century to exploit the identification of Polishness with Catholicism. However, in interwar Poland, political Catholicism was unable to attain a hegemonic position in political life. Especially after the seizure of power in May 1926 by the charismatic military hero Józef Piłsudski, political forces advancing a Catholic agenda, whether of a Christian Democratic or of a National Democratic character, were marginalized. The relations between the Church and the authorities were correct but hardly cordial, and a significant portion of the Episcopate, or Church hierarchy—though not the primate, Cardinal August Hlond (appointed in June 1926)—retained its sympathy for the National Democrats. Among parish priests, too, support for the Endecja was widespread.[2]

With regard to the Jews, the position of the Church was typical of pre-Second Vatican Council Catholicism. Hlond articulated this position in a pastoral letter of 1936:

The Jewish problem is there and will be there as long as Jews remain Jews. . . . It is a fact that Jews are in opposition to the Catholic Church, that they are freethinkers, the vanguard of godlessness, Bolshevism, and subversion. It is a fact that they exert a pernicious influence on public morality and that their publishing houses are spreading pornography. It is true that Jews are swindlers, usurers, and that they are engaged in fostering immoral earnings. It is true that the effect of the Jewish youth upon the Catholic is—in the religious and ethical sense—negative. This does not apply to all Jews. There are very many Jews who are believers, honest, righteous, merciful, doing good works. The family life of many Jews is healthy and edifying. And there are among Jews [individuals who are] morally quite outstanding, noble and honorable people.[3]

This was the mainstream position, with its classic statement of anti-Judaism coupled with its grudging concession that not all Jews could be held responsible for the negative behavior of the majority. There was also within the Church a more strongly antisemitic element that espoused essentially racist positions derived from populism and nationalism, which were best represented by the periodical *Rycerz Niepokolanej* and the daily *Mały Dziennik*. Since Catholic papers accounted for nearly a quarter of the entire Polish press and the Church had great influence on the minds of the population, particularly on the peasantry, it must be seen as one of the major forces behind the spread of antisemitism in interwar Poland.[4] In contrast, those circles within the Church that espoused progressive and humanistic attitudes, such as the center at Laski near Warsaw, which published the periodical *Verbum,* and the Association of Catholic University Students (Odrodzenie) in Lublin were inevitably small, isolated, and not influential. Moreover, although the Odrodzenie opposed and condemned the antisemitic violence of the Endecja, it was not always free of anti-Jewish prejudice.[5]

During the Second World War, the Church was savagely persecuted by both the Soviets and the Nazis. Monasteries and convents were closed, many members of the clergy were imprisoned, and as many as 20 percent of their number were murdered. Under such circumstances, the Church emerged from the war with its moral authority greatly strengthened.

Given its views and the harassment to which it was subjected, it is not surprising that the Church as an institution did not provide much support for Jews under the Nazi occupation. The only initiative it adopted in the first years of Nazi rule seems to have been intervention on behalf of converts. (This intervention was not always efficacious: a list of converts was handed to the Gestapo so that the converts could be exempted from wearing the identifying Star of David. When the Warsaw ghetto was established, the Gestapo made use of the list to ensure that all those on it were confined within the ghetto walls.) Throughout the implementation of the genocide, the Catholic hierarchy in Poland made no public statement on the fate of the Jews.[6] However, other Catholic groups, both political and social, did express opposition. As a rule, they condemned the Nazi extermination of the Jews as a barbaric, anti-Christian act and sympathized with the Jewish tragedy in generally human terms. Some members of these organizations, especially those belonging to the Front for the Rebirth of Poland, were also involved in rescue activities. At the same time, when discussing pre-1939 Polish society and the postwar future of Poland, they continued to refer to the Jews as opponents of Poland and of Catholicism. Such statements, whether mildly worded or more harsh in tone, could also be found in the various publications of the Labor Party and the Christian Democratic Labor Party.[7]

One area in which many individual priests and nuns were active was the rescue and placement of Jews in convents. In all, two thirds of the female religious communities in Poland took part in hiding Jewish children and adults. The fact that this took place on a large scale may suggest that it had the support and encouragement of the Church hierarchy.[8] It may also suggest that the ethos of providing aid to the most needy was a fundamental Catholic principle, regardless of the ideological position and political sympathies held by the individual or the hierarchy.

The transition to the postwar situation was fraught with its own set of issues. The Church's initial reaction to the establishment of Communist rule was hesitant and even confused.[9] Given the exhaustion of Polish society after 1945, it sought to avoid outright conflict with the new rulers of the country, aware that certain Communist reforms, including land reform, nationalization of industry, banks and commerce, and the annexation of the formerly German western and northern territories, were popular. Indeed, this period of accelerated social and economic change was difficult for the Church, with Polish society becoming increasingly secularized and many upwardly mobile peasants and workers appearing to leave the fold. At the same time, the Church succeeded in retaining much of its traditional influence, which it was able to employ in helping to stabilize the regime of Władysław Gomułka after 1956 and in performing a similar role for Edward Gierek after 1970. This strategy, the brainchild of Poland's extremely astute primate, Cardinal Stefan Wyszyński, preserved for the Church a central role in Polish public life:

> The Church . . . was transformed from a victim into a mediator, and thus became an actor in the politico-historical processes, a co-creator of change in society, its consciousness and its bonds with prewar Poland. As circumstances developed, by continuing this role of mediator it became ever more and more the partner of the authorities.[10]

The Church retained its influence by relying on its traditional base. It did not favor new initiatives such as rethinking its position on controversial topics, including its attitude toward the Jews. Moreover, it soon became clear that the war had neither brought an end to antisemitism nor seriously compromised the Church's anti-Judaic ideology. Since the Nazis had persecuted the Polish radical Right as fiercely as they did all other manifestations of Polish resistance, the Church's anti-Judaic tradition was not tainted by "Germanism" and emerged almost unscathed from the war. After the worst outbreak of anti-Jewish violence in postwar Poland— the pogrom in Kielce in July 1946, in which 42 Jews were killed by a mob—a Jewish delegation went to see Wyszyński, then bishop of Lublin. After asserting that popular hatred had been kindled by Jewish support for Communism, which had also been the reason why "the Germans murdered the Jewish nation," Wyszyński went on to comment that the question of the use of Christian blood by Jews had never been completely clarified, thus lending a kind of credence to the ritual murder rumors that had accompanied the pogrom.[11]

As is clear from Wyszyński's remarks, the war also strengthened the association of Jews with Communism in the eyes of Church dignitaries.[12] It is true that, in

1967, Wyszyński prayed publicly for the safety of Israel and protested against the anti-student campaign (with its strong anti-Jewish themes and aims) that had been orchestrated by Mieczysław Moczar, the leader of the nationalistic faction in the Communist party. But in general, the Church in Poland was little affected by the major efforts made by the Vatican during the pontificates of Pope John XXIII and of Pope Paul VI to transform its relations with Jews and Judaism.[13] The Polish Church's failure to implement the principles of Vatican II was an outcome of a deliberate policy pursued by Wyszyński. Although he had been a member of the pre-1939 Association of Catholic University Students, Wyszyński was not primarily interested in pursuing internal Church reforms, in developing a more progressive Church, or in adopting new approaches to individualistic and intellectual forms of religiosity. Instead, he concentrated his efforts on the preservation of the Church as an autonomous institution within the Communist system. Thanks to this strategy, the Polish Church succeeded in maintaining both its moral authority in society and its position as Poland's key national institution. However, a certain tension developed between Wyszyński and members of the group of progressive Catholic intelligentsia associated with the weekly *Tygodnik Powszechny*, who were much more open to the reforms introduced by the Vatican in the 1960s.[14]

With the growth of anti-communist opposition in the late 1970s, the Church's influence increased. As Gierek's promises of economic well-being proved empty and the government's popularity fell, the tide of secularization began to recede. The Church offered an ideology that was philosophically and morally richer, broader, and also more profound, being rooted both in the national traditions of Poland and in the culture of the West. Thus, religious observance and loyalty to the Church became increasingly widespread, not only in the traditionally Catholic countryside but also among the bulk of urban workers. Yet this was not only the result of disillusionment with the materialism fostered by the Gierek regime; it also reflected a more deep-seated rejection of Communism, precisely among those people who were expected to be its strongest supporters. Wyszyński's strategy bore fruit, and the Church became an important element in the growing opposition to the regime.[15]

The position of the Church was greatly strengthened by the election to the papal throne of Cardinal Karol Wojtyła in October 1978. This event had an electrifying effect on Poles. They had long thought of themselves as the stepchildren of Europe, the exponents of Western beliefs and values in a difficult geographic situation, who had been let down in 1939 and abandoned by the West in 1944–1945. That one of the principal institutions of the Western world (for many Poles, *the* principal institution) had elected a Pole as its first non-Italian head in nearly 450 years seemed an unprecedented act of reparation and a clear legitimation of the Poles' own view of their historical role. National self-confidence increased dramatically, as did the belief that major political change was now inevitable. In the summer of 1979, Pope John Paul II visited his homeland and was met with almost hysterical rejoicing. More than 1.5 million people attended an open-air mass at the national shrine, the Jasna Góra monastery in Częstochowa. For the two weeks of the pope's visit, it was as if the Communist authorities had ceased to exist. A submerged Poland—

Catholic, national, and self-assertive—demonstrated that it had the support of the overwhelming majority of the nation.

This was one of the principal factors in the emergence in 1980 of the first Solidarity movement, which mounted what became the most serious challenge to Communist rule since its establishment. Compromise between the popular movement and the weak and discredited government proved impossible, and martial law was imposed in December 1981. During the period of repression, the Church attempted to mediate between the government and the underground opposition, playing a key role in facilitating the round-table talks that brought about the negotiated end of the Communist regime in 1989. The Church's role as a powerful force behind both the anti-communist political opposition and the downfall of Communism itself was unquestionable. A new alliance emerged between the Church and the left-wing secular intelligentsia, including Solidarity leaders of Jewish origin such as Adam Michnik and Jan Lityński.[16] The religious revival and the new religious interest of the intelligentsia was noted in Church circles. Cardinal Józef Glemp, Wyszyński's successor as primate, has described this process in a characteristic way:

> Before the Second World War, the intelligentsia adopted mostly an unfavorable, indifferent, or opportunistic stance. There were also in that group some who sympathized with Communism.
>
> After the war the new generation of intelligentsia surrendered relatively easily to Marxist ideology. They joined the party without playing a leading part. The disappointment came only later. Many then protested against the methods of the system. Later the adherents of the Marxist ideology joined Solidarity. Others preferred to stay apart and simply turned in their party cards. Embittered, they regarded their life, or at least a considerable part of it, as wasted. This applied, above all, to the creative intelligentsia who did not know the Church or knew it simply from folk traditions. Against that background, there appeared a new attitude on the part of the intelligentsia toward the Church. This was expressed in respect for its deeper spiritual life and for its role in maintaining patriotic attitudes.[17]

The "Closed" versus the "Open" Church

After 1989, with Poland now a democratic republic, the divisions within the Church, formerly masked by the need to preserve unity in the face of the Communist authorities, came into the open. These differences were also reflected in the clearly antithetical positions taken on such issues as antisemitism and conducting dialogue with Jews and with Judaism. In 1985, Tadeusz Mazowiecki, then a leading figure of both the Solidarity movement and the Catholic progressive intelligentsia (and later, prime minister), presciently raised a number of problems that he felt the Church would soon have to face. Among them was "the question of whether th[e] rendezvous of Polishness and Christianity will be shaped into a kind of Polish-Catholic triumphalism and narrowness, or whether it will be a meeting of open Polishness with open Catholicism."[18]

Mazowiecki's description of the two poles of Catholicism in Poland was widely accepted in the 1990s. In liberal Catholic circles, these poles came to be described as the "open" Church and the "closed" Church.[19] The two groups differed widely on a number of issues, including the modernization of the Church, its position within the state, and its relations with other Christian and non-Christian religions. Advocates of the "open" Church have strongly criticized traditional forms of religiosity, claiming that, to some degree, such Catholicism lacks universal Christian values. Furthermore, they have frequently condemned the nationalist orientation of the "closed" Church as a deformation of Christian principles, accusing traditionalists of making the Church into a "besieged fortress." On a number of occasions, particularly with regard to Jewish issues, they have also accused the "closed" Church of failing to reject the anti-Judaic traditions condemned by Vatican II. For its part, the hard core of the "closed" Church has described the "open" Church as its internal enemy, one that has betrayed Catholic principles and is run by left-wing Catholic groups along with Jews, Freemasons, and those who serve them.[20]

While the "closed" Church is seen by its critics as a backward-looking body that represents, to varying degrees, the traditional, conservative, and folkish type of religiosity based on the pre-1939 model of Polish Catholicism,[21] it considers itself to be the true defender of the faith and of Polishness. It is characterized by its great reluctance to accept any criticism, which it views, by definition, as an attack on both the Church and the Polish nation. Antisemitic motifs can be found in its pronouncements, although these have decreased in number since 2000, perhaps as a result of Vatican influence.[22]

The views of the "closed" Church are expressed most strongly and frequently in a number of periodicals, including *Niedziela*, *Ład*, *Słowo-Dziennik Katolicki*, and the widely circulated *Nasz Dziennik*.[23] It also owns radio stations such as Radio Niepokalanów and Radio Maryja. Its most outspoken representatives among the bishops have been Edward Frankowski, Sławoj Leszek Głódź, and Ignacy Tokarczuk. Other well-known priests who can be considered representatives of the "closed" Church are Father Henryk Jankowski, chaplain of the Solidarity movement in the 1980s (and a former close personal associate of Lech Wałęsa) and Father Tadeusz Rydzyk, a Redemptorist, who is the founder and director of Radio Maryja. The "closed" Church also has a significant foothold at the Catholic University of Lublin—previously a stronghold of liberal views—as well as in some of the new private Catholic institutions of higher education that have mushroomed since the early 2000s.[24]

In contrast to the "closed" Church, the "open" Church is a more easily identifiable body. It consists mainly of the lay Catholic intelligentsia and some members of the higher and lower clergy. Former Prime Minister Mazowiecki and Bishop Tadeusz Pieronek, the ex-secretary of the Polish Episcopate, are among its leading representatives. Its main forums are lay Catholic journals such as the weekly *Tygodnik Powszechny* and the monthlies *Znak* and *Więź* and the network of Catholic Intelligentsia Clubs, with the exception of that in Lublin, which is a stronghold of the "closed" Church.[25] The Jesuit monthly *Przegląd Powszechny* can also be considered as representing its views, as is true of the Dominican monthly *W drodze*.

The position of the hierarchy, in which there are representatives of both groups as well as some who take a middle position, has been to maintain the unity of the Polish Church while at the same time upholding the basic principles of the Second Vatican Council, affirming the need to update the Church and to supersede its anti-Judaic traditions. It has been reluctant to take action against conservatives within the Church on the grounds that this might jeopardize its unity; for the most part, it has regarded the activity of the liberals as a provocative and unnecessary irritant.

In the remainder of this essay, we will examine the position of these different sections of the Church on a number of key issues of Jewish interest. First is the developing dialogue with Jews and Judaism. Second is the need for the Church to articulate a view on its anti-Judaic past and on antisemitic manifestations within both the Church and wider Polish society. Third is the controversy aroused by Jan T. Gross' scholarly account of the massacre of the Jews of Jedwabne by their Polish neighbors in the summer of 1941. Finally, there is the debate aroused by the showing in Poland of Mel Gibson's film, *The Passion of the Christ.*

Dialogue With Jews and Judaism: Achievements and Failures

The creation of formal institutions for Catholic-Jewish dialogue predated the end of Communism, since it was in 1986 that the Episcopal Sub-commission for Dialogue with Judaism (later renamed the Episcopate Committee for Dialogue with Judaism) was established. The objective of the dialogue, which was modeled on earlier frameworks set up in Western Europe and in North America, was to reshape Catholic attitudes toward Jews and Judaism and to eliminate anti-Jewish prejudices. This was a belated application to Polish conditions of the theological principles of the Second Vatican Council, which upheld the view that Jews were Catholics' "elder brothers in spirit" with whom "Christianity has a special bond." In the words of the papal encyclical *Nostra Aetate,* "Jews are the people of God who have not been disowned by the new election and the new covenant . . . [and] are not burdened with the responsibility for the death of Christ."[26]

As might have been expected, the liberal elements in Polish Catholicism were strong advocates of the establishment of this dialogue. They had long championed the concept of ecumenism and dialogue with agnostics and non-believers, as well as with other Christian and non-Christian religions. The best-known participants in dialogue with the Jews and Judaism are Archbishop Henryk Muszyński, Archbishop Józef Życiński, and Bishop Stanisław Gądecki; other outspoken champions of dialogue are Prof. Rev. Michał Czajkowski, and the late Stanisław Musiał, a Jesuit priest. Other, less-known names that are nonetheless worthy of note are Dr. Rev. Grzegorz Ignatowski and Father Stanisław Obirek (also a Jesuit).

Those identified with more conservative positions in the Church have had much greater reservations about this dialogue. For the most part they have ignored it. This was the position adopted in the 1990s by the weekly *Niedziela.* Published in Częstochowa, this important and widely read publication has a significant readership among the higher clergy; dialogue with Jews and Judaism has hardly been mentioned in its pages. Even the visit to Israel by Pope John Paul II in the spring of 2000 was reported in the margins, without any positive commentary regarding either his visit to Yad Vashem or his various meetings with Israeli Jewish officials.[27]

Members of the "closed" church have also expressed hostility to dialogue on theological grounds. According to *Nasz Dziennik*, a daily that is closely connected to Radio Maryja:

> In liturgical texts we now often hear the word "Israel" cited in all possible versions. "Jesus in the synagogue" now replaces the term "Jesus in the Temple." In a recent television program, the "privileged spokesman" Rev. Michał Czajkowski described Jewish religious law as the foundation of our celebration of the Sabbath. Don't we Catholics have our own religious laws? Do we really need to refer to the Jewish laws?[28]

It should be stressed that, given the tiny number of Jews currently living in Poland, the Christian-Jewish dialogue is hardly that of equals. Inevitably, the Jewish voice is very weak in comparison to that of Catholics. In addition, members of other Christian churches have also contributed to this dialogue, particularly the Evangelical Church, whose priests have regularly participated in conferences and other religious activities concerning Jews and Judaism. Indeed, on March 19, 2000, the Tenth Synod of the Evangelical Lutheran Church issued its own mea culpa for anti-Jewish prejudice ("Polish Lutherans view acts of intolerance of and prejudice against Jews from their own perspective, that is the perspective of a minority that has also experienced prejudice and intolerance").[29]

The Christian-Jewish dialogue in Poland has been accompanied by a number of important initiatives. These include the organization of a conference titled "Jews and Christians in Dialogue," held in Krakow in April 1988; the setting up in 1991 of the Polish Council of Christians and Jews; the establishment of the Institute for Catholic-Jewish Dialogue, affiliated with the Catholic Theological Academy in Warsaw; the exchange of lecturers in 1994 and 1995 between theological colleges in Poland and the United States, set up by Archbishop Muszyński and Rabbi A. James Rudin, director of interreligious affairs of the American Jewish Committee; and the establishment of a "Day of Judaism" on January 17 of each year whose aim is to "promote the recognition of the connection between Judaism and Christianity" by means of prayers and liturgical texts (including a special prayer dedicated to victims of the Holocaust) that are circulated each year to every Polish parish.[30]

To date, what has this dialogue achieved? In terms of the "rediscovery of the elder brother" in institutions of Catholic higher education, there have been some tangible achievements, such as the introduction of a new program in Jewish theology and ethics. In theological universities and seminaries, students and future priests now learn about Judaism as a religion with its own religious trends, spiritual insights, and integrity. This no doubt will result in growing interest in Israel and other Jewish communities.

Also in the last decade, a significant number of Christian and Catholic writings, including Vatican documents on Jews and Judaism, have been translated into Polish. Furthermore, a number of important publications by Polish priests have appeared, including *Lud Przymierza* by Rev. Czajkowski and two collections of essays by Rev.

Ignatowski, *Kościoły wobec antysemityzmu* and *Kościół i Synagoga*, in addition to the semi-autobiographical work by Rev. Romuald Jakub Weksler-Waszkinel, *Błogosławiony Bóg Izraela* (Blessed God of Israel).[31] All these works have emphasized the permanent values of Jews and Judaism.

In addition, anti-Judaic views condemned by the Second Vatican Council have been eliminated from new catechisms and religious textbooks. This does not mean that all new religious textbooks (intended for both the clergy and the lay Catholic communities) have been written according to the Vatican II recommendations. As Lucylla Pszczółowska has shown, many catechisms and religious textbooks published in the 1980s, while not reprinting anti-Jewish views, nonetheless failed explicitly to criticize them. This, she notes, is also true of many sermons.[32]

Certainly the dissemination of ideas aimed at reshaping Catholics' attitudes toward Jews and Judaism is the most difficult task facing advocates of the Christian-Jewish dialogue. This is a task that can fully be realized only when the traditional long-term negative patterns of thinking about Jews and Judaism are successfully challenged. In his comments concerning the third annual celebration of the Day of Judaism in 2000, Bishop Gądecki conceded that it was not celebrated at all in some dioceses, indicating that "there are problems with the transformation of the thought patterns of Catholics and there is a visible lack of understanding" of the day's objectives.[33]

Although it addresses the problem of antisemitism, the Christian-Jewish dialogue has tended (following the directives of Vatican II) to define it in religious and theological terms—that is, as a sin against God and Christianity—rather than as an ideology with damaging impacts not only on Jewish communities but also on intercommunal relations between Jews and non-Jews. One such statement reads: "Antisemitism is a betrayal of Christian faith, the defeat of Christian hope and the death of Christian love. It is a mortal sin. It is a blow against Jesus the Jew, the son of God and Redeemer of mankind."[34] As the Canadian scholar Iwona Irwin-Zarecka notes, such an interpretation inhibits the critical examination of the Polish Catholic Church's anti–Jewish legacy, particularly issues such as the historical role of the Church in disseminating anti-Jewish attitudes and prejudices and the role of religious antisemitism in provoking anti-Jewish violence. In her opinion, referring to antisemitism in the "religious language of sin and atonement may very easily lead to the closing of the critical inquiry" into the causes and nature of the sin.[35]

To be sure, self-critical inquiry has been advocated by some of the participants in the dialogue, among them the late Stanisław Musiał (1938–2004). In "Bloodthirsty Jews" and "The Path of Crucifixion of the Jews of Sandomierz," Musiał examined the ritual murder accusation in the Polish context.[36] He also expressed indignation concerning frescos depicting an alleged ritual murder that were (and are) still on display in the Cathedral and the Church of St. Paul in Sandomierz.[37] "There is no room for iconography depicting alleged ritual murder in Polish cathedrals and churches," he wrote. "As a Catholic and a priest, I wish to belong to a Church that does not tolerate lies in its chapels."[38]

Another positive development is the emergence of a new theme in the dialogue, namely, Christian moral responsibility for the Holocaust. The soul-searching on this subject that is often found in Western Christian writings has generally been

absent in Poland, although Musiał and Ignatowski have displayed it in their writings.[39]

The Struggle against Antisemitism in the Church and Beyond

Certainly, in spite of the efforts of those engaged in dialogue with Jews, other
elements within the clergy and even in the Church hierarchy have evinced far less
concern about the still widespread antisemitic stereotypes. Thus, during a press
conference of the Polish Roman Catholic Delegation in Paris in April 1990, Cardinal Glemp claimed that "antisemitism in Poland is a myth created by the enemies
of Poland."[40] Similarly, Józef Michalik, then bishop of Gorzów (and now chairman
of the Bishops' Conference), declared during the election campaign of September
1991 that "[a] Catholic should vote for a Catholic, a Muslim for a Muslim, a Jew
for a Jew, a Freemason for a Freemason, and a Communist for a Communist"—a
remark that seemed to indicate that Catholics had no business voting for a non-
Catholic candidate.[41]

The hierarchy was also slow to react to manifestations of antisemitism in the
lower clergy. The most notorious case involved the former Solidarity chaplain,
Father Henryk Jankowski of St. Brigida Church in Gdańsk, tarnished by his provocative, ultra-right-wing views. In April 1995, the traditional Easter decoration of
Jesus' grave in his church included the Star of David along with the swastika, as
well as emblems of the Soviet secret police (NKVD), the Polish Communist secret
police (UB), and various past and contemporary left-wing Polish political parties.
When the leaders of two of these parties (the Social Democratic Labor Party and
the Union of Labor) protested, Cardinal Glemp claimed that this constituted an
attack on the Church and an infringement of freedom of speech.[42] The Polish
primate apparently saw nothing offensive or inappropriate in equating the Star of
David with symbols of Nazism, Stalinism, and Communism. Although the display
itself was dismantled, photographs of it were sold during Easter in the Church
shop.[43]

In a sermon he gave the following year, on July 29, 1996, Jankowski again made
use of an antisemitic theme. He claimed that American Jewry constituted a major
threat to Poland and criticized Włodzimierz Cimoszewicz, the incumbent prime
minister, for apologizing to the Jewish people during the official ceremony commemorating the 50th anniversary of the Kielce pogrom, which had been held earlier
that month. A year later, at a Mass held on August 26, 1997, Jankowski asserted
that "the Jewish minority cannot be tolerated within the Polish government." These
observations were repeated two months later, when he called on the Poles "to keep
a watchful eye on the hands of the Jewish minority, which wants to gain full control
over the Polish government."[44]

In November 1997, following protests by various Western and domestic organizations and media, Jankowski was forbidden to deliver sermons by his superior,
Archbishop Gocłowski, on the grounds that he had introduced too many political
elements into his religious addresses. This ban did not refer to his open incitement

of antisemitism. Attempts to prosecute him on grounds of inciting interethnic hatred were unsuccessful. However, in the summer of 2004, Jankowski was accused of misconduct and the corruption of young parishioners; in November, he was dismissed from his position.[45]

Another focal point of right-wing and antisemitic agitation within the Church is Radio Maryja, established in December 1991 by Father Tadeusz Rydzyk, which soon became the fourth-largest private radio station in Poland. According to available data, the adult audience of Radio Maryja represents 14 percent of the population. This is no ordinary radio station. Affiliated with Radio Maryja is an extensive network of social and religious activities, including the recently established Institute of National Education in Lublin and the College of Social Culture and Media Studies in Toruń. Radio Maryja also enjoys the support of mainstream Catholic politicians, among them thirty MPs and senators.[46]

In the period of 1995 to 1997, when Jankowski was most active, the number of anti-Jewish statements broadcast on Radio Maryja also reached its peak. Jews were portrayed as a serious threat to the Polish state, nation, culture, and spirituality. Well-known foreign entrepreneurs such as George Soros were included on the list of Jews wishing to destroy Poland and Christianity, and various Polish politicians and public figures were frequently labeled as either Jewish or as "servants of the Jews."[47] In 1995, the station also came out strongly against the presidential candidacy of Aleksander Kwaśniewski, a politician affiliated with the former Polish United Workers' Party, going so far as to claim that Kwaśniewski's mother, who died at the time, should be denied burial in a Catholic cemetery because her family was actually Jewish.[48] In the fall of 1997, Rydzyk was finally criticized by Cardinal Glemp for the overly political content of his radio station. As in the case of Jankowski, the primate failed to criticize or condemn the specifically anti-Jewish character of Radio Maryja's broadcasts.

There is disagreement as to the influence of this station on the Catholic community at large, with some claiming minimal social impact and others pointing to its potentially damaging social consequences.[49] Those who claim that Radio Maryja has a marginal impact because it appeals to older, impoverished, and uneducated members of society ignore the fact that, in the context of Polish family life, many members of this social group are directly involved in bringing up children and young people, hence the influence of their worldview reaches beyond their own generation.

The failure to react more strongly to these phenomena is a clear indication of the ambivalent position of some Church officials and members of the higher clergy with regard to dialogue with Jews and Judaism and their lack of commitment toward the eradication of anti-Jewish prejudice within their own institution. It also implies that the perceptions of the Jews held by Jankowski and Rydzyk cannot be viewed as being marginal; rather, such views are, to a certain extent, deemed acceptable among some members of the clergy. For example, two bishops openly and publicly supported Jankowski: Bishop Michalik stated that Jankowski's views were the exemplification of patriotism, Polishness, and Catholicism, whereas Bishop Marian Kruszyłowicz termed the press reports on Jankowski's antisemitic sermons to be a provocation directed against the Church.[50] Jankowski also received a number of supportive letters from clergy, which were later published in two books by Peter Raina.[51]

Perhaps the most disturbing case of support for Jankowski was that of Waldemar Chrostowski, a renowned expert in the theology of Judaism and one of the co-founders of the Polish Council of Christians and Jews. Chrostowski has claimed that, "in the name of truth, objectivity, and justice," Poles of Jewish ethnic origin cannot be trusted and therefore should not play an active role in public life. Moreover, in the context of Polish-Jewish relations, he asserted, the Jews are themselves to blame for antisemitism, since they were responsible for the imposition of Communism upon the Polish people.[52]

Public condemnation by clergymen of Jankowski's statements and of the activities of Radio Maryja was limited. In fact, Bishop Pieronek, then secretary of the Episcopate, was the only senior Church official who condemned them explicitly for their antisemitic character, whereas Archbishop Józef Życiński indirectly criticized Radio Maryja. In his various sermons, Życiński called for "respect for others and dissociating oneself from those who, in the name of religion, incite ethnic hatred against the others."[53] Życiński also denounced "searching for Jewish blood in people's biographies" as a sign of "neopaganism."[54] Outright condemnation of Jankowski's antisemitism was left to the redoubtable Musiał.[55] In his articles, he also castigated Church officials for their lack of a proper reaction to antisemitic incidents and claimed that anti-Jewish statements were widely tolerated. Musiał was highly praised as "the voice of conscience" by some Polish intellectuals, including Jan Nowak-Jeziorański and Piotr Wandycz, as well as by members of the Polish Jewish community. However, his voice did not elicit significant response from the clergy. In reply to his articles in *Gazeta Wyborcza*, one reader, a nun from Toruń, described Musiał as a lone voice sounding opinions that many other clergymen were afraid to express, for fear of jeopardizing their own standing.[56] Yet these voices have gradually become louder. Father Tomasz Dostatni, chief editor of the Dominican publishing house W drodze, has acknowledged the strength of anti-Jewish views within the clergy,[57] as has Catholic journalist Jarosław Gowin.[58]

One factor strengthening the position of those opposed to antisemitism in the Polish Church has been pressure from the Vatican and from the late Pope John Paul II. Several years ago, as the millennial year 2000 drew near, the Vatican issued a number of statements expressing remorse for anti-Jewish prejudice and actions— or inaction, as in the case of widespread Catholic passivity during the Holocaust. Condemnation of all forms of anti-Jewish prejudice was accompanied by calls for a new and positive relationship between Jews and Christians. On August 25, 2000, following the lead of the Vatican and emulating other national churches, the Polish Bishops' Conference issued a letter "on forgiveness and reconciliation with the Jews, the adherents of non-Christian religions and non-believers," which was read out in all of Poland's parishes (more than 10,000 in number) during Mass on Sunday, August 27. This letter asked the Jews for "forgiveness for the standpoint of those of our members who despise those of other religions or who tolerate antisemitism"—the first unequivocal condemnation of antisemitism by the Polish hierarchy.[59] This followed an earlier Episcopal letter of January 20, 1991 that portrayed the Jews in accordance with the guidelines of the Second Vatican Council, which began with the following affirmation:

> Poles are linked by special ties with the Jewish nation, since, as early as the first centuries of our history, Poland became the homeland for many Jews—the majority of Jews living all over the world at present derive from the territories of the former and present Republic of Poland. . . . [T]he Pope, the Holy Father, [has] said . . . : "There is one other nation, one other special people, the people of the patriarchs, Moses and the prophets, the legacy of the faith of Abraham. These people lived with us for generations, shoulder to shoulder on the same land that somehow became the new land of the Diaspora. Horrible death was inflicted on millions of sons and daughters of this nation. . . . The murderers did this on our soil, perhaps in order to defile it. But earth cannot be defiled by the blood of innocent victims, earth becomes a holy relic as a result of such deaths.

The letter went on to discuss the fact that many Poles saved Jewish lives during the war, enumerating the number of trees planted in their honor in the Avenue of Righteous Gentiles at Yad Vashem. Nevertheless, it continued:

> We are aware that many of our compatriots still nurse in their memory the harm and injustice inflicted by postwar Communist rule, in which people of Jewish origin participated as well. But we must admit that the source of inspiration for their actions cannot be seen in their Jewish origin or in their religion but came from the Communist ideology from which Jews, too, suffered much injustice. We also express our sincere regret at all cases of antisemitism that have occurred on Polish soil. We do this because we are deeply convinced that all signs of antisemitism are contrary to the spirit of the gospel and, as Pope John Paul II has recently underlined, will remain totally contrary to the Christian vision of human dignity. . . . We Christians and Jews are united by the belief in one God, the Creator and the Lord of the whole Universe who created man in His own image, we are united by the ethical principles that are embodied in the Decalogue, which may be reduced to the commandment of the love of God and the love of one's fellow man. We are united by our veneration for the Old Testament as the holy scripture and our common traditions of prayer. And we are united by the hope for the final coming of the Kingdom of God.[60]

The Jedwabne Controversy

The Episcopal letters and their condemnation of antisemitism changed the climate within the Church, their effects being evident during the complex and often acrimonious debate surrounding Jan T. Gross' *Neighbors: The Destruction of the Jewish Community in Jedwabne*. When published in Polish in 2000, this work brought to widespread attention the facts regarding the massacre of the Jewish community of a small town in northeast Poland in the summer of 1941.[61] Gross' book prompted the most profound discussion on Polish-Jewish relations and antisemitism in Poland since the end of the war. This discussion is still underway; to date, the Church hierarchy has attempted to hold fast to the positions articulated in *Nostra Aetate* and in the bishops' letter while at the same time endeavoring, not very successfully, to keep more anti-Jewish elements in the Church under control.

Apart from Czajkowski and Musiał, who, as seen, consistently voiced the strong-est attacks against Church-tolerated antisemitism, the liberal ranks of the Polish Church include Archbishop Życiński (the Metropolitan of Lublin) and Archbishop Muszyński (the Metropolitan of Gniezno). In the matter of Jedwabne, they ex-pressed sympathy for Czajkowski and Musiał's views, in contrast to Cardinal Glemp, whose stated opinions often approximated those held by Poles who stress German responsibility while downplaying Polish guilt. Życiński set out his position in an article characteristically titled "The Banalization of Barbarity." In it, he argued that the massacre of Jedwabne demonstrated that the barbarism of Nazism could infect those who were not German:

> The drama of Jedwabne bears a bitter lesson of truth about mankind. It is particularly bitter for those who consider the barbarity of Nazism as nothing other than a local variety of genocide, horrifyingly alien to the commendable remainder of humanity. It transpires that the truth about human nature is much more complex. The victims of barbarous aggression can easily grow accustomed to it, and end up applying new ag-gression against the innocent. The spiral of evil knows no ethnic restrictions, and we cannot consider any environment to be immune to the radiation of primitivism. This bitter truth affords protection against ideological delusions whereby some people at-tempt to extol blood ties or cultural affinities. These values cannot be worshipped as contemporary deities because human susceptibility to evil transcends all the borders of the categories we hold dear.[62]

He concluded by stressing the need for an act of expiation:

> Today, we need to pray for the victims of that massacre, displaying the spiritual soli-darity that was missing at the hour when they left the land of their fathers. In the name of those who looked upon their death with indifference, we need to repeat David's words: "I have sinned against the Lord,"[63] regardless of whether any protest from the onlookers might have been efficacious in that situation.

Similar views were expressed by Muszyński in an interview with *Tygodnik Pow-szechny* in March 2001, in which he admitted that "some Polish residents of Jed-wabne" were indeed "direct perpetrators of the crime" [the words of the inter-viewer]. Muszyński noted that "those who are connected to [the direct perpetrator] by religious or national ties—though they bear no personal guilt—cannot feel themselves to be free of moral responsibility for the victims of this murder" and expressed the hope that efforts toward finding "a proper and dignified way of memorializing this shameful slaughter will be found, as will some form of redress for the evil that was done."[64]

Both Życiński and Muszyński were greatly influenced by Michael Schudrich, the American-born rabbi of the Jewish communities of Warsaw and Łódź, who played a major role in keeping down the emotional temperature and who went out of his way to be mindful of Polish sensitivities. In an interview with the Catholic Information Agency, published in *Rzeczpospolita* on March 14, 2001, he explicitly rejected the concept of collective guilt:

> The guilty party in a murder is the person who committed the murder. It is he who should be judged, if not in this world, then certainly in the next, and it would be better for him if it were in this world than in the next, for there it will be worse. But there

is the Jewish concept of *'eglah 'arufah* [cf. Deut. 21:1–9]. Why should the elder of the nearest town pray for the man who perished at the hand of an unknown assailant? It wasn't even in his jurisdiction, and yet, though not guilty, he takes on the responsibility for what has happened. There is a shadow and it falls on everyone. The person who committed murder is individually responsible for the act. However, another person can seek forgiveness and this does not mean he bears the same guilt as the perpetrator.

Schudrich stressed the primary responsibility of the Germans for the Holocaust, asserting that it "was planned and carried out from beginning to end by the Germans, in which representatives of other nations participated," and further arguing that Polish antisemitism was neither as strong as Jews sometimes believed nor as marginal a phenomenon as was believed by many in Poland. Asked by his interviewers, "Do you believe that Jews should apologize to the Poles for the sins of their Jewish ancestors?" he responded:

Humans must apologize for every committed wrong. That is also the duty of Jews. We must recognize that we were not only victims, but that we had amongst us people who wronged others. The Jews currently must open their eyes wider regarding their own history in the last few decades. . . .

We Jews must admit that there were Jews who actively worked for the Communists and even the Hitlerites and who committed crimes against Poles, and also against Jews. They never claimed, however, that they were acting in the name of the Jewish nation. Nonetheless the time has come that if we Jews want the Poles to feel and understand our pain, then we must understand and feel the pain of the Poles.

Schudrich also made a number of suggestions regarding how the memorial service on the 60th anniversary of the massacre could be conducted, calling for joint prayers that would commemorate the victims and lead to a request for forgiveness.

Poland's primate, Cardinal Glemp, did not rise to the occasion. From the outset, he ruled out a commemorative service of the sort proposed by Schudrich. In an interview on Warsaw's Radio Józef on March 4, 2001, he remarked sarcastically that "toward the end of February, in the course of several days, a number of high-ranking politicians contacted me with virtually identical proposals: on such-and-such day, the Catholic Church should undertake massive prayers in Jedwabne in repentance for the crimes and ask for forgiveness for the genocide, lest we incur anger." Although Glemp proposed a joint service in Warsaw with representatives of the Jewish community (as had also been suggested by Schudrich), the provocative stance he took in a subsequent interview worked against his proposal. In this interview, conducted on May 15 with representatives of the Catholic Information Agency, Glemp took issue with Muszyński's claim that the situation of Jews often worsened during Easter week. "This statement strikes me as improbable," Glemp said. "The first time I ever heard about this rise in anti-Jewish feeling was in Mr. Gross' book. Clearly, the book was written 'on commission' from someone."[65]

Glemp then went on to make a number of pointed observations:

Before the war I had no contact with Jews, because there were very few where I lived. Polish-Jewish conflicts did occur in those times, but they had an economic basis. Jews were cleverer, and they knew how to take advantage of Poles. That, in any case, was the perception. Another cause of dislike for Jews was their pro-Bolshevik attitude. This

was a very basic resentment, but it did not stem from religious motives. In Poland
before the war, matters of religion did not play any significant role as far as dislike for
Jews was concerned. Jews were disliked because of their odd "folk customs." The same
sort of dislike based on folk customs can be found today, for example, among fans of
different soccer teams in the city of Łódź.[66] Is there any point in looking for religious
motives in this?

Moreover, Glemp said,

I also cannot understand why Poles are unceasingly slandered, especially in the American press, and why we are constantly accused of antisemitism, as though it were
somehow different in form from what it is in other countries. In all this, Jews continually exhibit their dislike toward Poles. I cannot really understand why they do so.
For—in comparison with Europe—Jews had relatively the best situation with us, here
in Poland. They felt at home here. Why therefore are there so many unjust accusations
today? Think how this hurts Jews who genuinely love Poland and who live in friendship
with Poles![67]

In conclusion, Glemp accused "Jews" of causing harm to Poles by closely coop-
erating with the Bolsheviks and made reference to their allegedly prominent role
in the Communist secret police.

As could be expected, this interview prompted a sharp response from Musiał:

It seems to me that the case of Jedwabne, and the moral responsibility that Catholics
have incurred toward Jews in history, can be fully stated on half a page of a schoolchild's notebook. One can say simply: "This is the way we were. There is nothing we
can say to justify it. We apologize to you and to God for all of this with all our hearts
and all our souls. We want to change. We ask you: help us to be better."
    That's all. Plus a large number of penitential psalms.[68]

Like Glemp, Bishop Stanisław Stefanek of the Łomża diocese (to which Jedwabne
belongs) failed to rise to the occasion. In his sermon on March 11, 2001, delivered
in Jedwabne, he referred to what he described as the "unusual attack on Jedwabne"
and the "aggressive, biased modern campaign, which has reached wide circles."[69]
A similar position was taken by the local priest of Jedwabne, the late Rev. Edward
Orłowski, who became the chairman of the Committee to Defend the Good Name
of Jedwabne and who was responsible for calling upon the local population not to
take part in the official commemoration of the Jedwabne massacre, which was held
on July 10, 2001.[70]

Recent Developments

Since 2001, the divisions revealed in the Jedwabne debate have continued to plague
the Church. In January 2003, for instance, Rabbi David Rosen of Jerusalem appeared as a guest speaker at the sixth annual Day of Judaism ceremony, which was
held in Białystok and Tykocin under the patronage of Archbishop Wojciech
Ziemba. Rosen, who spoke on the topic of "Covenant and Mercy" in the Jewish
tradition, was followed by Father Henryk Witczyk of the Catholic University of
Lublin, who addressed the same topic from the Christian perspective. Witczyk

posed the question of whether and in what manner "all Israel" would be saved, calling on Jews to pay attention to three relevant sections of Paul's Epistle to the Romans (Rom. 11: 25–32). This talk aroused protest, particularly in the pages of *Tygodnik Powszechny*. One writer, Father Romuald Jakub Weksler-Waszkinel, characterized Witczyk's lecture as a return to the practice of calling for the conversion of the Jews.[71]

Theological disputes of this sort are perhaps an inevitable concomitant of a more open dialogue, and other encouraging developments should also be noted. One of these was the publication in the United States of "Dabru emet" (Speak truth), a declaration by some of the leading American Jewish theologians supporting interfaith dialogue, who called upon the adherents of each faith to respect each other's beliefs and interpretations of Scripture. Rabbi Michael Signer of Notre Dame University, in explaining the significance of this document to Sławomir Żurek of *Tygodnik Powszechny*, emphasized the point that, for those who signed it, Christians "are devotees of the God of Israel who believe that the Hebrew Scriptures, which they share with Jews, contain a partial revelation. Jesus is for them the Messiah sent by the God of Israel. I am deeply convinced that they remain in a covenantal relationship with the God of Israel, even though they are not Jews. In a word, they are the beloved children of God and I feel a close relationship with them."[72]

Another positive event was the publication of Czajkowski's "What Unites Us? An ABC of Christian-Jewish Relations," an eloquent plea for genuine dialogue between the two faiths. "The two religious communities, the Christians and the Jews, are linked to each other and are intimately dependent on each other," he wrote. "He who cuts himself off from Judaism cuts himself off from his Christian faith and destroys in it something essential."[73] This was not the only such publication in the new genre of writing about the Christian-Jewish dialogue; similar works by Musiał and Gądecki were also published in the early 2000s.[74]

In November 2002, the Episcopate endorsed a resolution to restore and preserve monuments of Jewish culture. One of the first fruits of this initiative was the restoration and return of Jewish gravestones to the Jewish cemetery in Sobieny Jeziory, near Warsaw. The local priest, Rev. Dr. Roman Karwacki, had discovered that, during the Second World War, the Nazis had made their local headquarters on church premises and had repaved a road using the gravestones. With the help of parishioners and the Social Committee to Commemorate the Memory of the Jews of Otwock and Karczew (headed by Zbigniew Nosowski of *Więź*), Karwacki transferred the gravestones to their original location.[75]

To date, efforts to rein in Radio Maryja have been only partially successful. Both the commission established by the Episcopate and attempts on the part of Cardinal Glemp to attain some degree of control over the "Rydzyk empire" have had little impact. In fact, with the inauguration in September 2003 of an affiliated television station known as Trwam ("I endure"), this group seems stronger than ever.[76] The establishment of a rival radio station (Radio Józef) under the auspices of the Episcopate, and the attempt to counter Rydzyk's organization by building up the Polish branch of Catholic Action (reestablished in 1996, it today has only 35,000 members), have not accomplished much.[77] Radio Maryja continues to receive kid-glove treatment both from the Church and from state authorities who have, over the years, overlooked its numerous infractions of the law. To a certain extent, Radio Maryja's "immunity" reflects the fact that there are those in the Church hierarchy who see some positive value in the station's activities.

The latest example of support for Radio Maryja by representatives of the upper clergy is the position taken by Bishop Głódź in the February 2005 dispute between Lech Wałęsa and the radio station. In a letter published in *Gazeta Wyborcza,* Wałęsa had criticized Rydzyk for spreading allegations that many former Solidarity members, including Wałęsa himself, had collaborated with the Communist regime. Wałęsa called upon the Church to take Rydzyk to task. Bishop Głódź, however, attacked Wałęsa for his criticism of Radio Maryja.[78] The following month, the Bishops' Conference failed to take a firm stance on Father Rydzyk in spite of Wałęsa's call, and despite Archbishop Życiński's earlier public condemnations of Rydzyk as a propagator of antisemitic and anti-Christian values.[79] At this conference, it became apparent to what extent Głódź's positive attitude toward Rydzik had influenced others in the Church.

The worst recent case of failure to deal with antisemitism within the Church has been the bookshop—located in the crypt of All Saints' Church in Warsaw—that is operated by the right-wing publishing house "Antyk" (its name means "anticommunist"). Antyk was established in 1997 by Marcin Dybowski, a right-wing politician and publisher who unsuccessfully ran for the senate in that year. In a message placed on his internet site, Dybowski informed the public of his intention to publish "the works of Feliks Koneczny [a prewar antisemite], old papal encyclicals against Freemasonry, modernism, and liberalism, as well as books of a patriotic character that defend Polish traditions, Latin civilization, and the Catholic Church." The bookshop sells prewar and contemporary antisemitic tracts, including *The Protocols of the Elders of Zion.* Reports on the bookshop were carried in *Rzeczpospolita, Gazeta Wyborcza* and *Więź,* and an attempt was made to prosecute the owner on the grounds of inciting racial hatred.[80] In addition, a young theology student, Zuzanna Radzik, waged an unsuccessful campaign to have the bookshop relocated—a matter that was eventually taken up by *Tygodnik Powszechny.*[81] According to its editor, Father Adam Boniecki: "That the location [of the bookshop] is a cause for scandal, that it throws a shadow on the good name of the Church, that it undermines the credibility of Catholics in dialogue with Judaism—is obvious. . . . We have to pose the question—would the matter be handled with such delicacy and tolerance if the tenant, for example, was selling pornography?"

Boniecki's criticism was directed against the diocese of Warsaw. The diocese initially refused to deal with the matter; its chancellor, Father Grzegorz Kalwarczyk, rhetorically asked whether the citizens of Krakow (where *Tygodnik Powszechny* is published) might not have more serious matters with which to concern themselves. In June 2003, the Warsaw district prosecutor's office decided against prosecuting the bookshop owner, on the grounds that antisemitic opinions expressed in books published before the Second World War "arose in a specific situation in which, inter alia, the demographic structure and the prognosis of its further development was unfavorable for persons of Polish nationality." Such opinions, in other words, had "a patriotic character." With regard to a number of vitriolic publications attacking Jan Gross' work on Jedwabne that were sold in the store, the prosecutor's office held that, although the language used in these works may have been extreme, it did not constitute incitement. This decision was upheld on appeal in October 2003.[82]

Soon thereafter, an open letter signed by a number of prominent lay and clerical Catholic figures, including Boniecki; the former foreign minister, Władysław Bartoszewski; Tadeusz Mazowiecki; Leon Kieres; and Jan Nowak-Jeziorański was sent to Cardinal Glemp. It referred first to Pope John Paul II's condemnation of antisemitism and then continued: "We do not understand how the propaganda of hatred can be allowed on holy ground. We are shocked at the toleration of its presence, which can only be understood as Church approval for the content of this material."[83] Glemp responded that the matter "has been investigated by the procurator, and I do not want to impose my will by limiting the freedom of the press." A firmer position was taken by Archbishop Życiński: "The sale of antisemitic literature in churches is repugnant to the Church and Christ. When Christ drove the money changers from the Temple, it was not because their activity was in conflict with the law. . . . He did it because it was incompatible with the sanctity of a holy place."[84]

Dybowski's claim was that he could not be expected to be familiar with the contents of every book that he published. Furthermore, he was merely selling books that "arouse and foster patriotism, support Catholicism . . . books critical of the EU, books critical of the plundering of the finances of Poland and the destruction of the economy."[85] The local priest, Father Zdzisław Król, claimed that he was disgusted by antisemitism but was not conscious of "any excesses" in the bookshop. He had accepted money from the bookshop to renovate the crypt and would be happy to take action if someone would reimburse the church for losses due to the closure of the store. He subsequently claimed (incorrectly) that the antisemitic books had been removed. An offer of financial assistance from *Tygodnik Powszechny*, whose editor quietly went about raising money to meet the cost of the renovation, was also turned down.[86]

The Debate over *The Passion of the Christ*

Differences of position on Jewish issues were also revealed by Mel Gibson's 2004 film, *The Passion of the Christ*, which had its European premiere in Poland and attracted an audience of several million. The film was less shocking to Polish religious sensibilities than to those in Western Europe and the United States because of the essentially Counter-Reformation character of Polish Catholicism, which accomodates rather graphic images of the death of Jesus. Scenes very similar to those depicted in the film can be seen at many Polish sites of pilgrimage—a good example is the Stages of the Cross at the shrine in Kalwaria Zebrzydowska near Krakow. One perceptive Polish reviewer saw the film as an attempt to return to a visual-based or iconic version of Christianity that was characteristic of the Middle Ages and the Counter-Reformation, in preference to the text-based Christianity originating in the Reformation and, in our day, to the changes introduced into the Catholic Church by the Second Vatican Council.[87] Similarly, Gibson's film could be regarded as a return to a folk-based rather than intellectual version of Christianity. In any event, even many "open Church" Catholics were deeply moved by the film. Among them were former prime minister Tadeusz Mazowiecki and Adam Szostkiewicz. The latter regarded *The Passion of the Christ* as stressing an essential element in Christianity, namely, "that one cannot ignore the Cross—the symbol of suffering, but also of redemption . . . the issue is not violence, but sin, whose consequence is violence." Szostkiewicz also argued that the violence in the film "is artistically justified and is not more extreme than in many other films that have been widely praised."[88]

The Church hierarchy, for its part, saw the film as an important tool for evangelization in the face of the perceived inroads of secularization and mass culture. Bishop Wiesław Mering of Wrocław, interviewed in *Tygodnik Powszechny* on July 3, 2003, observed: "I have not the slightest doubt that this film is—in the positive sense—an inspirer of religious feeling . . . I have no doubt that Gibson's film can bring believers nothing but benefit." Gibson, he claimed, had no "intention of arousing hostility to the Jews. . . . I saw nothing in the film that could offend Jews." Many bishops described viewing the film as "compulsory." The Catholic Information Agency strongly promoted the film, and leading Polish biblical scholars cooperated in providing the Polish subtitles.

In this, of course, they were only following the lead of the Vatican. Cardinal Dario Castrillon Hoyos, Prefect of the Congregation for the Clergy, did criticize some aspects of the film in an interview with *La Stampa*. Yet he asserted that all priests should see the *The Passion of the Christ*, which was "a triumph of art and faith" that "brings people closer to God," and he denied that it was antisemitic.[89] Although another cardinal, Walter Kasper (president of the Papal Commission for Religious Relations with the Jews), later stated that Hoyos was only expressing his personal opinion, it was generally believed that the film had been approved by Rome.[90] Such a view was strengthened by the report that, after seeing the film, the pope himself had commented: "This is how it was." Though later denied by the Vatican, the denial was not widely credited.[91] Lending further endorsement to the belief that the Vatican approved the film was the pope's beatification, in September 2004, of Anna Katharina Emmerich, whose gory visions of Jesus' last hours of suffering had provided Gibson with his main inspiration in making the film.

Both *Tygodnik Powszechny* and *Więź* opened their pages to serious discussion of the film, partly because they were concerned about its antisemitic potential. *Tygodnik Powszechy* organized a debate after its first showing in Krakow. Among those who participated were the paper's editor (Boniecki), the film-maker Agnieszka Holland, the co-chair of the Polish Council of Christians and Jews (Krajewski), and the philosopher Władysław Stróżewski. The debate appeared in the paper on March 14. In response to a question as to whether the film "restores the weight and burden of the Cross,"[92] Boniecki replied that it was "difficult to deny" that the film showed how Jesus "was crucified, died and was buried, martyred under Pontius Pilate." At the same time, he said, it placed at its center "the appalling character of [his] tortures [which it presents as] the mystery of our faith, the mystery of the death of the Christ, the Son of God. The burden and uniqueness of the Cross of Christ does not lie in the fact that He was subjected to atrocious tortures." Boniecki continued: "The call to organize 'Retreats with Gibson' or to treat watching the film as a religious experience alarms me enormously. . . . We are dealing here with a mystery that cannot be portrayed literally on the screen." Finally, Boniecki was greatly disturbed by the antisemitic potential of the film:

> The Church has reflected for two millenia on the texts [which describe the Crucifixion] and the culmination of these reflections was Vatican II. I don't know if Gibson is attended by the Holy Spirit, but I believe that the Church is so attended and that this is what led to the formulation "God is faithful to the covenant with his people."[93]

Holland, the film-maker, condemned the film even more strongly. Although she did not expect much from it, "I honestly did not expect it would be as bad as it is. It is a film filled with evil energy. The problem is not so much that it is kitsch, because kitsch is a recurring phenomenon that also characterizes many religious works of art. The danger lies in the fact that *The Passion* reveals an abyss of force, misunderstanding, violence, which in my view is far from the content of the Gospels."[94]

Three reviews appeared in the April 2004 issue of *Więź*. The most favorable was that of Tomasz Wiślicki, who, after criticizing some of the "kitschy elements" in the film, concluded: "Mel Gibson has brought before us an exceptionally important and frequently . . . neglected aspect of the Martyrdom of Our Lord: its appalling, cruel, bodily literalness. . . . This is sufficient for me to regard his film as especially important and necessary." Katarzyna Jabłońska was more doubtful. On the one hand, she praised the portrayal of Mary and did not see any "antisemitic tendencies" in the film, expressing concern that the controversy over it would "create more hostility toward certain Jewish circles than its actual content." On the other hand, the film left her cold, not so much because of its "escalation of cruelty" or its emphasis on the mystery of Good Friday rather than Easter Monday, but rather because "Gibson has made of the Passion a great Hollywood-style spectacle." She was also troubled by some of the statements in support of the film ("Those who criticize this film are criticizing the Gospels"; "Everyone gets from this film what he deserves, what he is able to take in"). "I am willing to believe Mel Gibson when he says that he made *The Passion* as an act of faith," Jabłońska wrote. "I cannot accept the statement that it was made by the Holy Spirit."[95]

The most hostile review was that of Czajkowski. His piece was titled "I prefer the Gospel," and it started by asserting boldly: "The film *The Passion* is not the Gospel of Jesus Christ—it is the Gospel according to Mel Gibson and Katharina Emmerich." He was convinced, moreover, that the film would increase antisemitism:

> If all my knowledge of the martyrdom of Jesus and the responsibility for his death was derived from this film, I would be in no doubt: some Roman mercenaries were cruel, but without the Jews these cruelties would not have occurred, this dreadful flagellation, this long road to the cross, the death on the cross . . . I regard this film as damaging and insulting to Jews. Some of them have compared it to Passion Plays that have also brought them many misfortunes, their own, centuries-long Passion. After the Shoah, Jews are entitled to be sensitive to such matters. We Christians should also look at this film through the eyes of the descendants of the victims of the Shoah.[96]

In contrast, *Nasz Dziennik* and *Niedziela* not only strongly endorsed the film but also attacked its critics in tones that were clearly antisemitic in connotation. One extreme case was an article published in *Niedziela* by Włodzimierz Rędzioch, who claimed that critics of the film represented anti-Catholic forces, organized by anti-Christian Jews, and that Jewish filmmakers and producers from Hollywood regularly made "anti-Christian" movies such as Martin Scorcese's 1988 film, *The Last Temptation of Christ,* and Antonia Bird's controversial film of 1995, *Priest*. In fact, Rędzioch argued, the offended and injured party in the debate over Gibson's movie were the Christians and their faith rather than the Jews and their faith.[97]

The Passion of the Christ has had an undeniable impact in Poland and has strengthened the position of conservatives in the Church. Thus, when the "Monty Python" parody *The Life of Brian* was released on DVD in Poland (its reissue was clearly a riposte to Gibson's film), Chrostowski darkly referred to it as a "conspiracy of certain circles"—a code phrase for "liberals" and "Jews."[98] And in May 2004, Gibson—together with Tadeusz Rydzyk of Radio Maryja—was awarded the first Julian Kalenty prize for "multi-media in the service of evangelization," presented by the Catholic Film Association. Gibson won the award for "using the most modern methods of expression that contemporary cinematography has at its disposal to mobilize people at the beginning of the twenty-first century to understand again the significance of the sacrifice of Jesus Christ." Rydzyk received his award for his "outstanding contribution to the work of evangelization through the uses of the most modern and varied means of social communication: radio, television, the press, the internet, and through his creation of the Higher School of Social and Media Culture."[99]

Conclusion

While the Polish Church of the early 1990s at first displayed visible discomfort with the country's new democratic system, it also showed considerable skill in turning the fledgling democracy to its own advantage. It has learned much from its initial political mistakes. In the early years of democracy, the Church antagonized some Poles by its demand to restore religious education to the public schools, by its pronounced opposition to abortion, and by its attempts to enshrine its own status in relations with the state in some form of concordat.[100] It also unsuccessfully threw its weight behind Lech Wałęsa's presidential campaign in 1995, warning the electorate against "choosing for highest positions in the fatherland people who during the period of the totalitarian state were involved in exercising power at the highest party-governmental level." Its defeats in these areas have inspired new cautiousness; as the new head of the Catholic Information Agency, Marcin Przeciszewski, explained in July 2001:

> I do not see in the Polish Bishops' Conference any particular desire to engage in political life, as was the case under the totalitarian system and in the first half of the 1990s. But then there came the cold shower of the electoral catastrophe of 1993 and

the victory of Kwaśniewski and then came the experience of what was happening on the right of the political spectrum. The main involvement of bishops in politics today is at the diocesan level, perhaps because they can exert much more influence on local politics, and that is what counts.[101]

What this has meant is that the hierarchy has valued unity above all in dealing with social and political problems. It regards the expression of critical views, whether on the Right or the Left, as dangerous to this unity and at best an unnecessary irritant. The selection of Archbishop Michalik (now Metropolitan of Przemyśl) as Chairman of the Bishops' Conference in March 2004 has strengthened this caution. Michalik was identified in the early 1990s with the "closed" Church. He has recently attempted to moderate his position by distancing himself from his earlier opinions, criticizing the activities of Radio Maryja and of Rydzyk, and appealing for the cooperation of "both believers and nonbelievers." He has also stressed the need for unity within the Church. Speaking after his election, he observed: "Christians must aspire to unity with Christ and with their fellow man. . . . We are not following a common path, we are divided, at odds, we divert each other from the good path. The lack of unity is the greatest contemporary challenge for the Church and the nation."[102]

Yet Michalik also described the liberal *Tygodnik Powszechny* as a threat to the Church in Poland—as dangerous as Radio Maryja—and he did not take part in the discussion of Poland's entry into the European Union because, as he put it, he was not prepared to take either side in this dispute. Moreover, in an interview published in *Niedziela* on April 4, 2004, he restated his full support of and attachment to the "folkish" traditional form of Polish Catholicism, although he also acknowledged the possibility of making such religiosity more sophisticated and spiritual.[103]

Michalik's deputy is Bishop Gądecki, a more liberal figure representing the "open" Church, who has been a consultant for the Papal Commission for Religious Relations with the Jews as well as chairman of both the Council for Religious Dialogue and the Committee for Dialogue with Judaism (the last group is affiliated with the Polish Bishops' Conference). One bishop described the choice of these two men as "an attempt to marry fire and water," while others simply note that the selection indicates the existence of two opposing forces within the Church, with the outcome of this encounter still unknown.[104]

The desire to preserve the status quo is also reflected in the decision to allow Cardinal Glemp to retain the office of primate after he reaches the normal ecclesiastical retirement age of 75. Glemp has succeeded, even if only partially, in restricting the activities of Radio Maryja.[105] But he has not been able to create effective press organs of its own for the hierarchy.

Describing the Episcopate, Adam Szostkiewicz wrote:

> The clash between the conservatives and the liberals, which is beloved by the media, is overplayed. Appearances to the contrary, the bishops have views that are very close on important matters. . . . We are talking here of a traditional Church—perhaps the only one of its type in Europe. There are no open disputes in the Polish Episcopate about doctrine, politics, or the teachings of the pope. There is loyalty toward the pope, one's

superiors and the state authorities (provided that they do not harm the vital interests of the Church).[106]

This strategy has been successful in the short run. At a time when economic difficulties and corruption scandals have undermined the faith of many Poles in conventional politics, the Church has retained its hold on society. The positive assessment of the Church has risen from 55 percent in 1997, while the negative assessment has fallen from 35 percent. Moreover, in the most recent poll, 60 percent of those interviewed expressed trust in their local parish priest, which indicates the importance of the Church in individuals' daily lives.[107] In addition, a poll conducted in October 2003 revealed that 56 percent of the respondents felt that the government should follow the social teachings of the Church.[108]

The lessons that the Church had learned from its earlier mistakes were clearly evident in the referendum over Polish entry into the European Union, in which the Church was able both to maintain its unity and to marginalize the anti-European elements within its ranks.[109] What this means with regard to Jewish issues is that while one can expect the Church hierarchy to uphold the teachings of Vatican II, it cannot be expected to take strong action against manifestations of antisemitism within its ranks; moreover, it will continue to show little understanding or sympathy for more liberal positions.

The liberal Jesuit Father Stanisław Obirek, talking about Poland's entry into the European Union, wrote optimistically about the Church's future, saying: "I believe that membership in the EU will cleanse Polish religiosity and strip it of the dangerous triumphalism incited not only by Radio Maryja but also by a section of the hierarchy intoxicated by the sociological success of the Church." A much more pessimistic view was expressed by the conservative Marcin Król in an article in *Respublica Nowa*. In his view, the Polish Church resists the fact that it exists in the modern world. It can change this world, he wrote, but not with the methods of the past. In the meantime: "The Church has been unable to leave the comfortable quiet of [the] curiosity shop."[110]

That is why the Church has such difficulty in dealing with phenomena such as Radio Maryja. In Król's view, its position is the result of the continued belief of many Polish Church faithful in a simple folk version of Catholicism, in which there is less interest in eschatology and more in the efficacy of belief and prayer. "In a period when an ever-growing number of people are educated and think for themselves," he reiterated, choosing to base the Church's position on "simple faith" is ultimately shortsighted.

The continuing link between traditionalist religion and right-wing nationalism was evident in the official welcome extended recently to Roman Giertych, the right-wing leader of the nationalistic League of Polish Families, at the renowned religious and national shrine at the Jasna Góra monastery in Częstochowa, despite Archbishop Życiński's previous statements condemning any political activities at the shrine.[111] Another worrisome sign were the voices raised against the proposal to bury Czesław Miłosz either in the crypt of poets at the Wawel or in the crypt of honor at the Pauline Church on the Rock (na Skałce) in Krakow following the Nobel laureate's death in August 2004. Opposition to burying him in a national shrine was voiced by *Nasz Dziennik,* Radio Maryja, and the reestablished right-wing Catholic and nationalistic All-Polish Youth organization. Although not as loud and widespread as the clerical opposition in interwar Poland against the official burial of Stefan Żeromski, the well-known socialist writer, the portrayal of Miłosz as an irreverent poet with a dark Communist past, who had dared to brand the interwar Catholic newspapers *Mały Dziennik* and *Rycerz Niepokalenej* as antisemitic, suggests that the heritage bequeathed from the past is difficult to eradicate in some segments of the Church and among its followers.[112]

In the short run, one has to be skeptical about any significant changes in the present situation. The death of Pope John Paul II on April 2, 2005 has introduced new challenges and anxieties for the Church in Poland. Lay members of the "open" Church such as Stefan Wilkanowicz of the monthly *Znak* and representatives of the upper clergy such as Bishop Pieronek are concerned about the strength of the legacy of John Paul II and its future in the Church in Poland, and have voiced their criticism of the current theological and intellectual trends in the Catholic clergy.[113] Only further passage of time will tell whether Father Obirek's optimistic prognosis will be fulfilled.

Notes

1. The strong connection between Polish, Catholic, and national identities and its impact on contemporary religiosity were pointed out in important sociological studies published in the early 1990s. See, for instance, Ewa Nowicka (ed.), *Religia a obcość* (Krakow: 1991); Lucjan Adamczuk and Witold Zdaniewicz (eds.), *Religijność Polaków 1991* (Warsaw: 1993).

2. On the close links between the Endecja and the Roman Catholic Church, see, for example, Witold Mysłek, *Kościół katolicki w Polsce w latach 1918–1939* (Warsaw: 1966), 201–205; Ronald Modras, *The Catholic Church and Antisemitism: Poland, 1933–1939* (Chur: 1994), 79–87.

3. Quoted in Bohdan Cywiński, *Z dziejów Kościoła katolickiego w Polsce niepodległej* (Warsaw: 1980), 210.

4. Data concerning the percentage of the Catholic press in interwar Poland is cited in Andrzej Paczkowski, *Prasa polska 1918–1939* (Warsaw: 1980), 222–223.

5. On Odrodzenie and its attitudes toward Jews and Judaism, see the pioneering study of Michał Jagiełło, *Próba rozmowy: Rodowód,* vol. 1 (Warsaw: 2001), 140–150. The presence of anti–Jewish perceptions among members of this group has also been discussed in the progressive lay Catholic weekly *Tygodnik Powszechny.* See the interview with the late Stefan Świeżawski, a leading member of the prewar Odrodzenie, *Tygodnik Powszechny* (special section) (Dec. 1997), 5. On the history of the center at Laski, where the dominant religious and spiritual trend was shaped by the writings of Jacques Maritain and St. Thomas, see the collection of essays edited by Tadeusz Mazowiecki, *Ludzie Lasek* (Warsaw: 1987).

6. Until recently, historians had not found any Church documents pertaining to attitudes toward Jews that were issued during the Second World War. The first such document, "The Church Report of June and July 1941," was discovered in the archives of the Polish government-in-exile in London by the historian Krzysztof Jasiewicz. An excerpt appears in his book, *Pierwsi po diable: Elity sowieckie w okupowanej Polsce 1939–1941* (Warsaw: 2002); also in the historical journal *Karta,* no. 40 (2004), 150–153. This unsigned report (which was most likely sent to the Polish government-in-exile by a member of the Catholic hierarchy) depicts the Jewish population as the enemy of Poland and Catholicism. In tone, it closely resembles the position of the most radical sections of the pre-1939 Church.

7. For excerpts about Jews from various Catholic publications during the Second World

War, see Paweł Szapiro (ed.), *Wojna żydowsko-niemiecka: Polska prasa konspiracyjna 1943–1944 o powstaniu w getcie Warszawy* (London: 1992).

8. This is the view of Ewa Kurek-Lesik in *Gdy Klasztor znaczył życie* (Krakow: 1992).

9. There is a new and growing literature on the history of Church-state relations in the Communist period. Among the most important works are Antoni Dudek, *Państwo i Kościół w Polsce 1945–1970* (Krakow: 1995); Antoni Dudek and Ryszard Gryz, *Komuniści i Kościół w Polsce, 1945–1989* (Krakow: 2003).

10. Jan Jershyna, "The Catholic Church, the Communist State and the Polish People," in *Polish Paradoxes*, ed. Stanisław Gomułka and Antony Polonsky (London: 1990), 89–90.

11. Michał Borwicz, "Polish-Jewish Relations, 1944–1947," in *The Jews in Poland*, ed. Chimen Abramsky, Maciej Jachimczyk, and Antony Polonsky (Oxford: 1986), 195.

12. Letter to the *Times Literary Supplement*, 28 March 1997.

13. For the Jewish perspective on the Roman Catholic Church's efforts to transform its relations with Jews and Judaism, see, for example, Norman Solomon, "A Critical Commentary on the Common Bond," *Jewish–Christian Relations* 18, no. 3 (1985), 67–73.

14. The majority of works about Wyszyński emphasize only the positive sides of his legacy; see for example, Peter Raina, *Kardynał Wyszyński*, 2 vols. (Warsaw: 1999). For a more critical evaluation of Wyszyński's legacy that depicts both his achievements and his weaknesses, see, for example, Roman Graczyk, "Kardynał Wyszyński—sam wobec historii," *Gazeta Wyborcza* (25 May 2001), online at http://wyborcza.gazeta.pl/info/artykul.jsp?xx=288672&dzial=0101201016.

15. Jershyna, "The Catholic Church, the Communist State and the Polish People," 92.

16. Perhaps one of the most important accounts of the rapprochement between the Church and the secular intelligentsia is Adam Michnik's *Kościół, lewica, dialog* (Warsaw: 1998).

17. Quoted in "Droga Kościoła w Polsce Ludowej," *Przegląd Katolicki* (24 May 1987).

18. Tadeusz Mazowiecki, "Questions to Ourselves," *Dialectics and Humanism* no. 2 (1990), 13. This essay was originally published in *Przegląd Powszechny* 6 (1985).

19. Jarosław Gowin, *Kościół w czasach wolności, 1989–1999* (Krakow: 1999); idem, *Kościoł po komunizmie* (Krakow: 1995); Joanna Michlic, " 'The Open Church' and 'the Closed Church' and the Discourse on Jews in Poland between 1989 and 2000," *Communist and Post-Communist Studies* 37 (2004), 461–479. See also the following essay in this volume by Geneviève Zubrzycki.

20. On the position of the "closed" Church toward the "open" Church, see, for example, Jan Turnau, "Arka Noego," *Gazeta Wyborcza* (17–18 Jan. 1998), 21.

21. Gowin, *Kościół w czasach wolności*, 344–350.

22. According to Stanisław Obirek, chief editor of the Jesuit journal *Życie Duchowe* (which endorses the principle of dialogue with Jews and Judaism), the efforts of Pope John Paul have been conducive to reducing anti–Jewish statements among some segments of the Catholic clergy in Poland. Obirek's claim is cited by Michał Okoński, "Żeby istniał żal," *Tygodnik Powszechny* (9 April 2000), 3.

23. *Ład* and *Słowo-Dziennik Katolicki* have recently ceased publication.

24. See Gowin, *Kościół w czasach wolności*, 335–343.

25. In its various activities, the Catholic Club in Lublin, chaired by Ryszard Bender, disseminates antisemitic and populist political views. In December 2004, Archbishop Życiński denied this club the right to use the adjective "Catholic" in its name and strongly condemned both its activities and its chairman. See the report by Tomasz Nieśpiał, "Porozumienie Kik-ów poparło abp. Józefa Życińskiego," *Gazeta Wyborcza*, http://srwisy.gazeta.pl/kraj/2029020,34317,2562722.html.

26. See Piotr Królikowski, "Jewish Culture, Religion and History in the Teaching and Religious Instruction of the Catholic Church of Poland," *From the Martin Buber House* 21 (1993), 35–36.

27. See issues of *Niedziela* from March and early April 2000.

28. This statement, originally published in *Nasz Dziennik*, was cited in *Polityka* (8 April 2000), 114.

29. Cited in *Tygodnik Powszechny* (26 March 2000), 2.

30. On the importance of the connection between Judaism and Christianity as expressed in the celebration of the Day of Judaism, see Grzegorz Ignatowski, *Kościół i synagoga* (Warsaw: 2000), 52–66.

31. Michał Czajkowski, *Lud Przymierza* (Warsaw: 1992); Grzegorz Ignatowski, *Kościoły wobec antysemitizmu* (Łódź: 1999); idem, *Kościół i synagoga;* Romuald Jakub Weksler-Waszkinel, *Błogosławiony Bog Izraela* (Lublin: 2000). Similar messages could also be found in earlier articles written by Father Jacek Salij, "Mroki egocentryzmu," *Tygodnik Solidarność* (12 April 1991), 15, and "Did the Jews Crucify Jesus?," *Więź* (special English-language issue titled *Under One Heaven—Poles and Jews* [1998]), 111–118.

32. Lucylla Pszczółowska, "Antisemitism and Religious Formation," *Więź* (special issue 1998), 118–123. This article originally appeared in Polish as "Antysemityzm a formacja religijna," in ibid. (June 1988), 142–145.

33. Bishop Gądecki's statement was reported in *Tygodnik Powszechny* (25 May 2000), 2.

34. Michał Czajkowski, "The Sin of Antisemitism," *Więź* (special issue), 150.

35. Iwona Irwin-Zarecka, *Neutralizing Memory: The Jew in Contemporary Poland* (Oxford: 1989), 181.

36. Stanisław Musiał, "Żydzi żądni Krwi," *Gazeta Wyborcza* (29–30 July 2000), 22; idem, "Droga krzyżowa Żydów Sandomierskich," ibid. (5–6 Aug. 2000), 21–22; both articles were recently republished in a collection of essays authored by Musiał, titled *Czarne jest czarne* (Krakow: 2004).

37. For a discussion of the presence of iconography depicting ritual murder by Jews in the Cathedral and the Church of St. Paul in the Sandomierz diocese, see "Sąd nad obrazem," *Gazeta Wyborcza* (27 Oct. 2000), 18–19; Andrzej Osęka, "Troska o mord rytualny," ibid. (10–12 Nov. 2000), 25; Anna Landau-Czajka, "The Last Controversy over Ritual Murder? The Debate over the Paintings in Sandomierz Cathedral," *Polin: Studies in Polish Jewry*, vol. 16, *Focusing on Jewish Popular Culture in Poland and its Afterlife*, ed. Michael C. Steinlauf and Antony Polonsky (London: 2003), 483–490.

38. Musiał, "Droga krzyżowa Żydów Sandomierskich," 22.

39. See Stanisław Musiał, "Ciężar antysemityzmu," *Tygodnik Powszechny* (29 March 1998), 9; Ignatowski, *Kościół i synagoga*, 66–96.

40. This statement was issued on April 15, 1990 and reported in *Gazeta Wyborcza* (16 April 1990), 2.

41. Reported in *Gazeta Wyborcza* (30 Sept. 1991). During the presidential election campaign in September 2000, Michalik made a political statement with a similar, but less explicit, content. This was done despite the official Church's line of distancing itself from any political involvement in the presidential election. See *Tygodnik Powszechny* (10 Sept. 2000), 2.

42. Rafal Zakrzewski, "Fakt, który nie zaistniał: prymas odpowiada ministrowi Żochowskiemu," *Gazeta Wyborcza* (19 April 1995), 1.

43. For reports of Jankowski's anti–Jewish statements in the Polish press, see, for example, Roman Daszczyński, "Skandalista Henryk Jankowski," *Gazeta Wyborcza* (31 Oct. 1997), 4; Grażyna Borkowska, "Obelgi ks. Jankowskiego," ibid. (29 July 1996), 2. See also *The World Report of Antisemitism 1996* (London: 1996), 192–193.

44. These remarks were mainly directed against the Union of Freedom (Unia Wolności) party, and particularly against one of its members, Bronisław Geremek, who was at that time appointed foreign minister.

45. During the months prior to his dismissal, Jankowski charged that an Israeli-Jewish-Communist conspiracy in the media was out to destroy him. See, for example, "Homilia wygłoszona w niedzielę, 8 sierpnia przez księdza prałata Henryka Jankowskiego w bazylice sw. Brygidy w Gdańsku," *Nasz Dziennik* (13 Aug. 2004), 12.

46. Krzysztof Olejnik, "Utopia Rydzyka," *Wprost* (8 April 2000), 36.

47. See, for example, Mikołaj Lizut, "Kto się boi Sorosa?," *Gazeta Wyborcza* (14 May 1997), 17; idem, "Rozmowy nie dokończone," ibid. (24 Oct. 1997), 3.

48. *The World Report of Antisemitism 1996*, 194.

49. On the phenomenon of Radio Maryja and different interpretations of its impact on society, see, for example, Gowin, *Kościół w czasach wolności*, 373–390; Jacek Kurczewski, "Polska partia Rydzyka," *Wprost* (11 May 1997), 26–28; Ewa Wilk, "Rodzina ojca Rydzyka," *Polityka* (13 Dec. 1997), 116–120; interview of Archbishop Życiński in *Gazeta Wyborcza* (14 May 2004), online at http://serwisy.gazeta.pl?wyborcza/2029020,34474,2074696 .html.

50. See the report by Marek Beylin, "Moja Gazeta Wyborcza," *Gazeta Wyborcza* (7 Nov. 1997), 5; Gowin, *Kościół po komunizmie*, 300.

51. Peter Raina, *Ksiądz Jankowski nie ma za co przepraszać* (Warsaw: 1996), 20–25; idem, *Ks. Jankowski znów atakuje* (Warsaw: 1998), 45–50.

52. Waldemar Chrostowski, "Tęcza malowana na czarno," *Tygodnik Powszechny* (11 Jan. 1998), 8. For other anti-Jewish comments, see the collections of conversations with Chrostowski titled *Rozmowy o dialogu* (Warsaw: 1996) and *Rozmowy, dialog w cieniu Auschwitz* (Warsaw: 1999).

53. This comment was made in a sermon preached to a group of pilgrims in the national Marian shrine at the Jasna Góra monastery in Częstochowa. See the report in *Gazeta Wyborcza* (10–11 Nov. 1997), 5.

54. Quoted in *Tygodnik Powszechny* (25 Jan. 1998), 2.

55. Stanisław Musiał, "Czarne jest czarne," *Gazeta Wyborcza* (15–16 Nov. 1997), 20–21; idem, "Grzech antysemityzmu," *Tygodnik Powszechny* (11 Jan. 1998), 9.

56. See a sampling of public responses to Musiał's first article in *Tygodnik Powszechny* (6 Dec. 1997), 4.

57. Interview by Ewa Berberyusz in *Gazeta Wyborcza* (16–17 May 1998), 29.

58. Gowin, *Kościół w czasach wolności*, 345.

59. Adam Boniecki, "List o przebaczeniu i pojednaniu," *Tygodnik Powszechny* (3 Sept. 2000). For lengthy excerpts from the Bishops' Conference letter, see, for example, ibid., 2.

60. Bishops' Conference letter, ibid.

61. Jan Gross, *Sąsiedzi: Historia zagłady żydowskiego miasteczka* (Sejny: 2000); the English version, published by Princeton University Press, appeared a year later.

62. Józef Życiński, "Banalizacja barbarzyństwa," *Więź* (March 2001). This article was also published in English in a special issue of *Więź* (2001) titled *Thou Shalt Not Kill: Poles on Jedwabne*, ed. William Brand.

63. A reference to David's responsibility for the death of Uriah (II Sam. 12:13).

64. Muszyński's interview appears in translation in *The Neighbors Respond: The Controversy over the Jedwabne Massacre in Poland*, ed. Antony Polonsky and Joanna Michlic (Princeton: 2003), 155–165.

65. The interview with Glemp appears in translation in ibid., 166–172.

66. A reference to the fact that the fans of one of the town's soccer teams refer to those of the other as "kikes" (*żydy*).

67. Glemp interview in Polonsky and Michlic (eds.), *The Neighbors Respond*.

68. Response by Musiał, ibid., 173–178.

69. Stanisław Stefanek, "Moralny obowiązek dochodzenia do prawdy," *Nasz Dziennik* (13 March 2001), 4–5. In his editorial column of the important Catholic weekly *Niedziela*, Michalik frequently presented a position similar to that of Stefanek; see Józef Michalik, "Piromani 'Wyborczej,' " *Niedziela* (24 June 2001), http://www.geocities.com/jedwabne/ piromani_z_wyborczej.htm

70. Joanna Michlic, "Coming to Terms with the 'Dark Past': The Polish Debate about the Jedwabne Massacre," *ACTA* 21 (Jerusalem) (2002), 18.

71. Witczyk's comments led to the discussion about how to conduct Christian-Jewish dialogue in *Tygodnik Powszechny*. See Stanisław Krajewski, "Dzień przezwyciężania judaizmu?" *Tygodnik Powszechny* (26 Jan. 2003), 4; idem, "Ponad dyplomacją," ibid. (9 Feb. 2003), 4; Henryk Witczyk, "Dzień poznawania judaizmu," ibid. (2 Feb. 2003), idem, "Pomieszanie poziomów," ibid. (23 Feb. 2003), 5; Michał Czajkowski, "Pomieszanie z popłątaniem?," ibid. (2 March 2003), 1; and Romuald Jakub Weksler-Waszkinel, "Dzień przepraszania Żydów," ibid. (9 Feb. 2003), 4.

72. Ibid. (12 Oct. 2003). For a discussion of "Dabru emet" and the shaping of Jewish-Christian relations with the participation of priests and members of the Jewish community in Poland, see "Bóg Sema i Jafeta," *Znak* (Jan. 2003), 65–84.

73. Michał Czajkowski, *Co nas łączy? ABC relacji chrześcijańsko-żydowskich*, (Warsaw: 2003); idem, *Nie wstydzę sie Ewangelii: Z ks. Michałem Czajkowskim rozmawia Jan Turnau* (Krakow: 2004).

74. See Stanisław Gądecki, *Kto spotyka Jezusa spotyka Judaizm: Dialog chrześcijańsko-żydowski w Polsce* (Gniezno: 2002); Stanisław Musiał, *Dwanaście koszy ułomków* (Krakow: 2002).

75. Tomasz Urzykowski, "Oddaję, co nie nasze," *Gazeta Wyborcza* (Stołeczna), (14 July 2003), 2; Maja Jaszewska, "Trzecie pokolenie sprawiedliwych," *Tygodnik Powszechny* (27 July 2004), 5.

76. On the "Rydzyk empire," see Janina Blikowska and Agnieszka Pukniel, "Telewizja Maryja," *Wprost* (27 April 2004), 30; Cezary Gmyz, "Gdzie jest 'Dwużydzian Polaków,' " ibid. (1 Feb. 2004), 22–25.

77. According to Bishop Piotr Jarecki, one of the main leaders of the reestablished Catholic Action, the organization does not wish to support the nationalistic vision of the Pole-Catholic. See Andrzej Goszczyński, "Front katolików," ibid. (16 Dec. 2001), 38–39.

78. See the report by Reverend Tomasz Słonimski, "Radio Maryja źle uczy modlić," *Gazeta Wyborcza* (27 Feb. 2005), online at http://serwisy.gazeta.pl/kral/2029020, 34474,257513.6.html; see also Lech Wałęsa's letter (addressed to "bishops and the faithful of the Roman Catholic Church in Poland), ibid. (23 Feb. 2005), online at http://wiadomosci.gazetapl/2029020,55670,2567404.html.

79. See Jan Turnau, "Najwyższa pora na ojca Rydzyka," ibid. (10 March 2005), online at http://serwisy.gazeta.pl/wyborcza/2029020,34474,2593456.html and Grzegorz Józefczyk's report, "Abp. Życiński Radiu Maryja," ibid. (25 Feb. 2005), online at http://serwisy.gazeta.pl/kraj/2029020,34317,2571480.html.

80. See, for example, Maciej Geller and Jerzy Jedlicki, "Z nadzieją—mimo wszystko," *Tygodnik Powszechny* (6 April 2004); letters to the editors, ibid. (13 April 2004); Marcin Dzierżanowski, "Podziemie antysemickie: Antyżydowskie publikacje w księgarni przy warszawskim kościele," *Życie Warszawy* (23 July 2003).

81. See Zuzanna Radzik, "Piwnice wciąż gniją," *Tygodnik Powszechny* (30 March 2003), 3.

82. Krzysztof Burnetko, "Antyk—ciąg dalszy nastąpił," *Tygodnik Powszechny* (30 Nov. 2001), 11.

83. The letter was published in *Gazeta Wyborcza* (3 Dec. 2003).

84. See the report "Lekceważenie miłości bliźniego," *Gazeta Wyborcza* (5 Dec. 2003), 4.

85. *Tygodnik Powszechny* (2 Aug. 2004).

86. Ibid. (27 June 2004).

87. Adam Krzemiński, "Witajcie w średniowieczu," *Polityka* (13 March 2004).

88. "Adam Szostkiewicz: to więcej niż film," *Polityka* (13 March 2004).

89. Quoted in *Tygodnik Powszechny* (28 Sept. 2003).

90. Quoted in *Polityka* (6 March 2004).

91. *Tygodnik Powszechny* (7 March 2004).

92. Ibid. (14 March 2004) (question posed by Joanna Petry-Mroczkowska in ibid. [7 March 2004], 1).

93. Ibid., 17.

94. Ibid.

95. Katarzyna Jabłońska, "Naturalistycznie zamiast realistycznie," *Więź* (April 2004), 116.

96. Michał Czajkowski, "Wolę ewangelię," ibid., 120.

97. Włodzimierz Rędzioch, "Film antysemicki czy antykatolicka krytyka? Amerykański Rabin Daniel Lapin broni filmu Gibsona," *Niedziela* (7 March 2004), 13. For an extremely positive evaluation of the film (without references to Jews or Judaism), see, for example,

Adrian Galbas, "Pasja czyli o miłosierdziu pokonującym każdą samotność," *Niedziela* (28 March 2004), 11.

98. Quoted in *Polityka* (29 May 2004).

99. *Tygodnik Powszechny* (23 May 2004).

100. See the interview with Tadeusz Mazowiecki, "Na początku jest pustka," *Gazeta Wyborcza* (17 Sept. 2004), online at http://servisy.gazeta.pl/wyborcza/2029020,34474, 2291717.html.

101. *Polityka* (14 July 2001), 7.

102. *Tygodnik Powszechny* (28 March 2004), 1.

103. *Niedziela* (4 April 2004), 12.

104. Cezary Gmyz, *Wprost* (28 March 2003); Mikołaj Lizut, "Abp Michalik następcą kardynała Glempa," *Gazeta Wyborcza* (18 March 2004), online at http://www2.gazeta.pl/info/elementy/druk.jsp?xx=1973969&plik=&tablica=document.

105. A call for more consistent and more effective dealings with Radio Maryja on the part of the hierarchy was voiced by Adam Boniecki in his article "Przypadek Savonaroli: Dziesięciolecie Radia Maryja," *Tygodnik Powszechny* (16 Dec. 2001), 4.

106. Quoted in *Polityka* (13 March 2004), 5.

107. See Mikołaj Lizut, "Jak oceniamy polskich księży," *Gazeta Wyborcza* (10 August 2004), http://serwisy.gazeta.pl/kraj/2029020,34308,2220807.html.

108. Ibid.

109. For the statement of Polish bishops on Poland's entry to the European Union, see "Słowo biskupów polskich w sprawie wejścia Polski do Unii Europejskiej," *Niedziela* (1 June 2003), 8.

110. Marcin Król, "15 lat za wolności: Kłopot z kościołem," *Respublica Nowa* (Feb. 2004).

111. See Kaja Malecka, "Dorobkiewicze partyjni pouczają Kościół," *Rzeczpospolita* (16 Aug. 2004), A5.

112. See the short note about Miłosz's death in *Nasz Dziennik* (16 Aug. 2004), 2; see also Zubrzycki, " 'Poles-Catholics' and "Symbolic Jews,' " 79–80.

113. See Stefan Wilkanowicz, "Jego trudny testament," *Wprost* (3 April 2005), online at http://www.wprost.pl/drukuj/?)=75315 and Roman Graczyk's interview with Bishop Tadeusz Pieronek, "Pieronek: kościołowi w Polsce brakuje wizji," *Gazeta Wyborcza* (9 April 2005), online at http://serwisy.gazeta.pl/wyborcza/2029020,34474,2645765.html.

"Poles-Catholics" and "Symbolic Jews": Jewishness as Social Closure in Poland

Geneviève Zubrzycki
UNIVERSITY OF MICHIGAN

The logic of normal, correct, and healthy antisemitism is the following: "Adam Michnik is a Jew, therefore he is a hooligan, a thief, a traitor, a bandit, etc. . . . ." Magical antisemitism, however, works this way: "Adam Michnik is a thief, therefore he is most probably a Jew.
—Adam Michnik

I'm not an antisemite. That's how they are representing me everywhere. That's not true. I love Jews. I just don't want my homeland, Poland, to be ruled by Jews.
—Kazimierz Świtoń[1]

In the summer of 1998, self-defined "Poles-Catholics" erected hundreds of crosses just outside Auschwitz, in the backyard of what had been, from 1984 to 1993, the notorious Carmelite convent.[2] This action was spurred by rumors to the effect that an eight-meter-high cross popularly known as the "papal cross" would soon be removed from the grounds.[3] Antoni Macierewicz, a well-known right-wing political figure, characterized the intended removal as "religious defamation and national humiliation," and Cardinal Józef Glemp's comments, whenever the papal cross and Auschwitz were brought up in interviews, were interwoven with antisemitic nuances. In mid-March, some parishes initiated special masses "for the respect and protection of the papal cross" alongside prayer vigils for the "defense" of crosses in Poland. At the annual, Jewish-sponsored "March of the Living" in April that year, banners and posters proclaiming "Defend the Cross," "Keep Jesus at Auschwitz" (in English), and "Polish Holocaust by Jews, 1945–56" were displayed on the fence of the former convent yard—"the gravel pit," as it was still known, hearkening back to its function during the Auschwitz era.

In June, Kazimierz Świtoń, ex-Solidarity activist and former deputy of the right-wing Confederation of Independent Poland, initiated a hunger strike that lasted 42 days.[4] Świtoń demanded a firm commitment from the Catholic Church that the papal cross would remain. This demand was not met, whereupon he appealed to his fellow Poles to plant 152 crosses on the grounds of the gravel pit, both to commemorate the execution of 152 ethnic Poles on that site in 1941 and to "protect and defend the papal cross." This appeal proved successful: during the summer and fall of 1998, the site was transformed into the epicenter of what became known as

the "war of the crosses" as individuals, civic organizations, and religious groups
from every corner of Poland (and from as far away as Canada, the United States,
and Australia) answered the call. By August 21, there were 135 crosses on the site.
A month later, 236 crosses were in place—96 of them measuring four meters or
more in height. By the time the Polish army finally removed them in May 1999,
there were a total of 322 crosses at the gravel pit.

The 14-month "war" was marked by debate, legal procedures, numerous declarations from public officials, and accusations and counteraccusations that embroiled
the government and the opposition, Polish public intellectuals, Polish Jewish activists, groups from the extreme Right, the Catholic Church, and a schismatic brotherhood claiming to represent "true" Catholicism in defense of the Polish nation.
Meanwhile, a group of U.S. Congressional representatives and the Israeli government demanded the removal of all the crosses, while members of the Polish and
Jewish diasporas added their own grains of salt to the boiling stew.

It took the relevant authorities several months to find a solution to the crisis. At
first, the government stood on the sidelines, evoking the principle of separation of
Church and state as defined in the Concordat of 1997 in arguing that the papal
cross was the property of the Catholic Church, which was responsible for the use
of its religious symbols.[5] The Church countered that the crosses stood on government property and that the Catholic Church had no monopoly over the symbol of
the cross, which belonged to the entire Christian community of believers. Over
time, however, as a growing number of crosses appeared at the gravel pit, the crisis
became more acute. The government was subjected to pressure from the United
States and from Israel precisely at a time when it was engaged in delicate negotiations regarding Poland's application for membership in NATO. The Church was
troubled both by the fact that many Catholics had disregarded the Episcopate's
request (in late August) to stop planting crosses, and by the persistent involvement
of a schismatic group in the affair. In the end, concerted attempts were made to
regain control of the gravel pit.[6] Following many legal battles and the passage of
a law regarding "the protection of the grounds of former Nazi camps" on May 7,
1999, a 100-meter zone was established around Auschwitz, giving the government
the legal means to evict Świtoń from the gravel pit, where he had been encamped
for nearly a year. The Church arranged for the crosses to be relocated in a nearby
sanctuary.

The papal cross, however, remained. Thus there was no resolution of the initial
conflict concerning the presence of that specific cross. For this reason, Świtoń's
"cross-planting" can be regarded (and is so regarded by Świtoń) as a success. By
escalating the conflict and radicalizing the demands—from the retention of one
cross to the retention of hundreds—the papal cross' defenders successfully altered
the terms of any proposed compromise. In fact, by the end of the affair, removal
of the papal cross was not even considered an option; at most, the removal of
Świtoń and the 300-odd crosses was the principal objective of most of those involved.

Fought on several fronts, the war of the crosses was structured along two main
axes. The first, and more apparent, revolved around the contested meaning of
Auschwitz and the problematic presence of a Christian symbol at that site, and was

played out between Poles and Jews.[7] The second concerned the contested meaning of the cross and, more broadly, that of the nation in post-Communist Poland, which became a matter of serious debate among Poles. While the war of the crosses was without doubt an interreligious and interethnic (and, as noted, even an international) conflict, it was also an *intranational* and *intrareligious* crisis. It divided ethnoreligious from civic-secular nationalists; it divided certain members of the clergy and of the Episcopate from others; and it also drove a wedge between the institutional Church and the self-defined Poles-Catholics who were responsible for planting the crosses. In short, it became *the* occasion for Poles to debate the relationship between Polish national identity and Catholicism.[8]

As I have shown elsewhere, the fall of Communism and the building of a legitimate state *of* and *for* Poles has necessitated the specification of what Polishness "is" and has brought about the examination of its association with Catholicism.[9] In this context, the post-Communist period has been shaped by a society-wide debate in which some call for the maintenance of a "Catholic Poland, united under the sign of the cross," while others demand the confessional neutrality of the state and advocate a civic and secular definition of national identity. Thus, the place of religion, religious symbols, and the role of the Catholic Church in public life have all been fiercely debated in the last decade. "Jews" occupy a privileged place in this debate, serving as a trope by which the relationship between Polishness and Catholicism is defined.[10] In this essay, I address the ways in which various Catholic groups articulate, both in discourse and via their ritual use of symbols, the relationship between religion and national identity, and how Jewishness is constructed as a symbol through (and sometimes, against) which Polishness is (re)defined.[11]

Catholicism and the Church after Communism

According to most popular and some academic representations of the Catholic Church under Communism, the institution was solidly unified against the party-state, with the two monoliths confronting each other like sumo wrestlers in a stadium packed with the Church's cheering fans. The Church, so the story goes, was not merely indivisible; its historic symbiotic unity with "the nation" and with civil society (in the 1980s, under the banner of Solidarity) was unbreakable. Wyszyński, Wojtyła and Wałęsa—the priest, the pope and the prophet, the "Holy Trinity" of the fight against the Communist regime and its atheist state—symbolized the strength of the Catholic Church and its bond with civil society and the nation. There is, of course, some measure of truth in this picture, not to mention a genuine aesthetic appeal. The need for unity under adversity pushed aside differences of opinions, strategies, and styles, such that divisions within the Church, as within Solidarity or society more broadly, were in fact kept to a minimum. Ironically, while the party-state's attempt to "divide and conquer" failed,[12] the process of building a sovereign and democratic state led to certain cleavages between the Church and civil society, as tensions that had been glossed over in the past were brought under scrutiny. The decade following the fall of Communism witnessed an unprecedented drop of popularity of the Church, a rise in anticlericalism, and a crisis within the Church: the monolith was breaking into a colorful, clashing mosaic, but the whole was less than the sum of its parts. At the same time, there was also a noticeable rise in antisemitism. As I will show, these two phenomena were related.

The Declining Significance of the Catholic Church

Several surveys conducted by the Centrum Badań Opinii Społecznej (CBOS) indicate significant attitudinal changes toward the Church and its role. Positive appreciation of the Church's activities has fluctuated from a high of 90 percent in 1989 to an all-time low of 38 percent in 1993.[13] During the 1990s, almost three quarters of Polish society felt that the political influence of the Church was too great, regardless of which parties were represented in the parliament.[14] This seismic shift in attitudes cannot be explained by the secularization thesis, since the change in attitude has not been accompanied by an increase of religious indifference or a drastic decrease in religious participation: according to recent data, 96 percent of Poles declare themselves to be "believers," and 58 percent go to church at least once a week.[15]

The drop in approval may instead be explained by the fact that many Poles have *changed their expectations* of the Church since the fall of Communism, finding in the new political constellation a number of other, and sometimes competing, elements for the construction of their social identities. Polish national identity can now express itself through channels other than religion, and there exists a plurality of institutions through which Poles can make their voices heard. This new institutional pluralism has important implications, foremost among them the end of the moral and social monopoly of the Catholic Church. I have suggested elsewhere that the advent of a legitimate, democratic state provoked the rupture of the model of relations between the Church and civil society.[16] The new dynamic was characterized by a growing critique of the Church and by the Church's attempt to compensate for the loss of its social influence both by trying to increase its institutional power and by intervening in the political sphere.[17]

From Monolith to Mosaic

As noted, the "recovery of independence" (*odzyskanie niepodległości*), as the transition from Communism is commonly termed, prompted tensions not only between civil society and the Church, but also within the Church itself. Old cleavages resurfaced and new fissures were created. In consequence, a more expansive (though still restricted) "menu of Catholicisms" became available for clergy and the faithful. Over the last decade, four main orientations have evolved within the Church and among Catholics: "open," or liberal; "purist"; traditional-conservative; and "closed," or integrist Catholicism.[18] Key typological axes include the groups' conceptualization of the relation between Polishness and Catholicism; the role of the Church in the public sphere; Church-state relations; "Europe" as threat or promise; and last, but not least, the Church's attitude toward Jews and antisemitism.

By far the most popular orientation is that of the traditional-conservatives. Theirs is the Catholicism of "continuity," supported by Cardinal Glemp and the majority of clergy as well as by political figures such as Lech Wałęsa. It is characterized by its active engagement in the life of "the nation" (with the nation cast as a divine community and the Church as its guardian), and by pressure for the public demonstration of faith. During the Communist era, this model of traditional religiosity and national activism on the part of the Church was successful in resisting state-sponsored atheism; it also provided a mobilizing narrative of the nation as intrinsically and primordially Catholic. For traditionalists, the fall of Communism meant the return to "normalcy," which they understood as a pre-Second World War model of Church-state relations, with Catholicism holding the status of a quasi-state religion.[19]

According to traditional-conservative Catholics, the specificity of the Polish way of life resides primarily in the tight relationship between religion and national identity. However, the *Polak-katolik* model is envisaged not as a reality that must be preserved at any cost, but rather as a summons and an invitation: by being better Catholics, Poles become better, "truer" Poles.[20] Following this logic, which was codified in the writings of Roman Dmowski (the nationalist leader, whose classic *Thought of the Modern Pole* [1933] was re-edited in the 1990s with a preface added by Cardinal Glemp), non-Catholics are not "true" Poles, and Jews are irremediably "alien"—that is, "strangers" among the Poles.

Traditional-conservatives did not oppose Poland's so-called "return to Europe," but they argue that Europe would be stronger if it renewed its bonds with Catholicism. Accordingly, they see it as their mission to re-evangelize the Continent, with Poland as the *Antemurale Christianitatis*, the rampart of Christianity. No longer must Christians halt the advance of the (external) infidel; rather, Europe must be brought back to its forgotten values. A corollary to this is that Poland's integration into a "de-Christianized Europe" brings with it a threat to Polish and Christian values: in the wake of Communism's collapse, it is the West and its corrupted values that endanger this last European bastion of Christianity. Poland, then, must also remain Catholic in order to protect Europe *from itself*.

Contrary to the traditional-conservative model of Catholicism that accentuates the *public* dimension of faith and politicizes religion, "purists" focus on its *private* aspects: on the deepening of faith, on its active internalization. According to them, traditional Catholicism is overly associated with secular emotions and has become a political religion. They warn against the conflation of nation and religion: instead of emphasizing Polish Catholic exceptionalism, as do the traditionalists and the integrists, the purists stress the universality of Catholicism. They also consistently promote the principles of Vatican II: namely, ecumenism and attempts to modernize the Polish Church. Purists, therefore, should not be characterized as resistant to change; rather, the changes they endorse are those related to a universalist construction of faith-based Catholic renewal. Despite their multiple critiques of traditional Catholicism, they do not reject it altogether, but rather aim at modifying it so that it can better adapt to the exigencies of the contemporary moment. The purist model has a strong base in the Church hierarchy and is particularly popular among the younger generation.[21] It is also well positioned within the episcopate represented by Archbishops Damian Zimoń, Józef Życiński, Henryk Muszyński and Tadeusz Pieronek.

"Open" Catholics are primarily those associated with "liberal" Catholic publications and groups: *Tygodnik Powszechny*, *Znak*, the Catholic Intelligentsia Club, and *Więź*. These loose formations actively embraced Vatican II even when the reigning Polish Catholic authority at the time, Cardinal Wyszyński, remained somewhat reluctant to implement its principles in the Communist context. "Open" Catholicism is much more elitist than the traditional and integrist orientations, which both have strong populist accents. Its clerical supporters have included Józef Tischner (1931–2000), Stanisław Musiał (1938–2004), Stanisław Obirek, and Michał Czajkowski, and it is also embraced by lay intellectuals. Within the Episcopate, however, it enjoys only marginal appeal, and it is often attacked by traditional and integrist Catholics. The "open" Catholics' critique of traditional-conservative Catholicism is harsher than that of the purists. They are committed to creating a dialogue with the secular media, and they are frequent contributors to *Gazeta Wyborcza*.

Following Vatican II, "open" Catholics see dialogue with people of other faiths (or those without faith) as their duty, and thus actively support pluralism. *Znak*, *Tygodnik Powszechny*, and *Więź* frequently publish articles on Judaism and advocate a rapprochement and reconciliation with their "older brothers in faith." Their contributors and publishers have also been at the forefront in denouncing antisemitism both within Polish society and within the Church itself.[22] Father Musiał was certainly the Church's most outspoken persona undertaking this mission: he was actively involved in the negotiations for the relocation of the Carmelite nuns away from Auschwitz, and he openly criticized the Church's "soft" stance on antisemitism. Aside from his vociferous condemnation of the war of the crosses and of the Church for "putting its head in the sand," Musiał sharply criticized the Church hierarchy for not taking more severe action against Father Henryk Jankowski, the renowned Solidarity chaplain who has since become notorious for both his stridently antisemitic sermons and his controversial Easter Sepulchers. Musiał's groundbreaking article, "Black is Black," provoked a mini-scandal within the Church, exposing and furthering tensions between the four main groups of Catholics.[23] The ensuing debate between Musiał and Father Waldemar Chrostowski (a traditional-conservative priest who defended the Church's position vis-à-vis Jankowski), which filled the pages of the Catholic press, was paradigmatic of this split.[24]

Finally, there is the group of Catholics at the opposite end of the continuum: integrists, or "closed" Catholics, personified by Jankowski and Father Tadeusz Rydzyk, the founder and director of the controversial Radio Maryja. Integrists represent a large though not dominant segment of Polish Catholicism in Poland. At the same time, they are probably its most vocal component, and they occupy public space with immense semiotic force. Radio Maryja ("the Catholic voice in your home") and various print publications such as *Nasz Dziennik* (Our daily) and *Nasza Polska* (Our Poland)[25] exert a significant influence on the image of Catholicism in Poland by affixing the terms and relative positions that appear in public debate. The voice of Radio Maryja in Polish homes is that of anti-communism, anti-liberalism and antisemitism, with Jews representing both Communism and liberalism.[26] Like the traditionalists, but more strident in their message, integrists see the nation as a divine creation, not as the product of historical processes. As a result, the state, which is the guardian of the nation, must be confessional in order to preserve the divine order. As Dmowski put it, the equation between Polishness and Catholicism is God-given, and must be protected by the state.

Integrists are the group that compacts Polishness and Catholicism most tightly. "Closed" Catholics see themselves as "true" Catholics and "true" Poles, whereas "open" Catholics are, in their eyes, "washed out" Catholics and "bad" Poles, or even crypto-Jews. Jerzy Turowicz (1912–1999), for example, who for nearly half a century was editor-in-chief of the Catholic weekly *Tygodnik Powszechny*, was often suspected of being a Jew by "closed" Catholic circles, who in this way could understand his "selling out" to "Jews"—a reference to Turowicz's contacts among left-leaning intellectuals and his promotion of Christian-Jewish dialogue in the pages of his weekly.

The language used by "closed" Catholics is one of exclusion, hence their label (which was given to them by "open" Catholics). Tellingly, the adjective they use when referring both to "open" Catholics and to the secular center-Left is "Polish-speaking" (to denote a person) and "Polish-language" (to denote a publication). These adjectives pejoratively distinguish such people, associations, and publications from "authentically" Polish ones. In addition, people who identify or are associated with Radio Maryja commonly refer to *Gazeta Wyborcza* as *Gazeta koszerna*, the "kosher newspaper." This nickname relates to the Jewishness of Adam Michnik and of some of the newspaper's contributors, but also, more broadly, to the paper's center-Left orientation and to its position in support of Christian-Jewish dialogue, which "closed" Catholics see as "pro-Jewish" and "politically correct."

For integrists, the post-Communist period is a continuation of totalitarianism—totalitarianism with a new, liberal face, which "Europe" has come to symbolize. Even following Poland's entry into the European Union, Radio Maryja remains locked in its crusade against Poland's so-called "return to Europe."[27] The European Union is perceived as a potential "new internationale" (referring to the Soviet Union's former global aspirations), an unambiguous evil, one additional step toward a world order that will encircle and strangle Polishness. The position of the far Right and so-called national-Catholics (associated with "closed" Catholicism) is thus *isolationist*. Europe's *Antemurale Christianitatis* is redefined in peculiar fashion: now that the Iron Curtain has been lifted, Poland should seek to erect a different kind of barrier, not on its Eastern border in order to protect Europe from the pagan East, but rather on its Western edge, to protect itself from Europe and its degenerate Western values (consumerism and secularization) or lack of values (ethical relativism).

The Broken Monolith and the War of the Crosses

The differences and divisions within Polish Catholic society were brought to light very clearly during the war of the crosses. During the crisis, the hierarchy's position on the papal and the other crosses was neither unified nor consistent. The Episcopate expressed various opinions, and Cardinal Glemp's declarations fluctuated from open approval to condemnation of the cross-planting.

Consider, to wit, Glemp's words about the papal cross at the beginning of the summer of 1998, when people were mobilizing for its defense but were not yet erecting additional crosses at the gravel pit:

> The Polish people [*lud*] have been put up on the cross. That is why they love this cross, [which is] a sign of love in suffering wherever it is: in the shipyards, in Warsaw or in Oświęcim. In Oświęcim the cross has been standing and will stand. . . . The Eiffel Tower did not and does not please everyone, but this is no reason to remove it.[28]

The three Polish sites enumerated by Cardinal Glemp are closely associated with the nation, with Polish martyrdom and resilience. All three are symbols of the moral victory of Poles under occupation: Oświęcim and Warsaw during the Second World War, and the Gdańsk shipyards under Communism (where the dissident Solidarity movement had its genesis). The Polish nation is identified here with Christ, in continuation with Polish Romantic thought: its history and destiny are intimately linked to the cross. Most striking, however, is the analogy drawn by Glemp between the cross at Auschwitz and the Eiffel Tower in Paris, which shows the extent to which he misunderstood, downplayed, and belittled the Jewish position. As will be seen, both in his early allocutions and through his later prolonged silence on the matter, Cardinal Glemp implicitly and sometimes even explicitly justified the war of the crosses.

Once the war of the crosses was fully engaged, the harshest critique of the Church's position came from Father Musiał:

> The shameful cross game at Auschwitz continues. What is going on here does not have anything to do with God or with the commemoration of the victims. For almost 45 years after the war this place did not interest either Catholics or patriots. . . . There is in this country an Authority [whose] mission and raison d'être require it to put an end to this battle of the crosses at Auschwitz. Everything, however, points to the fact that this Authority has buried its head in the sand, and what is worse, wants national and world public opinion to interpret this gesture of silence as a sign of virtue, discernment, and civic consideration. . . . It is high time for the Church in Poland to awaken and raise its voice against the abuse of religious symbols for extra-religious goals. In truth, those against Christ's Cross are not the ones demanding that the crosses be removed from the gravel pit . . . , but rather those who planted the crosses, and those who want them to remain. Christ's cross is not a tight fist. And that is what the crosses at the gravel pit in Auschwitz are.[29]

A few days later, in a message perceived by many, including Świtoń, as supporting the retention of the papal cross,[30] Cardinal Glemp replied that the Church had no monopoly over the symbol of the cross, and therefore could not authoritatively intervene:

> The cross is not the property of the Catholic Church, but is linked with Christianity, and as a symbol it is understood and recognized in Western civilization as a sign of love and suffering. Conceived in that way, not only the Episcopate, but all those who accept with faith . . . this cross, have the right to its use and its defense.[31]

Although Glemp stressed the right to defend the cross as a *Christian* symbol, he also indirectly justified its political instrumentalization by attributing responsibility for the crisis to the "Jewish side":

> This is Polish land, and any imposition by others is taken as interference with sovereignty. . . . Mr. Świtoń and his group . . . are often singled out as the cause for the escalation of tensions. We have to say, in the name of truth, that this group did not come out of nowhere, but rather in reaction to the constant and increasingly strident Jewish demands for the rapid removal of the cross.[32]

Cardinal Glemp also directly and contemptuously denounced Father Musiał's position:

> Some are decidedly for the defense of the cross, others are supporters of the Jewish position, such as . . . Father Musiał, editor of *Tygodnik Powszechny*. The one-sided condemnation of the Episcopate [for its not satisfying] the Jewish side—cannot bear fruit, mostly because it is unfounded. . . . We have to ponder how the planting of new crosses can be used in the process of agreement and unification. The affair must find a positive resolution on the condition that people at the service of a one-sided solution, such as Father Musiał, for example, will not inflame [popular feelings] with their apodictic judgments.[33]

In this expressly personal rebuttal, Glemp accused Musiał of supporting the "Jewish option" instead of defending the cross, as a Catholic priest should. The same week, however, Archbishops Muszyński and Zimoń, purists according to the typology adopted here, characterized the cross-planting action as both a provocation and a harmful manipulation of the religious symbol for political purposes. "Those who are using the cross as an instrument in the fight against anyone," declared Muszyński in an appeal to stop planting crosses, "are actually acting as *enemies of Christ's cross*."[34] In response to this new twist, only four days after his declaration, Cardinal Glemp issued a new statement in which he charged that the cross-planting had been orchestrated by "irresponsible groups." Their action, he said, diminished the symbol of the cross: "The gravel pit, this way, loses its gravity." The primate appealed to those concerned to stop planting crosses at the gravel pit, and he asked bishops to "try to control the rise of this un-Church-like action."[35] Similarly, Bishop Pieronek characterized the groups involved in the action as "anti-Church."[36]

Finally, at the end of August, the Episcopate of Poland issued a long-awaited official declaration in which, echoing the position of the purists within the hierarchy, it condemned the cross-planting:

> As shepherds of the Church, we address our words to the faithful, expressing our gratitude to those who have suffered for the cross during the unlawful Communist period. . . . At the same time, we categorically underline that it is forbidden for anyone to overuse the holy sign of the cross and turn it *against the Church in Poland*, by creating agitation and conflict. We declare that the action of planting crosses at the gravel pit has been undertaken *without the permission of the relevant diocesan Bishop, and even against his will*. . . . Planting crosses *on one's own initiative* at the gravel pit is provocative and is contrary to the dignity that such a place requires. . . . *Organized in such a fashion*, the action equally hurts the memory of the murdered victims and the well-being of the Church and the nation, in addition to inflicting pain on the dif-

ferent sensibility of our Jewish brothers. The cross, which for us Christians is the highest sign of love and sacrifice, can never serve as an instrument in the fight against anyone.[37]

Note here that the primary reasons for condemning the cross-planting were that it had negative repercussions on the Church and had been undertaken without the hierarchy's permission and even against its expressed will. It is revealing that, in this statement, the Jewish perspective occupies the last position in the list of concerns. The action was said to hurt the memory of the victims, the Church, and the nation, and only then was it observed to offend the "different sensibility of our Jewish brothers." Thus, events at the gravel pit were essentially placed in the framework of an *internal affair*: a conflict between the Catholic Church and disobedient Catholics, which was harmful to both the Church and the Fatherland.

In the wake of this declaration, it was decided that the papal cross would remain but that the other crosses should be removed. Plans were undertaken by the Church to find an appropriate site for the crosses' relocation, and it was suggested that any person or group who had brought a cross to the gravel pit could reclaim it. As noted, the crosses were finally removed only much later, in May 1999, when they were transferred to a Franciscan sanctuary in Harmęże, a small village about ten kilometers from Oświęcim. For Father Musiał, the declaration of August 1998, while welcome, came too late and did not go far enough.[38]

Although the framing of the war of the crosses as an "un-Church like action" could be interpreted as a tactical device (Poles were certainly more likely to rally on behalf of the Church rather than in support of the Jews), it also reflected the Episcopate's real concern regarding Catholic disobedience, especially as the conflict continued to escalate and as a schismatic group became involved in events at the gravel pit. I refer here to the Society of Saint Pius X, founded in 1970 by Archbishop Marcel Lefebvre, who refused to submit to the teachings of Vatican II and who was subsequently excommunicated by John Paul II in 1988. The Society participated in at least three rituals at the gravel pit over the course of the summer, celebrating Tridentine masses, erecting its own cross (second highest, after the papal cross) and blessing all of the newly delivered crosses.[39] Before the official declaration of the Episcopate, Lefebvre's society had celebrated two masses at the site (on July 21 and on August 15, the Feast of Assumption). This may have provided an additional incentive for the Church to finally react to the war of the crosses, and it clearly had an impact on the framing of the events as an internal crisis.

The attitude of the Church's hierarchy toward the war of the crosses evolved through the summer from implicit approval to indifference, to apprehension, and, finally, to condemnation. These changes in perception and response went hand in hand with the drama's unfolding. The various reactions were also associated with specific types or groups of Catholics: an embrace of the cross-planting by "closed" Catholics; implicit approval or indifference by conservative-traditionalists; apprehension by purists; and strong condemnation by "open" Catholics such as Father Musiał. Whereas Cardinal Glemp supported the action at its beginning, its condemnation by archbishops Muszyński and Zimoń forced him to publicly revise his position. Although traditional-conservative Catholicism is the most prominent orientation within the Polish Catholic Church, purists and to a certain extent even marginalized "open" Catholics such as Musiał were able to shape the Church's official response to the controversial event.[40]

By the end of the summer, the Church's hierarchy attempted to restrict the semantic orbit of the cross and regain the discursive and ritual control of the symbol. The bishops convened in order to emphatically promote a "correct theology of the cross," since it had become apparent that "a deeper reflection about the meaning of the cross [was] lacking."[41] Muszyński characterized this incorrect theology of the cross as "a great problem internal to the Church." According to him, "the cross is a sign of love, forgiveness and unity, and not exclusively the symbol of a rather narrow conception of identity that can then be freely exploited in the fight with others." In his view, it had been easy to mobilize Poles around the symbol "because of their emotional attachment to the cross, attacked and destroyed by two totalitarian regimes"; traditionally, it was seen as "a beautiful patriotic-religious symbol, worshiped as such."[42] Father Andrzej Zuberbier, a respected theologian, noted that the war of the crosses revealed the problem of different understandings of the cross within the Church itself with greater clarity than did the question of the different understandings of that cross by Christians and Jews.[43]

Archbishop Muszyński underlined both the Christian meaning of the cross and its special significance in Poland—a double signification, which he viewed as the root of an inevitable tension with Jews:

> For us Christians, the cross will always be the greatest holiness, the sign of salvation and the symbol of the highest love freely accepted for saving the world. From the beginning of Polish history, the cross also became deeply inscribed in our forefathers' land, so that there is no way to understand Poles and the Polish nation without the cross and resurrection, of which the cross is the symbol, the condition and sign. Conceptualized in this way, the cross deserves to be defended always and everywhere because it is the most complete symbol and sign of the whole of Christianity. One cannot forget, however, that our non-Christian Jewish brothers associate with the cross a completely different content. They expect the same respect for their convictions as we Christians do. The content of those cannot be reduced to a common denominator. The instrumental exploitation of the symbol of the cross and its Christian meaning in the fight with whomever is, however, the negation of Christianity and of the cross.[44]

While the Christian and Jewish views could not, in his opinion, be reconciled, he pointed out that the war of the cross actually constituted the "depravation of the cross," and he attempted to prevent the pope's words concerning the need to "defend the cross" from becoming a slogan (illegitimately) used by the Defenders of the Cross. As in the Episcopate's declaration, the following statement shows the extent to which the controversy was framed as one detrimental to the Church and the nation and only secondarily to the "Christian-Jewish dialogue":

> The reference to the words spoken in Zakopane by the Pope, "defend the cross," in order to justify the action of the crosses at the gravel pit constitutes an abuse, and is the evident deformation of the actual intentions of the Pope, just as it is the instrumentalization of the cross, which is made into a tool for one's own, unclear interests that affect the good of the Church, our Homeland and the Christian-Jewish dialogue.

. . . One must really be completely deprived of a sense of realism to think that the Holy Father desires that the defense of the cross be used in the fight against whomever.[45]

All these efforts were in vain. The Episcopate's condemnation of the cross-planting, and its active promotion of a "correct" theology of the cross, had no real effect on those who continued to bring crosses to the gravel pit throughout the fall. In fact, two priests even consecrated the crosses as well as a small chapel built by Świtoń—an act that supplied the Defenders of the Cross with fresh ammunition. The group could now argue that not only the papal cross, but also all the other crosses, must not be removed.

According to Świtoń and the Defenders of the Cross, the Church had no monopoly over the symbol—a position, it will be recalled, that Cardinal Glemp himself had articulated in an early declaration. What was more, they argued: "*We* are the Church." In an interview conducted almost two years after the conflict's resolution, Świtoń explained this statement:

> Our Church did not defend [the cross]. Because the Church is divided: there's the administration and there's the People of God. . . . But the real Church . . . is the People of God, just like Christ founded it, and not the administration, bureaucrats who are priests, bishops, or cardinals.[46]

In this explanation, Świtoń distinguishes between the institutional Church—the administration and its bureaucrats who did not come to the defense of the cross—and the People of God, a "truer" church, faithful to its mission of guarding the nation. Although the statement "we are the Church" is reminiscent of the democratic, post-Vatican II definition of the Church as a "community of believers," Świtoń's comment more forcibly brings to mind the Weberian distinction between Church and sect, between a routinized and institutionalized movement and a charismatic movement whose objectives have not been bent by the needs of the institution.[47] What defines Świtoń's "People of God" is their "true" Polishness. According to Świtoń, "a Pole who does not defend the cross stops being a Pole." Moreover, the hierarchy of the Catholic Church in Poland was no longer Catholic, since its members had stopped defending the cross *as the symbol of Polishness.*[48] The statement "*we* are the Church," therefore, places the no-longer "Catholic" Church (because not nationalist enough) in contrast to a truer Church, the People of God—defined here as "true Poles," that is, those who defend the cross as a symbol of Polishness.

"By defending the cross," Świtoń told me, "I was defending Polish identity. Polish identity. Because Poland without the cross would not be Poland. Mickiewicz already said it a hundred something years ago: 'Only under this cross/ Only under this sign/Poland is Poland and a Pole is a Pole.' "[49] Indeed, many crosses at the gravel pit bore these verses as part of their inscriptions, which are commonly attributed to the Romantic national bard. One cross, however, in either a creative inversion or a Freudian slip, proclaimed instead: "Only under the Cross/ Only under this sign/Poland is Poland/and a *Catholic is a Pole*" (emphasis added). These formulations might be the best contemporary articulations of the fusion of Catholicism and Polishness within a single category, that of *Polak-katolik.*[50]

For Świtoń, for the Defenders of the Cross, and for many other national-Catholic groups, Catholicism is so closely associated with the Polish nation that there is no perceived tension between the universalist reach of the religion and its nationalist interpretation. The supra-national dimension of Catholicism is simply absent from the logic of this discourse, and although the cross defenders borrow freely from some of the rhetoric of Vatican II, their interpretation is far removed from post-Council teachings. In fact, the Council of Lay Catholics, a national organization, came to the defense of the Church and denounced the usurpation of the language of Vatican II for what it perceived to be political ends:

> The fanatic agitators from the Oświęcim gravel pit declared that *they* are the Church. We categorically protest against such a caricatured vision of Catholicism. The teachings of the Second Vatican Council about the Church as the People of God are very dear to us. That is why we do not agree with its perversion, when, in the name of a private conception of Christianity, the slogan "we are the Church" is used in the fight against the ecclesial hierarchy. The National Council of Lay Catholics expresses solidarity with the pastors of our Church, and deplores the actions of those persons who insult the bishops, disrespecting their mission in the Church. We appeal to all Catholics—lay and religious—for whom the words "we are the Church" are not the call for fighting anyone but rather the expression of the deepest identity: Let us give . . . the testimony of our position and of the word that "to be in the Church" means to live according to the commandment of love.[51]

Note that it is the illegitimate use and claim to ownership of Catholic rhetoric that prompted the reaction of this lay Catholic group, not the nationalist and antisemitic sentiments and actions such rhetoric suggests and invites. Once again, the discourse of the Defenders of the Cross is perceived and interpreted as a direct attack on the Church, and is as such denounced.

The meaning of the war of the crosses changed as the crisis persisted and deepened. It was at first interpreted by diverse communities of discourse as a conflict over the meaning of Auschwitz/Oświęcim and narrated as a "war" waged by Poles to keep the memory of "Oświęcim" alive. The normative evaluations of the event, we have seen, diverged greatly—while some denounced the takeover of the gravel pit as a despicable antisemitic gesture, others saw in the event the just and legitimate fight of Poles for their nation and its symbols. Once the schismatic Society of St. Pius X became involved, however, the event's interpretation and narration were altered. Reconfigured as primarily a crisis of Catholicism and more specifically an attack on the Church and on the good name of the nation, different communities of discourse, previously split in their normative evaluation of the event, converged to unanimously condemn the action. By the fall of 1998, voices such as that of Father Musiał had been muted: the war of the crosses was progressively reframed as a problem not originating from within Polish society or even within the Church, as the Jesuit priest had suggested, but rather outside of it and developing without, in spite of, and even against it. The culprits in the war of the crosses were forces *external* to the Church—Jews and disobedient Catholics—who caused *internal* damage to the Polish Catholic body.

Jewishness as Social Closure

I began this article by discussing what the transition from Communism has implied for the Catholic Church, and then went on to analyze the various orientations within the ecclesial institution and the broader Catholic landscape. The empirical analysis of a single event, the war of the crosses, highlights divisions within the Church and the different ways in which Catholics of different groupings articulate the relationship between national identity and religion, as well as their relationship to Jews and antisemitism. In this last section, I discuss the role of "Jews" in shaping the discourse of what Polishness is and is not.

The war of the crosses shattered the myth of Polish society's homogeneity: Poland's population is 97 percent ethnically Polish and 95 percent Catholic, but the question of what Polishness and Catholic identity "are" is polysemous and contested. Contrary to the myth of Poland's intrinsic Catholicism, and of the Church's monolithic moral authority in that country, the lines of division run deep within Polish society and within the Church itself. The Pole-Catholic association is produced only by determined cultural work on specific symbols, events, and their meanings. This cultural "work," moreover, is carried out by specific social groups and performed through various media and on a variety of staging grounds to create communities of discourse. Their formulations are in turn disseminated—though not necessarily assimilated—throughout the population at large.

It should already be clear to the reader that Świtoń and his followers were not mainstream figures. Although the drama's main characters, they remained marginal in the social and political landscape. Their views are close to those expressed in the national Catholic daily *Nasz Dziennik*, tied to Radio Maryja, and to those of *Nasza Polska*, a far-Right weekly.[52] They are part of a subculture feeding on elaborate conspiracy theories, according to which international Jewry and Freemasonry are out to destroy Poland from within and from without in order to facilitate the Jews' return to Poland, the Promised Land. Nevertheless, the war of the crosses *did* mobilize support, and the issues it raised were not themselves marginal, but rather became a lightening rod for mainstream commentary and discussion of Polishness; its traditional association with Catholicism; antisemitism; and the state of Catholicism in post-Communist Poland.

Debates about the cross within Poland not only concerned whether religious symbols should or should not be present at Auschwitz or its immediate proximity— an issue that is at the core of theological arguments between Christians and Jews— but what the cross in Poland *means*. In other words, the debate about the cross(es) at Auschwitz was a debate about the appropriateness and legitimacy of the fusion of national and religious categories of identifications in the post-Communist context. The discussion rarely involved Poles and Jews in direct dialogue, although Jews remained the implicit (and often explicit) external and internal "Other" in exchanges between Poles. As noted, Jews and Jewishness served as a key trope in the discussion of Polishness, as well as of the role of Catholicism in defining and shaping the latter. This trope also appeared clearly in the discourses surrounding the writing of the Polish constitution's preamble and especially during the document's ratification process.[53]

Significantly, under Communism, Catholicism and the cross marked the group's boundaries: "us," the nation, against "them," the alien, atheistic Communist regime. Catholicism managed to coalesce different groups against the party-state, including atheists and Jews. In post-Communist Poland, however, the cross is used by ultranationalist Catholics *within* civil society to define the boundaries between "true" Poles and "non-Poles": in addition to Jews (Poland's traditional internal "Other"), "bad Catholics," "cosmopolitan secularists," and Freemasons have also become categories of symbolic exclusion from the nation. Often, the last two are also code words for "Jews." Religion is used by these groups to define the symbolic boundaries of the "Polish nation," where the determination of who truly belongs depends to a great extent on one's commitment to a very specific—and narrow—vision of Polishness: that of the *Polak-katolik*. These ideological criteria do not determine legal membership to the Polish community (formal citizenship), but are central in defining socio-cultural membership.[54]

Through a complex chain of associations, a "Jew" is anyone who does not adhere to a strictly exclusive ethno-Catholic vision of Poland. Even certain bishops are accused of being "crypto-Jews," and the civic nation, according to the editor of *Nasza Polska*, is an invention of Jews.[55] Among "closed" Catholics, the European Union is similarly held to be the product of Jewish machination aimed at the institutional and structural annihilation of nation-states. From this perspective, Poland is ruled by "Jews," that is, by *symbolic* Jews. Any opponent to the ethno-Catholic vision of the nation is accused, through a series of associations and double-entendres, of being a "Jew." Jewishness, in this context, itself becomes a symbol standing for a civic and secular Poland. Adam Michnik defines this peculiar phenomenon as "magical antisemitism" (see the epigraph to this essay).

Thus Polishness, as a category, is understood not only in ethnic terms, following the German Romantic model of nationhood, but also in an ideological-political sense.[56] Certain Poles, because of their political allegiances and ideological positions (mostly with the liberal Left), are deemed "un-Polish," "anti-Polish," or else are dismissed as "fake Poles" or "Jews" by the conservative far Right. The recent controversy surrounding the funeral of Nobel laureate Czesław Miłosz is a good example of this phenomenon.[57]

Miłosz, whose cosmopolitan outlook made him anathema to the Right, died in Krakow on August 14, 2004. In the days leading up to his funeral, right-wing groups vociferously condemned the arrangements being made: how could this "undeserving" Pole be given final honors in St. Mary's, one of Poland's most impressive churches? And how could he be laid to rest in the Church on the Rock (Kościół na Skałce), alongside some of the nation's greatest patriots?

Plans were made to stage protests outside St. Mary's church in the Krakow market square. Some even planned to disrupt the funeral procession from St. Mary's to the Church on the Rock by lying down on the ground, their bodies forming the shape of the cross. It took no less a personage than Pope John Paul II to quell the agitation. In a telegram read by Cardinal Macharski during the funeral, the pope emphasized the Catholic faith of the deceased, addressing him directly: "You write that . . . your concern was ensuring that you do not abandon the Catholic orthodoxy in your creative work. I am certain and confirm that you have succeeded." John

Paul was surely aware of the controversy surrounding the funeral, which is why his text was so emphatic: "I repeat these words today as a memento, along with a prayer and a Mass celebrated for his soul." After this authoritative intervention, order returned to the streets of Krakow, and the poet's last promenade in his adoptive city proceeded with the proper *gravitas*.

As the war of the crosses and subsequent events demonstrate, Catholicism in post-Communist Poland is no longer a uniting and inclusive force aimed at building an open society, but rather is often understood as excluding (even post-mortem!) those who are not considered worthy of full membership. Whereas such symbolic exclusion is typical of places where the nation is understood in civic terms, and where, therefore, one's national identity—at least ideally—is determined by his or her adhesion to the principles of the social contract,[58] it seems unlikely and ill-befitting a place where the nation is primarily understood in *ethnic* terms. In Poland, national identity is perceived as being primordial, transmitted through birth, flowing through one's veins. In line with this conception, national identity can neither be chosen nor escaped; it is constitutive of the self. How is it possible, given this understanding of national identity, to encounter *ideological forms of exclusion* from the ethnic nation? How is the tension between these two modes of social closure, one based on blood and culture, the other based on ideological orientations and political bonds, to be reconciled?

In the Polish case, the answer is that ideological difference is "ethnicized," such that an "un-Polish," or "Polish-speaking" (that is, "non-Polish") liberal intellectual advocating a civic-secular Poland becomes a "Jew."[59] "Magical antisemitism" is activated against a specific set of values, whether capitalism or Communism, since each of these threaten a traditional, conservative way of life and religious values. Both Communism and Western-style capitalism are associated with cosmopolitanism, and both are associated with Jewishness. "Jewishness" becomes an ethno-religious category opposed to the *Polak-katolik*, and serves to exclude "unwanted ideological elements." Hence, we witness the strange phenomenon of antisemitism in a country virtually without Jews.[60]

Under Communism, the notions of *żydokomuna* (Jewish "cabal") and later, of a Zionist plot, were used to purge Polish society of "undesirable social elements." The antisemitic campaign of 1968 purged the old Communist guard, but also rid the country of a significant contingent of young students, a reservoir of proto-opposition. Whereas most of those targeted in 1968 were actually Jewish, the purges and repression also included several "Jews." This logic of exclusion was not used by the Communist elite alone; it also pervaded the opposition. In a familiar logic, Communists could not be "Poles" but were rather believed to be disproportionately "Jewish": the *żydokomuna* phantom haunting Poland. Thus, in spite of the party-state's success in establishing a homogeneous nation-state for the first time in Polish history, the Polish People's Republic was not considered to be "Poland." Hence Solidarity's mission, which followed the motto taken from a popular song, "So that Poland be Poland . . ."

Conclusion

"Defenders of the cross" at Auschwitz were actively engaged in what Pierre Bourdieu, David Kertzer, and others have described under the rubric of "symbolic violence."[61] Neither direct coercion nor direct persuasion, symbolic violence instead entails the establishment of categories and divisions that inform social reproduction. The cross, in this light, is the key symbol in the making of Polish-Catholic hegemony: it establishes the categories that promote social divisions. Even those who reject the cross at Auschwitz articulate their mutiny in terms of that very symbol. Everyone speaks in its shadow, whether raising their lips in reverent praise, or pursing them to spit in disgust.

Yet even within these structuring categories, there is the radical malleability both of the symbol of the cross and of its moral valuation. Under Communism, it was regarded by a great number of Polish citizens as "good" because it marked the line dividing atheist colonizers from "authentic Poles" and marked an area of (relative) freedom from the state. Engaging in religious practices or articulating religious discourse in the public sphere were activities that, de facto, created a "plural" society in place of the totalizing society the Communist party-state endeavored to impose. In the post-1989 context, that signification is no longer persuasive. The cross is a multivocal symbol, and far from creating social cohesion, it serves both to sharpen existing divisions within Polish society and to exacerbate social conflicts. It is now used *within* civil society to define the boundaries between "true" Poles and "non-Poles": "bad Catholics," Jews, secular-cosmopolitans and Freemasons. As we have seen, "Jewishness" itself becomes a symbol that stands for a civic-secular Poland oriented toward Europe, and it serves as a potent mode of social closure.

Although the most reactionary groups in Poland attempt to sustain the symbolic potency of the cross, "planting" it before a new "Other"—the civic-secular-internationalist West (a.k.a. "Jews")—the majority of Poles reject this effort.[62] Indeed, for many Poles, the cross has come to stand not for a free and independent Poland, but for right-wing oppression within the nation. In this way, the cross' symbolic vector is reversed from national "freedom" to national "constraint," from being "progressive" to being anachronistic and reactionary.

Notes

1. Adam Michnik, "Wystąpienie," in *Kościół polski wobec antysemityzmu, 1989–1999: rachunek sumienia*, ed. Bohdan Oppenheim (Krakow: 1999), 73; interview with Kazimierz Świtoń, 25 April 2001. All translations in this essay, unless otherwise noted, are mine.

2. In 1984, Carmelite nuns established a convent in a building that, while being outside Auschwitz per se, overlooks the former camp and was used to store Zyklon B during the war. After protests from (non-Polish) Jewish groups objecting to the presence of the nuns at that site, an agreement was reached and ratified in Geneva in 1987 between representatives of the Catholic Church and European Jewish leaders. The accord stipulated that, by 1989, the convent would be moved from the proximity of Auschwitz. For various reasons, the nuns failed to move by that date and tensions escalated as a group of Jews from New York, under the leadership of Rabbi Avraham Weiss, occupied the grounds of the convent in July of that year and were forcibly ousted from its premises. Protests and resistance followed in

Poland, many times in the form of declarations by the head of the Polish Catholic Church, Cardinal Józef Glemp, which were often unashamedly antisemitic in content and tone. The Carmelite nuns finally relocated in 1993, when John Paul II personally intervened in the conflict by asking them to leave. For detailed accounts of the Carmelite convent dispute, see Władysław Bartoszewski, *The Convent at Auschwitz* (New York: 1990); Marek Głównia and Stefan Wilkanowicz (eds.), *Auschwitz: konflikty i dialog* (Krakow: 1998); and Carol Rittner and John K. Roth (eds.), *Memory Offended: The Auschwitz Convent Controversy* (New York: 1991). For a conservative, pro-Polish view, see Peter Raina, *Spór o klasztor sióstr karmelitanek bosych w Oświęcimiu* (Olsztyn: 1991).

3. The cross was originally part of an altar located three kilometers away, on the grounds of Birkenau, the camp adjacent to Auschwitz. In 1979, Pope John Paul II conducted a Mass there, hence its popular designation as the "papal cross." After being stored in a local church's basement for a decade, the cross was brought one night, without fanfare, to the site of the convent. A local priest and a group of former (Polish Catholic) Auschwitz prisoners were responsible; although religious considerations may have played a role, it is clear that the act was also, and perhaps mainly, politically motivated, and clearly related to the Carmelite controversy.

4. Born in 1931, Świtoń organized the first Committee of Free Professional Unions in the People's Republic of Poland (Komitet Wolnych Związków Zawodowych) in 1978. He was a member of Solidarity between 1980 and 1989 and a deputy in the Sejm from 1991 to 1993. During the late 1970s and throughout the 1980s, he participated in a number of hunger strikes.

5. A concordat is an agreement negotiated by the Vatican with a given state, which regulates the relations between the secular power and the Catholic Church in that state. In Poland, an agreement of this kind was reached in July 1993 and was ratified four years later. Some saw in the official reestablishment of diplomatic relations with the Vatican (broken unilaterally by the Communist regime in September 1945) a return to the "normalcy" that Communism had interrupted. Others viewed it as an outdated project that threatened the separation of Church and state. The Concordat was the focus of vigorous debate in the 1990s. In addition to controversial issues related to it, such as the question of religious instruction in public schools and the recognition by the state of Church marriages, the actual validity of the Concordat was questioned, since it had been negotiated before one of the two parties involved—the Republic of Poland—had acquired its legal foundations. Debate on this question was structured along two familiar poles: pro-Church, conservative center-Right Catholic versus liberal, center-Left secularists.

6. The war of the crosses was complicated by a number of complex legal issues originating in the fact that, in the course of negotiating with the Carmel convent in 1993, the government had purchased the building and its grounds. Before the sale took effect, however, the nuns had rented out the property for a 30-year period to the Association for the Victims of the War (Stowarzeszenie Ofiar Wojny). This contract could not easily be annulled. The leader of the association, Mieczysław Janosz, allowed Świtoń and the pilgrims free access to the grounds.

7. On the various meanings of Oświęcim/Auschwitz, see Emanuel Taney, "Auschwitz and Oświęcim: One Location, Two Symbols," in Rittner and Roth (eds.), *Memory Offended*, 99–112; Tomasz Goban-Klas, "Pamięć podzielona, pamięć urażona: Oświęcim i Auschwitz w polskiej i żydowskiej pamięci zbiorowej," in *Europa po Auschwitz*, ed. Mach Zdzisław (Krakow: 1995), 71–91; Peter Novick, *The Holocaust in American Life* (New York: 2000); Jeffrey C. Alexander, "On the Social Construction of Moral Universals: The 'Holocaust' from War Crime to Trauma Drama," *European Journal of Social Theory* 5, no. 1 (2002), 5–86; Antoni Sułek, "Wokół Oświęcimia: spór o krzyże na tle wyobrażeń Polaków o sobie i Żydach," *Więź* (Nov. 1998), 61–70; Marek Kucia, "KL Auschwitz in the Social Consciousness of Poles, A.D. 2000," in *Remembering for the Future*, ed. Elisabeth Maxwell (London: 2001); Geneviève Zubrzycki, " 'We the Polish Nation': Ethnic and Civic Visions of Nationhood in Post-Communist Constitutional Debates," *Theory and Society* 30, no. 5 (2001), 629–

669; and Jonathan Huener, *Auschwitz, Poland, and the Politics of Commemoration, 1945–1979* (Athens, Ohio: 2004). For an excellent analysis of the meaning of Auschwitz and its mythologization by Israeli and diaspora Jews, Soviet Russians and Poles, as well as the multiple and often contradictory philosophical preoccupations raised by Auschwitz, see Jonathan Webber, "The Future of Auschwitz: Some Personal Reflections" (First Frank Green Lecture, Oxford Centre for Postgraduate Hebrew Studies, 1992). On Holocaust memorial sites in Communist and post-Communist Poland, see James E. Young, *The Texture of Memory: Holocaust Memorials and Meaning* (New Haven: 1993).

8. My focus here is exclusively on the lines of conflict within the Catholic Church and among Catholics. For an analysis of the Polish Christian-Jewish axis of the controversy, see my *The Crosses of Auschwitz: Nationalism and Religion in Post-Communist Poland* (Chicago: 2006).

9. Ibid.; see also idem, " 'We the Polish Nation' "; Rogers Brubaker, *Reframing Nationalism: Nationhood and the National Question in the New Europe* (Cambridge: 1996).

10. The quotation marks indicate the symbolic and discursive nature of the category. It is the *image* of Jews and *representations* of Jewishness that are used to define Polishness, not real, existing Jews—even when actual Jewish persons are referred to or are verbally and symbolically abused, as was a frequent occurrence during the war of the crosses.

11. The evidence for this examination includes official Church documents, sermons and homilies, pastoral letters, editorials, and letters to the editor that were written during the war of the crosses. I reviewed newspapers (dailies, weeklies, bi-weeklies, and monthlies) representing diverse ideological and political orientations: *Nie, Polityka, Gazeta Wyborcza, Wprost, Tygodnik Powszechny, Nasz Dziennik*, and *Nasza Polska*, in addition to two Jewish publications, *Midrasz* and *Słowo Żydowskie*. I consulted the reports published in *Rzeczpospolita*, which is Poland's most ideologically neutral newspaper, in order to reconstruct the events that took place, and I analyzed reports appearing in *Katolicka Agencja Informacyjna* (hereafter: *KAI*), which publishes official declarations of the Episcopate and commentary from individual priests, bishops, and other members of the clergy. I also conducted field interviews with priests and with Catholic intellectuals, as well as with Kazimierz Świtoń, who initiated the cross-planting action. Participant observation among members of the Covenant in Defense of the Papal Cross at Auschwitz also yielded significant data. This group has been meeting by the fenced area surrounding the papal cross (just outside the Auschwitz-Birkenau Museum) every day since 1993. Among other things, its members pray on behalf of the papal cross and for the prompt return of the Carmelite nuns to the site.

12. Communist strategies to divide the Church from within and thereby diminish its social support included the internment of Cardinal Wyszyński (1953–1956), the establishment of the "Priests-Patriots" organization to collaborate with the Communist party (1949–1955), and the creation, in 1945, of Pax, an association that, until 1989, recognized the regime and the leading role of the Communist party.

13. Approval of the Church's activities stabilized toward the end of the 1990s to the mid-50 percent range, and has gone up by a few percentage points since the beginning of the new century (see surveys conducted by the Centrum Badań Opinii Społecznej [hereafter: CBOS]: *Kościół w III Rzeczypospolitej* [Warsaw: 1999]; *Stabilizacja opinii o wpływie Kościoła na życie w kraju* [Warsaw: 2004]). The period from 1989 to 1993 was marked by important ideological debates and controversies concerning, among other things, the character of the state, the return of mandatory religious instruction in public schools, and abortion. At the beginning of 1993, a new debate entered the public sphere with regard to a proposed law concerning the respect of Christian values in the media, which was passed in March of that year. This law was interpreted by many as the return of censorship. In popular culture, references to the Church and to the clergy as the "black mafia" or the "black totalitarian regime" (replacing the "red" regime of the Communists) became common at that time.

14. Jarosław Gowin, *Kościół w czasach wolności 1989–1999* (Krakow: 1999), 35.

15. CBOS, *Religijność Polaków na przełomie wieków* (Warsaw: 2001). Approximately

50 percent of the population participate in religious services once a week, and 8 percent participate *several* times a week. Another 15 percent go to church once or twice a month. In 2001, therefore, about 73 percent of Poles were involved in religious practices at least once a month.

16. Geneviève Zubrzycki, "De la nation ethnique à la nation civique: enjeux pour l'Église catholique polonaise," *Social Compass* 44, no. 1 (1997), 37–51.

17. Political intervention on the part of the Church was particularly pronounced from roughly 1989 to 1993, after which the Church became subtler in its interventions and its social approval, as we have seen, once again increased. In the initial post-Communist period, Church officials publicly endorsed various political candidates and parties, posting lists of the "right" candidates for whom "good Catholics" should vote, as well as lobbying strongly for issues dear to the Church. Although the Church's involvement in political life was perceived as necessary under Communism, this was not the case in a fully sovereign and democratic Poland. Over time, the Church, which had been used to playing a significant role in *oppositional* politics, was forced to modify its intervention. See CBOS (1999) for statistical data regarding social approval of the Church as this corresponded to specific debates in the public sphere, and Gowin, *Kościół w czasach wolności 1989–1999* for an analysis of the evolution of the Church in the 1990s.

18. This typology was initially inspired by that of Gowin; see *Kościół w czasach wolności 1989–1999* and idem, *Kościół po komunizmie* (Krakow: 1995).

19. The constitutions of 1921 and 1935 guaranteed that "the Roman-Catholic faith, being the religion of the overwhelming majority of the nation, holds in the state a primary position among the religions equal under the law" (see Gowin, *Kościół w czasach wolności 1989–1999*, 16).

20. Gowin, *Kościół po komunizmie*, 235.

21. Gowin, *Kościół w czasach wolności 1989–1999*, 350–356.

22. See, for example, *Więź*, "Pod Wspólnym Niebem" (Special Issue, 1998); Oppenheim (ed.), *Kościół polski wobec antysemityzmu,* and the numerous articles appearing in the pages of *Tygodnik Powszechny. Tygodnik*'s publishing house, Znak, is also very involved in this dialogue, both through its publications and via a special webpage, "Forum: Jews-Poles-Christians" that is explicitly devoted to Polish-Jewish and Christian-Jewish dialogue. Among other things, this site features reviews of the Polish press, personal testimonies, editorial comments and responses, book promotions, and a calendar of events organized by various associations and cultural centers. The site appears (in Polish) at *www.forum-znak.org.pl;* in English, at www.forum-znak.org.pl/index-en.php.

23. "Czarne jest czarne," *Tygodnik Powszechny* (16 Nov. 1997); a translation appears in *Polin: Studies in Polish Jewry* 13 (2000), 303–309. See also the essay by Joanna Michlic and Antony Polonsky that appears in this symposium, "Catholicism and Jews in Post-Communist Poland," 35–64.

24. A few weeks after the publication of Father Musiał's article, Father Waldemar Chrostowski published a critique titled "A Rainbow Painted in Black" ("Tęcza na czarno," *Tygodnik Powszechny* [1 Nov. 1998]). Musiał's response, "The Sin of Anti-Semitism," was published on the same page, along with a short endorsement of Musiał's position by Stanisław Krajewski, the co-chairperson—together with Chrostowski—of the Commission of the Christian-Jewish Dialogue. Shortly thereafter, Chrostowski resigned from the Commission; he was later replaced by Father Michał Czajkowski, an "open" Catholic.

Since then, Chrostowski, a traditional-conservative Catholic close to Cardinal Glemp, has been active in denouncing "Jewish excesses" and "Jewish anti-Polonism," from the Judaization of Auschwitz to the (American) Jewish attempt to prevent Mel Gibson's *The Passion of the Christ* from being adequately promoted. He refused to be interviewed by me in 2001 because he does not trust "American milieus." An account and discussion of the "Black is Black" debate can be found in Oppenheim (ed.), *Kościół polski wobec antysemityzmu.*

25. Note here the emphasis on "our," as opposed to an implied "their." The Catholic far Right attempts to recreate the distinction between "us, the nation," and "them, atheist Com-

munists"—a foreign power imposed from outside and above. This dichotomous frame, however, is expanded in the post-Communist era: it is now "us, true Poles" versus "them, fake Poles and Jews." In the post-Communist context, "them" becomes anyone who does not share or advocate an ethno-Catholic vision of Poland: "bad" Catholics, "Jews," "secularists," and Freemasons. This issue is explored in depth later in this essay.

26. For a theorization of antisemitism's "double sidedness," see Moishe Postone, "Anti-Semitism and National Socialism," in *Germans and Jews since the Holocaust: The Changing Situation in West Germany,* ed. Anson Rabinbach and Jack Zipes (New York: 1986), 301–314.

27. In May 2004, after Poland had already officially joined the European Union, Radio Maryja began re-broadcasting interviews with "experts" who predicted the end of national independence (and various other ills) should Poland ever join the EU.

28. Cardinal Glemp's remarks can be found in *KAI* (24 March 1998), 1.

29. Quoted in *Tygodnik Powszechny* (9 August 1998).

30. Interview with Świtoń, 25 April 2001.

31. *KAI* (11 Aug. 1998), 1.

32. Ibid.

33. Ibid.

34. Ibid., 3 (emphasis in original).

35. Quoted in *Rzeczpospolita* (11 Aug. 1998).

36. Quoted in *Wprost* (23 Aug. 98), 19–20.

37. The declaration, titled "Oświadczenie Rady Stałej Konferencji Episkopatu Polski w sprawie krzyży w Oświęcimiu," was issued on August 26 1998, following the Conference of the Episcopate; the said declaration was published a week later. See *Tygodnik Powszechny* (6 Sept. 98), 11; emphasis added.

38. Interview with Father Stanisław Musiał, 10 May 2001. Other prominent "open" Catholics, however, were satisfied by the Episcopate's resolution. Stefan Wilkanowicz, the editor-in-chief of the monthly *Znak* and co-chairperson of the International Commission of the Auschwitz-Birkenau Museum, reiterated in an interview conducted in April 2001 that, for Christians, the site could not be left without the cross; the absolute proscription of religious symbols (as demanded by the Jewish side) was simply untenable for Christians. That said, Wilkanowicz stressed that it need not be the papal cross, eight meters high and visible from inside the former camp. Rather, Wilkanowicz would deem appropriate a small monument (including the cross) to commemorate those Christians who died at Auschwitz.

39. A Tridentine mass is a mass celebrated in Latin, with a strict ritualistic code. The Second Vatican Council replaced the Tridentine mass with the New Mass, celebrated in vernacular languages. Although the public celebration of Tridentine masses is not banned, it is restricted by most bishops.

40. The final text of the declaration is ambiguous, which may result from the fact that such documents are written through a more or less democratic and consensual process. A small group of bishops usually drafts a first version, which is then discussed, rewritten, and resubmitted until it is deemed "acceptable" by all members. The final product, in consequence, is nearly always a compromise.

41. *KAI* (1 Sept. 1998), 4.

42. Ibid.

43. Quoted in *Tygodnik Powszechny* (2 Aug. 1998), 1.

44. *KAI* (11 Aug. 1998).

45. Ibid.

46. Interview with Świtoń, 25 April 2001.

47. Max Weber, *Economy and Society,* 2 vols. (Berkeley: 1978).

48. Świtoń also explained to me that the hierarchy was not defending the cross because many of its members were not, "in truth," Poles. He told me a story that I have heard many times in my conversations and interviews with ultra-nationalist Catholics: namely, that Jewish children during the Second World War were rescued and hidden by—and therefore survived

thanks to—Catholic nuns who raised them as "good Polish children." These children grew up to become Catholic, and some even entered the priesthood. However, they never really ceased to be Jewish; their allegiance remains to their "true" Jewish identity and nature, with their superficial Catholicism and "insider" status allowing them to attack at the Church from within.

49. Interview with Świtoń.

50. For a classical ethnography of the *Polak-katolik* stereotype, see Stefan Czarnowski, "La culture religieuse des paysans polonais," *Archives des sciences socials des religions* 65, no. 1 (1988), 7–23; for an analysis of the Catholicization of the national tie, a process that was accentuated and generalized only under socialism, see Paul Zawadzki, "Le nationalisme contre la citoyenneté," *L'Année sociologique* 46, no. 1 (1996), 169–185; for an analysis of the contemporary significance of the *Polak-katolik* stereotype in processes of inclusion and exclusion, see Ewa Nowicka, "Polak-katolik: o związkach polskości z katolizmem w społecznej świadomości Polaków," *Nomos* (1991), 117–138.

51. Document issued on 22 Aug. 1998, printed in *KAI* (25 Aug. 1998), 28–29.

52. According to research conducted by Ośrodek Badań Opinii Publicznej (OBOP) in February 1999, *Nasz Dziennik* has a circulation of 300,000 and an Average Issue Readership (AIR) of 170,000—that is, approximately 0.6 percent of Poles above the age of 15 read the newspaper. See OBOP, "Index Polska—Badania czytelnictwa prasy," at www.obop.com.pl .index_polska9902.htm; see also Ośrodek Badań Prasoznawczych, *Katalog Mediów polskich 1999/2000* (Krakow: 2000). In comparison, *Gazeta Wyborcza*, Adam Michnik's center-Left daily, has a circulation of 570,000 (720,000 on Saturdays), with an AIR of 2 million—that is, it is read by 7.2 percent of Poles above the age of 15. Since the fall of Communism in Poland, it has consistently been the most popular and influential nationwide daily (its circulation is actually higher than any other paper in Eastern Europe). See Grzegorz Ekiert and Jan Kubik, *Rebellious Civil Society: Popular Protest and Democratic Consolidation in Poland, 1989–1993* (Ann Arbor: 1999), 15.

53. Zubrzycki, " 'We the Polish Nation.' "

54. Edward A. Shils, "Primordial, Personal, Sacred, and Civil Ties," in his *Center and Periphery: Essays in Macrosociology* (Chicago: 1975), 111–126; Morris Janowitz, "Observations on the Sociology of Citizenship," *Social Forces* 59 (1980), 1–24.

55. During the debate regarding the naming of the constituent entity in the Constitution's preamble ("We, the Polish *nation*," or "We, Polish *citizens*"), Stanisław Krajski declared that the civic nation was an invention of Jews: "Not everyone knows that one of the inventors of this new 'meaning' of the word "nation" is Tomasz Wołek, editor-in-chief of the daily *Życie*. Who is Tomasz Wołek, and what is *Życie*? To this question, we can answer indirectly by noting that the assistant editor-in-chief is a certain Bronisław Wildstein" (quoted in *Nasza Polska* 23 April 1997); also see Zubrzycki, " 'We the Polish Nation.' "

56. Of course, even though its ideologues insist on its primordial character, the ethnic nation, like any other form of nation, is a social construction. Whereas the civic nation is conceived as a construct, the ethnic nation is conceived of as a *given*. This is not, however, what I am underlining here. Rather, I am pointing out the ideological criteria used by the Right in determining one's Polishness (or lack thereof) and the tension such criteria entails for the (ideally) ethnically defined nation. For a discussion of ethnic and civic nationalism, see Brubaker, *Citizenship and Nationhood in France and Germany* (Cambridge, Mass.: 1992); Dominique Schnapper, *La communauté des citoyens: sur l'idée moderne de la nation* (Paris: 1994); Bernard Yack, "The Myth of the Civic Nation," *Critical Review* 10, no. 2 (1996), 193–211, reprinted in *Theorizing Nationalism*, ed. Ronald Beiner (New York: 1999), 103–118; Kai Nielsen, "Cultural Nationalism, Neither Ethnic nor Civic," *The Philosophical Forum* 28, nos. 1–2 (1999), reprinted in Beiner (ed.), *Theorizing Nationalism*, 119–130; Zubrzycki, " 'We the Polish Nation' "; idem, "The Classical Opposition between Civic and Ethnic Models of Nationhood: Ideology, Empirical Reality and Social Scientific Analysis," *Polish Sociological Review* 3 (2002), 275–295.

57. For a good summary description of the controversy surrounding Czesław Miłosz's

funeral (in English), see http://letters.krakow.pl/local/milosz_funeral.html. The event also received front-page coverage in the *New York Times* (26 Aug. 2004).

58. The American case is the paradigmatic example of ideologically defined national identity, where "being" American means supporting a specific set of values and practices, and where, therefore, it is possible to be "un-American" by supporting, say, Communism during the McCarthy era or, more recently, by criticizing the Bush administration after the events of September 11, 2001. See Seymour Martin Lipset, *Continental Divide: The Values and Institutions of the United States and Canada* (Washington, D.C.: 1990) for an analysis of this mechanism.

59. In the case of Miłosz, Jewishness was not invoked. Rather, his "non-Polishness" was attributed to his proclaimed attachment to Lithuania, the homeland of his childhood. Accordingly, Miłosz was described in the right-wing press and chat rooms as a "Poland-hating Lithuanian."

60. It is very difficult to establish the number of Jews in Poland. Estimates vary greatly, ranging from 1,055 individuals (2002 Polish census) to 40,000 (*American Jewish Year Book* [2003]). The wide variation in these data is the outcome of different measures of "Jewishness": self-declaration in the census versus ancestry or formal membership in Jewish organizations. The numbers have steadily grown in the last decade, as better sources for estimating them have become available, and as the Jewish community has witnessed a cultural, religious, and institutional renaissance.

In 1989 and 1990, the *American Jewish Year Book* estimated the total Jewish population of Poland to be 5,000, of whom nearly 2,000 were "registered"—that is, were formally affiliated with one or more religious or secular Jewish organizations. This figure was widely cited in Polish publications throughout the 1990s. During that decade, however, the total number of Polish Jews was reestimated to be closer to 10,000 (see *American Jewish Year Book* [1992, 1995]). By the beginning of the new millennium, the number of Polish Jews affiliated with religious or secular Jewish organizations totaled 7,000–8,000. Moreover, between 10,000 and 15,000 people showed interest in rediscovering their Jewish ancestry, and as many as 40,000 Polish citizens were now thought to have "some" Jewish ancestry (ibid., 2002, 2003).

The numbers cited by Piotr Kadlčik, the president of the Jewish community in Warsaw and president of the Union of Jewish Communities in Poland, are slightly more conservative: according to him, there are now 4,000 to 6,000 "registered" Jews and approximately 20,000 to 25,000 Polish citizens of Jewish descent who do not maintain a formal connection to any Jewish institutions (radio interview, available at http://fzp.jewish.org.pl/english.present .html). For Polish census data, see www.mswia.gov.pl/mn_narod_żydzi.html; for other Polish estimates, see Sławomir Łodziński, "Dyskryminacja czy nierówność: problemy dyskryminacji osób należących do mniejszości narodowych i etnicznych w Polsce po 1989 roku," in *Integracja czy dyskryminacja? Polskie wyzwania i dylematy u progu wielokulturowości*, ed. Krystyna Iglicka (Warsaw: 2003).

61. Pierre Bourdieu, *Pascalian Meditations* (Cambridge: 2000); David I. Kertzer, *Rituals, Politics, and Power* (New Haven: 1988).

62. Zubrzycki, *The Crosses of Auschwitz*.

Communist! Fascist! New York Jews and Catholics Fight the Cold War

Joshua Zeitz
PEMBROKE COLLEGE, UNIVERSITY OF CAMBRIDGE

In 1949, a seventh-grade social studies teacher from Brooklyn named May Quinn found herself at the center of a gathering political storm.

Quinn was no stranger to controversy. In 1943, more than a dozen of her public school colleagues had filed an official complaint alleging that she promoted "intolerance and un-Americanism" in her classroom. She stood accused of ridiculing Jewish students and teaching that Hitler had achieved certain positive goals in Germany. In an attempt to clear her name, Quinn had sued her fellow teachers for libel, and lost, whereupon the local school superintendent suspended her without pay and relayed her case to the Board of Education. Ultimately the Board absolved Quinn of serious charges and reinstated her with a fine of two months' pay, but not before the city's supportive Irish Catholic community had made her a cause célèbre. The Holy Name Society of the parish church near Quinn's school, for instance, charged that the accusations against her originated with "a subversive or Communistic group now operating in this part of the city," while the Kings County (Brooklyn) Board of the Ancient Order of Hibernians saluted Quinn's "loyal Americanism" and lambasted her persecutors. Meanwhile, local and city-wide Jewish groups united unsuccessfully to demand that Quinn be dismissed from her teaching post.

After the Board's decision, Quinn fell from public view until December 1949, when school officials again censored her for telling students that "Negroes were happy before they knew about racial discrimination" and for suggesting that, "I would not go where I was not wanted." These statements sparked a renewed public controversy pitting the city's Catholic and Jewish communities against each other.[1]

At issue was not just ethnic wrangling over coveted public school teaching positions, or neighborhood scuffling of the sort long familiar to New Yorkers. More fundamentally, Jews were "demand[ing] an education free of fascism," and Catholics were outraged by "Communists [who] need reinforcement from Russia to oust Miss Quinn."[2] The highly charged rhetoric exposed the deep cultural divisions that drove much of early Cold War politics in postwar New York: many Catholics and Jews viewed the world as sharply bifurcated, with democracy locked in an epic struggle against either Communism or fascism.

In the years immediately following the second Quinn controversy, the *Brooklyn Tablet*, the official organ of the Brooklyn diocese, explained to its readers that antisemitism was a stock "Communist slogan" invoked to sully the reputation of anti-communists such as the "Catholic public school teacher, Miss Mary A. Quinn." Prompted by its intensely anti-communist editor, Patrick Scanlan, the *Tablet* had even spearheaded a defense committee for Quinn that raised $10,000 in small contributions from the paper's readership.[3]

While Catholic supporters of May Quinn labeled her critics Communists and denounced their tactics as divisive, Jewish activists—particularly local chapter members of the Jewish War Veterans (JWV) and the American Jewish Congress—considered conducting "letter-writing and telegram campaign[s]" to convince the larger New York community that Quinn was "a symbol of the broader issue of proper democratic teaching in the schools."[4] Jewish parents were particularly incensed that Quinn might receive another slap on the wrist, in comparison to the treatment accorded to a Jewish teacher named Minnie Gutride, who had allegedly hosted a Communist party function at her home several years before. In December 1948, the Board of Education's investigators had informed Gutride (a widow whose husband had served with the Abraham Lincoln Brigade in the Spanish Civil War) that if she refused to supply information about her past political activities, or if she insisted on soliciting legal counsel from the left-wing Teachers' Union (TU), she would be charged with insubordination—a transgression punishable by immediate dismissal. Confused and depressed, Gutride penned an emotional response to Superintendent William Jansen in which she denied any wrongdoing. That same evening, December 21, 1948, she took her life.

In light of the Quinn affair the following year, some Jewish New Yorkers bristled anew at the injustice suffered by one of their own, a woman whose only "crime" had been—*perhaps*—hosting a legal assembly in her living room. As one historian has noted, many Jews suspected that "[i]n the eyes of the Board of Education, racist and/or antisemitic utterances . . . posed a far less significant danger to the social fabric of the schools than the perceived threat of subversion."[5] Thus, when protesters squared off outside P.S. 220 in early 1950, their placards reflected a fundamental division between many devout Catholics, who understood the controversy as a case of Communist aggression against American unity, and many Jews, who viewed Quinn as an agent of the "fascist" threat to American democracy. For these Jews, the moral imperative was clear: "Parents want [a] human relations program. . . . Oust May Quinn"; "Veterans' Wives demand Dismissal of May Quinn"; "Dismiss Intolerance/Bigotry/May Quinn." Catholic protesters, for their part, proclaimed: "Oust Communist Teachers! Chivalry is not dead. Observe all these brave men against a lone woman. . . ."[6]

Although ethnicity and religion were clearly at issue in the Quinn affair, scholars are of two minds concerning the extent to which they were driving forces behind early Cold War domestic politics. In the early 1950s, leading sociologists and historians attributed anti-communist extremism to a sense of "status anxiety" shared by working-class Catholics and "old family, Anglo-Saxon Protestants."[7] However, subsequent studies have sought to discredit the idea that Catholics were exceptionally conservative or ardent in their opposition to Communism.[8] While political observers once speculated that anti-communism might have served as a cover for Catholic antisemitism in the late 1940s and early 1950s, recent scholarship takes a skeptical view of this notion, reminding readers that leading anti-communist politicians such as Joseph McCarthy scrupulously avoided appeals to religious prejudices (indeed, McCarthy's chief adviser—Roy Cohn—was Jewish). Moreover, most Jews were no less opposed to Communism than were Catholics or Protestants.[9]

At the same time, studies that minimize the ethnoreligious dimension of anti-communist politics in the early Cold War era may focus too much on political figures such as McCarthy and Cohn at the expense of examining political culture at the grassroots level. In metropolitan New York, cultural divisions between Catholics and Jews greatly influenced the debate over anti-communist politics. At the heart of that dialogue were conflicting fears about which "ism" most imperiled American democracy—fascism or Communism. Whereas many Jews came to believe that being Jewish and being liberal were nearly synonymous, a considerable number of Catholics held fast to an ethnoreligious culture that inspired a wide distrust of ideas falling under the broad rubric of liberalism.

In some ways, the tendency of Catholics and Jews to invoke cries of "fascist" and "Communist" reflected the unique political landscape of metropolitan New York in the 1940s and 1950s. Because "popular front"-style politics persisted longer in Gotham than throughout the rest of the country, the region's strongest voices for racial and economic equality were often tinged by past affiliation with the Communist party. This made all the difference to Catholics, whose disdain for Communism and radicalism often took precedence over their support for the rights of racial minorities and the working class. And in the case of Jews, the sustained allegiance of many of them to popular-front politics led them to characterize conservative politics as potentially "fascist."

In effect, Jews and Catholics in New York City clung to the political lexicon of the Depression era long after other Americans abandoned it for the new language of the Cold War. They continued to disagree about which totalitarian ideology—fascism or Communism—posed the greater threat to the United States. Because of this conflict, the New Deal electoral coalition of Catholics and Jews in metropolitan New York, apparently strong during the 1930s, broke down easily and frequently during the postwar years. Notably, New Yorkers often articulated their disagreements about totalitarianism in the language of authority and dissent, revealing ever-deeper layers of ideological discord between the city's Jewish and Catholic communities.

In the aftermath of the Second World War, many American Jews believed that pacifism, internationalism, and social democracy were integral to the survival of civilization. Although scholars tend to believe that American Jews were disinclined to discuss the Holocaust until the 1960s,[10] many New York Jews dwelled on it much earlier and considered it a clarion call for New Deal-style liberalism. Scholars agree that American Jews were an especially loyal, if small, segment of the postwar liberal coalition.[11] In the turbulent atmosphere of the early Cold War, their almost reflexive liberalism featured a tolerance of political dissent, strong support of social welfare measures, a faith in internationalism, and a commitment to dismantling legal and social barriers based on race, religion, or ethnicity.

Little wonder, then, that more than a few rabbis in metropolitan New York used their Rosh Hashanah and Yom Kippur homilies to trumpet a closely allied set of values. In a typical sermon, Rabbi Ben Zion Bokser of the (Conservative) Forest Hills Jewish Center told his congregants that "the great men of Jewish history earned their laurels by being meddlers. . . . Every movement of protest against social abuse has received vital reinforcement from the Jewish community." Bokser argued that Jews must demand "better working conditions, better housing, a fair wage, decent treatment for the sick and aged," and should continue not only to "giv[e] vital support to the struggle against racial and religious prejudice" but also to "meddl[e] with the abuses of the economic system."[12]

The merger of Judaism and liberalism apparent in sermons such as these point to a great self-contradiction among New York Jewry: its widespread professed dedication to a religion that few claimed to practice formally. Although more than 78 percent of New York's Irish and Italian Catholics attended Mass at least once each week, studies conducted in the late 1950s and early 1960s found that only 6 percent of second- and third-generation Jews in New York attended Sabbath services on a weekly basis. Only 20 percent attended one or more religious services a month, while the great majority (70 percent) attended religious services either once a year, or "a few times each year"—usually on the High Holidays (Rosh Hashanah and Yom Kippur).[13] Nonetheless, because they so often encountered overtly political themes on those few occasions when they did set foot in a synagogue, New York Jews could reflexively explain their commitment to liberal causes as an outgrowth of Jewish tradition.

Years later, Ruth Messinger, who grew up in postwar Manhattan and forged a successful career in city politics, was frequently asked about the origins of her "strong degree of social concern [and] willingness to talk about . . . increasingly unpopular issues that have to do with protection of poor people and minorities. . . . My instinct is always to say, 'Because I'm Jewish.' That is not a useful answer to most reporters and not exactly the way I want it written up, but that is very much the way I feel."[14]

In another Rosh Hashanah sermon, this one delivered in 1961, Rabbi Israel Mowshowitz of the (Conservative) Hillcrest Jewish Center offered a figurative interpretation of the biblical story of Joseph and his release from an Egyptian prison. "There are prisons far more confining and oppressive than those built with brick and mortar," he argued. "Joseph was confined in a self-imposed prison . . . the prison of prejudice." According to this reading,

> Joseph had a strong compulsion to find fault with his brothers. . . . He thought of them as competitors and looked at them with the microscope of criticism in order to expose their every weakness. . . . Poor Joseph. . . . He thought he would grow at the expense of his brothers. He meant to build himself up by tearing his brothers down. He did not give himself the opportunity to draw close to them, to learn to understand them, and to share life's hopes and dreams with them. He was a prisoner of his own prejudices. . . .

Mowshowitz went on to bemoan the tendency of prejudice to "bind" and "confine" humans. "We do not like a race or a people or an individual when we see them [from] afar, and therefore we conspire against them. . . . One of the tragedies of our time is that prejudice has enslaved the minds of millions." In this way, subtly wedding the theme of intellectual cosmopolitanism to a moral imperative to blot out race and religious hatred, Mowshowitz called on his congregants to break "through the prison of prejudice."[15]

Although synagogue attendance was highest for the High Holidays, Passover was perhaps even more widely celebrated among otherwise nonobservant Jews. A synagogue bulletin of 1963 noted:

> The *Seder*, the Passover observances and the Prayer Book all keep alive the memory of the event known as "the going out of Egypt." This has become one of the greatest Jewish doctrines. It declares that God is on the side of the slave and the oppressed. Tyranny may flourish for awhile, and may even appear all-powerful. But God hates the oppressor and sooner or later overthrows him. Egypt seemed unconquerable, but it fell before God's punishment.[16]

In 1945, Rabbi Jacob Pressman of the Forest Hills Jewish Center re-worked the traditional parable of the "four sons." In a newsletter published for members of his synagogue then serving in the armed forces, Pressman proposed a new approach to the familiar verses from the Haggadah. He urged his readers to honor the "wise son"—a "modern Moses, daring to lead the world out of its wickedness of ignorance, hate, and mistrust. . . . He has learned that only in the freedom of ALL people—Jews, Chinese, Negroes, Indians—can there be an assurance of freedom for ANY people."[17]

On the grassroots level, lay Jews echoed their rabbis in finding contemporary meaning in the historical drama of Passover. In April 1946, an officer of the Jewish War Veterans, Manhattan Post No. 1, wrote that

> two world-shaking wars [have been] fought to make the victory for human freedom complete. But victory for what? Victory to go back to the internal prejudices and dissensions [*sic*] that mock and divide us? Of course not! Our boys in the armed forces did not die for dear old Intolerance. Jewish war veterans had fought to secure for all Americans "the right to live, worship and work in full freedom, with equal opportunity for all"—regardless of race, color or creed.[18]

And in April 1954, only nine years after the end of the Holocaust and one month before the Supreme Court's ruling in *Brown v. Board of Education of Topeka*, Rabbi Morris Goldberg of Temple Shaare Zedek (Manhattan) drew an explicit connection between Passover and the postwar drive for civil rights:

> The MOSES of history is the constant leader whose life and experience made us realize the value of freedom. . . . We are all G-d's children and the Almighty plays no favorites. Pesach directs us to think of freedom as everyone's desire. Just as no nation could live "half slave and half free," so the world must now recognize that all men must be free. "Let my people go," is still the message today, even as it was in the days of Moses.[19]

If the struggle for civil rights offered the most obvious application of biblical wisdom to contemporary politics, Jewish leaders also urged their coreligionists to broaden the definition of "freedom." Rabbi Israel Levinthal, the spiritual leader of the (Conservative) Brooklyn Jewish Center, argued in April 1954 that:

> Political freedom, the right to express one's will at the polls, is an essential phase of freedom, but not enough. There must be economic freedom—freedom of opportunity to earn a livelihood; social freedom—freedom from all hate and prejudice; religious freedom—freedom to worship as one sees fit; intellectual freedom—freedom to think as one wills and to express these thoughts as one sees fit, so long as these thoughts do not endanger the ethical and moral life of the people.[20]

In the early postwar years, such rhetoric was unquestionably a confirmation of the liberal agenda: a commitment to full employment, civil rights, and the expansion of the welfare state.[21]

Students in New York Jewish schools were likely to learn that internationalism, as best manifested in support for the United Nations, was a linchpin of Judaism. "A number of Jewish schools joined in the celebration of United Nations Day," the *Jewish Education Committee Bulletin* reported in November 1950. "They stressed the continuous striving for peace which has characterized Jewish tradition and has been reflected in Jewish history and literature throughout the ages." The Jewish Education Committee recommended that all schools incorporate a similar observance into their schedules, perhaps along the suggested lines of a short sketch titled " 'Isaiah and the United Nations' . . . a fantasy in the form of a dream in which appropriate quotations from Isaiah are introduced into a mythical session of the United Nations Assembly."[22] Similarly, the Scarsdale women's division of the American Jewish Congress declared October 1954 to be a "commemorative period in which we reaffirm our unswerving belief in the principles of the United Nations Organization. We know that the only answer to recurring war is negotiation; and that the only instrument for negotiation that exists in the world today is the United Nations Organization."[23]

In the late 1940s and 1950s, religious and secular leaders in the American Jewish community developed a complex understanding of racial or religious prejudice, which they characterized as "unitary," that is, stemming from the same socio-psychological roots as antisemitism and all other forms of bigotry. To combat one without targeting the others was scientifically unsophisticated and futile; all forms of prejudice were held to be equally menacing to democratic institutions.

Driving these perceptions was a series of academic inquiries into the roots of bigotry that was commissioned by the American Jewish Committee. Particularly influential was *The Authoritarian Personality* (1950), a volume drafted by a team of social scientists headed by Theodor Adorno, a leading member of the Institute of Social Research (ISR) in New York. Essentially a reincarnation of the famed Frankfurt School, the ISR brought together leading left-wing Jewish intellectuals who had fled Germany during the 1930s.[24] Although they muted their Marxist tendencies and concentrated primarily on the psychological ingredients of fascism and bigotry, the authors of *Studies in Prejudice* (the series name) also identified economic insecurity as a leading motivator behind all forms of group hatred. To most Jewish leaders, the study's lessons were unmistakable. In the words of Bruno Bettelheim and Morris Janowitz, two ISR scholars, the economic goals of social action are . . . clear: An adjusted annual wage to do away with fears of seasonal employment, stabilization of employment, and an extension of social security. In the absence of comprehensive and successful attempts in that direction, it remains doubtful whether programs oriented specifically toward interethnic issues are at all relevant for changing interethnic relations.[25]

The prescriptive sections of *Studies in Prejudice* essentially read like a page from Harry Truman's Fair Deal. Each championed a modest expansion of the welfare state and the encouragement of economic growth, rather than a substantial redistribution of resources.

Bettelheim and Janowitz's study also concluded that those who were most susceptible to the lure of intolerance were likely to hold in contempt such established social institutions as the federal government and the university system. This finding lent credence to a suspicion among Jewish community leaders that McCarthyism and European fascism shared common derivations. A telling example of this intellectual association was Rabbi Israel Levinthal's warning in 1952 that McCarthy's tactics—"the method of the smear . . . the half truth . . . innuendo . . . twisting the meaning of words"—were no different from the means employed by Joseph Goebbels in Nazi Germany.[26]

It is nearly impossible to determine how widely known or correctly understood the *Studies in Prejudice* series actually was. Certainly its main themes were to some extent disseminated among the American reading public in 1950, when the *New York Times Magazine* ran an article about *The Authoritarian Personality*. Statements such as those of Rabbi Louis Levitsky—that "antisemitism is but one aspect of hate, and . . . it can be lessened only to the extent to which hate in general is reduced"—suggest a certain popular familiarity with the themes underscoring the ISR's publications. Significantly, Levitsky's larger point was that in order to ensure "that what happened in Germany will [not] happen here," American Jews needed to throw themselves into the work of interfaith relations.[27]

Such examples run contrary to scholarship arguing that the Cold War "muted" the Jewish community's discourse on the Holocaust or that American Jews were generally reluctant to discuss the Holocaust before Adolf Eichmann's arrest and trial in 1960. For instance, at a Hanukah ceremony in Manhattan in 1955, participants lit candles in "honor of the vivid memory of the heroes of the Warsaw ghetto [whose] courageous struggles against the brutal Nazis will be remembered for ages," and in commemoration of "the hardy group of Jewish pioneers who landed on American shores . . . and whose struggle for religious freedom, for civil rights, are now part of American history."[28]

Sensitivity to the history of German fascism also had immediate political repercussions. In the McCarthy era, some mainstream Jewish organizations felt at special liberty to isolate political conservatism as inimical to Jewish interests and values. Thus the Scarsdale women's division of the American Jewish Congress dedicated one of its regular Wednesday morning discussion groups in 1954 to investigating "the menace of reactionary thinking in this country" and posed the ominous question: "Do you think that you know everything about McCarthy and his cohorts? You don't! Come and learn more!"[29]

Like their colleagues in Scarsdale, members of the women's division of the

American Jewish Congress in Brooklyn understood radical anti-communism as hostile to the broad liberal agenda they supported in the name of Jewish values and interests. At a banquet in 1954, members of the chapter performed a musical skit that reflected the Jewish community's overriding hostility toward Joseph McCarthy and his supporters:

> . . . Oh, Joe McCarthy, oh Joe McCarthy,
> You're a master when it comes to treachery,
> Tell me, in our bag of tricks
> Are there photos we can fix . . . ?[30]

In contrast to the Jewish community's concerns regarding the anti-communist excesses of the McCarthy era, anti-communism supplied the main political theme of New York's Catholic subculture in the early Cold War years. It was not merely discussed, but formed the ideological backbone of official Catholic teachings and religious devotions.

One of the great ironies of Catholic anti-communism is that it claimed the same theological and intellectual moorings as did its left-wing counterparts—for instance, the small but influential Catholic Worker movement. Whatever they disagreed on, conservative Catholic clerics such as Francis Cardinal Spellman and radical laypersons such as Dorothy Day and Paul Maurin shared a common affection for Leo XIII, the 19th-century pope whose encyclical *Rerum Novarum* (Of new things, 1891) anchored both official and dissident Catholic social philosophy for the better part of the next seven decades.

Known also as "On the Conditions of the Working Class," the encyclical censured both Communism and classical liberalism for their violation of core Catholic values. This was the opening volley in the Church's struggle against Communism, alongside its much weaker critique regarding unfettered market forces. As historian Charles R. Morris has explained: "Basic Catholic principles [held] that there is an externally ordained social order that humans can understand rationally through natural law. Society is organized in a hierarchy, running from the Church through the State and through subsidiary associations such as labor unions down to the family." According to this worldview, "[s]ociety is an organism; each component is bound by a complex of duties and obligations to every other." Catholic doctrine thus held that "individuals derive their identity from a thick web of social relations" and that "the modern tendency to elevate the rights of individuals" was "at variance" with Christian reality. Thus *Rerum Novarum* flayed both Communism and classical liberalism for their inherent materialism and focus on the individual.[31]

In theory, *Rerum Novarum* and *Quadragesimo Anno* (In the fortieth year, 1931)—a companion encyclical issued by Pope Pius XI—demanded that capital recognize the reciprocal nature of its relationship with labor. Employees were entitled to decent working conditions, free time for family and religious pursuits and, most importantly, a "family wage" sufficient to keep mothers out of the workplace. In return, workers were enjoined to respect their obligations to employers: to execute their duties faithfully, to disavow violent confrontation, and to go on strike only when absolutely necessary. Both encyclicals demanded that government re-

spect the rights of labor and capital in kind—that the worker not be unduly deprived of his earnings by excessive taxation, and that the factory or shop owner
not be deprived of ownership and direction of his enterprise. As Morris aptly
explained, the Catholic social encyclicals "grew out of [an] organic theory of society."[32]

In reality, though, the Church placed disproportionate stress on the anti-
communist element of the two social encyclicals, especially in the 1930s and 1940s,
when Depression-era politics and Soviet expansion forced a widespread reappraisal
of Catholic social philosophy. In the United States, for instance, the Association of
Catholic Trade Unionists (ACTU) was established as an organization dedicated to
aiding the development of labor unions and promoting a quasi-corporatist ethic
among unionized workers. But by the mid-1940s in cities such as New York, the
ACTU had evolved into little more than a red-baiting organization that sought to
discredit all but the most conservative of labor unions.

So too with official Church spokesmen and organs, particularly diocesan newspapers, whose denunciations of Communism grew louder as their criticism of capitalism grew softer. As they lined up squarely against Communism, these same
Catholic leaders and institutions voiced growing concerns about Franklin Roosevelt's New Deal, whose statist approach to governance seemed to smack of socialism. Their opposition to economic liberalism grew more determined as the
1940s wore on.

Such concerns led Father John Flynn, the president of New York's St. John's
University, to warn in 1950 that "the present government program of nationalizing
things like credit, education, agriculture, medicine, and welfare organizations" resulted in "a great amount of federal tax." This, he added, was placing America "on
the road of totalitarianism and nationalization."[33] In this way, the specter of Communism pushed Catholic leaders into a conservative stance, despite the fact that
the postwar welfare state promised considerable dividends to working-class Catholics.

As noted, the Church's animus toward Communism dated back to the 19th century. It intensified in the 1930s, when Spanish Republicans (or Loyalists) opposed
to General Francisco Franco's Fascist army slaughtered upwards of 7,000 clergymen, subjecting some to highly symbolic acts of torture such as eye-gouging, crucifixion, and burning at the stake. Members of the Roosevelt administration and
leading American liberals voiced support for the Spanish Republicans and also lent
encouragement to the left-wing, anti-clerical Mexican government, which was engaged at the time in a long-running conflict with conservative Catholic rebels.
Though neither the Spanish Republicans nor the Mexican government was under
Communist control, Communists were closely allied with both—especially with
Spanish Republican forces, which received considerable material aid from the Soviet Union.[34]

Many American Catholics came to believe that the Church was under Communist
siege and that "popular front" liberals at home were little more than Communist
dupes. According to this view, which became increasingly widespread in Irish and
Italian communities, liberals applied a hypocritical double standard in denouncing
the violent excesses of Italian and Spanish Fascism even as they winked at brutal

anti-Christian campaigns perpetrated by Communists and fellow travelers. Public opinion polls revealed in 1946 that 46 percent of Catholics nationwide viewed Franco unfavorably, while 14 percent viewed him favorably and 40 percent had no opinion. This hardly signaled resounding Catholic support for Spanish Fascism, but it contrasted sharply with corresponding opinion in the Jewish community, where only 2 percent viewed Franco favorably and 78 percent viewed him unfavorably.[35]

For at least some Catholic leaders, anti-communism was also an expression of protest against the condescension—real and imagined—expressed toward them by Protestant members of the cultural and political elite. This was especially so for Irish Catholics, who had long bridled at the cultural disdain they had encountered upon first arriving on American shores in the mid-19th century. The Cold War supplied Irish Catholics with a long-awaited opportunity to turn the tables. Once anti-communism had become a defining American creed, establishment figures in the U.S. State Department and in academia found themselves on the defensive, forced to explain to an unbelieving public how the Soviet Union had developed its atomic bomb; why China had fallen to the Communists; and how it was that so many state secrets were finding their way to Moscow. Irish Catholics' anti-communist credentials were unimpeachable. Not so those of the New Dealers, Fair Dealers, and "popular fronters," who, many Catholics maintained, always seemed to enjoy looking down their noses at Irish America. As Daniel Patrick Moynihan— a product of New York's Irish community—famously observed, "the Irish achieved a temporary advantage from the McCarthy period. . . . In the era of security clearances, to be a Catholic became prima facie evidence of loyalty. Harvard men were to be checked: Fordham men would do the checking."[36]

In the early Cold War period, the *Irish Echo* consistently singled out Secretary of State Dean Acheson for especially harsh criticism, as when it claimed in 1951 that "[h]is honey-combed Red Department prepared the ground for red aggression in the Far East [and his] bitter anti-Irish policy plays into the hands of the Soviets in Western Europe." In 1954, the *Echo* accused the "Democratic party, or certain sections of it," of having "entered into a pact with the British government to sabotage American foreign policy in the interests of Britain and Russia."[37] To those Irish Americans who were both ardently anti-communist and intensely interested in the fate of the "six counties" (Northern Ireland), the pro-British disposition of leading liberals brought into sharper relief the apparent difference between loyal Catholics and traitorous Protestants.

Further contributing to the intensification of Catholic anti-communism was the Soviet Union's repression of Christian churches in Eastern Europe. In midwestern cities such as Chicago and Detroit, both home to large numbers of immigrants from behind the "Iron Curtain," a close political identification with Soviet-bloc countries probably accounted for a substantial part of the Catholic animus toward Communism. This was less the case in New York City, where the vast majority of Catholics were Irish, Italian, or German in origin. Still, Catholic institutions and periodicals encouraged New York parishioners to show solidarity with their persecuted coreligionists in Europe.[38] Consider, for instance, the headlines appearing in the *Brooklyn Tablet* over a period of barely two months: "Mockery of Court Trial in Yugoslavia is Described in Report on Bishop Cule's Case"; "Statistics Show Success of

Reds: But Church in Hungary Lives On"; "Romanian Church Life Strangled: Support of Communism Demanded; Nuns in Fear of Starvation"; "Reds in Romania 'Retire' Bishops and Abolish See"; "Hungarian Reds Jail More Clergy"; "Cardinal Prays; Reds Attack Him."[39] After surveying the literature on American Catholic politics, Charles Morris concluded that scholars "typically miss the religious component of the Catholic stance" on Communism. "To Catholics," he noted, "Stalin was the Antichrist, a satanic figure of biblical proportions."[40]

A good example of this marriage of religion and anti-communist fervor was the popular cult that developed around "Our Lady of Fatima." Catholic lore held that in 1917, the Virgin Mary appeared before a shepherd's daughter, Lucia, in the Portuguese town of Fatima, and said: "I come to ask the consecration of Russia to my Immaculate Heart. . . . If [Catholics] listen to my request, Russia will be converted, and there will be peace. If not, she will scatter her error through the world, provoking wars and persecution of the Church." The Virgin Mary's anti-communist prescription demanded that all Catholics say the rosary prayer each day for the conversion of Russia and that on five successive, first Saturdays of the month they take communion. Of course, not all Christians were so diligent, leading at least some Catholics to understand the Second World War and the Cold War as a result of their failure to heed the Blessed Mother's word.[41]

In the late 1940s, Pope Pius XII encouraged popular devotions and pilgrimages to Fatima. Fulton Sheen, an American bishop and host of a popular television show in the 1950s, was so convinced of Lucia's story that he made ten trips to Fatima and 30 to Lourdes (a French town that was the site of the first modern-day Marian apparition in 1858). As Morris explained, "Mariolatry was a central feature of 1950s Catholicism"—and, more particularly, Catholic anti-communism. When a farmer's wife in Wisconsin reported in 1950 that she had seen the Virgin Mary, who demanded that she pray for Russia, more than 100,000 people trekked to her farm to await a second apparition. *Scapular* magazine, a popular Catholic periodical, enrolled a million American Catholics in its "Blue Army of Fatima" to pray for the Soviet Union and to keep "First Saturdays." Catholic intellectuals were no less affected than the rank and file. "Our Lady herself has told us at Fatima that 'we must pray the Rosary,' " explained clergymen at Notre Dame to their students. "She promised the conversion of Russia if we said the Rosary. Will any student belittle the Russian threat?"[42]

New York Catholics were every bit as devoted to Mariolatry as their coreligionists across the country. In November 1945, between 25,000 and 30,000 Catholics attended a spontaneous evening vigil near the Grand Concourse in the Bronx, where nine-year-old Joseph Vitolo, Jr. knelt at the very spot where he claimed to have seen Mary's apparition several days earlier. On this particular occasion, the Virgin Mary's entreaty was apolitical; she asked simply that Joseph pray.[43] But the episode revealed the deep religiosity that ran through New York's Irish and Italian communities. For the better part of the 1950s, anti-communism and Mariolatry were mutually inextricable. When New Yorkers joined the Blue Army of Fatima, or took in Bishop Sheen's wisdom on the subject, they were participating in a worldwide religious and political devotion. To be a practicing Catholic was to be actively anti-communist.

Throughout the 1940s and 1950s, fear of Communism pushed the Church and many of its parishioners to the right of America's political spectrum. First and foremost, this involved a rejection of anything resembling economic radicalism. In 1949, some 57,000 Catholic schoolchildren from Brooklyn marched down Flatbush Avenue to commemorate "Loyalty Day," a Catholic counter-holiday staged annually on May Day. There they heard Rev. Ralph J. Garvey reaffirm the community's emphasis on deference and obedience. "[T]he security of American ideals rests in God," he announced, "God known, God respected, God obeyed." Ridiculing the competing May Day pageant staged by the left flank of organized labor, Garvey told the children that "[r]ight here on these streets . . . this morning we have seen something more than a demonstration of patriotic devotion. We have seen a challenge flung into the teeth of those who would destroy our American way of life and over-throw our American form of Government!"[44]

The Church provided its working-class constituents with alternative expressions of labor solidarity. In 1951, 88 parishes in the Brooklyn diocese, representing almost 30 percent of the total, staged special Labor Day celebrations. The diocese distributed 50,000 copies of the National Catholic Welfare Conference's statement on "social justice" and urged parish priests to draw special attention to the clause urging "recognition of our common responsibility to cooperate under God, establishing the rule of social justice in American economic life." The Church unequivocally asserted that "working people . . . posses a God-given dignity" that no employer was entitled to violate, but at the same time, its emphasis on cooperation and moderation contrasted sharply with the city's more combative labor movement.

At the same time, the Church carefully proscribed non-Catholic forms of labor politics. Many Irish and Italian Catholics followed the Church's lead and rejected New York's left-wing and liberal allies of organized labor, particularly the Liberal party and the American Labor Party (ALP).[45] Catholic prelates such as Francis Cardinal Spellman, the archbishop of New York, and Church organs such as the *Brooklyn Tablet* regularly scored leading left-wing unionists as Communists or fellow travelers, and in so doing suffered little if any loss of allegiance among their mostly working-class Catholic parishioners.

Local politics intensified the aversion to liberalism that increasing numbers of Catholics came to exhibit at the polls. In New York City, more than in other parts of the country, Communists and fellow travelers played a critical and lasting role in the development of liberal and left-wing politics after the Second World War. "Popular front"-style politics persisted in fact, if not in name, well into the 1950s, despite the political ravages of McCarthyism.[46] Joshua Freeman has found that "[w]hile the defeat (and self-destruction) of the [Communist Party]-left" after 1949 "transformed working-class New York in numerous ways, much didn't change. The Communist Party itself all but disappeared . . . but onetime CP members and sympathizers, and the worldview they shared, continued to influence working-class New York for decades to come. . . . Nowhere did left-wing and left-leaning ex-Communists have more influence than in New York."[47]

Because one-time Communists and fellow travelers enjoyed a strong position in New York's liberal-Left coalition, many Irish and Italian Catholics proved consistently wary of liberal institutions and public figures. Irish and Italian voters largely refused the overtures of ALP and Liberal candidates, even though their unions were often strongly allied with both parties. They also demonstrated considerable skepticism toward Democratic candidates running for statewide and national office (notably, Herbert Lehman and Adlai Stevenson). Ironically, New York's "labor" candidates found more support among the city's increasingly white-collar Jewish population than in highly unionized, working-class Italian and Irish neighborhoods.

The persistence of "popular front"-style politics in New York drove the Catholic Church and many of its Irish and Italian devotees to reject the city's most articulate and genuine proponents of civil rights. On the one hand, Catholic doctrine was unambiguous: racism was a violation of Christian doctrine, since Christ resided in all people, irrespective of race, when they took the Eucharist. Cardinal Spellman took several opportunities to reiterate this doctrine publicly, including a speech he delivered before 30,000 Catholics in 1945. He decried bigotry and celebrated American GIs who "may dislike one another's personalities, attitudes, beliefs, and actions, but nevertheless patriotism lifts them above disunion." The archbishop affirmed that "real Americans [fight] the spread of bigotry," a sentiment he reiterated in 1959, when he reminded the U.S. Civil Rights Commission that anti-discrimination "is what the Church has always and must always believe and teach."[48]

But in the 1940s and 1950s, rooting out Communism was the central concern of the Church and many of its followers; this state of affairs precluded widespread cooperation with New York's most vocal opponents of racism. In the minds of many Irish and Italian Catholics, these individuals were Communists or fellow travelers, and their advocacy of black rights was viewed as a cynical ploy to disrupt social harmony.

In 1948, Patrick Scanlan, the influential editor of the *Tablet*, assured readers that "much of the shouting about discrimination against one or another racial [or] religious group is deliberately instigated and encouraged by the Communists and others who seek to further their own ignoble ambitions by creating disunity and conflict." Scanlan beseeched Catholic citizens to "recognize the 'tolerance racket' as a snare"—a cheap ploy to "promot[e] distrust and hatred among neighbors." That year, as Henry Wallace braved hostile and sometimes violent Southern audiences to take his egalitarian message into the heartland of Jim Crow, the *Tablet* launched vicious attacks not only on the candidate and his supporters, but on such diverse organizations as the NAACP, the New York Jewish Welfare Board and the American Jewish Congress, whose cooperation with "Red-front groups" such as the Youth For Wallace Committee greatly offended the Catholic officialdom.[49]

The *Tablet* also attacked the Southern Conference for Human Welfare and its prominent supporters—Henry Wallace, Melvyn Douglas, Harold Ickes, Dorothy Parker, "big names and radical minds"—and agreed with the House Committee on Un-American Activities (HUAC) that the group was "perhaps the most deviously camouflaged Communist front organization" in the nation. In warning Catholics that the Southern Conference "displayed consistent anti-American bias and pro-Soviet bias, despite professions . . . of love for America," the *Tablet* played directly into the hands of conservative Southern Democrats, some of whom dominated HUAC. These staunch defenders of Jim Crow were heavily invested in discrediting the Southern Conference, whose leadership included early civil rights stalwarts such as Virginia Durr and Clark Foreman, and whose primary activities included marshaling opposition to the poll tax, fighting anti-labor legislation in Southern legislatures, and publicizing brutal attacks against African Americans.[50]

Neither the *Tablet* nor its readership supported Jim Crow. In fact, Catholics consistently registered a more liberal position on race relations than did other non-Jewish whites. National polls in 1947 revealed that 58 percent of Catholics supported the Interstate Commerce Commission's ban on segregated transportation, compared with 53 percent of northern Protestants and 67 percent of Jews. In 1957, 63 percent of Catholics expressed support for open housing and employment laws, compared with 57 percent of northern Protestants and 66 percent of Jews. Many devout Catholics, such as Anne Hamill, the mother of writer Pete Hamill, instilled in their children a firm sense of racial and religious justice. "A bigot is a hater," Hamill later recalled his mother's saying. "A bigot hates Catholics. A bigot hates Jews. A bigot hates colored people. It's no sin to be poor, she said. It *is* a sin to be a bigot. Don't ever be one of them."[51]

Conservative Catholic newspapers went to great lengths to avow support for civil rights. In 1949, the *Irish Echo* called "Jim Crowism the most repulsive of social and civil blandishments on [the] national escutcheon," an "ugly impairment of the rights and privileges guaranteed in the United States Constitution to all American citizens." The *Echo* even applied a tactic it normally reserved for liberal Democrats when it claimed: "In Ireland there is a counterpart to Jim Crowism . . . which lives and flourishes with the consent and support of the British Government . . . the subordinate puppet Parliament of Britain at Stormont."[52] Dean Acheson and the Democratic party were not the only subjects fit for comparison with Great Britain. If in fact the *Echo* gave accurate voice to the concerns of conservative Irish Americans, it was not racial liberalism that many Catholics opposed, but rather liberalism's apparent collusion with Communism.

Every summer more than a thousand children attended integrated summer camps sponsored by the Catholic Youth Organization and its parent group, the New York Catholic Charities. The program's organizers "decided to test its sincere belief that among boys and girls, 14 years or younger, there is no natural race prejudice," explained the camp's director. "We have never had a fight at the camp over race." Between 1942 and 1957, more than 20,000 children benefited from the camps. The Brooklyn Catholic Youth Organization (BCYO) also won kudos from the diocese for its repeated attempts to force the American Bowling Congress to integrate its leagues. Catholic leaders emphasized the harm that racism did to the anti-communist cause. According to a BCYO spokesman, "the eyes of the world are turned to the United States to see if our principles of democracy are working in practice. Imperialism is a thing of the past. Will the millions of people in Africa, India and China turn to a democratic form of government or to something else?"[53]

Notwithstanding, the Catholic Church's war against racism took a back seat to its epic struggle against Communism. In the 1940s and 1950s, many of the strongest advocates of racial equality in New York were tinged by past and present association with the popular front. Accordingly, the Church often restricted itself to small battles, such as its campaign to integrate indoor bowling.

As Jerry Della Femina, a son of New York's Italian subculture, later recalled:

These were the salad days of 1947, 1948, and into the 1950s, the days of that hero of
the Church, Senator Joseph McCarthy. McCarthyism was on its way and if we didn't
heed the message, Godless Russia was going to swallow us up. Every Sunday we said
a prayer for the conversion of Russia. . . . The priest was constantly sending out letters
about atheists, Communists, Godless atheists, Godless Communists, and occasionally
a socialist, although nobody could figure out the distinction. . . . [54]

Similarly, Pete Hamill recalled how the culture of anti-communism "dominated"
his neighborhood: "I do remember seeing a Catholic comic book that showed Communist mobs attacking St. Patrick's Cathedral. And there was an extended discussion of a papal encyclical called *Atheistic Communism*. . . ."[55]

While the women of the American Jewish Congress sang satirical ditties about
Roy Cohn, Joseph McCarthy attended a special Mass conducted at St. Patrick's
Cathedral in 1954 for the Holy Name Society of the New York City Police Department. Cardinal Spellman made a dramatic entrance at the ensuing communion
breakfast, where he clasped the senator's hand and beamed for the crowd. Later he
told reporters that McCarthy was "against communism and he has done and is
doing something about it. He is making America aware of the dangers of communism." This was *after* the famous Army-McCarthy hearings that effectively signaled the end of the senator's career. Moreover, McCarthy continued to be honored
with an annual Mass at St. Patrick's; upon his death in 1957, the *Irish Echo* saluted
him as "a great American."[56]

Leading political figures sensed a growing rift between liberalism and Catholicism, particularly among the Irish. In 1949, George Combs, a high-ranking Democratic party operative in New York City, explained in a private interview: "Years
ago, here in New York, the Irish and the Jewish people stayed together politically.
. . . That's all gone. I think it's largely ascribable to the Fascist growth in Europe.
So there is a dangerous, disheartening, and rather tragic cleavage now between our
Irish friends and our Jewish friends—and I am afraid that is going to deepen as
time goes on."[57] Nevertheless, a sizable minority of Irish and Italian voters in the
1940s and 1950s remained reliably committed to the national Democratic party,
while others continued to ally themselves with the Left. Two examples of this
persistent ideological pluralism within the Catholic community stand out.

From its inception in the early 1930s, the Transport Workers Union (TWU) drew
its leadership, and about half of its membership, from a generation of Irish immigrants who came to the United States in the 1910s and 1920s. Many of them
were veterans of the struggle for Irish independence; some (including the union's
president, Mike Quill) had belonged to the Irish Republican Army (IRA) and had
fought against British troops. Once in the United States, they held to their faith in
radical activism. Ignored or opposed by conservative Irish institutions such as the
Society of the Friendly Sons of Saint Patrick, the Ancient Order of Hibernians,
and the Knights of Columbus, the TWU enjoyed critical support from the Communist party. In return, many union leaders adopted the party's social platform and
continued, even after their ideological split with the party in 1949, to steer Catholic
transport workers toward the Left. Well into the 1960s, most rank-and-file members

of the TWU were both practicing Catholics and supporters of the ALP and Liberal party, moving easily between the radical labor milieu and the more conservative, Irish immigrant subculture. And while conservative Catholics may not have admired Quill's politics, they nevertheless invited him to serve as master of ceremonies at Hibernian lodge dinners and as grand marshall in the annual Saint Patrick's Day parade.[58]

Another exception to the rule of Catholic conservatism was Vito Marcantonio, the radical congressman from the working-class neighborhood of Italian East Harlem. Throughout his long congressional career (1935–1937, 1939–1951), Marcantonio was excoriated by the Church with unusual fervor. Although "Marc" never actually joined the Communist party, he toed its line consistently on the House floor. With regard to foreign affairs, this stance translated to an agonizing series of policy flip-flops: voting against war preparedness between 1939 and mid-1941; vigorously supporting armament and militarism after Hitler's invasion of the Soviet Union in June 1941; and then opposing Harry Truman's containment policies in the late 1940s.

Like other Communists and fellow travelers, Marcantonio also championed a broad civil rights agenda. In the late 1930s, he served as chairman of the International Labor Defense—the Communist party's legal affiliate, which provided high-profile assistance to the "Scottsboro boys" (nine black youths who were accused of raping two white girls) in Alabama. During the Second World War, he emerged as the most outspoken congressional proponent of anti-lynching laws and the establishment of the Fair Employment Practices Committee (FEPC). In the late 1940s, he even refused to support Rep. Graham Barden's bill providing federal aid to public education, principally because it "abett[ed] the . . . perpetuation of Jim Crow and segregated school systems." (The Church also opposed the Barden bill, but its dissent was aimed at the legislation's prohibition of aid to parochial schools and more or less ignored the race question.[59])

No matter how intensely Church officials denounced Marcantonio, his constituents continued to return him to Washington. His biographer has concluded that "Italian Harlem knew Marcantonio's left-wing political beliefs and associations." But they voted for him anyway, even as they turned to more conservative candidates in other electoral contests. On one level, Marcantonio championed a broad agenda that many working-class Italians favored—tenants' rights, rent control laws, low subway fares, collective bargaining rights, an expansion of Social Security. But "more impressive" to Italian Harlem "was Marcantonio's conformity in most major ways to its lifestyle." Born in East Harlem, he never moved more than ten blocks from his boyhood home, and he shared the community's folkways and values. When he died in 1954 at the age of 51, Cardinal Spellman denied Marcantonio a Catholic burial mass, but tens of thousands of his constituents defied the archbishop and filed through a small Harlem funeral home to pay their last respects.[60]

Because New York's Jews and Catholics continued to speak in the outdated and exaggerated vernacular of the 1930s, political differences between the two groups often resulted in a complete breakdown of civility. Such was the case in the late summer of 1949, when a predominately Catholic mob in Peekskill, a small town

40 miles upstate from Manhattan, twice ambushed a benefit concert featuring the renowned left-wing political activist and virtuoso singer Paul Robeson. Four days before the scheduled event, the *Peekskill Evening Star* ran a blistering editorial complaining that

> every ticket purchased for the Peekskill concert will drop nickels and dimes into the till basket of an Un-American political organization. . . . The time for tolerant silence that signifies approval is running out. Peekskill wants no rallies that support iron curtains, concentration camps, blockades and NKVDs, no matter how masterful the decor, nor how sweet the music.[61]

Leading citizens took up the paper's challenge. Hundreds of protesters blocked a road leading to the picnic area where the concert was to take place. The mob hurled antisemitic and racist invective at the concert attendees, most of whom were New York City Jews or blacks, and created enough chaos to cancel the event.

A week later, Robeson returned—this time protected by 2,500 left-wing union men wielding baseball bats—to perform before an audience of 20,000 supporters. The concert went off without a hitch. At the show's conclusion, the police directed the city-bound spectators up a windy, gravel road where a mob several hundred strong lay in wait near the top of the hill. Folk singer Pete Seeger, who also performed that day, later recalled that the crowd yelled, "Go home, you white niggers," "Kikes!" and "Go on back to Russia," while some of the younger rioters smashed the fleeing vehicles with small boulders and dragged concert attendees from their cars, beating some of them unconscious.[62]

The fallout from the Peekskill riot was complex. Left-wingers such as Henry Wallace and Paul Robeson overplayed their hand and described the event as evidence that America was rife with "fascist" potential.[63] In contrast, some national Jewish groups, notably the Anti-Defamation League and the American Jewish Committee, revealed the limits of Jewish free-thinking by quickly attempting to distance themselves from the Robeson forces, fearing that criticism of the riot might compromise their place in the broad anti-communist political coalition.[64] On the grassroots level, New York Jews seemed much more enraged than their national leaders.

The Brooklyn Jewish Youth Committee issued a strong protest against the riots, which it compared to earlier events in Nazi Germany. Other local groups also expressed their opposition to the riots, including the Brownsville and East New York Jewish Community Council and both the Brooklyn Division and Brooklyn Women's Division of the American Jewish Congress—an organization whose national office was on record as firmly opposed to Communism and other brands of "totalitarianism."[65] Although the Jewish War Veterans, a stridently anti-communist organization, had initially spoken out against Robeson, it too condemned the riots. Shortly before Robeson's second scheduled appearance in Peekskill, the JWV's Westchester County commander threatened any member who had participated in (or even planned to participate in) the first wave of violence with an official "court martial" and ouster. "The lynch spirit evidenced, the mob violence practiced . . . the innocent people hurt and the property damaged must find nothing but revulsion in real Americans who are opposed to any form of wool-hatters, black shirts or 'super'-Americans," he told the press.[66]

Whereas for many Jews, including committed anti-communists, the riots conjured up imagery from Germany in 1938, leading Catholics were far more inclined to agree with the local commander of the Catholic War Veterans (CWV), who dismissed accounts of both riots as fictitious and labeled the concert attendees and their supporters "godless, ruthless and vicious."[67] Predictably, the *Brooklyn Tablet* also weighed in heavily against the Robeson forces and, focusing once again on Communism's illegitimate challenge to established authority, branded the concert an "active conspiracy to overthrow our government." Editor Patrick Scanlan echoed the official line of the Brooklyn diocese and the New York archdiocese, denying "that the Peekskill affair was in any way the result of anti-Semitism or anti-Negro prejudice." At the heart of the paper's argument was the familiar Catholic line on authority and dissent, as expressed by one of the *Tablet*'s columnists: "It is part of the Communist strategy to create a distrust of public officials by distortion and magnification of incidents such as these, and also to bring about incidents to harass those officials and distract them from their functions of serving the community."[68]

Scholarship on postwar America tends to find that religion and ethnicity lost their significance as social, political, or cultural forces at almost the very instant that Levitt and Sons paved over the first potato field on Long Island.[69] Group histories of American Jews and Catholics frequently conclude with such telling chapter titles as "Assimilation," "From Ghetto to Suburbs: From Someplace to Noplace?" "Conclusion: The End of Immigrant Memory—Who Can Replace It?" and "The End of Catholic Culture," lending credence to the popular (if not entirely accurate) view of postwar history as a swift trajectory from city to suburb, from working class to middle class and, hence, from pluralism to white homogeneity.

It was precisely this route that Philip Roth's fictive Seymour "Swede" Lvov followed. Swede, a second-generation Jew, "could have married any [Jewish] beauty he wanted," according to his curmudgeonly younger brother. "Instead he marries the bee-yoo-ti-full Miss Dwyer. You should have seen them. Knockout couple. The two of them all smiles on their outward trip into the USA. She's post-Catholic, he's post-Jewish, together they're going out there to Old Rimrock to raise little post-toasties."[70]

Such incidents as the Quinn affair and the Peekskill riots and their aftershock challenge this version of history and bring into sharp relief the lasting importance of ethnicity and religion in postwar urban politics. Raised in different subcultures and haunted by different fears, New York Jews and Catholics spoke the oppositional language of "fascism" and "Communism" throughout the 1940s and 1950s. Their inability to move beyond competing intellectual frameworks weakened Franklin Roosevelt's storied coalition of Catholics and Jews. And their clashes foretold the day, not far off, when New York's white ethnic voters would part ways at the ballot box.

Notes

This essay is based on a chapter of my doctoral dissertation, " 'White Ethnic New York': Jews and Catholics in Post-War Gotham, 1945–1970."

1. For a brief synopsis of the two Quinn controversies (1943, 1949–1950), see Joshua B. Freeman, *Working Class New York: Life and Labor Since World War II* (New York: 2000), 72–74.

2. Quotes appearing on placards held by protestors; photographs of these are found in the American Jewish Archives (Cincinnati) (hereafter: AJA), Brooklyn Jewish Community Council MS (hereafter: BJCC), box 11, folder 7.

3. *Brooklyn Tablet* (31 Oct. 1953); "Urges People Not To Be Led Like Lambs to Bigotry," ibid. (15 April 1950).

4. BJCC meeting minutes (18 Jan. 1950), BJCC, box 9, folder 1; minutes, Metropolitan Presidents Advisory Committee meeting (28 Dec. 1949), American Jewish Historical Society (hereafter: AJHS) (New York), American Jewish Congress MS (hereafter: AJCongress), box 80, Metropolitan Advisory Committee folder.

5. Ellen J. Broidy, "Enforcing the ABCs of Loyalty: Gender, Subversion and the Politics of Education in the New York City Public Schools, 1948–1954" (Ph.D. diss., University of California, Irvine, 1997), 128–143.

6. Photographs in BJCC, box 11, folder 7.

7. Richard Hofstadter, "The Pseudo-Intellectual Revolt—1954," in idem, *The Paranoid Style in American Politics and Other Essays* (Cambridge, Mass.: 1963), 54. Concurring studies include Seymour Martin Lipset, "Democracy and Working-Class Authoritarianism," *American Sociological Review* 24, no. 4 (Aug. 1959), 482–501; and Robert Sokol, "Power Orientation and McCarthyism," *American Journal of Sociology* 73, no. 4 (Jan. 1968), 443–452.

8. Donald Crosby, *God, Church, and Flag: Senator Joseph R. McCarthy and the Catholic Church, 1950–1957* (Raleigh, N.C.: 1978), esp. ch. 11; Richard Gid Powers, *Not Without Honor: The History of American Anticommunism* (New York: 1996). Powers argues that anti-communism was a broad-based movement whose fringe elements have received too much attention. By implication, Catholics were merely one constituent group in the anti-communist consensus. For a more equivocal opinion, namely, that "messianic ardor among [Catholic] parishioners and prelates . . . was found mainly on the Right," although most Catholics continued to vote for Democrats and support the New Deal welfare state in the 1950s, see Michael Kazin, *The Populist Persuasion: An American History* (New York: 1995), 174. For an opposing view, see Stephen J. Whitfield, *The Culture of the Cold War* (Baltimore: 1996), 91–99; and Michael Paul Rogin, *The Intellectuals and McCarthy: The Radical Specter* (Cambridge, Mass.: 1967), 238–239, 256.

9. Stuart Svonkin, *Jews against Prejudice: American Jews and the Fight for Civil Liberties* (New York: 1997), 116; Edward Shapiro, *A Time for Healing: American Jewry since World War II* (Baltimore: 1992), 34–36. An early study of Joseph McCarthy's appeal concluded that the Wisconsin senator was not an antisemite, though his movement did earn the support of some avowed Jew-baiters. See Richard H. Rovere, *Senator Joe McCarthy* (New York: 1959), 141.

10. The most forceful expression of this interpretation is to be found in Peter Novick, *The Holocaust in American Life* (New York: 1999), esp. 103–123. Novick writes: "Between the end of the war and the 1960s, as anyone who lived through those years can testify, the Holocaust made scarcely any appearance in American public discourse, and hardly more in Jewish discourse—especially discourse directed to gentiles" (ibid., 103). For more nuanced views, see Arthur Hertzberg, *The Jews in America: Four Centuries of an Uneasy Encounter, A History* (New York: 1989), 301–303; Jack Wertheimer, *A People Divided: Judaism in Contemporary America* (Hanover, N.H.: 1993), 28–29; and Howard M. Sachar, *A History of the Jews in America* (New York: 1992), 839.

11. Alan Fisher, "Continuity and Erosion of Jewish Liberalism," *American Jewish Historical Quarterly* 66 (1976), 332–333, 341; J. J. Goldberg, *Jewish Power: Inside the American Jewish Establishment* (New York: 1996), chs. 1–2. Goldberg finds that, well into the 1990s, Jews consistently supported liberal and/or Democratic party candidates in ratios far exceeding that of the general population. On issues other than capital punishment and

affirmative action, they also continued to register more liberal responses to political polling questions. Most studies reveal political divisions between Jews and Gentiles, even after using controls for socioeconomic status and residence. It was this phenomenon that led sociologist Milton Himmelfarb to quip that Jews earned like Episcopalians but continued to vote like Puerto Ricans (quoted in Marc Dollinger, *Quest for Inclusion: Jews and Liberalism in Modern America* [Princeton: 2000], 3).

12. Ben Zion Bokser, untitled (and undated) Rosh Hashanah sermon (emphasis added), found in Jewish Theological Seminary (hereafter: JTS), Joseph and Miriam Ratner Center for the Study of Conservative Judaism (hereafter: RCSCJ), Ben Zion Bokser MS, box 11, High Holiday sermons folder. The bulk of the dated materials in this folder suggest that Bokser wrote this document in the 1940s or 1950s. Ben-Zion Bokser assumed the pulpit at the Forest Hills Jewish Center in 1935 and, except for his tenure as army chaplain in the Second World War, remained there until shortly before his death in 1984.

13. Marshall Sklare (ed.), *America's Jews* (New York: 1971), 120–121. Three surveys conducted in 1959 revealed that 19 percent of all New York City Jews never attended synagogue, while 50 percent attended only a few times a year, primarily on the High Holidays. Corresponding national figures for Jews not residing in NYC were 12 percent and 50 percent. See Bernard Lazerwitz, "Jews in and Out of New York City," *Jewish Journal of Sociology* 3, no. 2 (Dec. 1961), 254–260.

14. Interview, Ruth Messinger, 25 Feb. 1982, New York Public Library/Jewish division, oral history library of the American Jewish Committee.

15. Israel Mowshowitz (Hillcrest Jewish Center, Flushing, New York), "Breaking the Shackles" (sermon delivered at the High Holiday Sermon Seminar, Jewish Theological Seminary, 1961), RCSCJ, Samuel Penner MS, box 6, folder 32.

16. *Congregation Shaari Israel Bulletin* (April 1963), RCSCJ, Congregation Shaari Israel MS, box 4, folder 1.

17. Rabbi Jacob Pressman (Forest Hills Jewish Center), "There Were Four Sons . . . ," *Forest Hills Home News for the Men and Women in the Armed Forces* 1, no. 4 (March 1945), RCSCJ, Ben Zion Bokser MS, box 15, Forest Hills correspondence folder, 1944/1945.

18. William L. Rubin (Senior Vice Commander, Manhattan Post No. 1), "Passover and Human Freedom," *Manhattan Post #1—JWV Bulletin* (Passover edition, April 1946), AJHS, Jewish War Veterans MS, box 3, printed materials of local JWV posts folder; also see "Passover and Freedom," in ibid.

19. Rabbi Morris Goldberg, "Let My People Go," *Shaare Zedek Newsletter* 4, no. 23 (27 March 1953); reprinted in ibid. 5, no. 25 (16 April 1954), found in RCSCJ, Shaare Zedek MS, box 2, folder 1. Other Jewish religious leaders also drew a parallel between Lincoln and Moses. In February 1945, Rabbi Jacob Pressman of the Forest Hills Jewish Center delivered a sermon titled "Let My People Go" on the occasion of Lincoln's birthday. See *The Message* (Forest Hills Jewish Center) 11, no. 20 (8 Feb. 1945), found in RCSCJ, Ben Zion Bokser MS, box 15, Forest Hills correspondence folder, 1944/1945.

20. Rabbi Israel Levinthal (Brooklyn Jewish Center), "Passover and the Freedom Ideal," *Brooklyn Jewish Center Review* (April 1954), RCSCJ.

21. By the early 1950s, the terms of Harry Truman's Fair Deal had survived their author's political life to define the liberal agenda. Highlights of the program were federal aid to education, establishment of a permanent Fair Employment Practices Committee (FEPC), legislation to promote full employment, a progressive tax structure, repeal of the Taft-Hartley labor bill, national medical coverage, resource development, and housing assistance programs. See Alonzo L. Hamby, *Beyond the New Deal: Harry S. Truman and American Liberalism* (New York: 1973), 296–310.

22. *JEC Bulletin* (New York) (Nov. 1950).

23. American Jewish Congress, National Women's Division, Scarsdale-White Plains-Harrison Chapter, *Bulletin* (Oct. 1954), AJHS, American Jewish Congress MS, box 131, South Shore correspondence folder.

24. The "Frankfurt School" was the popular designation of the Institute of Social Re-

search (ISR), founded in 1923. Many of the ISR's predominantly Jewish membership fled Germany in 1933 and relocated, first in Geneva and then in New York, where the ISR was relaunched as an affiliate of Columbia University. See Svonkin, *Jews against Prejudice*, 33.

25. Quoted in ibid., 40.

26. Ibid.

27. Louis Levitsky, "What's On My Mind," *Oheb Shalom Review* (1 Feb. 1950), RCSCJ, Louis Levitsky MS, box 2, folder 9. Along similar lines, officials of the American Jewish Congress reminded members in 1948 that "[t]he fight against Antisemitism is not separate and distinct from the fight against lynching, the poll tax and defamation and discrimination in employment, education and housing." See *American Jewish Congress*, South Shore Women's Division (Summer 1948), AJHS, AJCongress, box 131, South Shore correspondence folder, 1948–1949.

28. American Jewish Congress, West Side Chapter, "Hanukkah Living: A Candle Lighting Dramatization" (15 Dec. 1955), AJHS, AJCongress, box 131, National Women's Division, West Side Chapter folder.

29. American Jewish Congress, Scarsdale-White Plains-Harrison Chapter, *Bulletin* (March 1954), in ibid.

30. A dramatic moment in the "Army-McCarthy hearings" came when Joseph Welch, a Boston attorney who served as counsel to the U.S. Army, exposed one of Roy Cohn's exhibits as a doctored photograph. Cohn served as McCarthy's chief subcommittee counsel.

31. Charles R. Morris, *American Catholic: The Saints and Sinners Who Built America's Most Powerful Church* (New York: 1997), 150–151; see also Alan Brinkley, *Voices of Protest: Huey Long, Father Coughlin and the Great Depression* (New York: 1982), 86–89. Brinkley explores the early religious education of Father Charles Coughlin, who was greatly influenced by the social encyclicals—in particular, their censure of international Communism.

32. Ibid.

33. "Warns against Crushing Taxes," *Brooklyn Tablet* (22 April 1950); David O'Brien, *American Catholicism and Social Reform: The New Deal Years* (New York: 1968), esp. 97–119; Richard Camp, *The Papal Ideology of Social Reform: A Study in Historical Development, 1878–1967* (New York: 1969); Lawrence B. DeSaulniers, *The Response in American Catholic Periodicals to the Crises of the Great Depression, 1930–1935* (Latham: 1984). DeSaulniers demonstrates that Catholic periodicals—with a few notable exceptions—were highly skeptical of, or conflicted about, the growth of the New Deal welfare state.

34. The interethnic and interreligious tensions spurred in New York by these foreign conflicts in the 1930s is discussed in Ronald H. Bayor, *Neighbors in Conflict: The Irish, Germans, Jews, and Italians of New York City, 1929–1941* (Baltimore: 1978), 90–93.

35. Robert Frank, "Prelude to the Cold War: American Catholics and Communism," *Journal of Church and State* (Winter 1992), 39–56; Wilson Miscamble, "Catholics and American Foreign Policy: From McKinley to McCarthy," *Diplomatic History* (Summer 1980), 223–240; J. David Valaik, "Catholics, Neutrality and the Spanish Embargo, 1937–1939," *Journal of American History* (June 1967), 73–85; Leo Kanawanda, *Franklin D. Roosevelt's Diplomacy and American Catholics, Italians and Jews* (New York: 1982); John Stack, *International Conflict in an American City: Boston's Irish, Italians and Jews, 1935–1944* (Westbury, Conn.: 1979), 58–72.

36. Nathan Glazer and Daniel Patrick Moynihan, *Beyond the Melting Pot: The Negroes, Puerto Ricans, Jews, Italians, and Irish of New York City* (Cambridge, Mass.: 1963), 271.

37. "Food for Thought," *Irish Echo* (23 Dec. 1950); see also "Food for Thought," ibid. (11 Sept. 1954).

38. Whitfield, *Culture of the Cold War*, 94–96.

39. *Brooklyn Tablet* (18 and 25 Sept. 1948); ibid. (2 and 9 Oct. 1948); ibid. (6 Nov. 1948).

40. Morris, *American Catholic*, 299.

41. For a general history of the events at Fatima, see William T. Walsh, *Our Lady of Fatima* (New York: 1947).

42. Ibid., 229; Thomas A. Kselman and Steven Avella, "Marian Piety and the Cold War in the United States," *Catholic Historical Review* (July 1986), 403–424; *Life Magazine* (29 Aug. 1950).

43. John T. McGreevy, "Bronx Miracle," *American Quarterly* 52, no. 3 (Fall 2000), 405–443.

44. "Display of Loyal Youth Surpasses Borough Record," *Brooklyn Tablet* (7 May 1949).

45. "Labor Day Theme is Social Justice" and "Asks Religious Labor Day Rites," *Brooklyn Tablet* (1 Sept. 1951). The American Labor Party was dissolved in 1956.

46. Martha Biondi, *To Stand and Fight: The Struggle for Civil Rights in Postwar New York City* (Cambridge, Mass.: 2003).

47. Freeman, *Working Class New York*, 93–94.

48. Quoted in John T. McGreevy, *Parish Boundaries: The Catholic Encounter with Race in the Twentieth-Century Urban North* (Chicago: 1996), 69, 133.

49. "Practical Tolerance," *Brooklyn Tablet* (31 July 1948). For background on Wallace's dangerous campaign forays in the South, see Hamby, *Beyond the New Deal*, 206, 260–262.

50. *Brooklyn Tablet* (5 June 1948); Numan V. Bartley, *The New South, 1945–1980: The Story of the South's Modernization* (Baton Rouge: 1995), ch. 2.

51. Pete Hamill, *A Drinking Life* (New York: 1994), 11.

52. "Jim Crowism Rules in the Six Counties," *Irish Echo* (12 Dec. 1949).

53. "Negro and White Children at Same Camp to Test Theory No Bias Exists in Youths," *New York Times* (18 July 1947); "A Summer Appeal," *Irish Echo* (22 May 1957); "CYO Fight on Ban Against Negroes in ABC Defeated," *Brooklyn Tablet* (24 April 1948).

54. Jerry Della Femina and Charles Sopkin, *An Italian Grows in Brooklyn* (New York: 1978), 150; also see Alden Brown, *The Tablet: The First Seventy-Five Years* (New York: 1983), 52–65; Diocese of Brooklyn, *Revised Handbook of Regulations, Elementary and High Schools* (Brooklyn: 1946), 14, 37–38, housed in Archives of the Diocese of Brooklyn, Queens, NY. Brown explains that by the late 1940s, the *Tablet's* "focus of attention now was anti-communism, with little qualification. The *Tablet's* earlier criticism of American capitalism virtually disappeared" (*Tablet*, 44).

55. Hamill, *A Drinking Life*, 125.

56. "God Must be Angry," *Irish Echo* (11 May 1957); Whitfield, *Culture of the Cold War*, 96–97; Linda Dowling Almeida, "From Danny Boy to Bono: The Irish in New York City, 1945–1995" (Ph.D. diss., New York University, 1996), 309–311; "Vote Confidence in Sen. McCarthy," *Brooklyn Tablet* (29 July 1950).

57. Interview, George Combs (chairman, speakers bureau, William O'Dwyer mayoral campaign) (2 Nov. 1949), Oral History Project, Columbia University (hereafter: OHP-CL).

58. Joshua B. Freeman, "Catholics, Communists and Republicans: Irish Workers and the Organization of the Transport Workers Union," in *Working-Class America: Essays on Labor, Community, and American Society*. ed. Michael H. Fritsch and Daniel J. Walkowitz (Chicago: 1983), 256–276.

59. Interview, Vito Marcantonio (3 Nov. 1949), OHP-CL.

60. Gerald Meyer, *Vito Marcantonio: Radical Politician, 1902–1954* (New York: 1989), 53–86, 122.

61. Quoted in Svonkin, *Jews against Prejudice*, 137–138.

62. Ibid., 135–144; David King Dunaway, *How Can I Keep from Singing: Pete Seeger* (New York: 1981), 13–23.

63. "Robeson, Officials Differ on Disorder," *New York Times* (6 Sept. 1949); "Budding Fascism Seen By Wallace," ibid. (3 Sept. 1949).

64. Svonkin, *Jews against Prejudice*, 135–144.

65. "A Petition for the Protection of Full Civil Liberties" and "Can It Happen Here?" AJHS, AJCongress, box 134, National Women's Division (Brooklyn) reports folder; minutes of the meeting of the executive committee, Brooklyn Jewish Youth Council (20 Oct. 1949), AJA, Brooklyn Jewish Youth Council MS, box 4, folder 2.

66. Dewey Aide Urged Review for Robeson Row," *New York Times* (31 Aug. 1949). The term "wool-hatters" referred to a white supremacist group in Georgia.

67. "Gossip, Threats Divide Peekskill as Aftermath of Robeson Fight," ibid. (10 Sept. 1949).

68. "The Peekskill Affair," *Brooklyn Tablet* (24 June 1950); untitled column, ibid. (29 July 1950).

69. Two notable exceptions to the prevailing tendency to downplay the lasting importance of ethnicity and religion in the postwar period are McGreevy, *Parish Boundaries*; and Gerald Gamm, *Urban Exodus: Why the Jews Left Boston and Why the Catholics Stayed* (Cambridge, Mass.: 1999).

70. Philip Roth, *American Pastoral* (New York: 1997), 73. Also see Lawrence J. McCaffrey, *The Irish Catholic Diaspora In America* (Washington, D.C.: 1997), ch. 7; Morris, *American Catholic*, ch. 10; Jerre Manhione and Ben Morreale, *La Storia: Five Centuries of the Italian American Experience* (New York: 1993), part 8; Arthur Hertzberg, *The Jews in America: Four Centuries of an Uneasy Encounter* (New York: 1989), ch. 20. Another example of this tendency to view ethnicity as a prewar phenomenon is Herbert Gans, *The Urban Villagers: Group and Class in the Life of Italian Americans* (New York: 1962), 32–36. Gans emphasized class rather than ethnicity as a primary behavioral and associational determinant. "Generally speaking," he wrote, "the Italian and Sicilian cultures that the immigrants brought with them to America have not been maintained by the second generation. The over-all culture is that of Americans" (ibid., 33).

Toward a Structural Explanation of Jewish-Catholic Political Differences in the United States

Kenneth D. Wald
UNIVERSITY OF FLORIDA

In 1948, Wesley and Beverly Allinsmith published the first empirically based analysis of the political tendencies of American religious groups. Drawing on six nationwide surveys conducted by the Gallup organization in 1945 and 1946, the Allinsmiths ranked eight major religious traditions by their members' attitudes toward the government's responsibility for economic security, their support for increasing the power of workers, and their presidential vote in the 1944 election. Regardless of which issue they examined, the authors reported, Jews and Roman Catholics held similar political views on the major issues of the day and, together with Baptists, constituted the left wing among religious groups.[1]

Perhaps because they so relentlessly undermined preconceptions, the Allinsmiths' findings do not seem to have penetrated the scholarly discourse. Most casual observers seem to have assumed a natural political antagonism between liberal Jews and conservative Roman Catholics.[2] In part, this assumption reflects the difficult and uneasy historical relationship between the two religious traditions. As James Carroll demonstrated in his controversial *Constantine's Sword*, the historical record of Catholic mistreatment of Jews goes back to the very beginning of Christianity and continued largely unabated over the centuries.[3] By the time of the Holocaust, the murderous Nazi regime discovered no shortage of willing collaborators among the German Episcopate and enjoyed strong electoral support from some segments of the German Catholic population.[4] A contentious literature now suggests that the Vatican was complicit—if only because of its inattention—in Hitler's genocidal program.[5] Even in the comparatively tolerant postwar period, there was evidence of continuing animosity toward Jews from the highest levels of Catholicism in the United States.[6] As if these historical factors were not enough to drive a political wedge between the two groups, some scholars suggest that conflicting political imperatives were inherent in the ethos of each religious tradition. From this vantage point, Judaism was a non-ascetic, this-worldly religion that emphasized human reason, freedom of thought, social reform, and other progressive causes.[7] By contrast, it was argued, Catholicism emphasized the sinful character of temptations of

111

the flesh, stressed the need for social control, and trusted to the next world for human salvation. Each ethos was said to display an elective affinity with a political orientation: Judaism with the Left, Catholicism with conservatism. Almost by definition, the two groups were destined for opposite sides of the political spectrum.

Such accounts simply overlooked the persuasive evidence from the mid-20th century that Jews and Catholics were often ranged on the same side of the American political spectrum. Today, of course, when we look at conventional wisdom about Jews and Roman Catholics, the two groups appear to have much less in common politically. Roman Catholics, the single largest denomination (about 30 percent) in the electorate, have moved to the center of the American political spectrum. As a group, they tend to define the modal position on most political issues, and their partisan commitments shift from one election to the next.[8] Jews, however, remain seemingly fixed in their position as the bedrock of the liberal coalition in American politics. They are more committed to the Democratic party than any group except black Protestants and more liberal on social issues than any constituency except the unchurched. This pattern was already in evidence by 1960 when Jewish voters exceeded Roman Catholics in their support for John F. Kennedy, only the second Catholic (after Al Smith, in 1928) to run for president as the nominee of a major party.[9]

Despite a renewed scholarly interest in religion and political behavior, few have explored the diverging paths of Jews and Catholics. Scholars have tried to understand the bases for continuing Jewish political distinctiveness, and a number of studies have drawn comparisons between Catholics and American Protestants.[10] Yet Jews and Catholics have not been compared directly, perhaps on the assumption that there is little of interest to learn by contrasting the two communities.

What follows is a dissent from that view in which I offer reasons why scholars should explore political similarities and differences between Jews and Roman Catholics. The fundamental puzzle is why Jews and Catholics diverged politically at a time when their historical differences had become muted and the two groups had powerful reasons to forge a political alliance. Given the inherent complexity of the subject, no single essay can explore this peculiar pattern in a comprehensive way. My goals are much more modest: first, to explain why we might expect more similarity than difference between Jews and Catholics in American political life; second, to document the extent of contemporary political differences between Jews and Catholics in the United States and to determine whether these are real or spurious; and finally, to offer the beginnings of a structural explanation for these findings.

Jewish and Catholic Political Approaches

The apparent political divergence of Jews and Roman Catholics over the past half century raises interesting questions for scholars of religion and political behavior. To begin with, it seems odd that two groups with so much in common would drift apart so quickly. Both Jews and Catholics were predominantly mid-19th to early 20th-century immigrants to the United States who met with considerable suspicion, hostility, and discrimination from nativists who resented the economic and cultural challenges presented by the newcomers.[11] As ethnic immigrants, Jews and Catholics often found themselves confined to ghettos where crime, sports, and politics offered the quickest ways out of poverty. Both battled for recognition and admission to the citadels of education, business, and power, finding common political heroes in the New Deal and important allies in the labor movement and urban political machines. Both faced discrimination from a public school system imbued with the values and norms of Protestant Christianity. In time, with the aid of government programs such as the GI Bill, many Jews and Catholics attained positions of importance in society that would have been inconceivable to members of earlier generations. Yet despite the considerable progress experienced by both communities, they remain somewhat marginal and less than fully sure of their welcome in the United States. Only one Catholic has held the presidency, and a Jewish candidate has yet to claim even a major party presidential nomination. Both religious groups still maintain communal defense organizations against various forms of discrimination. In sum, Roman Catholics and Jews have often been positioned as "the Other" in the eyes of many Americans—strange bedfellows who at times have shared interests or common enemies.

Alongside their shared status as outsiders in a country dominated by Protestants, the two communities have also experienced parallel patterns of upward social mobility. When the Allinsmiths conducted their study, Jews had already achieved significantly higher levels of education, income, and occupational status than Roman Catholics. Indeed, the striking social differences between the two groups in 1948 made their political commonality all the more inexplicable. Yet in the intervening decades, Catholics significantly closed the gap in all three domains. By the mid-1970s, Andrew Greeley reported that Catholic averages on measures of education and socioeconomic status were no longer clearly distinguishable from those of Protestants.[12] While there continued to be a Jewish advantage, the differences were much smaller. This pattern deepens the mystery. With both a similar historical legacy as outsiders and subsequent entry into middle-class status, why have Jews and Catholics grown further apart politically?

Adding a twist to this mystery is the fact that the political divergence occurred amid a general modernization of Roman Catholicism that attempted to heal many of the longstanding tensions between Jews and Catholics. At the second Vatican Council from 1962 through 1965, Pope John XXIII and then his successor, Paul VI, embraced a series of changes in the Catholic understanding of the Church's role in the world. For the purposes of Catholic-Jewish understanding, the principal innovation was a repudiation of the foundation of Catholic antisemitism, the accusation of deicide against the Jewish people. In *Nostra Aetate* (Declaration on the relationship of the Church to non-Christian religions, 1965), the Church withdrew the deicide charge and reminded believers that "it decries all hatreds, persecutions, displays of antisemitism directed against the Jews at any time or from any source." This effort stimulated ecumenical outreach that attempted to heal the wounds between the two peoples.

Such factors notwithstanding, Jews and Catholics did not develop identical political profiles. At the same time that the Allinsmiths were discovering political similarities between them, Jews and Catholics were being pushed apart by the turbulent politics of the postwar period. For instance, they split over the anti-communist crusade pursued in the late 1940s and early 1950s by Wisconsin's senator Joseph McCarthy. McCarthy's fellow Catholics were much more enthusiastic recruits in the campaign against domestic subversion, real and imagined, than were their Jewish counterparts.[13] As time passed, the two communities also developed different political profiles on such issues as the civil rights movement (particularly when it came to Northern cities), the Vietnam War and antiwar demonstrations, abortion, and a host of issues involving human sexuality.[14] Jews were generally supportive of the civil rights movement, mainstays of opposition to the Vietnam War, and advocates of various forms of social liberalism whereas Catholics, in the main, were less enthusiastic about civil rights, strong proponents of the initial military engagement in Vietnam, and defenders of traditional morality from what they saw as threats produced by social change.

In the course of time, as most of these issues receded in importance, a new issue arose with the potential to unite Jews and Catholics. In the late 1970s, American politics was seriously perturbed by the emergence of a social movement known as the Christian Right. With deep roots in white evangelical Protestant churches, this campaign called for a restoration of "traditional morality" in American public policy.[15] The movement targeted such practices as gender equality, the decriminalization and subsequent drive for equality by gays and lesbians, liberalized divorce laws, restrictions on prayer in public schools, and increased legal access to abortion. Its leaders also called for tax support for sectarian schools and increased participation by religiously affiliated organizations in the administration of government programs. While these goals enjoyed some support among traditionalist Roman Catholics and Orthodox Jews, the history of antipathy between militant Protestants and members of what they decried as "alien" religions precluded an effective alliance. Indeed, while they might agree with the Christian Right on this or that issue, and while leading social conservatives often reached out beyond Protestantism, both Jews and Catholics were wary of the energized evangelicals. In fact as well as perception, activist evangelicals often held views that denied the authenticity of groups outside Protestantism.[16] Catholic bishops warned their flock not to forget that while members of the Christian Right held similar views on abortion, they differed from Church positions across a wide range of issues.[17] Jews, skeptical of the philo-Zionism embraced by evangelical Protestants, were even more concerned about the "Christian America" rhetoric that permeated the movement's discourse.[18] As Christian conservatives took center stage in the Republican party, becoming its most reliable electoral constituency and the incubator of the GOP's national leadership, many Jews and Catholics found renewed grounds for cooperation on the other side of the political spectrum.

The tendency of Jews and Catholics to look askance at the Christian Right may reflect fundamental differences between Protestantism and the two other religious traditions. In one of the classic sociological studies of American religion, Gerhard Lenski noted an important difference in the styles of cohesion between Jews and Catholics, on the one hand, and Protestants, on the other.[19] In his 1958 survey of metropolitan Detroit, Lenski observed that Jews displayed high levels of communal involvement while Catholics strongly adhered to the associational forms of their community.[20] Strong communalism was manifest in the development and mainte-nance of durable social ties among coreligionists, while associational behavior en-compassed high levels of church attendance and worship. Compared with Catholics, Jews were more likely to live among, interact, socialize, marry, and identify with other members of their community. Compared with Jews, Catholics were apprecia-bly more likely to attend church services and worship among their brethren. And compared with Jews and Catholics, Protestants scored strikingly lower on both measures of cohesion. They lacked the high rates of social interaction with core-ligionists that typified Jews and could not match Catholics in their church atten-dance habits. These findings echoed the argument of Emile Durkheim, first ex-pressed at the end of the 19th century, when he attempted to explain the lower rates of suicide among Jews and Catholics as compared with Protestants. The pat-tern was puzzling because all three traditions had strongly proscribed suicide on doctrinal grounds. According to Durkheim, the explanation lay in the fact that Jews and Catholics lived in tightly bound communities with strong social networks and religious institutions, and thus were bound by tighter norms of group solidarity than were the more individualistic Protestants.[21]

Durkheim's argument can be further generalized: the concept of religiosity ap-pears to tap very different markers in religious traditions such as Judaism and Catholicism, on the one hand, and Protestant Christianity, on the other.[22] The former two faiths are much more cohesive or community-oriented in nature, and mem-bership is usually defined principally by immersion in an encompassing social collectivity. Religious activity in such an environment often involves collective wor-ship and ritual behavior of a type that reinforces the sense of group cohesion by sacralizing collective identity. By contrast, Protestantism is usually defined as cog-nitive adherence to prescribed beliefs. Strong connection to Protestantism is typi-cally indexed by "right belief"—not surprising in a tradition that has long stressed the priesthood of all believers and rejected the need for intermediaries between the devout and the divine. In Protestantism, one joins a church voluntarily and voli-tionally, whereas Jews and Catholics typically belong as a consequence of heritage.

Such differences in styles of religiosity also seem to possess political relevance. According to studies of 19th- and early 20th-century American public life, the principal dividing line between Democrats and Republicans often reflected these different religious imperatives.[23] Pietistic Protestant religious communities were at-tracted to political reforms that stressed public rectitude, crusades for such disparate ends as temperance or prohibition, women's suffrage, non-partisanship, Sunday closing laws, restrictions on immigration, anti-evolutionism, and the like. These political efforts were often perceived, not entirely inaccurately, as attacks on the cultural practices of Jews and Catholics, in particular.

Something very similar to this cleavage appears to have persisted deep into the 20th century, when it often defined urban political conflict.[24] In our own day, Cath-olic social teaching on such fundamental questions as war, poverty, civil rights, and social injustice often bears the hallmark of a powerful communal strain that has historically been muted in the individualist Protestant tradition but finds an affinity with Jewish teaching about interdependence. To take but one example, it is not altogether surprising that the Catholic bishops and Jewish communal organizations were among the few voices raised in opposition to the more draconian elements of what was called "welfare reform" and have worked against neo-nativist efforts to restrict immigration to the United States.

As this review has suggested, then, the emergence of fundamental and wide-ranging political differences between Jews and Catholics at the beginning of the 21st century constitutes an interesting puzzle precisely because the two communities would seem to have so much in common. Can it be that these political differences are more apparent than real?

Possibilities

The research suggesting a political divergence between Jews and Catholics from the mid-20th century draws on comparisons of the "average" political attitudes and actions exhibited by the two populations. That is, such research looks at the overall distribution of attitudes within each group and assumes that the group differences reflect fundamental political disagreement. Table 1 shows one example of this kind of analysis. The data, drawn from parallel surveys of Jewish and Catholic samples in early 2000 by the Zogby International polling organization, exhibit a substantial difference in responses to a question about partisan loyalty. In accordance with what one of my teachers described as the test of "inter-ocular dynamism"—meaning, does the difference hit the observer between the eyes—the table attests to large differences in partisan loyalty: Jews are more than one and a half times as likely as Catholics to be Democrats and, correspondingly, less than half as likely to identify as Republicans. Using a conventional measure of statistical significance, we learn there is less than one chance in a thousand of drawing a sample with this kind of group pattern if there were no real difference between the Catholic and Jewish populations. The growth in the difference since the Allinsmiths' baseline study in 1948 only emphasizes the unraveling of whatever Jewish-Catholic political alliance may have existed back then.

However, the idea that Catholics, qua Catholics, think differently than Jews about political parties is not necessarily the explanation for the pattern in Table 1. Catholics may appear to embrace a different partisan option than Jews only because of what we call *compositional differences* between the two populations. It may be that Catholics differ systematically from Jews on background social traits and that these traits, rather than religion, account for the partisan difference revealed in Table 1. Suppose, for example, that Jews on average still report much higher levels of education than Catholics and that people with higher levels of education typically identify with the Democratic party. If that is so, we would consider the relationship between religion and partisanship to be spurious—a function of the relationship between education, on the one hand, and religious affiliation and partisanship, on the other.[25] We can test this hypothesis by comparing the two groups while taking account of educational differences, or, in statistical language, "controlling" for that factor. Doing so may reveal no genuine religious differences in politics, or may even show that the groups are closer together than they should be, based on com-

Table 1. Party Identification,
by Religious Affiliation

	Roman Catholic (n=802)	Jewish (n=483)
Republican	36.3	15.9
Independent	21.8	15.7
Democratic	41.9	68.3
Total (%)	100	100

positional differences. Alternatively, it may affirm that the simple differences in Table 1 do reflect something enduring about each group's political profile.

In fact, a host of background factors have been linked to political attitudes. What follows is an analysis of the Zogby data of 2000 to determine whether Catholic and Jewish political orientations are affected by age, gender, education, region, religious attendance (associationalism), size of community, generation in the U.S., religious integration of neighborhood and friendships (based on Lenski's communalism), ethnicity, and labor union membership. In addition, the models include a measure that indicates whether Jews differ from Catholics after taking account of all these differences in background traits. The tests were performed using several multivariate statistical models appropriate for the various measures of political attitudes and behavior.[26] For each political disposition, the average political difference between Jews and Catholics with no controls is compared with the difference that emerges once the critical background traits are controlled for. Rather than presenting a plethora of regression parameters in the body of the text, I summarize and report in my own words the findings from the multivariate model.[27]

Five measures of political orientation covering a broad range of contemporary political debate—which include both attitudes and behavior—are examined. The analysis begins with the aforementioned measure of partisanship and a measure of self-described political ideology. Previous research has demonstrated that such fundamental political orientations strongly predict positions on a host of political issues as well as influencing vote choice. For the third measure, I made use of a scale of pro-Democratic voting based on reported vote in 1996, intended vote in the 2000 congressional elections, and preferences revealed in several trial heats involving candidates for the presidency in 2000. The two remaining measures tap two major dimensions of contemporary political controversy in the United States. The first scale, a composite measure of attitudes toward what is sometimes called the "consistent ethic of life," comprises four questions about abortion and a fifth about euthanasia. If there is any one issue where Catholics should be differentiated from Jews, this would certainly be it. The other scale attempts to measure economic values by incorporating questions about the minimum wage, Social Security, government health insurance, taxation, government spending, and penalties for polluting industries. On these questions, Catholic and Jewish organizations have been much more in step with each other.

The data for these analyses are derived from two of the "Culture Polls" conducted by Zogby International from late 1999 through early 2000. During that period, Zogby simultaneously interviewed members of six distinct ethnoreligious groups by telephone from its headquarters in Utica, New York. The survey of 589 Jews, conducted in cooperation with the *New Jersey Jewish News,* took place beginning on December 14, 1999 and ending on February 7, 2000. The data were weighted by region, age, and gender to more closely approximate the resident Jewish population of the United States. A total of 1,006 Roman Catholics were also surveyed from March 17 through April 17, 2000. This sample was weighted by age and gender to render it more representative of the target population.[28]

Results

Party

As Table 1 demonstrated, Catholics and Jews were quite far apart on the measure of political partisanship. The multivariate model, which is not displayed here, showed that party affiliation varied as expected, with some important compositional qualities. For the entire sample, Democratic support was lower among residents of rural areas and suburbs than among people who lived in large cities. Conversely, women, nonwhite ethnics, and labor union members were more prone to identify with the Democratic party than were men, whites, and non-union respondents, respectively. Compared with college graduates, those with less than a high school diploma were significantly more likely to be Democratic. None of these findings was surprising because they confirm what has long been known about the social contours of partisanship in the United States. The interesting question is whether taking account of these differences eliminates the average partisan difference between Jews and Catholics. The answer is a resounding no. Even after taking account of all the relevant social background differences, Jews remain considerably more likely than Catholics to describe themselves as Democrats.

Ideology

Survey participants were asked to select the ideological label that most closely fit them. The choices were "very conservative," "conservative," "moderate," "liberal," and "very liberal." Table 2 shows that Catholics and Jews were significantly different on this scale. Catholics were nearly twice as likely to select one of the first two options and Jews, conversely, were one-and-a-half times as likely to pick one of the two liberal labels.

Regarding the social forces that affect ideology, the multivariate model reveals that members of several of the more Democratic-oriented groups—women, labor union members, those with a high school education (compared with those holding a college degree or advanced degrees), and residents of large cities—were also more likely to describe themselves as "liberal" or "very liberal." There were also some unique patterns that did not show up in the multivariate analysis of party loyalty. Respondents who were foreign-born were much more liberal than persons

Table 2. Political Ideology, by Religious Affiliation

	Roman Catholic (n=984)	Jewish (n=522)
Very conservative	4.3	3.1
Conservative	32.1	17.4
Moderate	32.4	29.5
Liberal	24.2	36.0
Very liberal	7.0	14.0
Total (%)	100	100

of fourth-generation status in the United States, a finding that undoubtedly reflects the influence of Hispanic Catholics among the former group. Those who reported having friendships outside their ethnoreligious group and who lived in mixed neighborhoods were also more liberal than those who were strictly endogenous in their choice of companions and places of residence. Lending some support to the idea of a "faith factor," the equation revealed that individuals who never attended religious services were appreciably more liberal than those in the highest attendance category (who attended religious services more than once a week). However, apart from the difference between people at the extremes of the attendance spectrum, there was no significant difference in ideology between persons who attended services at different frequencies.

When we turn to the Jewish-Catholic difference, the results are once again clear. As with partisanship, Jews remained distinctly different in ideology from Catholics even after controlling for variables that might affect the relationship. The direction is the same as indicated in Table 2: Jews were more liberal than Catholics.

Voting

The measure of Democratic voting is based on both actual and anticipated electoral decisions. Respondents were asked whom they had supported in the 1996 presidential election and for whom they intended to vote in the 2000 congressional races. Because the survey was conducted well before the presidential nominees of 2000 had been determined, respondents were also asked to indicate their preference in three presidential trial heats involving Al Gore, Bill Bradley, George Bush, and John McCain. Given the distance between the survey and the election date in late 2000, all of those who indicated that they were uncertain regarding their preference in the trial heats were classified as not voting Democratic even if they were Democratic partisans. While this voting measure bears a relationship to the psychological measure of partisanship that was earlier discussed, its inclusion of reported and intended behavior makes it arguably more useful as a measure of partisan disposition.

Given the strong influence of ideology and partisanship on voting, it is not surprising to find the same kind of patterns for actual vote choice as were observed for those two traits. Democratic voting—both actual and anticipated—is more pronounced among women, residents of large cities, nonwhites, and labor union members. As with ideology, higher levels of religious attendance and exclusively in-group friendships were associated with a lesser tendency to vote Democratic. Older and better-educated voters were more likely to report Democratic voting habits.

The simple comparison of Catholics and Jews on this scale, which ran from 0 (no support for Democratic candidates) to 5 (maximum support for Democratic candidates), showed a 1-point difference. Catholics averaged 1.6, versus a 2.6 average for Jews. In the multivariate analysis, this difference was maintained almost exactly. After taking account of all the background factors, Jews on average exceeded Catholics by 0.9.

Consistent Ethic of Life

If there is one issue that is thought to typify Catholic political distinctiveness in the United States, it is surely the debate over abortion. Despite efforts by some members of the hierarchy to broaden the agenda by incorporating a range of issues, American bishops have clearly assigned political priority to the abortion question.[29] However, American Catholics have not marched in lockstep with their leaders. On this question, as on so many others, Catholics have usually occupied the midpoint. Catholic women appear about as likely as women from other religious traditions to terminate a pregnancy, and the Catholic lay population strongly supports abortion when it involves threats to the life or health of the mother or involves a severely damaged fetus. Among American religious groups, evangelical Protestants—white and black alike—have exhibited the most intense opposition to abortion. For their part, with the exception of the ultra-Orthodox, American Jews have been among the strongest supporters of access to legalized abortion.[30]

To assess the differences between them, Catholics and Jews were compared on a composite measure of attitudes regarding the consistent ethic of life. The composite measure included a question about banning all forms of abortion; another about the banning of so-called "partial birth" abortion; a question about whether physicians should be required to notify the parents of minor girls who seek to end a pregnancy; and a fourth question in which respondents could array themselves on a scale from "always pro-life" to "always pro-choice."[31] These questions tap the major dimensions of the ongoing American debate about abortion. The composite scale was further augmented by a question about whether terminally ill individuals had the right to choose to end their own lives.

The simple comparison of Catholics and Jews yielded powerful differences. The attitudinal measure ranged from zero (for those who favored the most restrictive anti-abortion option for each question) to a maximum of 16 (for the most unalloyed supporters of choice). Roman Catholics averaged 6.8, versus a mean score of 11.4 for Jewish respondents. That difference was both large and statistically significant—but would it remain of such magnitude with controls for the relevant background factors?

Previous research on abortion suggests that the issue is often a template for views about the proper role of women in society.[32] While factors such as gender and education matter, the attitudes reported by individuals often reflect deeply held cultural tendencies as well. The multivariate analysis proved consistent with these expectations. Women, residents of large cities, and people with higher levels of education were more supportive of legal access to abortion than were their counterparts. Longer residence in the United States—probably a surrogate for age—pushed respondents in the pro-life direction. Cultural factors were equally if not more powerful than demographic variables. For instance, attendance at worship strongly promoted the pro-life perspective. Similarly, individuals who lived in neighborhoods dominated by their own socioreligious group, and who had only in-group friendships, were much more likely to reject liberalized abortion.

With controls for the usual factors vis-à-vis abortion, did the simple Jewish-Catholic group difference of 4.6 hold up? Indeed it did. Although the controls reduced the difference to 3.0, religious identification was the second most powerful influence on the composite measure. The persistence of Jewish/Catholic divergence on this measure is all the more remarkable because it discounts religiosity per se: simply identifying as a Jew or a Roman Catholic matters greatly, regardless of how deeply involved one is either communally or associationally.

Economic Values

If abortion was the issue with the best potential to divide Jews and Catholics, the scale measuring progressive economic values is arguably the least likely to differentiate between the two groups. This dimension underlay the common political stance of Jews and Catholics in the Allinsmiths' study at mid-20th century, and there is little sign of change at the elite level. The strong social justice motif in American Judaism has encouraged Jews to advocate generous social welfare programs. American Catholic bishops have also drawn on a similar tradition in Catholic social thought, criticizing market economics for its treatment of the poor and calling on the state to intervene with a variety of compensatory programs.[33] Moreover, although this has received comparatively little public attention, the Church has lobbied consistently against budget cuts that target social welfare programs and on behalf of a leaner allocation for military purposes. Hence we might not be surprised if there is convergence in Catholic-Jewish thinking on issues pertaining to economic values.

The scale of economic values includes questions about the minimum wage, government health insurance, defense spending, taxation, pollution control, and health care.[34] The multivariate analysis shows that men, people who have been in the United States for several generations, whites, and regular churchgoers were less disposed toward progressive economic causes, as opposed to members of labor unions, who (as expected) were much more supportive of a strong government role in the economy.

This variable yielded essentially the same pattern as was apparent on all the other indicators. In the simple bivariate comparison, Jews outscored Catholics by about 1.3 points on this measure. The difference was large enough to rule out chance variations in sampling. In the multivariate model, after imposing controls for all the background factors, the difference was still 1.2, with Jews again more prone to embrace progressive economic values.

Discussion

Two major findings of the empirical analysis stand out clearly and with little am-
biguity. First, across a wide range of political measures—core orientations to party
and ideology, behavior in the voting booth, attitudes toward economic and social
issues—Jews and Catholics are different. The political differences between them
are *not* reducible to socioeconomic or cultural background traits. In fact, the simple
differences between Jews and Catholics were usually unaffected by the more complex statistical models. Even taking into account the social profile of each community, something about "being Jewish" versus "being Catholic" makes a difference, politically speaking. Moreover, the direction of such difference is consistent
across the five measures. On each domain, Jews were more left-leaning than Roman
Catholics: they were more inclined to identify themselves as Democrats and liberals, cast votes for Democratic candidates, embrace the pro-choice side of the
abortion debate, and display progressive values on economic issues.

These findings were unexpected. As I argued at the outset, there were many
reasons to anticipate a Jewish-Catholic convergence in political views once extra-
neous traits that differentiated the two groups were controlled for. The two groups
have always shared a somewhat marginal status in the United States and have
become more alike in terms of socioeconomic qualities since mid-20th century.
The historical enmity between them appears to have eased considerably over the
postwar period. For the last two decades or so, they have shared a concern about
the growing influence of evangelical Protestants in the Republican party. Yet despite
these developments, the two groups have developed very different political profiles.

A full explanation of these patterns requires a much longer and deeper analysis
than can be provided here. But perhaps we can get a purchase on this difference
by thinking about the findings in terms of *self-interest.*

From the perspective of economic theories that are conventionally employed by
political scientists to make sense of political behavior, the evolution of Roman
Catholic politics in the United States makes a great deal of sense. As the Allinsmiths noted at mid-20th century, the ordering of the religious groups—Jews ex-
cepted—followed their socioeconomic status. That is, the larger the proportion of
manual workers and the lower the level of formal education and affluence in each
group, the greater the support for Democrats and for policies that favored the
working class. Hence, the pronounced liberal tilt among Catholics (and Baptists)
in the immediate postwar years reflected the predominance of people in those
groups who benefited directly from Democratic economic policies. Over the past
60 years, the Catholic population as a whole has enjoyed considerable upward
economic mobility and now matches the average American in terms of education
and economic comfort.[35] As a middle-class population, Catholics presumably have
less to gain from the more liberal political party and their leadership has strongly
pushed the community rightward on abortion and related issues. Given self-interest
and priestly guidance, it is hardly surprising that the politics of the community has
moved to a more conservative posture.

No such explanation suffices for the Jews. The Allinsmiths noted in 1948 that
Jews had the lowest proportion of manual workers and the highest proportion of

well-educated persons among the eight religious traditions in their study. By the iron law of economic self-interest, Jews should have been the most conservative group in the study. Sixty years later, the behavior of Jews remains just as puzzling to economic determinists. The Jewish community as a whole remains well above national averages on measures of educational attainment, occupational status, income, and wealth. Although Jews do respond politically to short-term changes in their economic situation, most of them continue disproportionately to support both a political party associated with the poor and deprived and the public policies that favor them.[36] In Milton Himmelfarb's memorable (albeit politically incorrect phrase), Jews earn like Episcopalians but vote like Puerto Ricans.

This pattern prevails despite concerted efforts to shift Jews to the political right. During the last 25 years, some self-described "neoconservative" voices in the community have argued long and hard that Jews do not belong on the Left in the United States.[37] Irving Kristol, Dennis Prager, Norman Podhoretz, and others have argued that, given American Jews' economic success, it makes more sense for them to support policies favoring low taxation and limited government—views that are much more pronounced among Republicans. They also contend that the Left has become hostile to Israel and that conservative Americans, who favor high levels of military spending, are now the Jewish state's best friends. These views have been widely expounded on the pages of *Commentary*, the publication of the American Jewish Committee, and have been voiced as well in such formerly left-wing outlets as the *New Republic*. The neoconservative perspective has also been the raison d'être for the founding of such publications as *National Interest* and *Azure*.

Since the events of 9/11, the critics of Jewish liberalism have added another argument to their arsenal, identifying militant Islam as the common global enemy of Jews, Israel, and the United States. Once Jews recognize that reality, it is argued, they will realize that their security and prosperity rests on a vigorous military response to terrorism, as exemplified by the U.S. attack on Saddam Hussein's Iraq. Indeed, Jewish neoconservatives were among the most public advocates of preemption even though the policy itself was clearly the brainchild of President George W. Bush, Vice President Dick Cheney, and Secretary of Defense Donald Rumsfeld (Protestants all). Citing Bush's position as the leader of the coalition against Iraq, as well as his virtually unqualified support for the policies of Israeli prime minister Ariel Sharon, the critics of American Jewish liberalism have renewed their call for American Jewry to move to the right.

This call for a political conversion does not seem to have yielded much fruit. Despite a major Republican outreach to Jews, the best polling data indicates that the Jewish community was deeply troubled by the Iraq war and remained solidly behind the Democratic nominee in the 2004 presidential race, Senator John Kerry of Massachusetts. Kerry's advantage (74 percent) over George W. Bush (25 percent) among Jewish voters in election-day exit polls confirmed pre-election polls conducted by Gallup and by Greenberg Rosner. These results indicate that Jews did not respond enthusiastically to the few former Democratic Jewish voices who endorsed the GOP.[38]

And so we remain with the paradox that was noted by the Allinsmiths in 1948: Jews remain to the left of the American public and, specifically, the Catholic com-

munity with whom they once shared a political affinity. Whereas Catholics have
moved in a direction consistent both with economic self-interest and, on the abor-
tion/life issue, with the guidance provided by their religious leadership, Jews continue to stand out in ways that make little sense, at least given the predominance
of self-interest models of political behavior.

Over the past few decades, a virtual cottage industry has emerged in an effort
to explain Jewish political behavior in the United States. To date, the research
spawned by this effort has been most effective at discovering what does *not* account
for American Jewish political behavior. In the classic work on the subject, *The
Political Behavior of American Jews*, Lawrence Fuchs argued that Jewish political
liberalism could be traced to specific religious values embedded in the tradition.
He argued that the Jewish emphasis on *ẓedakah* (charity/justice), human reason,
education, and internationalism all predisposed Jews to embrace progressive political causes.[39] Subsequent surveys have shown that Jews certainly believe that their
politics of social justice amount to a kind of applied Judaism.[40] Yet scholars have
recognized two central problems with this hypothesis. First, if the tendency toward
liberalism is intrinsic to Judaism, it should be manifest wherever Jews reside. However, a left-wing political orientation seems to be much more common among
American Jews than among their counterparts elsewhere: certainly the Jews of Israel
are much less liberal on a wide range of issues, and there is evidence that Jews in
Western Europe are often centrist if not right-wing in their basic political values.[41]
The second problem with Fuchs' argument becomes apparent when American Jews
are analyzed in terms of varying levels of religious adherence. If liberalism is
implicit in Jewish values and texts, we would expect the most religious Jews to be
the political standard-bearers of the community. In fact, there is persuasive evidence
that the commitment to liberal political values is lower among the most religious
segments of the community.[42]

An alternative theory holds that the European heritage of American Jewry best
accounts for the community's political uniqueness.[43] Oppression of Jews, it is argued, which was championed primarily by forces on the Right—the Church, the
monarchy, the aristocracy, the military—was often resisted by socialists, Communists and other adherents of left-wing political movements. In consequence, American Jews forged a long-lasting mental association that linked the Right with antisemitism and the Left with a much more sympathetic disposition toward Jews.
This link was reinforced when Democratic presidents appointed the first Jewish
Supreme Court justice in 1916 and the first significant concentration of Jews to
top-level policy positions during the New Deal. Democratic leadership of the war
against Hitler and support for the creation of Israel further reinforced this historical
tendency.

While such an argument makes a great deal of sense, it is not sufficient to account
for the prevalence of Jewish liberalism more than half a century after the end of
the Second World War and the establishment of the state of Israel. Scholars who
study political socialization—the acquisition of political attitudes and values—recognize that group-related experiences can be a powerful and persistent stimulus to
partisan loyalty. For example, Southern whites remained Democratic for nearly a
century after the Civil War, and blacks were Republican for nearly the same period

of time. These allegiances reflected Democratic opposition to the Civil War and Republican support for ending slavery. Over time, however, such "primordial" sentiments are likely to erode and become susceptible to political shocks. Almost at the moment that the national Democratic party embraced the cause of racial integration in 1948, Southern whites abandoned the party in large numbers. And when the Democrats signaled their support for the Civil Rights Act of 1964 (and the Republicans nominated a critic of the legislation as their presidential candidate), African Americans flocked to the Democratic banner almost overnight. Historical alliances, while powerful, require strong reinforcement if they are to persist.

This is precisely the problem with the "European heritage" explanation of contemporary American Jewish liberalism: the underlying cause has not been reinforced consistently, and it has weathered political shocks that might well have produced the kind of realignment long sought by neoconservatives. As Jews have become increasingly integrated in U.S. society—many are already third- or fourth-generation Americans—the influence of the European experience ought to have faded. Given some of the changes identified by the neoconservatives, especially the determined courting of Israel by conservative Republicans, one might well have anticipated much greater erosion in Jewish affiliation with the Left. Certainly Peter Medding expected as much in his classic discussion of the evolution of American Jewish organizations in the 1970s.[44]

Thus the question remains: Why have American Jews not moved to the right and caught up with Catholics in political attitudes? Why do they remain, politically, a people apart? While a full answer would draw on several strands of argument, I think that the core of American Jewish political behavior can best be explained by turning to structural explanations for religiously based political behavior.

As scholars are increasingly making clear, the rules and norms governing the public status of religion (what I have called the "regime" of religion and state) seem to matter greatly for how religious groups behave politically.[45] Consider the case of Muslims in Western Europe. In an intriguing three-country study of state accommodation to Muslim religious needs, Joel S. Fetzer and J. Christopher Soper found that the United Kingdom has been quite responsive to Muslim concerns on a range of issues, whereas France, under the doctrine of *laïcité* (secularism), has been most resistant, whether the issue has been Muslim schooling, zoning laws for mosques, or job discrimination.[46] Conditions in Germany fall somewhere between the British and French models. To account for this pattern, the authors test and reject theories based on the resources or mobilizing capacity of the Muslim population. Ultimately, they hypothesize that each nation's longstanding approach to religion best accounts for the outcome. With a long history of a state church and accommodation to personal religious needs, the United Kingdom has found it easiest to adapt to Muslim concerns. France, which is characteristically hostile to public religious expression, has treated Muslims pretty much as it has historically treated other religious groups. And in Germany, the same historical norms that have long governed the country's predominantly bi-religious population have allowed Muslims more scope than in France, although less than in the U.K.

Applied to the case at hand, it is important to consider the situation of Jews and Catholics in the United States with regard to the regime of religion and state. The

U.S. Constitution broke new ground with the revolutionary language incorporated in Article VI, that "no religious test shall ever be required as a qualification to any office or public trust under the United States." While less well known than the famous religion clauses of the First Amendment, this obscure provision effectively decoupled religion and citizenship in the new state. Americans were to be defined not by ethnicity, religion, national origin, or other ascriptive traits—the usual standards employed by nations—but by the simple matter of birth or naturalization. Jews did not have to struggle for emancipation, since it was woven into the legal fabric of the United States from the very beginning of its history. Jewish life was thereby considerably transformed, and in the 19th century, Jews flocked to the United States, sensing opportunity that was denied to them both throughout Western Europe and in the Muslim world. Despite the reality of discrimination, which long limited their chances for advanced education, economic mobility, desirable housing, and other benefits, Jews generally felt at home in the United States precisely because it did not condition membership in the nation on a common religion. Rather, it promised full citizenship and treated impediments to that goal as shameful shortcomings that should be remedied in time.

As they gradually acquired more confidence and political capital, Jews emerged as a strong voice defending secularism in public policy.[47] Under the banner of "strict separation," they led the postwar efforts to remove state-sponsored prayers and Bible-reading from the public school curriculum; to oppose the funding of sectarian education with tax money or the allocation of privileges or penalties based on religious affiliation; and to ensure that religious minorities were not disadvantaged because their practices differed from the majority. Under the U.S. regime, Jews have fought for the right to be openly Jewish without suffering penalties for their minority status. Hence they were (and remain) deeply disturbed by talk of "Christian America" or by policies that appear to grant official favor to Christianity. Such favoritism would undermine the Jews' own standing in a society that has always considered religion to be a private matter having no bearing on a citizen's treatment by public authorities.

One might have expected American Catholics to follow a similar path since they, too, faced serious handicaps from the Protestant majority. Beyond discrimination in jobs, housing, and other social practices, Catholics were occasionally subject to mob violence at the hands of Protestant gangs and were often portrayed as an alien force that was inimical to genuine American values. We tend to forget that the Ku Klux Klan of the immediate post-First World War era was perhaps more hostile to Catholics than to Jews or even African Americans.[48] Until Philip Hamburger made the argument so forcefully in his recent book, many Americans were also unaware of the degree to which the separationist doctrine in Church-state matters was driven by antipathy toward Roman Catholicism.[49] Protestants tried to limit state aid to private religious schools, or even to mandate public schooling, simply because most private education was Catholic-affiliated. Much as Jews, in the course of time, were accused of dual loyalty to Israel and the United States, Catholics, especially Catholic candidates for national office, were deemed unfit because they were said to owe their first allegiance to Rome.[50]

Although circumstances have changed, Jews continue to act like political outsiders, supporting parties and causes that are usually associated with disadvantaged minorities, whereas Catholics have moved to the center of the political spectrum. The outsider tag no longer seems to matter very much to most Catholics. I would suggest two reasons why they have found it much easier than Jews to assimilate politically. First, there is the matter of sheer numbers. Jews number barely more than 2 percent of the American public; Catholics, at around 30 percent, are today the single largest U.S. religious denomination. In many localities and states, Catholics are the dominant religious force. With such numbers, Catholics can understandably be less sensitive than formerly to their status as a minority: to the extent that public policy reflects religious values, those values will likely be congruent with Roman Catholicism. Jews, lacking a majority or even plurality, have no such assurance.[51]

Second, Catholics—as Christians—are closer than Jews to the religious "center" of American life. Even the leaders of the evangelical political revival have foresworn the narrow language of Protestantism in order to embrace what they sometimes describe as "Christian America." As part of this overwhelming religious majority and as a people who speak in Christian cadences, Catholics are part of the religious center in a way that Jews can never be. Comforting language about a "Judeo-Christian" heritage to the contrary, Jews remain perennially threatened by any effort to define the United States in religious terms.

As Leonard Fein has argued, the continuing embrace of liberalism by most American Jews can thus be understood from the perspective of self-interest.[52] While they may believe in their hearts that their political views are compelled by Judaism's prophetic teachings, American Jews also seem to feel that liberalism has been good for them. According to Fein, liberal societies that reduce racial and social tension are better places for Jews than are societies that institutionalize inequality and thereby breed social resentment and, in more extreme circumstances, violent political resistance. Therefore, Fein suggests, Jewish self-interest prompts them willingly to pay higher rates of taxation for public policies that both ameliorate the excesses of the market and erect a social safety net, averting conditions that have historically generated resentment toward Jews. The constitutional provisions that assured equal citizenship for Jews made them fierce defenders of the liberal order. They remain so to this day, in part because they still regard themselves as belonging with other outsiders in the United States.

Can the structural argument linking Jewish political distinctiveness to the regime of religion and state in the United States also account for the peculiar politics of American Jewry vis-à-vis its counterparts elsewhere? Can it explain why religiously observant Jews in the United States are less likely to embrace that distinctiveness? I believe that it can. On the first point, it is important to recall that the major Jewish centers of Europe (and prior to 1948, North Africa and the Middle East) were located in societies that formally privileged another religious tradition—Catholicism or Protestantism in Europe, Islam in Africa. While Jews may have achieved a degree of emancipation in the European societies and enjoyed a tolerated status as *dhimmis* in Muslim societies, they were clearly not on an equal footing with those belonging to the dominant religious tradition. Indeed, it may be said that Jews in those environments did not *expect* equality, precisely because national identity was defined by religious criteria that Jews could not meet except by abandoning their faith. If they did not believe they were entitled to such treatment, it probably rankled less that they were subject to disabilities. Hence, their politics developed in different ways than in America. In the extreme case of Israel, the only society with an explicit Jewish identity, Jews have shown themselves to be much less committed to a liberal order on religious equality than their American brethren.[53] British Jews, for their part, lack the strong commitment of their American corelig- ionists to the outsider perspective and thus can find common ground with the Conservative party even though it is identified with the traditional institutions of a monarchist society.

The denominational differences in American Jewish political behavior may also reflect structural patterns. As noted, American Jewry's fierce commitment to the constitutional order on religion has meant that most American Jews regard religion as an illegitimate basis for public policy. As I have argued, state recognition of religion appears to threaten their status as full citizens of the republic. This per- spective, however, does not necessarily hold for the more religiously observant segment of American Jewry. Perhaps reflecting both the theocratic tendency in Judaic thinking and their primary interest in maintaining traditional Judaism, the observant have been less concerned with public religious neutrality.[54] Policies that favor religious institutions, such as state aid to religious schools, are more consistent with the self-interest and core values of the Orthodox. Indeed, one might even speculate that state support for theism as manifested in school vouchers, the "under God" language of the Pledge of Allegiance, or the campaign for faith-based public service makes religious Jews feel more rather than less like other Americans. As Orthodoxy remains a minority among American Jewry, it does not define the central tendency of the community's political behavior, but it nonetheless adds to the value of the structural argument.

As has been shown, Catholics have much less investment than Jews in the reli- gious neutrality of the American constitutional order. With no such anchor, they have been much freer to define their political interests on the basis of other criteria. It follows that unless Jews lose their sense of outsider status or come to believe that their interests are better protected by a more explicitly religious political sys- tem, they are likely to continue to differ from Catholics on a wide range of political issues. Thus the political convergence detected by the Allinsmiths in 1948 now appears to be less a harbinger of intergroup political trends than a momentary alliance brought about by conditions that have since changed.

Notes

I am grateful to the University of Florida Research Foundation for providing the funds that enabled me to purchase the survey data from Zogby International.

1. Wesley Allinsmith and Beverly Allinsmith, "Religious Affiliation and Politico- Economic Attitudes: A Study of Eight Major U.S. Religious Groups," *Public Opinion Quar-*

terly 12 (1948), 377–389. Apart from Jews and Roman Catholics, the sample comprised Methodists, Presbyterians, Lutherans, Baptists, Episcopalians, and Congregationalists.

2. In American political discourse, the term "liberal" encompasses a set of values that includes social compassion, support for active government action to combat poverty and discrimination, and libertarianism in social behavior. Hearkening back to the Lockean heritage of the term, liberalism also denotes opposition to policies that appear to privilege specific religious institutions while simultaneously permitting individuals wide scope to express their religious identity without hindrance. Americans refer interchangeably to liberalism, the Left, and progressivism. I use these terms in that sense rather than with regard to their historical meanings.

3. James Carroll, *Constantine's Sword: The Church and the Jews* (Boston: 2001).

4. Guenter Lewy, *The Catholic Church and Nazi Germany* (New York: 1964); Courtney Brown, "The Nazi Vote: A National Ecological Study," *American Political Science Review* 76 (1982), 285–302.

5. Daniel Jonah Goldhagen, *A Moral Reckoning: The Role of the Catholic Church in the Holocaust and Its Unfulfilled Duty of Repair* (New York: 2002); Susan Zuccotti, *Under His Very Windows: The Vatican and the Holocaust in Italy* (New Haven: 2000).

6. Thomas Maier, *The Kennedys: America's Emerald Kings* (New York: 2003).

7. Michael Parenti, "Political Values and Religious Cultures: Jews, Catholics, and Protestants," *Journal for the Scientific Study of Religion* 6 (1967), 259–269; Lawrence H. Fuchs, *The Political Behavior of American Jews* (1956).

8. Kenneth D. Wald, *Religion and Politics in the United States*, 4th ed. (Lanham: 2003).

9. Lucy S. Dawidowicz and Leon J. Goldstein (eds.), *Politics in a Pluralist Democracy: Studies of Voting in the 1960 Election* (Westport: 1974), 9–14. The vote for Kennedy in predominantly Jewish areas was even higher than the total he registered in the mostly Irish Catholic wards of Boston.

10. Mark D. Brewer, *Relevant No More? The Catholic/Protestant Divide in American Electoral Politics* (Lanham: 2003).

11. John Higham, *Strangers in the Land: Patterns of American Nativism*, 2nd ed. (New Brunswick: 2002 [1955]).

12. Andrew M. Greeley, *Ethnicity, Denomination and Equality* (Beverly Hills: 1976), passim. The principal exception to this generalization is the large population of Hispanic Catholic immigrants in the United States. As a result of immigration law changes in 1965 and the porous Southern border with Mexico, the Hispanic population—about half of which is Roman Catholic—has grown appreciably and has imparted a much more liberal strain to the Church.

13. See Joshua Zeitz's article in this volume, pp. 88–110.

14. Jonathan Rieder, *Canarsie: The Jews and Italians of Brooklyn against Liberalism* (Cambridge, Mass.: 1985).

15. Clyde Wilcox, *God's Warriors: The Christian Right in Twentieth-Century America* (Baltimore: 1992).

16. Tom W. Smith, *A Survey of the Religious Right: Views on Politics, Society, Jews and other Minorities* (New York: 1996).

17. Scott Appleby, "Catholics and the Christian Right: An Uneasy Alliance?," in *Sojourners in the Wilderness: The Christian Right in Comparative Perspective*, ed. Corwin E. Smidt and James Penning (Lanham: 1997), 93–114.

18. Naomi W. Cohen, *Natural Adversaries or Possible Allies? American Jews and the New Christian Right* (New York: 1993).

19. Gerhard Lenski, *The Religious Factor* (Garden City: 1963).

20. Ibid., 41.

21. Emile Durkheim, *Suicide: A Study in Sociology* (New York: 1966).

22. Kenneth D. Wald and Corwin E. Smidt, "Measurement Strategies in the Study of Religion and Politics," in *Rediscovering the Religious Factor in American Politics*, ed. David C. Leege and Lyman Kellstedt (Armonk, N.Y.: 1993), 26–49.

23. Paul Kleppner, *The Cross of Culture* (New York: 1970); idem, *The Third Electoral System* (Chapel Hill: 1979).

24. James Q. Wilson and Edward C. Banfield, "Public-Regardingness as a Value Premise in Voting Behavior," *American Political Science Review* 58 (1964), 876–887.

25. Morris Rosenberg, *The Logic of Survey Analysis* (New York: 1968).

26. The statistical model of choice depends principally on the measurement level of the dependent variable. When a given variable can be ordered by degree but not differentiated more finely (as in the case of partisanship or ideology), it is customary to use one of the general likelihood models such as ordered probit or logit. But for what are called continuous variables with a real zero point and more precise gradations, such as the scale of abortion attitudes ranging from zero to 16, one can model the relationships with ordinary least squares regression. I have followed conventions in selecting the appropriate model for each political orientation under investigation.

27. Readers who wish further details should contact me at kenwald@polisci.ufl.edu.

28. While I am grateful to the Zogby Organization for collecting the data and making them available to me, I must insist that the analysis and interpretations are my own and do not necessarily reflect the views of the sponsor of the survey. The supplier of the data is in no way implicated in this report.

29. Timothy A. Byrnes, *Catholic Bishops in American Politics* (Princeton: 1991).

30. Wald, *Religion and Politics in the United States*, chs. 7–8.

31. Because survey participants and scholars may understand the political universe in different terms, it is important to check that the items in a composite scale do measure a common construct. This is conventionally assessed by calculating what are called reliability statistics. For this scale, the Cronbach's alpha is a robust +.77.

32. Kristin Luker, *Abortion and the Politics of Motherhood* (Berkeley: 1984).

33. Charles E. Curran, *American Catholic Social Ethics: Twentieth Century Approaches* (Notre Dame: 1982).

34. The Cronbach's standardized alpha was an acceptable +.63. This was achieved by converting each individual answer to a Z value such that the mean was 0 and the standard deviation was 1.

35. Greeley, *Ethnicity, Denomination and Equality*.

36. Lee Sigelman, "If You Prick Us, Do We Not Bleed? If You Tickle Us, Do We Not Laugh?," *Journal of Politics* 53 (1991), 977–992.

37. Edward Shapiro, "Right Turn? Jews and the American Conservative Movement," in *Jews in American Politics*, ed. L. Sandy Maisel and Ira N. Forman (Lanham: 2001), 161–194.

38. The 2004 exit poll data are available online at http://us.cnn.com/ELECTION/2004/pages/results/states/US/P/00/epolls.0.html.

39. Fuchs, *The Political Behavior of American Jews*.

40. Marshall Sklare and Joseph Greenblum, *Jewish Identity on the Suburban Frontier* (New York: 1967).

41. Charles S. Liebman and Steven M. Cohen, *Two Worlds of Judaism: The Israeli and American Experiences* (New Haven: 1990); W.D. Rubinstein, *The Left, the Right and the Jews* (London: 1982).

42. Steven M. Cohen, *American Modernity and Jewish Identity* (New York: 1983).

43. Arthur Liebman, *Jews and the Left* (New York: 1979).

44. Peter Y. Medding, *The Transformation of American Jewish Politics* (New York: 1989).

45. Kenneth D. Wald, "The Public Role of Private Religion in the United States," in *Religious Cultures/Communities of Belief*, ed. Jurgen Gephardt and David Martin (forthcoming).

46. Joel S. Fetzer and J. Christopher Soper, *Muslims and the State in Britain, France, and Germany* (New York: 2004).

47. Gregg Ivers, *To Build a Wall: American Jews and the Separation of Church and State* (Charlottesville: 1995).

48. Kenneth T. Jackson, *The Ku Klux Klan in the City, 1915–1930* (New York: 1967).

49. Philip Hamburger, *Separation of Church and State* (Chicago: 2002).

50. Allan J. Lichtman, *Prejudice and the Old Politics: The Presidential Election of 1928* (Chapel Hill: 1979).

51. Naomi Cohen, *Jews in Christian America* (New York: 1992).

52. Leonard Fein, *Where Are We? The Inner Life of America's Jews* (New York: 1988), 233–236.

53. Liebman and Cohen, *Two Worlds of Judaism.*

54. Martin Sicker, *The Political Culture of Judaism* (Westport: 2001).

Catholic (and Protestant) Israel: The Permutations of Denominational Differences and Identities in Mixed Families

Bruce A. Phillips
HEBREW UNION COLLEGE-JEWISH INSTITUTE OF
RELIGION, LOS ANGELES

An old "Borscht-belt" joke describes a Jew trying to pass as a Gentile so that he can join a restricted country club. When asked for his religion, the Jew replies: "I'm a goy." At the time this joke was popular, the distinctions between Catholics and Protestants were unimportant for Jews. Almost a century later, as American Jews have become intimately connected with Gentiles as spouses, parents, and children, the supposition of the original joke remains unexamined in the context of the mixed-married family. Are there, in fact, meaningful differences between Catholics, Protestants, and secular non-Jewish spouses?

Previous research has demonstrated differences between Christian and secular spouses in mixed marriages with Jews,[1] but what about intra-Christian differences? Uzi Rebhun hypothesized that because Catholicism is more "exclusivist" than American Protestantism, marriages between Jews and Catholics should be more "Christian" and less "Jewish" than marriages between Jews and Protestants.[2] (Catholicism is "exclusivist" because canon law requires, first, that the non-Catholic partner be married in the Roman Catholic marriage rite and second, that the non-Catholic spouse promise to raise any children of the marriage as Roman Catholics.[3]) Rebhun found that marriage to a Catholic had a greater negative effect on Jewish ritual observance and affiliation than did marriage to a Protestant.

More than a decade after the 1990 National Jewish Population Survey (NJPS) of 1990, there is reason to conjecture that Catholic-Protestant differences may be of less consequence than was previously believed. William D'Antonio, James Davidson, Dean Hoge, and Katherine Meyer conducted a series of surveys of American Catholics between 1990 and 1999.[4] They found religious practice to be lowest and marriage to non-Catholics to be highest among the youngest, "post Vatican II," Catholics.

There is also evidence of an underlying convergence of values between Catholics and Protestants that is reflected in voting trends. A recent study by the Pew Research Center concluded that denominational differences between Protestants and Catholics were no longer important, in terms of politics:

> [T]he important political fault lines in the American religious landscape do not run along demoninational lines, but cut across them. That is, they are defined by religious outlook rather than denominational labels. For instance, traditionalist Catholics are closer to traditionalist Evangelicals than to modernist Catholics in their views on issues such as abortion or embryonic stem cell research.[5]

An important factor for the Bush victory in the 2004 presidential election was that religiously traditional Catholics voted like religiously conservative Protestants.[6]

Given these trends, there is good reason to revisit Rebhun's earlier analysis. The continued intermarriage that took place during the 1990s also calls for an expansion of his analysis to determine the extent to which Catholic spouses resemble Protestant spouses in Jewish-Christian marriages.

In this essay, I approach the issue through an examination of four specific questions:

1. Who are the non-Jewish spouses in Jewish households?
2. Does the religion of the non-Jewish spouse influence how children are raised in mixed marriages?
3. Does the religion of the non-Jewish spouse influence the religious life of the mixed-married home?
4. To what extent and in what ways are "Jewish-Christian" adults (mostly the products of first- or second-generation mixed marriages) different from Christian spouses who have no Jewish ancestry?

Socio-Demographic Profile of Non-Jewish Spouses

The data used in the following analysis come primarily from the National Jewish Population Survey of 2000–2001, sponsored by the United Jewish Communities. For this survey, tens of thousands of households were screened to locate a sample of 5,126 Jewish households.[7] In addition, I have made use of data obtained from the National Survey of Religion and Ethnicity (NSRE), which surveyed 4,027 non-Jewish households. These data were used to profile non-Jewish Americans for comparisons with non-Jewish spouses in intermarriages with Jews. Both data sets were provided by the North American Jewish Data Bank at the Roper Center at the University of Connecticut. Where applicable data were not available, the 1990 NJPS was used along with some local Jewish population surveys.

Religious Origins of Non-Jewish Spouses

In almost half (45 percent) of the marriages involving Jews in the NJPS sample, one spouse was not Jewish. The non-Jewish spouses were split between those with no religion (45 percent) and those who identified as Christian (grouped among those with "no religion" were the relatively few spouses who identified with an

Eastern or New Age religion). Among the Christian spouses, Catholics slightly outnumbered Protestants (30 percent versus 25 percent)—which means that Catholics were overrepresented, since Protestants outnumber Catholics by 2-to-1 in the United States. Secular non-Jews (that is, the 45 percent reporting mainly "no religion") were even more overrepresented among the non-Jewish spouses; Barry Kosmin and his colleagues report that 14 percent of Americans have no declared religion.[8]

One reason for the overrepresentation of Catholics among spouses is an apparent affinity for Jews. In the early 1970s, Catholics were more approving of marriages between Jews and non-Jews than were Protestants (84 versus 63 percent).[9]

Birthplace and Geographical Distribution in the United States

One in five non-Jewish spouses was foreign-born. The percentage of the foreign-born among non-Jewish spouses of Jews generally reflected their proportion in the American population as a whole. The percentage of foreign-born Catholics among spouses (13 percent) was comparable to the percentage of foreign birth among Catholics in the NSRE (12 percent). Protestant spouses were only slightly more likely to be foreign-born than were Protestants in the NSRE (7 percent versus 5 percent). The secular and Eastern/New Age religion spouses, however, were almost twice as likely to have been born outside the United States than were their counterparts in the NSRE (18 percent versus 10 percent).

In addition to the apparent affinity for marriages to Jews among Catholics, the overrepresentation of Catholics among spouses is further explained by geography (Table 1). Like Jews, Catholics are concentrated in the Northeast. For example, Catholics make up the majority of the population in Massachusetts and Maine, and they comprise 40 percent of the population of Vermont, New York, and New Jersey.[10] As the table shows, the Catholic spouses of Jews were also regionally concentrated in the Northeast (59 percent). Protestant spouses were more likely to have been born in the South (35 percent of Protestant spouses versus 12 percent of Catholic spouses).

The geographic distribution of current residence (Table 2) resembles the region of birth. Mixed marriages of Jews and Catholics were concentrated in the Northeast (47 percent), whereas mixed marriages involving Protestants were most likely to be found in the South (38 percent). This table distinguishes between three cate-

Table 1. Region of Birth for Spouse

Region of birth	Religion of spouse		
	Catholic	Protestant	Secular/Eastern
Northeast	59	25	26
Midwest	12	19	27
South	12	35	21
West	17	22	27
Total (%)	100	100	100

Table 2. Region of Current Residence, by Religion of Spouse

	Region of current residence				
Religion of spouse	Northeast	Midwest	South	West	Total (%)
Catholic	47	11	21	22	100
Protestant	24	13	38	26	100
Secular/Eastern	29	14	24	32	100
Jewish (by birth and religion)	49	10	25	16	100
Jewish (by birth; identifies as secular)	26	32	15	27	100
Jewish (by choice)	19	20	37	25	100

gories of Jews: Jews from birth who also identify religiously as Jews; Jews from birth who identify as secular; and Jews by choice. There were virtually no differences between "born Jews" and Jews by choice. In-marriages between two Jews from birth were concentrated in the Northeast (49 percent); this situation reflects the lower rates of mixed marriage in that region.[11] In contrast, marriages to Jews by choice were most likely to be found in the South (37 percent) and least likely to be found in the Northeast (19 percent).

Table 3 further investigates the association between region and religion of spouse by comparing the region of birth for respondents and their spouses. In nearly half (48 percent) of all marriages to a Catholic spouse, both respondent and spouse were born in the Northeast, and in two out of three such marriages, at least one of the partners was born in the Northeast (computed from Table 3). In-marriages between two Jews by religion were similarly concentrated in the Northeast. In nearly three-fifths (59 percent) of such unions, both partners were born in the Northeast; in 80 percent, at least one partner was born in that region. Thus, mixed marriages to Catholics resembled endogamous Jewish marriages between two Jews from birth—in geographic terms, at least. Marriages to Jews by choice, in contrast, were associated with migration. As already observed, these marriages were concentrated in the South, yet the Jews by birth in these unions were largely born in the Northeast (43 percent). Many of the Jews by choice had also migrated south. Although, as noted, 37 percent of them lived in the South, only 22 percent of them were born in the South, whereas a third were born in the Midwest.

Although Jews married to Protestants were more likely to have been born in the South than Jews married to Catholics (22 percent versus 13 percent), more of them were born in the Northeast (37 percent), suggesting that they married after moving to the South, where Protestants outnumber Catholics. Marriages to Protestants were more geographically dispersed than Catholic intermarriages. The most typical combinations in Jewish-Protestant marriages were both partners born in the South (17 percent) and both partners born in the Northeast (18 percent). Secular non-Jewish spouses were born equally in all regions. In instances of marriages between two Jews from birth, most of the individuals were born in the Northeast; those married to Jews by choice were less likely to have remained in the Northeast. This pattern

Table 3. Region of Birth for Spouse, by Region of Birth for Respondent

Region of birth for spouses, by religion		Region of birth for respondent				
		Northeast	Midwest	South	West	All spouses
Catholic	Northeast	48	5	4	1	59
	Midwest	3	9	1	0	12
	South	3	2	5	1	12
	West	4	2	3	8	17
	All respondents	58	18	13	11	100%
Protestant	Northeast	18	3	2	2	25
	Midwest	5	11	2	1	19
	South	10	5	17	4	35
	West	4	4	1	12	22
	All respondents	37	22	22	19	100%
Secular non-Jewish	Northeast	20	1	1	5	26
	Midwest	6	14	4	4	27
	South	10	1	7	3	21
	West	3	4	1	19	27
	All respondents	39	20	11	30	100%
Jewish (by birth and religion)	Northeast	59	4	4	3	70
	Midwest	3	9	1	2	15
	South	5	1	3	0	10
	West	1	1	0	3	5
	All respondents	68	15	10	8	100%
Jewish (by birth; identifies as secular)	Northeast	38	5		5	47
	Midwest	19	9			28
	South	2	5	3		10
	West	3	3		9	15
	All respondents	62	22	3	13	100%
Jewish (by choice)	Northeast	19	6			26
	Midwest	9	13	7	3	33
	South	9	5	9		22
	West	6	3	1	9	19
	All respondents	43	27	17	13	100%

suggests the following: 1) Jews from the Northeast who were married to non-Jews were likely to have married after they had migrated; 2) they were more likely than intermarried Jews from other areas of birth to select spouses who were open to the idea of becoming Jewish.

Conversion

The NJPS of 2000–2001 did not ask specifically about the religion in which respondent and spouse were raised, only if they were "raised Jewish." Thus, data regarding conversion were obtained from the previous NJPS survey of 1990, which did inquire about the specific religion in which the respondent and spouse were raised; other data were supplied by several recent local studies.

Tables 4a, 4b, and 4c compare the religion of origin for non-Jewish spouses with their current religion. According to the NJPS of 1990 (Table 4a), spouses raised as Protestants were more likely to identify with Judaism (11 percent) than were spouses raised as Catholics (2 percent). They were also more likely to have had a formal conversion to Judaism as opposed to merely identifying as Jewish (Table 5), whereas the non-Jewish spouses raised in no religion were more likely to identify with Judaism.

Table 4a. Religion Raised and Current Religion for Spouse (NJPS, 1990)

Current religion of spouse	Religion in which spouse was raised				
	Jewish	Catholic	Protestant	Other	None
Jewish	98	2	11	8	13
Catholic	0	74	1	0	0
Protestant		1	58	8	13
Other	1	7	7	62	4
None	1	14	22	21	70
Don't know		2	1		
Total (%)	100	100	100	100	100

Table 4b. Religion Raised and Current Religion for Spouse (Chicago, 2001)

Current religion of spouse	Religion in which spouse was raised		
	Jewish	Catholic	Protestant
Jewish	98	10	14
Catholic	0	64	2
Protestant	0	2	56
Other/none	2	24	28
Total (%)	100	100	100

Table 4c. Religion Raised and Current Religion for Spouse
(San Francisco Federation Area, 2004)

Current religion of spouse	Religion in which spouse was raised			
	Jewish	Catholic	Protestant	Other/none
Jewish	99	4	3	18
Catholic	0	63	1	6
Protestant	0	5	47	3
Other/none	1	28	48	73
Total (%)	100	100	100	100

Similarly, according to the Chicago Jewish Population Survey of 2001 (Table 4b), spouses raised as Protestants were more likely than those raised as Catholics to identify as Jewish, though here the differences were smaller (14 percent versus 10 percent). In the San Francisco Federation Area Survey (Table 4c),[12] spouses born Catholic and Protestant were equally unlikely to identify with Judaism, in contrast with spouses raised in no religion. Nonetheless, in this survey there were significant differences between Protestants and Catholics with regard to the retention of original religious identity: San Francisco-area Protestants were more likely than the Catholics to have abandoned Christianity in favor of no religion (48 percent versus 28 percent). In all three studies, then, non-Jewish spouses of Catholic origin remained more loyal to their religion of origin than did spouses of Protestant origin.

The word "convert" was purposely avoided in the discussion above, since not all Jews by choice had a formal conversion. Table 5 reports formal conversion by a rabbi among Jews by choice. According to the NJPS of 1990, Jews by choice of Protestant origin were more likely than Jews by choice of Catholic origin to have undergone a formal conversion. In Chicago, however, Jews by choice who were Catholic in origin were more likely to have had a formal conversion. In San Francisco, where there were few Jews by choice to begin with, there were no differences. No significant conclusions can be drawn from this analysis because the impact of sample size and region on formal conversion cannot be disaggregated.

Table 5. Formal Conversion by a Rabbi among Jews by Choice, by Religion of Origin (% who had formal conversion)

Study	Respondent raised as:		
	Catholic	Protestant	Other/none
NJPS, 1990	67	83	67
Chicago, 2001	94	34	100
San Francisco, 2004	95	90	69

Race

The majority of non-Jewish spouses were white (Table 6). Although 29 percent of American Catholics were Hispanic in 2001,[13] only 4 percent of the Catholic spouses in the NJPS were identified as Hispanic. This is consistent with the finding reported above that Catholic spouses were overwhelmingly born in the Northeast, a region where Catholics of European origin predominate. Protestant spouses, too, were predominantly white, although 6 percent were African American. Interestingly, the Protestant spouses were as likely to be of Hispanic origin as the Catholic spouses. One of the recent trends in Hispanic religion is the increase in Hispanic Protestants as a result of both religious switching in the United States and selective migration of Protestants from Central and South America. Although the number of Hispanic spouses was small, the distributions in Table 6 suggest that Protestant Hispanics were overrepresented among non-Jewish spouses.

Secular spouses were the most racially diverse. Asians were most prevalent among spouses with no religion or a non-Christian religion. This pattern apparently mirrors national trends; Kosmin and his colleagues report that Asian Americans are the group most likely to describe themselves as secular. Thus, American Jews married to Asian Americans tend to be married to secular Asian Americans. One out of ten Jews by choice was identified as bi-racial. Perhaps they were more comfortable adopting a new religion because of their hybrid racial status. It is also possible that, being of mixed parentage, they were raised in no religion and thus were *adopting* a religion as opposed to *changing* religion.

Education

Education has long been associated with denominational identification.[14] From early in the 20th century, mainline Protestants such as Episcopalians and Methodists have been more highly educated than the more conservative or "strict" denomination Protestants such as Southern Baptists. Table 7 and Fig. 1 present the educational

Table 6. Race of Spouse, by Religion of Spouse

Race of spouse	Current religion of spouse			
	Catholic	Protestant	Other/ none	Jew by choice
White	90	87	84	86
African-American	1	6	2	4
Asian	1	1	6	<1
Native American	0	2	1	<1
Bi-racial or other race	4	1	4	10
Hispanic*	4	4	3	<1
Total (%)	100	100	100	100

*Hispanic identification was a separate question. Spouses identified as Hispanic are here categorized as such regardless of race.

Table 7. Educational Attainment of all Respondents and Spouses under Age 50

	Highest degree completed				
	High school or less	Some college	College graduate	Beyond college	Total (%)
Catholic spouses	23	24	32	20	100
Catholics (NSRE)	32	34	27	7	100
Protestant spouses	28	33	25	15	100
Protestants (NSRE)	41	34	20	6	100
Secular non-Jewish spouses	25	25	31	19	100
Secular (NSRE)	39	29	20	12	100
Jews (by birth and religion)	13	20	32	35	100
Jews (by birth; identify as secular)	25	32	25	18	100
Jews (by choice)	16	31	30	23	100

attainment by current religious identification for respondents and spouses under 50 years of age. Jews by birth and religious identification had the highest educational attainment: 67 percent had graduated college and fully 35 percent had at least some graduate or professional education. Jews by choice were the next most educated, which means that non-Jews who became Jewish resembled Jews by birth and religion in terms of educational attainment. Secular Jews had lower educational attainment than either Jews by birth/religious identification or Jews by choice, further demonstrating an association between Judaism and educational achievement.

Among the non-Jewish spouses, Catholics were more educated than Protestants: 52 percent of the former and 40 percent of the latter were college graduates. Further, more Catholic spouses than Protestant spouses had continued their education beyond college (20 percent versus 15 percent). The secular non-Jewish spouses were almost as highly educated as the Catholics. Thus, Protestant spouses stand out as having the lowest educational attainment. Although the NSRE analysis found that mainline Protestants were more highly educated than Protestants from strict denominations (data not shown), there were no educational differences between mainline and strict Protestants among the spouses in the NJPS.

All the non-Jewish spouses had higher educational attainment than did their religious counterparts not married to Jews. More than half of the Catholic spouses had graduated college, as compared with only a third of Catholics under the age of 50 in the NSRE. Similarly, 40 percent of the Protestant spouses had graduated college, as compared with only 26 percent of the Protestants younger than 50 years of age. The non-Jewish spouses who identified with no religion or with an Eastern religion were also more educated than other secular/Eastern-religion Americans under 50 years of age. Thus Jews tended to choose the most educated among Protestants, Catholics, and other non-Jews. Conversely, it may also be that the most educated non-Jews are the most open to marrying a Jew.

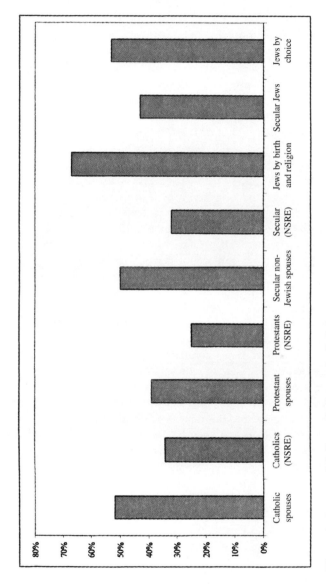

Figure 1. Percent of College Graduates, by Religion

Religious Practice in the Home

Marriage Ceremonies

The first religious decision a mixed (almost married) couple must make concerns the religious ceremonial aspects of their wedding. Under what religious auspices will the couple be married? What kind of clergy (if any) will perform the ceremony, and what kind of ceremony will it be? As Table 8 shows, the most popular choice for all mixed marriages was no clergy at all. That stated, Jews by religion were more likely than secular Jews to have been married by a rabbi. Among "dual-religion" couples (a Jew by religion married to a Christian), the ceremonies of those including a Protestant spouse were more Christian than those involving a Catholic spouse. Jews by religion married to Protestants tended to be married either by a rabbi (24 percent) or a minister (31 percent). Jews by religion married to Catholics were more likely than those married to Protestants to have a ceremony performed by a justice of the peace (49 percent versus 35 percent). They were also more likely to have been married jointly by a priest and a rabbi (15 percent versus 10 percent). Jews by religion married to secular non-Jews were the most likely to have been married in a nonreligious ceremony (53 percent) or by Jewish clergy (27 percent) and the least likely to have been married by Christian clergy either alone or with a rabbi (16 percent and 4 percent, respectively).

Consistent with their lack of religious identification, secular Jews, regardless of spouse, rarely had Jewish officiation. Secular Jews married to Catholics were more likely to have Christian clergy officiate (41 percent) than those married to Protestants (34 percent), but they were also more likely to have been married by a rabbi. One would expect that secular Jews married to secular non-Jews would mostly have had a non-religious ceremony, but this was not the case. Almost as many were married by non-Jewish clergy (44 percent) as by a justice of the peace (46 percent). There are multiple explanations for this, albeit all speculative. It could be that the secular non-Jewish spouse identified as a Christian at the time of the wedding. It could also be that the non-Jewish bride simply wanted a conventional "church wedding." There is evidence for this (data not shown): 68 percent of the secular non-Jewish brides had a church wedding, versus only 28 percent of the secular non-Jewish grooms.

Ritual Observance

The NJPS included questions about a variety of ritual observances (Table 9). Jews by religion practiced these rituals more often than did secular Jews. Controlling for religious identification of the Jewish spouse, the greatest differences were between couples in which the non-Jewish spouse was secular and those in which the non-Jewish spouse was Christian. For example, 40 percent of Jews by religion married to secular non-Jews reported lighting Shabbat candles, as compared with less than 30 percent of Jews by religion married to Catholic or Protestant spouses. Conversely, only 7 percent of the secular non-Jewish spouses married to Jews by re-

Table 8. Marriage Ceremony, by Religious Identification of Respondent and Spouse

	Jew by religion married to a:		
Ceremony performed by:	Catholic	Protestant	Secular non-Jew
Rabbi, cantor, or both	18	24	27
Non-Jewish clergy (minister/priest)	17	31	16
Both Jewish and non-Jewish clergy	15	10	4
Justice of the peace or other non-religious official	49	35	53
Total (%)	100	100	100

	Secular Jew married to a:		
Ceremony performed by:	Catholic	Protestant	Secular non-Jew
Rabbi, cantor, or both	8	0	3
Non-Jewish clergy (minister/priest)	41	34	44
Both Jewish and non-Jewish clergy	0	3	7
Justice of the peace or other non-religious official	51	63	46
Total (%)	100	100	100

ligion belonged to a non-Jewish religious organization, as compared with more than a quarter of the Christian spouses married to Jews.

Among dual-religion marriages, Jews by religion married to Catholics were more observant than Jews by religion married to Protestants. For example, 63 percent of Jews by religion married to Catholics attended a seder, as compared with 52 percent of those married to Protestants. Conversely, 37 percent of Protestant spouses belonged to a non-Jewish religious group as compared with 26 percent of Catholic spouses. Overall, however, the differences between Catholic and Protestant dual-religion marriages were small.

How Children are Raised

Arguably the most important aspect of the religious life of mixed-married Jews is how children are being raised. Three factors affected the religion in which children were being raised in mixed marriages: the religion of the Jewish spouse (Judaism versus no religion), the religion of the non-Jewish spouse (Catholic, Protestant, or no religion) and the gender of the Jewish parent. Table 10 reports how children were being raised within various religious configurations of respondent and spouse.

Households in which both the Jewish and non-Jewish parents were secular (or

Table 9. Ritual Observance, by Religious Identification of Respondent and Spouse
(% who observed each ritual)

	Jew by religion married to a:		
	Catholic	Protestant	Secular non-Jew
Observed any Jewish mourning ritual	73	71	69
Held or attended a seder	63	52	68
Lit Shabbat candles at least sometimes	27	25	40
Lit candles last Chanukah at least some nights	78	75	84
Had Christmas tree in home last Christmas	64	63	47
Increased level of Jewish activity compared to five years ago	29	23	27
Belongs to a synagogue	27	24	28
Non-Jewish spouse is member of a non-Jewish religious group	26	37	7

	Secular Jew married to a:		
	Catholic	Protestant	Secular non-Jew
Observed any Jewish mourning ritual	44	29	23
Held or attended a seder	17	18	19
Lit Shabbat candles at least sometimes	0	24	9
Lit candles last Chanukah at least some nights	22	34	23
Had Christmas tree in home last Christmas	92	83	66
Increased level of Jewish activity compared to five years ago	4	11	14
Belongs to a synagogue	1	4	0
Non-Jewish spouse is member of a non-Jewish religious group	52	51	23

of an Eastern or New Age religion) overwhelmingly raised their children in no religion at all. In dual-religion couples, Jewish mothers married to Catholics and secular non-Jews were the most likely to raise their children as Jews (65 percent and 60 percent, respectively). Jewish mothers married to Protestant fathers were the next most likely to raise children as Jews (47 percent). Mixed-married fathers who were Jewish by religion were less likely to raise Jewish children than were mothers who were Jewish by religion, regardless of the religion of the spouse. Jewish fathers married to secular non-Jews were more likely to raise children as Jews than those married to Christians. In mixed-married families with Jewish fathers, Catholic-Protestant differences were minimal.

Table 10. Religion in Which Child Was Being Raised (controlling for gender and religious identification of Jewish and non-Jewish spouses)

Religious combination of spouses	Religion in which child was being raised					
	Jewish	Other/none	Protestant	Catholic	Total (%)	N=
No religion in the household	5	74	15	6	100	149
Jewish mother and Catholic father	65	14		21	100	57
Jewish mother and secular (non-Jewish) father	60	27	13	0	100	32
Jewish mother and Protestant father	47	37	16	0	100	26
Jewish father and secular (non-Jewish) mother	42	40	18	0	100	19
Jewish father and Catholic mother	30	19	8	43	100	55
Jewish father and Protestant mother	27	20	53	0	100	33

"Jewish-Christians"

The NJPS interviewed more than 600 "Jewish-Christian" respondents. Most Jewish-Christians were the products of a mixed marriage in which they were raised as Christians by a non-Jewish parent, although some identified as Jewish by virtue of a Jewish grandparent. Respondents who identified with both Judaism and Christianity were included in the Jewish population estimates and reports published by the United Jewish Communities, the sponsor of the NJPS, whereas respondents who identified exclusively as Christian were excluded. Although Jewish-Christians probably do not belong in a profile of the American Jewish population, such individuals reveal a good deal about the long-range impact of intermarriage. They are of great interest in this analysis because their demographic profile and attitudinal responses indicate whether being raised as Catholic or as Protestant has an impact on adult Jewish identification.

In this analysis, Jewish Catholics are respondents with Jewish ancestry who identified themselves either as Catholic only or as both Catholic and Jewish. Similarly, Jewish Protestants identified themselves as Protestant only or as both Protestant and Jewish.

In the screening section of the NJPS questionnaires, respondents who were not Jewish by religion were asked if they considered themselves to be Jewish and on what basis. The majority of both Jewish Catholics and Jewish Protestants answered no, but respondents identified with Judaism and Christianity were more likely to consider themselves Jewish than those who identified only as Christian. Among respondents who identified with two religions, those who identified as both Jewish and Catholic were more likely to consider themselves Jewish than respondents who identified as both Jewish and Protestant (Table 11). Based on the weighting formula used in the NJPS, there were an estimated 329,000 Catholics and 511,000 Protestants who claimed such dual religious heritage. It is striking that relatively few adults identified as both Jewish and Christian: adult children of mixed marriages preferred a single religious identification.

Jewish Background of Mixed-Heritage Christians

Three quarters of both "Jewish Protestants" and "Jewish Catholics" were raised in mixed marriages with one Jewish parent (Table 12). Another 14 percent of the Catholics and 16 percent of the Protestants had only a Jewish grandparent. Between 8 and 12 percent of the "Jewish-Christians" said that both of their parents had been born Jewish. A closer inspection found that the Jewish-Christians with two Jewish parents were all raised as Christians, which is certainly puzzling. How is it that they had two Jewish parents? Some, as it turns out, were raised as messianic Jews by two messianic Jewish parents, but what explains the rest? An explanation may lie in the ambiguous wording of the question. Respondents were asked if their parents were *born* Jewish, rather than being asked what religion was practiced in the household when the respondent was growing up. In other words, respondents with a Jewish-Christian parent could have reported that the parent was "born" Jewish even though that parent identified as a Christian. In some cases, one of the two "born Jewish" parents was described as being "half-Jewish." Thus, Christian (but "half-Jewish") parents married to (probably secular) Jews were described as having been born Jewish.

The screening questions (used as a basis of determining whether the household should be defined as Jewish) asked if mixed-heritage Christians considered themselves to be Jewish. Table 13 shows that the Jewish parentage of Jewish-Christians had an impact on their self-conception as Jews. They were most likely to consider themselves Jewish when both parents were Jewish and least likely when they were of Jewish ancestry only. The pattern was the same for both Jewish Catholics and

Table 11. Estimated Population of Jewish-Christians and Their Religious Self-Definition

Respondent's religious identification	Considered self to be Jewish		Did not consider self to be Jewish			Total
	%	Estimated population	%	Estimated population	N=	Estimated population
Jewish and Catholic	78	2,895	22	831	9	3,726
Jewish and Protestant	57	13,450	43	10,125	22	23,575
Jewish and Orthodox (Greek, Russian)	36	5,936	64	10,335	16	16,271
Roman Catholic only	26	65,540	74	263,358	237	328,898
Protestant only	20	133,100	80	377,792	358	510,892
All Jewish-Christians	25	220,921	75	662,441	640	883,362

Table 12. Jewish Parentage of Jewish-Christians,
by Denomination

	Current religion of Jewish-Christians	
Parentage	Catholic	Protestant
Both parents born Jewish*	8	12
One parent born Jewish	76	74
Jewish grandparent only	16	14
Total (%)	100	100

*but respondent raised as a Christian

Jewish Protestants. The Jewish Catholics and Protestants were equally likely to report having a Jewish mother (data not shown).

Jewish-Christian as a Hybrid Identity

Jewish-Christians are a "hybrid" category with counterparts in the "mixed-race" population included in the U.S. census of 2000. For example, Kerry Ann Rockquemore and David Brunsma found that adult children of black-white intermarriages identified with both races, with one only, or else alternated in their identity on a situational basis.[15] The hybrid identity of Jewish-Christians is examined here in two ways. Demographically, the Jewish Catholics and Jewish Protestants can be compared with three different groups: other Jews, Catholic and Protestant spouses of Jews, and American Catholics and Protestants in general (using the NSRE).

In terms of education, Jewish Catholics closely resembled the American Catholic population as a whole more than they resembled Catholic spouses in mixed marriages with Jews. Only a third of both Jewish Catholics and American Catholics had completed college, as compared with half of Catholic spouses married to Jews (Table 14). The Jewish Protestants were more educated than American Protestants overall, but were comparable to mainline Protestants (data not shown) and less

Table 13. Jewish Identification of Jewish-Christians,
by Jewish Parentage (% who considered themselves
to be Jewish)

	Current religion of Jewish-Christians	
Parentage	Catholic	Protestant
Both parents born Jewish*	39	43
One parent born Jewish	21	27
Jewish grandparent only	11	15

*but respondent raised as a Christian

Table 14. Educational Attainment of Jewish-Christians and Christian Spouses
(respondents and spouses under 50 years of age)

	High school or less	Some college	B.A. degree	Beyond B.A. degree	Total (%)
Catholic spouses	23	24	32	20	100
Jewish Catholics	30	36	22	11	100
Catholics (NSRE)	32	34	27	7	100
Protestant spouses	28	33	25	15	100
Jewish Protestants	32	36	23	9	100
Protestants (NSRE)	41	34	20	6	100
Secular (non-Jewish) spouses	25	25	31	19	100
Secular (NSRE)	39	29	20	12	100
Jews (identify as secular)	25	32	25	18	100
Jews (by birth and religion)	13	20	32	35	100
Jews (by choice)	16	31	30	23	100

educated than the Protestant spouses of Jews. There were no significant educational differences between Jewish Catholics and Jewish Protestants, but both were less educated than Jews by religion and birth or Jews by choice. In terms of educational achievement, Jewish-Christians had assimilated into the American mainstream.

The lower educational attainment of Jewish-Christians as compared with Jews by religion is part of a larger pattern. Mixed-parentage Jews (regardless of their religious identification) had lower educational attainment than Jews with two Jewish parents (Table 15). More than two thirds (70 percent) of adults with two Jewish parents had graduated college (or beyond), as compared with less than half (43 percent) of adults with one Jewish parent and only one in five (21 percent) adults of Jewish ancestry only. Being raised by Jewish parents was strongly associated

Table 15. Educational Attainment by Jewish Parentage
(respondents and spouses under 50 Years of Age)

	Parentage of self-identified Jews			Non-Jews by origin	
Education	Both parents Jewish	One parent Jewish or mixed-Jewish	Jewish ancestry only	Non-Jewish	Jews by choice
High school or less	12	23	40	25	16
Some college	18	34	39	27	31
College graduate	34	26	15	29	30
Beyond college	36	17	6	18	23
Total (%)	100	100	100	100	100

with secular educational achievement. Beyond the scope of this analysis is the question of why the non-Jewish spouses were more educated than their children.

Attitudinal Differences between Jewish-Christians and Jews

The demographic differences between Jewish-Christians and Jews by religion were only partially matched by attitudinal differences. Table 16 compares the mean scores for a variety of attitudinal items included in the NJPS. All items but the first had a high score of 5 and a low score of 1. A score of 5 corresponds to an answer of "very important" or "strongly agree." A score of 1 corresponds to "not at all important" or "strongly disagree." For the first item (respondent's positive or negative assessment vis-à-vis "being Jewish"), a score of 6 corresponds to "very positive." It should be noted that these items were only asked of Jewish-Christians who considered themselves Jewish, which may have biased them in a more positive direction.

Both Jews by birth and religion and Jews by choice scored relatively high on all the items, but the mean scores of Jewish-Christians varied. Jews by religion and Jewish-Christians responded positively to statements related to a sense of Jewish belonging and affirmation. Both agreed that they felt positive about being Jewish, that being Jewish was important to them, and that they had a clear sense of what being Jewish meant to them. They both said that learning Jewish history and culture was part of how they were Jewish. Their responses were similar to statements about sharing a common Jewish fate. They agreed that remembering the Holocaust and fighting antisemitism were part of how they were Jewish. They also agreed that caring about Israel was part of how they were Jewish and, moreover, that Israel is the spiritual center of the Jewish people. They both believed in a common destiny shared by Israeli Jewry, world Jewry, and American Jewry. They equally disagreed that being Jewish estranged them from American society.

Where did Jews by religion (either born or converted) differ from Jewish-Christians? Mainly in the areas of Jewish community and the content of Judaism. Jews by religion scored more positively on the centrality (to their sense of being Jewish) of Jewish holidays, Jewish observance, the support of Jewish organizations, and being part of a Jewish community. Jewish-Christians, on average, were more neutral in these areas. There was an even more marked difference with regard to emotional attachment to Israel. Although Jewish-Christians and Jews by religion agreed on the importance of Israel, Jewish-Christians had much less emotional attachment to Israel than did Jews by religion.

The greatest difference between the two groups concerned Jewish continuity. Jews by religion said that giving their children a Jewish education was important to them, as was having grandchildren raised as Jews. Jewish-Christians did not consider these important, which is consistent with their own background.

In sum, Jewish-Christians and Jews by religion were most similar in their sense of abstract Jewish connection, such as sharing a common fate. While Jews by religion scored more positively on these items than did Jewish-Christians, both groups, overall, were positive. In contrast, Judaism and Jewish community were less important to Jewish-Christians than to Jews by religion, and Jewish continuity

Table 16. Attitudinal Differences among Jewish-Christians, Jews by Birth and Religion, Secular Jews, and Jews by Choice

	Jewish Catholics	Jewish Protestants	Jews (by birth and religion)	Secular Jews	Jews (by choice)
Sense of being Jewish					
Now, please tell me, how do you feel about being Jewish? (positive or negative)*	5.2	5.4	5.7	5.2	5.5
How important is being Jewish in your life?	3.5	3.6	4.2	3.1	4.3
I have a clear sense of what being Jewish means to me	3.9	4.1	4.6	4.0	4.6
Personally, how much does being Jewish involve learning Jewish history and culture?	3.8	4.0	4.2	3.7	4.5
I feel like an outsider in American society because I am a Jew	1.6	2.0	1.8	1.7	2.1
Holocaust and antisemitism					
Personally, how much does being Jewish involve remembering the Holocaust?	4.2	4.3	4.5	4.3	4.6
Personally, how much does being Jewish involve combating antisemitism?	3.9	3.8	4.2	3.9	4.3
Israel and common destiny with other Jews					
Israel is the spiritual center of the Jewish people	4.3	4.4	4.2	3.8	4.3
Personally, how much does being Jewish involve caring about Israel?	3.8	4.0	4.0	3.4	4.2
Israel and world Jewry have a common destiny	3.8	4.1	3.9	3.4	4.2
Jews in the United States and Jews in Israel share a common destiny	3.6	4.1	3.8	3.3	4.1
Universal aspects of Judaism					
Personally, how much does being Jewish involve leading an ethical and moral life?	4.0	4.2	4.4	3.9	4.8
Personally, how much does being Jewish involve believing in God?	4.4	4.5	4.1	3.4	4.6
Personally, how much does being Jewish involve making the world a better place?	3.9	4.0	4.2	3.6	4.6
Personally, how much does being Jewish involve having a rich spiritual life?	3.7	4.2	3.8	3.3	4.4
Personally, how much does being Jewish involve attending synagogue?	2.7	2.5	3.2	2.2	3.6
Jewish content and community					
Personally, how much does being Jewish involve celebrating Jewish holidays?	3.3	3.1	4.1	3.0	4.3
Personally, how much does being Jewish involve observing halakhah?	3.0	2.8	3.4	2.5	4.0

Table 16. (continued)

Personally, how much does being Jewish involve being part of a Jewish community?	3.1	2.8	3.6	2.6	4.0
Personally, how much does being Jewish involve supporting Jewish organizations?	3.1	3.0	3.6	2.7	3.9
How emotionally attached are you to Israel?	2.4	2.7	3.6	2.5	3.6
Jewish continuity					
Personally, how much does being Jewish involve giving your child(ren) you might have a Jewish education?	2.7	2.9	4.0	2.8	4.4
Importance of grandchildren being raised Jewish	1.9	2.0	3.7	2.0	3.4

*This item was scored 1–6

was of little relevance to Jewish-Christians. The responses of the Jewish-Christians were either comparable to or more positive than the responses of secular Jews. Like Jewish-Christians, most of the secular Jews were of mixed parentage. The similarity in attitudes between Jewish-Christians and secular Jews suggests that identifying as a Christian is a less significant factor than simply having mixed parentage.

Political orientation is not inherently a Jewish issue. Historically, however, American Jews have been, and continue to be, liberal and Democratic. Perhaps the most striking attitudinal difference between Jewish-Christians, secular Jews, and Jews by religion is political orientation. Jews by religion were much more likely to describe themselves as "liberal" and as Democrats than were Jewish-Christians and secular Jews (Tables 17 and 18). Interestingly, Jews by choice were also more likely than Jewish-Christians and secular Jews to describe themselves as liberal and Democratic. It might be that they picked up these attitudes in the process of becoming Jewish—or perhaps they were attracted to Judaism because of its perceived liberal worldview.

Finally, and not surprisingly, Jewish-Christians married to non-Jews overwhelmingly raise their own children as Christians, with gender differences being insignificant in this regard (Table 19). Whether Jewish-Christians will pass on their own sense of connection to a larger Jewish destiny remains to be seen.

Conclusion

To the extent that there are differences, mixed marriages involving a Catholic spouse are more "Jewish" than mixed marriages involving a Protestant spouse, whereas marriages to secular non-Jews are more "Jewish" than either of these. Although the gender of the Jewish (by religion) parent was the most important

Table 17. Political Orientation of Jewish-Christians, Jews by Religion, Secular Jews, and Jews by Choice (respondents under 50 years of age)

Political orientation	Jewish Catholics	Jewish Protestants	Jews (by birth and religion)	Secular Jews	Jews (by choice)
Conservative	34	41	19	23	26
Moderate	30	25	20	22	26
Liberal	36	34	61	55	48
Total (%)	100	100	100	100	100

Table 18. Political Orientation of Jewish-Christians, Jews by Religion, Secular Jews, and Jews by Choice (respondents under 50 years of age)

Political party identification	Jewish Catholics	Jewish Protestants	Jews (by birth and religion)	Secular Jews	Jews (by choice)
Republican	30	34	14	16	22
Democrat	36	29	59	36	44
Other	34	38	27	48	34
Total (%)	100	100	100	100	100

Table 19. How Jewish-Christians Married to Non-Jews Raise Their Children

Gender and religion of Jewish-Christians	Religion in which children were being raised				Total	N=
	Judaism	Other/none	Dual religion	Christian		
Mother is Jewish Catholic	1	9	1	89	100	186
Mother is Jewish Protestant	2	15	1	82	100	207
Father is Jewish Catholic	10	4	0	86	100	18
Father is Jewish Protestant	3	8	0	89	100	45

factor in raising Jewish children, Catholic spouses were more likely to do so than Protestants. Further, Jews raised as Catholics were more "Jewish" as adults than those raised as Protestants. Catholic and Protestant spouses of Jews were more educated than American Catholics and Protestants in general, although they were apparently not passing on this educational advantage to their children. Neither were secular, non-Jewish spouses.

Based on the NJPS of 2000–2001, there are almost a million Jewish-Christians in the United States. Only a quarter of them said that they considered themselves Jewish, but it is possible that some of those who did not consider themselves Jewish were thinking in religious terms. They did, after all, agree to be interviewed. The significance of this population for American Jewry is unclear. Some Jewish-Christians may be attracted back to Judaism, while others might become advocates for Jewish issues such as Israel. The very existence of this population attests either to the positive feelings that Americans have for Jews, to the salience of Judaism in American society, or to both.

Finally, to a certain extent, the theme of the old joke still applies. Differences between Catholic and Protestant spouses were less significant than were differences that separated Jews from non-Jews.

Notes

1. Bruce Phillips, *Re-Examining Intermarriage* (Brookline: 1996).

2. On these data, see Uzi Rebhun, "Jewish Identification in Intermarriage: Does a Spouse's Religion (Catholic vs. Protestant) Matter?" *Sociology of Religion* 60, no. 1 (1999), 71–88.

3. Patrick Viscuso and Kristopher L. Willumsen, "Marriage between Christians and non-Christians: Orthodox and Roman Catholic Perspectives," *Journal of Ecumenical Studies* 31, nos. 3–4 (Summer-Fall 1994), 276.

4. William V. D'Antonio, James D. Davidson, Dean R. Hoge, and Katherine Meyer, *American Catholics: Gender, Generation, and Commitment* (Walnut Creek: 2001).

5. Pew Research Center, *Trends 2005* (Washington, D.C.: 2005), 28.

6. See Paul Kengor, "Kerry Loses His Faith," *The American Spectator* (5 Nov. 2004), online at www.spectator.org/dsp_article.asp?art_id=7355.

7. In addition to the 4,522 households included in all reports issued by the United Jewish Communities (which conducted the NJPS of 2000–2001), I include an additional 604 households in which the respondent was not sufficiently Jewish to be counted as part of the Jewish population. See United Jewish Communities, *Strength, Challenge and Diversity in the American Jewish Population* (New York: 2003).

8. Barry Kosmin, Egon Mayer, and Ariela Keysar, *American Religious Identification Survey* (New York: 2001), 38.

9. Jon P. Alson, "Review of the Polls," *Journal for the Scientific Study of Religion* 15, no. 1 (1976), 77.

10. Kosmin et al., *American Religious Identification Survey*, 38.

11. United Jewish Communities, *Strength, Challenge and Diversity in the American Jewish Population* (New York: 2003).

12. This survey covered Marin County, Sonoma County, San Francisco County, San Mateo County, and the northern part of Santa Clara County.

13. Kosmin et al., *American Religious Identification Survey*, 35.

14. Richard H. Niebuhr, *The Social Sources of Denominationalism* (New York: 1929); Barry Kosmin and Seymour Lachman, *One Nation under God* (New York: 1993), ch. 2.

15. Kerry Ann Rockquemore and David L. Brunsma, *Beyond Black* (Newbury Park, Calif.: 2001), ch. 3.

Mini-symposium
Holocaust Memory and Judgment

What Is Holocaust Literature?

David G. Roskies
THE JEWISH THEOLOGICAL SEMINARY OF AMERICA

On September 25, 1968, the Humanities Section of the Library of Congress made the following new entry to its subject catalogue: "Holocaust, Jewish (1939–1945)." Three years later, to facilitate geographic subdivision, the heading was slightly revised.[1] So many questions arose, however, regarding both the specific time span of the Holocaust and the use of the qualifier "Jewish" that in October 1995, the Cataloguing Policy and Support Office (CPSO) of the Library of Congress issued a survey on subject headings and classification numbers relating to the Holocaust. Among the respondents to the survey was the United States Holocaust Memorial Museum (USHMM), which convened a mini-conference to deliberate on the eight options allowable under LC cataloguing guidelines. The choices were:

1) Holocaust, Jewish (1939–1945)
2) Holocaust, 1939–1945
3) Holocaust, 1933–1945
4) Holocaust
5) Holocaust (Nazi genocide)
6) Jewish Holocaust, 1939–1945
7) Jewish Holocaust, 1933–1945
8) Jewish Holocaust

The first question debated was the accuracy and even necessity of the dates. Although historians have argued that the Holocaust "began" with the Nazi seizure of power on January 30, 1933, when Adolf Hitler was sworn in as chancellor of the German Republic, options (3) and (7) were challenged because the events of the period 1933–1939 were the antecedents of the Holocaust, not the Holocaust itself. Appending any dates, one respondent objected, implied that there could be other "Jewish holocausts." Did not the very qualifier "Jewish" obviate the need for a chronology? No, it did not, for insofar as "Holocaust, Jewish" was an "event" heading and a subset of the broader term "World War," it required that dates be provided; it followed, therefore, that the corresponding dates of the Second World War were the most logical choice.[2]

The second point of contention was the use of a qualifier. There was general consensus that to define the Holocaust as "Nazi genocide" (option 5) was both

157

confusing and offensive, for it could be read as suggesting that Nazis, not Jews, were the victims. There were compelling arguments, however, in favor of retaining the qualifier "Jewish." It was likely that, in the future, "holocaust," whether upper or lower case, would be applied more broadly to describe atrocities against other ethnic groups. "Jewish" clearly identified the heading for the general public. In the final analysis, the seven alternative headings were rejected and the original subject heading, "Holocaust, Jewish (1939–1945)" was upheld as being at once the most inclusive, because universally recognized, and the most exclusive.

The inverted structure had the added advantage of retaining "Holocaust" as the key term. Just as the volume of published works on the Holocaust had grown exponentially in the 27 years since the subject heading was first adopted, so too had the number of works of Holocaust denial. Asked whether the current heading, "Holocaust, Jewish (1939–1945)—Errors, inventions, etc.," ought to be retained, the respondents were unanimous in selecting a new analytic breakdown under the following three headings:

- Literature: Holocaust denial literature, D804.35
- Phenomenon: Holocaust denial, D804.355
- Criticism of the literature: Holocaust denial literature—History and criticism, D804.355

Now that the Library of Congress has adopted "Holocaust, Jewish" as a discrete subject of human inquiry and has made it coterminous with the Second World War, all routes lead to and from its catalogue. Personal narratives, diaries, *yizkor* (memorial) books, psychological studies of survival in the concentration camps—in short, the documentary sources that form the bedrock of Holocaust memory—are all housed in the D Section under the broad rubric of History. Those wishing to take a more expansive view can begin their search with DS102 (1. Jews—Persecution—History; 2. Jewish Literature; 3. Holocaust, Jewish), followed by DS135, which contains, for instance, both the rescued diaries and the oversized yizkor books. The fastest-growing branch of Holocaust writing, personal narratives of Holocaust survivors (now numbering in the thousands) and the growing body of criticism of the same, are assembled in D804.3, while D810 is reserved for books with a focus on survival in the concentration camps. Adhering to long-established practice, however, works of the literary imagination pertaining to the Holocaust are assigned a completely different classification number. "Holocaust Literature," PN56H.55, is housed alongside PN56.D4 (Death and Literature) and PN.W3 (War and Literature). This by no means exhausts the relevant categories, for "Human Liberty in Extremis" is catalogued under HM271, "Passive Resistance" can be found under HM278, and "Art of the Holocaust" is classified variously under the letter "N."

Classification is the beginning of knowledge. When this new subject heading was adopted, revised, and reviewed is therefore just as important as the classification itself. Clearly, by 1968, the term "Holocaust" had gained such currency, at least in the English-speaking world, that a qualifier, "Jewish," was already deemed necessary, even though a layperson might view this as a tautology at best, an insult at worst. A little over a quarter century later, with the Holocaust enshrined in the nation's capital and Holocaust consciousness assuming universal significance, a full-scale professional review was now called for, which did more than affirm the original classification. It drew a bright line between the validation, the affirmation, of the "Jewish Holocaust" and its denial. By 1995, in other words, the Holocaust had become an article of faith.

But the very attempt to classify and delimit a subject raises a host of new questions. Note that the search for "Holocaust Literature" can lead to any number of different classifications: to DS102, D804.15, and D810.J4, even before one reaches the PN section, often located on another floor. This would suggest that Holocaust literature defies generic boundaries and crosses disciplines. And indeed, despite the best efforts of the Library of Congress, major works defy easy categorization, either as literature or as history. Documentary novels written by survivors in the immediate postwar period are catalogued as historical documents (DS126), and therefore might be overlooked by students of literature. An eyewitness account of the Second World War does not take sufficient note of the Jews to merit its becoming part of the Holocaust canon. Memoirs of the Holocaust routinely defy the neat distinction between the antecedents—responses to the rise of Hitler, the Nuremberg Laws, Kristallnacht—and the event itself. Overtly theological responses to the Holocaust are catalogued in BM645.H6, among the classics of rabbinic literature. Children's literature, a reader's first exposure to the meaning of history, is catalogued in D804.34 for nonfiction or in PZ for fiction. The children of Holocaust survivors the world over now claim insider status, as a distinct and definable "second generation." Does their testimony follow seamlessly from the narratives of those who survived the ghettos, the camps, the years in hiding? Does one catalogue Art Spiegelman's *Maus* under comic books, psychology, personal narrative, fiction, or fantasy?[3]

What, then, *is* Holocaust literature? Where does it belong, and how is it changing? Is it to be read as a genre of literature about death or war, atrocity or trauma? Does this vast outpouring of writing invite comparison with responses to other Jewish catastrophes or with other forms of Jewish resistance? Is it sui generis, to be measured against itself alone and demanding a new interpretive lens? How may its verbal art be related to the other arts—memorial, graphic, photographic, cinematic, homiletic? What temporal, spatial, ethnic, political, philosophical, and linguistic coordinates define this event called the Holocaust, if that is the name it still goes by?

War, Literature, Memory

Until modern times, death lay within the purview of religion. Whatever aspect of *Death in Literature* one follows, it is appropriate to begin, as does the anthologist Robert F. Weir, with Israelite, Mesopotamian, Greek, Christian, Hindu, or Confucian sources. Within the Hebrew Bible, for example, he finds that the Psalms, Job, and Ecclesiastes offer a wide range of human responses to the inevitability of death and ideas about immortality. Under the rubric of "Death by Killing," Weir places mass murder, which, for the most part, he locates within the purview of modernity.

Trench warfare, the Nazi concentration camps, and the atomic bomb define for Weir the three major stations of mass death in a secular, industrial age. To document the fate of Jewish women—"the living dead"—in Stuthof, Weir chooses a brief excerpt from *Journey Through Hell*, by Reska Weiss, the title itself suggesting that the Nazi concentration camps were the closest approximation of Hell on earth.[4]

Accessing the subject of war and literature is relatively easy. One can proceed by war, by country, or by language. The *Iliad* and *Odyssey* are to Greek what the Gallic Wars are to Latin. But in the modern era, epics of war have been downsized. Tolstoy's is still a wide-screen war in Technicolor, focusing on the triumph of General Kutuzov over the one they contemptuously called Buonaparte. In Babel's *Red Cavalry* (1924–1925), where the Polish campaign is doomed from the start, the moon above and the gonorrhea below make for easy bedfellows. Like Babel (on instructions from Gorky to dirty his hands with life), other modern writers signed up to fight—Hemingway in the First World War, Malraux in China, Orwell in Republican Spain.

The First World War was the great divide, separating the war zone from the home front, the "lost generation" from everyone else. Millions of young men went "over the top," many of them to certain death, defining an experience that was both unique and everywhere the same, and it was literature that provided the master narratives, even while the war was still being waged. The first antiwar classics, Henri Barbusse's *Under Fire* (1916) and Andreas Latzko's *Men in War* (1918), were followed by Jaroslav Hašek's *The Good Soldier Shvejk* (1921–1923; the original *Catch 22*), and Ludwig Renn's *War* (1928), culminating, of course, in Erich Maria Remarque's *All Quiet on the Western Front* (1929).

Those who sat out the war could wrestle with its meaning only after the fact. "After such knowledge," asks T. S. Eliot in "Gerontion," "what forgiveness?" On an ordinary June day in 1923, the suicide of an ex-soldier named Septimus Smith disturbs the dinner party given by Clarissa Dalloway, in *Mrs. Dalloway* (1925). Following the example of Paul Fussell's ground-breaking study of *The Great War in Modern Memory* (1975), literary scholars have tracked a cumulative response to the war within English culture by identifying certain commonalities, synoptic signposts such as "the irony of situation" and a return to myth.[5] Reaching for broader coordinates is Robert Wohl who, in *The Generation of 1914*, argues for "a unity of experience, feeling, and fate that transcended national borders," even while recognizing that "the story of the generation of 1914 has to be told from a national point of view."[6] Indeed, the war's most lasting legacy was the very construct of a "generation," the sense that one historical experience could so transform its participants as to single them out forever among the rest of humanity. After the war, they would see themselves as a revolutionary cohort, moved by a "spirit of intolerance, revolt and heroic unrest," in the flowery prose of the dashing young Italian Fascist, Curzio Malaparte (1898–1957). This generation, Malaparte claimed, had surpassed for all time in patient and unacknowledged heroism "all generations, including those which gave us our myths, our heroes, and our lives."[7]

Though in the league of beleaguered nations the English lost far fewer men than either the French or the Germans, no one national point of view is necessarily ranked above any other, Wohl's assumption being that only if all nations are taken together, as equals, can the cultural historian arrive at their collective biography. More catholic still is Samuel Hynes, who imagines "that if all the personal recollections of all the soldiers of the world's wars were gathered, they would tell one huge story of men at war"—hence, the title of his tome, *The Soldiers' Tale*.[8]

Inclusive though these synoptic narratives may be, they exclude the national perspective of the Jews. With a world torn in half, Jewish soldiers were thrown into battle against other Jews. Whether inducted into the Russian or Austro-Hungarian armies, they experienced virulent antisemitism within their own ranks and returned to a home ravaged by pogroms. By the 1920s, the Jewish memory of the war was kept in a double set of books: one for combatants, another for civilians: part apocalypse, part jeremiad. Rare was the writer, like Isaac Babel, who tried to portray both at one and the same time, and when Babel tacked on a new ending to *Red Cavalry*, in which Lyutov the Cossack is seen riding off into the sunset, he forced into the backdrop the death of his "brother," the Jewish Red Army soldier Ilya Bratslavsky.[9]

Whether one separates the various literatures of the First World War (the French, the British, the German, the Italian, and, sooner or later, the Jewish) in an attempt to reconstruct a national point of view, or one studies the literature of the Great War in its entirety, seeking to reconstruct the "Lost Generation," the "Fallen Soldiers," the "Heroes' Twilight," the "Rites of Spring," the "Sites of Memory," or the "Sites of Mourning," the attempt to fashion a master narrative rests on three principles: (1) one can speak of a unity of experience, feeling, and fate that transcends national borders; (2) war, like every other human experience, is refracted through the lens of a particular culture; and (3) because culture is a social construct, the representation of one war will progressively, retroactively, or dialectically affect the representation of another.[10] Representation, in turn, is broken down into discrete periods—prewar, wartime, postwar—as cultural historians take their source material to represent "what contemporaries thought and said."[11] Since each period is presumed to have its own point of view, a reader schooled in the literature of war should be able to situate a given work within a periodization of public memory. Remarque's book, for example, "coarse as it now seems" when compared to Barbusse's documentary novel *Under Fire* (which was written while the war was still going on), is significant for "what it tells us about the state of mind of people some ten years after the armistice."[12] Twenty years later, as Europe once again braced for war, the memory of the Great War was enlisted to mean something vastly different for Germans and Italians than it did for the French and British.

Those who speak for the experience of war are first and foremost the soldiers who fought it. Wartime writing enjoyed and continues to enjoy pride of place, whether or not these writings were censored, prettified, or turned into propaganda—what Edmund Wilson, in his study of the American Civil War, called "patriotic gore"—for there are always letters and diaries to balance the progress of the war as depicted in the press and the media. Ex-soldiers turned poets, playwrights, and novelists are likewise granted a certain privilege. Some became writers by virtue of their wartime experience. Others, having seen what they saw, would never again write as they had before. When the synoptic soldiers' tale is bracketed by symbolic events that occurred before and after the war, they allow the cultural historian

Modris Eksteins to conclude that "our whole modern consciousness, the whole complex of moral, aesthetic, and social attitudes we label as 'modernism,' was born out of the Great War."[13]

Shelved so close at hand, but a few decimals away, the literature and scholarship of the First World War has much to teach us about the literature of the Holocaust. It can teach us about the evolution of generational consciousness; how specific acts of war that occurred at the intersection of time and place come to stand in for the vast and unfathomable destruction; how history is refracted through a cultural lens; and how, in manifold ways, literature both shapes public memory and is shaped by it.

The Generations of 1914 and 1945

Precisely because public memory of the Holocaust is so public, and so beholden to developments in the geopolitical sphere, it is easier to chart its ebb and flow than to perceive the lines that divide one period of Holocaust literature from another. Casting a backward glance to the literature and memory of the First World War is therefore both a welcome and a necessary exercise.

Common to the two world wars is a profound generational consciousness. The inmates of the Nazi ghettos and concentration camps, thrown together from all parts of Europe, certainly can be said to have shared "a unity of experience, feeling, and fate that transcended national borders." As recorded in their native tongues, that unity of experience found its first expression in the writings and artwork preserved in the various ghetto archives (in Warsaw, Lodz, Vilna, Kovno, Terezin, and elsewhere); buried on the grounds of concentration and internment camps; given to peasants for safekeeping; or otherwise discovered after the war. Unity of experience was expressed most powerfully in the variety of Yiddish periodicals published in the DP (displaced persons) camps in Germany, Austria, and Italy, where the vast majority of the 220,000 inmates were young adults, lone survivors from among a multigenerational folk that once numbered in the millions.[14] Here was born the first sustained effort to transcribe eyewitness accounts, to gather documents, and to record songs. Here, young men and women fiercely debated the political lessons of Jewish powerlessness even as they reconfigured themselves into new families. Although, by 1950, all had dispersed to the four corners of the earth, most adopting new languages, their very absorption into a civilian population that knew next to nothing about the war and was already preoccupied with other matters would steel their resolve never to forget.

At commemorative gatherings, whether organized by the *landsmanshaft* (hometown association), the kibbutz, the community, the political party to which survivors still swore allegiance, or by other organizations and agencies, the focus was always on forms of resistance. The emerging master narrative told of heroism and self-determination in the face of all odds. Certain epic poems became popular at such gatherings, among them Abraham Sutzkever's "Teacher Mira" and Binem Heller's "It Is the Month of Nissan in the Warsaw Ghetto."[15] Children were always present to light the six memorial candles, to perform in a choir, and to represent the next generation. Depending on the venue, the evening ended either with the singing of "Hatikvah," Hirsh Glik's "Song of the Partisans," or the anthem of the Jewish Labor Bund.

How widespread were these gatherings? What do they signify? To what extent did public memory help alleviate the private memory, the personal experience, of the survivor-participants? What was the extent of their involvement? In these matters, historians are deeply divided. In Israel today, the minority holds that the survivor community was vitally and deeply engaged in the task of family and nation-building from the moment its members were ferried or smuggled ashore. The majority view—underscored by the literary and cinematic image of the survivor decades later—is that they were cowed into silence, their private experience forced underground.[16]

Elsewhere in the postwar world, where no name for the Holocaust as yet existed (let alone, public forums for its commemoration), a very different master narrative emerged, which focused on the coming of age of a sensitive young person thrust into the brutal realities of war. Instead of one young man's education under fire— Remarque's *All Quiet on the Western Front*—which bespoke a brotherhood of despair at the senseless carnage of war, *The Diary of a Young Girl* in hiding offered hope to all people. As edited for postwar consumption, Anne Frank's diary (1947) conveyed great optimism and celebrated the symbiosis of Gentiles and Jews. The success of *The Diary of Anne Frank* in France, according to David Weinberg, "had more to do with the evocation of Christian ideals of martyrology than with its association with the persecution of a young Jewish girl."[17]

The reception of *The Diary of Anne Frank* ("the most famous book by a Jewish author after the Bible"[18]) also anticipated two ways in which the plight of Jewish women, in particular, was to become emblematic of the Holocaust as a whole. The first was as an ecumenical love story. Anne, like every young woman in hiding, is ripe for love. Thus it was possible to maintain the dramatic integrity of Anne's story, when adapted for the stage or screen, while downplaying her Jewishness. Taken one step further, in movie after movie, in language after language, and with every conceivable twist of plot, the love of a Christian male for a condemned Jewish woman became the redemptive message of the Holocaust. Because the Jewish woman in question ended up being shot or dragged off to the transport despite all efforts to save her, her death served to expiate the guilt of the Christian world.[19]

Second, to the extent that all Jews were victims, all Jews figuratively were also women. With fathers rendered impotent and husbands rounded up and killed, every home or hideout turned into a battlefield in which the resourcefulness of women was decisive. The heroism of the Holocaust was the heroism of small deeds, of parental sacrifice, bonding, loyalty, love. In the wake of Anne Frank, the master narrative of the Holocaust would include many women, whether as diarists (the diaries and letters of Etty Hillesum), as heroines (Hannah Senesh [Szenes], Justyna, Mussia Daiches), as eyewitness chroniclers (Rachel Auerbach, Charlotte Delbo, Liana Millu, Sara Nomberg-Przytyk, Gisella Perl, Nechama Tec, Giuliana Tedeschi, Gerda Weismann Klein, Reska Weiss), as poets (Nelly Sachs, Irena Klepfisz, Gertrud Kolmar, Rivka Miriam, Kadia Molodowsky, Reyzl Zychlinsky), as novelists (Ida Fink, Naomi Frankel, Ilona Karmel, Anna Langfus, Elsa Morante, Chava Rosenfarb), and as metonymns. Later still, when the focus of Holocaust memory turned ever inward, the madness of women and female hysteria would become a master trope of Holocaust fiction and film.[20]

Thus, in the public sphere, all victims of the Holocaust were not taken together, as equals, and no collective biography would speak for them all. What evolved instead were various forms of collective remembrance and commemoration—of the ghetto, the partisan brigade, the DP camp, and by extension, the people as a whole. Since in the Jewish scheme of things, the commemoration of the dead must be rooted in time, it was important to agree upon a symbolic date. While the *landslayt,* the compatriots, met on the anniversary of the liquidation of the ghetto, the former inmates of Bergen-Belsen (both the concentration and DP camp) would gather on the anniversary of the liberation. These were local, grassroots initiatives. To mourn on a national level, however, required a consolidation and consensus, for the very enormity of the Holocaust forged a link in the chain of earlier catastrophes, each of which had its sanctified place in the liturgy of remembrance. In 1947, the Chief Rabbinate of Jewish Palestine ruled that the 10th of Tevet, a traditional day of fasting, be adopted to memorialize the victims of the Holocaust whose date of death was unknown. Others argued on behalf of the anniversary of the Warsaw ghetto uprising, since this was a universally compelling story projecting the image of a New Jew, Molotov cocktail in hand, who reached back in time to the Maccabees. The government of Israel decided, in 1951, that the 27th of Nissan would be observed as Holocaust and Ghetto Uprising Remembrance Day. Only two groups dissented: the Orthodox, who continued to observe the 10th of Tevet, and the Bundists who, *pour épater les orthodoxes*, stubbornly convened on April 19, the secular date of the uprising, even when this coincided with Passover.[21]

The other unit of remembrance was the lone individual, who "graduated" from the ghetto to survive years in hiding, prolonged deprivation, forced labor, torture, death marches—the seven gates of Hell. Yet if every story was different, and the suffering obeyed a strict hierarchy, how and when could commemoration happen? With inexorable logic, the memory of the individual victims of the Holocaust eventually coalesced into a fixed *place*. Auschwitz became to the Holocaust what the "troglodyte world" of the trenches was for the First World War: the part that stood for the apocalyptic whole. Aided by works of cultural criticism, social psychology, fiction, and film, modern memory placed Auschwitz at the heart of the epistemological darkness: Auschwitz as the axis of a new world order, Auschwitz as a pan-European dystopia, Auschwitz as the birthplace of a new language—what Tadeusz Borowski called crematorium Esperanto.[22] For Western intellectuals, Auschwitz became the telos, the sum and substance of the Holocaust, the ultimate, and exclusive, reference point. Once Auschwitz was adopted as a master metaphor, the Jews—crammed into cattle cars at one end of the journey and their sticking mass of blue bodies dragged from the gas chambers at the other—ceased to be bearers of a distinct cultural identity. They became the Unknown Victims of the Second World War. With the myriad points on the Holocaust compass reduced to one; with all personal effects plundered or destroyed upon arrival at Auschwitz; and with all the inmates—men and women, Gypsies and Jews, the Kapos and *musselmen*—dressed in identical striped uniforms, there emerged a master narrative of absolute extremity.[23]

The named survivors were the ones who spoke for the nameless victims, and in the late 1970s, they in turn began to merge into a single composite identity. By now, there were a sufficient number of survivor testimonies published, translated, and catalogued (in D804 and D810) to invite a collective biographer to step forward. Based on English translations of eyewitness accounts from the Nazi and Soviet concentration camps, Terrence Des Pres drew a group portrait of *The Survivor* (1976), whose emaciated, brutalized body could withstand the "excremental assault," survive nightmare and waking, survive "radical nakedness" through a kind of biological imperative. Countering this Darwinian scheme was Lawrence L. Langer, whose "aesthetics of atrocity" centered on the "choiceless choice," the denial of all human initiative or volition in the death camps.[24] Either way, the inmate upon arrival was severed from spouse and children, then stripped of clothes, personal belongings, and name, so that reading the testimony of the camp survivors, the cultural critic came away with a new set of universal principles that transcended or subverted the existing moral, religious, and rational order. The modernist consciousness born, according to Eksteins, out of the trenches could now be replaced by a postmodern consciousness born out of Auschwitz.

Defined by its uniqueness, the Generation of 1914 could have no heirs. Besides, those born in the wake of the First World War were barely old enough to read and absorb what their parents had experienced before they too were either drafted or deported. They became "first-generation" combatants, collaborators, and casualties, and if they ended up under Communist rule after the war, they were robbed of all consciousness, save for class consciousness. For the Generation of 1945, the situation was different. By the time those survivors who had lacked a fixed memorial date, a place of common origin, and a coherent story had merged into a global network of Holocaust survivors and had organized their first widely publicized gathering in Jerusalem in the summer of 1981, a self-professed "second generation" had already come into being. The effect this had on literature and cultural production, as we shall see, was profound and unprecedented.

Two separate and equal master narratives could not be sustained in the public memory of the Holocaust, the one collective and heroic, the other individual and equivocal. They could not be sustained over time, certainly not at the point when achieving a national consensus of any kind was becoming untenable in the United States, Israel, France, Germany, and the Communist bloc countries. Thus the unit of remembrance began to shrink: from the martyrs and fighters to the Jews of a specific locale or political persuasion; from the Jews of a specific locale or political persuasion to a discrete generation; from a discrete generation to the Holocaust as an assault upon the individual human body, male and particularly female; and finally, to the Holocaust as a species of trauma inflicted upon the human mind. In due course, the unit of remembrance became the survivor, as individual or aggregate.

The construct of "memory" was likewise disassembled. From communal, collective, and collected memories, one arrived at Holocaust testimony, testifying to events too terrible for words, which were best deciphered with the tools of psychoanalysis. What distinguished one survivor from another was the extent to which the memory of one's wartime trauma was buried, divided, besieged. What distinguished the Holocaust from all other atrocities was the degree to which "Holocaust memory" was the most shameful, degrading, and therefore, the least accessible.[25] And since trauma had secondary manifestations, devastating in their own right, the children of survivors were next in line. It could take up to two generations for the hidden transcript of their suffering to come to light. Like Curzio Malaparte, they could claim a kind of patient and unacknowledged suffering, surpassing "all generations, including those which gave us our myths, our heroes, and our lives."

Those scattered or ingathered individuals who lay claim to its covenantal scars are those who speak for the Holocaust.

The Literary Phases of Public Memory

What is Holocaust literature? Looking back more than two generations later, we conclude that Holocaust literature comprises all forms of writing, both documentary and discursive, and in any language, that have shaped the public memory of the Holocaust and been shaped by it. The publication of *Holocaust Literature*, a 1500-page encyclopedia, edited by S. Lillian Kremer, covering 309 authors and written by an international team of 122 scholars, presents the perfect opportunity to do for this literature what has been done so ably for the public memory of the Great War.[26] Since each entry also lists the author's entire oeuvre and samples the critical response to the author's Holocaust-related works, it should be possible, on the basis of this encyclopedia alone, to chart where this literature comes from, where it presently stands, and how it is changing; that is, to present, for the first time, a periodization of Holocaust literature worldwide. Conversely, with the help of computer-generated appendixes, it should be possible to break this vast body of writing down genre by genre, ghetto by ghetto, camp by camp, nation by nation, culture by culture. Any author should be locatable both in time and space. This alone would go very far toward demystifying the Holocaust and charting the complicated course of Holocaust memory.

Would that it were so! Rather than moving from the past to the present; rather than rescue for the English-speaking reader those writers who perished; rather than proceed systematically from within each subculture; rather than provide a descriptive compendium, this encyclopedia proceeds from the present and works backwards: that is, the selection of authors, the allocation of space, and the litcritical jargon bespeak current intellectual fashion, mostly in the North American academe. A strong feminist agenda drives the selection of authors. A writer who lives in postcolonial Australia or Brazil, even if she has authored but a single Holocaust-related book, is more likely to be included than a writer who perished in Auschwitz or Bialystok. Since the success of a writer in English or in English translation is the yardstick of literary merit, members of the "second generation" (however loosely defined) enjoy an easy advantage over their European-born parents. Yiddish writing, if assigned at all, is consigned to the margins. The Hebrew poet Rivka

Miriam (b. 1952), by virtue of being a woman and a child of survivors, has three pages devoted to her lyric verse. Her father, Leyb Rochman, whose major contributions to Holocaust literature will be discussed in the pages that follow, must await a second edition. Beholden to current literary fashion, to current curricula, and to the current state of foreign language instruction, *Holocaust Literature* (henceforth: HL) fails to provide the most elementary overview of the field. Read as a cultural document, however, it provides sad and eloquent testimony to its latest phase.

If one begins at the beginning, rather than at the end, what emerges is a cumulative, though truncated, process of public memory, which has evolved in five phases: wartime memory (1938–1945); communal memory (1945–1960); displaced memory (1960–1978); personalized memory (1978–1991); and essential memory (1991–present).[27] Each of these will now be discussed.

Wartime Memory: 1938–1945

In 1944, Anne Frank heard a member of the Dutch government-in-exile broadcasting from London: after the war, he promised, the Dutch people would document the Nazi occupation by publishing diaries and other firsthand accounts. Anne promptly pulled out her diary and began work on a more polished, literary version.[28]

At least four lessons emerge from this piece of bio-bibliographical data. First, whether or not diaries prove to be most typical of literary production during the Holocaust, it is true that wartime writing as a whole was turned inward.[29] Second, at a certain point in the progress of the war—different for different parts of occupied Europe—even the most inward-looking writer-diarist-chronicler might make the decision to turn outward. Third, however distant readers of the imagined future might be, they comprised an audience already familiar to the writer; or in the words of Sara Horowitz, "implicit in the chronicles and diaries is the vision of a posterity resembling the writers'."[30] Constructing a postwar future helps both the writer and reader unlock the hermetic wartime present. And fourth, since every item of wartime writing is located somewhere on that continuum, an accurate reading must begin with the precise date of composition or final revision. One year, one month, can make all the difference.

In addition, the centripetal direction of wartime writing may be precisely gauged through any of the following: the use of codes and cryptic language; the close interplay of genre and audience; the degree of rootedness in time and place; the reemployment of prewar tropes and literary traditions; or the search for meaning.

Codes and Cryptic Language

In the ghettos and camps, where survival itself was outlawed, the cryptic arts became a universal asset.[31] Before the war, only the Jewish underworld and klezmer musicians (an unsavory bunch) possessed a secret argot, although in the normative realm, Jewish merchants also employed a super-Hebraicized Yiddish, called *yehudi-*

beloy-shprakh, to gain an edge over their Gentile customers.[32] In wartime, however, to live was to lie, to smuggle, and to constantly look over one's shoulder. Mail was heavily censored and the use of the Hebrew alphabet was generally banned. Letters and postcards that arrived in Warsaw from the outlying regions, for example, letters pleading for assistance, hastily written postcards warning of imminent deportation—these were written in a venerable in-group code.[33] The historical diaries of public intellectuals such as Emanuel Ringelblum and Herman Kruk likewise adopted a cryptic style. The identity of authors whose documents were preserved in the Warsaw ghetto's Oyneg Shabes archive—itself a code name meaning "Pleasure of the Sabbath"—was carefully protected; so too in all publications of the Jewish underground press. These pseudonyms would later bedevil postwar historians.[34]

Whereas the uninitiated or hostile eyewitness perceived street life in the Nazi-ruled ghettos as primitive, anarchic, a throwback to the Dark Ages, there were ghetto intellectuals who greeted the reappearance of a street culture amid the squalor and terrible congestion as a welcome sign of folk vitality, proof that these urban masses had not lost their ability to roll with the punches. Sh. Shaynkinder (?–1943) recorded the cries of ghetto peddlers and street urchins to demonstrate how group solidarity could be forged in extremis. How? Through the employment of cryptic speech, punning, dialect, diglossia, and the Hebraic-Judaic stratum of Yiddish. Shaynkinder neglected to decode the sales pitch of a peddler hawking used books (whose every phrase was a double entendre), simply because the meaning was obvious to anyone, young and old, who crowded the ghetto streets.[35]

Shaynkinder's modest reportage has survived because it supported the research goals of the Oyneg Shabes archive, which was conceived and coordinated by the historian Emanuel Ringelblum (1900–1944; HL 1005–1010). Thanks to Ringelblum's organizational skills, each Jewish courtyard in Warsaw, and later in the ghetto, supported its own varied menu of cultural activities in addition to maintaining hygiene, civility, and group sanity.

The Interplay of Genre and Audience

Most forms of self-expression that flourished in the Nazi ghettos were addressed to a specific, live audience: sermons and petitionary prayers, halakhic responsa, eulogies, classroom compositions, political and documentary journalism, public lectures and colloquia, scholarship, theatrical reviews and cabaret skits, cantatas, epic and lyric poetry, novels and short stories, proclamations, the graphic arts, and music. In most ghettos, however, theatrical performances could be staged only with the support of what the historian Lucy Dawidowicz termed the "Official Community," that is, the Judenrat, under the predatory eyes of the Gestapo and SS.[36] Such programmed recitals, lectures, and plays were carefully scripted. In the Lodz ghetto, the poet and prose writer Shaye (Isaiah) Spiegel (1906–1990; HL 1189–1192) nearly forfeited his life for daring to stage a heartrending lullaby, "Close Your Eyes," written in response to the death of his only daughter.[37] No less encrypted were the aboveground publications produced under German auspices by the various Judenräte. When Herman Kruk (1897–1944), the chronicler of the Vilna ghetto, cited the weekly editorials of the official *Geto-yedies*, he did so with a mixture of sarcasm and scorn, yet these editorials were the work of a Hebrew pedagogue named Zemach Feldstein (1885–1945), whom the Union of Writers and Artists entrusted, along with Kruk, to write a full-scale history of the ghetto. Reread dispassionately, these same editorials reveal a message of hope with deep roots in Jewish consciousness and culture.[38]

The choice of language in wartime was likewise determined by one's immediate audience—other party members, those who paid admission, passersby on the street—or by the gulf between the public and private sphere. Thus, the public persona of Zelig Kalmanovitsh (1885–1944) in the Vilna ghetto, as befitted a founder of the famed YIVO Institute, was that of a Yiddishist intellectual. In Yiddish, he lectured on Peretz and Ahad Ha'am and delivered an occasional sermon. In private, however, Kalmanovitsh kept his diary in Hebrew, replete with scriptural and talmudic passages to underscore his scathing criticism of the whole Yiddish secular enterprise.[39] With the outbreak of the war, the Hebrew neo-Romantic poet Yitzhak Katzenelson (1886–1944; HL 617–620) from Lodz switched to producing poetry, drama, and literary criticism almost entirely in Yiddish for the sake of his newly adopted audience in the Warsaw ghetto. But with an eye to the last surviving remnant in Palestine, Katzenelson composed his strongest personal indictment, the so-called *Vittel Diary*, in Hebrew.[40] In the first days of the Great Deportation, the beginning of the end of Warsaw Jewry, the Hebrew pedagogue and popular historian Abraham Lewin (1893–1943) abruptly switched from Yiddish to Hebrew when keeping his ghetto diary.[41] Most stunning was the career of Emanuel Ringelblum, whose every waking hour was dedicated to preserving the inner Jewish dialogue: between past and present, the elite and the folk, Hebrew and Yiddish. Yet when Polish Jewry was no more, Ringelblum, oblivious to the conditions in his underground bunker, completed his most sustained piece of historical research, *Polish-Jewish Relations during the Second World War*, written in Polish for a postwar audience.[42]

Rootedness in Time and Place

Ghetto writings are rooted in time and place in a way that postwar accounts cannot replicate. They "simply plunge the reader into the midst of daily life and death."[43] Most alive to the passage of time, best able to recapitulate the changes in the conditions of ghetto life, and most accurate in charting the growing awareness of the Final Solution is a hybrid genre at once personal and reportorial, factual and full of artifice—reportage. Peretz Opoczynski (1895–1943) had mastered this genre before the war, becoming the scribe of urban poverty and neglect in Warsaw.[44] Working as a letter carrier in the Warsaw ghetto by day—an enervating and thankless job that he described in one of his finest reportorial fictions—he managed to produce carefully wrought vignettes of ghetto life by describing a single ghetto courtyard or profession and tracing its changing fortunes and misfortunes over a specific time frame, ranging from one day (in the life of ghetto smugglers) to several years.[45] Josef Zelkowicz (1897–1944) from Lodz also led a double life. He collaborated on the official—and officious—*Lodz Ghetto Chronicle*, the pride and joy of Mordechai Chaim Rumkowski, King of the Ghetto, while producing satires, internal travelogues, and numerous other writings in a sardonic, idiomatic style. "In Those Nightmarish Days," Zelkowicz's day-by-day, hour-by-hour account of the *Szpere*, the Great Deportation of September 1942, is unrivaled in its immediacy and rhetorical power.[46]

Typically, the purpose of a reportage is to reach readers directly, to seduce them in two simultaneous ways: as writer-chronicler, an eyewitness who records exactly what he saw and heard, and as omniscient narrator, "free to formulate broad, transcendent truths, generalizations, and value judgments."[47] Ghetto reportage was a species of engaged journalism written for an imagined, highly literate, mass reader. In her memoirs, Rachel Auerbach describes how Opoczynski produced his ghetto reportage as if he were writing under deadline, knowing full well that none would see the light of day until after the war.[48] Neither the authors nor most of the imagined readers of these pieces were to survive.

Prewar Tropes and Literary Traditions

To the Jews of Eastern Europe, schooled in collective memory, enforced ghettoization was seen as a return to the Middle Ages. Or was it? This question was fiercely debated in the pages of the underground press in the Warsaw ghetto and in the writings of the Oyneg Shabes. With extraordinary prescience, the modernist Yiddish poet Jacob Glatstein (1896–1971; HL 427–432) had opened the debate in April 1938. In a poem titled "Good Night, World," he railed against the Western democracies for their abandonment of the Jews, calling upon his fellow Jews to return, of their own free will, to the figurative "ghetto," there to reconsecrate themselves to cultural renewal. "Good Night, World" launched Glatstein's career as a national Jewish poet.[49]

Glatstein intuited that a radical reaffirmation of one's core values could help compensate for the loss of one's freedom, livelihood, security, and life. In Berlin, under the Nazis, Rabbi Leo Baeck (1873–1956) studied a page of Talmud every morning, followed by some Sophocles in Greek. Later, in Terezin, Baeck read Goethe and Schiller and delivered public lectures on Herodotus and Thucydides.[50] In Warsaw, the philosopher-critic Hillel Zeitlin (1872–1942) sat in his ghetto tenement translating the Psalms into Yiddish. And on May 2, 1943, after his expulsion from the Hungarian literary scene, after being deprived of his livelihood, after being twice inducted into forced labor as a Jew, Miklós Radnóti (né Glatter, 1909–1944; HL 974–978) converted to Christianity, thus affirming his own core identity as a Hungarian.

Search for Meaning

Among writers, the search for meaning *in extremis* was a search for metonymies. The parent-child relationship became a universal trope, whether in lullabies (by Spiegel, Leah Rudnitsky [1913–1943]), in theater songs (by Leyb Rosental [1916–1945], Henryka Lazowert [1910–1942]), in the prose poems of Yoysef Kirman (1896–1943), or in the epic poems of Simkhe-Bunem Shayevitsh (1907–1944; HL

1156–1158), culminating in the martyrdom of Janusz Korczak (1878–1942) and the children of his orphanage, who assumed iconographic significance before the war had ended (in the writings of Yehoshue Perle and Katzenelson). In wartime writings, as in life, the child was inducted into a reality too terrifying even for the adult to comprehend, but the very presence of a Jewish child signaled the possibility of regeneration. Rosental calls his spunky child protagonist Yisrolik ("little Israel") in the hit song of that name, and cast his own daughter, Khayele, to perform it in the Vilna ghetto. Abraham Sutzkever (b. 1913; HL 1234–1240) makes the theme of regeneration explicit both in *The Grave Child*, his epic poem about the birth of a child on the grounds of the Vilna Jewish cemetery, and in the concluding lines of his personal lament, "To the Child," written to commemorate the murder of his first-born son.[51] The sight of a child being operated upon in the ghetto hospital concludes a short story by Leyb Goldin (1906–1942) titled "Chronicle of a Single Day" (1941), a superb example of psychological realism that focuses relentlessly on a single bowl of soup. Arke, the cynical, super-intellectual narrator, reads this operation as an oracular sign of human self-transcendence.[52]

Contrariwise, in the eyes of some, the sight of starving children, beggar children, dead children, on the ghetto streets was an indictment of the community at large, proof that Jewish solidarity had collapsed and that Jewish agency was bankrupt. But seen even in this dark light, the metonymy of the abandoned ghetto child did not signify a choiceless choice. Surely something could still be done to rouse the conscience of a demoralized body politic!

Among members of the intelligentsia, the search for meaning was a search for historical archetypes. This was true both of Chaim A. Kaplan (1880–1942; HL, 599–601), a Hebrew pedagogue and teacher of Bible, who punctuated the ghetto portion of his diary with many scriptural passages, thus providing a metahistorical and morally devastating countercommentary on his own life and the life around him, and of Rabbi Shimon Huberband (1909–1942), charged by Ringelblum with the task of documenting Jewish religious life in the Warsaw ghetto. Huberband compiled a fact sheet of Jewish martyrdom, which he then used as the basis to redefine the halakhic meaning of *kidush hashem*.[53] Even the Communist writer Yehudah Feld[wurm] (1906–1942) titled his collection of short stories *In the Days of Haman II* to create an obvious linkage between present and mythic past.[54] After escaping to the Aryan side in March 1943, Rachel Auerbach (1903–1976; HL, 85–87), one of Ringelblum's closest associates, abandoned the ongoing chronicle of the living ghetto in order to commemorate the six weeks during which the Jews of Warsaw were erased from the earth. "Yizkor, 1943" is both a personal lament and a secular liturgy, perhaps the first Holocaust liturgy written from a woman's perspective.

Among the members of the "countercommunity," the political underground, the search for meaning was a search for actual precedent. The first book published in Nazi-occupied Warsaw, in July-August 1940, was a 101-page mimeographed anthology, *Suffering and Heroism in the Jewish Past in the Light of the Present*, compiled by Eliyohu Gutkowski (1900–1943) and Yitzhak (Antek) Zuckerman (1915–1981) to steel the resolve of the surviving leadership of the Zionist youth movement, Dror.[55] Bundists, too, tried to mobilize for the future by invoking past exemplars of self-sacrifice, from the Paris Commune of 1848 to the revolutionary struggle against the tsar. A complete reconstruction of the youth movement culture in the Warsaw ghetto would begin with the search for a usable past as revealed in the pages of the underground press, and end with its actualization within the ranks of the Jewish Fighting Organization.

In the end, the search for meaning was a race against time. All wartime writing must be read with close attention to the dates, for "images succeeded one another with cinematic speed," as Ringelblum wrote in his retrospective essay on the achievements of the Oyneg Shabes archive, the Great Deportation being the moment of truth, the caesura, the event that divided Time Before/After.[56] The closer one gets to the enactment of the Final Solution, the more telescoped time becomes. Perhaps, also, the greater the need to write.

Few were the writers who survived long enough to redirect their efforts from looking inward to looking outward. Having made it that far, they were now faced with three overwhelming challenges: (1) For whom would they write if every last Jew in Europe was condemned to death? If the surviving remnant was concerned only with its own survival, whom was there left to mobilize? (2) Inasmuch as the writer's own survival was in question, what would become of his writing? (3) Who would wreak revenge for this unprecedented crime, the systematic murder of an entire people? The writings that date from 1943–1944 are filled with overwhelming grief, sorrow, and rage.

It is all the more remarkable, then, to read the buried writings of the *Sonderkommando*. How could men who oversaw the murder of their own people, who gave them instructions about where to undress and where to leave their belongings, who shaved their heads and led them to the baths, whose job it was to pull the dead from the gas chambers, pry open their mouths to extract their gold teeth and feed the bodies into the ovens, men whose own days were numbered—how could these accursed men have the wherewithal to write and the ability to hide their writings? Zalmen Gradowski (1910–1944) was one of them. Not knowing who would discover his chronicles, he addressed the title page in five languages. Careful to keep his own identity a secret, he labored to reconstruct his journey from ghetto to concentration and death camp. Oh, the myriad ways a person condemned to death can misread the signs! In another reportage, he identified the Czech family transport to be the part-that-stands-for-the-whole; such intelligent and resourceful Jews, who had been allowed to live together, were duped together, and were gassed together. That all these crimes would be avenged—of this Gradowski had no doubt whatsoever. After securing different hiding places for his writings, he led and perished in the one-day revolt of the *Sonderkommando* on October 7, 1944.[57]

Jewish writing of the Second World War was indeed "a literature of resistance."[58] Perhaps that is how it ought to be catalogued.

Communal Memory: 1945–1960

The giving and collecting of testimony about the Holocaust occurred in five settings: the courtroom; the DP camps; sessions of historical commissions; annual commemorations of the Warsaw and other ghettos; and the Jewish mass media. Genocide was declared a crime against humanity, and more eyewitness testimony was gathered about the Holocaust than about any other instance of mass murder in history. Yet the purpose of this testimony was to establish the guilt of the Nazi party, the SS, the Gestapo, and the captains of German industry, rather than to document the suffering of the Jews. Perhaps that explains why the first Jew to give testimony at Nuremberg, on February 27, 1946, was the 33-year-old poet Abraham Sutzkever. (The trial was then in its fifth month.) He spoke for 38 minutes. He testified in Russian, one of four official languages, and not, as he had fervently hoped, in Yiddish. Though not nearly as eloquent as he might have been in Yiddish or in Polish, his testimony had a visible effect on the gum-chewing Julius Streicher, who puffed at him from the dock "like a green frog"; on Hans Frank, who took off his dark glasses just long enough to measure him "with his bloody eyes"; and on Alfred Rosenberg, who busied himself taking notes. The witness from Vilna twice refused the Chief Justice's request to sit down. "I spoke standing up," Sutz-kever recorded in his diary, "as if I were reciting Kaddish for the victims."[59]

Let us call it *témoignage*, this first stage of giving direct eyewitness account before a tribunal of peers. But how complex the postwar reality had already become! Assuming that some tribunal, whether real or constructed, was interested in hearing the testimony of a Jew, there was no guarantee of being able to speak in (any of) one's native tongues—or of seeing it published. In the Byzantine and treacherous world of Soviet realpolitik, Vasilii Grossman (1906–1964; HL 487–490) was granted permission to print his reportage "Ukraine without Jews" only in Yiddish, not in the Russian original. During his brief sojourn in Moscow, Sutzkever succeeded in republishing his politically correct memoir, *Fun vilner geto* (From the Vilna ghetto) (1945, 1946), which played up the role of Communists in the FPO (the United Partisan's Organization) and of Vilna Jews in the Soviet partisan brigades. But by 1947, Stalin viewed the Jewish Anti-Fascist Committee as a hotbed of Zionist imperialism and halted the imminent publication of the Soviet *Black Book*, edited by Grossman—a prelude to the liquidation of Soviet Yiddish culture.[60]

Historical commissions were set up almost as soon as the fighting stopped. On November 7, 1945, as a member of the delegation of the Polish State Committee for the Investigation of Nazi War Crimes on Polish Soil, Rachel Auerbach visited Treblinka and published her historical account of the camp, its machinery, and its victims. She also prepared eyewitness accounts for publication, a guide for the taking of testimony, as well as an analytic questionnaire on specific topics. In September 1946, together with Hersh Wasser (the secretary of the Oyneg Shabes archive), she succeeded in unearthing the first portion of the archive, where her own ghetto writings lay buried. When Auerbach moved to Israel in 1950, she became founder and director of the Department for the Collection of Witness Testimony at Yad Vashem in Jerusalem, and oversaw its rapid expansion. Both in Poland and Israel, testimonies were recorded in the native language of the informant.

For all this frenetic activity, whether in the Communist-bloc countries or in the free world, there appeared but a tiny window for disseminating and publishing eyewitness accounts about the fate of the Jews. A window that opened on the day of liberation closed in 1947–1948. "Publishers are not philanthropists," the historian

Annette Wieviorka reminds us; no wonder, then, that between 1915 and 1928, a total of 304 French works appeared that were inspired by the First World War as compared to about a hundred for the period between the liberation of Paris and the end of 1948.[61] Those who wrote about the Great War were certain of finding a receptive audience in the millions of former soldiers, she goes on to explain, whereas the survivors of the deportations were comparatively few in number. Only when the window of opportunity was reopened, decades later, would the number of Holocaust-related books far exceed those on the Great War, as a new, nonsurvivor audience was drawn into the story.

Market forces were but one factor of many that militated against an outpouring of testimony. France, like Italy, the Netherlands, West and East Germany, Austria, the Communist-bloc countries, and the Soviet Union, was "caught awkwardly between past and future."[62] Everywhere there was a legacy of betrayal, collaboration, disastrous defeat, and Fascism, which the myth of the Résistance (or the Russians' Great Patriotic War) could alleviate but not erase. In Italy, as elsewhere, the "trauma of national identity [was] forged through ignoring and forgetting."[63]

Only by negotiating a highly polarized and politicized landscape could the former inmates and deportees succeed in finding a sympathetic publisher. As is well known, Primo Levi (1919–1987; HL 749–758) had his first work, *If This Is a Man* (1947), turned down by several prestigious publishers before he found the small (and short-lived) publishing house of the antifascist activist Franco Antonicelli. Although Charlotte Delbo (1913–1985; HL 258–264) completed the first two parts of her memoir about Auschwitz in 1947, they were not published until 1965 and 1970, respectively. Returnees whose work was published during this early period tended to downplay the specific fate of the Jews, "to deny the existence of a semitic type," not to flaunt Jewish martyrdom, but to underscore their patriotism instead. "As the *Marseillaise* had marked the departure, so it did the return."[64] Reading French testimonies about the internment camp at Drancy, Wieviorka reports, one comes away with the impression that Christianity was a far more important cultural presence than Judaism. Oftentimes, the universal and universalist message was proclaimed on the very title page: Robert Antelme's *The Human Species* (1947; HL 46–49), David Rousset's *The Concentrationary Universe* (1946; HL 1048–1052), Elio Vittorini's *Men and Non-Men* (1945), Carlo Levi's *Christ Stopped at Eboli* (1945), and, of course, Primo Levi's masterpiece.[65] Antelme (1917–1990) and Rousset (1912–1997) had both been arrested as members of the French Resistance. Their primary identification in Buchenwald, Auschwitz, Dachau, and elsewhere was with other political prisoners. Their cognitive map of the camp experience was governed by Marxist theory and class struggle. This found a receptive audience on the Left Bank of the Seine.

Because the opportunity to have such works published was so brief, the date of a work's composition and eventual publication are of great significance, for they signal the degree to which early Holocaust testimony did not so much shape public memory as it was shaped by it. Preoccupation with dates also signals the need for old-fashioned textual history: What changes did Levi introduce into the second edition of his work that was published in 1958? At what later point did he Judaize the work by appending the poem "Shema" (the first edition of *Survival at Auschwitz* does not begin with this poem)? How do the passage of time and the mediation of translation affect our reading? Is it correct to group all these works together under the rubric "Holocaust, Jewish (1939–1945)"?

Beholden to the few available publishers and to the politics of postwar memory, these early works of testimony and documentary fiction are also time-bound in matters of style. Call it neorealism, call it the plain style—when former inmates adopted a hard-boiled, semi-poetic realism to render their experiences in the camps, they did so to counteract the years of Fascist propaganda, doublespeak, pagan blood lust, and programmed hysteria. Primo Levi's low-keyed meditation on the nature of man, his "ethical-cum-ethnological reflection," was by no means unique. It bespoke the critical sensibility of other Italian writers who came of age in the Second World War.[66]

What of the writers who had come of age in the First? Curzio Malaparte's *Kaputt* was "a tremendous, ambiguous, and loathed success in Italy" when it appeared in 1944, as befitted so lush, extravagant, and horrific a panorama of occupied Europe.[67] Malaparte was everything that Levi was not: a card-carrying Fascist who had accompanied Mussolini on the march to Rome; overtly Proustian both in the way he rediscovers his lived experience through sensory perceptions and striking imagery and in his comfort level among members of the aristocracy; a writer preoccupied with blood and soil. One major Sign of the Apocalypse for Malaparte is the fate of European Jewry: naked Jews marching off to their deaths in the Krakow ghetto; Jewish children being shot for sport in the Warsaw ghetto; Jews literally being butchered to death in Iasi, Romania, by local army and town officials; Jewish girls with exactly 20 days to serve as prostitutes before being executed on the 21st. Where Levi's narrator struggles to regain a sense of selfhood, of basic humanity, Malaparte ends with an epiphany of blood in the catacombs of Naples, a spontaneous mass rite whose effect will be to wipe clean the rot of Europe. Where German behavior and language remain indecipherable for the scientist Primo Levi, Malaparte the adventurer, the man about town, luxuriates in the beauty of the Fascist mind and recoils from its horror.

Levi's obscurity and Malaparte's notoriety in the late 1940s are now reversed, of course. By viewing Holocaust literature through the lens of language, however, and by further refining that lens to distinguish between one period and another, we discover that the Holocaust entered public memory much earlier than we thought and through a greater diversity of perspectives. The tension between secular humanism and apocalypticism in postwar Italy, rooted in the larger struggle of Fascism and anti-Fascism, has its counterpart in other national literatures as well. All postwar memory is communal, but restoring these communal synapses now requires sustained historical research.

In Yiddishland and the Land of Israel

Meanwhile, back in Paris, another national literature was being created, which spoke of nothing else but the destruction of European Jewry and of the civilization that was destroyed. For the Yiddish-speaking refugees, statelessness was an advantage, not a liability, when it came to finding a venue for their harrowing tale of destruction and survival. Yiddish was (still) the universal language of the Jews. There was a thriving Yiddish press everywhere from Paris to Buenos Aires, from Johannesburg to Montreal; from Mexico City to New York; even (sporadically) in Tel Aviv. That press did not wait for a public furor to erupt over German reparations, the trials of Israel Kasztner, Adolf Eichmann, Klaus Barbie, Ivan the Terrible, or the scandal of Swiss gold. The public memory of the Holocaust—called simply *der khurbn*, the Catastrophe, or *der driter khurbn*, the Third Catastrophe (after the destruction of the two Temples)—defined one's Jewish consciousness. It coexisted with the daily news wherever Yiddish was spoken and read.

Does this mean that Yiddish Holocaust writing of the immediate postwar era was artless and unmediated? If everyone spoke the same language and shared the same past, presumably no great effort was required to produce *témoignage* before a "tribunal" of Yiddish-speaking peers. How, then, with the mass media inundated with eyewitness accounts, could any single work stand out among so many others if not by literary means? The conditions that prevailed in Yiddish, paradoxically, were much closer to those of a "normal" postwar literature, where the readership was hungry to learn what really happened; where, but for an accident of history, the same fate might have befallen the reader; where many a reader felt deep down that more could have been done on behalf of the dead—who therefore deserved at least to be remembered. Under "normal" postwar conditions, then, a great work could shape public memory the moment it appeared.

The chair of the Yiddish Writer's Union in Paris between 1946 and 1948 was Chaim Grade (1910–1982; HL 457–463), a different kind of survivor, who had fled eastward into the Soviet Union, abandoning his mother and wife. The crucible of memory, loyalty, and guilt for Grade the poet, essayist, and novelist would henceforth be Vilna, not only its secular Yiddish culture, but also its great Torah sages and radical asceticism. These two sides of his personal past were brilliantly pitted against each other in his first work of autobiographical fiction, "My Quarrel with Hersh Rasseyner" (1952), the lion's share of which takes place in Paris.

While living in Paris, Leyb Rochman (1918–1978) and Mordecai Strigler (1921–1998) committed their wartime memories to writing. Rochman's *And in Your Blood Shall You Live* (1949) and Strigler's multivolume *Extinguished Lights* were serialized in the Yiddish press before they appeared in book form. Whereas the *landslayt* from the Polish town of Mińsk Mazowiecki underwrote the publication of Rochman's book, Strigler was able to publish his memoir and other documentary volumes in the Argentinian Yiddish library, *Dos poylishe yidntum*, an ambitious and well-edited series of reprints and original works about the civilization of Polish Jewry. Capitalizing on his close contacts in Palestine, Strigler saw one volume of his writings appear simultaneously in Hebrew.[68] Later, Rochman would reinforce the intimate bond between the survivor and the survivor community by editing the *yizkor* book of Mińsk Mazowiecki, which, like all such works, first constructed an idealized image of the home that was destroyed and then devoted its last, lengthy and terrifying section to a description of the slaughter.[69]

In *And in Your Blood Shall You Live*, Rochman became the first survivor to describe the elemental confrontation of Jews and Christian Poles with all the props removed, a pagan world in which even children take part in the Jew-hunt, a world where the only thing that could save a Jew was his or her sexual attraction to a Polish peasant. Models of heroism were to be sought among the most debased and marginal members of Polish society. Most brilliantly, Rochman plays two time sequences against one another. Survival Time in the various hideouts, one more primitive than the next, is rendered slowly; it is the durational time of the diary, measured with painstaking effort and frequently the subject of self-analysis. In contrast, the Time of the Slaughter is broken up into four major episodes recounted out of sequence, since Black Friday (August 21, 1942, the final liquidation of the ghetto) represents the heart of darkness, which those in hiding must keep buried, lest it overwhelm their ability to persevere.

Within 20 years, a standard chronicle of survival would emerge in the West: a plot depicting youthful protagonists whose story usually begins with the outbreak of the war and always ends with the liberation. This subgenre invites comparison with the First World War memoir so skillfully described by Fussell.[70] Rochman's fictionalized diary was among the earliest such chronicles from the Second World War, and its revelatory power was widely acknowledged. I. B. Singer (1904–1991; HL 1163–1172) not only reviewed the book favorably; he was later inspired by Rochman's tale of Polish captivity to write *The Slave*. Aharon Appelfeld (b. 1932; HL 50–60), a protégé of Rochman's, would openly acknowledge his own debt.[71]

Mordecai Strigler emerged from the war looking "like a slum-bred thirteen-year-old boy," in the words of war correspondent Meyer Levin (1905–1981). "He had an intellectual face, widening upward from a delicate chin to a broad forehead; he wore glasses."[72] All his copious wartime notes and manuscripts were lost, and reconstructing them from memory was neither feasible nor desirable. In order for his experiences in Majdanek, in Werk Ce (the infamous munitions factory at Skarżysko-Kamienna), and in Buchenwald to reach a wider audience, Strigler decided to adopt a thin fictional cloak, and he defended this decision in a belabored, three-part introduction to his cycle of documentary novels.[73] Fiction, he argued, would mitigate some of the horror, while a literary approach to his real-life protagonists would help deepen their psychological profile. To ensure that the reader not mistake this as mere "literature," historical documentation precedes and punctuates the story.

Rochman and Strigler, rooted in communal memory, scrupulous in their attention to time and place, define the normative, "neoclassical" response in postwar Yiddish literature. As in Italy, however, so in Yiddishland there emerged an apocalyptic voice whose intent was to intensify the horror by situating the Holocaust within its own geography, by representing real personal experience through the veil of hallucination and nightmare, and by rendering the historical transtemporal. Enter: Ka-Tzetnik 135633 who, when asked his name by his Red Army liberators replied: "My name was burned along with all those others in the Auschwitz crematorium." Like Malaparte, Ka-Tzetnik thrived on notoriety, and like *Kaputt*, Ka-Tzetnik's novels of atrocity, *Salamandra* (1946), *House of Dolls: The Chronicles of a Jewish Family in the Twentieth Century* (1955), and *They Called Him Piepel* (1961) would double as pulp fiction. Unlike Malaparte, who luxuriated in his fund of personal and sensual memories, Ka-Tzetnik defined himself solely in terms of his experience of absolute extremity in the Holocaust. The public would learn only decades later of one Yekhiel Feiner-Dinur (1909–2001; HL 621–624), an Expressionist poet of middling talent who had emerged from the ranks of Polish Orthodoxy.[74]

Though recent scholarship has demonstrated that Ka-Tzetnik invented very little, that "Metropoli" was a (thin) fictional cloak for Warsaw, "Kongressia" for Lodz and the unnamed Ghetto was Sosnowicz in Upper East Silesia, the poetics of horror rendered reality into nightmare and history into myth.[75] The authorial self was a cipher. The ghetto and *Lager* were a closed system. The branding of Jews, both male, and especially female, marked a new and demonic covenant, a permanent defilement that could never be eradicated. The world is split between good and evil: Jews versus Germans, Vevke the Saint versus Monyek the Devil, Fella the Survivor versus Daniella the Victim, and so on. When Daniella throws herself on the electrified barbed wire at the conclusion of *House of Dolls*, questions of causality are suspended. Since no human initiative will make any difference, her fate is preordained. If there exists a metonymy for Auschwitz, it is pure womanhood defiled. Clarissa the *Feldhure* can never birth again.

From Ka-Tzetnik's fiction, the nonsurvivor community in Palestine learned to demonize the Judenrat and to lump all its members together as willing collaborators. Earlier in the 1940s, the Hebrew press had offered a morally nuanced map of the various ghettos. But with the arrival of ex-fighters from the ghettos and partisan brigades, the most vocal of whom were later to join the left-wing Mapam (which had split off from David Ben-Gurion's ruling Mapai party), the battle lines were drawn between heroic fighters and passive martyrs. Occupying a gray zone in between were ghetto officials like Adam Czerniakow, Mordechai Chaim Rumkowski, Jacob Gens, Israel Kasztner, Michal Weichert, and "Monyek the Devil" (an obvious stand-in for Moshe Merin, the head of the Judenrat in Bendin). From then until the present day, all memory of the Holocaust in the Hebrew public sphere was contested memory: between Right and Left, religious and secular, Ashkenazim and Sephardim, the elite and the folk. A straight line leads from Ka-Tzetnik's morality plays to those of Joshua Sobol (b. 1939; HL 1182–1188) four decades later.[76]

Within the Yiddish- and Hebrew-speaking survivor community, Ka-Tzetnik's apocalyptic approach and purple prose were just as normative as the writings of Rochman and Strigler. Although this may be hard for contemporary Western readers to believe, Ka-Tzetnik's *House of Dolls* first appeared in serialized form in the American Yiddish press alongside the standard fare of sensational potboilers—this, in the staid 1950s! In children's literature, too, what happened to the Jews of Europe was considered appropriate reading material for the young. There one can find perhaps the earliest instances in Holocaust literature of mixing fact and fantasy.[77] Once we place Yiddish and Hebrew writing at the center of the "Holocaust, Jewish, 1939–1945" rather than at its periphery, we see that, very early on, the literature about the destruction of European Jewry occupied a variegated role with cumulative impact within public memory, this role comparing favorably with the place of the Great War in European memory.

In literature as in life, the norm was a chorus of competing voices from every conceivable part of the Holocaust compass, Auschwitz enjoying no special privilege. The norm was that, given the choice, Yiddish and Hebrew readers strongly preferred reading a documentary novel about the Holocaust rather than actual documents rescued from the Holocaust. From such seasoned writers as Rochman, Strigler—and for that matter, John Hersey (1914–1993; HL 524–527)—to the rookie Eliezer Wiesel, every journalist in the 1940s and 1950s understood this preference and catered to it. On the one hand, they chose fictional modes of enhanced authenticity, such as confessions, autobiographies, memoirs, and diaries, lest, as Strigler worried out loud, these novels be read as "mere" fiction. These true tales of the ghettos and camps, on the other hand, fed the readers' hunger for more documentary fiction.[78] Not only can aesthetic preferences be inferred from studying the way in which Rochman, Strigler, Grade, and Ka-Tzetnik each adopted literary techniques to make their story more readable, but also, and more relevant, reader response can be gauged rather precisely from two controversies that erupted in the pages of the Yiddish press.

On March 17, 1952, the revered Yiddish poet H. Leivick (1888–1962; HL 732–737) published a lengthy article in the New York daily *Der tog* in which he compared "Two Documents" that had recently appeared in scholarly publications: one, an anonymous chronicle of the Great Deportation from Warsaw, in the Warsaw-based *Bleter far geshikhte*, and the other, the Vilna ghetto diary of Zelig Kalmanovitsh, translated from the Hebrew, in the *Yivo-bleter*. Leivick was so scandalized by the first document (in which the anonymous author poured out his wrath on the Judenrat and the Jewish ghetto police, thus desecrating the memory of the martyrs) that he pronounced it a forgery, a product of the Jew-hating, Polish Communist regime. Kalmanovitsh's diary, in contrast, he held up as a model of balance and empathy that correctly viewed all the victims in the same sacred light.

Rising to the challenge, the historian Ber Mark (1908–1966) published a monograph-length rebuttal in the next issue of *Bleter far geshikhte* in which he revealed the just-discovered identity of the anonymous author: none other than Yehoshue Perle (1888–1944), a popular and prolific Yiddish novelist. All undergrounds, Mark reminded the erstwhile revolutionary H. Leivick, operated in secrecy, the Oyneg Shabes archive being no exception. Perle's abhorrence of the Judenrat, the Jewish police, and the Jewish bourgeoisie, Mark averred, was shared by Ringelblum, most members of the archive, and all members of the Jewish Fighting Organization—and, with neo-Nazism on the rise in the capitalist West, Perle's moral reckoning was more relevant than ever. Kalmanovitsh, in marked contrast, represented the despicable ideology of "culturism," which validated the ghetto, further isolated the Jews, and lulled the masses into passivity. Had Kalmanovitsh's mentor, Jacob Gens, the head of the Vilna Judenrat, survived the war, he would have been tried and convicted as a German collaborator.[79]

Thus, the battle lines were drawn: on one side were those who believed that the way to keep memory alive was by reopening old wounds; on the other, those for whom the memory of the martyrs was sacred. Communal memory was politically engaged memory. The debate pitted Left against Right, hard-nosed historians against the guardians of the flock. The clear winner in this particular dispute was Mark. Yet this proved to be a Pyrrhic victory, for the series of Yiddish wartime writings that he managed to publish from 1948 to 1955—novels, short stories, reportage, prose poems, diaries, and a variety of other genres that, even suffering from postwar political censorship in Poland, ought to have formed the primary canon of Holocaust literature—was morally unassimilable for their intended audience in the West. They languish in obscurity to this very day.

Several years before the Leivick-Mark controversy, a story "written especially for *Di yidishe tsaytung*" of Buenos Aires appeared on September 25, 1946 in honor of the High Holiday season. Its author was Zvi Kolitz (1918–2002), who happened to be in town as part of his fund-raising mission on behalf of the Revisionist Zionist movement. The story was called "Yosl Rakovers vendung tsu got" ("Yosl Rakover's Appeal to God"). "In one of the ruins of the ghetto of Warsaw," a prefatory note explained, "among piles of charred rubble and human bones, there was found, concealed and stuffed in a small bottle, the following testament, written during the Warsaw ghetto's last hours by a Jew named Yosl Rakover."[80] Apart from the hackneyed device of a found document and the by-now standard use of the Warsaw ghetto uprising as the pivotal event of the Holocaust, Kolitz cast a Gerer Hasid in the title role; this, to proclaim his faith in a seemingly absent God on the High Holidays. Rakover, implausibly, is also portrayed as an independent ghetto fighter; this, to espouse the credo of Revisionist Zionism: the need for armed resistance and the absolute dichotomy between the merciful God of Israel and the merciless God of Love. A theologically expurgated version of the story appeared a year later in an English-language collection of Kolitz's *Stories and Parables of the Years of Death*, the changes apparently introduced by the translator without Kolitz's knowledge.[81]

In 1954, an anonymous typescript of the original Yiddish story arrived in the Tel Aviv office of *Di goldene keyt*, the Yiddish literary quarterly edited by Abraham Sutzkever. "Yosl Rakover redt tsu got" ("Yosl Rakover Speaks to God," as it was renamed) was published as an authentic document from the Warsaw ghetto, but with stylistic improvements, as per Sutzkever's usual practice. Jacob Glatstein, among many others, hailed the newly discovered testament as "a part of our monumental Holocaust literature [*khurbn-literatur*], which will remain for all the generations." This was too much for the Holocaust historian and former ghetto fighter Michel Borwicz (1911–1988). Disappointed that Sutzkever provided him with so poor an explanation of the manuscript's provenance, Borwicz decided to expose the story's manifold historical inaccuracies and obvious literary gildings. In the face of public protest, Borwicz proclaimed it a fake, and published his findings in a Paris-based literary journal.[82]

The public protested because, as Borwicz understood, the need to believe was simply too great. The Yiddish-reading public had responded viscerally to a "sacred testament" that fully met its expectations and slaked its spiritual thirst. Since, by the time the issue went to press, the truth of Kolitz's authorship had already come to light, Borwicz appended an afterword in which he expressed the hope that the public would soon develop a hermeneutics of reading that would distinguish between the literature *of* the Holocaust and the literature *on* the Holocaust. In any event, he concluded happily, the controversy surrounding Yosl Rakover's pseudo-epigraphic testament was now over.

Of course, it had barely begun, for a French translation appeared in 1955, the same year as Borwicz's exposé, and was heralded by the philosopher Emmanuel Levinas (1906–1995; HL 759–762); it was then published in German, Hebrew, and once again in English. "Yosl Rakover Speaks to God" remains a revered—and controversial—text to this very day.[83]

Communal memory, then, was *témoignage*—real or constructed—mediated by a set of core values, whether political or theological. The unassimilable facts of the Holocaust were reinterpreted in the light of credos, archetypes, and myths; or, as we have just seen, mediated by various fictional means. Most popular were texts that purported to be true but defied historical analysis; that could be excerpted, edited, anthologized, translated, performed, and retranslated. What "Yosl Rakover Speaks to God" and the "Letter of the Ninety-Three Bais Yaakov Girls of Krakow" shared with *The Diary of a Young Girl* was that their authors, who had (presumably) perished, bespoke faith in the future.[84]

Call it a liturgical impulse. It was shared by religious and secular alike, in "godless" America as well as in the Holy Land. For the Orthodox, history was never more than raw material, a sermonic text, proof to the faithful of God's hidden hand. As Mendl Piekarz has demonstrated in exhaustive detail, Orthodox apologists worked overtime to preserve the sacred memory of all their murdered flock.[85] That the same liturgical impulse was operative among secular, Yiddish-speaking Jews should likewise come as no surprise. The Yiddish-reading public was traumatized by its losses, its secular gods smashed and discarded. Staunch secularists of yesteryear became guardians of the sacred flame. Thus, in 1948, Shmuel Niger, the preeminent Yiddish literary critic of his day, published *Kidush hashem*, subtitled "A collection of selected, oftentimes abbreviated reports, letters, chronicles, testaments, inscriptions, legends, poems, short stories, dramatic scenes, essays, which describe acts of self-sacrifice in our own days and also in days of yore." That year, the former Vilna partisan, Shmerke Kaczerginski (1908–1954), published the definitive edition of *Songs of the Ghettos and Concentration Camps*: definitive by virtue of size, H. Leivick's imprimatur, and inspirational chapter headings.[86]

Aesthetics was another core value. A particularly beautiful volume of this period was *Martyrs: Poetry of Those Tortured to Death* (1947), published on blue-grey stock in a numbered edition by Machmadim Art Editions. Each selection from the work of a Polish-Yiddish poet was set to music by the modern composer Henech Kon, with paintings by Isaac Lichtenstein.

A similar anthological impulse was apparent in other languages as well: Marie Syrkin's *Blessed Is the Match: The Story of Jewish Resistance* (1947), for example, or the indefatigable Leo W. Schwarz's *The Root and the Bough: The Epic of an Enduring People* (1949). When Jacob Apenszlak reissued *De profundis: Ghetto Poetry from the Jewish Underground in Poland* (1945), he did not reveal in his introduction the controversy that had arisen among the members of the Jewish National Committee back in 1944 over which poems by (the non-Jewish) Czesław Miłosz (1911–2004; HL 846–848) to accept.[87] Through the art of anthologizing, it was possible to erase the terrible divide between the living and the dead; to set their words to music; to harmonize the martyrs with the fighters.

Could a non-witness also bear witness? "*In Treblinke bin ikh nit geven*," wrote Leivick with false modesty, "I was never in Treblinka / nor in [the death camp of] Maidanek. / But I stand upon their threshold, / at their very edge."[88] The mark of a great poet in Yiddish- and Hebrew-land was one who could give individual voice to national mourning. As Leivick's maudlin rhyme "Majdanek"/"ganek" [lit. "porch"] testifies, real poetic greatness was reserved for those who struggled to find the proper voice. In Yiddish, Jacob Glatstein was that poet. In *Memorial Poems* (1943), perhaps the first book of poems in any language devoted to the Holocaust, the arch-modernist, the rootless cosmopolitan, the New York intellectual, donned various masks, one more "communal" than the next: a Jew with a yellow star; a bleeding Jewish Jesus standing on the butcher block; the great hasidic master, Nahman of Braslav, confiding in his scribe; EveryJew pleading before an absent God.[89]

In Hebrew, that poet was Uri Zvi Greenberg (1896–1981; HL 471–477), who wrote very little from September 1939, when he fled Warsaw (where he had been working as a Yiddish journalist), until 1943, when the Palestinian Jewish community began to absorb what had happened in Europe. In any event, he had no real audience, since both the literary establishment and the left-wing kibbutz movement ostracized him for his Revisionist views. But by the time he emerged from his self-imposed isolation in 1945, Greenberg was immediately acclaimed as "the Jeremiah of our generation," his poems were mainstreamed in the influential daily *Ha'aretz*, and a nation-state in the making hung on to his every word.[90]

Streets of the River: The Book of Dirges and Power (1951) was the first and only book of Holocaust poetry designed to be a *sefer*, a sacred tome. All the secular props were here discarded. The poet-prophet abjured the term *shoah*, which implied a natural disaster emancipated from the master drama of Christian enmity, and he refused the easy consolation of coupling *shoah* with *gevurah*, the martyrs with the fighters. The destruction of a people was a catastrophe of cosmic proportions, requiring a new poetic language—No Other Instances! he proclaimed—a new accounting with God, a last encounter with the dead, and a final reckoning with the goyim. This *sefer* stood alone, in part because Greenberg would allow no other book of his to be published until the day he died; in part because it was published by the Schocken Press, in its distinctive, archaic typeface; and finally, because it made the same maximal demands of the reader as it did of the poet.[91] It also marked the end of an era, for the next generation of Hebrew poets, even if they knew some Yiddish, would not champion its speakers, and, eschewing the mantle of prophecy, would never presume to turn their poems into prayers.

In sum, from 1945 to 1960, nowhere—not in France or Italy, neither in the United States nor in Israel, not even in the Soviet Union—was there a conspiracy of silence.

Displaced Memory: 1960–1978

The second period of postwar memory also begins with a trial. *The Man in the Glass Booth*, as the playwright Robert Shaw (1927–1978) described him, was judged for all the world to see. And all the world—from Germany to Hungary, from Argentina to Israel—was now a stage for replaying what really happened in the "Holocaust," as it was henceforth to be called. What really happened at the trial of Adolf Eichmann, by contrast, became so enmeshed in public memory that it assumed a design of its own. The British historian Hugh Trevor-Roper proclaimed to the world that the trial had been the brainchild of David Ben-Gurion, whose intent was to showcase Israeli power and to demonstrate that Israel alone stood up for justice. Although Ben-Gurion himself said as much at a special Independence Day address in May 1961, the "old man" actually had no interest in bringing Eichmann to trial, never once attended the proceedings, and wished it would go away so that he could attend to weightier matters of state. David Grossman (b. 1954; HL 481–486), then seven years old, "remembers," as do many other Israelis, being glued to the radio every single night to hear highlights from the day's proceedings. In point of fact, the trial was broadcast only four times a week for a mere 25 minutes, and even this was a hard-won concession by the staff at Israel Radio. Turning down lucrative offers from every major television network, from NBC to the BBC, the government agency in charge gave the concession to a local amateur, with predictable results. Thanks to the surviving footage, we do see, standing tall, the partisan-poet-novelist Abba Kovner (1918–1987: HL 701–707) declaiming his call-to-arms from the Vilna ghetto, and Ka-Tzetnik being carried from the courtroom in a dead faint after giving testimony regarding "the planet of Auschwitz."[92]

The very fact that the Eichmann trial was covered by every major news agency, with snippets of it televised abroad, marked a turning point in the public memory of the Holocaust. For Americans, it brought home the face of Nazi evil.[93] In Israel, the trial was doubly cathartic. For the survivors, as poet Haim Gouri (b. 1923; HL 450–453) recalled many years later, it "legitimized the disclosure of one's past. What had been silenced and suppressed gushed out and became common knowledge."[94] For those who had arrived before the deluge, leaving their loved ones to perish, the trial provided a much-needed public arena within which they could confront their profound sense of guilt. Could we have done more to save them? Years later, the resounding answer would be: Yes.

Who indeed was to blame? As she sat in the press gallery, listening without earphones to the defendant's testimony in German, Hannah Arendt (1906–1975; HL 67–75) felt indignant at the chief justice's heavy-handed manner. Was not the mindless evil of the Germans the root cause of the Holocaust, she asked herself, and perhaps also the studied complicity of the Jewish leadership? Like another German Jewish refugee, Bruno Bettelheim (1903–1990; HL 148–151), Arendt was intent upon wresting universal significance from the tribal experience of the Jews, and thus she threw down the gauntlet to American Jewish intellectuals, heretofore disengaged.[95]

In the wake of the Eichmann trial, the Holocaust was displaced morally, temporally, geographically, linguistically, and nowhere more profoundly than in works of the literary imagination. The languages in which the Holocaust was lived were now replaced by the languages in which it was relived. For the first time in the annals of war, speaking—and writing—"with an accent" became the sign of an authentic witness.[96] Certainly this had not been the case in the literature of the Great War. The coarse humor of Jaroslav Hašek was as palpably Czech as the pathos of Remarque was quintessentially German. As we have just seen, those eyewitnesses who came forward in the first decade-and-a-half after the Second World War still answered to the expectations of their native audience, whose limited tolerance for tales of unmitigated horror was severely tested. In the 1960s and 1970s, by contrast, there emerged a cohort of middle-aged writers who could make themselves heard only in their *acquired* language and before an adopted audience. Those who could gain a hearing before a panel of judges and from the vast unseen audience that lay beyond were those who spoke for the Holocaust.

Ruth Wisse calls them "Writers in Search of Language," and in a lucid chapter surveys the career of four survivors of East-Central Europe—Piotr Rawicz (1919–1982; HL 983–986), Elie Wiesel (b. 1928; HL 1315–1325), Jerzy Kosinski (1933–1991; HL 697–700), and Aharon Appelfeld—who needed to reinvent themselves after the war because they could not return to their native land or language.[97] How shall such displaced writers be read? One's first impulse is to read these strangers in terms of one another, and to situate them in a separate "concentrationary universe." Wisse, however, models a different approach. As a first interpretive step, she tries to understand their transition from refugee to landed immigrant status.

"This book is not a historical record," protests the narrator at the conclusion of Rawicz's *Blood from the Sky* (1961). True, the author has gone to great lengths to cover his biographical tracks, to shock and confuse the reader, so perhaps he means what he says? Taking note of where the narrator is sitting when he pronounces these bitter words—in a Parisian café in the early 1960s—Wisse discovers the source of his rage, which is turned both inward, at a Jew who has ceased to be one, and outward, at his debased, super-intellectual, French audience. Similarly, the manifold changes that Wiesel made when translating *Night* (1956, 1958) from Yiddish into French are understood by Wisse to be a response to the two great influences on Wiesel's intellectual development, François Mauriac and Albert Camus. Rather than explain the "trope of muteness" in Kosinski's *The Painted Bird* (1965) as the essential condition of the Jew-in-hiding, the hunted bird, she seeks an explanation in "the author's cultural autism," the essential condition of a Jew who was robbed of his Jewishness at birth.

Appelfeld, too, stands both inside and out, both perpetual immigrant and new *'oleh*. As other critics have pointed out, the very transience of Appelfeld's characters, the poverty of their speech, and the failure of Zionism to rescue the survivors from their oedipal struggle are precisely what allowed Appelfeld's early stories to swim with the New Wave of Israeli fiction.[98] Along with Amos Oz, A. B. Yehoshua, and other writers of his generation, Appelfeld adopted the plain style, in opposition to the high pathos and ideological certainties of the Zionist founders. As in the early days of Primo Levi, the moral authority of the survivor depended on his ability to carve out a new cultural space. And recognition for Appelfeld came much more quickly than it had for Levi. One year after *Smoke*, Appelfeld's inaugural collection, *In the Fertile Valley* (1963) was published under the Schocken imprimatur. This prestigious house had just launched the career of another rising star named Yehudah Amichai (1924–2000; HL 25–30).

The displacement wrought by the Second World War was so far-reaching that even those who continued to write in their native languages sought refuge among speakers of a foreign tongue, among whom they could never be fully at home. This was the fate (in alphabetical order) of Paul Celan (né Antschel, 1920–1970; HL 215–223), Edgar Hilsenrath (b. 1926; HL 554–558), Jakov Lind (b. 1927; HL 772–

778), and Peter Weiss (1916–1982; HL 1303–1306), not to mention those who became political exiles and chose never to return, including Henryk Grynberg (b. 1936; HL 499–503) and Arnost Lustig (b. 1926; HL 779–784). With the exception of Celan and Lustig, these writers made their debut in the 1960s.

So the strangeness of these strangers derived from several sources. They bore witness to what happened over there. Some, but by no means all, had blue numbers tattooed on their arms. They spoke with a foreign accent or with a limited vocabulary. And the story they told—of who did what to whom—was both familiar and strange. No longer was it Ka-Tzetnik's *Chronicles of a Jewish Family in the Twentieth Century*, Malaparte's indictment of Europe, or Levi's search for a basic humanity. It was the Holocaust telescoped, fragmented, and individualized; the story, as Amichai put it, *Not of This Time, Not of This Place* (1968).

World literature as a whole was in open revolt against mimesis, with Borges, Cortázar, and magic realism all the rage, "Kafkaesque" becoming a household term, and Tolkien a cult classic on college campuses. Writing on the Holocaust—still the province of those old enough to remember—was keeping pace. Ushering in the Sixties were two epic novels that viewed the war and the fate of European Jewry through the perspective of a boy: Günter Grass' *The Tin Drum* (1959) (HL 464–467) and André Schwarz-Bart's *The Last of the Just* (1959) (HL 1122–1126)—the one a boy who refused to grow up, the other a boy who bore the genetic code of Jewish martyrdom.

The search for meaning gained new momentum, with veteran writers such as Romain Gary, S. Y. Agnon, Leyb Rochman, I. B. Singer, Abraham Sutzkever, and Elie Wiesel adopting a variety of antirealistic means. Can Germany ever rid itself of its Jewish ghosts? asks Romain Gary (né Kacew, 1914–1980; HL 399–403). The answer is his black comedy, *The Dance of Genghis Cohn* (1967), starring former executioner Schatz and the dybbuk of a Jewish nightclub comedian. What will remain of Polish Jewry and its millennial-old civilization? ask S. Y. Agnon (1888–1970) and Leyb Rochman. The name of the martyred community, answers Agnon, inscribed into a religious hymn composed by the greatest of medieval poets, Solomon ibn Gabirol ("The Sign," 1960).[99] An apocalyptic landscape, answers Rochman in his *With Blind Steps Over the Earth* (1968), where a returning survivor is split into two and even plundered books can speak. Can the dead come back to life? ask I. B. Singer (1904–1991; HL 1163–1172) and Abraham Sutzkever. In Singer's "The Cafeteria" (1968), a survivor of various hells peeks through the hole in the fabric of reality and sees . . . Adolf Hitler. Similarly, in the deranged reality of Sutzkever's fantastical tales, *Messiah's Diary* (1975), *Where the Stars Spend the Night* (1979), and *Prophecy of the Inner Eye* (1989), the luminous-murderous past invades everyday events through chance encounters and late-night visitations. Who is responsible? asks Elie Wiesel, and gives the answer in a series of dialogues-in-novel-form—*Dawn* (1960), *The Accident* (1961), *A Town Beyond the Wall* (1962), and *The Gates of the Forest* (1964)—that pits victim against executioner, witness against bystander, teacher against disciple.

Was Wiesel's Gregor the same as his Gavriel? Was Gavriel perhaps the Prophet Elijah in disguise, or one of the Seven Beggars? Characters who just yesterday seemed to have some grounding in reality were now seen wearing ancestral garb and speaking in tongues. Increasingly, Wiesel turned to the stylization of hasidic narrative. So when Edmond Jabès (1912–1991) was exiled from Egypt in the wake of the Suez Crisis, settled in France, and published *The Book of Questions* (1964), the story of two survivors, Sarah and Yukel, as interpreted by a host of imaginary rabbis, the French public did not know what to make of it. Jacques Derrida, another Jewish exile, was among the few who expressed his deep admiration.[100]

The return to Judaic, non-Western modes of self-expression was both a way of proclaiming one's artfulness, artistry, and artifice, and of reclaiming the Holocaust for the Jews. Whereas Strigler had earlier apologized to his readers for not writing straight history, and Kolitz had laid bare his devices, in the next period of Holocaust literature, the public already knew—or thought it knew—who did what to whom, and was anxious for its writers and intellectuals to tackle the bigger questions. The 1960s and 1970s saw the beginning of sustained theological writing on the Holocaust—by Emil Fackenheim (1916–2003; HL 323–327), Arthur A. Cohen (1928–1986; HL 235–240), Irving Greenberg (b. 1933), and Richard L. Rubenstein (b. 1924)—and the first attempts at compiling Holocaust liturgies.

Cast ashore in the New World, fictional landed immigrants cut a grotesque figure: Sol Nazerman, the anti-hero of *The Pawnbroker* (1961), by Edward Lewis Wallant (1926–1962; HL 1283–1287); Adam Stein, in *Adam Resurrected* (1968), by Yoram Kaniuk (b. 1930; HL 593–598); and Artur Sammler in *Mr. Sammler's Planet* (1970), by Saul Bellow (1915–2005; HL 124–134). Sammler's daughter, Shula, is emotionally crippled by her experiences; his son-in-law, Eisen, is a brutalized man-of-iron; Bruch, a survivor of Buchenwald, is appropriately named "Hernia"; and Artur himself—named after Schopenhauer, the philosopher of nihilism, who preached that organs of sex are the seat of the Will—Sammler is the "collector," anthropologist, observer, his one good eye a symbol of suffering and survival, leaving him one blind eye to look inward. It is Sammler who crawled out of a mass grave and (contra Tolstoy) had to kill to stay alive, but as an elitist intellectual who loves English cultivation and restraint and carries his umbrella around everywhere, he is also a man of reason, a believer in human survival who wants a rational human community in which men are accountable. Mr. Sammler, in short, represents the basic conflicts within Jewish life at the height of the sexual revolution and the antiwar movement in America. Little noticed in this novel (so devilishly designed to offend everyone) is that, after talking back to all the demagogues, Sammler finds his true voice—not the subdialects he has perfected for other peoples' benefit, not Oxford English à la H. G. Wells, not Angela's confessional style, not his nephew Elya's family memory, either, but a prayer for the soul of Elya, an internal monologue, one of the most moving passages in contemporary American fiction. This oddball Jewish refugee understands the meaning of a flawed and diminished life, and he knows how to mourn.

Unhinged from its source languages, from its geography, from the constraints of reality, from the need to forge a consistent group narrative, something remarkable happened to the literature of the Holocaust in this third period of its development. It became displaced temporally as well. Try though the Library of Congress might to delimit the temporal scope of the "Holocaust, Jewish" to the years of the Second World War, the writer-survivors had designs of their own. One was the Israeli poet and scholar of medieval Hebrew poetry, Dan Pagis (1930–1986; HL 913–917). In 1970, he published this 7-line poem, destined to become, along with Celan's "Todesfuge," a poem of almost scriptural authority:

> Written in Pencil in the Sealed Railway Car
>
> here in this carload
> i am eve
> with abel my son
> if you see my other son
> cain son of man
> tell him that i[101]

Here Pagis, with absolute precision, displaces space into time. The universal reach of the Nazi genocide is immediately apprehendable because the grafitti discovered (by whom?) inside the sealed railway car, of the kind that transported millions of Jews to their deaths, is addressed to Cain, the world's first murderer, related, through a brilliant pun, to Ezekiel, the prophet of the resurrection, the only "Son of Man [Adam]" in the Hebrew Bible. And what is this writing? Is it a memorial, an act of defiance, an apocalyptic warning, akin to Daniel's writing-on-the-wall; an amulet, perhaps, an invocation of God's name designed to guard its bearer against evil? Why then have a mother and son been shipped off to their death, which is far worse than "just" a brother killing his own brother, for in *this* carload something has happened that eclipses everything that happened before—although as in Genesis, only Cain is left on earth, which suggests that every reader of this poem is a member of the Cain-anite race, carrying the curse of perpetual wandering and murder. For every survivor is Cain, and Cain is every survivor, which in turn suggests that this poem too was "published" (for someone had to provide the title!) out of guilt, his brother's blood crying out to the poet-publisher, and by extension, to each one of us.[102]

As in Appelfeld, as in Amichai, as in Natan Zach, as in the whole modernist school of Israeli literature, the Hebrew language is used here against the grain, stripped of its biblical and rabbinic locutions (except for the weird redundancy of "cain son of man"), a language at once colloquial and strange—like the Holocaust survivor in our midst, like the memory of the dead. As Sidra Ezrahi noted, Pagis relinquished "the mimetic project in his poetry," renounced chronology, dispensed with "the available strategies for structuring experience through the myths . . . by which a community remembers," and finally, in the most courageous act of all, "surrendered the 'privileged' status of the survivor."[103]

In this poem, Dan Pagis, a survivor from Romania, writing in an adopted language, literally inscribed the Holocaust into the beginning of the human saga, albeit merely in pencil. "Holocaust, Jewish" was the same for him as "History, Human."

In the same year, his *landsman* and contemporary, Elie Wiesel, writing in English, his *second* adopted language, took exactly the opposite approach. "By its uniqueness," Wiesel concluded, "the holocaust defies literature." When it comes to giving testimony about the dead, "writing itself is called into question."[104] For Pagis, the very act of writing—however primitive and truncated—testified to the possibility of dialogue, defiance, memorial. For Wiesel, all prior writing on the Holocaust, presumably including his own, merely underscored the mystery, the unknowability, of the Event.

Making the calculation that one generation, that is, a quarter-century, had elapsed since the liberation of the camps, Wiesel used the occasion to issue a manifesto on behalf of all survivors. An indifferent, disbelieving, and hostile world had cowed the survivors into silence, he proclaimed. "They were afraid of saying what must not be said, of attempting to communicate with language what eludes language, of falling into the trap of easy half-truths." "One generation after," these survivors had finally come of age, as would their offspring, in due course, so that "from here on," there would be a change. "From now on, one will speak differently about the holocaust. Or not at all."[105] An abyss of silence and "easy half-truths" lay between "Holocaust, Jewish (1939–1945)" and the Generation of 1970. Wiesel, like Malaparte and other apocalypticists before him, reserved the right either to reveal the "full truth" of the Holocaust or to swear a collective vow of silence.

Instead, he left for Washington.

Personalized Memory: 1978–1991

Five events usher in this next period in the public memory of the Holocaust, all of them, not coincidentally, occurring in the United States:

1) The President's Commission on the Holocaust, chaired by Elie Wiesel, presents its *Report to the President* (September 27, 1979);
2) Gerald Green's made-for-television drama, *Holocaust*, airs in North America and Europe (1978);
3) The Holocaust Survivors' Film Project begins in New Haven (1979);
4) The Holocaust Library is launched in New York City (1978); and
5) Helen Epstein publishes *Children of the Holocaust* (1979).

The *Report to the President*, presented to Jimmy Carter, is a remarkable document.[106] Theoretical positions on the meaning and roots of the Holocaust, which until then were the province of specialists, appear on its pages as national policy. Emil Fackenheim's dictum, his "614th commandment" not to grant Hitler a posthumous victory, is presented to Carter as an article of faith. So, too, is the shame of President Franklin D. Roosevelt's America, for not doing more "to prevent the Holocaust."—by no means a commonplace in American historiography—and so, too, Raul Hilberg's and Richard Rubenstein's analyses of Nazism as "a thoroughly modern expression of bureaucratic organization."[107] The *Report to the President* contains veiled references to Watergate and openly criticizes the U.S.S.R. and the Communist bloc for having effaced the particular fate of the Jews. "The universality of the Holocaust," writes Wiesel in his oracular mode, "lies in its uniqueness: the Event is essentially Jewish, yet its interpretation is universal." (Note that like the Ineffable Name of God, the Holocaust is best referred to as the "Event.") Consistent with his own manifesto of 1970 is Wiesel's definition of the survivor "as a messenger and guardian of secrets entrusted by the dead."[108]

The *Report to the President* documents the enshrinement of the Holocaust within the civil religion of the United States of America. Beyond the wildest dreams of Rabbi Irving Greenberg when he created the Zakhor Holocaust Resource Center in 1975, the President's Commission on the Holocaust now called for Days of Remembrance of Victims of the Holocaust to be proclaimed in perpetuity and to be held annually. Later called Holocaust Remembrance Week, the date would be fixed each year in accordance with the Jewish calendar. To complete the transformation of the Holocaust into a second Sinai, the source of a new ecumenical revelation, the Commission recommended the establishment of a National Holocaust Memorial/Museum in the nation's capital.

Meanwhile, until the Museum was actually built, the real business of public memory was conducted not in smoke-free offices, not in academic seminars, but in popular culture, which increasingly meant on the big and little screen. A survey of the feature and documentary films made about the Holocaust reveals a powerful synergy between literature and film. The vaudevillian shtick of Chaplin's *The Great Dictator* (1940) situates it ever so firmly within Wartime Memory. The high-mindedness of Alexander Ford's *Border Street* (1948), the Alain Resnais/Jean Cayrol documentary, *Night and Fog* (1955), and Stanley Kramer's *Judgment at Nuremberg* (1961) is the mark of their "communal" aesthetics. Try screening any of them outside their country of origin and the *Tendenz* of each is glaring.[109] The period I have called "Displaced Memory" witnessed a series of daring art films, from Sidney Lumet's *The Pawnbroker* (1963), Andrzej Munk's unfinished masterpiece, *The Passenger* (1963), Jurek Becker's original screenplay for *Jacob the Liar* (1967, finally filmed in 1974), and the heady New Wave of Czech cinema, which brought us Ján Kadár's *The Shop on Main Street* (1966), to Vittorio de Sica's lush production of *The Garden of the Finzi-Continis* (1970), to Marcel Ophuls' fiercely polemical *The Sorrow and the Pity* (1970). As in literature, there were filmmakers who believed that the way to keep memory alive was by reopening old wounds (Lumet, Munk, Ophuls), and those for whom the memory of the martyrs and fighters, the lovers and losers, was sacred (Ford, Forman, de Sica, Becker).

Against this backdrop, Gerald Green's television mini-series, *Holocaust*, may seem like a giant step backward. Wiesel and other crusaders were predictably outraged at what they saw as a Holocaust soap opera.[110] But 220 million viewers in the United States and Europe watched it, including half of all adults in West Germany (HL 469). Certainly they would remember the portrayal of SS officer Erik Dorf as anything but banal.[111]

Such things are difficult to document, but seeing the Weiss and Dorf families, the one Jewish, and therefore good, the other German, and therefore morally ambiguous, in the privacy of one's own home, with or without commercial interruption, may have broken the last taboo associated with the destruction of European Jewry. This was, after all, in the wake of the Vietnam War, when Americans and audiences worldwide had the experience of viewing death and destruction up close as an "everyday" event. The same audience could now approach another terrible subject on the small screen with something like familiarity. Once the Holocaust became normalized and standardized, it became possible, indeed mandatory, to teach it to one's children. In the 1980s, Holocaust curricula were introduced into state schools in the United States, Germany, France, and elsewhere.

If the Weiss family saga was appropriate for television, then why should every survivor not have the opportunity to videotape his or her personal testimony? The Holocaust Survivors' Film Project began as a grassroots phenomenon. In 1981, the videotaped testimonies were deposited at Yale University and became the core collection of the Fortunoff Video Archive for Holocaust Testimony, now numbering 4,200 interviews. A driving force behind the merger was the English literary critic, Geoffrey Hartman (b. 1929; HL 520–523), who had been evacuated from Germany on the *Kindertransport* and who had begun to reclaim his Jewish past.

The radical minimalism of these videotapes is the source of their power. One person (or at most two) in a bare room (or in a living room), staring at a camera and talking to a total stranger in English. Interviews were allowed in any language—but who still believed in a Yiddish or Polish Jewish posterity? Talking to a total stranger, the informants were really thinking of their own children; their children, who were not raised on their songs, taught their prayers, or encouraged to delve into their past. Since the informants believed that the purpose of these interviews was to record one's Holocaust experiences, there was no point wasting the stranger's time with stories about life before the war—unless it pertained to antisemitism or premonitions of disaster. Stick to the war, end with the liberation, and try to keep it personal.

The more primitive the camera work, the greater the illusion of truthfulness. Later, when Steven Spielberg and Hollywood professionals took over the job, the key to verisimilitude would lie in the close-up and the skillful editing. A catch in the voice, eyes momentarily averted from the screen, groping for the right word— these would signal that some deep wound had just been opened. Still later, thanks to advances in digital technology and the huge financial resources that Spielberg invested in the Survivors of the Shoah Visual History Foundation (1994), videotaped interviews with aging survivors speaking varieties of immigrant English would become the central repository of Holocaust memory, replacing the written word.

The net result of Gerald Green's *Holocaust* is that the unfathomable, ineffable Event took on a poignant and personal face. In public, that face became increasingly self-confident. Not only were survivors prominent among the 32 signatories (not including Wiesel) of the *Report* of the President's Commission on the Holocaust; not only were they willing and able to organize themselves into a worldwide network, but they were also prepared to take over the means of production. Under the energetic leadership of Alexander Donat (né Michal Berg, 1905–1983), a Holocaust Library was established "to offer to the reading public authentic material, not readily available, and to preserve the memory of our martyrs and heroes untainted by arbitrary or inadvertent distortions." The statement of purpose began by proclaiming: "The *Holocaust Library* was created and is managed by survivors" and ended with an appeal for the moral reconstruction of today's hate- and violence-stricken world by means of retelling the "holocaust story." Inaugurating the series was a reissue of Donat's *The Holocaust Kingdom: A Memoir* (1963), no longer "readily available."

One generation begat another, though not in the image of Donat, the ghetto fighter and crusader. When the first encounter groups of children of Holocaust survivors, led by Eva Fogelman and Bella Savran, began to meet in private homes in Boston in the spring of 1976, another "holocaust story" emerged.[112] Beneath the facade of new lives, new families, and new prospects, this was a story that told of unending trauma. Wanting to protect their children from the past, fearful of bonding to those closest to them, lest they (too) be taken away, the survivors' fear of loving, their repressed mourning, their psychic closing off, had engendered a powerful sense of identification with suffering on the part of their children, coupled with depression, rage, and self-loathing. This and more came to light in a series of publications. The first, published by Bloch Publishing Co. and therefore not widely known, was *Living After the Holocaust: Reflections by the Postwar Generation in America*, edited by Lucy Steinitz and David M. Szonyi (1976). There followed an article titled "Heirs of the Holocaust," by Helen Epstein (b. 1947; HL 308–310), which appeared in the *New York Times Magazine* on June 19, 1977, culminating in her very influential book, *Children of the Holocaust: Conversations with Sons and Daughters of Survivors* (1979). Just as the parents had banded together to find and support one another, so too did their children, by founding an International Network of Children of Holocaust Survivors. What had begun as group therapy quickly burgeoned into a movement that was very much in the public eye. Thus was born a Second Generation, unlike any seen before.

Singled out from among their cohort by a historical experience not their own, the residue of the terror experienced by their parents—what the kabbalists called the *reshimu*—clung to the offspring, marking them for life. Because the catastrophic damage of the Holocaust was felt most profoundly in the psychic realm, the way of "working through" the trauma was not by means of memorializing the lost culture, seeking meaning through analogies and archetypes, or by calling for vengeance—not, in short, through any of the sanctioned means perfected over millennia—but rather by therapeutic means, facilitated in a group setting.

What bound the children to their parents most powerfully was the myth of suppression. Wiesel's manifesto of 1970 became the rallying cry not of one generation, but of two. If an indifferent, disbelieving, and hostile world had cowed the survivors into silence, because "they were afraid of saying what must not be said, of attempting to communicate with language what eludes language;" and if "one generation after," these survivors and their offspring had finally come of age, then by banding together to break the silence, they would now force the world to listen. This mandate was doubly liberating, because it turned former victims and their disaffected children into a revolutionary cohort, and it started the memory clock all over again. Who spoke for the Holocaust were all those who bore its psychic scars and were now prepared to bare them.

And preferably—to do so in English.

Much has been written on the Americanization of the Holocaust and the Holocaust in American life, by sympathetic and hostile critics.[113] Less obvious is the way in which American literary and academic tastes began to shape and delimit the canon of Holocaust literature, both looking back and going forward. If, in the period of Displaced Memory, the refugee-writers became landed immigrants, in this, the next phase, they became naturalized American citizens. Consider the career of Aharon Appelfeld, who became known to the American public solely as a novelist, and would himself later play a pivotal role inside a novel by Philip Roth. Consider the career of Yoram Kaniuk, whose *Adam Resurrected* (1968) languished in obscurity until 1976, when Susan Sontag hailed its translation as a literary masterpiece. Kaniuk's portrayal of Israel as a gigantic insane asylum was one to which she was already predisposed. Consider, finally, the fate of *The White Hotel*, the third novel written by D. M. Thomas (b. 1935; HL 1262–1265). First published in Britain in 1980, it "looked similarly fated for obscurity" when, in the spring of 1981, it was celebrated by critics in the United States and became a bestseller (HL 1262). What Appelfeld, Kaniuk, and Thomas had in common was their intense focus on the pathology of the Jews. Where they differed was in their prognosis for a possible cure.

Also in this period, suicide became emblematic of the displaced writer-survivor. Few Jewish writers had taken their own lives in wartime—one thinks of Stefan Zweig (1881–1942) in faraway Brazil and the mysterious circumstances of the death of Walter Benjamin (1892–1940) while trying to cross the Pyrenees to freedom. Ghetto chroniclers routinely commented on the low rate of suicide—at least in the period before the mass deportations. Suicide in the wake of the Holocaust represents a second point of closure. The suicide of a shell-shocked soldier such as Virginia Woolf's fictional Septimus Smith, or of a real-life Holocaust survivor, lays bare the lie of liberation. It reveals, with terrible finality, what can never be revealed. Celan (1970), Rawicz (1982), Levi (1987), Bettelheim (1990), and Kosinski (1991) took their own lives. So did Sarah Kofman (1934–1994; HL 680–683), upon completing her autobiography.[114] The rediscovery of Tadeusz Borowski (1922–1951; HL 177–180) by Philip Roth in his influential series, *Writers from the Other Europe*, established Borowski's suicide-by-gas as the grisly prototype.[115] In the wake of the Holocaust, choosing how and when one dies is also a choice.

Film emerged in this period as a highly personalized medium, a means of private exorcism made public. The political scandal of casting Vanessa Redgrave in the lead role of Fania Fenelon (1909–1983; HL 335–337) in Arthur Miller's adaptation of *Playing for Time* (1980) very nearly eclipsed the heroine's saga of survival. In an exquisitely deft manner, Louis Malle (1932–1995) waited for the final moments of *Au Revoir les Enfants* (1987) to acknowledge his own role in the story of a Jewish child hidden in a French Catholic boarding school. Gila Almagor (b. 1939; HL 14–16) not only wrote but also starred in her quasi-autobiographical *The Summer of Avia* (1985; filmed 1989) and in its upbeat sequel, *Under the Domim Tree* (1992; filmed 1994). In Israel, where the personal is always political, the official "coming out" of the Second Generation occurred in 1988, when director Orna Ben-Dor Niv released her film *Because of That War*, the very title signifying a dramatic shift in national perspective: from the War of Independence to "that" unmentionable war. On screen, for the first time, parents spoke openly to their children of their fears; two survivors of Auschwitz, one from Warsaw, the other from Salonika, compared horrors; and two of Israel's most popular performers, Yehudah Poliker and Ya'acov Gilad, discovered that, beyond their love of music, what drew them together was the wartime experience of their parents. To celebrate that bond, they perform rock music composed about the camps, perhaps the first new songs written about the Holocaust in any language since the late 1940s.[116] Looking back on this period, it becomes clear that the apotheosis of Holocaust-film-as-personal-indictment was Claude Lanzmann's *Shoah* (1985). Whether on-camera or off, Lanzmann the interrogator (b. 1925) relentlessly pursued his "willing and unwilling subjects."[117] In Lanzmann, the Second Generation found its Avenger and Grand Inquisitor.

When the focus of public memory shifted away from what had happened Over There to what was happening on the Other Side, to those ships full of survivors who had managed to arrive at a safe haven, new laboratories were needed to distill their story and that of their children: in group therapy, in front of a camera, in the corridors of power, at international gatherings. This new inward focus, confessional and proceeding from the present, reaped unexpected rewards for the literary imagination. Even if the Holocaust was unknowable, there was hope at least of knowing something about one's parents. Even if their true story had been suppressed, or made into slogans learned by rote at school, or had became part of the collective neurosis, an attentive and artistically inclined child could tease it out of them, and what could not be learned in fact could be imagined, reenacted, transfigured. And so it was that two exceptionally fine works of Holocaust literature appeared in 1986, both written from the perspective of an only child of survivors, by authors practiced in fantastical genres—one in comix, the other in children's literature. The publication of each was a watershed event: Part I of *Maus*, by Art Spiegelman (b. 1948; HL 1199–1207), and the four-part experimental novel *See: Under Love*, by David Grossman (b. 1954).

How to signal to a postwar generation the enormity of the event? By turning the Holocaust into the crucible of culture. *Maus* is part fable, part animal Haggadah (an archetypal tale that must be continually retold and illustrated), part political allegory (remember *Animal Farm*), part spoof on the American cartoon (in 1:133, his father confuses him with Mickey Mouse!), and several parts avant garde comix. *See Under: Love* begins with nine-and-a-half-year-old Momik reliving the life of Sholem Aleichem's *Motl, the Cantor's Son*, complete with Yiddish dialogue.[118] Now a grown-up writer, Shlomo (Momik) Neuman (the "new man") luxuriates in a meandering, modernistic Hebrew prose, followed by a no less fantastical sojourn in Auschwitz, where Grandfather Anshel Wasserman speaks and writes in turn-of-the-century baroque Hebrew, which in turn gives way to the neutral, academic prose of an encyclopedia. No linguistic or stylistic register, no one generation, no one level of reality can get at the truth. No matter how resourceful and creative Art and Shlomo may be, there are gaping holes and missing documents: Vladek Spiegelman has destroyed his wife Anja's diaries, which she had kept for Artie's sake; Shlomo struggles to recover Bruno Schulz's lost masterpiece, *The Messiah*. Both Momik and Artie suffer mental breakdowns before our very eyes.

The parents "bleed history" into their children. Not directly—what can these children possibly understand?—but through the denial of love and emotional overload, through silence and cryptic signals, which the child must labor over a lifetime to decipher. If the child is an avid reader, a gifted artist, or a seasoned listener, he is able eventually to translate the pain and personal struggle into an equally complex cultural medium. Through the artistic layering, the discordant elements, the disjunction, the active reader, in turn, experiences the texture of a deeply buried past. Grossman's narrative may be the more redemptive of the two, not because he only imagined the childhood that Spiegelman lived, but because it was the experience of growing up in Israel, in the shadow of the Shoah, that bled the fear and collective neurosis into his system.[119] Be that as it may, in this period of personalized memory, the medium is very much the message. After finishing Part II of *Maus*, the next thing one wants to read is Elisabeth Kübler-Ross's ruminations on death and Melanie Klein's writings on the angst of love and guilt between parents and children; whereas for those who make it to the end of *See Under: Love*, the next thing on their list is Sholem Aleichem and Bruno Schulz.

Essential Memory: 1991-Present

The myth of suppressed memory that galvanized the Generation of 1970 and its offspring; the emotional reunions and gatherings; the desperate desire on the part of so many survivors to go public—these were exclusive domains that others could enter only at their peril. With the official opening of the United States Holocaust Memorial Museum (in April 1993) and the collapse of the Soviet empire (in 1989–1991), a significant shift occurred in the public memory of the Holocaust. Suddenly, a new territory opened up—real places on a real map, accessible to all. Any serious confrontation with the Holocaust would henceforth involve making a pilgrimage to one or more essential shrines. Whoever visited the Holocaust museum in Washington, D.C. would remember the tower of photographs that Yaffa Eliach (b. 1937; HL 294–297) assembled from her native town of Eyshishok, and anyone with the means to do so would now plan a visit to the abandoned or reinhabited homestead. The government of a united Germany would even pay all expenses and roll out the red carpet. Jewish high school seniors from across the globe began to take part in the March of the Living, carefully orchestrated so that all groups first met at the entrance to Birkenau. Failing that, one's European roots could be traced via the internet, where everyone was free to create a virtual *landsmanshaft*. A grassroots movement sprang up, its mission to translate all *yizkor* books into global English.

For those who never left the Old World, however, the memory clock, smashed or hidden away, now started ticking anew. In Eastern and Central Europe, there was no operative myth of suppression, limited to a singular group of sufferers. Under Communist rule, *all* memory of the past was suppressed. The Holocaust was no less taboo than the Great Purges; Soviet guilt for the massacre of 4,500 Polish officers at Katyn no less than Nazi guilt for the massacre of 33,774 Jews at Babi Yar in the first two days alone; not to speak of Polish guilt for Jedwabne, Romanian guilt for Iasy and Bucharest, and the mass collaboration of Ukrainians both at home and abroad. In Poland, cradle of the resistance, the Solidarity movement made the rehabilitation of the Polish-Jewish past part of its political mandate.

Once again, dates become all-important. Who could have known that Vasilii Grossman completed his epic novel, *Life and Fate,* which stunningly equated Nazism and Communism, in 1960? Because the push and pull, the carrot and stick, of Communist rule was nowhere the same, it was possible for Imre Kertész (b. 1929; HL 632–635) to publish his autobiographical novel, *Sorstalanság* (Fateless) in 1975, although his real coming out as a novelist did not occur until 1989, and an English translation would not appear until 1998—without which he would not have been awarded the Nobel Prize for Literature in 2002.

In the first postwar period, the public response to the publication of authentic (and invented) documents from the Holocaust was sometimes intense, and always immediate. But for a society that languished under totalitarian rule, the time lag could be enormous, and the impact of rediscovery—all the more powerful. Such was the case, we learn from Monika Adamczyk-Garbowska (HL 846–847), with the second of two poems that Miłosz submitted for publication back in 1944. "A Poor Christian Looks at the Ghetto" was rejected by the Jewish National Committee in Warsaw for being too pessimistic and for needlessly provoking the Polish reader. Virtually forgotten, it was rediscovered over four decades later by the Polish critic Jan Błoński. Appearing in a Catholic (that is, dissident) weekly on January 11, 1987, Błoński used the poem to open a fierce public debate on Polish-Jewish relations under the Nazi occupation. Among the many responses to Błoński's challenge was the documentary novel on the Warsaw ghetto, *Umschlagplatz* (1988), by Marek Rymkiewicz (b. 1935; HL 1063–1066), a poet, literary scholar, and dissident. The answer to the Big Lie were the small, irreducible facts.

Until the collapse of the Soviet Union, the catharsis that attended this open confrontation with the past was very much a local phenomenon. Then, sometime in the early 1990s, all public memory of the mass murder of the Jews consolidated around a single loan-word, "Holocaust." Why not choose an equivalent term from within the existing lexicon, such as Martyrdom, Destruction, Catastrophe, or even the Event? Consider the challenge of spelling "holocaust" in the Cyrillic alphabet: there is no Russian equivalent for the letter *h*; Heinrich Heine is fondly known as Geinrich Geine; yet here the *h* is rendered *kh*, which is both acceptable to the Russian ear and which echoes another Jewish loan-word, *khanukah.* More subtly, the diphthong *au*, equally impossible in Russian, is flattened into yet another *o*. Thus, while the Cataloging Policy and Support Office of the Library of Congress, in 1995, did not even list "Shoah" as a viable option in its 1995 survey, precisely because "holocaust" was already universally recognized, throughout Central and Eastern Europe, "Holocaust" was the term of choice precisely because it had no prior resonance, because it sounded utterly foreign, ineffable, untouchable, exceptional. In many an East European capital, there would eventually be a museum dedicated to the HOLLOW-COST.

Art Spiegelman had only a tape recorder and a single informant—his father, still living in Rego Park, N.Y. In contrast, child survivors and children of survivors now embarked upon a Passage to Poland armed with a video camera. The first intrepid travelers, among them Marian Marzynski and Eva Hoffman (b. 1945; HL 567–572), spoke Polish and knew what they were looking for. Marzynski wanted his pound of flesh, whereas Hoffman set out to prove that shtetl Jews were as much Polish as Jewish.[120] The next generation of young Jewish filmmakers went in search of personal identity, and what they found, in the first post-Communist decade at least, was a country in black-and-white, looking exactly like the iconic photographs of Roman Vishniac. Whether they discovered a covenantal or accursed landscape, these filmmakers returned with a marketable commodity: a 60- to 90-minute film that PBS networks were eager to air during Holocaust Remembrance Week. In this way did the personal Holocaust-and-shtetl odyssey become part of American civil religion.

From now on, all roads lead to the sacralization of the Holocaust in public memory. Spielberg, Benjamin Wilkomirski, W.G. Sebald, and Melvin Bukiet can serve as pilgrims in this progress.

The Holocaust is sacred only if non-Jews, who make up the bulk of the world's population, acknowledge it to be so.

Purely on artistic grounds, Steven Spielberg was right to choose *Schindler's Ark* (1982), by the prolific Australian novelist and playwright, Thomas Keneally (b. 1935; HL 628–631), because the story of Oskar Schindler was true, it pitted good against evil, the dialogue was great, and it had a happy end. Spielberg underscored the film's facticity by filming in black-and-white and by paying meticulous attention to historical and geographical detail. The street-by-street blockade of the Krakow ghetto is a tour-de-force of documentary realism: never again would a filmgoer confuse ghetto, labor camp, and concentration camp. At the same time, however, the perspective of Keneally's novel was rooted in the author's Catholicism, which Spielberg exploited by turning the (rather dissolute) life of Oskar Schindler into a Christian parable of sin-death-and-resurrection—ending in Jerusalem! Small wonder that *Schindler's List* tours are now a staple of the Polish tourist trade, a made-for-Hollywood pilgrimage site.

Benjamin Wilkomirski (né Bruno Dössekker, 1941; HL 1330–1334) illustrates the new essentialism of Holocaust memory because he, like Zvi Kolitz before him, gave his generation exactly the (fictional) Holocaust they wanted. Writer/readers of the 1950s, such as Sutzkever, Glatstein, and Levinas, needed to believe that there was still a People Israel who had fought side-by-side in the Warsaw ghetto and held the God of History accountable for the incalculable losses. That eternal dialogue was reason enough to go on living as a Jew. Fifty years later, with the "Holocaust experience" now understood as a species of individual psychic trauma, Wilkomirski turns every abused child into a concentration camp victim in miniature. More than that. The Swiss-born Bruno Dössekker reinvents himself as his Holocaust double, Binjamin Wilkomirski from Riga, the better to fabricate a horrific past out of whole cloth. The very fragmentariness of his "memoir" reveals how tortuous is the process of retrieving lost memories, of recovering one's lost identity. That the reissue of "Yosl Rakover Talks to God" (1999) and the first edition of Wilkomirski's *Fragments* (1995/6) share the same publishing house and translator suggests: (a) that neither publishers nor the public have as yet learned to distinguish between the literature of and on the Holocaust, and (b) that competing essential messages can coexist, so long as they come in small packages: the one about reclaiming a diminished God, the other about reclaiming a battered self.[121]

The farther the Holocaust recedes into the past, the more it becomes the function of fiction and film to discover new ways of buttressing its truth. The lost souls whom W.G. Sebald (1944–2001; HL 1132–1134) excavates in *Die Ausgewanderten* (1992; trans. as *The Emigrants* in 1996) and its sequel, *Austerlitz* (2001)—are they real? It would certainly seem so, given Sebald's strategic use of photographs, his painterly attention to the physical landscape, and his Proustian ability to render the passage of time. If nothing else, he is a much finer dissimulator than Keneally, Kolitz, or Wilkomirski. I, for one, believed every word, until something caught my attention on the last page of *Austerlitz*: the narrator, who has labored so long to retrace every step of his subject, suddenly defers to another author, the South African Jewish writer Dan Jacobson (b. 1929). Is it because a writer of Holocaust fiction must account for his sources? Or is it because a German interloper must defer to the Jews? Or pander to the Jews?[122]

Melvin Jules Bukiet (b. 1953; HL 194–198) is no panderer. He is the in-your-face promoter of the 2Gs, as he provocatively calls the children of Holocaust survivors, the Malaparte of Manhattan. In the ferocious preface to *Nothing Makes You Free*, his anthology of *Writings by Descendants of Jewish Holocaust Survivors* (2003), Bukiet establishes a draconian cut-off: any Jew born in Europe before the liberation is still a survivor; any Jewish offspring born a day later is a fellow-sufferer, privy to exclusive nightmares of entrapment. Irena Klepfisz (b. 1941; HL 670–673) is out; Eva Hoffman is in. Bukiet's generational scheme carries almost biblical sanction: the return to YHWH, who visits the sin of the parents unto the children—for who-knows-how-many generations to come. It is also a return to a Freudian god, this oedipal displacement of the survivors by their own descendants.[123] Christ, too, proffers his blessing, for although Bukiet vehemently denies the Holocaust any redemptive meaning—*Nothing Makes You Free*—the suffering of the second generation is a form of Romantic agony, the suffering that justifies the seclusion and heightens the sensibility of a writer or a poet.[124]

Grouped together from the four corners of the earth, their collective presence in Bukiet's anthology bespeaks a memory held sacred in every country and community that cherishes both its resident survivors and self-identifying members of the Second Generation. In her encyclopedia, taking a more catholic approach than Bukiet, S. Lillian Kremer's working hypothesis is that an engagement of some sort with the Holocaust is what makes a writer Jewish—or an honorary Jew. And since the "moral imperative to remember," "bearing witness," and "identity and self-definition" are an absolute good, they must each contribute to what she calls "Tikkun."[125]

Let us call it Holocaust. Whatever one's cause, doing it in the name of the Holocaust will render it sacred. Whatever is morally repugnant shall be called another Holocaust. Whatever murderous instincts one harbors—these are expressed by denying the Holocaust. The Library of Congress did well to add a new classification for Holocaust denial, D804.355, and to hire new catalogers, who can read Arabic.

Reprise and Conclusion

How should Holocaust literature be read?

The same way, to start with, that literary and cultural historians read the Great War: by looking for a unity of experience, feeling, and fate that transcends national borders; by examining how the Holocaust is refracted through the lens of a particular culture; and by taking what contemporaries thought and said in order to establish how the representation of the Holocaust in one period progressively, retroactively, or dialectically affected the representation in another. Periodization is the beginning of historical understanding.

Some (short) time after he left for the forests with the second group of Vilna partisans, Abraham Sutzkever fashioned a legend about his fellow-fighters: that they had melted down the lead plates of the Rom printers' Vilna Talmud in order to make bullets.[126] With this symbolic shorthand, Sutzkever turned history into memory, the failure of the uprising and the liquidation of the ghetto into a mandate for action. Without analogies, says this meta-narrative, without a shared past, without a spiritual baseline, these young Jews could not have mobilized against the enemy. Many other authentic wartime documents, as we have seen, bear out this critical insight, but none so memorably as Sutzkever's mini-epic. So completely had his world been destroyed, however, that within a year or two, the poem was being understood literally, as Sutzkever himself came to embody the one rescuable piece of the past: the new Jew, the partisan-poet.

It is not enough, therefore, to know when something was written—and rewritten. The next question to answer is how the poet has changed, and the readership as well. During the war, the poems of Sutzkever that shaped public memory, that were most prized, that earned him (and his wife, Freydke) an airlift to freedom, were rhymed and metered, neoclassical epic verse that disassembled the unfolding horror into its recognizable, archetypal parts. Whether or not these particular poems "speak" to us in the present, whether or not they lend themselves to translation, they are our point of departure when reconstructing the literary past. To understand why Sutzkever labored over his most ambitious epic poem, *Secret City*, for three years (1945–1947) in three cities (Moscow, Lodz, Paris), we begin in the Soviet Union, where his image as a partisan-poet was created, and with the precarious situation of Jews and Jewish culture in the postwar period, which together can explain why it was that the great Soviet-Yiddish writer, Der Nister (Pinkhes Kahanovitsh, 1884–1950), burst into tears when Sutzkever read him the poem's opening cantos, in 1946.[127] Much closer to contemporary tastes are Sutzkever's "Epitaphs" (written in the Vilna ghetto, Moscow, and Lodz, between 1943 and 1946), in which Sutzkever "projects with virtuoso variance the voices of twenty-seven Nazi victims" (HL 1237), one of which was almost chosen to greet all visitors to the National Holocaust Museum in Washington (see below).

Within postwar Yiddish culture as a whole, the shock waves were seismic, no matter how far away one lived from the epicenter. The lyric voice of women was subsumed into a genderless voice of national lamentation.[128] Most startling was the wholesale self-censorship of the past. It is one thing when Soviet-Yiddish writers were compelled to eliminate all traces of petty-bourgeois nationalism in the 1930s if they wished to see their work (re)republished. It is quite another when, in the 1940s and 1950s, the leading American Yiddish modernists disavowed their modernism in light of the Holocaust.[129] In a letter to Leyb Feinberg of February 4, 1946, Anna Margolin (1887–1952) recanted the naughty, self-deprecating last line of her famously provocative poem, "I Was Once a Young Man," "a line which I could not lift my hand to write in the present era of our great catastrophe."[130] In the Yiddish world, the war was not over—and its tremors were felt not only forward but also backwards in time.

Each period of public memory has its own inner logic. Flashing forward, let us compare two personae born out of the Holocaust: Ka-Tzetnik and Benjamin Wilkomirski. Wilkomirski's fragmented "memoir," credible and compelling as it now seems when compared to Ka-Tzetnik's overwrought novels, is significant for what it tells us about the state of mind of people some 50 years after the liberation of the camps.

The Holocaust was not "hardly talked about for the first twenty years or so after World War II," as Peter Novick and many others would have us believe. In fact, in each period, the Holocaust was discovered anew, for different reasons, by a different public. The public memory of the Holocaust proceeded in fits and starts, differently in Communist-bloc countries from those of the free world, differently for the speakers of one language from the speakers of another. The first 20 years—indeed, the first ten—were probably the most protean: in the authentic wartime writings that were unearthed; in the sheer quantity of eyewitness testimonies that were recorded; in the quality of the writing; in the diversity of styles, genres, and languages. I say "probably," because work on this period has barely begun.

Can the Holocaust be "emplotted," the historians are anxious to know.[131] "Displaced Memory" is itself a literary trope, a synoptic signpost for a specific phase, as we have seen, in the public memory of the Holocaust, a composite of writer-survivors, each in search of a literal and literary language, coupled with the external portrayal of the survivor—Sol Nazerman, Adam Stein, Artur Sammler, and Rosa Lublin—who arouses so little sympathy in the reader.[132] Read from a distance and measured solely against each other, these diverse writings define a unity of experience, feeling, and fate that transcends national borders.

There follows the "emplotment" of a generational consciousness, what I have called Personalized Memory. The literary evidence confirms what the student of sociology already knows: the highest concentration of Holocaust survivors lived in the two great postwar Jewish communities—Israel and the United States—two countries that emerged victorious from the Second World War, where self-empowerment, the master narrative of military victory, the desire to start anew, did not square with Jewish victimhood. Only three and four decades later, after terrible wars had been fought and terrible losses incurred, did the former victims and former victors form a new alliance. These people from the ghettos and camps knew how to mourn. Maybe they also knew how to "work through" the collective trauma. And if not they, then surely their children, those who grew up to be therapists and writers, at any rate. So that when David Grossman and Art Spiegelman burst onto the scene, in 1986, they spoke not only for their generation. They modeled not only a Holocaust narrative freed from generic constraints. They bespoke a convergence that had occurred in both survivor communities: the solitary was rendered communal; the communal—solitary.

There was, however, another survivor community not yet spoken for: the Jews of the Soviet Union, the so-called Jews of Silence (or did Wiesel *really* mean the silent Jews of the West?). The great protest poem by Yevgenii Yevtushenko (b. 1933; HL 1348–1351), "Babi Yar" (1961), stands alone because, like its subject, all memory of the Soviet past lay buried in an unmarked mass grave. Real memory work in the Soviet Union was conducted in private; how and when we are only now discovering.[133] We do know that Yiddish writers used all possible means to get the word out, exploiting Aesopian language, the relative freedom of Poland, the largesse of fellow travelers abroad, to produce a literature at once cryptic and communal.[134] In the light of Soviet realities, we may have to modify our working definition of Holocaust literature as comprising "all forms of writing, . . . which have shaped the public *and private* memory of the Holocaust and been shaped by them."

The historian Saul Friedländer notes that despite the "huge increases in references to the Holocaust from the late sixties onward, . . . no enduring, compelling narrative of mythical dimensions seems to have emerged" anywhere in the Jewish world.[135] But as this review of the literary-historical record has just demonstrated, the huge increases in references to the Holocaust from the late 1960s onward constitute their own mythic metanarrative, a story of burial and retrieval, displacement and replacement, denial and affirmation, which nation after nation, generation after generation have discovered anew. And this jagged, uneven course, with its multiple gaps in cultural transmission, its constant push-and-pull between remembering and forgetting, its power to scandalize unabated, is what is most enduring, compelling, and mythic about the "Holocaust, Jewish" in public memory.

Instances of scandalous memory are a way of measuring these gaps, when an uncensored piece of the Holocaust narrative violates the horizon of expectations of a specific public. I have already mentioned the controversy surrounding Perle's "The Destruction of Warsaw," written in 1942 and published in 1951. But there are other examples. In 1987, Gerer hasidim in Brooklyn bought up and burned copies of the English translation of Shimon Huberband's *Kiddush Hashem: Jewish Religious and Cultural Life in Poland during the Holocaust* because Huberband, acting on Ringelblum's instructions, had documented the moral depravity of young Gerer hasidim in the Warsaw ghetto. So far as I know, the Hebrew publication of *Kidush hashem* (in 1969) passed without protest, but revealing "to the goyim" the dark side of Orthodox behavior in wartime was anathema.[136]

Similarly, Antek Zuckerman, guardian of the flame and heroic ghetto fighter, did not escape posthumous censure from two distinct generations of Israeli readers. Although the most stringent measures were taken to vouchsafe the accuracy and honesty of his memoirs, including the stipulation that they be published only after he died, there were Israeli reviewers of the older generation who reacted with outrage at his description of Emanuel Ringelblum as . . . a boring lecturer. Yet in a novel by Roni Givati (b. 1940) *Between Silences* (1987), the narrator, engaged in a search for her own identity, is scandalized by Zuckerman's inability to confront the repressed fears and feelings that she prizes most dearly.[137] So Zuckerman stands convicted on both counts: for not protecting the honor of the dead, and for revealing too little of his own inner struggle. Understanding why, when, and where these scandals erupt does more than help us track the jagged evolution of public memory of the Holocaust, however. For whenever the threshold falls too low, it is the task of the artist to provoke scandal. Inspired by Grossman's *See Under: Love*, other native-born Israeli writers proclaimed their artistic freedom by finding new stories to tell and new ways to tell them: the story of a place called Kiryat Hayim, for example, just outside of Haifa, where "every" adult is a survivor of the Holocaust, and learning its secrets becomes a built-in rite of passage; where ordinary Jews become extraordinary storytellers by virtue of their wartime experience. This is what happens in *Our Holocaust* (2000), a first novel by Amir Gutfreund (b. 1963).[138] Should there, moreover, prove to be works of Holocaust literature that provoke scandal *in perpetuity*, such works may qualify as classics.

Scandalous memory signals its sacred alternative. Despite well-meaning attempts to ascribe sanctity to the literature of the Holocaust—by comparing it to midrash, by seeking parallels between the Hebrew Bible and the Holocaust as translation phenomena—Holocaust literature is a resolutely secular enterprise, never more so than when it waxes liturgical.[139] Yosl Rakover gives the game away not because he fails to identify his bunker, not because so late in the uprising no one waged battle against German tanks with a self-made "bottle of gasoline," but because no Gerer hasid in Poland ever wrote the way he did. To decipher the weekly sermons that Rabbi Kalonymus Kalman Shapira, an intellectual (as opposed to political) leader of Polish hasidism, delivered in the Warsaw ghetto on the meaning of suffering, faith, and evil requires fluency in Scripture, Talmud, the liturgy, and the Zohar.[140] It does not translate into a bestseller. The real-life Yosl Rakovers of Poland—young men, some of them with rabbinic ordination, all deeply conversant with the traditional forms of Jewish self-expression—did in fact leave "messages in a bottle" designed to be read by the outside world. Yekhiel Feiner, Zalman Gradowski, Shimon Huberband, Leyb Rochman, and Mordecai Strigler all adopted a secular vocabulary and Western literary forms to do so.

After the war, outreach was the last thing that ultra-Orthodox Jews were concerned about. Just listen to Hersh Rasseyner! We can eavesdrop on his vehement "quarrel" with Chaim Vilner because the surviving secular Yiddish community needed, above all, to renew the inner Yiddish dialogue of "two Jews talking."[141] Grade's dramatization of ideas is so eminently readable, in turn, because Hersh and Chaim are picking up where Alyosha Karamazov and the Grand Inquisitor left off. Meanwhile, within the depleted ranks of ultra-Orthodoxy itself, the work of "communal memory" was carried out in media that excluded the outside world and precluded eavesdropping. Since research in this area has barely begun, we must wait and see if and how this changes the master narrative of public memory of the Holocaust. But we do know this: when, in 1982, Yaffa Eliach published *Hasidic Tales of the Holocaust*, carefully edited, stylized, and rehistoricized personal narratives from the hasidic community of Brooklyn, she effectively invited ultra-Orthodoxy back into the mainstream at the very moment when Holocaust memory worldwide was becoming personalized. There followed a flood of fake Holocaust diaries (published in Lakewood, N.J.) and other enhanced memoirs of truly miraculous survival.

Within ultra-Orthodoxy, thriving today as never before, messianism looms much larger than catastrophe. By contrast, the Holocaust is ever-present in two cultures that were mortally wounded by the war: Polish Jewish and secular Yiddish culture. Even if Ida Fink (b. 1921; HL 348–356) were not such a brilliant writer, even if she were not a woman, she would stand as a symbol of what was lost: the dream of a Polish-Jewish symbiosis, the last and most fervent hope of Emanuel Ringelblum and of so many others. It is thanks to Ida Fink, Henryk Grynberg, and the recovery—virtually, or so it seems, on a weekly basis—of lost Jewish identities among native Poles, that a distant echo of this cultural dialogue can still be heard.[142] One measure of Poland's independence is the place that writings from and on the Holocaust occupy therein. As I write these words, Aharon Appelfeld's novels are first appearing in Polish translation. How Jewish ghosts will reinhabit the New Europe, of which Poland is now a part, will certainly affect the place of the Holocaust in public memory.

But before Polish, the first language that a student of Holocaust literature must learn is—Yiddish. In Yiddish alone, the Holocaust has never lost its centrality. In Yiddish alone there exists an unbroken, cumulative, variegated, internally coherent, and transnational body of writing on the Holocaust. In Yiddish alone can the full catastrophic impact of the Holocaust be gauged, far and beyond the borders of Europe, more lasting by far than the traumas of individual survivors and their children. Whatever essentialist claims are currently in vogue, Yiddish is their corrective.

Thus far, almost nothing has been said about the autonomy of the writer. In the zeal to classify and periodize, to improve upon the Library of Congress, literary works of genius and the testimony of victims "rendered . . . extraordinary against their will"[143] have all been lumped together. But there are major distinctions to be drawn: between those who became writers by virtue of their wartime experience, those who had written previously, but who wrote differently after the war, and those whose approach to art, reality, and history determined their response to Hitler. Writers in the first two categories are strongly favored by Holocaust professionals and their disciples, intent as they are to map the rupture in human values after Auschwitz, to do for the Holocaust what literary and cultural historians have done so ably for the Great War. They lock onto the generation that speaks for the rupture, and hearken unto its voice. In the forefront of modern Hebrew and Yiddish literature, however, stand two poets who could never be anything but poets, who created their own space and established their own precedent. Uri Zvi Greenberg was shaped as a writer and political activist by the apocalyptic violence of the First World War. His perspective on the cataclysm of 1939–1945 was therefore transgenerational, global, metahistoric, yet it remained grounded in minute observation, introspection, empathy, existential terror. He never flinched from the face of evil. However difficult, indeed scandalous, his writing now appears, it endowed the murder of Europe's Jews with cosmic and, ultimately, redemptive significance.

Sutzkever's response to the rupture of the Holocaust was no less defiant than

Greenberg's. As founder and editor of *Di goldene keyt*, the gold standard of Yiddish letters for more than 40 years, he became one of the main purveyors of Holocaust memory. As one who, immediately after the liberation of Vilna by the Red Army in 1944, personally oversaw the retrieval of hidden materials from the ruins of the ghetto, Sutzkever exercised moral ownership.[144] One such document was a monograph by Naftoli Vaynig (1897–1944) on the neo-Romantic poet Leyb Naydus (1890–1918). A model of Yiddish academic prose, it was awarded a literary prize in the ghetto, in 1943. There were several anniversaries that would have merited its postwar publication: the liquidation of the Vilna ghetto, for one; the anniversary of Vaynig's death for another. Instead, Sutzkever held onto this precious manuscript for more than 50 years, finally publishing it on the 100th anniversary of Naydus' birth.[145] Sutzkever refused to abdicate his lifelong role as the champion of great poets. He refused to make the destruction the crucible of his culture. If Naftoli Vaynig, after spending two years in hiding, could return to the ghetto (where he lived in abject poverty, even by ghetto standards) in order to labor over the work of a dead poet whose decadent themes, luxurious rhymes, and formal complexity were at the farthest possible remove from the realities of 1943, then great art would triumph over death, and the chain of Jewish creativity would not yet have been broken.

Elie Weisel, who became a writer by virtue of his wartime experience, defined the survivor of Hitler's Holocaust as "a messenger and guardian of secrets entrusted by the dead." For Abraham Sutzkever, only the Muse was the guardian of secrets, and as always, she spoke in meter and rhyme. Now, after Hitler, she also spoke for the dead, 27 of whose voices the poet transcribed in his "Epitaphs." Here is one of them:[146]

> Survivors: your legacy of gladness should be tentative,
> Some of us still flicker in the straits of death.
> Don't forget to keep our dying in your breath.
> Don't forget, your martyrdom now will be to live.

This poem was translated in 1990 by the American Jewish poet C. K. Williams, and was to have been inscribed at the entrance to the United States Holocaust Memorial Museum in Washington. Two scriptural passages were chosen instead.

How should Holocaust literature be read?

In its original languages. In all genres. From the beginning.

Notes

1. Lenore Bell, personal communication (26 April 2004).

2. Lenore Bell, "LC Holocaust Headings Survey: Analysis of Results" (12 June 1996). I would like to thank Ms. Bell, the head of the Hebraica team in the Regional and Cooperative Cataloguing Division at the Library of Congress, for her assistance.

3. On the manner in which Spiegelman "pushes generic boundaries," see Sara R. Horowitz, "Auto/Biography and Fiction after Auschwitz: Probing the Boundaries of Second-

Generation Aesthetics," in *Breaking Crystal: Writing and Memory after Auschwitz,"* ed. Efraim Sicher (Urbana: 1998), 276–282.

4. Robert F. Weir, *Death in Literature* (New York: 1980), 211–212.

5. Paul Fussel, *The Great War in Modern Memory* (New York: 1975).

6. Robert Wohl, *The Generation of 1914* (Cambridge, Mass.: 1979), 3.

7. Curzio Malaparte, *L'Europe vivente*, ed. Enriquo Falqui (Florence: 1961), 152; *La Conquista dello Stato* (15 March 1928), quoted in Wohl, *The Generation of 1914*, 179.

8. Samuel Hynes, *The Soldiers' Tale: Bearing Witness to Modern War* (Harmondsworth: 1997), xii–xiii.

9. Efraim Sicher, " 'The Jewish Cossack': Isaac Babel in the First Red Cavalry," in *Studies in Contemporary Jewry*, vol. 4, *The Jews and the European Crisis 1914–1921*, ed. Jonathan Frankel (New York: 1988), 113–134; David G. Roskies, *Against the Apocalypse: Responses to Catastrophe in Modern Jewish Culture* (Cambridge, Mass.: 1984), chs. 3–6; Simon Markish, "The Example of Isaac Babel," in *What Is Jewish Literature?*, ed. Hana Wirth-Nesher (Philadelphia: 1994), 207–211; Jillian Davidson, "A 'Secular Catastrophe' in Eastern Europe: The Great War and the Reconstruction of Modern Jewish Memory" (Ph.D. diss., Jewish Theological Seminary, 2004).

10. Bernard Bergonzi, *Heroes' Twilight: A Story of the Literature of the Great War* (London: 1980); Modris Eksteins, *Rites of Spring: The Great War and the Birth of the Modern Age* (Boston: 1989); George Mosse, *Fallen Soldiers: Reshaping the Memory of the World Wars* (New York: 1990); Jay M. Winter, *Sites of Memory, Sites of Mourning: The Great War in European Cultural History* (Cambridge: 1995).

11. Wohl, *The Generation of 1914*, 3.

12. James Joll, "No Man's Land," *The New York Review of Books* (27 April 1989), 54.

13. Following Joll's wording, ibid., 53.

14. Research on this important subject has hardly begun. See Ayelet Kuper Margalioth, "Yiddish Periodicals Published by Displaced Persons, 1946–1949" (Ph.D. thesis, Magdalen College, Oxford, 1997); Gershon Greenberg (ed.), *Sheerit hapelatah vehashoah: reshimat maamarim usefarim 'al hashkafah be'inyanei haemunah hayehudit leaḥar shoat yehudei eiropah (1944–1949)* (Ramat Gan: 1994); Zachary M. Baker (ed.), *Jewish Displaced Persons Periodicals From the Collections of the YIVO Institute* (Bethesda: 1990).

15. Abraham Sutzkever, "Teacher Mira" (1943), in *Selected Poetry and Prose*, trans. from the Yiddish by Barbara Harshav and Benjamin Harshav (Berkeley: 1990), 160–162; Binem Heller, "In varshever geto iz khoydesh nisn," in his *In varshever geto iz khoydesh nisn* (Tel Aviv: 1973), 31–33.

16. For the minority view, see Hanna Yablonka, "The Formation of Holocaust Consciousness in the State of Israel: The Early Days," in Sicher, *Breaking Crystal*, ch. 3; Dalia Ofer, "The Strength of Remembrance: Commemorating the Holocaust during the First Decade of Israel," *Jewish Social Studies*, ns 6 (2000), 24–55; Boaz Cohen, "Holocaust Heroics: Ghetto Fighters and Partisans in Israeli Society and Historiography," *Journal of Political and Military Sociology* 31 (2003), 197–213. For the majority view, see Tom Segev, *The Seventh Million: The Israelis and the Holocaust* (New York: 2000 [1991]); Anita Shapira, "Hashoah: zikaron perati vezikaron ẓiburi," in her *Yehudim ḥadashim, yehudim yeshanim* (Tel Aviv: 1997), 86–103, and various literary works surveyed in this essay.

17. Anne Frank, *The Diary of a Young Girl: The Definitive Edition*, ed. Otto H. Frank and Mirjam Pressler, trans. Susan Massolty (New York: 1995); David S. Wyman, "France," in *The World Reacts to the Holocaust*, ed. David S. Wyman (Baltimore: 1996), 20.

18. Ruth R. Wisse, *The Modern Jewish Canon: A Journey Through Language and Culture* (New York: 2000), 220.

19. Much has been written on this subject. See, for example, Annette Insdorf, *Indelible Shadows: Film and the Holocaust* (New York: 1983), ch. 7; and more recently, Esther Fuchs, "Gender and Representation: Love Stories in Holocaust Films," in *The Representation of the Holocaust in Literature and Film*, ed. Marc Lee Raphael (Williamsburg, Va.: 2003), 29–45.

20. See Risa Domb (ed.), *New Women's Writing from Israel* (Essex: 1996); Dalia Ofer and Lenore J. Weitzman (eds.), *Women in the Holocaust* (New Haven: 1998); Esther Fuchs (ed.), *Women and the Holocaust: Narrative and Representation* (New York: 1999). For a lucid discussion of gender inversion as a measure of atrocity, see Sara R. Horowitz, "Gender, Genocide, and Jewish Memory," *Prooftexts* 20 (2000), 158–190. In the ghettos, Horowitz demonstrates, gender inversion was sometimes seen as a sign of hope.

21. See Ofer, "The Strength of Remembrance," 26, 31–34. The controversy became even more complicated when the Likud party came to power in 1977 and proposed that the Ninth of Av, when Jews mourn the destruction of both Temples, be merged with Holocaust Remembrance Day.

22. Tadeusz Borowski, *This Way for the Gas, Ladies and Gentlemen* (1945–1948), trans. Barbara Vedder, with an introduction by Jan Kott (Harmondsworth: 1976), 35.

23. The connection between trench warfare and the concentrationary universe is made, implicitly, by Paul Fussell, in his authoritative *Norton Book of Modern War* (1991), where we find a long and detailed excerpt from Rudolf Höss' memoir, *Commandant of Auschwitz* (1951), followed by a brief meditation on the death camps by the French writer Marguerite Duras (1985). Since the Jews, ingathered at Auschwitz, were voiceless victims, it suffices to have a Nazi Commandant and a French novelist speak on their behalf.

24. See Lawrence L. Langer, "Auschwitz: The Death of Choice," in his *Versions of Survival: The Holocaust and the Human Spirit* (Albany: 1982), 67–129; idem, *Admitting the Holocaust: Collected Essays* (New York:1995), index, s.v. "Choice."

25. See, esp., Lawrence L. Langer, *Holocaust Testimonies: The Ruins of Memory* (New Haven: 1991).

26. S. Lillian Kremer (ed.), *Holocaust Literature: An Encyclopedia of Writers and their Work*, 2 vols. (New York: 2003). For an overview of recent encyclopedias of the Holocaust, see Naomi B. Sokoloff, "The Holocaust and the Encyclopedic Imagination—See Under: Grossman," in Raphael, *The Representation of the Holocaust in Literature and Film*, 139–143.

27. This attempt at periodization was inspired by the work of historian Robert G. Moeller at the University of California, Irvine, who is tracking the place of the Holocaust in German public memory. For a different periodization, see Saul Friedländer, "Afterword: The *Shoah* between Memory and History," in Sicher, *Breaking Crystal*, 345–357. Less polemical and more focused is Friedländer's now-classic essay, "Historical Writing and the Memory of the Holocaust," in *Writing and the Holocaust*, ed. Berel Lang (New York: 1988), ch. 5.

28. Mirjam Pressler, foreword to *The Diary of a Young Girl: The Definitive Edition*, v.

29. See Marie Syrkin, "Diaries," in *Encountering the Holocaust: An Interdisciplinary Survey*, ed. Byron L. Sherwin and Susan G. Ament (Chicago: 1979), 226–243.

30. Sara Horowitz, "Voices from the Killing Ground," in *Holocaust Remembrance: The Shapes of Memory*, ed. Geoffrey H. Hartman (Oxford: 1994), 50.

31. The standard reference works are Israel Kaplan, *Dos folksmoyl in natsi-klem: reydenishn in geto un katset*, 2nd rev. ed. (Tel Aviv: 1982), and more generally, Nachman Blumental, *Verter un vertlekh fun der khurbn-tkufe* (Tel Aviv: 1981).

32. Shmuel Lehman, "Ganovim un gneyve: rednsartn, fragn, gramen, anekdotn, un mayses," in *Bay undz yidn: zamlbukh far folklor un filologye* (Warsaw: 1923), 45–91; Roskies, *Against the Apocalypse*, 164–170.

33. *Archiwum Ringelbluma: Kospiracyjne Archiwum Getta Warszawy*, vol. 1: *Listy o Zagladzie*, ed. Ruta Sakowska (Warsaw: 1997), passim.

34. W.H. Iwan, "Vegn di psevdonimen fun di mitarbeter funem untererdishn geto-arkhiv (Ringelblum-arkhiv)," *Bleter far geshikhte* 4, no. 3 (1951), 87–88. An indispensable source for the deciphering of anonymous and pseudonymous works from the Warsaw ghetto is *'Itonut-hamaḥteret begeto varshah, 1939–1944*, ed. Joseph Kermish, 6 vols. (Jerusalem: 1979–1997).

35. Sh. [Shaynkinder], "Af di gasn," in *Tsvishn lebn un toyt,* ed. Leyb Olicky (Warsaw:

1955), 97–99; poorly trans. in *To Live with Honor and Die with Honor: Selected Documents from the Warsaw Ghetto Underground Archives,* ed. Joseph Kermish (Jerusalem: 1986), 677–679. For an analysis, see David G. Roskies, "Bialik in the Ghettos," *Prooftexts* 25 (2005), 82–99.

36. Lucy S. Dawidowicz, *The War Against the Jews 1933–1945* (New York: 1975), ch. 11.

37. On the provenance of Spiegel's "Makh tsu di eygelekh" see Gila Flam, *Singing for Survival: Songs of the Lodz Ghetto, 1940–45* (Urbana: 1992), 148.

38. See Herman Kruk, *The Last Days of the Jerusalem of Lithuania: Chronicles from the Vilna Ghetto and the Camps, 1939–1944,* trans. Barbara Harshav (New York: 2002); David G. Roskies, "Tsum moment: Dr. Tsemakh Feldshteyns editoryaln in vilner geto, 1942–1943," *YIVO-bleter,* ns 3 (1997), 114–205.

39. See Roskies, *Against the Apocalypse,* 199–201; Wisse, *The Modern Jewish Canon,* 201–205. The controversy that erupted upon the publication of this diary is discussed later in this essay.

40. Yitzhak Katzenelson, *Yidishe geto-ksovim varshe 1940–1943,* ed. Yechiel Szeintuch (Tel Aviv: 1984); Shlomo Even-Shoshan (ed.), *Ketavim aḥaronim begeto varsha uvemaḥane vitel* (Tel Aviv: 1988). The entry on Katzenelson in HL, by Ziva Shavitsky, is woefully inadequate.

41. Abraham Lewin, *A Cup of Tears: A Diary of the Warsaw Ghetto,* ed. Antony Polonsky, trans. from Yiddish and Hebrew by Christopher Hutton (Oxford: 1988).

42. Emanuel Ringelblum, *Polish-Jewish Relations during the Second World War,* ed. Joseph Kermish and Shmuel Krakowski, trans. from the Polish by Dafna Allon, Danuta Dabrowska, and Dana Keren (New York: 1976). For a riveting account of Ringelblum's last days, see the intellectual biography of Ringelblum cum history of Oyneg Shabes that Samuel Kassow is soon to publish with Indiana University Press. I wish to thank Professor Kassow for his critical reading of my essay.

43. Horowitz, "Voices from the Killing Ground," 45.

44. Peretz Opoczynski, *Gezamlte verk,* ed. Sh. Tenenboym, with a biography of the author by Rina Oper-Opoczynski (New York: 1951).

45. Peretz Opoczynski, *Reportazhn fun varshever geto,* ed. Ber Mark (Warsaw: 1954). A fuller, uncensored edition exists in Hebrew only: *Reshimot,* ed. Zvi Szner, trans. Avraham Yeivin (Israel, n.p.: 1970). For the few available English translations, see "The Letter Carrier," trans. E. Chase, in *Anthology of Holocaust Literature,* ed. Jacob Glatstein, Israel Knox, and Samuel Margoshes (Philadelphia: 1969), 57–70; "Smuggling in the Warsaw Ghetto, 1941," in *A Holocaust Reader,* ed. Lucy Dawidowicz (New York: 1976), 197–207, and "House No. 21," trans. Robert Wolf, in *The Literature of Destruction: Jewish Responses to Catastrophe,* ed. David G. Roskies (Philadelphia: 1989), sec. 73. David Suchoff is currently preparing a scholarly edition of the ghetto reportage of Opoczynski and Zelkowicz, to be published by the New Yiddish Library.

46. Lucjan Dobroszycki (ed.), *The Chronicle of the Lodz Ghetto* (New Haven: 1984). Zelkowicz's reportage (in English) is found in Alan Adelson and Robert Lapides (eds.), *Lodz Ghetto: Inside a Community under Siege* (New York: 1989), and Jozef Zelkowicz, *In Those Terrible Days,* ed. Michal Unger, trans. (from the Hebrew!) by Naftali Greenwood (Jerusalem: 2002).

47. Hanan Hever, *Sifrut shenikhtevet mikan: kiẕur hasifrut hayisreelit* (Tel Aviv: 1999), 25. For our purposes, it is important to note that Hever is describing the famous reportage of Israel's War of Independence.

48. Rachel Auerbach, *Varshever tsavoes: bagegenishn, aktivitetn, goyroles 1933–1943* (Tel Aviv: 1974), 174–175.

49. See Ruth R. Wisse, "Language as Fate: Reflections on Jewish Literature in America," *Studies in Contemporary Jewry,* vol. 12, *Literary Strategies: Jewish Texts and Contexts,* ed. Ezra Mendelsohn (New York: 1996), 129–147.

50. Albert H. Friedlander, *Leo Baeck: Teacher of Theresienstadt* (New York: 1968), 3, 215–219.

51. See Roskies, *Against the Apocalypse*, 232–240.

52. The story, translated by Elinor Robinson, appears in Roskies (ed.), *The Literature of Destruction*, sec. 74.

53. See *Scroll of Agony: The Warsaw Diary of Chaim A. Kaplan*, trans. from Hebrew by Abraham I. Katsh, 2nd rev. ed. (New York: 1981), which supersedes Katsh's edition of 1965, but unfortunately excludes Kaplan's prewar diary, begun in 1933 and as yet unpublished; also see Shimon Huberband, *Kiddush Hashem: Jewish Religious Life in Poland during the Holocaust*, trans. from the Yiddish by David E. Fishman (New York: 1987).

54. Yehudo Feld, *In di tsaytn fun homen dem tsveytn*, ed. Leyb Olicky (Warsaw : 1954).

55. See *'Itonut hamaḥteret begeto varshah*, 1:44–52. The Warsaw ghetto was sealed off on November 15, 1940.

56. Emanuel Ringelblum, "Oyneg Shabes," trans. Elinor Robinson, in Roskies (ed.), *The Literature of Destruction*, 391.

57. Ber Mark (ed.), *Megiles oyshvits* (Tel Aviv: 1977); *The Scrolls of Auschwitz*, trans. from the Hebrew by Sharon Neemani (Tel Aviv: 1985). Mark smuggled the precious microfilms to Israel, where they were published posthumously. With this and similar acts, he sought to expiate his complicity with the Polish Communist regime. See Khone Shmeruk's impassioned "Letter to the Editor" in *Di goldene keyt* 140 (1995), 214–216. Another rescued manuscript by Gradowski is *In harts fun genem: a dokument fun oyshvitser zonder-komando, 1944*, which made its way to Israel, where it appeared in a tiny private edition put out by Chaim Wolnerman, with a preface by David Sfard and a photograph of the author, as per Gradowski's last wish (Jerusalem: ca. 1977). See Nathan Cohen, "Diaries of the *Sonderkommando*," in *Anatomy of the Auschwitz Death Camp*, ed. Yisrael Gutman and Michael Berenbaum (Washington, D.C.: 1994), ch. 24.

58. Wisse, *The Modern Jewish Canon*, 197.

59. Abraham Sutzkever, "Mayn eydes-zogn farn nirnberger tribunal: togbukh-notitsn" (1966), in *Baym leyenen penimer: dertseylungen, dermonungen, eseyen* (Jerusalem: 1993), 161–164.

60. See Joshua Rubenstein and Vladimir P. Naumov, *Stalin's Secret Pogrom: The Postwar Inquisition of the Jewish Anti-Fascist Committee* (New Haven: 2001).

61. Annette Wieviorka, "On Testimony," in Hartman (ed.), *Holocaust Remembrance*, 26.

62. Robert S.C. Gordon, "Primo Levi's *If This Is a Man* and Responses to the *Lager* in Italy 1945–47," *Judaism* (Winter 1999), 51.

63. Ibid. For rich documentation, see the relevant entries in Wyman (ed.), *The World Reacts to the Holocaust*.

64. Annette Wieviorka, "Jewish Identity in the First Accounts by Extermination Camp Survivors from France," in *Yale French Studies*, vol. 85, *Discourses of Jewish Identity in Twentieth-Century France*, ed. Alan Astro (New Haven: 1994), 147, 143.

65. See Gordon, "Primo Levi's *If This Is a Man*," 52, for the Italian titles.

66. Ibid., 52, 55. On the plain style, see Naomi Diamant, "Writing the Holocaust: Canons and Contexts," *Prooftexts* 11 (1991), 105.

67. Curzio Malaparte, *Kaputt*, trans. from the Italian by David Moore (New York: 1946). The quotation is from William Barrett, "To Save Their Own" (a review of Malaparte's subsequent work, *The Skin*), *New York Times* (21 Sept. 1952). *Kaputt* was reissued in 1966 in a mass-market paperback edition with a provocative cover; that is, as a mainstream work of war fiction.

68. Leyb Rochman, *Un in dayn blut zolstu lebn* (Paris: 1949); pub. in English as *The Pit and the Trap: A Chronicle of Survival*, trans. Moshe Kohn and Sheila Friedling (New York: 1983); Mordecai Strigler's *Maydanek* (with a preface by H. Leivick), together with *In di fabrikn fun toyt*, Verk *"tse"* (2 vols.), and *Goyroles*, comprise his *Oysgebrente likht* (Buenos Aires: 1947–1950). *Maydanek* appeared in Hebrew as *Nerot shekavu* (Tel Aviv: 1948), in the midst of Israel's War of Independence.

69. *Seyfer minsk-mazovyetsk*, ed. Efraim Shedletzky [Rochman's brother-in-law; Rochman figures in the four-person editorial board] (Jerusalem: 1977). For the same synergy, see *Kolbuszowa Memorial Book*, ed. I.M. Biderman (New York: 1971), in which Bertha

Ferderber-Salz (1903–1997; HL 338–339) served on the eight-member memorial book committee.

70. Fussell, *The Great War in Modern Memory*, 104, 310.

71. See review of *Un in dayn blut zolstu lebn* by Yitskhok Varshavski [I.B. Singer], *Forverts* (9 Oct. 1949); see also Aharon Appelfeld, introduction to *The Pit and the Trap*. To date, there is no detailed comparison between Rochman's novel and the original diary that he kept while in hiding (housed in the Yad Vashem Archives).

72. Meyer Levin, *In Search: An Autobiography* (New York: 1950), 241. My thanks to Leah Strigler for finding me this source. Levin, responsible for the English translation of *The Diary of Anne Frank*, a man "obsessed" with the Holocaust, is inexplicably absent from HL.

73. Mordecai Strigler, "Araynfir tsum bukh," "Nokhvort fun mekhaber tsum araynfir," "A shmues fun mekhaber mit eyner fun zayne hoypt-heldins," in idem, *In di fabrikn fun toyt*, 7–67. This last, "A Conversation of the Author with One of His Main Heroines," is part apologia, part confession, part meditation. It provides a rare portrait of the author's moral, sexual, and religious turmoil while living and writing in Paris.

74. Dan Miron, "Bein sefer le'efer," *Alpayim* 10 (1994), 196–224; Omer Bartov, "Kitsch and Sadism in Ka-Tzetnik's Other Planet: Israeli Youth Imagining the Holocaust," *Jewish Social Studies*, ns 3 (1997), 42–76. Ziva Shavitsky's entry on Ka-Tzetnik in HL is 20 years out of date and is replete with errors.

75. See Yehiel Szeintuch, "K. Tzetnik: mavo leheker yezirato bashiv'im hashanim ha-aharonot," *Dapim leheker hashoah* 14 (1997), 109–148. See, esp., n. 14, where Szeintuch cites the original preface to *Salamandra*, which Ka-Tzetnik later omitted. Szeintuch is soon to publish a critical edition of *Salamandra* in its Yiddish original.

76. See Ofer, "The Strength of Remembrance," esp. 41–42; Boaz Cohen, "Holocaust Heroics." No comparable studies have as yet been done on the Yiddish press, although comprehensive, multivolume bibliographies were produced by Yad Vashem and YIVO. On the tragic fate of Michal Weichert (1890–1967), director of the Jewish self-help network in occupied Europe, see Dov Sadan, "A tragish dilema," preface to vol. 4 of Weichert's *Zikhroynes* (Tel Aviv: 1970).

77. See Diane K. Roskies, *Teaching the Holocaust to Children: A Review and Bibliography* (New York: 1975), 33; Yael Darr, "Hama'avar mi'sipur shel yishuv' le'sipur shel medinah' basifrut hayeladim ha'ivrit, 1939–1948" (Ph.D. thesis, Tel Aviv University, 2002).

78. See James E. Young, "Holocaust Documentary Fiction: The Novelist as Eyewitness," in Lang (ed.), *Writing and the Holocaust*, ch. 13. Young has a fine critical eye for how documentary fiction works, but he evinces no interest in where it comes from. It is no accident that two of his central authors are Vassilii Grossman and Anatoli Kuznetsov, both from the U.S.S.R., where documentary novels were and continue to be extremely popular.

79. See Ber Mark, "Yudenratishe 'ahves-yisroel' (an entfer afn bilbl fun H. Leyvik)," *Bleter far geshikhte* 5, no. 3 (1952), 63–115, with facsimiles of the anonymous manuscript. Similar debates were raging in the state of Israel at exactly this time. See Dalia Ofer, "Israel," in Wyman (ed.), *The World Reacts to the Holocaust*, 864–873; Yablonka, "The Formation of Holocaust Consciousness in the State of Israel," 123–129.

80. Zvi Kolitz, "Yossel Rakover's Appeal to God" (a new translation with afterword by Jeffrey V. Mallow and Frans Jozef van Beeck), *Cross Currents* (Fall 1994), 362–377. My thanks to Dr. Mallow for sending me this translation and afterword and for providing me with a xerox copy of the Yiddish original.

81. Zvi Kolitz, *Tiger Beneath the Skin: Stories and Parables of the Years of Death*, trans. Shmuel Katz (New York: 1947); Mallow and van Beeck, "Afterword," 373–374.

82. Mikhl Borwicz, "Der apokrif u.n. 'Yosl Rakover redt tsu got,'" *Almanakh* (Paris) (1955), 193–203. The quotation from Glatstein's review is cited in ibid., 199. The moment Kolitz's authorship became known, Sutzkever issued an "explanation," published in Glatstein's regular column in the Labor Zionist *Yidisher kemfer*. Sutzkever claimed to have shown the manuscript to Nachman Blumental and Rachel Auerbach, both of whom had vouched

for its authenticity. See "An oyfklerung fun A. Sutskever," *Yidisher kemfer* (18 Feb. 1955), 12, 14. Note that this controversy raged in Yiddish-speaking communities across three continents.

83. See Albert H. Friedlander (ed.), *Out of the Whirlwind: A Reader of Holocaust Literature* (New York: 1968), where a postscript identifies Rakover as a real person whose tragic fate was known to the author; Zvi Kolitz, *Yosl Rakover Talks to God*, trans. from the German by Carol Brown Janeway, ed. Paul Badde (New York: 1999).

84. On the legend of the 93 Bais Yaakov girls, which literally made its way into the Jewish liturgy, see Judith Tydor Baumel and Jacob J. Schacter, "The Ninety-three Bais Yaakov Girls of Cracow: History or Typology?" in *Reverence, Righteousness and Rahamanut: Essays in Memory of Rabbi Dr. Leo Jung*, ed. Jacob J. Schacter (Northdale, N.J.: 1992), 93–130.

85. Mendel Piekarz, *Sifrut ha'edut 'al hashoah kemakor histori* (Jerusalem: 2003). This book, a collection of unedited essays, is marred by a strident tone, a polemical thrust, and a completely hermetic approach to the subject. Piekarz's anger creates a time-warp effect, reminiscent of the very period he is examining.

86. See David G. Roskies, "The Holocaust According to Its Anthologists," in *The Anthology in Jewish Literature*, ed. David Stern (Oxford: 2004), 335–350.

87. *Z otchłani: Poezja ghetta i podziemia w Polsce* (New York: 1945). I shall return to these poems later in this essay.

88. H. Leivick, "A Treblinke-kandidat," in idem, *In treblinke bin ikh nit geven (lider un poemes)* (New York: 1945), 11. Thanks to Avner Holtzman, we now know how Holocaust testimony made its way into Hebrew fiction of the Yishuv even before the war had ended. See " 'They Are Different People': Holocaust Survivors as Reflected in the Fiction of the Generation of 1948," *Yad Vashem Studies* 30 (2002), 337–368.

89. There are several translations of Glatstein's Holocaust-related poems into English. Among the most accessible are those in *The Penguin Book of Modern Yiddish Verse*, ed. Irving Howe, Khone Shmeruk, and Ruth R. Wisse (New York: 1989), 430–457 and *American Yiddish Poetry: A Bilingual Anthology*, ed. Benjamin and Barbara Harshav (Berkeley: 1986), 278–319.

90. This paragraph and the next are a bald summary of Dan Miron, *Akdamot leUZG* (Jerusalem: 2002), chs. 18–20. Hanoch Guy's entry on Greenberg in HL is woefully inadequate.

91. For a modest sample in English translation, see Roskies (ed.), *The Literature of Destruction*, sec. 95.

92. See Ofer, "Israel," 873; Hana Yablonka, *Medinat yisrael neged Adolf Eichmann* (Tel Aviv: 2001); Ora Herman, "Shidurim miplaneta aheret: mishpat Eichmann, hamimshal, ukhlei hatikshoret haelektronit" (master's thesis, The Hebrew University, 2004).

93. This is the subject of *Touching Evil* (1969), by Norma Rosen (b. 1925; HL 1014–1020).

94. Haim Gouri, "Facing the Glass Booth," in Hartman (ed.), *Holocaust Remembrance*, 155.

95. Hannah Arendt, *Eichmann in Jerusalem: A Report on the Banality of Evil* (New York: 1963) (earlier serialized in the *New Yorker* [1962]). Cf. Bettelheim's "Individual and Mass Behavior in Extreme Situations" (1943), later expanded into *The Informed Heart: Autonomy in a Mass Age* (Glencoe, Ill.: 1960).

96. See Alan Rosen, *Sounds of Defiance: The Holocaust, Multilingualism, and the Problem of English* (Lincoln: 2005). As Rosen demonstrates, already in the first postwar decade, John Hersey and David Boder were keenly aware of the problem of linguistic verisimilitude, yet still refused to allow their Jewish subjects to speak with an accent.

97. Wisse, *The Modern Jewish Canon*, 204–219. It was Sidra DeKoven Ezrahi, if I am not mistaken, who first identified the phenomenon of displaced literature, which the interpretive community of other academics came to see as an essential feature of Holocaust writing. See her *By Words Alone: The Holocaust in Literature* (Chicago: 1980).

98. Alan Mintz, "Appelfeld's World," in his *Ḥurban: Responses to Catastrophe in Hebrew Literature* (New York: 1984), ch. 6; Hever, *Sifrut shenikhtevet mikan*, 63, 66–67.

99. Agnon's story, translated by Arthur Green, appears in Roskies (ed.), *The Literature of Destruction*, sec. 97. The exclusion of Agnon from HL is astonishing. Holocaust literature in Hebrew begins with Agnon's *A Guest for the Night* (1939), a semi-autobiographical novel that reinterprets the Jewish catastrophe of the Great War in the light of the catastrophe that is sure to come. It ranks with Glatstein's poetry and prose as the great harbinger of doom— and of ambiguous hope. See Dan Laor, "Did Agnon Write about the Holocaust?" *Yad Vashem Studies* 22 (1992), 17–63; Wisse, *The Modern Jewish Canon*, ch. 5.

100. Edmond Jabès, *The Book of Questions*, trans. R. Waldorp (Middletown: 1976); see also Berel Lang, "Writing-the-Holocaust: Jabès and the Measure of History," in Lang (ed.), *Writing and the Holocaust*, 245–260.

101. Dan Pagis, *Points of Departure*, trans. Stephen Mitchell with an introduction by Robert Alter (Philadelphia: 1981), 23.

102. I am drawing here on the course notes of my late colleague, Zvia Ginor, who routinely presented her students with 25 different interpretations of this poem.

103. Sidra DeKoven Ezrahi, "Conversation in the Cemetery: Dan Pagis and the Prosaics of Memory," in Hartman (ed.), *Holocaust Remembrance*, 126.

104. Elie Wiesel, "One Generation After," in his *One Generation After* (New York: 1972), 16, 15.

105. Ibid., 13, 17.

106. The report is published by the Superintendent of Documents, U.S. Government Printing Office (Washington, D.C.), Stock Number 052-003-00707-0.

107. Ibid., 4.

108. Ibid., iii, iv.

109. See, for example, Alan Mintz, *Popular Culture and the Shaping of Holocaust Memory in America* (Seattle: 2001), ch. 3.

110. See, for example, Lawrence L. Langer, "The Americanization of the Holocaust on Stage and Screen" (1983), in his *Admitting the Holocaust*, 175–177.

111. In France, according to David Weinberg, the screening of *Holocaust* was preceded by intense controversy, and its impact on Jewish youth was profound. Debórah Dwork and Robert-Jan van Pelt credit the miniseries with integrating the Holocaust into everyday life in the Netherlands. See Wyman (ed.), *The World Reacts to the Holocaust*, 25, 73.

112. See Eva Fogelman and Bella Savran, "Therapeutic Groups for Children of Holocaust Survivors," *International Journal of Group Psychotherapy* 29, no. 2 (April 1979), 211–235.

113. For an extremely hostile view, see Peter Novick, *The Holocaust in American Life* (Boston: 1999). Novick traces change in the public memory of the Holocaust to the influence of Zionist leaders and the Jewish, pro-Israel establishment in general.

114. For the link between autobiography and suicide in the lives of Zweig and Kofman, see Michael Stanislawski, *Autobiographical Jews: Essays in Jewish Self-Fashioning* (Seattle: 2004), chs. 4–5.

115. For a list of other writers whom Roth's series rehabilitated, see HL 1298.

116. See Ilan Avisar, "Personal Fears and National Nightmares: The Holocaust Complex in Israeli Cinema," in Sicher (ed.), *Breaking Crystal*, 154–156.

117. Horowitz, "Auto/Biography and Fiction after Auschwitz," 282.

118. In an otherwise admirable English translation, Betsy Rosenberg consistently gets the Yiddish wrong: an unintended semiotic sign of what has been lost.

119. For a study that situates Grossman in time and place, see Iris Milner, "Writing and the Holocaust: Problematics of Representation in Second-Generation Literature in Israel," *The Journal of Israeli History* 22, no. 1 (Spring 2003), 91–108.

120. Marzynski's *Shtetl*, which was aired on PBS in April 1996, inspired Eva Hoffman's *Shtetl: The Life and Death of a Small Town and the World of Polish Jews* (Boston: 1997). For a discussion, see David G. Roskies, "The Shtetl in Jewish Collective Memory," in idem, *The Jewish Search for a Usable Past* (Bloomington: 1999), ch. 4.

121. The convergence of the two works was noted by Blake Eskin, "Yosl Rakover's Creator Talks to a Reporter," *Forward* (3 Dec. 1999).

122. Anne Michaels (b. 1958; HL 831–834) does the same thing in her novel, *Fugitive Pieces* (1996). For an attempt to separate the freedom of the creative writer from the demands of historicity specific to the Holocaust, see Cynthia Ozick, "The Rights of History and the Rights of Imagination," in *Quarrel and Quandary: Essays* (New York: 2000).

123. See Ruth Franklin, "Identity Theft: True Memory, False Memory, and the Holocaust," *The New Republic* (31 May 2004).

124. I owe this insight to Iris Milner, in "Writing and the Holocaust," 97.

125. Grouped under "Healing: religious and secular," which she glosses as "Tikkun (repair)," is a motley of writers as diverse as Emil Fackenheim and Yoram Kaniuk, Aaron Zeitlin and Primo Levi. Fifty-five writers are listed under "Jewish second generation," which for some reason includes Elie Weisel, plus another seven names under "German second generation."

126. Abraham Sutzkever, "The Lead Plates of Rom's Printing Press," trans. Neal Kozodoy in *The Penguin Book of Modern Yiddish Verse*, 678–689. See also HL 1236.

127. Abraham Sutzkever, personal communication, 23 July 2004. For the Soviet context, I am indebted to Hannah Polin, "*Geheymshtot* and the Construction of Sutzkever's Public Persona" (senior honors thesis, Columbia College [3 May 2004]).

128. For this, and other reasons, the poetry of Malka Heifetz-Tusman (1896–1987) stands out as a notable exception.

129. This subject remains unexplored. The best available source is Harshav and Harshav (eds.), *American Yiddish Poetry: A Bilingual Anthology,* if one reads the marginal notes with care.

130. Cited by Avraham Novershtern in " 'Who Would Have Believed that a Bronze Statue Can Weep': The Poetry of Anna Margolin," in Anna Margolin, *Lider* (Jerusalem: 1991), xv (n. 12).

131. See Saul Friedländer (ed.), *Probing the Limits of Representation: Nazism and the "Final Solution"* (Cambridge, Mass.: 1992).

132. On two works of Cynthia Ozick (b. 1928; HL 902–912), "The Shawl" (1980) and *Rosa* (1983), which inspired an enormous body of criticism, see Wisse, *The Modern Jewish Canon*, 314–317.

133. See Catherine Merridale, *Night of Stone: Death and Memory in Twentieth-Century Russia* (New York: 2000); Zvi Gitelman, "Soviet Union," in Wyman (ed.), *The World Reacts to the Holocaust*, 306–321.

134. See Chone Shmeruk, "Yiddish Literature in the U.S.S.R.," in *The Jews in Soviet Russia since 1917*, 3rd ed., ed. Lionel Kochan (Oxford: 1978), ch. 12.

135. Friedländer, "Afterword: The *Shoah* between Memory and History," 346.

136. Cf. the censored version of Yitzhak Katzenelson, *Vittel Diary*, trans. Moshe Cohn (Kibbutz Lohamei Hagetaot: ca. 1964) with his *Ketavim aharonim begeto varsha uvemahane Vittel*, ed. Shlomo Even-Shoshan. My source on the destruction of Huberband's *Kidush Hashem* is David E. Fishman, who edited and translated the book into English. Scandalous memory and attempted cover-ups in the Orthodox world are treated at length by Piekarz, *Sifrut ha'edut 'al hashoah kemakor histori*, esp. chap. 4. Piekarz mentions the offending passage in Huberband (on pp. 33–34) but does not cite any angry responses.

137. See Yitzhak [Antek] Zuckerman, *A Surplus of Memory: Chronicle of the Warsaw Ghetto Uprising*, trans. and ed. Barbara Harshav (Berkeley: 1993); Iris Milner, "Writing and the Holocaust," 95–96.

138. In Hebrew, *Shoah shelanu*, 2nd ed. (Ganei-Aviv: 2002). In his "Afterword," the author reveals how he transgressed the historical truth in order to enliven the dead.

139. Naomi Seidman sees a (questionable) connection between Jewish Hellenism and the process whereby certain translations of Holocaust literature achieve canonical status. See her article "The Holocaust in Every Tongue," in Raphael (ed.), *The Representation of the Holocaust in Literature and Film*, 93–111. On "the midrashic trope," see Sara R. Horowitz, "Auto/Biography and Fiction after Auschwitz," in Sicher (ed.), *Breaking Crystal*, 286–292.

140. See Nehemia Polen, *The Holy Fire: The Teachings of Rabbi Kalonymus Kalman Shapira, the Rebbe of the Warsaw Ghetto* (Northvale, N.J.: 1994).

141. See Ruth R. Wisse, "Two Jews Talking: A View of Modern Yiddish Literature," in Wirth-Nesher (ed.), *What Is Jewish Literature?*, 129–142.

142. See Monika Adamczyk Garbowska and Antony Polonsky (eds.), *Contemporary Jewish Writing in Poland: An Anthology* (Lincoln: 2001); Louis Begley (b. 1933; HL 117–123), "An Orphaned Writer," *The American Scholar* 73 (Summer 2004), 41–49.

143. Wisse, *The Modern Jewish Canon*, 193.

144. See David E. Fishman, *Embers Plucked From the Fire: The Rescue of Jewish Cultural Treasures from Vilna* (New York: 1996).

145. N. Vaynig, "Naydus etyudn," *Di goldene keyt* 129 (1990), 57–86; ibid. 130 (1990), 86–126.

146. Abraham Sutzkever, "Epitafn, 21," in his *Lider fun yam-hamoves: fun vilner geto, vald, un vander* (New York: 1968), 194. I found this text in my files. For a different translation, see Ruth Wisse, "Sutzkever—An Appreciation," *The B'nai B'rith International Literary Award 1979–5739 Presented to Abraham Sutzkever* (New York: 1979), n.p. In the Yiddish original, the rhyme scheme is abab.

Moshe Sharett and the German Reparations Agreement, 1949–1952

Yechiam Weitz
UNIVERSITY OF HAIFA

The Israeli government's decision to conduct direct negotiations with Germany[1] on postwar reparations (*shilumim*), which was the outcome of months of discussion, caused great controversy both within the Knesset and among the general public. The opposition was fierce and, at times, violent.[2] On the Left, both the Zionist-oriented Mapam party and the non-Zionist Maki (Israeli Communist party) voiced their disapproval. For Mapam, such negotiations desecrated the memory of the Holocaust victims. For Maki, they were the ultimate proof that Israel was subjugating itself to the imperialist-capitalist bloc, which Maki regarded as the direct successor of the Nazi-Fascist axis. At the other end of the political spectrum, the Herut party, led by Menachem Begin, viewed any negotiations with the Germans (the "modern Amalek") as a profound blow to national honor.

In between these two extremes were the religious parties—Zionist as well as the non-Zionist ultra-Orthodox—all of whom were partners in the coalition government formed in October 1951, and without whose support the government's proposal to open negotiations with Germany would not receive the necessary majority vote in the Knesset.[3] Within the religious parties, opinions were divided. Among those supporting negotiations were Moshe Shapira and Yosef Burg (Hapoel Hamizrachi), and David Zvi Pinkas of the Mizrachi party; among those emphatically opposed was Minister of Welfare Meir Levin, the leader of Agudat Israel.[4]

Negotiating with Germany on economic matters had long been a contested issue among Zionists. During the 1930s, after the Nazi rise to power, the Zionist leadership in Palestine had conducted talks with the German government concerning the transfer of assets of German Jews immigrating to Palestine. The central figure in these negotiations was Chaim Arlosoroff, head of the political department of the Jewish Agency, who was assassinated in Tel Aviv in June 1933 and succeeded by his deputy, Moshe Sharett (then Shertok).[5] Prior to the murder, radical elements within the Revisionist movement had conducted a vicious campaign against Arlosoroff, maintaining that he was selling the honor of the Jewish people in his "negotiating with the devil." Following the Holocaust, such accusations sounded an even harsher note. At the same time, it was undeniable that the newly established state of Israel, a haven for Holocaust survivors, was in desperate need of material aid. This fact heightened the bitter tension between emotional recoil from financial dealings with Germany, on the one hand, and a necessary pragmatism, on the other.

Most supporters of negotiations belonged to the Mapai leadership. Motivating them was the catastrophic state of Israel's economy, then on the verge of collapse.[6] But ideological arguments and matters of principle also played a role in shaping their outlook. There was a feeling that Israel might "miss the boat" if it did not demand reparations from the Germans: because of the Cold War, Germany stood likely to be reinstated into the family of nations. Enabling the Germans blithely to inherit the assets of Holocaust victims was, it was argued, morally repugnant. Under the circumstances, a claim for reparations could by no means be construed as forgiveness for unpardonable crimes.

The burden of dealing with the reparations issue at the policy level was borne in the main by a group of four individuals. First among them was Prime Minister David Ben-Gurion, who viewed the decision to conduct negotiations as a political commitment that must be undertaken by a sovereign nation. Ben-Gurion's primary role was to provide political and public backing for those engaged in the endeavor on a daily basis, notably Foreign Minister Moshe Sharett.[7]

Representing both the world Zionist movement and diaspora Jewry was Nahum Goldmann, then interim president of the World Jewish Congress.[8] Goldmann played two important roles in the negotiations. In his capacity as the leading representative of the Jewish people at large, he participated in the establishment of a Claims Conference that, at its inaugural session, decided to assign Israel first priority in claims made against Germany (with additional claims to be filed on behalf of Jews living outside Israel). Goldmann's second role was of a more personal nature: in discussions with German Chancellor Konrad Adenauer, he helped clear the way to the reparations agreement.

The third personage was David Horowitz, director-general of the Ministry of Finance and financial adviser to the government from 1948 to 1952. In preliminary economic negotiations with Germany in 1950, a key role had been played by Eliezer Kaplan, the minister of finance. The following year, however, Kaplan became critically ill and his involvement drastically diminished. Horowitz took his place and, together with Maurice Fischer, the Israeli envoy in Paris, was the first Israeli to meet secretly with Adenauer (in Paris, in 1951).

The fourth member of this group was Sharett, the subject of this study. Until his ouster from the foreign ministry in June 1956, it was primarily Sharett—and not Ben-Gurion—who conducted Israel's charged and difficult relationship with Germany.

At this time, Sharett was firmly entrenched in the front rank of Israel's political leadership. Of all Mapai leaders of the pre-state period, he was the only one, apart from Ben-Gurion himself, who continued to hold a senior position in the government.[9] Sharett's major source of political authority and status lay in his professional capacities; he did not have a power base in the party or in the Histadrut labor federation. Unlike most of his colleagues in Mapai who had made their way up by means of these apparatuses, he had risen within the Jewish Agency bureaucracy (the pre-state executive body); the public at large identified him with Israel's foreign policy. The fact that he was appreciated more for his professional efforts than for his party affiliation was both a source of strength and a potential weakness.

Sharett worked closely with the civil servants in his bureau and presented their arguments to the political echelon, both in the cabinet and in the Knesset. The fact that he had headed the Yishuv's diplomatic service for nearly two decades, first as head of the Jewish Agency's political department and then as Israel's foreign minister, enabled senior officials in the ministry to view him not as an outsider but as an outstanding and accepted leader who was prepared to listen to, and take account of, their opinions.

Apart from having a major role in the direct negotiations with Germany, Sharett was an important figure in the public information campaign designed to prepare the political system and public opinion for the anticipated change in Israel's previous policy of absolute boycott of Germany. He also played a significant role on the political and diplomatic level in negotiations with the Allied powers. Sharett was actively involved in the German question, both publicly and behind the scenes, throughout the entire period it was on the public agenda. His stand on this emotional issue was clear: as a sovereign state, Israel could not afford to ignore the political and diplomatic fact of Germany's existence. This was even more the case when the issue of contention was reparations.

The First Deliberations: The Naftali Committee and Its Aftermath

The question of German reparations was first discussed by the government in the summer of 1949.[10] The issue was raised by Finance Minister Eliezer Kaplan, who informed the cabinet of a question that had been posed to him by a committee (the Restoration Committee) that had been established abroad to deal with the matter of Jewish property stolen during the Holocaust. The question was: Would it be possible to handle sums of money that individuals living in Israel would receive as reparations from the Germans, and to transfer them to Israel in the form of goods to be acquired in Germany? Kaplan noted that the answer to this question could bring about a change in Israel's position on Germany. "Until today, there has been opposition to importing goods from Germany, and we have allowed only new immigrants to bring their money in the form of goods from Germany," Kaplan noted. "The question is, will we [now] allow [veteran immigrants] to bring in goods?" After some deliberation, the government decided in the affirmative.[11]

Several months later, at the beginning of 1950, the government once again faced the issue. The matter was placed on the agenda when a government committee, appointed by Kaplan and Sharett to investigate "matters concerning transfer from Germany," presented its decisions and recommendations. Headed by member of the Knesset (MK) Peretz Naftali of Mapai, the committee included representatives of several government ministries.[12]

At its final session early in January 1950, the Naftali Committee adopted several proposals, all of which were based on the fundamental premise that direct negotiations between Israel and the German government were inevitable. Only such direct contacts were likely to produce "arrangements of a general nature" with

Germany, which would facilitate a significant economic transfer.[13] The committee believed that adopting a decision of this nature was "desirable not only from the practical viewpoint of the transfer of assets" but also from the standpoint of Jewish and Israeli national honor: it was deemed preferable to negotiate openly and directly with Germany rather than relying on evasive substitutes such as "informal talks" between Israeli and German officials.[14] Sharett, as noted, was in agreement. Commenting on the efforts to gain reparations for Holocaust survivors, he remarked that such matters "cannot be carried out without contact; you cannot close your eyes to avoid seeing the contact, and it is impossible, in this matter, to have it both ways."[15]

In discussing the committee's report at a meeting of the cabinet, Sharett argued that, as a sovereign state, Israel could not adopt a posture of "standing aside and refusing to dirty its hands," adding that, in any case, there was nothing wrong in the attempt to regain Jewish property. This point prevailed, as indicated by the final cabinet decision (against the opinion of Minister Dov Joseph), "to empower the Ministry of Finance and the Ministry of Foreign Affairs, with the concurrence of the prime minister and of the Jewish Agency, to carry out arrangements to obtain reparations from and claims against Germany, via direct contacts with the German authorities. The public must be provided with the necessary explanations concerning this matter."[16]

To all intents and purposes, this cabinet decision of February 1950 opened the first chink in the wall of boycott. It was a more far-reaching decision than the one adopted by the government in the summer of 1949, since it openly referred to the emotionally charged issue of "direct contact" with Germany. Notwithstanding, the decision was limited: what the government authorized was direct contacts solely for the purpose of recovering assets and gaining reparations for private individuals, rather than negotiations on behalf of an overall economic arrangement with Germany.

Shaping the Foreign Ministry's Position on Reparations

The issue of reparations was once again brought before the cabinet at its session of October 30, 1950. Since its previous discussion of the issue, Germany's status had changed. The outbreak of the Korean War on June 25 had accelerated its integration into the Western bloc, a process that was a cornerstone of Adenauer's policy to speed the Western Allies' recognition of (West) German sovereignty and thus bring to an end the military occupation.[17] Less than a month after the outbreak of hostilities in Korea, the three occupying Western powers declared an end to the state of war with Germany—a declaration that expressed a willingness on the part of the West to allow Germany to be rehabilitated among the community of nations. On October 23, 1950, the occupying powers asked Israel to concur with its declaration regarding the end of hostilities.[18]

Germany's economy at this time was improving rapidly, which meant that it would be able to bear the payment of reparations. Between 1950 and 1954, Germany's economic growth rose by an annual average rate of 8.4 percent; Israel's foreign ministry kept abreast of these economic developments.[19]

Several months prior to the cabinet session in October, Kurt Mendelssohn, the director of the customs and excise section of the finance ministry, had been dispatched to Germany by Kaplan and Sharett.[20] His formal mandate was merely to check the possibility of obtaining reparations for German (as opposed to all European) Jews. However, in the course of conducting discussions with senior officials in the German government, Mendelssohn also sought to ascertain the prospects and possible scope of reparations from Germany for all Jewish assets. The report he later submitted emphasized that the only way to tackle the issue would be by means of contacts between Israeli and German officials. Leading figures in the German government had shown interest in him and in his ideas: "This is the first time they met with an official spokesman [of Israel], and they understood that the state could coordinate and conduct negotiations about a global settlement. They apparently take great political interest in direct negotiations with the state of Israel." From this, Mendelssohn concluded that the handling of claims from Germany must be left "in the hands of our, that is, strictly Israeli, bodies" rather than being transferred to the world Jewish organizations. The reason for this was that "our state has absorbed 80–90 percent of Jewish refugees in general, and of those who could present such claims, in particular."[21]

Mendelssohn's conclusions were presented and discussed at a meeting of senior foreign ministry officials held on August 1, 1950.[22] Those present maintained that there were two clear alternatives: either Israel was prepared to "erase from the history of the Holocaust this aspect of the Nazi atrocities" (that is, the plunder of Jewish property), or else it must persuade Germany "to make a great historical gesture toward the Jewish people by a one-time payment of a sum that would be proportionate to the adversity it has inflicted." Participants at the meeting believed that the Germans would be prepared to make such a gesture—for which there was no formal basis in postwar legislation governing war reparations—because of "the strong desire of Germany to rejoin the family of nations."[23] In a follow-up meeting, a committee (again headed by Peretz Naftali) was established in order to prepare a proposal regarding the setting up of an Israeli delegation in Germany.[24]

Concurrent with the work of the two committees headed by Naftali, senior members of the foreign ministry, both in Israel and abroad, had reached the conclusion that the Jewish state could not bury its head in the sand, pretending to ignore Germany and its official representatives.

An example of the dilemmas faced by Israel's foreign service vis-à-vis relations with Germany was a delicate problem raised by Shmuel Tolkowsky, Israel's first diplomatic representative in Switzerland. In the summer of 1950, President Chaim Weizmann and Chancellor Adenauer were guests in the same hotel in Buergernstock, a holiday resort near Lucerne.[25] "The spectacle of the three flags [Israeli, German, and Swiss] flying above the president's hotel . . . aroused in me . . . deeply mixed feelings," wrote Tolkowsky. In addition, the possibility of a chance meeting between Weizmann and one of the chancellor's aides greatly perturbed the foreign ministry staff, and Tolkowsky did everything in his power to prevent such a meeting. Yet, at the same time, he himself made contact with Ernst Ostermann, Adenauer's secretary and a member of his entourage. Tolkowsky cabled a report concerning this meeting to Jerusalem:

> Upon your instructions to [Gershon] Meron [director of the economic division in the foreign ministry], I spoke with the private secretary of the man [Adenauer]. He stated that there was no intention of anything more than a courtesy visit and that [Adenauer] did not intend, and even now does not intend, to discuss the concrete issues, either with the president or with our government. This, despite the fact that I made clear to him that I have the authority to respond to his ideas. He said that there is indeed a desire to find a solution to the problem, and that his government is trying to overcome the great obstacles that exist, and that they will contact you once again through [Kurt] Mendelssohn when the time is appropriate. The impression is that the secretary's master truly wishes to come to an arrangement regarding relations.

Further on in the cable, Tolkowsky touched on a sensitive matter. "Despite his affirmations that [Adenauer] has no intention of discussing the matter now, I ask myself whether it may be a pity to miss a unique opportunity to speak, on neutral soil, with the man himself, whom we have as yet not succeeded in meeting face to face."[26]

After receipt of this cable, Meron asked Tolkowsky to sound out the German position vis-à-vis a goodwill gesture, in the sum of 10 million German marks, that Adenauer had proposed in the course of an interview conducted in November 1949 with Karl Marx, the editor-in-chief of the *Allgemeine Zeitung der Juden in Deutschland* (Ostermann had mentioned this proposal in the course of his conversation with Tolkowsky).[27] In reply, Ostermann outlined the legal and economic difficulties that had led to the proposal's being struck from the agenda.[28] Meron brought the Tolkowsky correspondence to Sharett's attention, adding his own notation: "It is my opinion that this . . . makes it clear that without on-the-spot negotiations, there is no hope that our demand will be met."[29]

Government Deliberations on the German Issue, Fall 1950 and Early 1951

The question of relations with Germany was raised at three sessions of the cabinet in the fall of 1950 and in early 1951. The first session dealt with the Western powers' proposal to end the state of belligerency with Germany. Sharett used this opportunity to lay before the government the foreign ministry's position on the matter, which had taken shape in the course of the year. He opened his survey by reporting that two requests had been received relating to Germany; the first, involving ending the state of war with that country and the second, a "special request" to support Germany's candidature for membership in the International Wheat Organization. On the latter, Sharett said, his first reaction was that Israel should abstain during the voting, but on second thought, he had come to the conclusion that Israel must support this request, since "only a short while ago we knocked on the doors of the world's nations asking for their support, and now we must not be opposed."[30]

The main part of Sharett's survey was devoted to the reparations issue. He expressed his fear that Israel might miss its last opportunity to demand reparations, as Germany was now making its way back into the family of nations. Israel's boycott of Germany, Sharett stressed, was one of those policies "that seems to make sense, but in fact cannot be sustained—at any rate, cannot be sustained for any great length of time." The government summed up its discussion with a "balanced" decision: not to acquiesce in the Western powers' request to end the state of belligerency with Germany, but to agree that Germany be allowed to join the International Wheat Convention.[31] This compromise decision was indicative of the government's wavering between the necessity of accepting the fact of Germany's new international status and its fears concerning Israeli public reaction.

Shortly thereafter, relations with Germany came up at two consecutive cabinet sessions: on December 26, 1950, and a week later, on January 3, 1951. The initiative for the discussion came from Walter Eytan, the director-general of the foreign ministry. In a letter to Ze'ev Sharef, the cabinet secretary, Eytan proposed two points for discussion. The first was whether Israel should exploit the dialogue with the Western powers concerning its request to end the state of belligerency with Germany "in order to present a comprehensive memorandum about our demands and concerning the responsibility that rests upon the Western powers to ensure that Germany will meet the claims of the Jewish people."[32] Eytan also suggested a discussion on "a decision in principle about contact with the German authorities for the purpose of furthering our claims." Eytan stressed that "true progress can be achieved only if the government of Israel enters into negotiations not only with the occupying powers in Germany but also with the German authorities in West and East Germany."[33]

This proposal met with widespread opposition from a number of cabinet members, including representatives of Mapai such as Dov Joseph. However, other ministers tended to agree with the director-general's assessment. Moshe Shapira of the United Religious Front, for example, suggested that direct negotiations with Germany did not imply "any recognition of Germany," since only the economic aspect would be involved. At the second cabinet meeting, two resolutions came up for a vote. The first, which proposed beginning direct negotiations with Germany and dispatching an official delegation to the German authorities, ended in a tie, with five ministers in favor and five opposed. The second resolution, that "the representatives of Israel will approach the central governments of the occupying powers in order to secure reparations from Germany and the return of Jewish property," was passed. Thus Sharett was given responsibility for carrying out a task to which he was himself opposed.[34]

Playing for Time: Two Diplomatic Messages

Following the government's decision, Sharett sent two letters to the Western powers (the United States, France, and Great Britain), and the Soviet Union. The first, dated January 16, 1951, dealt with the question of individual reparations, while the second, dispatched on March 12, took on the wider issue of reparations to the

Jewish people.[35] Reporting to the cabinet on February 8, Sharett touched on a new issue—namely, immigrant absorption—that had not come up in earlier discussions. Israel, he said, had to "emphasize the fact that we have absorbed . . . more than half a million refugees, but their absorption still calls for massive investments and we still must be prepared to absorb immigrants from Iraq and Egypt, and from North Africa and Romania." Sharett then returned to the question of reparations and direct relations with Germany, asking rhetorically: "What if we present . . . a demand [for reparations] and they invite us to negotiate over it, and let us say that they say to us, 'all right, your demand has been accepted,' what then?" Sharett supplied his own answer:

> In my opinion, our reply in that case must be: we can move ahead with the settlement of our relations with Germany. In other words, it is unthinkable that we will present such a claim to Germany, even if by other means [that is, through a third party], while at the same time declaring that even if our claim is accepted, this does not mandate settling our relations with Germany and that we will continue the struggle against Amalek forever.[36]

As noted, a letter signed by Sharett went out on March 12, in which the state of Israel presented itself as the sole representative and inheritor of the millions of individuals who were murdered in the Holocaust, with a demand that East and West Germany together be made to pay reparations in the sum of 1.5 billion dollars. The following day, Sharett addressed both the Knesset plenum and the Knesset Committee on Foreign Affairs and Defense. His remarks included key points that were later to guide government policy on Germany.[37]

Sharett first raised the moral and ideological aspects of the issue. On the one hand, he maintained, no monetary reparations could ever atone for the Nazis' sins, as "there can be no atonement for torture and there can be no atonement for death." Yet, on the other hand, "it is inconceivable that the German nation should continue to enjoy the benefits of what they stole while the burden of rehabilitating the victims, those who were rescued in time or who survived the Holocaust, will be placed on that same Jewish nation." Sharett's conclusion was that "they are obligated [to pay for] the rehabilitation; we say that the majority of the victims found refuge here, and therefore it is Israel, first and foremost, that is entitled to the reparations."[38]

Sharett then explained the logic behind the sum demanded as reparations: it reflected neither the extent of the damage that had been inflicted on the Jewish people, nor the sum needed to rehabilitate all Holocaust survivors. Rather, it was the amount necessary to rehabilitate those who had reached the shores of Eretz Israel. (This "Zionization" of the claim for reparations formed part of the larger, ongoing "nationalization" by Israel of the Holocaust in general.)[39]

Sharett spoke quite candidly about direct negotiations with Germany. Replying to questions posed by committee members, he referred to Israel's ostracism of Germany and reiterated his position that such a policy could not be sustained for any length of time. While in theory it was possible to postpone facing the issue for another generation or two—"to strike [the question of a change in policy] off the agenda of the generation that lived through these events and witnessed the horror"—in practice, "we encounter Germany wherever we go. . . . We will be with them everywhere, so that . . . our moral veto against their entrance [into the family of nations] will be absolutely worthless."[40]

Sharett equivocated somewhat in presenting these dilemmas in public, although he offered a much more clear-cut stand to his colleagues in the government. This ambivalence can be explained by the situation in Israel's internal politics at the time—in particular, the precarious state of Mapai. Sharett's party had suffered a harsh blow in the municipal elections held on November 14, 1950. The aggregate results for the country as a whole showed that Mapai had received only slightly more votes than the General Zionists, a party that overnight became the second-largest in Israel and, as such, a contender for political supremacy.[41] These results sent a shock wave through the political system, leading to two significant events: the fall of the government in a Knesset vote in February 1951, and the First Knesset's consequent decision to dissolve itself. Elections for the Second Knesset were set for July 30. For many months, there was no stable government; it was only in October that a new government, again headed by Ben-Gurion, was finally installed. Until then, the interim government, because of its temporary status, could not adopt clear, difficult, and painful decisions. Only after the establishment of the new government was it formally decided to open direct negotiations with Bonn on reparations. During the preceding months, Sharett trod the borderline between professional diplomat and politician.

Sharett's Stand on Direct Negotiations

Not long after the dispatch of the government's two letters to the occupying powers, Sharett set down his thoughts on direct negotiations with Germany in a dispatch that he intended to send, in April 1951, to the heads of Israeli diplomatic delegations abroad.[42] In a memorandum in his own handwriting, which he titled "Have We Missed the Opportunity to Demand Reparations?," he noted the reasons behind the dispatch. After the Israeli claim had been presented to the occupying powers, he wrote, the public "had doubts about the prospects of its realization."

Sharett observed that, at first glance, the Israeli claim for reparations might seem "quite fantastic, both because of its fundamental character, which is unprecedented in international relations, and also because of its monetary dimensions, which are much above that which, to date, have been deemed practical." Nonetheless, Israel was justified in its action. In the case of certain claims, Sharett argued, the failure "is not in [the claim's] not being achieved, but in [its] not ever being presented." Moreover, the letter sent to the occupying powers was only the first step in a long and involved process that, in the long run, was capable of realization. According to Sharett, the Zionist experience with such processes "has been most instructive." For instance, "the demand for Jewish independence . . . [which] despite all the odds . . . was achieved."[43]

Furthermore, Sharett asserted, far from "missing the boat," it might well be "that we have picked the right time [to present the claim]." To what was Sharett referring? A joint meeting of the four deputy Allied foreign ministers was about to be convened in order to prepare a conference to be attended by the foreign ministers of the United States, Great Britain, France, and the Soviet Union. At this conference, (West) Germany's status was to be changed: from an occupied country, it would become a member of the Western bloc whose military units would become part of a European army.[44] Sharett argued that, precisely at this point, right before the reestablishment of German sovereignty, there were good prospects of persuading the Allied powers to present Germany with the conditions for reparations. Germany itself, Sharett emphasized, might also be prepared to acquiesce in Israel's demand, "because when it has almost attained its objective, it is worthwhile [for Germany] to make a special effort to remove obstacles from its path."[45]

Moreover, it might be possible to get around the restrictions placed upon the payment of German reparations that were agreed upon at the Yalta and Potsdam conferences.[46] These arrangements, "a Procrustean bed for us," had been formulated in order "to cover the damages incurred during the war by the Allied states." They were not appropriate for Israel's unique condition: "We are demanding reparations not for war damages but for the theft and destruction of property during the war and the period preceding it." In addition, Israel was "demanding reparations on such a scale as can never be covered from existing equipment; it is only natural that it should be levied from current production and paid over a number of years."[47]

This argument led almost naturally to Sharett's final, and reiterated, point: Germany's improving economy. Though there was no certainty that Israel would receive part or the entire amount it was demanding, "in any case there are better prospects of receiving substantial payments . . . when the German economy is recuperating and its production is rising steeply."[48]

The Path to Adenauer's Declaration of September 27, 1951

Sharett's memorandum hints at his intention to open a direct path to Bonn—a step he had already advocated to the government at a meeting held on February 15. First attempts to follow such a path were taken prior to July 15, the date on which the occupying powers formally rejected (as expected) Israel's demand for reparations.[49] On April 6, the Israeli consul in Munich, Eliahu K. Livneh, sent a confidential letter to Jewish Bundestag member Jakob Altmaier (a member of the Social Democratic opposition party), in which he proposed that a meeting be arranged between Adenauer and Israeli representatives during the chancellor's forthcoming visit to Paris.[50] "The purpose of the *confidential* meeting," he wrote, "will be to explore the possibility of future negotiations between the two states—the issue itself and the form it will take."[51] Livneh suggested further that the German consul general in Paris contact his Israeli counterpart to work out the details of the proposed meeting. Two days later, Altmaier replied to Livneh, informing him that he had shown the Israeli request to the chancellor, whose reply was positive: he was willing to meet with two Israeli representatives.

Sharett sent a "top-secret" telegram to David Horowitz, then in Washington. Since Israel had been directly approached by Bonn, "including a certain proposal from Adenauer . . . instructions have been sent to check if Germany accepts our stand, in principle, and if so, to arrange a meeting with Adenauer in Paris for an exploratory talk." Sharett wrote Horowitz that "should the meeting be set [for a date] after your arrival in Paris, you will participate in it, but we did not see fit to delay it lest A[denauer] cut short his stay there and we will miss the opportunity."[52] Toward the end of the message, he outlined why he decided to turn to negotiations with Germany: "Faced with the great uncertainty of a positive reaction from the Powers, we thought it would be unwise to reject Bonn if it makes an overture to us." In addition, it was necessary to find a unique manner of demanding reparations, "and not be part of the general reckoning [of the German debt] to the Allies, which the Committee of Three is now trying to resolve in London." Our reckoning, he wrote, "is separate and unique and we must not retreat from this stand." Here he reiterated his thinking on the need to depart from the Potsdam paradigm, which could be done only if Israel negotiated directly with the Germans.[53]

The secret meeting between Adenauer and the two Israeli representatives, David Horowitz and Maurice Fischer, took place on April 19, 1951. When Adenauer expressed willingness to begin direct negotiations with representatives of Israel, Horowitz and Fischer presented two conditions: public admission by Germany of the collective guilt of the German nation for its crimes against the Jewish people, and acceptance of the Israeli demand for reparations in the amount of 1.5 billion dollars as the basis for negotiations. Adenauer immediately agreed to the first condition; as for the second, he maintained that Germany would present no serious obstacles.[54]

From Israel's point of view, this was a decisive step forward: a public German admission of guilt and contrition was necessary in order to prepare public opinion in Israel for the removal of the taboo against direct negotiations with the Germans. The first draft of Adenauer's declaration was completed in July 1951, and in September, a final text was agreed upon by both sides. On September 27, Adenauer read the proposed reparations agreement to a special session of the Bundestag in Bonn. The declaration was approved, not by a vote of raised hands, but by the members' standing up as a sign of respect. With this vote, a decisive step was taken toward direct negotiations.

In the interim period between the meeting in Paris in April and Adenauer's declaration in September, senior officials in the foreign ministry, including Sharett, were occupied with preparing the ground for Israeli public and world Jewish acceptance of the dramatic volte-face from absolute boycott to direct and formal negotiations with Bonn. A meeting devoted to this question was convened in June, with the participation of Sharett and Horowitz. The latter opened the discussion. "We made one mistake," he maintained, "and that is that we set out on the path of diplomacy before securing the support of the home front, in other words, Jewish public opinion."[55] Horowitz devoted most of his presentation to American public opinion, claiming that, in the final reckoning, "it is the American taxpayer who will have to bear the burden," namely, that of financing German reparations to Israel.[56] As part of their campaign to forestall the danger of Communism in Europe, he explained, the Americans were doing what they could to maintain a high standard of living in Germany, whereas the Germans were exploiting the situation by continuing to amass a deficit in their balance of payments. Israel's strategy must be to point to the dynamic improvement in Germany's economy, Horowitz stressed.

To this end, he suggested creating "unceasing coverage by the press" so that "the matter does not come off the agenda." He also made two concrete proposals: first, the convening of a "special world Jewish convention" and second, the preparation of a "world Jewish petition." Most participants in the meeting supported the former proposal but opposed the latter. Sharett was among those vehemently opposed to the petition, which, he said, "will be, at best, a demonstration and will not lead to practical results." In contrast, "the idea of a Jewish convention is an important idea whose possibilities must definitely be explored."[57] To a great extent, this meeting was the first step toward the creation of the Claims Conference, which was established in New York on October 25 of that year. On several occasions, Sharett stressed that the initiative had come from the Israelis. He spoke of this during a government session, on the eve of the convention that created the Claims Conference: "This was our initiative; it did not cross the mind of the Jewish organizations. No Jewish organization thought it necessary to mobilize and convene the Jewish people on this matter."[58]

October–December 1951: Moving toward a Decision

Adenauer's declaration in the Bundestag opened a new episode in the history of the negotiations. This episode, which could be titled "The Struggle for a Majority Vote," went on for about three and a half months, until the Knesset approved the government's proposal by a narrow majority, which in effect opened the way for direct negotiations with Bonn. Until Nahum Goldmann's meeting with Adenauer in London on December 6, 1951, the government's willingness to engage in direct negotiations was still conditional, since no confirmation had as yet been received from Germany regarding the sum that would serve as the basis for negotiations.[59] During this time, the government tried to downplay public discussion of the issue.[60]

In his meeting with Goldmann, Adenauer agreed that the financial basis for negotiations would be 1.5 billion dollars, the sum specified in Sharett's letter of March 12, 1951 to the occupying powers. The German commitment removed the last doubts on the part of the government concerning negotiations, and from that date onward, its campaign to achieve a parliamentary majority went into high gear.

Opponents of negotiations hoped to kill two birds with one stone—by undermining negotiations with Bonn, they would also bring down the government. With this in mind, the government needed to shore up the domestic political front in order to avert a parliamentary defeat. Such a defeat, it was believed, would be catastrophic not only for Israel's economy but also for its domestic politics and public morale.

Sharett's major task during this period was to inform the public of the government's complex, and at times deliberately vague, position on the issue of reparations. Another of his tasks was to try to clarify the critical question of Germany's true intentions concerning the sum of the reparations. Speaking at a press conference on October 26, Sharett sounded an ambiguous note. On the one hand, he did not conceal his support for the decision to open negotiations with the Germans; on the other, he refused to clearly admit the government's willingness to enter into such negotiations. When asked if the government was prepared for direct negotiations with Bonn, he replied that it had decided "to do all that was necessary to achieve [payment of] reparations," but since then had not adopted any new decision. Despite his refusal to clarify whether "all that was necessary" included direct negotiations, Sharett, upon his own initiative, reminded his audience of the sharp controversy that had surrounded the "transfer agreement" that, in his own words, had been concluded "while Hitler was still alive." He stressed that, without this agreement, "Israel could not have achieved its industrial, military, agricultural, and economic strength." From this comment, a correspondent for the daily *Ha'aretz* concluded that "the government is prepared to conduct direct negotiations with the Germans."[61]

Meanwhile, Sharett urged the cabinet, several of whose members were wary of angry public reaction and consequent defeat in the Knesset, to decide quickly on this issue. His stance was expressed most clearly during the cabinet session held in late December, only a few days before the scheduled debate in the Knesset. Sharett informed his colleagues of a fact that had been kept secret, namely, that Germany was under heavy pressure "to include, in its budget, sums for the occupying powers, as [a form of] participation in the defense of the West." The Germans were keeping this matter secret, he continued, because public knowledge of these two parallel obligations, for Western defense and for Jewish reparations, would not be to the benefit of either. However, he emphasized, "they informed [us] that they are intent upon settling our matter. This message was passed on to us in Adenauer's name, and he asks that we show understanding for the difficulties involved in this situation." He therefore asked the government to decide immediately, lest Israel miss the last opportunity to receive reparations from the Germans.[62]

January 1952: Sharett in the Knesset Debate on *Shilumim*

The debate in the Knesset, one of the most dramatic and stormy ever conducted in that house, began on January 7, 1952, a week after the cabinet meeting. On that same day, Sharett appeared before the Knesset Committee on Foreign Affairs and Defense and summarized the issue of direct negotiations with Germany.[63] He also responded to a question concerning a public referendum, which was proposed by MK Yitzhak Ben-Aharon, of Mapam. According to Ben-Aharon, "the majority that the government has in the Knesset does not give it authority to take a decision, on its own responsibility, in this matter. . . . I believe that . . . the government . . . must turn to the people for such authorization."[64] Sharett categorically rejected Ben-Aharon's proposal. He admitted that the issue being debated was unique and extraordinary, but the idea of a referendum "is an absolutely undemocratic means that does not enable the voting public at large a full understanding of the problem . . .

making it prey to all sorts of demagogic tricks, and [therefore the voters'] decision will be unreasoned and irresponsible."[65]

It was originally planned that Sharett would open the Knesset debate, but at a later stage it was decided to have Ben-Gurion do so, with Sharett serving as the closing speaker. Alluding to the well-known biblical "J'accuse" (I Kings 21:19), Ben-Gurion put Israel's case primarily in moral terms: "The murderers of our people shall not inherit its goods!"[66] For his part, Sharett, whose closing address brought to an end three days of debate, combined pragmatic elements with moral principles. Indeed, the two could not easily be separated, since the pragmatic arguments contained elements of principle, while the moral arguments had pragmatic ramifications. His address may be construed as an expansion upon what he had told the cabinet almost two years earlier, in February 1950, when he noted the substantive contradiction between the wish to maintain an absolute boycott against Germany and the desire to receive "reparations from those wicked persons . . . for all they have done to us."[67]

Sharett opened his address by referring to the statement he had made to the Knesset on March 13, 1951, after the government's letter had been sent to the occupying powers, and to the debate that had then ensued.[68] In that debate, he claimed, "there was almost no controversy over the question whether these reparations are due to us and whether we must . . . demand them." Sharett asked rhetorically:

> What would have happened had Israel's claim been deemed acceptable by the Western powers? Who would have conducted negotiations on behalf of Israel, for instance, on the question whether payment would be in currency, in engines, or in goods; and if in engines and goods, which engines and which goods? Would Israel then have said to the occupying powers: "If you do this for us and we stand aside, our hands will not be defiled . . . you will defile yourselves, we will not"? Could anyone accept such a demand?

And he continued:

> We open the gates to every Jew who comes to us with only a shirt on his back after all of his property has been stolen from him. In similar fashion, we must open wide the gates, and this with our own hands, to bring in all of that property whose owners did not have the good fortune of bringing it with their own hands, because they were murdered.

He concluded his address with a statement that indicates to what extent he believed that a decision in favor of negotiations was a corollary of the fact that Israel had become a sovereign state: "We are an independent state today. What a defeat [for the Nazis] when the heirs to that Nazi regime sit down in some neutral capital to negotiate with the representatives of an independent Jewish state, whose very existence points to the utter defeat of the Nazi objective."[69]

In the vote that followed Sharett's speech—which was certainly one of the highlights of this lengthy and tormented debate—the government's decision was approved by a majority of 61 in favor, with 50 opposed and nine abstentions.

Conclusion

This is the point at which to ask whether Moshe Sharett's position on the issue of negotiations with Germany can be related to his overall convictions, and to what extent his policy reflected his personality and political behavior.

It seems clear that the decisions he made and his manner of expressing them reflected his conception of Zionism as "a return to history's vale of tears," by which he meant an unmitigated assumption of political responsibility. But it is also characteristic of his inclination to measure events, including harsh and emotional ones, using a rational yardstick. He did everything in his power to dissociate himself from populism or cheap sentimentalism. The historian Israel Kolatt is convinced that this aspect of Sharett's character was shaped during his years of education in England, where he acquired "a systematic, clear, and empirical approach."[70]

This rational approach did not conflict with Sharett's ethical standpoint or moral values. From his point of view, the alternatives to rationalism were romantic pretenses, blind acceptance of illusions, or mysticism. This viewpoint was clearly reflected in his attitude toward negotiations with Germany, but was also evident in other issues that he was called upon to handle over the course of his public career. One such issue had been the proposed partition of Palestine, as suggested by the British Peel Commission of 1937. Sharett's behavior on that occasion bears a great deal of similarity to his handling of the negotiations with Germany. Both were emotionally charged issues that centered on essential questions of national interest and "national honor," and both called for a difficult decision based on a clear-cut conception of what Jewish sovereignty, or the aspirations to sovereignty, must entail. In both cases, Sharett demonstrated his conviction that even the most emotion-laden issues must be decided on the basis of cold logic. In each instance, he also argued that the achievement of Jewish aspirations required, at times, difficult and unpopular decisions.

In a speech delivered in August 1937, "Partition as the Lesser of Evils and a Great Opportunity," Sharett presented arguments in favor of accepting partition— arguments that he would return to years later when defending his stand on direct negotiations with Germany. The analogy between the two cases begins with his presentation of the situation: "The choice we now face is not a choice between two good [alternatives] but between two bad [ones]." Although one is not obliged to choose the most difficult option, "we must not run away from difficulties." It was necessary to choose "the path of greatest achievement, and it may well be that this is the most difficult path, and not the easiest one." Furthermore, he expressed his opposition to what he termed "that Zionist mysticism that obstructs our ability to reap the benefit from the real opportunities with which we are presented."[71]

Moshe Sharett, as foreign minister and later as prime minister of Israel, played a central role in the development of Israeli-German relations. His stands and pronouncements on this charged issue reflect the intense drama of the years that followed the annihilation of European Jewry. The process of defining and defending a policy of realistic pragmatism was, and continues to be, a central aspect of Israel's political culture, which Sharett did so much to shape.

Notes

This essay was translated by Yohai Goel; an expanded version appears, in Hebrew, in the journal *Cathedra* 115 (2005).

1. Unless otherwise indicated, "Germany" will refer in this essay to the German Federal Republic (West Germany).

2. Yechiam Weitz, "Hadegel hahalufi: kishrei yisrael 'im germaniyah bitnu'at haherut, 1951–1967," *Zion* 67, no. 4 (2002), 435–464.

3. The government that was constituted in October 1951 had a narrow majority of 65 (out of 120) Knesset members, comprising 45 representatives of Mapai, 5 of ethnic minorities affiliated with Mapai, and 15 members representing the religious parties. See Yechiam Weitz, "The Road to Wassenaar: How the Decision on Direct Negotiations between Israel and Germany was Approved," *Yad Vashem Studies* 28 (2000), 311–350.

4. Within Mapai, the major coalition member, there were also several groups opposing negotiations, including a group of Holocaust survivors.

5. Arlosoroff's murder was never solved, although the Israeli Left long maintained a tradition of holding right-wing Revisionist Zionists responsible. More recent information points, however, to German agents and to Nazi propaganda minister Joseph Goebbels—whose wife, before her marriage, had been romantically involved with Arlosoroff. See S. Teveth, *Rezah Arlosoroff* (Tel Aviv: 1982), 35–36.

6. Nachum T. Gross, "The Economic Regime during Israel's First Decade," in *Israel—The First Decade of Independence*, ed. S. Ilan Troen and Noah Lukas (New York: 1995), 231–245.

7. For Ben-Gurion's stand on this issue, see Yechiam Weitz, "Haderekh legermaniyah haaheret: David Ben-Gurion veyahaso legermaniyah, 1952–1960," *'Azmaut—hamishim ha-shanim harishonot*, ed. Anita Shapira (Jerusalem: 1998), 245–266.

8. In 1956, he was elected president of the World Zionist Organization, a position that had not been filled since the deposal of Chaim Weizmann in 1946. He served in this capacity until 1968.

9. During the first few years of statehood, a new generation of Mapai leaders gradually came of age. At the time of the *shilumim* controversy, however, its members had not yet achieved top-ranking positions. Levi Eshkol, for instance, joined Israel's third cabinet in October 1951 as agriculture minister, the first step in his meteoric rise to the upper echelons of government. As Gabriel Sheffer notes, during 1951 and 1952, Ben-Gurion and Sharett "remained alone at the apex of the political Israeli pyramid" (Sheffer, *Moshe Sharett—Biography of a Political Moderate* [Oxford: 1996], 632).

10. Minutes of cabinet meeting (7 June 1949), Israel State Archives (hereafter: ISA). See also Weitz, "Haderekh legermaniyah haaheret," 247–248.

11. The only member voting against the decision was Dov (Bernard) Joseph, then in the dual role of agriculture minister and minister in charge of supplies and rationing.

12. See Sheffer, *Moshe Sharett*, 524.

13. Decisions of the Committee on Matters concerning Transfer from Germany (6 Jan. 1950), ISA-Foreign Ministry (hereafter: ISA-FM), 2417/1A. The decisions bear the signature of the committee chairman, Peretz Naftali.

14. Ibid.

15. Minutes of cabinet meeting (15 Feb. 1950), ISA.

16. Ibid.

17. Henry Ashley Turner, *The Two Germanies since 1945* (New Haven: 1987), 67–80.

18. Yehudit Auerbach, "Ben-Gurion and Reparations from Germany," in *David Ben-Gurion—Politics and Leadership in Israel*, ed. Ronald W. Zweig (London: 1991), 276–277.

19. Turner, *The Two Germanies*, 59–60. On the foreign ministry's interest in the West German economy, see Eliyahu K. Livneh to the foreign ministry (24 May 1951), ISA-FM, 2417/4.

20. See the minutes of a meeting chaired by Peretz Naftali (10 May 1950), ISA-FM 2417/1A.

21. Summary of talks conducted with West German authorities regarding reparations for Israeli residents, ISA 2482/13 [undated].

22. For a report on the meeting, see *Documents on the Foreign Policy of Israel*, vol. 5, *1950*, ed. Yemima Rosenthal (Jerusalem: 1988), 452–455; cf. ISA-FM 2539/1.

23. Ibid.

24. Ibid., 455 (n. 4).

25. See Tom Segev, *The Seventh Million: The Israelis and the Holocaust* (New York: 1993), 199; Niels Hansen, *Aus dem Schatten der Katastrophe: Die deutsch-israelischen Beziehungen in der Ära Konrad Adenauer und David Ben-Gurion* (Dusseldorf: 2002), 67.

26. Tolkowsky to Sharett, ISA 2417/1A (23 July 1950).

27. Meron to Tolkowsky, ISA 2417/2 (2 Oct. 1950).

28. Tolkowsky to Meron, ISA 2417 (10 Jan. 1951).

29. Meron to Sharett, ibid. (30 Jan. 1950).

30. Minutes of cabinet meeting (30 Oct. 1950), ISA.

31. Ibid. At the end of the discussion, Ben-Gurion, who had not participated in it, maintained that Israel must adopt a realistic stand vis-à-vis Germany. "There are already *ḥaluzim* [that is, a vanguard of leftists] in Israel who say that the Germans in East Germany are 'kosher,' reliable, and progressive. The same thing will happen with West Germany. One has to face reality."

32. ISA 2417/2 (17 Dec. 1950); cf. *Documents on the Foreign Policy of Israel*, 5:xix.

33. *Documents on the Foreign Policy of Israel*, 5:xix. Abba Eban warned Sharett on September 8, 1950 that the conference of Western foreign ministers, which was shortly scheduled to discuss matters relating to Germany, might be the last opportunity for Israel to press its claim (ibid., 529).

34. Weitz, "Haderekh legermaniyah haaḥeret," 249.

35. Minutes of cabinet meeting (8 Feb. 1951), ISA.

36. Ibid.

37. Knesset session (13 March 1951), *Divrei hakneset* 8:1320–1323. The figure of 1.5 billion dollars required explanation, considering the fact that a cautious estimate of the value of stolen Jewish property was closer to 6 billion dollars. Sharett explained that this was the amount of money needed by Israel to absorb and rehabilitate some 500,000 refugees from Europe, on the basis of an estimated \$3,000 per refugee. Further, Sharett noted, the government of Israel was claiming reparations because it "sees the state of Israel as the legal heir of the rights of the slaughtered millions, and is entitled and duty-bound to demand compensation in their name." The rationale for this was that the victims had been persecuted merely because they belonged to the Jewish people, which was now embodied in the state of Israel.

38. Session of the Knesset Committee on Foreign Affairs and Defense (13 March 1951), ISA 7562/8A.

39. See, for instance, minutes of cabinet meeting (7 June 1949), ISA, at which Ben-Gurion stressed that Israel should be the only representative of Jewish Holocaust victims.

40. Ibid.

41. Mapai received 92,052 votes (27.3 percent of those cast), whereas the General Zionists received 24.5 percent. See Yechiam Weitz, "Hamahapakh shelo hayah," *Panim* 9 (Spring 1999), 91–99.

42. "Kavei hadrakhah laneziguyot," Brief no. 16 (Tel Aviv) (17 April 1951), ISA-FM 2417/6II. I have been unable to ascertain whether this dispatch was actually sent. On April 19, Sharett sent it to Chaim Yahil, director of the foreign ministry's information division. In a memorandum he appended to the letter, Sharett wrote that after reading what he had written, "I have a serious doubt about whether what I wrote should be made public." What gave rise to this feeling was the fact that "there are considerations and premises here that, if made public, would give too much exposure to the 'speculator' aspect of our claim." He ended the memorandum with the sentence: "My inclination is to shelve it."

43. "Kavei hadrakhah laneẓiguyot."

44. The formal declaration ending Germany's status as an occupied country took place in Bonn on September 24, 1951. The three high commissioners representing the Western powers notified Adenauer of the change in status, on condition that West Germany be prepared to play a role in European security.

45. "Kavei hadrakhah laneẓiguyot."

46. At the Yalta Conference in February 1945, the principle laid down was that reparations could be demanded of Germany only in goods, not in financial assets. At the Potsdam Conference held in July of that year, it was further decided that reparations would not exceed a set percentage of all the goods produced by Germany. These decisions reflected the lessons learned from the reparations that the victorious Allies had imposed on Weimar Germany after the First World War, which were a factor in the collapse of that first German democracy. See Nana Sagi, *German Reparations: The History of Negotiations* (Jerusalem: 1980); Turner, *The Two Germanies*, 10.

47. "Kavei hadrakhah laneẓiguyot."

48. Ibid.

49. See, for instance, Nicholas Balbakins, *West German Reparations to Israel* (New Brunswick: 1971), 89; Yeshayahu A. Jelinek (ed.), *Zwischen Moral und Realpolitik: deutsch-israelische Beziehungen 1945–1965: eine Dokumentensammlug* (Gerlingen: 1997), 19.

50. Livneh filled this post from March 1949 until the consulate was closed down on July 1, 1953. On the consulate and its special status, see Yeshayahu A. Jelinek, "Like an Oasis in the Desert: The Israeli Consulate in Munich, 1948–1953," *Studies in Zionism* 9 (1988), 81–98.

51. Quoted in Jelinek (ed.), *Zwischen Moral und Realpolitik*, 152–153 (doc. 13).

52. *Documents on the Foreign Policy of Israel*, vol. 6, *1951*, ed. Yemima Rosenthal (Jerusalem: 1991), 231–232. Sharett ended his telegram with the warning: "All this is top secret, I repeat, top secret."

53. Ibid.

54. Neima Barzel, "Yisrael vegermaniyah, 1945–1956: Hitpatḥut yaḥas haḥevrah veha-medinah beyisrael legermanyiah be'ikvot hashoah" (Ph.D. diss., University of Haifa, 1990), 190–208.

55. Minutes of a meeting held at the home of the foreign minister (19 July 1951), ISA-FM 2417/2.

56. See Sheffer, *Moshe Sharett*, 541.

57. Minutes of meeting at home of foreign minister (19 June 1951).

58. Sharett maintained that the initiative had begun in the summer of 1951, even before Adenauer's decision. He made this claim at a meeting of the Knesset foreign affairs and defense committee on January 7, 1952 (see Weitz, "The Road to Wassenaar," 318 [n. 19]) and even earlier, at a meeting of the government on October 25, 1951. To the government, Sharett declared that "it transpires that this convention, which we initiated before we knew of Adenauer's speech [in the Bundestag], is being convened following Adenauer's speech" (meeting of the government [25 Oct. 1951], ISA). On September 2, representatives of the Israeli government and those of Jewish organizaitons met in New York to discuss the establishment of a joint body having a dual purpose: supporting Israel's claim vis-à-vis the German government, and the struggle on the reparations issue among the Jewish people. The Israelis insisted that the Israeli ambassador, Abba Eban, be the one to address the constituent convention of the Claims Conference. See Ronald W. Zweig, *German Reparations and the Jewish World: A History of the Claims Conference* (London: 1987), 14–29.

59. See Weitz, "The Road to Wassenaar." Pinhas (Felix) Shinnar, representing the foreign ministry, spoke with Goldmann on several occasions in Tel Aviv prior to the meeting. In a memorandum to Sharett, he reported that "Dr. Goldmann intends to conduct [the discussion with Adenauer] against a historical and political background, without going into details" (Shinnar to Sharett [28 Nov. 1951], ISA 534/6).

60. At a press conference held on October 26, 1951, for instance, Sharett referred only

vaguely to the possibility of direct talks with Germany; see "Sharett 'al hatokhniyot lehaganat hamizrah hatikhon," *Ha'aretz*, 28 Oct. 1951.

61. Ibid.

62. Minutes of cabinet meeting (30 Dec. 1951), ISA.

63. Minutes of the committee on foreign affairs and defense (7 Jan. 1952), ISA 2547/12.

64. Ibid.

65. Ibid.

66. Cf. Elijah's admonition to Ahav, 1 Kings 21:19.

67. *Divrei hakneset* 10:953–961.

68. On the debate following Sharett's statement, conducted on April 2, 1951, see *Divrei hakneset*, 8:1547–1561.

69. Quoted in diary of David Ben-Gurion (11 Jan. 1952), Ben-Gurion Archives, Sdeh Boker. In his diary, Ben-Gurion summed up Sharett's address in the following words: "The summing up of the debate by Moshe was exemplary."

70. Israel Kolatt, "Moshe Sharett: medinai ziyoni ben haarez," *Bitfuzot hagolah* 75 (1975), 92.

71. Speech to the 20th Zionist Congress in its session as a political committee (9 Aug. 1937), quoted in its entirety in *Bamaavak lemedinah: hamediniyut haziyonit 1936–1948*, ed. Joseph Heller (Jerusalem: 1985), 201–207.

The Clandestine Zionist Press in the Dachau-Kaufering Concentration Camp: Selected Documents from *Niẓoẓ*, 1944–1945

Dov Levin
THE HEBREW UNIVERSITY

The following documentary materials derive from handwritten bulletins and other writings distributed during the Second World War among young Zionists from Lithuania.[1] Members of this group succeeded in maintaining activity and underground publication efforts from the period of the Soviet occupation of Lithuania (1940–1941), to their incarceration in the Kovno (Kaunas) ghetto under Nazi occupation, and through their internment as slave laborers in Kaufering (one of the subcamps of Dachau),[2] which lasted until May 1945.

The selections presented here derive from the final months of the war. Whereas a great deal of scholarly attention has been devoted to Holocaust-era diaries, legal and underground periodicals appearing in the ghettos, and other writings produced by Jews in wartime Europe, the unique efforts by young Lithuanian Zionists to maintain communication among themselves under any and all circumstances has received scant notice.[3] Yet it is noteworthy that this clandestine press played a significant role in galvanizing a nucleus of young activists for a postwar political role. Of particular interest is their (mistaken) perception that ideological or historical differences between Zionists of various prewar factions had become irrelevant in the context of the Holocaust. This perception was an outcome of their particular experience and their status as a "remnant" (*sheerit hapeleitah*), as they themselves put it. As such, they felt a morally compelling responsibility to bring the message of unity to the rest of the Zionist movement and world Jewry.

The Irgun Brit Zion (IBZ) (Allied Zionist Organization) began its career as a clandestine Zionist youth group in Kovno in June 1940, soon after the new Soviet regime abolished all non-Communist organizational activities. The group, composed mainly of high school students and graduates, drew upon the memberships of prior existing youth groups and put out a Hebrew-language newsletter called *Niẓoẓ* (Spark).[4] The first issue came out in December 1940; in all, seven issues appeared until the outbreak of the German-Soviet war in June 1941. In response to the Soviet occupation, Zionist youth activity in Lithuania acquired a distinctly anti-communist coloration, but steered toward a common political center and an emphasis upon Jewish nationalism as its prime tenet.

Under the Nazi occupation, many Zionists (especially the radical socialist-Zionists from the Hashomer Hazair movement) participated in armed resistance alongside the Soviet-controlled partisans in the surrounding forests. Other Zionist youths focused instead on immediate refuge and rescue activities, such as arranging hiding places both outside and within the ghetto. Those who established themselves within the partisan resistance succeeded in distributing a clandestine publication called *Igeret* (Newsletter) and also laid the groundwork for a network intended to smuggle members out of Europe to Palestine. During the first two years of the German occupation, these efforts resulted in the rescue of some 1,500–2,000 Jews, many of whom managed to reach Palestine.[5]

In the ghetto, meanwhile, former members of such groups as Hanoar Haziyoni, Maccabee Hazair, Bnei Akiva, and Gordonia closed ranks within the IBZ and continued to put out *Nizoz*. Numbers 8 through 35 appeared over the course of the following three years, edited by Shlomo Frankel (Shafir).[6] In its ideological platform, drafted in early 1942, the IBZ castigated the existing structure of the Zionist movement for its internal divisiveness, which the group saw as part of the overall failure of the Zionist movement to capture the hearts and minds of the Jewish population.[7]

Surviving members who were present in Kovno during the final liquidation of the ghetto in July 1944 were sent to Dachau-Kaufering. In all, they numbered several dozen, which included as well individuals who had come from the socialist-Zionist youth movements. In the camp, they formed a new clandestine association known as the Hitahdut Hanoar Haleumi (United National Youth). Those who took charge of the group's activities moved quickly to engender a sense of purpose and discipline by establishing a reliable chain of communication between the leadership and the members in the various camps (doc. 2). Shafir, along with a core of about ten co-workers, produced a successor to the original *Nizoz*—a handwritten monthly bulletin circulated in eight copies, which reached an estimated 150–200 readers in the camps. *Nizoz* is apparently the only Hebrew-language publication in Europe to have been produced almost without a break throughout the entire war.

As revealed in their writings, ideological constancy played an important role in strengthening the Zionists' resolve and inner defenses, particularly as the day of liberation drew near. The imminent transition from ghetto and concentration camp to life in the outside world challenged their convictions and consciousness in two ways. First, the Zionist faith they had struggled to maintain had lost one of its central purposes—namely, the rescue of European Jewry, whose destruction they themselves had witnessed. Second, in preparing themselves for liberation, they understood that they would be required to shift from spiritual resistance to political implementation of their ideals. Would their ghetto- and camp-bred unity suffice? As they put it in May 1945 (doc. 7): "We know that this is no longer a hypothetical exercise." In forging a conscious bridge between their lives as prisoners and the future that awaited them, they formulated an awareness of themselves as "gatekeepers" of the Jewish national spirit. This role seemed all the more critical, in their view, because they were far from sanguine about the realistic chances of advancing rapidly toward the establishment of a Jewish state (doc. 3). Thus, as we read in the bulletin from December 1944 (doc. 1), readers were asked to identify themselves as heirs of the Maccabean tradition, because theirs was a spiritual resistance unmatched by fellow Jews living in freedom.

Alongside the Zionists in Dachau-Kaufering were a number of pro-Communist factions, which supported immediate repatriation to the (once again) Soviet-ruled Baltic republics. When asked by the Allied liberators of Dachau in May 1945 to express their preference, Lithuanian Jewish inmates overwhelmingly replied that they wished to return to Lithuania (115 out of 183). In contrast, only 30 asked to be evacuated to Palestine, with a similar number expressing a desire to emigrate to the United States. While ideology may have been one factor, many inmates of the camp were most of all eager to return to their former homes in order to search for any possible survivors from their families.[8]

Particularly noteworthy is the eulogy for Franklin D. Roosevelt (doc. 6), which alludes to an analogy between the American president and Moses. From a historian's point of view, the chief interest here lies in the contrast in perspective between this expression of admiration and affection for FDR—from inside the "Holocaust planet"—and the now-prevailing critique of Roosevelt and his attitude toward the destruction of European Jewry.

Documents

1. *Niẓoẓ* no. 3 (38), 11 December 1944
Bulletin of the Irgun Brit Ziyon [IBZ] Branch in Kaufering Concentration Camp, fifth year, Hanukah 5705
" *'Od lo avdah tikvateinu"*[9]
Communique

Dear comrades! At this moment in time, when our fellow Jews in the free world and in the homeland [in Palestine] are celebrating the holiday of the heroic Maccabees and the [historic] liberation of our land and our nation, while we, in contrast, mark six months of languishing under the overseers of this concentration camp,[10] we once again conclude that it is we who are truly capable of safeguarding our national heritage, as our movement has always done, if we but continue, even now, to uphold the tradition; if we but strengthen the awesome bond that unites us; if our plight in this camp touches us only outwardly [but does not affect us inwardly]. Particularly as we recall Jewish heroism in the land of Israel, the [Maccabees'] war for freedom and liberation, we are again filled with hope for redemption and the ultimate victory of the Jewish people. This is not the first time that [Jews] have been subjected to a decree of destruction.

There is no distinction between Antiochus Epiphanes and Adolf Hitler. The antisemitic movement that reached its highest development in Nazism and that has brought about the physical extinction of 6–7 million European Jews is historically rooted in the period in which Judah the Maccabee battled against the Hellenistic conquerors and their cause.

And just as 2,000 years ago a mere handful of rebels succeeded in withstanding an enemy many times their own strength, thus we ourselves are assured of the survival of a remnant from among us—[we need have] only endurance and courage!

Therefore, if in recent months our national work has suffered setbacks due to our own and the surrounding circumstances, we now declare our resolution to take up our task with renewed energy. For the dawn is coming, both in the east and in the west: the nations of Europe have awakened, and we must be ready for our own people's historic moment.

We have every faith that this bulletin will reach each and every member of our group in the various camps.

Members of IBZ! Take heart! Never doubt that "the eternal hope of Israel lives forever" ["neẓaḥ yisrael lo yishaker"]. With greetings from the IBZ—prepare yourselves for the liberation!

IBZ Command, first night of Hanukah 5705

2. Directive no. 1 (December 1944)

As we resume our activity, we issue the following directive:

1) Every member shall remain in touch via a liaison with the central group leadership.

2) In each camp, all members constitute a single group.

3) Each group shall have one leader, responsible for liaison with the central group leadership.

4) Each directive is sent from the central leadership to each group liaison, who will transmit it to his own group.

5) All matters of personal assistance or safety of the members are to be handled through the group liaison.

6) The group liaison shall be responsible for distributing the *Niẓoẓ* bulletins to his group.

IBZ Command, Hanukah 5705

3. *Niẓoẓ* no. 4 (39), 28 January 1945
Bulletin of the Hitahdut Hanoar Haleumi (United National Youth)
Kaufering Concentration Camp, fifth year, 15th of Shevat 5705
Declaration

In the midst of the gigantic catastrophe that has struck our people in this war, while we, the surviving remnant of the communities of Europe, remain in German captivity, imprisoned in concentration camps, we hereby express once more the Jewish people's will to live. Despite the inhuman conditions in which we live, we do not surrender; we pursue the path assigned to us. Full of bitter grief over the destruction of European Jewry in general and of our own fellows in the national movement in particular, we have reached the following conclusions based upon reflection and analysis of the tragedy that has befallen the Jews since 1 September 1939:

1) The "Jewish Question" as debated throughout the world and in Zionist ranks up to the outbreak of the war is no longer relevant, having been "resolved" by Adolf Hitler through fire and sword, wielded by Germany's armed forces.

2) There can be no doubt that the Jews of the U.S.S.R. are headed for national extinction, be it by the design of the Soviet regime or by their own voluntary actions.

3) American Jewry does not now, nor will it in the foreseeable future (for at least several generations), constitute a Jewish problem demanding urgent relief.

4) No international political constellation likely to emerge in the postwar period is apt to bring about a political resolution of the Jewish question in the land of Israel.

5) There is no justification [therefore] for the existence of separate and distinct nationally conscious [Zionist] organizations among the survivors [of European Jewry].

Knowing firsthand that world Zionism is losing its goal and function as a movement of national salvation for the great masses of the Jewish people, who no longer exist, we nevertheless will not despair of our Zionist faith, since we take into account that Zionism is not merely a political movement, but a movement of national, social, and cultural rebirth for the Jewish people. Hence, we still fervently believe that only the land of Israel is capable of serving as a national and spiritual center for the ongoing existence of the Jewish nation and its culture—both in view of its unique historical character as the national Jewish homeland [*hamoledet ha'ivrit*], and in view of its significance as the largest remaining center of refuge. We therefore declare our task to be as follows:

- to set about creating, here in the concentration camp itself, the framework needed to group together all nationally conscious youth, united and determined to establish the links [among us] in preparation for our liberation;
- to strive toward a thorough revision of the social structure in the Jewish homeland;
- to strive toward a cultural-spiritual Hebrew revival and the creation of a new Zionist weltanschauung [*torat hayim*] in Israel's national homeland in the land of Israel.

Central Bureau of Hitahdut Hanoar Haleumi

4. Our Program (1945)

1) Hitahdut Hanoar Haleumi hopes to forge a union of all Jews who see Zionism as the sole solution for the Jews and for Judaism, and for whom the establishment of a national home for the Jews in the land of Israel is a necessary precondition for the fulfillment of Zionist aspirations.

2) Hitahdut Hanoar Haleumi therefore demands the merger of all Zionist parties as have existed until now, in order to effect a concentration of all our national efforts, aimed both within our ranks and beyond them.

3) We demand the punishment of all nations that have participated in the persecution and destruction of the Jews over the past twelve years, and a special international tribunal to try those leaders responsible for its execution.

4) We demand complete compensation for the survivors on the part of the European nations, as shall be determined by an international court.

5) Hitahdut Hanoar Haleumi demands an international resolution of the "Jewish Question" corresponding to the spirit of our point no. 1, as one of the first postwar priorities, to be carried out by means of an evacuation of the Jews of Europe.

6) Hitahdut Hanoar Haleumi aspires to the social and cultural regeneration of the Jewish people in the land of Israel ['*am yisrael beerez yisrael*].

7) Hitahdut Hanoar Haleumi views its tasks in the concentration camps as:

(a) strengthening the spiritual and cultural resolve among us;
(b) preserving our inner integrity, among young people in particular;
(c) coordinating the various surviving groups.

Central Bureau of Hitahdut Hanoar Haleumi

5. Reflections on Passover 5705 in the Concentration Camp (April 1945)[11]

And so here we are in the midst of Passover. Today is the last of the [four] interim days of the holiday. Here I sit in the camp's recuperation barrack, looking out the window. All that I see is divided into small, equal squares, formed by the fence that has enclosed me for the past four years. The sky is cloudy. A cool wind is blowing. The landscape is bleak. Here and there one sees a bit of "green" already, but most of all, one sees the toil performed by the hands of the Israelites as they bear granite stones from here to there. Mindless, infantile work, intended only to exhaust the legs of the laborer, to mortify the flesh of that remnant of Israel that has been relegated to this spot.

Today, the 3rd of April in the year '45, as we begin to sense, as an echo begins to penetrate—an echo of that breath of freedom that the free world is beginning to draw—we are still locked away over here in the Middle Ages. With some hope, yes; but without the means to liberate ourselves.

All Europe is already free. A third or more of Germany is free; but we, 8,000 Jews in a distant corner of Upper Bavaria, still live the lives of slaves.

One's soul is wracked with bitter pain and grief to think about it. After four years of being driven from place to place, imprisoned, starved, frozen, subjected to all sorts of hard labor, persecution of the worst sort, this is how we will finish. All that we have been through will have been for naught. One is overcome with rage that there is nothing we can do about it. We—our lives and our deaths—lie in their hands. As they near their own end, they begrudge us food supplies but demand maximum labor.

Rain begins to fall. The skies darken even more. Germans of the O.T.[12] pass along the fence, escaping from the rain. Only the Israelites are left to toil in the open, without coats, starving, wrapped in grief. But hope for a brighter future nests in their hearts.

6. On the Death of Roosevelt, by "Aryeh" [Leyb Garfunkel]
Niẓoẓ, no. 7 (42)
Dachau-Kaufering Concentration Camp, fifth year, 25 May 1945

He died on the threshold of a world renewed, freed from the clutches of the brown monster;[13] he—whose best efforts and abilities were focused on defeating that monster.

Strictly speaking, he was president of the world's greatest democracy, but in truth he was the leader and champion of all the world's democracies. Just when all and sundry had started to believe that its light had dimmed forever, that it had lost its power, that it had no more creative force left, he showed that democracy still had something to say to the world; that it was still capable not only of defending itself, not only of protecting [the free world] that already existed, but also of assaulting and defeating its foes. And then, just weeks or perhaps just days before the final victory, when the monster, which symbolized every evil and every pestilence in the world, had already begun its death throes, on the very eve of the Allies' success, he closed his eyes forever and departed from us. Nor was this unprecedented, for as we know, there is nothing new under the sun and in this respect, too, apparently, it has happened this way before . . .

7. Last Generation of Enslavement and First Generation of Redemption
Niẓoẓ, no. 7 (42), 25 May 1945
Editorial

Were we to make a final accounting to ourselves, after five years of Zionist activity, and ask ourselves, "Have we indeed done all we could have done for our nation in the extraordinary circumstances of our lives during these past years?," we know that this is no longer a hypothetical exercise. For in the near future we will have to account for our actions before world Zionist opinion. We have not borne the flag of Zion aloft for five years in vain, but rather in the sure knowledge that this was the only way to ensure the survival of the Jewish people.

Notes

1. Original copies of the documents discussed herein were preserved by Dr. Shlomo Shafir and may be found in a special collection of the Yad Vashem Archive, M1P/24.

2. After 1943, hundreds of forced labor camps were built as annexes to major concentration camps, among which was the Dachau complex at Landsberg-Kaufering in Bavaria. During 1944–1945, inmates worked at tunneling into caves and mountainsides to create underground bunkers (meant to house bomb-proof factories for German weaponry and aircraft). Kaufering itself comprised 11 subsidiary camps, each of which contained several

thousand prisoners, mostly Jews. See Edith Raim, *Die Dachauer KZ-Aussenkommandos Kaufering und Mühldorf Rüstungsbauten und Zwangsarbeit im letzten Kriegsjahr 1944/45* (Landsberg: 1992).

3. For background, see Dov Levin, *Bein nizoz leshalhevet: Irgun Brit Ziyon bemilhemet ha'olam hasheniyah* (Ramat Gan: 1987); cf. idem, "Meigra rama lebira 'amikta—pe'ilut ziyonit bamahteret belita hasovyetit," *Masuah* 6 (1978), 57–101; idem, "Yehudei haarazot habaltiyot: pe'ilutam haziyonit vegoralam bashoah uleaharehah," *Gesher* 140 (1999), 73–83; idem, "Letoledot 'irgun brit ziyon' bemilhemet ha'olam hasheniyah," *Masuah* 19 (1991), 95–104; idem, "Nizoz shel mahteret usheerit hapeleitah," *Ha'itonut shelanu* 7 (1991), 9–16.

4. There is, perhaps, some irony in the fact that "The Spark" (*Iskra*) was also the name of Lenin's legendary Bolshevik journal.

5. Rozhka Korczak, first among these former partisans to make it to Palestine, arrived even before the war ended, on December 12, 1944.

6. Shlomo Shafir is the recently retired editor of *Gesher*, a journal published by the World Jewish Congress.

7. See Levin, *Bein nizoz leshalhevet.*

8. Central Zionist Archive, S-25/5233; cited by Yoav Gelber, *Nosei hadegel*, vol. 3 (Jerusalem:1980), 364. The prevailing opinion shifted drastically once some of the survivors actually returned to Lithuania, were received with no great warmth, and discovered that none of their family members were left alive. See Dov Levin, "Livtei shihrur," *Shvut* 2 (1976), 58–59, 71–73.

9. "We have not abandoned our hope . . ."—from the words of "Hatikvah," the Zionist anthem.

10. Most of the IBZ members had earlier been interned at Dachau's "Camp No. 1" (*Lager* 1), but many of them were transferred to "Camp No. 2" in November 1944, where conditions were somewhat less severe.

11. Written by the late Zerubavel Rosenzweig, a former student at the Real-Gymnasia of Kovno, who had taken part in underground Zionist student activities with the IBZ during the initial period of Soviet occupation (1940–1941) and was subsequently active in the Kovno ghetto under German occupation. The manuscript is in his widow's possession.

12. A reference to "Organization Todt," the war production labor office.

13. Brown, of course, was the color of the Nazi uniform (hence the use of the term "brownshirts" for Fascists).

Essays

Zola's Novel of the Dreyfus Affair: Between *Mystique* and *Politique*

Jeffrey Mehlman
BOSTON UNIVERSITY

An enigma: one of the leading and most enduring novelists of the 19th century finds himself gloriously embroiled in one of the great historical ventures of his age; he then proceeds to write a long novel in which the circumstances of the historical sequence are transposed into fiction; an accidental death turns that novel into the last the author would pen, the culmination of a life in fiction. And yet that novel—which we can now call by its name, *Vérité*, which Emile Zola began writing in 1901—is among the least read of his works, one that did not, to my knowledge, make its way into a popular edition until the centenary of the Dreyfus affair. This then is an initial enigma, but one that immediately deserves to be complicated— or perhaps supplanted—by a second and stranger one: to wit, *Vérité* is in large measure deserving of the relative oblivion into which it has fallen. It is a mediocre novel, at best, so that the true enigma is not that Zola's fictionalization of the Dreyfus affair could have fallen into oblivion but that this exemplary encounter between literature and history should have resulted in such a fiasco. It is as though the road to literary hell, in this case a cloyingly saccharine hell, might indeed be paved with the very best intentions.

Or perhaps, for Zola, the Dreyfus affair was in some respects a "novel" from the outset. Given the fact that his first reflection upon being told of the ceremonial degradation of Dreyfus, as he observed, was "to make use of the scene in a novel," might it not be that the unsatisfactoriness of his completed novel of the affair spoke to some limitation in his very engagement in the matter? Here we touch on the intriguing question of Zola's detractors during the affair, not all of whom were anti-Dreyfusards. For Charles Péguy, of course, the true hero of the affair was Bernard Lazare, unjustly obscured by Zola: "Nothing," he wrote, "is so deserving of extreme indignation as the primacy unjustly attributed to Zola: it is absolute." And he goes on to suggest ironically that, in the heat of combat, the kettledrum is, of course, more important than the artillery.[1] Yet another Dreyfusard observer, Julien Benda, recalled a disappointing discussion with Zola at the time of the affair: "I left convinced that the true values of Dreyfusism lay elsewhere than with this decent man, who seemed to me adept principally at exhibitions of self-abnegation."[2] Zola, it would appear, stood accused of self-dramatization in the affair, a propensity that might shed some light on the sentimental intoxication with abstract ideals of the sort encountered in *Vérité*.

Perhaps the best description of the novel would be as an attempt to superimpose the ethos of *politique* (to use Péguy's term), the political dogmatism into which the *mystique* of the affair eventually degenerated, onto a plot line that reads like a precise transposition of the events of the affair in its heroic phase. Indeed it is that shift—to a drama of dogmatic anticlericalism—that dictates the very terms of the transposition. What follows is a speculative attempt to wrest a measure of *mystique* from the *politique* that has all but stifled it in Zola's 700-page tome.

Zola's Dreyfus is a hyperconventional Jewish schoolteacher, Simon, in the communal school of a generic provincial town, who stands convicted—by rumor, indifference, prejudice, and clerical fraud—of the rape and murder of his own nephew, Zéphirin, an angelic, if infirm, schoolchild. Zola's *évangile*, or "gospel," as he called it, pits a heroic surrogate for the author, the elementary school teacher (or *instituteur*) Marc Froment (brother of Luc, Jean, and Mathieu), against the forces of ecclesiastical darkness, takes us through the equivalent of both Dreyfus trials, the identification of the actual culprit (a churchman), and the final rehabilitation of Simon, in a utopian France now become an *instituteur's* paradise. Indeed it is a utopia in which Marc-Zola, now a patriarch, feels prompted to remind the generations of *instituteurs* he has spawned that he is, in his words, not a god.

We turn from the sublime (or merely gaseous) puffery of the novel's conclusion to Zola's ingenious solution to a problem posed at the outset of the novel: how to insert the equivalent of the notorious *bordereau*, the slip of paper used to incriminate Dreyfus, into a case involving not treason, but rape? For it is the speculation around the interpretation of what was perhaps the most studied document of the 19th century in France, the *bordereau* allegedly offering to sell French military secrets to the German military attaché, that opens up the most intriguing possibilities, I would argue, for the literary theorist.[3] What, then, is Zola's solution? Alongside the sullied corpse of the angelic schoolchild, in his first-story room with the window wide open, a rolled up wad of paper, plainly used as a gag (or *tampon*), is found. When the Jesuit Philibin enters the room and unrolls or unravels the paper, he finds a bit of newspaper combined with a single sheet: "a thin white sheet, crumpled and spotted."[4] That strip of paper turns out to bear a bit of calligraphy; it is a mutilated writing sampler (*un modéle d'écriture*) of the sort used by teachers to instruct their charges in handwriting. It bears a *paraphe*, an indecipherable set of initials, perhaps a mere flourish, in one corner. When Philibin hands the writing sampler over to the authorities, a second corner, apparently bitten off by the gagged victim in his struggle, is missing. It is agreed that the rapist must have been a teacher who had the sampler in his pocket along with his newspaper, and stuffed the two together in his victim's mouth in a desperate and careless effort to silence him. The case will be solved when the teacher making classroom use of that specific text—whose meaning, of course, is indifferent—is identified. Witnesses, however, are not forthcoming and it is only when the missing corner, bearing the imprint of a sinister teacher in the church school, one Brother Gorgias (corresponding to Esterhazy) is found in the personal effects of Brother Philibin (standing in for

Colonel Henry), who had in fact "heroically" torn off the incriminating corner lest the Church be compromised in the incident, that the case against the Jew Simon is revealed to be groundless. The indentations of the torn corner complement precisely those of the writing sampler: "the fragment aligned itself exactly with the tear of the model."

Concerning this scenario, two comments:

1) The centrality that is accorded the mutilated text in the mouth, apparently unattributable, its letters stripped of or indifferent to their meaning, impeding speech, gagging into silence: such are the intriguing elements of the para-Freudian discourse that has flourished in recent years in the American academy as deconstruction. *Para*-Freudian? Consider that the mutilated text in the mouth has become the emblem of a child's inability to negotiate his own passivity in relation to an adult sexuality beyond his ken. It is a motif that resonates tellingly with the vexed origins of psychoanalysis in Freud's "seduction theory." Consider, additionally, that the matching up of complementary fragments of a torn sheet (or broken tessera) lies at the divided heart of the *sum-bolon*—from which Jacques Lacan's much-vaunted analogue for the unconscious, the *symbolique*. Regarding all this, Marc's task is one of domination, to submit the enigmatic text to the regimen of Truth and thereby disarm it. For once that task is accomplished, the Church, sworn enemy of Truth, can be thwarted, indeed destroyed, and, in Zola's image, Catholicism's "sacred heart" undone, will go the way of the Phallus and other crude fetishes of dead religions.

2) Zola's writing sampler, the *modéle d'écriture*, however inventive, was in significant ways a borrowing from an important source in the affair. For it was the remarkable argument of the principal witness for the prosecution in the first Dreyfus trial, the handwriting expert Alphonse Bertillon, that in writing the *bordereau*, Dreyfus himself had made use of his own "writing model," a template (or *gabarit*) placed beneath the relatively transparent sheet on which the incriminating letter was written. Why should he do this? According to the ingenious Bertillon, Dreyfus had traced his message so that he would be able to claim that it had been forged in the event he had been caught with the letter on his person. The *gabarit* consisted of a chain comprised of the word *intérét* repeated over and over, with the final "t" coinciding with the initial "i," then of a second identical chain shifted 1.25 millimeters to the left. A double chain, then, a divided proto-writing or *archi-écriture*, which generates the identity of a "natural writer" (Dreyfus), subverts that identification as forged, and then subverts that very subversion, since that very "forgery" was, according to Bertillon, a mystification.

If all this seems like a heady exercise in post-structuralism *avant la lettre*, it is because Bertillon, head of Paris' "service d'identité judiciare" and star witness for the prosecution, in many ways thought of himself as a "structuralist." Whereas Bertillon's graphological predecessors had studied handwriting as the *expression* of character or identity, Bertillon restricted himself to refining techniques for better delineating the idiosyncrasies of different modes of handwriting, which were themselves said to be our surest touchstones of identity: handwriting, then, not as the expression of identity, but as identity itself. In practice this entailed the establishment of a laboratory of textual superimposition, which I have discussed elsewhere.[5]

Bertillon's methodological loyalties, however, were divided between handwriting identification, which he refined, and a second technique for identifying juridicial subjects, one which he all but introduced in France, fingerprint analysis. For the status of the plurilinear pattern called "handwriting," in Bertillon's perspective, was ultimately no different from that of the intricate "arabesque" of a fingerprint: "the outline of the thousand small capillary striations formed through the random agglomeration of sweat glands lining the finger tip of each individual." It is as though, for Bertillon, there was an identificatory chip inscribed on—or just beyond—one's digital extremities, a chip taking on the qualities of what the Freudians call a "partial or component object," a perpetually oscillating index of identity whose very vibrations play havoc with the possibility of identity itself.[6]

It is time, no doubt, to close this parenthesis in Zola's novel, the mutilated text in the mouth, and to close it in part because the novel itself, in the person of its new-evangelical protagonist, would have us bracket, even foreclose, the question of the writing model: "even if this writing sampler, crumpled and rolled into a gag . . . was there as an indecipherable enigma, all-powerful Reason [*la toute puissante raison*] dictated that one had to look elsewhere."[7] In the name of Truth, then, the novel would bracket the question of *écriture* and repress the adepts of a *sacré coeur* Zola imagines as destined to the same oblivion as . . . the phallus. Marc's battle, moreover, is fundamentally sexual. For much of the novel deals with the Church's insidious hold on women, the fundamental "disunion" at the heart of French sexuality, a conflict created by the Church's simultaneous distrust, devastation, and enlistment of the women of France on its behalf.[8] To fight the good fight is to win womankind back from the Church, to submit it to the wisdom of right-thinking males, and such is indeed the accomplishment of Marc—with regard to the women in his family—in *Vérité*.

That "good fight," however, culminating in the apotheosis of the patriarch, bent on eradicating the "rift" at the heart of sexuality, on consigning the *sacré-coeur* phallus to oblivion, is in its very structure, and beyond the tendency to self-glorification already alluded to, narcissistic. For that structure is specular. Consider, for instance, that the Catholics of *Vérité* stand convicted of bilking the faithful through the sale of fraudulent spiritual favors. Their crime, that is, is the hoary theological sin of "simony." None of that would be particularly significant if Zola had not named his Dreyfus surrogate Simon. So the "Simonists," supporters of Simon, wage their war against a band of "simonists" (French: *simoniaques*), practitioners of simony, as though the very language of the novel were intent on underscoring, against the author's own argument, a perilous symmetry. Indeed, even Zola's distinction between a marginally acceptable Gallican church and a fundamentally corrupt and rapacious Ultramontane international seems to mirror, incredibly, the distinction between assimilated *Israélites* and unassimilable *Ostjuden/juifs*. For the novel's onslaught against Catholicism ("source of every lie and all misery")[9] is so unrelenting as to figure as no more than the flip side of his adversaries' antisemitism. Marc, one feels, initially identifies the culprit in the rape case as a churchman on grounds no more probative than those of the equally intuitive anti-semites who have, they feel, ample grounds for suspecting the Jew Simon. Equally troublesome is the degeneration of the writing into sheer formulaic cliché as the novel moves into its utopian phase, toward what Zola does not blush to call "the future city of perfect solidarity."[10] Sentimental solemnities abound; predictable dichotomies between past and future, Church and School, error and Truth, all underwrite the meliorist vision that sustains the protagonist in his progress toward apotheosis.

The closer the novel moves to Truth, the more hackneyed its formulations; the closer it moves toward eradicating the "poison" of Catholicism, the more dogmatically intolerant its posture—so much so that one suspects that it was precisely such intolerance (a bizarre outcome for the Dreyfus affair) that may have been a principal factor contributing to the novel's subsequent unreadability. And finally, the closer the protagonist moves to apotheosis, the less the novel seems to see beyond the nobility of his cause. This culminates in a remarkable line, at novel's end, to the effect that the Jews have long since disappeared, since the Catholics themselves are on the way out.[11] The happy end of the Dreyfus affair in Emile Zola's fictional transposition is, paradoxically, a world without Jews.

Finally, the reader is left gasping for anything that will resist the progress of Truth, shatter the novelist's narcissism. Fortunately, Zola gives us a character happily (or miserably) resistant to the progress of the author's Manichean scheme: Brother Gorgias, the counterpart to Esterhazy, sometime rapist, heretical masochist, and a man imbued with so authentically religious a spirit that he proves too hot for even the Church to handle. "At that precise moment, Brother Gorgias was truly resplendent with mocking impudence and heroic mendacity. . . . He even aspired to the palms of martyrdom; each of his pious ignominies would earn him a new joy in heaven. . . ."[12] The cliché of Dreyfusard historiography is that Esterhazy was a character out of Balzac, but as *Vérité* makes clear, he is in fact a first-rate character out of Zola.

I would like to take this reference to Zola's heretical masochist (wallowing, once the statute of limitations has run out, in self-vilification) as an occasion to open a second parenthesis in our reading of the novel, to speak briefly of the one authentically heretical mystic to have written about the affair. Let Gorgias' masochism serve as a pretext for inserting into Zola's text the piece to which Léon Bloy gave the devastating title: *Je m'accuse.*

Bloy was one of the wild men of the fin de siècle, a flamboyant mix of scatology and eschatology whose persona was somewhere between religious mystic and stand-up comic. I have commented elsewhere on Bloy's affinities with Jacques Lacan, and was gratified to see Elisabeth Roudinesco acknowledge Lacan's special affection for Bloy in her biography of Lacan.[13] *Je m'accuse* is Bloy's journal, during a stay in Denmark, of both the Dreyfus affair and his reading of a previous Zola *évangile, Fécondité.*

The title *Je m'accuse* refers to Bloy's self-reproach for having sullied the myth of Antaeus in an earlier allusion to Zola, but is attractive in this context because of its implicit critique of both the relentlessly *accusatory* tone and the fundamentally *accusative* attitude toward language in, say, the novel *Vérité*. Accusative: discourse has as its direct—and only suitable—object Truth itself, against which Bloy proposes the reflexive or masochistic flipping back onto the subject of *je m'accuse.* All of which —*Je m'accuse* and its onslaught against the "religion of life" preached in Zola's several *évangiles*—brings us back to Freud, who was his contemporary, and to the primary masochism said to devastate the incipient vitalism of Freud's Eros-bound ego psychology.[14] All this, moreover, in a rhetoric—Léon Bloy's—that has left a decided imprint on Lacan in his critique of the ego psychologist in Freud. Decidedly, the grafting of *Je m'accuse* onto the heretical-masochistic sequence (Gorgias-Esterhazy) in *Vérité* opens onto some intriguing perspectives.

Bloy might have appreciated the graft, as a first quotation from *Je m'accuse* makes clear: "Insofar as I am an artiste I am *for* the scoundrel [*crapule*] Esterhazy and *against* the scoundrel [*crapule*] Urbain Gohier."[15] (Gohier was an ardent Dreyfusard and an ardent antisemite, who ended his career writing for the collaborationist weekly *Au pilori*, but that is another story . . .).[16] The artist, that is, will side with originality against cliché, independent of issues of justice. Bloy was convinced that Dreyfus was innocent, but felt that the real meaning of the affair was as an anticipation of Apocalypse:

> All of this transcends infinitely the Jewish captain and resembles the initial tremors of the Cataclysm. Ever since the obscene and stupid trial at Rennes came to a conclusion, how could one doubt that the misfortunes of that man were but a pretext for the two varieties of dog that have been competing over France vicious bite by bite [*coups de gueules*]?[17]

With dogs (or *crapules*) on both sides, it is as though Bloy were, above all, sensitive to the vileness of anti-Dreyfusards *and* Dreyfusards, a symmetry spelling devastation for France. That specularity is given its most striking formulation in a wish that he be given, in Denmark, a subscription to both *L'Aurore* and *La Croix*: "I would then have possession of the two extremities of the cow's intestine [*boyau de vache*] with which the most noble people ever to exist is being strangled."[18]

Dreyfus, a wretched innocent, had become a pretext for France to tear itself apart in a fit of mimetic rivalry. But Bloy subjects the thesis of Dreyfus' innocence to a curious twist in a letter (to an anonymous soldier) of April 25, 1899:

> To bring this filthy Dreyfus matter to an end, I do indeed find myself obliged, despite the extraordinary infamy of most of his friends, to regard it as quite probable that that unfortunate man is expiating, on Devil's Island, the crime of another, or several others, and that the high command of our army has been entrusted, for quite some time now, to some altogether remarkable individuals [*de bien jolis garçons*]. It is a matter of derision and shame the whole world over.[19]

And yet, given the mystic's assumption that the world itself is a divinely—though enigmatically—ordered Text, there must be a rationale behind whatever it is that Dreyfus seems to be expiating. For he was rich: "What was the origin of his wealth, and what use did he make of it? Just as he is paying for others, in his jail, who knows if someone else is not paying for him, in an even more frightening way, in the recesses of some cave?"[20] The argument that, as a bourgeois, Dreyfus, the class enemy, was inevitably guilty (even if he did not commit treason) was used extensively by the Left, and would survive in its resistance to the politics of antifascism in the 1930s, and even into the alliance of the left-wing journal *La Vieille Taupe* with the Holocaust "negationism" of Robert Faurisson in the 1980s. Alain Finkielkraut has written eloquently on the subject.[21] But Bloy was not a man of the Left. The logic of a general economy of displacement—in which everyone ends up serving for or displacing someone else—is in fact a version of Bloy's reading of the Communion of Saints, in which "no one knows his own name, no one his own face, because no one can identify the mysterious person (who is perhaps already devoured by worms) whose place he *essentially* occupies."[22] The texture of reality is of a cascade of displacements or substitutions, and the restricted economy (which would stop at the proposition: Dreyfus is paying for Esterhazy), aside from plunging France into the first stages of civil war or Apocalypse, is above all blind to that general economy—or cascade—of substitutions that is the divinely (dis)ordered Text of reality itself.

The restricted economy (the Dreyfusard–anti-Dreyfusard symmetry) had proved a gold mine for Zola: whence the indignation of Bernard Lazare, "who was in reality the first, the only one to take an interest in Dreyfus, who saw Zola suddenly spring from between his paws *when the affair was ready*, ripe for the plucking and who, after the victory, did not even get a mention."[23] Worse still, for Bloy, the affair had ushered in a flood of clichés so grotesque in their repetitiveness that Bloy, beside himself, ends one entry in his journal with a call to embrace his "hero": "Emile! viens que je te baise!"[24] Emile Zola, the Vasco da Gama of the commonplace, "the Michelangelo of turd": such is the Zola served up by his adversary Léon Bloy.

But, it will be objected, it is one thing to resist the degeneration of the Dreyfusard *mystique* (in Péguy's terms) into sordid or dogmatic politics, and a very different one to pump that very *mystique* with the stuff of mysticism proper, the scatological-eschatological perspective from which Bloy saw the affair. And I am prepared to indulge that cavil. For which reason, in compensation, I would suggest that we extend the other term of Péguy's dichotomy—*politique*—to its extreme, and pose, however briefly, the question of what the Dreyfus affair has become more recently, in our age of political correctness. A first stop might take us to a wonderful novel of Romain Gary, *Gros-Câlin*, in which a poor soul of a narrator, a Parisian office worker, falls in love with a Guyanese looker, who also, unbeknownst to him, happens to be a Guyanese hooker. Her name: Mlle. Dreyfus:

> She's a black from French Guyana, as her name indicates, which is very often adopted in those parts by vintage types, for reasons of local color and to encourage tourism. Captain Dreyfus, who wasn't guilty, stayed there for five years in jail, for no particular reason, and his innocence ended up splattering over everyone.[25]

In brief, if so many black families have adopted the name Dreyfus in French Guyana, it is because it is part of a politically correct racket: "That way, no one dares lay a finger on them."[26]

And then, finally, there is the American baseball novel by Peter Lefcourt published a few years back under the title *The Dreyfus Affair*.[27] Randy Dreyfus is a champion shortstop. You may recognize some of the other members of the infield: Bernie Lazare is the catcher; Rennie Panizzardi is on third. The team's manager is Charlie Gonse. A crisis arises when Dreyfus falls in love with his second-baseman,

D. J. Pickett (for which we are perhaps to read Picquart). Dreyfus' love is recip-
rocated, and when the two are accidentally discovered (and videotaped) necking in
a Neiman Marcus changing room, all hell breaks loose. They are suspended from
the game by the baseball commissioner, and it is only thanks to the press campaign
of a dyspeptic sportswriter named Milt Zola that they are reinstated in the game.
All of which is jejune enough, and would perhaps not even be worth noting were
it not for the fact that the only way to fully script this version of the Dreyfus affair,
in which there is no culprit (since I'm O.K., you're O.K.), is to attribute the role
and name of Esterhazy to the baseball commissioner himself. In the age of political
correctness, in which there are no misdeeds, the only villain—Fritz Esterhazy—is
the bigot who imagines that such a thing as a misdeed might exist.

Such was *The Dreyfus Affair*, a best-selling novel in the United States in 1993.
And it is against that tendential degeneration of the affair's *politique* into a particularly bland form of political correctness, that I have risked the apparently reactionary gesture of comparing the affair's very *mystique*, as portrayed in Zola's
novel, with Bloy's mystical vision.

Notes

1. Charles Péguy, *Oeuvres en prose 1898–1908* (Paris: 1959), 1491.
2. Julien Benda, *La Jeunesse d'un clerc* (Paris: 1936), 80.
3. Jeffrey Mehlman, "Pierre Menard, Author of *Don Quixote*," in idem, *Genealogies of the Text: Literature, Psychoanalysis, and Politics in Modern France* (Cambridge: 1995), 67–81.
4. Emile Zola, *Vérité*, 2 vols. (Paris: 1928), 20.
5. Mehlman, "Pierre Menard, Author of *Don Quixote*."
6. For a discussion of Freud and Bertillon, see Carlo Ginzburg, "Morelli, Freud, and Sherlock Holmes: Clues and Scientific Method," in *History Workshop* 9 (1980), 5–36.
7. Zola, *Vérité*, 55.
8. Ibid., 490.
9. Ibid., 529.
10. Ibid., 564.
11. Ibid., 605.
12. Ibid., 311.
13. Elisabeth Roudinesco, *Jacques Lacan: esquisse d'une vie, histoire d'un systéme de pensée* (Paris: 1993); see also Jeffrey Mehlman, "The Suture of an Allusion: Lacan with Léon Bloy," in idem, *Legacies of Antisemitism in France* (Minneapolis: 1983) 23–33; idem, "The Paranoid Style in French Prose: Lacan with Léon Bloy," in idem, *Genealogies of the Text*, 139–153.
14. On primary masochism in Freud and its relation to Freud's vitalism, see Jean Laplanche, *Life and Death in Psychoanalysis*, trans. J. Mehlman (Baltimore: 1974), chs. 5–6.
15. Léon Bloy, *Oeuvres complétes* (Paris: 1947), 24:62. All of the following quotes are from volume 24.
16. See Simon Epstein, *Les Dreyfusards sous l'Occupation* (Paris: 2001), 127–133.
17. Léon Bloy, *Oeuvres complétes*, 121.
18. Ibid., 77.
19. Ibid., 37.
20. Ibid., 38.
21. Alain Finkielkraut, *Lavenir d'une negation: réflexion sur la question du genocide* (Paris: 1983).

22. Cited in Mehlman, *Genealogies of the Text*, 142.
23. Bloy, *Oeuvres complétes*, 54.
24. Ibid., 68.
25. Romain Gary, *Gros-Câlin* (Paris: 1974), 15.
26. Ibid.
27. Peter Lefcourt, *The Dreyfus Affair: A Love Story* (New York: 1992).

Franz Boas' Linguistic Paradigm and the Paradox of Jewish Group Existence

Amos Morris-Reich
THE HEBREW UNIVERSITY

Franz Boas (1858–1942), a German Jew by descent and a founder of academic American anthropology, denied that there was anything that could be designated as Jewish culture or Jewish group existence. In his resolute fight against racism in general and racist anthropological theories in particular, he repeatedly contended that the Jews were—anthropologically speaking—a deeply assimilated and racially diverse group.[1] Most of the work that deals with Boas and his position on the Jews specifies his biographical background as the key to understanding how or why he developed such a position.[2] Far less attention has been paid to other factors, in particular the way in which Boas' own anthropological paradigms, applied throughout his research, could not have constituted the Jews as anything other than deeply assimilated in character. Moreover, whereas those who have dealt with Boas' statements on the Jews have concentrated primarily on his pioneering work on race, little attention has been paid to the fact that Boas never related to Jews in his work on general culture or, more specifically, on language.

Why did Boas not extend his argument about the Jews' assimilated character to the sphere of language? Did not the history of diverse communities of Jews around the world testify to an extraordinary degree of linguistic assimilation (Yiddish, Judeo-Persian, Judeo-Arabic, Judesmo, and the like)? As long as one focuses solely on Boas' background, this question does not seem relevant; indeed, it is difficult to see how Boas' German Jewish descent can provide an answer here. The answer, I believe, is to be found in the conflicting principles that guided Boas' anthropology.

Throughout his long career, Boas moved increasingly from viewing race and culture as independent, or contingently related, variables to viewing culture as the real ground of specific difference. In the sphere of race, Boas' categories *deconstructed* racialist theories, repeatedly revealing their scientific arbitrariness and demonstrating their lack of scientific foundation. In the sphere of language, in contrast, his categories *constructed* group identities, revealing that the identity of primitive groups was found in, and in fact was founded upon, their language. In the sphere of race, the deeply assimilated nature of the Jews served his overall anthropological goal; in that of language, it ran counter to it. When one shifts the perspective from the author (Boas) to the construction of the object (the Jews) under terms derived from Boas' disciplinary paradigm, his references to the Jews—or rather, lack of them—reveal a critical difference between his work on race and his work on culture. To make the focus of my argument clearer, I wish to introduce a term from the metaphysical notion of individuality: "specific difference." Specific difference comprises the common features that help distinguish a given entity from a larger group, and at the same time, make it part of a smaller group, the members of which can be distinguished as individuals. The specific difference of the Jews is what distinguishes them from a larger group (humanity). According to Boas, the Jews' specific difference was that of a deeply assimilated group. However, it was only in the sphere of race—as opposed to culture—that he made this claim explicit. Considered in this light, Boas' statements on the Jews are subordinated to his general anthropological goals, not to his biography.

Race, notes Rachel Caspari, "was the major theoretical foundation of anthropology; physical anthropology was virtually synonymous with the study of race."[3] However, she continues, while essentialism is one of the attributes entailed by the concept of race, biological determinism is not.[4] Thus, it was possible for Boas to reject biological determinism without rejecting the concept of race in toto and to operate with the category of race without accepting the principle of "fundamental racial difference."

According to Boas:

> Numerous attempts have been made to give a scientific status to the feeling of racial difference and particularly to the claim of Nordic superiority. In these attempts use is made of historical data, of descriptions of national character and of psychological tests to which individuals of different races have been subjected. In none of these discussions, however, do we find a concise and definite answer to the question of what constitutes a race.[5]

Elsewhere, he writes: "Racism as a basis of social solidarity as against the cultural interest of mankind is more dangerous than any of the other groupings [that is, forms of social cohesion] because according to its claims the hostile groups are biologically determined, and therefore permanent." Moreover, to prove the credibility of a racist theory, "we should have to prove that each 'race' is so strongly inbred that anatomical characteristics which determine behavior would be inherited by all its members, or at least that they are so common that they will give a certain stamp to the behavior of the whole group."[6]

In this comparative context, Boas studied a number of physical traits, and their variation, among children of East European immigrant Jews in America.[7] Apart from this early work, his only other discussion devoted primarily to Jews was an article, first published in January 1923, which was titled "Are the Jews a Race?" (it was later reprinted in his *Race and Democratic Society*). In this essay, Boas forcefully rejects the claim that the Jews constitute a race. Yet it is possible to observe that above and beyond disclaiming a "Jewish race," Boas is aiming at something more comprehensive. The Jews, who are certainly the focal point of the article, are not seen here as the object of *research*—that is, Boas is not trying to observe anything new about them—but rather as the object of *explanation*. That is, Boas uses the case of the Jews to deny the scientific validity of antisemitism and other racialist theories.

The Jews, according to Boas, so clearly lack the necessary characteristics of a race (not to speak of a "pure race," which, even had such a thing ever existed, no longer did), that they make the best case for discrediting such erroneous and dangerous theories. Racist theories, according to Boas, are in fact used to support nationalistic theories of the *nation*, thus confusing two terms that Boas understands as fundamentally dissimilar. In this sense, Boas' use of the term "Jew" may be designated as rhetorical.

Boas argued that Jews living in widely differing geographical areas tended to share bodily build and other racial markers with the populations among which they lived, rather than with Jews living elsewhere. "The dispersion of the Jews all over the world," Boas states, "has tended to increase considerably the intermixture. A comparison of the Jews of North Africa with those of Western Europe and those of Russia, not to speak of those of Southern Asia, shows very clearly that in every single instance we have a marked assimilation between the Jews and the people among whom they live."[8] As a result: "The Jews of North Africa are, in their essential traits, North Africans. The Jews of Europe are in their essential traits, Europeans, and the black Jews of the East are in their essential traits members of a dark-pigmented race."[9] From these observations, Boas concludes: "The assimilation of the Jews by the people among whom they live is much more far-reaching than a hasty observation might suggest. In stature as well as in head form and in other features there is a decided parallelism between the bodily form of the Jews and that of the people among whom they live."[10]

According to Boas' parameters, it is easier to make a convincing point regarding the Jews than it would be regarding black or Asiatic groups. In the latter cases, he would have had to enter upon a much longer and more detailed explanation as to why there are, indeed, races (albeit no "pure races"), since blacks, as a group, and Asiatics, as a group, do in fact share certain physical racial markers. By denying that the Jews are a race, Boas wishes to make clear that any attempt to claim the purity of a *nation* on the basis of the purity of a *race* is twice mistaken, both because of its erroneous definition of race and because of its incorrect definition of a nation. With this, Boas comes to his real point of interest: "It is a fiction to speak of a German race" since "[n]ational groups and local types have nothing in common."[11] *In this project, the signifier "Jew" is a powerful tool in Boas' hands.*

In his pioneering treatment of language found among groups without a system of writing (termed primitive), Boas subverted the 19th-century concept of language and initiated a working paradigm that was further developed by Edward Sapir, Benjamin Whorf, and others.[12] Nineteenth-century Western linguists paid special attention to the texts and manuscripts of written language. This approach inevitably resulted in a limited, ethnocentric perspective on language, since it restricted study to those cultures and languages with a long written tradition—that is, largely their own Western cultures—whereas historical philologists confined themselves mainly to the diachronic study of language. On his arrival in the United States in 1887,

Boas challenged the linguistic work done among the Native American "Indians" on at least three grounds. First, he called into question the empirical value of the existing research and was crucial in transforming the study of language among Native Americans into a professional academic field. Second, rather than comparing Native American and Indo-European languages, he introduced what he called "analytical" terms of description. And finally, he came out strongly against evolutionary presumptions in the study of language among primitive groups.

Prior to Boas, the study of North American aboriginal languages had been done mainly by missionaries who were eager to convert the "Indians" to Christianity, or else (at best) by untrained amateur anthropologists. The majority of "linguistic studies" of Indian languages in Boas' day were actually comparisons of compounded lists of words with the vocabulary of Indo-European languages and the comparison of native grammatical structures with those of Indo-European languages. The findings regularly pointed to the "inferiority" of the Indian languages (based, among other things, on their having a smaller vocabulary, a simpler syntax, and a lack of abstract notions such as were found in European languages).[13] These results, in turn, reaffirmed the supremacy of European languages (and races)—an assumption that stood at the starting point of such research.

Boas' simple demand was that the student of a tribe, a group, or a language *know* the language he or she was studying and be minimally disciplined in the area of linguistics. This demand, which from our contemporary standpoint may seem self-evident, was in fact a call for a comprehensive modification of the standards of study of Indian languages: a demand to move away from a conception of language study that was centered on the Indo-European languages.

"Our needs become particularly apparent," Boas wrote in his 1911 introduction to the *Handbook of American Indian Languages,*

> when we compare the methods that we expect from any investigator of cultures of the Old World with those of the ethnologist who is studying primitive tribes. Nobody would expect authoritative accounts of the civilization of China or of Japan from a man who does not speak the languages readily, and who has not mastered their literatures. The student of antiquity is expected to have a thorough mastery of the ancient languages. A student of Mohammedan life in Arabia or Turkey would hardly be considered a serious investigator if all his knowledge had to be derived from second-hand accounts. The ethnologist, on the other hand, undertakes in the majority of cases to elucidate the innermost thoughts and feelings of a people without so much as a smattering of knowledge of their language.[14]

Boas fought not only to raise academic standards to a level comparable to other areas of ethnology, but also to institutionalize the anthropological discipline (with the support of students from Columbia University, where he held a chair, and from the Bureau of American Ethnology). What he described as a program for a "descriptive analytical" treatment of languages was in fact a demand for the establishment of a new, and inherently counter-evolutionary, paradigm for the study of languages among primitive groups. Under this paradigm, grammatical categories were to be formulated as if a native speaker, "without knowledge of any other language, should present the essential notions of his own grammar without reference to the current classifications of Indo-European languages."[15] In this way, Indo-

European languages would no longer serve as a privileged point of reference for the study of other languages, and the differences between languages would not be formulated in hierarchical terms.[16]

Since he was dealing with groups that possessed no system of writing and therefore no corpus of written texts, Boas based his descriptive-analytical analysis on spoken language. Language was accounted for, not in terms of detailed philological and etymological analysis, but in terms of practically learned, physically produced *sounds*. Thus, Boas' paradigm came to identify the existence of a given language with the people who spoke it. According to Boas, it "seems reasonable to suppose that the number of languages that have disappeared is very large."[17] When a language has no written record, its survival is dependent on, and identical with, the life of those who speak it. A language "lives" as long as it is spoken. Implicitly, assimilation of the group's members will cause the actual disappearance of the language as well as the group. For instance: "Tonkawa is now spoken by only six persons—all of them past middle age. . . . The language is not being learned by any of the younger people, and, with the death of the present speakers, will become extinct."[18]

It is interesting to note that, in the section on language in his *General Anthropology* (in the course of discussing the form out of which two modern forms of a word are derived), Boas only twice refers to a language (Latin) that did not exist as a spoken language in his present day. Latin is one case in which the intricate connection implicit in Boas' paradigm between a spoken language, the psychological world of experience, and the culture of a group is not strictly maintained, perhaps because of Latin's status as the source of many contemporary European spoken languages.

In the sphere of language, Boas was aiming at something very different than the deconstruction of racialist theories of identity in an attempt to deflate the significance of race. In subverting the evolutionary conception of language and arguing for strict empirical standards, Boas came to advocate a holistic paradigm concerning the nature of language and its relation to the life of the group. Language was used as an alternative to racialist theories: via his treatment of language as the basis of primitive groups' consciousness, Boas was in fact constructing their very identity.

"There are two kinds of people," Boas is famous for telling his students, "those who have to have general conceptions into which to fit the facts; those who find the facts sufficient. I belong to the latter category."[19] However, what Boas regarded as strictly empirical actually led to important supra-empirical axioms concerning the nature of language and its relation to the life of its speech–community.

Boas continually argued for the centrality of the individual and against the reification of culture.[20] He repeatedly stated that the "identification of an individual with a class because of his bodily appearance, language, or manners has always seemed to me a survival of barbaric, or rather of primitive, habits of mind."[21] However, the study of language, which in its essence is *supra-individual*, represents a case in which Boas' project stood in clear opposition to what he said (or thought) he was doing. Louis Dumont puts this matter most succinctly when he states that the study of language "emancipated the researcher from his compulsory reference to the human individual and embodied the promise of an unmediated grasp of the society itself."[22]

Boas did not come up with his notion of language *ex nihilo* but was rather continuing a long line of German-Romantic thought. This tradition, which held language to be the constitutive criterion for identifying group identity, was initiated by Johann Herder and developed by Wilhelm von Humboldt and, later, by Moritz Lazarus and Heymann Steinthal, both of whom Boas esteemed highly.[23] In relation to the anthropological study of language, Boas can be seen as carrying on the specific legacy of Herder and Lazarus. "Herder," writes R. G. Collingwood, "was the first thinker to recognize in a systematic way that there are differences between different kinds of men, and that human nature is not uniform but diversified."[24] According to Herder, language "can only be learnt in a community. It is synonymous with thought . . . every language is different from every other." It follows that "each community has its own mode of thought,"[25] and language "expresses the collective experience of the group."[26] Boas' study of language gave new substance to Herder's anthropological line of thought.

Donald Levine observes: "Thanks to Boas, the Herder/Humboldtian notion of intuiting the genius of a culture's distinctive configuration th[r]ough careful study of its language [became] central to much of later cultural anthropology."[27] Boas connected group consciousness and group identity with language on two levels. First, he developed a thesis concerning the structure and meaning of language in human life, and second, he argued on the basis of specific characteristics of existing languages. That is, Boas differentiated between language as a universal human invariable, and the study of distinct, variable languages. Concerning language in general, Boas argued: "If ethnology is understood as the science dealing with the mental phenomena of the life of the peoples of the world, human language, one of the most important manifestations of mental life, would seem to belong naturally to the field of work of ethnology."[28] This is because language classifies human experience: "Since the total range of personal experience which language serves to express is infinitely varied, and its whole scope must be expressed by a limited number of phonetic groups, it is obvious that an extended classification of experiences must underlie all articulate speech."[29] Yet Boas, the anthropologist of distinct *languages*, writes: "In various cultures these classifications may be founded on fundamentally distinct principles."[30] Elsewhere he states that "the principles of classification which are found in different languages do not by any means agree."[31] *Therefore, language classifies experience; different languages classify experience differently.*

Boas demonstrates his view on two different linguistic levels. The first is the lexical level. "In the life of the Eskimo," Boas writes in one of his famous examples, "*snow* means something entirely different as falling snow, soft snow on the ground, drifting snow or snowdrift."[32] Lexically, there are different words for classifying what in English is designated generally as snow (or rain, in his English equivalent). "On the whole," Boas writes in the introduction to *Handbook of American Indian Languages* (in what Roman Jakobson termed "one of the most daring, most fertile and innovatory ideas ever uttered by Boas"),[33] "the categories which are formed always remain unconscious."[34] However, over and above the lexical level, Boas argued that the obligatory classification of experience may be found in grammar.

According to Boas: "Language without both vocabulary and grammar is impossible." As he explains:

> Grammar . . . determines those aspects of each experience that *must* be expressed. When we say that "The man killed the bull," we understand that a definite single man in the past killed a definite single bull. We cannot express this experience in such a way that we remain in doubt whether a definite or indefinite person or bull, one or more persons or bulls, the present or past time, are meant. We have to choose between these aspects, and one or the other must be chosen. These obligatory aspects are expressed by means of grammatical devices. The aspects chosen in different groups of languages vary fundamentally. To give an example: while for us definiteness, number, and time are obligatory aspects, we find in another language location near the speaker or somewhere else, source of information—whether seen, heard, or inferred—as obligatory aspects. Instead of saying "The man killed a bull," I should have to say, "This man (or men) kill (indefinite tense) as seen by me that bull (or bulls)."[35]

In examples of this kind, Boas demonstrated the unconscious power of the classification of experience extant in grammar. "When we consider for a moment what this implies," Boas notes (in line with von Humboldt's understanding of language), "it will be recognized that in each language only a part of the complete concept that we have in mind is expressed, and that each language has a peculiar tendency to select this or that aspect of the mental image which is conveyed by the expression of the thought."[36] Boas is by no means trying to argue that there are no universal aspects shared by the grammar of languages the world over (such as the relation between subject and predicate, noun and adjective, verb and adverb, and the like).[37] He simply maintains that "the methods by means of which these and other relations are expressed vary very much."[38]

Any given language represents the mental world of the *group* and has itself been shaped and determined by the *group's* "universe of experience."[39] *Spoken* language, therefore, represents the group's mental world of experience.[40] Furthermore, although Boas never states this explicitly, his analyses of primitive groups' languages always take for granted that the consciousness of the group's members is based on one language. In this, too, Boas followed a long line of Romantic thought. Friedrich Schleiermacher, for instance, believed that "[o]nly one language is firmly implanted in an individual. Only to one does he belong entirely, no matter how many he learns subsequently. . . . For every language is a particular mode of thought and what is cogitated in one language can never be repeated in the same way in another. . . . Language, thus . . . is an expression of a particular life."[41]

Through language, Boas establishes distinct "cultures" and "geniuses" in the restricting framework of what he terms "historical particularism."[42] In this, too, he was importing German thought into American anthropology. Johann Gottlieb Fichte, for instance, expressed the same understanding concerning the dependency that exists between language and group identity. In his *Addresses to the German Nation* (1806), Fichte stated that language "is the most important criterion by which a nation is recognized to exist, and to have the right to form a state on its own." Very much in Boas' line of treatment of the linguistic aspect of group existence,

Fichte concluded that "we give the name of *people* to men whose organs of speech are influenced by the same external conditions, who live together, and who develop their language in continuous communication with each other."[43] Boas, for his part, notes: "On the whole the degree of specialization will depend upon cultural interests. Categories that are culturally unessential will not be found; those culturally important will be detailed."[44]

In sum, Boas' paradigm associates the mental life-experience of a given group with its spoken language; thus, Boas *derives group identity from (spoken) language*.

At this point, we need to shift our perspective from the author (Boas) to the object (the Jews). In addressing the Jews as an analytical object, Boas does not necessarily deal with historical data, but rather with the embedded interconnection between Jewish realities and deeply seated, mostly Christian-European, stereotypes of the Jews' language (or lack thereof). It is historically true that in Boas' time (as is the case today) there was no one language in use by Jews everywhere. Consequently, a crucial element in the Jews' anthropological character—which, in Boas' view, was tightly connected to the group's culture—was subverted. Yet this view was based on at least two widely held but erroneous assumptions.

The first, held by most Europeans, Christians and Jews alike, was that Hebrew, the Jewish language par excellence, was a "dead" language. In the Zionist version of this myth, Eliezer Ben-Yehuda single-handedly "resurrected" Hebrew.[45] (The late Israeli humorist Ephraim Kishon captured the theoretical impossibility of "resurrecting" Hebrew as a mother tongue when he noted that Israel was the only place in the world in which parents learned their mother tongue from their children.) Second, Boas and most others believed that those few who did know Hebrew were familiar with it primarily from written texts. In fact, in Eastern Europe, Hebrew existed together with Yiddish in a bilingual system that served the great majority of Jews.[46] Moreover, especially in its Hebrew-Aramaic "rabbinic" form, Hebrew was primarily an aural/oral language for the mass of Jews (except for the very small religious intelligentsia), even if it was not the daily language spoken by the majority of Jews anywhere in Europe or the Americas.

Whether or not he was willfully ignorant of the realities of Jewish life in Eastern Europe, it seems clear that Boas was unaware of the extent to which various forms of spoken Hebrew remained in use. He shared the common assumption that Hebrew had not served as a spoken language for many hundreds of years, most certainly not as *the* spoken language of a people, and thus, perforce, was a "dead" language rather than one in which Jews compressed their present daily experiences into something constituting a distinct "world."

If not Hebrew, what about the other languages spoken by Jews? Although Jews naturally spoke the languages of their respective countries, these could hardly be taken as representing a distinctly *Jewish* world of experience.[47] (Indeed, according to these terms, if all Jews would speak only the languages of their respective countries and if there were no Jewish languages in existence, Boas could represent the Jews as having lost all vestiges of their Jewish individuality. There would be no distinct Jewish "world" and their assimilation would be complete.) In fact, apart from the languages of their respective countries, Jews also maintained distinctive

Jewish languages. Yet such languages, particularly Yiddish, were most often considered to be either "dialects" or "jargons" rather than true languages.[48] There is great irony in the fact that Boas declined to view Yiddish as a distinct language, as his historical particularism could in fact furnish such a representation. However, were he to do so, he would be compelled to recognize Yiddish as a fused, or amalgam, language—a phenomenon ruled out by his postulates. Only a generation later, Max Weinreich used historical particularism to argue that Yiddish was a fused language and that this assimilated nature was the essence of Jewish languages.[49] The difference between Boas and Weinreich is conceptual: Boas refused to concede that the "form" of a language could be fused.

The question of fused language is much disputed in the history of linguistics, and Boas himself is not fully consistent in his writings on interlanguage relationships. On the one hand, arguing against views that languages are "pure," he contends that all languages undergo borrowing through contact. On the other hand, arguing against the theory of an original, common *Ursprache*, he stresses each language's particularity. Boas also differentiates between various levels of linguistic influence. Whereas words and sounds are readily loaned, what Humboldt called a language's "inner form" cannot easily amalgamate. Boas, who speaks of the "borrowing of traits," does so in terms of diffusionism. In his article "The Aims of Ethnology," he states that "there is no people whose customs have developed *uninfluenced* by foreign culture, that has not borrowed arts and ideas which it has developed in its own way."[50] Thus, he speaks of a language that is influenced by or that borrows from other languages, not of a language that in its very kernel is a fusion of disparate languages. Consequently, it is inaccurate to understand this as a theory of hybridization of cultural identity, as does Michel Espagne.[51]

It is true that in his 1917 "Introduction to the International Journal of American Linguistics," Boas stresses the (one-way) influence exerted by European languages on the Native American languages not only in vocabulary but also in phonetics and grammar.[52] However, Boas states in the introduction to *Handbook of American Indian Languages:* "As long, however, as the inner form [of language] remains unchanged, our judgment is determined, not by the provenience of the vocabulary, but by that of the form."[53] And in his "Classification" of 1929, Boas states: "So far as I know the actual process of a transfer of grammatical categories from one language to another has never been observed."[54] This framework distinguishes between *influence* (hence "dissemination of traits") and basic *structure* or *inner form*. While Boas the person might have been able to view Yiddish as a distinct language, his postulates would refuse to recognize its inner form as an amalgam of two (or more) genetically unrelated inner forms.

Moreover, were Boas to recognize Yiddish (or other Jewish languages) as a distinct language, he would be forced to recognize in it a Hebrew component. However, this component connects genetically with the components of other equivalent languages. This would force him to recognize a Jewish linguistic (and therefore cultural) common denominator, which in turn would lead to recognizing the Jews' cultural specific difference. Boas wished to avoid this.[55]

Boas was probably unaware of the quarrel that took place in the beginning of the 20th century, mainly in Eastern Europe, between supporters of Hebrew and supporters of Yiddish concerning which language best expressed the living Jewish tradition and was most suitable for the Jews' future.[56] On the basis of his linguistic paradigm, Boas should have supported the Yiddishists. However, as noted, he never discussed Jewish languages; just as significant, the implicit Boasian monolingual assumption is unsuitable for the case of the Jews.[57]

Given that Jews did not share a single spoken language, what "genius" could they possess? What mental existence could be symbolized in a language (Hebrew) that was not spoken? Alternatively, how could languages such as Yiddish and Judeo-Arabic be included in Boas' historical particularistic framework while denying their Hebrew component?

Acknowledging a specifically "Jewish" language, I believe, would have led Boas to a number of difficult questions concerning his own paradigm of language. He would have been compelled to find theoretical solutions to issues that extended beyond the particular case of the Jews. He would have been forced to make explicit those implicit connections between spoken language and the "world" of the group as the foundation of its distinct cultural identity. Above all, he would have been forced to reassess and readapt his conceptual scheme to account for a group that was located in widely dispersed geographical areas of the globe, sharing (according to his view) neither common biological traits nor a common language, and yet still regarded, both by others and by themselves, as a unique and clearly identifiable group.

Whereas Boas made extensive use of the signifier "Jew" in his deconstruction of racist theories, his avoidance of reference to the Jews in his work on language is particularly problematic. If (because of his assimilated background) Boas' real aim was to deny the Jews' identity as a people, he could easily have extended his arguments on the racially assimilated nature of the Jews to encompass their linguistic character. Did not Jews speak the language of the surrounding non-Jewish populations among which they lived? Was not Hebrew a "dead" language for centuries? And as for other distinctly "Jewish" languages, were they not, as the Jews themselves, deeply assimilated into their surrounding languages?

It is at this stage that a basic "Boasian paradox"[58] reveals itself as both a problem and as a solution to the problem. If group existence is *derived* from language, any mention of a "Jewish" language (or languages) implicitly—but necessarily—recognizes Jewish group existence. Boas, it is true, could have claimed that even linguistically, as in the sphere of race, Jews are highly assimilated. Yet this homological attribute (physical assimilation/linguistic assimilation) bears *contrary consequences* in the two different spheres of research (physical anthropology versus cultural anthropology), because Boas in these two areas has *contrary aims*. This paradox, which reveals itself by an analysis of Boas' references to the Jews, does not only bear on the representation of the Jews; it is also significant vis-à-vis the most fundamental, implicit Boasian hypothesis concerning the connection between language and group identity. Had Boas referred to the Jewish case in his discussions of language (as he had in the sphere of race), he would have argued against his own wider anthropological aims. Any mention of Jewish languages would interfere with his general anthropological aim: to recognize, through language, the culture of illiterate groups. This would have compelled him to rethink and reformulate anthropology's most fundamental assumptions concerning the connections between language and group identity: that is, he would have encountered a group identity that did not necessarily depend upon monolingual exclusivity. Or, put in the negative: he would have encountered languages that express no "world."

Everything testifies to the fact that Boas (as an author) had decided a priori that Jews were not a racial, cultural, or national group, and his entire treatment of the Jewish case testifies that, for this reason, he did not recognize a distinctly Jewish language. However, it is precisely for this reason that the difference between his references to the Jews in the sphere of race and his silence about them in the sphere of language is so significant. It shows that Boas subordinated any allusion to the Jews to his comprehensive anthropological project. On this point—not Boas' denial of Jewish group existence, but rather how this denial is framed by, subordinated to, and interlaced with his general anthropological considerations—I believe that the biographical thesis falls short. If his first priority was to deny Jewish culture at any expense, Boas might have referred to the assimilated linguistic character of the Jews. By recognizing "race" and "culture" as differing guiding principles in Boas' work, one finds a motivation and source of coherency stronger than his biography, furnishing as it does a more nuanced reading of his references to the Jews (or lack of them).

Arguing about the Jews in the same vein as he did in physical anthropology would have run counter to his general treatment of language and would have culminated, for Boas, in one of two unhappy alternatives. On the one hand, since one starts from recognition of a group's distinct identity by treating its language, Boas might have been compelled to acknowledge a heterogeneous individuality (an oxymoron, in his paradigm). Alternatively—and, in certain respects, even worse for Boas—he would have been forced to acknowledge that his linguistic paradigm was inherently faulty, given that the Jews' "linguistic situation" raises theoretical difficulties that are probably unsolvable within his postulates.

Perhaps there is a third alternative? Could not Boas have simply acknowledged the Jews' "linguistic situation" as unique, an exceptional case that could not be integrated within his paradigm? The answer, of course, is that he could not. Boas' ideal of science always remained that of 19th-century natural science, that is, an ideal of laws that are universally valid. All that is needed in order to invalidate a law is to find its exception. In Boas' case, this meant that his anthropology had to apply not merely to primitive groups, but universally. To resolve the difficulties raised by the Jews' "linguistic situation" would necessitate a fundamental rethinking of the paradigm's implicit connections between language, the life of the group, and the group's psychological world of experience—in short, the core of that which makes its "genius."

By way of conclusion, I would like to place Boas' "Jewish linguistic paradox" in the context of his anthropological epistemological framework. In *The Mind of Primitive Man* (1911), Boas disjoined the racial, geographical, and linguistic aspects of the anthropological group, in clear contradiction to Anglo-American anthropology of his time.[59] Later, in fact, after his "cultural turn," Boas accorded group culture supremacy over the other aspects of group identity. One way of stating culture's supremacy over biology was by asserting that the biological unit is much broader than the linguistic one;[60] hence, the unique-particular was to be found not in the biological but in the cultural realm. However, here too the basic epistemological framework remained unchanged: Boas' individual remained (in Louis Dumont's terminology) "holistic." That is, every single human being, from the moment of birth, was formed in relation to an already existing and distinct culture—the group, or culture, held priority over the individual.

One must not overlook the fact that it is precisely this framework that gives meaning to Boas' assertion that the Jews had for centuries been highly assimilated. In Boas' framework—one that celebrates the "individuality" of a culture—the claim that a group is highly assimilated amounts to an attempt to disown the culture's existence, because it aims at demonstrating that a group's culture is no longer unique.

"It is impossible to trace with any degree of certainty the steps by which the homogeneous groups became diversified and lost their unity," Boas writes typically, "or by which the opposing groups came into closer contact."[61] That is, from our present situation, we will never be able to deduce the *origin* of the group's distinct identity. However, in contradistinction to the otherwise extraordinary cautiousness that Boas maintained in relation to the groups he studied, he projected the Jews' assimilated character, or lack of distinct identity, onto the Jews' origin. "Even in antiquity," Boas states, "while the Jews still formed an independent state, they represented a thorough mixture of divergent racial types." "[T]hree elements (the Armenian type of Asia minor, the Arab type of the Arabian Peninsula, and the Kurdish type of Asia minor) were represented in the ancient Jews. . . . Even in antiquity, therefore, we cannot speak of a Jewish race as distinct from other races in Asia minor."[62] (Note that even when he breaches his own cautious method, Boas does not extend his argument to the sphere of culture and language.)

Even Boas' attempt to project the Jews' lack of difference or distinct identity to their very origin could not break the "hermeneutic circle" that his own cultural paradigm establishes in the relation it poses between individual and group. Given Boas' anthropological holism, a Boasian attempt to deny the Jews' group existence presupposes that the Jews had once constituted a unique group. Boas could not deny the Jews' present existence as a cultural group without presupposing their (past) group individuality and so he remained silent. In the end, Boas subordinated his allusions to the Jews to the principles that guided his anthropological project as a whole. In this instance, Franz Boas the anthropologist held the upper hand over Franz Boas the German Jew.

Notes

I would like to thank Marcelo Dascal, Sander Gilman, Eli Lederhendler, Ezra Mendelsohn, Paul Mendes-Flohr, Gabriel Motzkin, Michael Silverstein, and Amitai Touval for commenting on earlier versions of this essay.

1. Since Boas' day, the depiction of the Jews as highly assimilated became standard in anthropological accounts. See, for example, Clyde Kluckhohn, *Mirror for Man: Anthropology and Modern Life* (New York: 1949), 110; Melville J. Herskovits, "Who Are The Jews?," in *The Jews: Their History and Culture*, ed. Louis Finkelstein, 4 vols. (New York: 1949), 2:1158.

2. Leonard Glick notes that "Boas's published writings on assimilation were deeply influenced by his German Jewish background. In particular, his unwillingness to recognize Jewish cultural identity as reality." Moreover, "Boas's personal history and its influence on his intellectual career were greater than anyone has heretofore suggested" (Glick, "Types Distinct from Our Own: Franz Boas on Jewish Identity and Assimilation," *American Anthropologist* 84, no. 3 [1982], 545–546).

According to Ellen Messer, "He [Boas] was very self-consciously a product of his background and particular upbringing" (Messer, "Franz Boas and Kaufmann Kohler: Anthropology and Reform Judaism," *Jewish Social Studies* 2 [1986], 132). Cf. Julia Liss ("German Culture and German Science in the *Bildung* of Franz Boas," in *Volksgeist as Method and Ethic: Essays on Boasian Ethnography and the German Anthropological Tradition*, ed. George W. Stocking, Jr. [Madison: 1996)], 169):

> Boas' anger and resistance did not lead, however, to a heightened attachment to his own Jewishness. Instead, he seems to have been aware of his ethnicity only as a result of external designation rather than through any subjective identity. For this reason, his experience contributed to what might seem otherwise a paradoxical orientation: he grew increasingly impatient with prejudice, especially that deriving from generalizations about racial or physical characteristics, while at the same time trying to prove himself as part of the mainstream culture.

See also idem, "Patterns of Strangeness: Franz Boas, Modernism, and the Origins of Anthropology," in *Prehistories of the Future: The Primitivist Project and the Culture of Modernism*, ed. Elazar Barkan and Ronald Bush (Stanford: 1995), 117–118; Hasia Diner, *In the Almost Promised Land: American Jews and Blacks, 1915–1935* (Westport: 1977), 142–149.

Geyla Frank puts the issue as follows: "I will begin historically by asking what influence the Jewish background of founder Franz Boas had in shaping the field. In what ways does Boasian anthropology reflect a Jewish 'subject position' or Jewish 'subject positions'? And 'Is anthropology in some sense a Jewish science?' " (Frank, "Jews, Multiculturalism, and Boasian Anthropology," *American Anthropologist* 99, no. 4 [1997], 731–732). Even when Frank relates to the ways in which Jews did not fit Boas' anthropological notions, she refers back to his biography:

> [T]he Jews did not easily fit Boas' concept of culture as a temporally and spatially bounded set of traditions shared by a community with its own language, more or less separable from its neighbors. Boas' experience with political anti-Semitism in Germany in the 1880s, when the recent emancipation and civil rights of Jews were being eroded, affected this definition (Frank, "Melville J. Herskovits on the African and Jewish Diasporas: Race, Culture and Modern Anthropology," *Identities* 8, no. 2 [2001], 179).

Michel Espagne argues that Boas unconsciously substituted the study of American Indians for the study of Jews, and that a combination of political liberalism and faithfulness to Judaism constituted Boas' intellectual horizon. See his article "La question des imbrications culturelles chez Franz Boas," *Revue germanique internationale* 17 (2002), 147–160.

Whereas the biography of a man need not necessarily be separated from or contrasted with his professional work, the two are not identical. Thus, in contrast to Frank, Liss, Glick and, in a different way, Espagne, I focus primarily on Boas' paradigm and the ways in which it construes and understands its research object. By this I do not mean to argue that Boas' subjectivity played no role in his anthropology; one must constantly look at the interplay between them. However, I argue that even Boas' subjectivity was submitted to anthropological categories of thought.

3. Rachel Caspari, "From Types to Populations: A Century of Race, Physical Anthro-

pology, and the American Anthropological Association," *American Anthropologist* 101, no. 5 (2003), 65.

4. Ibid., 67.

5. Franz Boas, "Race: What It Is," in idem, *Race and Democratic Society* (New York: 1969), 22–23. Originally published as "What is a Race?" in *The Nation* (28 Jan. 1925).

6. Franz Boas, "Racism," in idem, *Race and Democratic Society,* 29–30.

7. Franz Boas, *Changes in Bodily Form of Descendants of Immigrants: Partial Report on the Results of an Anthropological Investigation for the United States Immigration Commission* (Senate document no. 208, 61st Congress, 2nd session) (Washington, D.C.: 1910), 1–7.

8. Franz Boas, "The Jews," in idem, *Race and Democratic Society,* 40.

9. Ibid.

10. Ibid., 41.

11. Boas, "The 'Aryan'," in ibid., 48–49.

12. See Edward Sapir, *Language: An Introduction to the Study of Speech* (New York: 1921); idem, "Language," in *Encyclopedia of the Social Sciences* (1933), 9:353; idem, "The Status of Linguistics as a Science," in idem, *Selected Writings of Edward Sapir in Language, Culture, and Personality* (Berkeley: 1949); Benjamin Whorf, *Language, Thought, and Reality: Selected Writings* (Cambridge, Mass.: 1956); Leonard Bloomfield, *Language* (New York: 1933). See also Clyde Kluckhohn, *Mirror for Man,* 145–167.

13. For the standpoints Boas confronted, see Marvin Harris, *The Rise of Anthropological Theory: A History of Theories of Culture* (New York: 1968), 250–262. Harris offers examples of the racist-evolutionist standpoints prevalent at the time (in which race, language, and culture were fully conflated), which Boas so fiercely opposed.

14. Franz Boas, introduction to *Handbook of American Indian Languages,* reprinted in *Language, Culture, and Society: A Book of Readings,* ed. Ben G. Blount (Prospect Heights, Ill.: 1995), 17.

15. Boas to Dr. W. Thalbitzer, quoted in *The Shaping of American Anthropology, 1883–1911: A Franz Boas Reader,* ed. George W. Stocking, Jr. (New York: 1974), 178. In fact, his "analytical" framework makes clear that *any* language can in principle serve as (an arbitrary) reference point for the analysis of another language's grammatical forms. Indo-European languages could just as easily be analyzed according to grammatical forms found in Indian languages.

16. According to Dell Hymes and John Fought:

> Institutionally, intellectually, an effective, sustained tradition of description of language can be said to begin with him [Boas]. The tradition was systematic, synchronic, universalistic, but in retrospect it seems a precursor of structuralism proper, not an instance of it, if by "structuralism" one means an approach that defines the status of elements explicitly and consistently in terms of internal relations (Hymes and Fought, *American Structuralism* [The Hague: 1981], 82).

Boas is thus placed between a tradition of European historicism and American structuralism (although clearly striving toward the latter).

17. Franz Boas, "The Classification of American Languages," in idem, *Race, Language, and Culture* (New York: 1940), 212.

18. One should add that the distinction between "dead" and "living" languages, that is, the very idea of treating language as something that can be either dead or alive, goes back to Fichte, based on Herder's theory of the origin of languages—testifying to an infusion of Romantic influence on Boas' paradigm.

19. Franz Boas, quoted in Clyde Kluckhohn and Olaf Prufer, "Influences during the Formative Years," in *The Anthropology of Franz Boas: Essays on the Centennial of His Birth,* ed. Walter Goldschmidt (San Francisco: 1959), 22. This anthology also appeared as a special issue of *American Anthropologist* 61, no. 5, pt. 2.

20. Franz Boas, *Anthropology and Modern Life* (New York: 1928), 162, 235–236.

21. Franz Boas, "An Anthropologist's Credo," *The Nation* 147 (1938), 203. See also his

"Autobiography" in Clifton Fadiman, *I Believe: The Personal Philosophies of Certain Eminent Men and Women of Our Time* (New York: 1939), 24.

22. Louis Dumont, *German Ideology: From France to Germany and Back* (Chicago: 1994), 141.

23. Matti Bunzl, "*Völkerpsychologie* and German-Jewish Emancipation," in *Worldly Provincialism: German Anthropology in the Age of Empire*, ed. Glenn Penny and Matti Bunzl (Ann Arbor: 2003), 47–85. Bunzl convincingly demonstrates how Lazarus' and Steinthal's linguistic legacy was continued in Boas' work.

24. R.G. Collingwood, *The Idea of History* (Oxford: 1993), 90–91.

25. Johann Gottfried Herder, quoted by J. Breuilly, *Nationalism and the State* (Manchester: 1993), 57.

26. Quoted in Isaiah Berlin, *Vico and Herder: Two Studies in the History of Ideas* (London: 1976), 169. See also Maurice Olender, *The Languages of Paradise: Race, Religion, and Philology in the Nineteenth Century*, trans. Arthur Goldhammer (Cambridge, Mass.: 1992), 46.

27. Donald N. Levine, *Visions of the Sociological Tradition* (Chicago: 1995), 199. For a detailed study of Boas' German scientific and humanistic sources, see Kluckhohn and Prufer, "Influences during the Formative Years," 4–28. See also Matti Bunzl, "Franz Boas and the Humboldtian Tradition: From *Volksgeist* and *Nationalcharakter* to an Anthropological Concept of Culture," in Stocking, Jr. (ed.), Volksgeist *as Method and Ethic*, 17–78. See also Marvin Harris, *The Rise of Anthropological Theory: A History of Theories of Culture* (New York: 1968), 250–289; Adam Kuper, *The Invention of Primitive Society: Transformations of an Illusion* (London: 1988), 125–151; George W. Stocking, Jr., "Romantic Motives and the History of Anthropology," in *Romantic Motives: Essays on Anthropological Sensibility* (History of Anthropology, vol. 6), ed. George W. Stocking, Jr. (Madison: 1989), 5.

28. Boas, introduction to *Handbook of American Indian Languages*, 20. According to Hymes and Fought (who deal more precisely with the meaning of "mental" or "psychological" in this context):

> mental did not mean "psychological" in the sense of belonging to the domain of the discipline of psychology; Boas was patently discussing the domain of the discipline of ethnology. He was expressing a general conception known in German as that of the *Geisteswissenschaften*, and "mental" here is an equivalent of *Geist*—in other words, he was defining ethnology as equivalent to the cultural sciences (Hymes and Fought, *American Structuralism*, 81).

29. Franz Boas, *The Mind of Primitive Man* (New York: 1965), 189. For the Humboldtian sources of this notion, see William A. Foley, "Linguistic Relativity and the Boasian Tradition," in idem, *Anthropological Linguistics: An Introduction* (Malden, Mass.: 1997), 193–197.

30. Boas, *The Mind of Primitive Man*, 190.

31. Ibid.

32. Franz Boas, "Language," in idem et al., *General Anthropology* (New York: 1938), 130 (emphasis in original). Boas similarly uses concrete illustrations to elucidate principles of classification and numerals.

33. Roman Jakobson, "Franz Boas' Approach to Language," *International Journal of American Linguistics* 10 (1944), 4.

34. Franz Boas, introduction to *Handbook of American Indian Languages*, 23.

35. Boas, "Language," 127, 132–133.

36. Boas, *The Mind of Primitive Man*, 38.

37. "From this point of view, the occurrence of the most fundamental grammatical concepts in all languages must be considered as proof of the unity of fundamental psychological processes" (Boas, introduction to *Handbook of American Indian Languages*, 27). In fact, the lexical and grammatical aspects collapse in Boas' linguistic relativity. Since every language has a structure of its own (as Sapir later claimed), each individual element—even if phonetically similar to an element in another language—is, by the mere fact that it is an

element in a different structure, inevitably different. See P. H. Matthews, *Grammatical Theory in the United States from Bloomfield to Chomsky* (Cambridge: 1973), 6.

38. Boas, "Language," 133. Sapir and Whorf went much further in this direction than Boas. One should add that Boas at no time endorsed a theory of cultural determinism out of language. As Lucy writes:

> In the end, it seems that Boas's two desires, to assert the psychic unity of man and to avoid premature generalization at the theoretical level, kept him from going further along this line of thought to the claim of significant differences in thought among different linguistic-cultural groups. Nonetheless, most of the elements necessary for such an argument are already present in his work (John A. Lucy, *Language Diversity and Thought: A Reformulation of the Linguistic Relativity Hypothesis* [Cambridge: 1992], 16).

39. Boas, "Language," 127. See also ibid., 125.

40. Julia Kristeva quotes Boas: "It does not seem likely that there is any *direct* relation between the cultures of a tribe and the language they speak, except in so far as the form of the language will be molded by the state of culture, but not in so far as a certain state of culture is conditioned by the morphological traits of the language." She then concludes that "Boas did not, however, agree with the theory of linguistic relativity" (Kristeva, *Language—the Unknown: An Initiation into Linguistics*, trans. Anne M. Menke [New York: 1989], 49). Kristeva, I believe, misunderstands the Boas quote, which is in fact aimed at defending himself against linguistic *determinism* and cultural relativity (of which linguistic relativity was an important component). Boas was very careful to avoid linguistic determinism (or geographical-linguistic determinism, as can be found in Rudolf Bastian's work, which deeply influenced Boas). William A. Foley makes this clear, noting that "linguistic categories may express (at least partially) those of thinking, but never the other way around: linguistic categories do not determine thought" (Foley, *Anthropological Linguistics*, 195). See also Kluckhohn and Prufer, "Influences during the Formative Years," 19.

41. Quoted in Elie Kedourie, *Nationalism* (London: 1966), 63. Summarizing the dilemma that haunted Boas concerning Jewish language, Kedourie concludes (based on Fichte's understanding of the matter): "first, that people who speak an original language are nations, and second, that nations must speak an original language" (ibid., 67). The other side of the coin is that every individual must be assigned to *one* language. As William Adams observes: "Each Indian 'belonged' to one and only one culture in the same way that he or she was a speaker of one and only one mother-tongue" (Adams, *The Philosophical Roots of Anthropology* [Stanford: 1998], 313).

42. Boas maintained that each language evolved historically. In the controversy over the origin of native American languages, Boas rejected theories of a common origin (*Ursprache*), nor was he willing to regard the languages as a "linguistic family"—rather, according to him, each language developed in its local setting and reflected a specific psychological environment. See Boas, "The Limitations of the Comparative Method" and "The Classification of American Languages," in idem, *Race, Language and Culture*, 270–280 and 212.

43. Quoted in Kedourie, *Nationalism*, 64.

44. Boas, "Language," 141; idem, "The Classification of American Languages," 214.

45. See Ron Kuzar's account of the question of the revival of Hebrew and Ben-Yehuda's allegedly crucial role in it in *Hebrew and Zionism: A Discourse Analytic Cultural Study* (Berlin: 2001). The very idea that a language that died could be resurrected is probably alien to Boas' anthropological thought, which, as has been seen, was concerned with spoken languages that, once vanished, left no trace. My thanks to Marcelo Dascal, who pointed out this differentiation in private communication.

46. I would like to thank Eli Lederhendler and Ezra Mendelsohn for their elucidating remarks on the realities of Jewish languages in Eastern Europe. There are various historical accounts—see, for instance, the second part of Benjamin Harshav's *Language in Time of Revolution* (Berkley: 1993), 81–180. See also Shaul Stampfer, "What Did 'Knowing Hebrew'

Mean in Eastern Europe?," in *Hebrew in Ashkenaz: A Language in Exile*, ed. Lewis Glinert (New York: 1993), 129–140.

The Jews were hardly distinctive in their being bilingual. In Europe, for instance, Latin lived side by side with national languages. In both cases, the written language was learned via a spoken language but was not in itself used as a daily spoken language. However, in the European case, the language used for ritual and writing was universal, whereas the languages used for daily communication were national—the daily spoken language was what united each national group. In the case of the Jews, the language used for daily communication varied widely in accordance with geography and served to differentiate different groups of Jews. Hebrew, though, was the language all Jews used in ritual and in writing. See Hava Turniansky, *Sefer masah umerivah leR. Aleksandr beR. Yitzhak Pfaffenhofen (1627)* (Jerusalem: 1985), 126–134. More precisely, the written language was *loshn koydesh*, which is not identical with Hebrew. See Abba Ben-David, *Lashon mikra velashon hakhamim* (Tel Aviv: 1967), 153–164.

47. Several authors have attempted to argue for a distinct Jewish English language. For definitions, see Joshua Fishman, "The Sociology of Jewish Languages from a General Sociolinguistic Point of View," in idem (ed.), *Readings in the Sociology of Jewish Languages* (Leiden: 1985), 4; Chaim Rabin, "What Constitutes a Jewish Language?," *International Journal of the Sociology of Language* 30 (1981), 19–28. It is possible to argue that there are certain distinct patterns of use in English among Jews. However, it is difficult to see how one could argue that it is a distinct language with a distinct "inner form," in accordance with Boas' stronger definitions.

48. Sander L. Gilman and others have repeatedly pointed to the significance of the problematic reputation of Yiddish at the turn of the century in Europe. See Gilman's extensive discussions in *Jewish Self-Hatred: Anti-Semitism and the Hidden Language of the Jews* (Baltimore: 1986) and idem, *Difference and Pathology: Stereotypes of Sexuality, Race, and Madness* (Ithaca: 1985), 176–186; Jacob Toury, "Die Sprache als Problem der jüdischen Einordnung in den deutschen Kulturraum," in *Gegenseitige Einflüsse deutscher und jüdischer Kultur von der Epoche der Aufklärung bis zur Weimarer Republik* (Tel Aviv: 1982), 75–95. When reading Boas, one must also keep in mind that the issue of differentiating a language from a dialect was closely attached to nationalist asseverations. This question engaged, for instance, Pan-Slavist Russian contemporaries of Boas, who invented classifications of Slavonic tongues in order to prove their ultimate parentage link with Russian; and German nationalists, who claimed that Dutch was really a dialect of German, thus making Holland a part of the German nation. See Kedourie, *Nationalism*, 123.

49. Max Weinreich, *History of the Yiddish Language*, trans. Shlomo Noble (Chicago: 1980), 29, 166, 350. Weinreich states: "The essence of a Jewish language, we postulate here, is the fact that it is a fusion language" (ibid., 166).

50. Franz Boas, "The Aims of Ethnology," reprinted in idem, *Race, Language, and Culture*, 631.

51. Espagne, "La question des imbrications culturelles chez Franz Boas." Boas' diffusionist view of influence is also evident in his 1938 last word on the subject (Boas, "Language," 136–139). For a detailed account of German geographical diffusionism, see Woodruff D. Smith, *Politics and the Sciences of Culture in Germany, 1840–1920* (Oxford: 1991).

52. Franz Boas, "Introduction to the International Journal of American Linguistics," in idem, *Race, Language, and Culture*, 201.

53. Ibid., 202.

54. Boas, "The Classification of American Languages," 220 (emphasis added). Anyone acquainted with Boas' manner of argumentation must be aware that his negative statement is not suggested as an opening to find a language or historical occurrence that proves the opposite. His categorical assertions were made by way of negative, empirical statements. However, studies conducted after his day showed that the syntax of languages, not just the vocabulary, undergo processes of hybridization (the amalgamation of French and Haiti's native languages being one famous example). I would like to thank Marcelo Dascal for elucidating this point.

55. Denying the evolutionist moment in Powell's account, Boas turned to particular languages, *conceptually* distinguishing between the diffusion of traits in a specific area and the genetic origin of distinct languages but arguing *empirically* that resulting similarities between languages could not be distinguished from the genetic ones. On empirical grounds, therefore, the question of language families remained undecided for Boas. Already in an early essay, "Classification of the Languages of the North Pacific Coast" (1894), Boas was inclined toward more intensive analyses of particular languages. His refusal to recognize a "Native American *Ursprache*" can also be seen as a metonymical contention of the "Arian *Ursprache*," whose implications for the representation of the Jews cannot be overstated. Boas rejected theories of a common origin (*Ursprache*), arguing that each language developed in its local setting and reflected a specific psychological environment. However, if Yiddish were recognized as a distinct language (rather than a dialect of German), Boas would be compelled to recognize a Hebrew component. See Boas, "Classification of the Languages of the North Pacific Coast" in idem, *A Franz Boas Reader*, 159–166.

56. Israel Bartal, "From Traditional Bilingualism to National Monolingualism," in Glinert (ed.), *Hebrew in Ashkenaz*, 141–150.

57. It fell to a later generation to formalize multilinguistic situations into different types and categories. See "The Use of Vernacular Languages in Education: The Report of the UNESCO Meeting of Specialists, 1951," reprinted in *Readings in the Sociology of Language*, ed. Joshua A. Fishman (The Hague: 1968), 688–716.

58. I am purposely using "Boasian paradox" rather than "Boas' paradox." The former implies that Boas was both *constructing the variables* for studying anthropological phenomena and employing these very same variables *as given*.

59. Boas, *The Mind of Primitive Man*. See also Elazar Barkan, *The Retreat of Scientific Racism: Changing Concepts of Race in Britain and the United States between the World Wars* (Cambridge: 1992), 81.

60. Boas, *The Mind of Primitive Man*, 31.

61. Boas, *Anthropology and Modern Life*, 94. The unanswerable question relates to the possible common origin of the different races of mankind.

62. Franz Boas, "Are the Jews a Race?" in idem, *Race and Democratic Society*, 39–41. It seems likely that Boas, confronting racialist theories of his day, was so eager to confront *present* theories of a Jewish race that he was willing to annul—against his own empirical premises—even the very *possibility* of a distinctive Jewish racial difference in origin.

Innovating the Past: The Emerging Sphere of the "Torah-true Historian" in America

Kimmy Caplan
BAR-ILAN UNIVERSITY

Students of the history and sociology of religion are familiar with the concept of religious historiography: the use of history within religious discourse, not as an autonomous discipline, but as a means of addressing central religious concerns. Use of the past may be religiously valid, for example, as an adjunct to other religious speech or literature dealing with the continuity of faith over time and in settings that are perceived as changing.

Religiously oriented approaches to the past vary from one faith community to another, but exhibit some common features. Often, it is said, the present is "guided" by the past and must therefore be understood in relation to the past. At the same time, religiously engaged history rejects the notion that the religious past can be legitimately objectified—that is, defined as "other" and clearly delineated from the present through the application of neutral, critical, or morally innovative norms and viewpoints.

This essay presents a preliminary study of the background of an emerging religious-historical discourse in American Jewish Orthodoxy—in particular, its haredi wing.[1] I argue that the emergence of a new discussion concerning the religious legitimacy of history is doubly innovative. First, by broaching the subject at all—and in English-language publications—scholars, rabbis, and educators affiliated with the haredi camp have taken cognizance of the changing cultural circumstances surrounding Orthodox life in America and have indicated that new discursive means are required to address those changes. Second, by forging ahead in published discussion among themselves, these writers and teachers have departed from established Orthodox semantic protocol, according to which spiritual initiative, innovation, and advice must originate with recognized rabbinical leaders of unrivalled authority. Acknowledging the secondary status of historical knowledge within the canonical traditions of rabbinic Orthodoxy, and thus providing an efficient rationale that absolves the highest spiritual leadership from dealing with historical learning, this emerging body of haredi opinion establishes the legitimacy for such learning and teaching at a secondary level of communal leadership.

Expressions of historical orientation may be culled from a large variety of texts extant among contemporary haredi Jews in America: publications of Artscroll, Feldheim, Torah Umesorah, and Targum presses;[2] the literature produced under the auspices of the various hasidic groups; the popular historical trilogy by Rabbi Berel Wein;[3] weekly pamphlets distributed in Orthodox synagogues; audio and video tapes; fiction and children's literature. This essay, however, is limited in scope, and I will deal specifically with some early examples of writing that called for an explicit historiographical agenda, which were published in the Agudath Israel journal, *The Jewish Observer*, from the 1960s to the late 1970s. As one leading figure in that discussion, Rabbi Joseph Elias, put it:

> Through it [later Jewish history] we can convey to our youth the principles which underlie and emerge from our past, and their application to the problems and issues of our time. Let it be well understood however: *we must see the present in the light of the past and not, reversely, project the passing ideas of* [our] *day, its confusions and uncertainties, into the past.*[4]

Methodological Considerations, Terminology, and Characteristics of Orthodox Historiography

As perceived by its adherents, Orthodoxy is the natural, authentic, and only legitimate continuation of traditional Judaism. Scholars in the field of Jewish social and religious history, however, have argued that it is a modern religious phenomenon in which the dissimilarities from traditional Judaism are as significant as the similarities between them.[5] The most basic and important difference between traditional and Orthodox Judaism lies in the contrast between simply being traditional and the need to consciously reinforce or even reinvent tradition.[6] As a modern response to the decline of traditional Jewish society, secularization, and the appearance of various Jewish religious movements and political ideologies, Orthodoxy has a strong tendency to consider itself a vulnerable minority that, in order to exist, has developed into a counterculture within Jewish society.

Recent historical studies of the various genres of European Orthodox and Israeli haredi historiography[7] identify five basic characteristics and historiosophical guidelines of this literature:

1) It is based on the view that all occurrences in this world are controlled by God and are part of a carefully designed plan, especially those events involving the Jewish people.[8]
2) It focuses primarily, if not solely, on Jewish history.
3) It tends to offer an alternative, or counterhistory, although this is not necessarily written as a conscious, direct response to academic or other histories.
4) Its main goal is to promote an educational-ideological agenda, be it religious or moral, that is directed toward contemporary society. In other words, the past is important insofar as it provides tools to understand present-day events and dilemmas, with the aim of strengthening individual and group belief in God. It also serves the need of Orthodox society for a structured, clear, and— most important—usable past.

5) On this basis, it is clear that "true" history can be written only by a God-fearing "true believer" who holds that the abovementioned guidelines take precedence over other considerations such as academic research models based on humanistic theories of causation, and who understands his or her educational responsibilities as an Orthodox scholar.[9]

The application to haredi groups in America of models developed in the study of European Orthodox and Israeli haredi discourse cannot be taken as a matter of course. My analysis is based on the shifts that have taken place within American Orthodoxy between the 1930s and the mid-1960s, primarily within haredi circles, which have augmented the relevance of the haredi paradigm within the American context in the second half of the 20th century.[10] Moreover, as we shall see, there are phenomenological similarities and continuities that bridge the gaps between these literatures. In particular, one notes a common basic approach to the past and to defining its proper relevance. There is also a basic uneasiness or opposition to the historiosophical approaches and guidelines to be found in academic or "other" works, as well as to the actual representations of the past in such works.

At the same time, there are specific elements in the American case and in the literature under study here that merit noting. For example, young Modern Orthodox and haredi Jews in the United States are far more likely than their Israeli counterparts to attend college or university, and thus are exposed to a greater degree to academic scholarship and modes of thinking. Consequently, the debate regarding historiography has practical as well as intellectual applications in the American Orthodox sector.[11]

Perhaps such environmental considerations also form the background for the sharply contested historiographical debates in American Orthodox circles that pit Modern Orthodox views against haredi perspectives. An example is Jacob J. Schacter, formerly of the Jewish Center in New York City, who currently teaches at Yeshiva University. In recent years, this Modern Orthodox rabbi (with a doctorate from Harvard) has engaged in a series of confrontations with American haredi rabbis, writers, and historians, arguing that, because of its ideological commitments and apologetic tendencies, haredi literature presents a distorted picture of the past.[12] Some of the figures to be discussed below are similarly involved in highly politicized skirmishes over historicizing versus hagiographical impulses, and while some may be said to be more confrontational, others comport themselves as fence-straddlers.

Here we might include a few sentences on the recent vociferous character of this debate, as evidenced by the furor over Rabbi Nathan Kamenetsky's *Making of a Godol*.[13] Kamenetsky found himself under severe attack from both American and Israeli haredi rabbis and religious leaders, who issued bans on purchasing or reading the book and who demanded that the publisher stop marketing it. (*Making of a Godol* was also burned at the Jerusalem branch of the Lakewood Yeshiva.) It appears that a main reason for their outrage is the fact that the author presented haredi spiritual leaders, such as Rabbi Aaron Kotler (head of the Lakewood Yeshiva), as "human"—that is, as people whose day-to-day behavior was not necessarily strictly in line with contemporary haredi educational goals.[14]

"Torah-True" Literature in English: Historiosophical Dilemmas in *The Jewish Observer*

The first issue of *The Jewish Observer*, published by Agudath Israel of America, a "sectarian Orthodox" (that is, haredi) organization,[15] appeared in September 1963, close to the beginning of the Jewish New Year (5724). Even though the publication had "limited success" during its first years,[16] it gradually became popular among mainstream American haredi circles and has therefore served as an important venue for the internal haredi discourse regarding history and its uses.[17]

Several editorials and articles in the first issues of *The Jewish Observer* were devoted to elucidating the aims of the journal (primarily to offer the "correct" way to perceive current events) and to defining its audience—whose voice, according to the writers, was unheard from within and misrepresented from without.[18] This process of self-definition and evaluation continued in the first issues of the second and third year.[19] While formulating a proper view of the past, as a part of this process, was rarely mentioned, it was raised in an article in the very first issue. According to Murray Friedman, then principal of the Yeshiva of Brighton (Brooklyn) and a few years later the administrative dean of the Rabbi Chaim Berlin Yeshiva: "Only a flowering of the best literary minds in our loyal camp can meet the colossal challenge of our time. It is our historical imperative to fashion a literary force of such magnitude and compass that it shall serve as a mighty counter-current to the storm winds of this distressed era."[20] His article, however, did not delineate operative principles for this literary force.

Similarly, in its campaign to combat the "negativism and hostility of forces in Jewry that are opposed to the centrality of Torah in Jewish life," the editorial opening *The Jewish Observer*'s third year defined the "major themes of a vibrant Orthodoxy" without relating to the issue of confronting and correcting the history written by "others."[21] While this issue does appear in numerous articles on specific topics and personalities throughout the first years of the journal, it is touched on only indirectly.

The need to grapple with history from an "Orthodox" point of view is raised directly, in various ways, from the middle of the journal's fourth year of publication (1967). Rabbi Elias addressed this topic through a review of a four-volume textbook written by Gilbert and Lillian Klaperman, *The Story of the Jewish People* (1961–1966), which was "widely used in Orthodox schools."[22] Critiquing the context and language in which certain topics were discussed (as well as those that were omitted), Elias concluded that the "Torah historian" is obliged to present the past according to fundamental principles, since "if he permits his values and judgments to be subject to the influence of his age, he will arrive at a distorted picture of both the Torah world and the secular world—and he will even project these distortions into that past from which he could have learned the truth."[23]

In a subsequent article, Friedman spelled out "some axioms for understanding our past."[24] He explained that the problem is not "data and dates," but rather that students of history find that "events fall into patterns [and] possess a meaningful context, and that this meaning not only relates to the past, but to the present and future as well." Consequently, the main problem is the subjectivity of the writer who is interpreting objective data. In other words, whereas several Orthodox historiographers focused on correcting facts and details published by other historians, Friedman was more concerned with the process of evaluating and contextualizing these "data and dates."[25]

Following this agenda, Friedman set forth his basic axioms:

1. There is no such thing as scientific objectivity.
2. "The course of human events is shaped by Providence."
3. "The history of the world was 'coded' from the very moment of creation."
4. "Any interpretation [of Jewish history] prior to the final Redemption must of necessity be tentative and subject to revision in the light of later events."
5. Jewish history can be properly studied only by those who have "eyes endowed with [transcendent] wisdom."
6. "[T]he history of Israel must be studied parallel with the emerging patterns of the Torah of Israel."[26]

Several months later, David Kranzler, then a doctoral candidate at Yeshiva University, addressed the importance of establishing "an archive for Torah Jewry."[27] In a note of communal self-criticism, Kranzler wrote that

> one day a historian will set out to record what Jewish life was like in our time, and even if he is properly objective, he will probably present a distorted picture of Orthodox [Jewish] life and its communal institutions. Should this happen—and there are signs that it has already begun—it will be because of the lack of primary resources to study what is undoubtedly the most dynamic sector of contemporary American Jewry.[28]

Kranzler pointed to three reasons for what he considered to be a void in Orthodoxy: its struggle for physical and spiritual existence; Orthodox Jews' "lack of self-assurance and self-awareness of their own achievements"; and an "almost total lack of historical perspective," given that Orthodoxy's "major concern has been to criticize history written by Jews who lack the understanding of Jewish tradition."[29] As noted, he proposed establishing an Orthodox Jewish archive and institute for oral history that would consist of four departments: an archive, a reference library, a photo collection, and an oral tape collection. Kranzler concluded his article by expressing the hope that the necessary funds could be raised for such a project.[30]

Whereas Friedman contended that, by definition, there was no such thing as objective history, Kranzler apparently felt that, given proper access to the facts, an objective history could be written. Furthermore, while both Friedman and Elias faulted academic historians for the way in which they presented and explained history in general and Jewish history in particular, Kranzler rebuked the Orthodox camp for failing to document itself properly. Kranzler was more concerned with gathering primary source material than with rebutting offending historical interpretations. (His later scholarly work reflects this concern. In addition to his involvement in founding and later expanding the Agudath Israel Archives in New York, Kranzler has written a number of books, most of them published by Orthodox-associated presses. These books, several of which deal with Orthodox Jewry during the Holocaust, are heavily documented, significantly more than most other haredi historical writings.[31])

Shmuel Steven Singer, at the time a student at both the Beth Midrash Yeshurun of the Samson Raphael Hirsch Yeshiva in New York and at the City College of New York, continued the discussion on the need for Orthodox Jewish historians. After citing several examples indicating that American Orthodox Judaism had begun to find itself, Singer observed that there was one area in which "Torah Judaism in America has not kept pace with its other accomplishments. There is today no society, association, or journal for the study of Jewish history in the light of Torah. There exists no school or institution in which the Torah historian can be trained." Consequently, with one or two exceptions, there were "no Orthodox Jewish historians in America today," Singer noted—even at Yeshiva University.[32] This was unfortunate, he went on, because academic-oriented Jewish historical works could easily undermine the faith of true believers, no less than the faith of "our untrained or even moderately observant co-religionists." In contrast, "works produced by religious historians strengthen the emunoh [faith] of even the strongest [believer]. . . . Does not the Orthodox Jewish historian paint a truer picture of the past"?[33]

Singer went on to raise an issue that had not been addressed by Elias, Friedman, or Kranzler—that of coping with the "numerous areas in which apparent contradictions exist between information given us by our sacred sources and current historical data," especially in the periods of the Bible and the Mishnah. He defined three possible ways to deal with these contradictions. The first, dismissed as impossible, was to reject traditional sources as untrue. The second, "to reject the historical evidence . . . as pure fabrication; [to regard] it as a plot to corrupt the believers," was judged by Singer to be an "unfortunately widespread" approach; in his view, although they were quite possibly biased, "historians do not usually plot against anyone," and their works "are still based on some factual background." This, then, leads him to the third option: to examine the facts and try to "separate the valid from the invalid." For instance, "whatever appears to contradict the Bible is false, and must therefore be rejected. At the same time, certain historical facts can legitimately be interpreted differently."[34]

Furthermore, in his opinion, Orthodox historians can serve an important role in shedding light on "many dark areas" in medieval and modern Jewish history. Without such guidance, yeshiva students are likely to remain in a state of ignorance that is "in many ways more dangerous." "There is so much he [the Orthodox historian] must do," Singer concluded, "But *where is he?*"[35]

Apparently, Singer himself seriously considered becoming a trained historian. In 1981, he submitted a doctoral thesis titled "Orthodox Judaism in Early Victorian London" to the Bernard Revel Graduate School of Yeshiva University (interestingly, he chose to use his "American" name, Steven, for this work).[36] He did not, however, pursue an academic career as a historian. Instead, he taught in several yeshivas in New York, served as a rabbi in Orthodox congregations in New York, Ohio, and Rhode Island, and worked in the kosher food division of the Union of Orthodox Jewish Congregations, while at the same time publishing articles and educational material aimed at Orthodox audiences.[37]

It was in the late 1970s and early 1980s that a group of haredi historiographers begin to produce written works that were put out by publishers such as Artscroll, Feldheim, and Mesorah. Although these "Torah-true historians" approach the writing of history in different ways, they appear to share the same basic dilemmas, challenges, approaches, and solutions that were noted by the founding generation of *The Jewish Observer*.[38]

"Torah-true" History and Historiography

The discussions in *The Jewish Observer* regarding the nature of history in general, and the principles that should guide "the true believer" when looking into the past, did not remain abstract formulations. During the journal's first decade, numerous historical articles were published, most of them dealing with European Orthodoxy, and its leaders. The Holocaust was also discussed,[39] as were the Orthodox (and, later, haredi) ideological struggles with secular Zionism and the state of Israel.[40]

Most of the articles on European Orthodoxy fall under one of two headings. The majority are historical accounts of Orthodox rabbis and leaders and their struggles with Reform Judaism[41]—which was also a major theme in 19th-century Orthodox historiography.[42] The second group of articles are those presenting words of wisdom from the writings of leading Orthodox figures.[43] Articles of a more contemporary nature deal mainly with the issues and challenges facing the "true" Orthodoxy in the United States, such as the American rabbinate, changes within neighborhoods, the *kolel* institution, and the functions of, and relationships between, various idealized figures within the Orthodox community (for example, "the rabbi" and the "ben torah" [Torah scholar]).[44] A good deal of attention was also paid to the fraternal struggle between haredi Jewry and Modern Orthodoxy and its leaders, the latter including such rabbis as Norman Lamm and Emanuel Rackman.[45]

Occasionally *The Jewish Observer* would publish words of wisdom penned by contemporary figures within American Orthodox and haredi circles. These were similar to the articles focusing on European Orthodox rabbis, the difference being that, in the former case, most of the authors were still alive when their articles appeared.[46] Although, according to popular contemporary haredi views, immigrant rabbis played a vital role in establishing and maintaining Orthodoxy on American soil, *The Jewish Observer* rarely featured articles about these rabbis during its first years.[47] One of the few, published in 1974, was devoted to Rabbi Jacob Joseph (d. 1902), the first—and, to date, only—chief rabbi of New York's Orthodox Jews.[48] It appears that, during the journal's first decade, the editors regarded abstract historiosophical pieces as not entirely useful, in and of themselves. Rather, Orthodox perceptions of history and historiography had to be expressed through specific personalities and events.

Religious Leaders Discuss Historiosophy, Historiography, and Ethics: Rabbis Shimon Schwab and Isaac Hutner

One issue that was not explicitly discussed during the first few years of *The Jewish Observer*'s publication concerned the moral or religious propriety of dealing with history. Put in the form of a question: Was not the act of delving into the past contradictory to some basic norms of Orthodoxy?[49]

Implicitly, of course, the discussions regarding the guidelines and methodology of the "Torah historian" do relate to this question. For example, the argument that the Torah historian's "right" to uncover the past is based upon the need to correct the way it is presented by "other" historians implies that historiography does present an issue of legitimacy, and that it is only in the modern context, with its unprecedented challenges, that it is to be considered a justifiable religious activity.

In other words, the pursuit of a sacred historiography was envisaged at first as a prophylactic spiritual endeavor that was sanctioned on the basis of extrinsic and instrumentalist considerations. Such a position underscored the essential distinction between historiography and "learning" proper, in the more accepted Orthodox sense of the word. It is noteworthy that those involved in writing about history in *The Jewish Observer*'s first decade were either rank-and-file haredi rabbis or educators, or individuals of a haredi orientation who were studying history at American universities—whereas the opinion of leading haredi rabbinical figures on the matter remained unheard. To be sure, they kept silent on other matters as well; nevertheless, this phenomenon is striking, given that one of the main principles guiding the haredi community is adherence to rabbinic leadership, especially on issues of fundamental importance. It seems as though the "proper" approach toward examining history was not viewed at the time as a fundamental issue.

Toward the second half of the 1970s, however, leading rabbis began to address historiosophical and historiographical issues. Here we will discuss two representative articles published in *The Jewish Observer*. The first was written by Shimon Schwab (1908–1995), who was born and raised in Frankfurt. In 1926, he went to Lithuania, where he studied first at the Telz Yeshiva and later at the Mir Yeshiva. In 1936, Schwab crossed the Atlantic to serve as rabbi of Congregation Shearith Israel in Baltimore. In 1958, he relocated to Washington Heights, New York, after accepting an offer to become the assistant rabbi to Joseph Breuer at K'hal Adath Jeshurun.[50] Over the years, Schwab gradually assumed more responsibilities, and on Breuer's death in 1980, he became rabbi of the congregation. Schwab's ideological and theological approach differed from that of his predecessor. Unlike Breuer, for example, he did not wholly subscribe to Rabbi Samson Raphael Hirsch's ideal of *torah 'im derekh erez*, which sanctioned the pursuit of secular knowledge.[51] By the 1970s, Schwab had become an important and influential leader among mainstream haredi circles in the United States.

In March 1974, *The Jewish Observer* published "A Parable *told by* Rabbi Simon Shwab [sic]."[52] In this parable, Schwab relates to Christopher Columbus' achievements in order to offer a lesson regarding the correct approach toward the state of Israel. Schwab opens by reminding readers that Columbus had

conceived the idea of sailing westward from Europe to reach the East Coast of India in order to prove his contention that the world was round. When he and his 120 men finally sighted land, they were fully convinced that they had indeed reached the other side of the Globe. All they really did was to land on some island in the Bahamas.

Columbus, he continued, "sincerely believed that he had set foot on Indian soil," and so mistakenly "named the red-skinned aborigines he encountered 'Indians.' " But this "turned out to be an embarrassing mistake," and only "a great many years later was the east coast of India finally reached by courageous navigators." Although Columbus discovered a new continent, "until he died it never dawned on him that he was caught in an error."[53]

"This," Schwab continues, "is by now history and familiar to every school child. Why rehash it? Because it may serve as a fitting parable to our own historic experience." In the second part of his article, Schwab explains why "our generation has fallen prey to an historic illusion," namely, that "the rise of the Jewish State in Eretz Israel [is] identical with the beginning of the messianic redemption."[54]

In line with previously mentioned views of history, Schwab's article exemplifies the approach that recalling a historical event is worthwhile only insofar as it can teach a lesson regarding the present. In the case of Columbus (and, so the parable seeks to teach, in the case of the state of Israel), the lesson is that mistakes in the interpretation of events do exist, even though many or even most contemporary observers do not perceive them.

Over the years, Schwab published numerous articles in K'hal Adath Jeshurun's bulletin. In 1988, these were collected in a book that was edited by students of Mesivta Rabbi Samson Raphael Hirsch.[55] One of these essays, originally published in 1985, is titled "Jewish History."[56] Schwab opens this article with the observation that Jews in ancient times did not document their activities for future generations and that,

> come to think of it, since the close of the Tanach [Bible] at the beginning of the Second Beis Hamikdash [Holy Temple], we have no Jewish history book composed by our Sophrim [scholars of the pre-Tannitic period], Tanaim [scholars of the Mishnah] and Amoraim [scholars of the Talmud].... Why did our great Torah leaders not deem it necessary to register in detail all the events of their period just as the Neviim [prophets] had done before them?

Pointing to the differences between "history and storytelling," Schwab notes:

> History must be truthful, otherwise it does not deserve its name. A book of history must report the bad with the good, the ugly with the beautiful, the difficulties and the victories, the guilt and the virtue. Since it is supposed to be truthful, it cannot spare the righteous, if he fails, and it cannot skip the virtues of the villain. For such is truth, all is told the way it happened.

Schwab goes on to argue, however, that an objective work of history "would make a lot of people rightfully angry." Furthermore, the writer of such a history "would violate the prohibition against speaking Loshon Horah [slanderous speech]," which applies both to the living and to the dead. Interestingly, the example he brings in this regard is one that is very close to him: the "history of Orthodox Jewish life in pre-Holocaust Germany." Schwab states: "There is much to report but not everything is complimentary. Not all of the important people were flawless as one would like to believe and not all the mores and lifestyles of this bygone generation were beyond criticism."[57]

Thus, according to Schwab, a person writing history faces a series of religio-ethical issues: "What ethical purpose is served by presenting a realistic historic picture? . . . What is gained by pointing out [people's] inadequacies and their contradictions?" Nothing more than "the satisfaction of curiosity." Whereas the real aim, Schwab argues, should be to become "inspired by their example" and to "learn from their experience." Hence, one must focus on "the good memories of the good people, their unshakeable faith, their staunch defense of tradition, their life of truth, their impeccable honesty, their boundless charity and their great reverence for Torah and Torah sages."[58] Schwab concludes:

> Rather than write the history of our forebears, every generation has to put a veil over the human failings of its elders and glorify all the rest which is great and beautiful. That means we have to do without a real history book. We can do without. We do not need realism, we need *inspiration* from our forefathers in order to pass it on to posterity. And Torah-true "historians" do just that.[59]

Schwab's words adhere to one of the aforementioned basic criteria of Orthodox and haredi historiography: learning about the past is important only insofar as it serves an educational, ideological, or religious purpose in the present. Knowing the past merely for the sake of knowing it is meaningless or even harmful.

Although Schwab argued that only a prophet "has the ability to report history as it really happened, unbiased and without prejudice,"[60] he did not claim that one cannot write an objective and balanced history. His point was rather that, while such a thing is possible, it does not serve the desired religious-educational agenda.[61] It is for this reason that a "Torah-true" Jew, by definition, cannot be a historian.

Another article relating to historiography, published in *The Jewish Observer* in 1977, was authored by Yitzchok (Isaac) Hutner (1907–1980), one of the most important leaders of the Lithuanian (mitnagdic) stream of American haredi Jewry. Hutner at the time was dean of the Chaim Berlin Yeshiva.[62] His article came in response to questions from school principals regarding the proper approach to history in general and to the Holocaust specifically.[63] In this article, Hutner explores the origins of the term "Shoah" and explains that, by singling out this event, "those who sought a new terminology missed its essence." Hutner argues that the Holocaust was "intricately related to the basic pattern of Jewish history itself."[64]

Hutner's views on this subject have been analyzed by two scholars, Yaffa Eliach and Lawrence Kaplan.[65] Eliach, who focused on the historiosophical foundations of Hutner's essay, summarized them as follows: 1) the Holocaust should be placed within the historical continuum of Jewish history, which includes destruction, exile, and redemption; specific terms for the Holocaust (for example, Shoah) should not be introduced to particularize the event; 2) it is important to internalize the notion that events such as the Holocaust are part and parcel of being the chosen people. The questions that have been raised regarding the Holocaust prove that this message had not been sufficiently reinforced in the haredi educational sphere.

According to Kaplan, two main underlying motifs influenced Hutner's writing: first, his ideological hostility to Zionism; and second, his concern to draw attention to incorrectly presented historical data while at the same time setting guidelines for what he regarded as a correct historiosophy.[66]

It is important to note that Hutner was not forced to enter the historical arena. In fact, his historiosophical approach leads to the conclusion that there is no inherent need to deal with historical details, since these are all part of the grand continuum of Jewish history. Hutner probably chose to relate to specific events and processes in modern Jewish history in order both to prove his own point of view and to refute historical scholarship.

In line with Schwab, Hutner sees the past as an educational tool for the present, but the two differ in their evaluation of critical historiography. Whereas Schwab argues that it is indeed possible (albeit undesirable) to write an objective history, Hutner's message seems to be that the historiography of "others" is ideologically motivated and seriously flawed in the way it understands and contextualizes the past.

Conclusion

Although this preliminary survey is in no sense exhaustive, I would suggest several tentative findings regarding the nature and characteristics of the American haredi approach to history. First and foremost, all of the sources explored here are of a popular nature, and none of them aims specifically at elite or especially sophisticated segments of the American haredi community. In addition, with a few exceptions, the personalities discussed were not haredi religious leaders of international or even national repute at the time, but rather rabbis or educators on the more local scene.

Second, the topic itself was apparently considered sensitive for haredi historiographers and "true believers" alike. It is indicative that it took more than a decade for leading rabbis to express their opinions on the usefulness (or otherwise) of history.

Third, American haredim writing about history do not represent a coherent cultural force or school of thought. Theirs is not an academic historiography—a cumulative literary body of knowledge about the past. Rather, it is a discourse about the past that is specifically relevant to haredi religious concerns that American haredi writers typically voice to an internal, popular, or middle-level readership.

The issue of potential readership as well as the religious identity and institutional affiliation of some of the writers in *The Jewish Observer* raises another important point. Whereas the borders between haredim and religious Zionists can be fairly clearly defined in the Israeli context (though even in Israel the two groups overlap at some points), the definition of "haredim" on the American Jewish scene, as well as the borders between them and the Modern Orthodox camp, have been far more amorphous. It is not clear, for example, whether Emanuel Feldman or educational/religious figures such as Joseph Kamenetsky should be considered haredim. Furthermore, defining Breuer's (and later, Schwab's) congregation of the 1960s and 1970s as haredi, rather than simply Orthodox, is not entirely precise. These vague boundaries and distinctions are reflected as well in the mixed readership of mainstream haredi publications, which include people who should most likely be classified as Modern Orthodox. In fact, the ongoing ideological struggle between mainstream American haredim and Modern Orthodoxy revolves around issues of definition.

Because of its polemical and confrontational tone, haredi historiography is often seen as targeting the non-haredi Jewish society. This is not actually the case. On one level, the aim of historical discussion appears to be to provide a religiously worthy and reliable alternative for haredim who are exposed to historiography written by "others." However, most haredim involved in this discussion are associated with one or another particular group within their camp, and it is therefore likely that their targets are their peers within the fold, as it were. In other words, in certain cases, haredi historiography aims directly at the haredi community, even though it also responds, whether directly or indirectly, to non-haredi historiography. An example of this is provided in the works of Aharon Sorski, a prolific Israeli haredi historian, which have appeared primarily in Hebrew, but also in English.[67]

As we have seen, several American haredi rabbis and educators are professionally trained historians. Beginning in the 1960s, some of them, such as David Kranzler, gained a reputation in their respective fields of scholarly interest, and held or still hold positions in academic institutions. Others combined academic historical writing with haredi historiography, and this dual track was apparently not perceived as being inherently problematic. It would appear possible for a haredi Jew in America to be an academic scholar adhering to the methods of the historical discipline and at the same time to engage in writing "Orthodox" history or historiosophical homilies in accordance with very different guidelines and assumptions. Such a combination rarely existed in Orthodox circles in 19th-century European Orthodoxy. Nor, with a few notable exceptions (such as Esther Farbstein, a leading haredi educator in the field of Holocaust education, who holds a master's degree from the Hebrew University and who has published several articles in academic publications) is it a factor on the contemporary Israeli haredi scene.[68]

While European, and especially East European, Orthodox historical literature was undoubtedly the primary source of inspiration for haredi historians in both the United States and Israel in the second half of the 20th century, it bears noting that, in large measure, American haredi historiography rarely mentions the early authors of this literature and their classic works, such as the four-volume work of Yaakov Halevi Lifschitz, *Zikhron Ya'akov*.[69] This lack of reference to the pioneers of Orthodox historiography may indicate a lack of self-awareness on the part of the writers as they reinvent their own "worldly" literature. Alternatively, as suggested in this essay, it may reflect the sense of innovation and renewal in haredi historiosophy and historiography that has been occasioned by life in 20th-century America.

Notes

This essay is part of a research project exploring American Jewish Orthodox historiography in the second half of the 20th century. A preliminary version was presented at the 33rd Annual Conference of the Association for Jewish Studies, Washington, D.C. on December 18, 2001. This project was supported by a research grant from the Van Leer Jerusalem Institute (2001–2003), for which I am most grateful. I wish to thank Richelle Budd Caplan, Jeffrey Gurock, Elliott Horowitz, Lawrence Kaplan, Eli Lederhendler, Jonathan D. Sarna, and Chaim I. Waxman for their helpful comments and criticism on earlier versions of the essay.

1. For a basic typology of the various groups within American Orthodoxy, see Charles S. Liebman, "Orthodoxy in American Jewish Life," *American Jewish Year Book 66* (1965), 21–99. Liebman did not use the term haredi, which was not yet in popular use at the time, but it would more or less fit his category of "sectarian Orthodox." Haym Soloveitchik has noted that "the term 'haredi' has gained recent acceptance among scholars because of its relative neutrality." Terms such as "ultra-Orthodoxy" and "right-wing Orthodoxy" have a value-added connotation (the former is most commonly used by social scientists). Moreover, haredim themselves generally (though not exclusively) define themselves as such. When relating to 19th-century European Orthodoxy or to later 19th and early 20th-century American Orthodoxy, I use the term "Orthodox" since the term "haredi" in this context would be anachronistic or irrelevant. See Haym Soloveitchik, "Rupture and Reconstruction: The Transformation of Contemporary Orthodoxy," *Tradition* 28, no. 4 (1994), 105, n. 1; Menachem Friedman, *Hahevrah haharedit: mekorot, megamot vetahalikhim* (Jerusalem: 1991); Samuel C. Heilman, *Defenders of the Faith: Inside Ultra-Orthodox Jewry* (New York: 1992), 11–13.

2. To the best of my knowledge, these presses have received very little scholarly attention. See Jeremy Stolow, "Communicating Authority, Consuming Tradition: Jewish Orthodox Outreach Literature and Its Reading Public," in *Religion, Media and the Public Sphere*, ed. Birgit Meyer and Annelies Moors (forthcoming).

3. Berel Wein, *Triumph of Survival: The Story of the Jews in the Modern Era 1650–1990* (Monsey: 1990), idem, *Herald of Destiny: The Story of the Jews in the Medieval Era 750–1650* (Brooklyn: 1993); idem, *Echoes of Glory: The Story of the Jews in the Classical Era 350 BCE–750 CE* (Brooklyn: 1995).

4. Joseph Elias, "Past and Present in the Teaching of Jewish History," *The Jewish Observer* (hereafter: *JO*) 4, no. 8 (1967), 18, emphasis in original. Quoted in Jacob J. Schacter, "Haskalah, Secular Studies and the Close of the Yeshiva in Volozhin in 1892," *The Torah U-Madda Journal* 2 (1990), 112. At the time his article was published, Elias was both the chairman of the *The Jewish Observer's* editorial board and a leading figure in the Torah Umesorah publishing company. On the history and development of Torah Umesorah, see Doniel Z. Kramer, *The Day Schools and Torah Umesorah: The Seeding of Traditional Judaism in America* (New York: 1984); cf. Joseph Kaminetsky, *Memorable Encounters: A Torah Pioneer's Glimpses of Great Men and Years of Challenge* (Brooklyn: 1995). Torah Umesorah, *The Jewish Observer*, and Agudath Israel should not be seen as institutionally interconnected, although they share worldviews and cooperate in various activities. See Kramer, *The Day Schools and Torah Umesorah,* 152–156.

5. Jacob Katz, "Orthodoxy in Historical Perspective," in *Studies in Contemporary Jewry*, vol. 2, *The Challenge of Modernity and Jewish Orthodoxy*, ed. Peter Y. Medding (Bloomington: 1986), 3–17; Moshe Samet, "The Beginnings of Orthodoxy," *Modern Judaism* 8, no. 3 (1988), 249–270.

6. See, for example, Michael K. Silber, "The Emergence of Ultra-Orthodoxy: The Invention of Tradition," in *The Uses of Tradition: Jewish Continuity in the Modern Era*, ed. Jack Wertheimer (Cambridge, Mass.: 1992), 23–85.

7. See, among others, Ada Rapoport-Albert, "Hagiography with Footnotes: Edifying Tales and the Writing of History in Hasidism," *History and Theory* 27 (1988), 119–159; David Assaf, *The Regal Way: The Life and Times of Rabbi Israel of Ruzhin* (Stanford: 2002), 11–27; Israel Bartal, " 'True Knowledge and Wisdom': On Orthodox Historiography," in *Studies in Contemporary Jewry*, vol. 10, *Reshaping the Past: Jewish History and the Historians*, ed. Jonathan Frankel (New York: 1994), 178–192; Haim Gertner, "Reishitah shel ketivah historit ortodoksit bemizrah eiropah: ha'arakhah mehadash," *Zion* 67, no. 3 (2002), 293–337; Nahum Karlinsky, *Historiyah shekeneged: igerot hahasidim meerez yisrael* (Jerusalem: 1998), 109–167.

8. For an illustration of an Orthodox opinion regarding God's role in American history,

see Zevulun Charlop, "God in History and Halakhah from the Perspective of American History," *The Torah U-Madda Journal* 1 (1989), 43–59. To be sure, this approach long predated the appearance of Jewish Orthodox historiography; see, for example, Ernst Breisach, *Historiography: Ancient, Medieval, and Modern* (Chicago: 1983), index: "God in history."

9. See, for example, Moshe L. Bernstein, "The Orthodox Jewish Scholar and Jewish Scholarship: Duties and Dilemmas," *The Torah U-Madda Journal* 3 (1991–1992), 8–37; Shalom Carmy, "To Get the Better of Words: An Apology for *Yir'at Shamayim* in Academic Jewish Studies," *The Torah U-Madda Journal* 2 (1990), 7–25.

10. See Liebman, "Orthodoxy in American Life"; idem, "A Sociological Analysis of Contemporary Jewry," *Judaism* 13, no. 3 (1964), 285–305; Jeffrey S. Gurock, "Twentieth-Century American Orthodoxy's Era of Non-Observance, 1900–1960," *The Torah U-Madda Journal* 9 (2000), 87–108; idem, *From Fluidity to Rigidity: The Religious Worlds of Conservative and Orthodox Jews in Twentieth Century America* (David W. Belin Lecture in American Jewish Affairs 7) (Ann Arbor: 1998); idem, *American Jewish Orthodoxy in Historical Perspective* (Hoboken: 1996), 299–313; William B. Helmreich, *The World of the Yeshiva: An Intimate Portrait of Orthodox Jewry*, 2nd ed. (Hoboken: 2000); George Kranzler, *Williamsburg: A Jewish Community in Transition* (New York: 1962); Steven M. Lowenstein, *Frankfurt on the Hudson: The German-Jewish Community of Washington Heights, 1933–1983* (Detroit: 1989); Solomon Poll, *The Hasidic Community of Williamsburg* (New York: 1962); Jonathan D. Sarna, *American Judaism: A History* (New Haven and London: 2004), 227–243.

11. Certain writers in *The Jewish Observer* express awareness of this issue: see, for example, Bernard Fryshman, "The Child You Lose May Be Your Own . . ." *JO* 9, no. 9 (1974), 8–16; "Readers Comment on 'The Child You Lose,' " *JO* 9, no. 10 (1974), 3–8.

12. See, for instance, Schacter, "Haskalah, Secular Studies and the Close of the Yeshiva in Volozhin"; idem, "Facing the Truth of History," *The Torah U-Madda Journal* 8 (1998–1999), 200–277.

13. Nathan Kamenetsky, *Making of a Godol: A Study of Episodes in the Lives of Great Torah Personalities* (Jerusalem: 2002).

14. See, for example, ibid., 802.

15. For basic details on Agudath Israel of America, see Liebman, "Orthodoxy in American Jewish Life," 76–79. Still to be written is an account of Agudath Israel's gradual move toward segregation and isolation, beginning in the 1960s and 1970s. This process was subject to internal debates; see, for example, Chaim D. Keller, "The Unbridged Gap: The Youth Culture vs. the Establishment," *JO* 7, no. 6 (1971), 10–16.

16. Liebman, "Orthodoxy in American Jewish Life," 78.

17. Nevertheless, it has not received scholarly attention, with the exception of Daniel Gutenmacher's "Agudath Israel of America and the State of Israel: The Case of the *Jewish Observer*," in *Israel and Diaspora Jewry: Ideological and Political Perspectives*, ed. Eliezer Don-Yehiya (Ramat Gan: 1991), 109–127. It should be noted that *The Jewish Observer* is an important source for understanding the internal discourse between haredi and Modern Orthodox/Yeshiva University circles.

18. See, for example, "A New Voice: Our Reason for Existence," *JO* 1, no. 1 (1963), 3, 12; Murray I. Friedman, "What is Our Historical Imperative?," *JO* 1, no. 1, 19–20; Yaakov Jacobs, "News Management—Jewish Style: How and Why the Flow of News to American Jews is Controlled," *JO* 1, no. 6 (1964), 6–8, 20.

19. "Entering Our Second Year: A Subjective Evaluation and a Progress Report," *JO* 2, no. 1 (1964), 3–5; "Entering our Third Year: A Restatement of Objectives and Reaction to Our Critics," *JO* 3, no. 1 (1965), 3–6.

20. Friedman, "What is Our Historical Imperative?," 20. Friedman's educational activities probably explain his involvement in writing about Hebrew day schools from an Orthodox point of view. See idem and Joseph Kaminetsky, *Hebrew Day School Education: An Overview* (New York: 1970).

21. "Entering Our Third Year," 5–6.

22. Elias, "Past and Present in the Teaching of Jewish History," 18–24. The content of textbooks used in Orthodox schools continued to disturb Elias over the years. See his "A Danger from Within: A Look at Some of the Textbooks We Are Giving Our Children," *JO* 11, no. 6 (1976), 11–14.

23. Elias, "Past and Present in the Teaching of Jewish History," 23. For other articles that address the threat of various nuances of language and negative associations, see Bernard Fryshman, "The McGraw Hill Anti-Sexism Memo," *JO* 10, nos. 5–6 (1974), 26–29; letter to the editor on this article and the author's response, *JO* 10, no. 7 (1975), 28–31; Yaakov Jacobs, "The Book Industry and Orthodox Judaism," *JO* 5, no. 6 (1968), 3–9; idem, " 'The Promise'—A Novel or a Polemic?," *JO* 6, no. 4 (1969), 8–11.

24. Murray I. Friedman, "The Patterns of Jewish History: Some Axioms for Understanding Our Past," *JO* 4, no. 10 (1968), 18–20.

25. Interestingly, Friedman does not address the possible subjective influences of scholars on their choice of data and the way in which they present them. On this issue, see, for example, Edward H. Dance, *History the Betrayer: A Study in Bias* (London: 1960), 9–15; Oscar Handlin, *Truth in History* (Cambridge, Mass.: 1979), 165–252.

26. This point reflects the influence of Rabbi Isaac Hutner, whose argument was based on the sages' statement that "Israel and the Torah are one and the same" ("yisrael veoraita had hu").

27. David Kranzler, "Needed: An Archive for Torah Jewry," *JO* 5, no. 2 (1968), 7–10.

28. Ibid., 7.

29. Ibid., 7–8. From the context of his article, it appears that Kranzler first confronted the issue of the lack of Orthodox historical documentation while working on his dissertation ("The History of the Jewish Refugee Community of Shanghai, 1938–1945"); he received his degree in 1971 from Yeshiva University.

30. Kranzler, "Needed: An Archive for Torah Jewry," 8–9.

31. See, for example, David Kranzler, *My Jewish Roots: A Step-by-Step Guide to Tracing and Recording Your Genealogy and Family History* (New York: Sepher-Hermon Press, 1979); idem, *Solomon Schonfeld, His Page in History: Recollections of Individuals Saved by an Extraordinary Orthodox Jewish Rescue Hero during the Holocaust Era* (New York: Judaica Press, 1982); idem, *Heroine of Rescue: The Incredible Story of Recha Sternbuch, Who Saved Thousands from the Holocaust* (Brooklyn: Mesorah Publications, 1984); idem (co-authored with Dovid Landesman), *Rav Breuer, His Life and His Legacy: A Biography of Rav Dr. Joseph Breuer* (Jerusalem: Feldheim, 1998). A more recent work by Kranzler, reviewed in vol. 20 of this journal, was published by Syracuse University Press (*The Man Who Stopped the Trains to Auschwitz: George Mantello, El Salvador, and Switzerland's Finest Hour* [Syracuse: 2000]).

32. Shmuel Singer, "Wanted: Orthodox Jewish Historians," *JO* 6, no. 4 (1969), 15. It should be noted that *The Jewish Observer* often ran articles critical of prominent individuals associated with Yeshiva University (among them, Samuel Belkin, Emanuel Rackman, and Norman Lamm); see, for example, Joseph Elias, "The New Halachah: Can Halachah Be Determined by Sociological Criteria?," *JO* 1, no. 9 (1964), 3–7; Emanuel Feldman, " 'Modern Orthodoxy' and Dialectical Jiujitsu," *JO* 10, no. 2 (1974), 22–27.

33. Singer, "Wanted: Orthodox Jewish Historians," 15.

34. Ibid., 15–16.

35. Ibid.

36. Steven Singer, "Orthodox Judaism in Early Victorian London, 1840–1858" (Ph.D. thesis, Yeshiva University, 1981). Serving on the committee evaluating Singer's thesis were Jeffrey Gurock, Paula Hyman, and Todd Endelman.

37. For Singer's candid and critical assessment of the religious state of Orthodox Jews in the American periphery, see his "Orthodox Judaism and the Smaller American Community," *Tradition* 22, no. 1 (1986), 59–65, quoted in Gurock, *From Fluidity to Rigidity*, 41, n. 4; see also Shmuel Singer, *A Parent's Guide to Teaching Children Mitzvot: A Halakhic Guide* (Hoboken: 1991).

38. Shimon Finkelman and Yonason Rosenblum are two of the leading figures in this group, both of whom have written a number of biographies of Orthodox religious figures. The following books by Shimon Finkelman were all published by Mesorah Publications in Brooklyn: *The Story of Reb Yosef Chaim: The Life and Times of Rabbi Yosef Chaim Sonnenfeld, The Guardian of Jerusalem* (1984); *The Story of Reb Elchonon* (1984); *Reb Moshe: The Life and Ideals of HaGaon Rabbi Moshe Feinstein* (1986); *Reb Chaim Ozer: The Life and Ideals of Rabbi Chaim Ozer Grodzenski of Vilna* (1987); *The Chazon Ish: The Life and Ideals of Rabbi Avraham Yeshayahu Karelitz* (1989); *5 Great Lives: The Steipler, R' Yaakov Kamenetsky, R' Moshe Feinstein, R' Yehudah Zev Segal, R' Shlomo Zalman Auerbach* (1998). Yonason Rosenblum's books (also published by Mesorah Publications) include *Reb Yaakov: The Life and Times of HaGaon Rabbi Yaakov Kamenetsky* (1993); *Rav Dessler: The Life and Impact of Rabbi Eliyahu Eliezer Dessler* (2000); *Reb Shraga Feivel: The Life and Times of Rabbi Shraga Feivel Mendlowitz, The Architect of Torah in America* (2001).

39. Examples include Joseph Friedenson, "Why Didn't They Fight Back?," *JO* 1, no. 1 (1963), 9–11; Asher Lazar, "The 'Dumb Child': An Episode from the Years of the Holocaust," *JO* 1, no. 4 (1964), 15–16, 20; Siegmund Forst, "Biographical Fragments and Aspects of the Life of Michael B. Weissmandel," *JO* 2, no. 8 (1965), 9–14; Moshe Prager, "A Warsaw Ghetto Tale," *JO* 2, no. 4 (1965), 19–21.

40. See, for example, Isaac Levin, "Rabbi Yitzchak Meir Levin zẓ"l [of blessed memory—in *The Jewish Observer*, this phrase often appears in Hebrew letters]: Spokesman for Three Generations," *JO* 7, no. 9 (1971), 11–17.

41. For a few examples, see Yechiel Y. Perr, "Beyond Relevance: HaGaon Reb Avrohom Jofen zẓ"l, *JO* 6, no. 9 (1970), 19–22; Nosson Scherman, "100 Years since the 'Chofetz Chaim,' " *JO* 8, no. 2 (1972), 3–8; Chaim Shapiro, "Reb Yisroel Yaakov: The Mashgiach of Baranovich," *JO* 6, no. 8 (1970), 15–19; idem, "My Year with Reb Boruch Ber zẓ"l," *JO* 1, no. 2 (1963), 23–24; Shmuel Singer, "A Victory Centennial: In the Battle for Supremacy between Orthodoxy and Reform in Hungary," *JO* 8, no. 5 (1972), 13–16. It should be noted that several anonymous articles of this nature also appeared, for instance, "Moreinu Yaakov Rosenheim zẓ"l," *JO* 3, no. 1 (1965), 12–15; "The Tchebiner Rav zẓ"l," *JO* 3, no. 1, 15–17; "The Lutzker Rav, Rabbi Zalman Sorotzkin zẓ"l, *JO* 3, no. 7 (1966), 18–21. Finally, most of these biographical sketches were reprinted in several volumes edited by Nisson Wolpin and published by Mesorah Publications. See *The Torah Personality: A Treasury of Biographical Sketches* (1980); *The Torah World: A Treasury of Biographical Sketches* (1982); *The Torah Profile: A Treasury of Biographical Sketches* (1988); *Torah Luminaries: A Treasury of Biographical Sketches* (1994); *Torah Lives: A Treasury of Biographical Sketches* (1995).

42. See, for example, Bartal, " 'True Knowledge and Wisdom,' " 186–187; Gertner, "Reishitah shel ketivah historit ortodoksit."

43. See, for example, Nathan Birenbaum, "From Freethinker to Believer," *JO* 4, no. 3 (1967), 7–13; Fabian Schoenfeld, "Fragments from the Teachings of the S'fas Emes," *JO* 1, no. 4 (1964), 13–15; idem, "Sfas Emes on Pesach," *JO* 2, no. 5 (1965), 16–18; Nisson Wolpin, "The Anatomy of Teshuvah," *JO* 6, no. 10 (1970), 3–6. Among the anonymous articles published were "From the Writings of Rabbi Samson Raphael Hirsch, *JO* 1, no. 4 (1964), 17–19; "Samson Raphael Hirsch on Chanukah," *JO* 2, no. 2 (1964), 20–23; "From the Chofetz Chaim's Seifer Hamitzvos—Understanding Mitzvos," *JO* 3, no. 3 (1966), 17–19; "Must We Still Mourn? A Prophetic Message by Samson Raphael Hirsch," *JO* 3, no. 6 (1966), 19–22; "Daf Yomi is a Bridge: An Address to the First Siyum by R' Meir Shapiro zẓ"l," *JO* 4, no. 10 (1968), 13–14; "Three Sefirah Pieces: Adapted from the 'Hagaddah Shem Mishmuel' of Rabbi Shmuel Borenstein, Sochoczover Rebbe zẓ"l," *JO* 7, no. 6 (1971), 8–10.

44. See Berel Wein, "The American Rabbinate—Revisited," *JO* 2, no. 6 (1965), 11–13; Bernard Weinberger, "The Miracle of Williamsburg: How a Community Managed to Halt a Population Shift," *JO* 2, no. 6, 16–20; idem, "The Yeshiva Bochur and College: A New Look at an Old Problem," *JO* 3, no. 4 (1966), 6–9; idem, "America's Orthodox Melting Pot:

An Amalgam of Jewish Types in Creating an 'American Style' Torah-true Jew," *JO* 4, no. 4 (1967), 7–9; H.D. Wolpin, "Kollel: U.S.A.—A Look Inside a New-Old Torah Institution," *JO* 3, no. 1 (1965), 9–12 (this is a rare case in *The Jewish Observer* during the years examined in which the author is female); "Rabbi, Rosh Yeshiva, Ben Torah: Three Articles on Their Inter-Relationships," *JO* 4, no. 7 (1967), 12–20.

45. See Shelomoh E. Danziger, "Modern Orthodoxy or Orthodox Modernism? An Analysis of Some New Trends in Modern Orthodoxy," *JO* 3, no. 8 (1966), 3–9 (see also Irving Greenberg's letter to the editor and Danziger's reply, both in *JO* 3, no. 10 [1966] 13–21); Elias, "The New Halachah"; Menachem Greenberg, "The Yeshiva World's Outlook on Torah and Secular Studies," *JO* 6, no. 4 (1969), 11–15; Yaakov Jacobs, " 'American Orthodoxy' Yesterday and Today: Some Implications of the Recent UOJCA Convention," *JO* 2, no. 3 (1964), 3–9; Chaim D. Keller, "Modern Orthodoxy: An Analysis and a Response," *JO* 6, no. 8 (1970), 3–15; "Opportunities," *JO* 3, no. 5 (1966), 18–19. For recent continuations of this internal debate, see, in chronological order, Yonason Rosenblum, " 'Torah Umadda': A Critique of Rabbi Dr. Norman Lamm's Book and Its Approach to Torah Study and the Pursuit of Secular Knowledge," *JO* 25, no. 2 (1992), 27–41; Yaakov Perlow, "The Clash Between Modernity and Eternity," *JO* 26, no. 10 (1994), 9–16; Lawrence Kaplan, "Letter to the Editor," *JO* 27, no. 3 (1994), 13 (a response to Perlow's article); Mayer Schiller, "*Torah Umadda* and *The Jewish Observer* Critique: Towards a Clarification of the Issues," *The Torah U-Madda Journal* 6 (1995–1996), 58–91. Finally, for some general observations regarding the complex and tense relationship between Rackman and the American haredi "yeshiva world," see Charles S. Liebman, "Emanuel Rackman and Modern Orthodoxy: Some Personal Reflections," in *Studies in Halakha and Jewish Thought*, ed. Moshe Beer (Ramat Gan: 1994), 23–33.

46. See Mordechai Gifter, "The Permanency of Maamad Har Sinai," *JO* 1, no. 8 (1964), 24–26; idem, "Human Law and Torah Law: A Comparison of Purposes," *JO* 2, no. 8 (1965), 3–6; idem, "A Dissident Speaks Out: A Statement by Harav Mordecai Gifter," *JO* 4, no. 1 (1967), 7–10; Chaim D. Keller, "Is the Jew Losing His Identity?," *JO* 2, no. 9 (1965), 16–18; Aharon Kotler, "The Primacy of Torah Study," *JO* 1, no. 6 (1964), 14–16.

47. See the following articles: "Sparks from a Sacred Flame: On the Occasion of the First Yahrzeit of the Gaon of Our Generation—Reb Aharon Kotler zẓ"l, *JO* 1, no. 3 (1963), 15–18; "Harav Chaim Mordecai Katz: An Appreciation," *JO* 2, no. 3 (1964), 11–15; "Ha'admo"r Rabi Avraham Yehoshua Heschel Mikupisheniẓ Zẓuk"l [zekher ẓadik vekadosh livrakhah]," *JO* 4, no. 6 (1967), 18–19 (the title in this article appears in Hebrew); "Rabbi Eliezer Silver zẓ"l," *JO* 5, no. 1 (1968), 14–15; Chaim Shapiro, "Last of a Species: a Personal Memoir of Horav Avrohom Kalmanowitz . . . on His Seventh Yahrzeit," *JO* 8, no. 3 (1972), 13–17. All but one of these articles appeared without a byline.

48. See Shmuel Singer, "A Chief Rabbi for New York City," *JO* 10, no. 1 (1974), 16–21. In the following issue, there are an unusual number of letters to the editor regarding this article. See *JO* 10, no. 2 (1974), 30–33. On Joseph's unsuccessful career in New York, see Abraham J. Karp, "New York Chooses a Chief Rabbi," *Publications of the American Jewish Historical Society* 44, no. 3 (1955), 129–199.

49. On history as an anti-traditional pursuit, see Yosef H. Yerushalmi, *Zakhor: Jewish History and Jewish Memory* (Seattle: 1982), 81–104.

50. On this congregation, see Lowenstein, *Frankfurt on the Hudson*. For basic biographical information about both rabbis, see Moshe D. Sherman, *Orthodox Judaism in America: A Biographical Dictionary and Sourcebook* (Westport: 1996), 36–37, 190–192.

51. See Lowenstein, *Frankfurt on the Hudson*, 157–159; Shnayer Z. Leiman, "R. Shimon Schwab: A Letter Regarding the 'Frankfurt' Approach," *Tradition* 31, no. 3 (1997), 71–78.

52. *JO* 9, no. 10 (1974), 24–26.

53. All quotations in ibid., 24.

54. Ibid.

55. Shimon Schwab, *Selected Writings: A Collection of Addresses and Essays on Hashkafah, Jewish History and Contemporary Issues* (Lakewood: 1988).

56. The essay originally appeared in *Mitteilungen: Bulletin of K'hal Adath Jeshurun* 46 (Dec. 1984-March 1985), 1–2; reprinted in Schwab, *Selected Writings*, 232–236.

57. Ibid., 233–234.

58. Ibid., 234.

59. Ibid., emphasis in original. See also Schacter, "Haskalah, Secular Studies and the Close of the Yeshiva in Volozhin," 111–112. For an attack on Schwab's approach, see Isaac Chavel, "On Haym Soloveitchik's 'Rupture and Reconstruction: The Transformation of Contemporary Orthodox Society': A Response," *The Torah U-Madda Journal* 7 (1997), 129–131.

60. Schwab, *Selected Writings*, 233.

61. This stands in contrast to Yaakov Halevi Lifshitz's outlook; see Bartal, "True Wisdom and Knowledge," 183. Lifshitz was personal secretary to Rabbi Isaac Elhanan Spektor (1817–1896) and was very active in Jewish public affairs. As will be noted, he authored a four-volume work of history and memoirs.

62. On Hutner's life and thought, see Hillel Goldberg, "Rabbi Isaac Hutner: A Synoptic Interpretive Biography," *Tradition* 22, no. 4 (1987), 18–47; Steven S. Schwarzschild, "An Introduction to the Thought of R. Isaac Hutner," *Modern Judaism* 5, no. 3 (1985), 235–278; idem, "Isaac Hutner," in *Interpreters of Judaism in the Late Twentieth Century*, ed. Steven T. Katz (Washington, D.C.: 1993), 151–166; Sherman, *Orthodox Judaism in America*, 97–100.

63. Yitzchok Hutner, " 'Holocaust'—A Study of the Term, and the Epoch it is Meant to Describe," *JO* 12, no. 8 (1977), 3–10.

64. Ibid., 4.

65. See Yaffa Eliach, "The Holocaust—A Response to Catastrophe within a Traditional Jewish Framework," in *The Historiography of the Holocaust Period: Proceedings of the Fifth Yad Vashem International Historical Conference*, ed. Yisrael Gutman and Gideon Greif (Jerusalem: 1988), 722–726; Lawrence J. Kaplan, "Rabbi Isaac Hutner's 'Daat Torah Perspective' on the Holocaust: A Critical Analysis," *Tradition* 18, no. 3 (1980), 235–249.

66. Kaplan, "Rabbi Isaac Hutner's 'Daat Torah Perspective' on the Holocaust."

67. See, for example, Aharon Sorski, *Chazon Ish: A Biography of Rabbi Abraham Isaiah Karelitz* (Bnei Brak: 1971); idem, *Reb Elchonon: The Life and Ideals of Rabbi Elchonon Bunim Wasserman of Baranovitch* (Brooklyn: 1982); idem, *Great Chassidic Leaders: Portraits of Seven Masters of the Spirit* (Brooklyn: 1991).

68. See Kimmy Caplan, "Have 'Many Lies Accumulated in History Books'? The Holocaust in Ashkenazi *Haredi* Historical Consciousness in Israel," *Yad Vashem Studies* 29 (2001), 254–264.

69. The first three volumes of Lifshitz's work were published (1924–1930); to the best of my knowledge, the fourth volume remains undiscovered.

Book Reviews

Antisemitism, Holocaust, and Genocide

Shmuel Almog, David Bankier, Daniel Blatman, and Dalia Ofer (editorial board), *The Holocaust—The Unique and the Universal: Essays Presented in Honor of Yehuda Bauer*. Jerusalem: Yad Vashem and the Avraham Harman Institute of Contemporary Jewry, 2001. xxxi + 194 pp. (Hebrew); 143 pp. (English).

Shmuel Almog, David Bankier, Daniel Blatman, and Dalia Ofer (editorial board), *The Holocaust—History and Memory: Essays Presented in Honor of Israel Gutman*. Jerusalem: Yad Vashem and the Avraham Harman Institute of Contemporary Jewry, 2001. xxxiii + 246 pp. (Hebrew); 123 pp. (English).

This two-volume festschrift contains 31 articles in Hebrew and English presented to Yehuda Bauer and Israel Gutman a few years after their official retirement from the Hebrew University. The laureates have long been recognized as founders of Holocaust study in Israel, and they are among the leading experts in the field worldwide. Each has his own credentials; together, they represent a sui generis cooperation between two scholars whose academic relations were initially those of a teacher and his student. Over time, Gutman and Bauer came not only to epitomize the saying that a teacher is not to be envious of his pupil, but actually to complement one another.

The extraordinary symbiosis between these two scholars probably originated from the synchronization, to some extent, between their personal biographies and their academic activities. Bauer, a native of Prague, was in Palestine during the Second World War. He entered the field of Holocaust study via the history of the Jewish community in Palestine (the Yishuv) during the war, including its reaction to the Holocaust. He went on to investigate a wide range of issues, among them the relationship of the Great Powers to the tragedy of European Jewry; the powerlessness of the Jews in the face of alienation; Jewish resistance; and rescue attempts during the war. He has also written about the flight (*berihah*) of Jews from Poland after the war and the concentration of the surviving remnant (*sheerit hapeletah*) in Germany; about the American Jewish Joint Distribution Committee (JDC) and its activities before, during, and after the war; and about genocide and the uniqueness of the Holocaust as a historical phenomenon.

Gutman spent the war in Poland: first in Warsaw, then in Majdanek, in Auschwitz, and on the death marches. He first focused his research on the fate of Polish Jews during the Holocaust, on the activities of the Jewish leadership in the ghettos, and on the Jewish resistance, and then widened his scope to cover the history of Polish Jewry before and after the Holocaust. His distinct imprint on the field lies in his studying and narrating the Holocaust from the perspective of Jewish sources. The large number of studies and monographs initiated and supervised by Gutman have sought to reconstruct both the inner world and the activities of Jews during the Holocaust. In Bauer's words, the basis of Gutman's work is "to see the Holocaust from Jewish points of view" (*History and Memory*, p. xvi).

Put somewhat differently, and in accordance with a long-established classification of Holocaust study, Gutman has portrayed the Holocaust from the perspective of the *victims*, as distinguished from that of the *perpetrators*, the *bystanders*, and the *rescuers*. However, the titles of the two-volume festschrift, *History and Memory* and *The Unique and the Universal*, either intentionally or implicitly propose other ways of defining and navigating the wide field of Holocaust research: not only the Holocaust as a unique and unparalleled historical event, but also its universal significance and the ways it is remembered and commemorated, and, in an even wider context, the Holocaust as a turning point in world history and culture and its impact on human civilization.

To map "the state of the art" of Holocaust study, it might be helpful to combine the established and conventional classifications with the directions denoted by the titles of the volumes dedicated to Bauer and Gutman (hereafter: B and G, respectively), and to apply them to the essays they include. Four essays concern the perpetrators, by Wolfgang Benz (B), Yehoshua Büchler (B), Eberhard Jäckel (G), and Szymon Rudnicki (G). Two contributions, by Jerzy Tomaszewski (G) and David Bankier (B), deal with the bystanders. Two others (both in Gutman's volume) concern the rescuers: that of Dov Levin on the rescue of Estonian Jews by the Soviets, and that of Shmuel Krakowski on rescue activities in Poland.

The essays devoted to the victims draw our attention to another matter not explicitly addressed by the editors, that of the chronological boundaries of the Holocaust as a historical event and its division into sub-periods. Thus, there is a contribution by Walter Zvi Bacharach on Jewish intellectuals in the Weimar republic (B), a number of articles on the fate of European Jews during the Second World War (Christopher R. Browning in [B] and Renée Poznanski, Shmuel Spector, and Sara Bender in the Gutman volume), and a cluster of essays dealing with Holocaust survivors (all in Gutman's volume) by Antony Polonsky and Monika Garbowska, David Engel, Daniel Blatman, Hagit Lavsky, and Hanna Yablonka. Shlomo Aronson's article (B) covers Israel Kasztner's activity both during and immediately after the war (during the Nuremberg trials) and his fate in Israel.

Three different essays, by Emil Fackenheim (B), Shmuel Almog (B), and Michael R. Marrus (G), grapple with philosophical, religious, and historiosophical matters (Marrus' piece also belongs to the section on victims). Dina Porat's innovative article about the diary of Anne Frank and the deniers of the Holocaust in the last four decades of the 20th century (B), which points to the relevancy of the Holocaust—or rather, its lessons—to this day, is in a class of its own.

Not surprisingly, most of the articles dealing with the perspective of the victims are included in Gutman's volume, whereas those that place the Holocaust in a universal and comparative context are found in Bauer's and are all in the English section, written by scholars from abroad. Vahakn N. Dadrian and Franklin H. Littell discuss various aspects of genocide, including problems concerning its detection and prevention; and Steven T. Katz offers "some reasons why . . . despite many historical and phenomenological similarities, . . . ultimately the Armenian tragedy and the *Shoah* are basically dissimilar in their structure and should be distinguished one from the other by the fundamental intentionality that caused each to occur" (B:101).

The interchangeable use of the terms "Holocaust" and *"Shoah,"* found not only in Katz's essay but also in the foreword and preface to each volume, draw our attention to the issue of terminology and lead us to Dan Michman's illuminating article, "One Theme, Multiple Voices: The Role of Linguistic Cultures in Holocaust Research" (B). In a clear and methodical manner, Michman analyzes Holocaust research conducted in three linguistic-cultural circles: the German, the English, and the French, and then examines Israeli historiography in relation to these three circles. This essay adds another brick to the edifice that Michman has been constructing as he seeks to synthesize a systematic picture of "the state of the art" of Holocaust research. In this regard, Michman quite properly credits the impact of Raul Hilberg's ground-breaking work of the early 1960s.

In similar fashion, four other essays seek to provide a more comprehensive discussion. Raya Cohen reconsiders armed resistance in the ghettoes (G); Dalia Ofer raises issues about the fate of children and youth during the Holocaust, focusing on firsthand accounts (G); and, in their respective pieces, Hava Eshkoli and Tuvia Friling tackle the extensive body of research on the Yishuv and the Holocaust (B). In his abovementioned article, Michman offers some instructive explanations concerning the current popularity of this last topic, although one might be tempted to argue with his remark concerning the effect of gender and marital status on the selection of research subjects (B:36, n. 93). Eshkoli and Friling represent different generational stages in Holocaust research: Eshkoli is the veteran member of a group of second-generation researchers who have followed Bauer in examining the attitude of the Yishuv leadership toward rescuing European Jews. Tuvia Friling's work constitutes the third stage of research in the field. Following the line of argument developed first by Bauer and then by Dina Porat, Friling does not merely relate to "what really happened" during the war, but also endeavors to explain and evaluate the claim that the Yishuv entrusted rescue operations during the Holocaust to backseat members of the Zionist leadership.

In both volumes, a collegial atmosphere prevails. Indeed, the contributors are either former students of the laureates, now well-established researchers in their own right, or else are contemporaries and friends. The introductory sections refer to Gutman and Bauer by their first names, and the overall tone is reminiscent of an intimate gathering—which in fact is characteristic of so many academic forums on the Holocaust held in Israel and abroad. An outsider might wonder whether this familiar atmosphere is sufficiently open to allow for fresh critical approaches.

According to the editors, these two volumes are neither a summation nor a conclusion, but rather one more milestone added to the many that Bauer and Gutman have set on the road of Holocaust research. Both Gutman and Bauer are still active in research, teaching, and lecturing. It is probably too much to expect that a festschrift would fully chart the field of Holocaust research, even as defined by the two scholars being honored. Nonetheless, a comprehensive bibliography of Gutman's and Bauer's writings, as well as a list of theses and dissertations carried out under their supervision, would have been helpful, and would also have served as another tribute to their enormous contribution. Another asset to the reader would have been abstracts of the articles, in Hebrew for the English section, and vice versa.

These comments (more in the nature of wishes) do not diminish the achievement represented by these volumes. The editors deserve our praise not only for summarizing some 40 years of Holocaust research, but also for setting directions for future study that, increasingly, will be conducted by teachers and students who have no personal experience of the Holocaust. For generations to come, the scholarly groundwork laid by Bauer and Gutman will doubtless continue to nourish academic and public discourse on the Holocaust, both in Israel and abroad.

AVIVA HALAMISH
The Open University of Israel

Jonathan Frankel, *Dam upolitikah: 'alilat damesek, hayehudim veha'olam* (Heb. version of *The Damascus Affair: "Ritual Murder," Politics and the Jews in 1840*). Jerusalem: The Zalman Shazar Center for Jewish History, 2003. 513 pp.

An Israeli student of Jewish history might well identify the 1840 blood libel against the Jews of Damascus as one of the pivotal events of modern Jewish history. An American student of Jewish history, in contrast, is more likely to be unsure what the term "Damascus affair" actually refers to. (I wonder where European students would fall in this dichotomy.) But no scholar with an interest in Jewish history can afford to miss the opportunity of reading Jonathan Frankel's seminal study, now translated into Hebrew, in which he transforms what we cannot help but think of as a mere case of absurd accusations into a major intersection of the basic contours of the modern Jewish experience. This is a remarkable achievement of scholarship that first excavates the details of events in Damascus and subsequently in the capital cities of the Middle East and Europe, and then broadens further as it delves not only into the political contexts of events, but also into the affair's religious and intellectual repercussions.

There is scarcely a book on any subject in the realm of modern Jewish history that can even approach this work in scope, erudition, scholarship, and profound rethinking of basic historical concepts of the period. The book builds its own momentum, moving gradually from the immediate drama of the missing Father Thomas and his servant through the arrests, torture, confessions, and subsequent retractions of a group of Damascus Jews. It then takes on a broader sweep, covering Mideast politics, the Jewish struggle for emancipation in Europe, and Frankel's take

on the connections of these events with the emergence of Jewish nationalism later
in the 19th century.

True, the reader will be tested at the outset. Frankel's attention to detail in describing the early events, with special emphasis on the rival diplomacy set into
action by the French and Austrian representatives, almost succeeds in discouraging
the reader from continuing. It is extremely difficult to follow who is who and what
their functions are as the narrative shifts between Damascus, Alexandria, Istanbul,
Paris, Vienna, and London. These chapters also jump around as they describe the
near-simultaneous ritual murder accusations in Damascus and Rhodes. It might
have been better to describe the Rhodes incident in one compact section, rather
than requiring the reader to negotiate between pages. Frankel, however, has his
reasons for imposing such a structure; by presenting the entire matrix of events,
he succeeds in demonstrating how a seemingly passing episode in Damascus snow-
balled into an international affair with lasting implications. Once Frankel moves
his focus to Europe, his text and style become more coherent and cogent. At a
time when historians are notably wary of the long-term significance of individual
events, Frankel's thought-provoking and comprehensive study of the Damascus
affair is itself a contribution of singular importance.

There is of course the occasional slip, so badly needed by a reviewer. In one
such lapse, he virtually gives the Rothschilds credit for the establishment of the
modern state of Israel in 1948 through their support of 19th-century settlements.
But even if this tribute is exaggerated, Frankel's documentation of the extent of
Rothschild involvement in the Zionist enterprise will be pivotal in any future examination of the Jewish activities of the family.

The Damascus Affair is marked by the continuous pursuit of contexts that
broaden the focus beyond the immediate. To begin with, Frankel explains the development of events in the context of Mideast power struggles, between Muham-
med Ali in Egypt and the seat of the Ottoman empire in Istanbul, and subsequently
between France and Austria as they vied for influence in the region: "[T]he Damascus affair had, throughout, developed under the shadow of the upheaval in the
Middle East . . . and the ever-increasing involvement of the European powers in the
region had combined to excite extreme expectations, hopes, fears, and hatreds in
both the East and the West" (p. 385).[1]

Frankel makes extensive use of European archives and newspapers to describe
the diplomatic rivalry between France and Austria, with the former intimately im-
mersed in the accusations against the Jews and the latter demanding a denunciation
of barbaric charges and acquittal of those accused. His description of the Crémieux-
Montefiore mission to Alexandria is one of the highlights of his narrative. By this
time, the reader is craving for detail, and Frankel supplies it with relish. Combining
recently uncovered Crémieux documents with published and unpublished Montefiore versions, Frankel shatters any delusions of a unified diplomatic thrust. Starting
with quarrels over quarters in the ship and then the scampering for faster and larger
press coverage, he shows in detail the conflicts between the two leaders and between their wives. Differences in age, personality, commitment to religious observances, and national rivalries all contributed to the tensions and bore implications
for the mission itself.

The respective positions of France and Austria in the affair must surprise and disturb the reader throughout, with the very cradle of emancipation actively supporting the blood libel and reactionary Austria steadfast in defense of the Jews. Frankel poses the question bluntly: "Was there not encapsulated in this apparent paradox the fundamental dilemma facing the Jews of Europe in the modern era?" (p. 440). His explanation is steeped in his particular expertise of the Russian context. Reactionary regimes, committed to maintaining order, protected the rights of Jews inherent in their own systems, while ostensibly liberal societies were apt to react negatively to the expanding Jewish presence in various walks of life, and many within those societies nurtured the image of the Jew as outsider. As Frankel maps the extensiveness of blood libel accusations in support of his thesis, he provides considerable evidence for a position that I personally had long dismissed: that of the continuity between older forms of Jewish hatred and 19th century antisemitic movements. However one chooses to integrate blood libels into modern times, it will now be very difficult to write these incidents off as mere aberrations within a more generally secularized trend.

Frankel's entry into religious polemics both internal and external is innovative, illuminating, and insightful. Jewish religious figures were shocked that they were left on their own to counter accusations of barbarism not only against individual Jews, but also against Judaism. Their disappointment echoes an ongoing theme, dating at least from the late 18th century and culminating in the 20th, that non-Jews who should have known better could become strangely mute when their voices were most urgently required.

Heinrich Graetz plays an important role in this discussion, but I do think that Frankel overemphasizes the religious component of his thinking, while not sufficiently recognizing his social consciousness. But more significantly, Frankel demonstrates that German Jews did not sit on the sidelines, as is often thought. He pinpoints the specific reason for that impression, stemming from the notable reticence of Gabriel Riesser, the preeminent German Jewish Liberal leader. The contrast with Crémieux, sufficiently secure in his emancipated status, and Montefiore, who was apparently quite comfortable with the less-than-full political equality of English Jews, underscores the objective insecurity of German Jews generally, and certainly of their leading spokesman, who proved reluctant to enter the international arena. Moreover, Riesser was less affected by the French involvement and the English objective of punishing its rival.

The press plays a central role in Frankel's presentation and interpretation, often stirring up events as well as reporting on them. Thus, the press serves not only as a primary source, but at times as an active agent. Frankel's comments on the relationship between the Damascus affair and the emergence of the European Jewish press are far more tempered than Baruch Mevorach's much earlier claims, to which I strongly objected a number of years ago, basing myself on an advanced mathematical model that demonstrated how events of 1840 could have had but a limited influence on, for example, the founding of Ludwig Philippson's *Allgemeine Zeitung* in 1837! Yet I differ even from Frankel's more moderate interpretation. I cannot speak of the French press at the time, but from my own reading of both the English and German Jewish press, it appears to me that the events in Damascus received far less attention than did the domestic affairs of emancipation and religious struggles in both communities. My argument with Mevorach was that he failed to appreciate that European Jews did not require an external shock to stimulate local political initiative, and that the Jewish press emerged precisely to pursue Jewish objectives even prior to the alarming news from the Middle East. No one who reads Frankel's monumental study can possibly maintain that European Jews acquiesced passively to the events around them. And few of us will leave the book thinking as we did beforehand.

ROBERT LIBERLES
Ben-Gurion University

Note

1. Quotes refer to the English version of the book, published by Cambridge University Press in 1997.

Daniel Jonah Goldhagen, *A Moral Reckoning: The Role of the Catholic Church in the Holocaust and Its Unfulfilled Duty of Repair.* New York: Alfred A. Knopf, 2002. 362 pp.

Michael Phayer, *The Catholic Church and the Holocaust, 1930–1965.* Bloomington: Indiana University Press, 2000. xviii + 301 pp.

One of the more important chapters in contemporary Jewish-Christian relations involves the criticism (the battering, from the Catholic point of view) sustained by the Roman Catholic Church with respect to its alleged indifference to, if not its conspiracy with, the Nazi government's program of brutalization and extermination of the Jews of Europe. Since the mid-1960s, scholars, including some who were nurtured in the Roman Catholic tradition, have begun to examine the history, politics, and theology of the Church. Their purpose has been to determine how a church that has laid claim to the highest moral and religious standards for 2,000 years could be found complicit in the perpetration of the crimes of the Holocaust.

These scholars' findings reveal that not only were there bishops and priests who were indifferent to the mass murder of European Jewry but, more crucially, that the Bishop of Rome himself, Pope Pius XII (1939–1958), may be said to have been the arch-villain whose wartime record, to this very day, continues to hover in the shadows. It was not until after his death that questions about his conduct during the Holocaust were first raised. Rolf Hochhuth's drama, *The Deputy*, first published in the United States in 1964, was the first such public condemnation of Pius' behavior with respect to the plight of the Jews. Although a work of dramatic imagination, Hochhuth's presentation of a self-centered and callous pontiff was soon reinforced by a number of probing works. One that comes to mind is Guenter Levy's *The Catholic Church and Nazi Germany* (1964). A decade later, Rosemary Radford Reuther of the Catholic Theological Seminary in Chicago published *Faith and Fratricide: The Theological Roots of Antisemitism* (1974), which argued that Catholic theology, liturgy, and even its New Testament foundations laid the groundwork for hatred of the Jews. In a more recent book, John Cornwell's *The Secret History of Pius XII* (1999), Pius again came under attack. Clearly, then, Michael Phayer and Daniel Jonah Goldhagen are not alone in presenting their critical views about the wartime pope's behavior.[1]

Phayer, a retired history professor from Marquette University, a Jesuit institution in Milwaukee, offers a sober and well-organized view of the subject. Well-versed in German archival and printed sources, he provides a thoroughly researched and clearly written exposition. Admitting that Pius' image of aloofness and coldness was rooted in an indifference to the extermination of the Jews, Phayer notes that the pope's public policies convinced many that he was an antisemite. At the same time, he argues, Pius XII seemed warm and compassionate in his personal contacts with both Gentiles and Jews (p. 222). Phayer also acknowledges that antisemitism was pervasive for centuries throughout Catholic Europe and was tied to Church teachings; but he goes on to differentiate between that tradition—which did not produce a Holocaust—and racial antisemitism, which emerged during the 19th century. The question, of course, is whether racial antisemitism and Nazism could have arisen in a semantic-theological void; popular images of Jews in Nazi propaganda were drawn from anti-Jewish stereotypes with which the Christian world had long been familiar.

Phayer deals extensively with Pius' insistence on remaining silent in the face of Nazi atrocities. Such silence, he suggests, was manifested not only with regard to the murder of the Jews but even earlier, beginning in 1939, when Poles, Serbs, and others were murdered by the Nazis (chs. 2–3). Germany's attempt to eradicate Poland's Catholic elite and other religious leaders was one of the great tragedies of the war. Yet the pope did not respond, and this, Phayer suggests, characterized Pius' style in the face of genocide in general.

Provocative and important as this insight might be, it again seems to beg the question of the specific relationship of the Church to Hitler's Jewish victims. By positing a doubtful universalism, Phayer weakens the force of his book.

Papal silence contributed to the tragedy of the Holocaust. First and foremost, it involved Pius' refusal to protest to the Nazi government regarding the murder of European Jewry. Although he knew more than most about the massive deportations and extermination program, Pius failed to keep his bishops informed about events and refrained from alerting the international diplomatic community. As Phayer observes, had Pius XII spoken out, his words might have motivated many of his faithful to protest, and fewer Jews might have died.

Phayer justifiably rejects the notion that the pope was concerned that open criticism of the Nazi government could have compounded its fury toward the Jews and somehow aggravated their already unimaginable suffering. Nor does he believe that Pius' affection for Germany (a country in which he had long resided as a Vatican diplomat) made him reluctant to condemn Germany; Pius XII hated the

Nazis.[2] Rather, argues Phayer, papal silence was generated by the pontiff's desire to be seen as neutral. He aspired to be a peacemaker, and his specific goal was to help bring about the defeat not only of Hitler, but also of Communism, and thereby to create a new Europe that would be safe for the Catholic Church. The survival of the Jewish people was not Pius' highest priority. Rather, in accordance with his concern for the fate of Christian Europe, Pius believed that Germany must emerge from the war both intact and strong.

Thus, the pope issued no encyclicals pertaining to deportations or mass exterminations. As Phayer records, any communication on such events was made through diplomatic channels to his nuncios. References to the Holocaust were never couched in outrage or compassion for the victims, but in formal legal language. Pius also took care to refrain from criticizing German bishops and to treat Hitler with deference. He did not wish to alienate Germany, fearing the possibility of a military takeover of Rome, or even worse, its destruction.

Such anxiety illuminates the pope's shameful behavior in 1943, when 1,000 Jews were dispatched from his very doorstep to Auschwitz. The pope's silence was an ominous signal of Catholic indifference to the Jews' fate. If the pope himself could stand by silently while the Jews of his Eternal City were led to slaughter, what could be expected of all the other faithful, to whom he was infallible?

Even after the war, throughout the years of the Cold War until his death in 1958, Pius XII's studied disregard of the Holocaust and the plight of its survivors continued. Phayer's careful explanation of the postwar years is a real strength of this volume. Especially striking is his description of the pope's continued affection for Germany and its people; Pius treated the Germans as victims and martyrs of Nazism rather than as perpetrators of the most heinous crime in history. According to Phayer, the pope's conciliatory stance was motivated by his dread of Communist expansion. Consequently, on all issues related to Germany and European politics, he acted as a calculating diplomat rather than as a moral leader. Even this, however, does not explain why it was that the Vatican befriended Nazi war criminals, providing them with documentation that enabled them to flee to Argentina and other countries beyond Allied control. Phayer is unable to inform us of the degree of Pius' personal involvement, but he surmises that it must have been considerable (p. 168).

By the same token, the pope did not raise his voice against postwar antisemitism in Germany, Poland, and elsewhere. Phayer stops short of attributing Pius' attitude to blatant antisemitism, arguing rather that the pope's behavior stemmed from his desire to bolster German and Polish resistance to the Communists, and his consequent fear of alienating them. The pope's Cold War began in 1945, a good three years before its "official" birth.

Although Phayer provides further insight into Pius XII, a more complete assessment must take into account the antisemitic factor: to conclude that the pope was anything other than antisemitic constitutes a gross misjudgment of his nature. The great changes in Christian-Jewish relations that were first launched by the Church with its *Nostra Aetate* encyclical of 1965 were not introduced until several years after Pius' death. To his credit, Phayer (who goes beyond Pius to analyze the work of the Second Vatican Council of 1962–1965), is one of the few historians to appreciate the impact of this event on the relationship between Catholics and Jews.

Although Daniel Jonah Goldhagen's *A Moral Reckoning* draws liberally upon the works noted earlier in this review, its author, to a greater or lesser extent, finds grounds to disagree with them all. His own book is far more radical, a jeremiad accusing Pius XII of utter failure as a Christian leader and demanding that the Church face up to its crimes against the Jews, pay a penalty for them, and reform its behavior. Historians, with their sober and measured methodology, do not ordinarily write such books. But Goldhagen is not a historian. He is a Harvard University political scientist who offers a compelling moral message both to the academic community and to the Christian world.

Although his heaviest guns are reserved for Pius XII, Goldhagen, like Phayer (and, in this regard, succeeding rather more than the latter), professes to be a critic of the Church as a whole. Unlike Phayer, he does not hesitate to accuse the Church of antisemitism. He traces this hatred to such theological notions as deicide and supersessionism, the displacement of Judaism by the Church, the "new Israel." Such Christian thinking, Goldhagen believes, molded the Church as an antisemitic institution and taught its faithful that the Jews were to be demeaned. That Catholics would willingly join in the slaughter of Jews is thus hardly surprising to Goldhagen. Whereas historians (including Phayer) have distinguished between Church-inspired anti-Judaism and Nazism (the latter perceived as a product of pagan, non-Christian forces alien to the Church), Goldhagen reduces the distinction to one of method: both the Nazis and the Church aspired, in one way or another, to rid the world of Jews.

Contrary to the defenders of Pius XII who insist that he was not an antisemite, Goldhagen charges that the pope's silence was selective. For example, he did not remain silent when baptized Jews were deported or when the disabled were sent to their deaths. He excommunicated all those who joined the Communist party, though he never excommunicated a single Nazi killer—including Adolf Hitler. Pius believed Communism to be the principal evil, and he equated Jews with Bolshevism. In this sense, Goldhagen argues, the leader of the Church held views on the Jews that differed little from those of the Nazis.

Although Goldhagen is uncompromising in his judgment of the Church of Rome, his greatest and most original contribution lies in his bold, almost utopian recommendations concerning how the Church should go about "repairing" itself. According to him, the Roman Catholic Church must view itself as a political entity, for it is in this fashion that it has related to Jews for the past two millennia. It follows that Jews may examine the Church's behavior just as they scrutinize any other political entity. They may justifiably demand restitution for their material and psychological suffering, and they are entitled to see justice meted out to those members of the clergy who actively participated in the Holocaust.

Another issue posed by Goldhagen concerns what the Church can do to prevent a repetition of such crimes against the Jews. His recommendations do not include building upon the achievements of the Second Vatican Council, which he dismisses as virtually ineffective. Likewise, he has little use for the *Nostra Aetate* encyclical of 1965. Goldhagen does not see this initiative as a first step in revolutionizing the relationship between the Church and the Jewish people. In this sense, his thinking about Vatican II differs considerably from that of Phayer and many others.

Not all of Goldhagen's recommendations are unreasonable. There is much to be said for his demand that the Church compensate the Jewish people by offering them national support. The Church, Goldhagen believes, must stand by the state of Israel and reject all forms of anti-Zionism along with antisemitism. In addition, Goldhagen demands that the Church publicly admit its culpability, show a genuine contrition, and ask for forgiveness for its abominable behavior. Actually, in recent years (since *Nostra Aetate*), the Church has begun to fulfill these demands. For Goldhagen, however, it has not gone the full, required distance. He wants the Church to admit without equivocation its 2,000-year practice of antisemitism and its implication in the Holocaust. He expects Church leaders to acknowledge that its teachings conditioned the faithful to accept the idea of Jewish extermination. He also finds abhorrent the Church's efforts to turn the Holocaust into a Christian tragedy by declaring itself a co-victim with the Jews, as in the case of the beatification of Edith Stein, a convert to Catholicism who perished at Auschwitz.

Goldhagen recommends not only that scholars should probe the Vatican archives, but that they should be dispatched to examine the records of all the national Catholic churches in the period before, during, and immediately after the Holocaust.[3]

Among his less realistic recommendations is the proposed convening of a Third Vatican Council whose task would be to examine all the sources of its faith that have generated hostility toward Jews, including a repudiation of New Testament texts held to contain pernicious, anti-Jewish doctrines. Indeed, Goldhagen goes so far as to suggest the excision from the Christian Bible of any reference that accuses the Jews of crucifying the Christian Savior. Equally difficult, and quite as utopian, is his request that the Roman Catholic church assume responsibility for reforming its own institutional structure. For the Church to assume the role of a true moral agent, Goldhagen asserts, it must divest itself of its political and diplomatic responsibilities. It must give up its foreign alliances, concordats, and dispatching of nuncios throughout the world in its quest for political influence. Goldhagen sees power and morality as incompatible.

Different though these two books are, they do share an important similarity both with each other and with the numerous other recent books on similar themes. Both are the product of the post-Vatican II era; were it not for *Nostra Aetate*, it is possible that neither could have been written.

EGAL FELDMAN
University of Wisconsin, Superior

Notes

1. Concurrently with Phayer's book, three other works appeared in the year 2000: John Cornwell's *Breaking Faith: The Pope, the People, and the Fate of Catholicism;* Gary Wills' *Papal Sin: Structures of Deceit;* and Susan Zuccotti's *Under His Very Windows: The Vatican and the Holocaust in Italy.* Two additional works were published the following year, James

Carroll's *Constantine's Sword: The Church and the Jews*; and David Kertzer's *The Vatican's Role in the Rise of Modern Antisemitism*.

2. See Charles R. Gallagher, "A Newly Discovered Report from 1930 Reveals Cardinal Pacelli's Anti-Nazi Stance," *America* (1 Sept. 2003), 8–10.

3. Notwithstanding his disclaimers, several Catholic thinkers since the Second Vatican Council have begun to tinker with ideas similar to those proposed by Goldhagen. See Egal Feldman, *Catholics and Jews in Twentieth-Century America* (Urbana: 2001), chs. 8 and 10.

Dina Porat and Yechiam Weitz (eds.), *Bein magen david litlai zahov: hayishuv hayehudi beerez yisrael veshoat yehudei eiropa 1939–1945: kovez te'udot* (Between the Star of David and the yellow star: the Jewish community in Palestine and the Holocaust, 1939–1945: documents). Jerusalem: Yad Vashem and Yad Yitzhak Ben-Zvi, 2002. 457 pp.

The prevailing negative stereotype in Israeli popular and scholarly discourse regarding the attitude of the Yishuv and its leaders toward European Jewry during the Holocaust is built on several weighty charges. These are, however, highly questionable.

First, it is alleged that the classic Zionist tenet of *shlilat hagolah* (negation of the Exile) provided an underlying ideological dimension that weakened Zionist involvement in the plight of Europe's Jews in principle, and in practice might have hobbled potential rescue efforts by pitting Zionism against rescue.

Second, we find the zero-sum hypothesis of mutually negating pragmatic considerations: a small community with meager resources at its disposal, it is argued, could not cope simultaneously with two enormous tasks—rescue and state-building; therefore, supposedly, this stand-off between two alternatives prompted the Yishuv leadership to forego rescue and to focus instead on laying the groundwork for a Jewish state.

Next there is the characterization of David Ben-Gurion as an unyielding personality for whom, given his leadership style, it was quite in character to make "tough" decisions. Thus, so the argument goes, he decided to maintain his predetermined course in building the Yishuv even if this meant turning his back on the Jews in Nazi Europe.

We have to factor in, as well, a number of other cognitive and historical issues. There is, for example, the appalling gap between the massive number of victims— including a million and a half children—and the paltry number of those rescued, which is difficult to absorb rationally, and certainly difficult to accept. One might point, as well, to the elaborate trap in which the Jewish people found itself, hemmed in by the absolute determination of the Germans to carry out the Final Solution, on the one hand, and the wartime policies adopted by the Allies, on the other; the utter sense of helplessness that the Jews experienced—the Yishuv included; the sheer complexity, both political and logistical, of any conceivable, large-scale rescue endeavors, which seemed to doom such efforts from the start; and, indeed, the failure of those rescue attempts that were made, despite the fact that the Yishuv recruited its finest and its ablest men and women for the task.

As if all this were not enough, the negative judgment rendered on the Yishuv's performance is also overlaid by latter-day political debates concerning the character of Israeli society, the lasting psychological scars of the process of state-building, and the problematic new debate over collective memory and its scholarly representation—a debate that takes place in a distinct tone of discomfort, fuelled by a lack of consensus, bordering on despair, about our national future.[1]

In light of the foregoing, there is no doubt that the Yishuv's behavior during the Holocaust presents issues that must be dealt with, if they are ever to be laid to rest, and toward that end the meticulously edited volume presented by Dina Porat and Yechiam Weitz makes a significant contribution. It offers the informed reader a rich variety of documentation and conceptual tools through which to address these emotionally laden questions, which comprise one of the most painful debates in Israeli historiography.

As its title ("Between the Star of David and the yellow star") implies, the reader will find among some 200 documents published in this volume material related both to "here"—the realm of the Jewish Yishuv—and "there"—Nazi Europe—as well as some of the implications of the interface between them. The book ranges from the time of the war itself to later perceptions of the events; from the tragically failed attempts at rescue to the debates generated by attempts to analyze, account for, and explain them—or, if you will, the efforts to portray these failures as signaling one of the "original sins" (perhaps the worst of them) of the Zionist movement. In the words of author Natan Shaham, in his own contribution to the volume, "the smell of smoke clings to every word."[2]

The book contains four chapters as well as a methodological introduction and a series of informative appendices. The first chapter deals with the initial war years, from 1939 to 1942, and traces the epistemological process that shaped the Yishuv's awareness of what was happening in Europe. The questions relevant for this period are: what information reached the Free World, including the Yishuv, about the mass killings that begin systematically from the summer of 1941, and what took place as that information was absorbed?

The second chapter encompasses the years from 1942 to 1945. Published statements of the time officially confirmed that the Nazis' deliberate, systematic, and total program of genocide was quite different from pogroms of the past. In those three years, the Yishuv tried to extricate itself as quickly as possible from the anguished paralysis occasioned by this news and sought ways to grapple with the enormity of the disaster. This chapter documents the Yishuv's attempts to frame some kind of policy, including programs of assistance and rescue. Here the reader will find details about relief work (dubbed, in the parlance of the time, "minor rescue"—*hahazalah haketanah*): sending parcels of food and medical supplies, money, and forged papers to Jews in occupied Europe, or smuggling Jews out of high-risk zones to areas that were still relatively safe, all of which was calculated to enable Jews to survive the war as long as possible. "Major rescue" (*hahazalah hagedolah*) consisted of plans to evacuate Jews from the occupied zone entirely. The editors present four such plans—one plan for the rescue of children and three ransom attempts: the so-called "Transnistria plan" (intended to rescue Jews forced into that deadly no-man's land by the Romanian authorities); the "Europa plan," also known as the "Rabbis' plan," which developed from previous attempts by Slovakian Jews to ransom themselves; and the aptly named "blood for goods" plan to rescue Hungarian Jews, which was connected with the missions of Joel Brand and Bandy Grosz in the spring-summer of 1944 (and which would later fuel the uproar over the Grunwald-Kasztner trial). This chapter contains, as well, documents regarding the Yishuv leadership and its role in trying to convince the Allies to bomb the camps or the transit lines leading to them—a topic that has figured prominently in recent debates.

The next two chapters deal with the activities undertaken by the Yishuv toward the end and in the immediate aftermath of the war. In chapter 3, the editors present material documenting the emerging characterization of the surviving Jews—the "surviving remnant" (*sheerit hapeletah*), as they came to be called—who, as a group, were deemed to share certain traits or characteristics and to possess needs that had to be attended to. Here, too, are documents related to the initial discussions over possible immigration "reservoirs" elsewhere (that is, from countries other than Europe)—discussions that are pertinent both to the polemical claims about the alleged "instrumental" attitude of the Yishuv leadership toward European Jewry during the Shoah and also to the late "discovery" of Middle Eastern Jewry, after the Yishuv's leaders realized that there would not be enough Ashkenazi Jews left to successfully fulfill the Zionist mission. The final chapter is devoted entirely to the Shoah and the self-image of the Yishuv: the various postures adopted regarding Jewish resistance in the Holocaust, the painful arguments about "sheep to the slaughter," the influence of the Shoah on the developing character of Israeli identity, and finally, the disturbing questions (as disturbing in retrospect as they were then) over "who shall be saved?" Who, that is, should be saved when it is not possible to save everyone?

What is missing throughout this valuable and diverse compilation is the external perspective: how did the Yishuv appear to others, especially as reflected in British and American documents? Both Britain and the United States were concerned about what would be done with those thousands of Jews whom the Yishuv sought to rescue. It became evident even before the war (at the Evian conference of 1938), and during the war (at Bermuda, in 1943), as well as afterward, that the Allies were not ready to deal with hundreds of thousands of refugees. Nor were they prepared to significantly alter their own immigration policy or the White Paper policy of 1939, which barred future Jewish immigration to Palestine (beyond the last-chance quota of 15,000 per year for five years, totaling only 75,000). Indeed, Britain stuck to the White Paper of 1939 even after November 1942, by which time it was known for sure that whoever did not make it out of Nazi-controlled Europe was sentenced to death.

External documentation, especially from Allied intelligence sources, sheds important light on the rescue activities undertaken by the Yishuv, on the central importance assigned to them, and the profound determination of those involved in this work on behalf of the Jewish Agency's political department and the Agency for Illegal Immigration (Hamosad le'aliyah bet). Such documentation largely refutes the notion that the Yishuv was busy with organizing kibbutz dance festivals, enjoying wartime prosperity at Tel Aviv cafés, and mainly ignoring the catastrophe befalling the Jews of Europe. It also demonstrates, though this is naturally hard to accept, that the Yishuv's rescue efforts failed despite the fact that it assigned the task to its most trusted and ablest personnel, people who were deeply committed to the Zionist movement and its Palestine agenda both before and after the war.[3]

Also missing are documents pertaining to the various wings of the Zionist Revisionist Right and the diverse Orthodox religious community. Material of this sort would certainly have enriched and completed the picture.

Bein magen david letlai zahov contains a wealth of different types of documentary material: telegrams, conference minutes, selections from the press, inter-office correspondence, letters sent from Palestine and from Europe to Palestine, newspaper cartoons, posters and flyers, poetry from the war years and beyond, and other literary material, with eminently clear and readable chapter introductions that provide the contextual information for approaching these texts. It gives us a portrait of a community that is at once stimulating and poignant: a view of the Yishuv as a living, breathing, society, confused and in pain, which saw itself as both a spearhead and last refuge of the nation, and which was unable, despite its deepest wish, to provide that sanctuary.

Tuvia Friling
Ben-Gurion University

Notes

1. See Tuvia Friling, introduction, to idem (ed.), *Teshuvah le'amit post-ziyoni* (Tel Aviv: 2003).
2. Natan Shaham, *Sefer ḥatum* (Tel Aviv: 1988), 141–143; reprinted in Porat and Weitz (eds.), 381–382.
3. See Tuvia Friling, *Heẓ ha'arafel: David Ben-Gurion, hanhagat huyishuv venisyonot haẓalah bashoah* (Sde-Boker: 1998), ch. 7.

Pamela Shatzkes, *Holocaust and Rescue: Impotent or Indifferent? Anglo-Jewry 1938–1945.* Houndmills, Basingstoke: Palgrave, 2002. xiii + 322 pp.

Eleanor Rathbone (1872–1946), the courageous Member of Parliament who fought consistently, often in vain, for those attempting to flee Nazi persecution, once wrote that she felt herself standing outside prison bars behind which fellow humans were being tortured: "We scrape at the bars with little files. A few victims are dragged painfully one by one through the gaps."[1] Her rueful acknowledgment of minor successes amid overwhelming need illuminates the tragic dilemma for would-be rescuers: the number of those who could be saved was always a mere fraction of those in mortal danger. Even before the war, the fate of Nazi victims, most of them Jews, was never a high priority for any government, including the British government, deeply anxious about its position in Palestine and its military weakness vis-à-vis the Axis. Still less were Jews a priority after September 1939, when every aspect of government policy was subordinate to the overriding aim of survival and ultimate victory in a global war. In that supreme struggle, older British traditions of asylum, of humanitarian concern, sometimes of sheer decency, gave way to military needs. This was the reality confronting the British Jewish community and its leaders from 1933 to 1945.

Pamela Shatzkes, who teaches at the London School of Economics and Political Science, presents with admirable clarity the political and social context within which British Jews lived and pursued their efforts on behalf of fellow Jews on the occupied Continent. Her meticulous examination of evidence, including the papers of Jewish organizations and their leaders, enables her to conclude that these often valiant efforts were nugatory, but not for lack of will or courage, let alone indifference to suffering. The inescapable fact remains that the overwhelming impulse of the British Jewish leadership, to succor their brothers and sisters, "was incompatible with Britain's perceived overall goal" (p. 238). Had the leaders fully and early enough comprehended the scope of Hitler's war against the Jews, pounded daily on every official door, argued their case with the eloquence of Churchill, flooded the media with protests, organized repeated mass demonstrations, they could not have budged official intransigence as to war aims and, it has to be said, at times indifference to the fate of the Jews. What was *pikuah nefesh*, life and death, for the Jewish leadership was seen by most officials as a tiresome distraction from the war effort, and a potential diversion of scarce resources needed to assure victory. Shatzkes usefully reminds us that even the few desperate efforts to exchange or ransom small numbers of Jews foundered on the Allies' adamant insistence on no negotiation with the Nazis, on unconditional surrender.

Despite these ineluctable realities, the Anglo-Jewish leaders, in particular Otto M. Schiff, chairman of the German Jewish Aid Committee, have been attacked by a number of "revisionist" historians who proceed from a view of these leaders as reactionary, prejudiced against any but middle-class Jews, apologetic, even pusillanimous. With all the benefits of hindsight, these writers castigate the leadership for its perceived inability to rise to the challenge of Hitler, for allegedly turning a blind eye to the catastrophe overwhelming Jews trapped in occupied Europe, for being insecure, craven, failing to counter with sufficient energy and self-confidence the arguments of government officials for whom protecting European Jews was never a central concern. In examining the papers of the organizations and leaders themselves, including the Central British Fund, the Board of Deputies, the British section of the World Jewish Congress, Agudat Israel, and the Schonfeld and Goodman papers, Shatzkes has made a signal contribution to the historical debate: some of these materials have only recently been made available, and collectively they permit an objective assessment of what actually happened, and against what background. She concludes that the mainstream organizations in fact mounted a valiant, praiseworthy effort against overwhelming odds. These efforts were destined to fail, not least for reasons of unfortunate timing: for example, the deportations of Hungarian Jewry were happening simultaneously with the desperate fighting after D-day in the summer of 1944; and confirmation of the Final Solution came to Jewish leaders just as the Allies were invading North Africa. Examining the personalities and careers of individual Jewish leaders, the author has consistently avoided the elementary historical error of hindsight that mars the work of several of the "revisionist" school, and as she writes in her introduction, "does not debate whether efforts were feasible in the light of what is known today," nor aim to tell us "what 'ought' to have been done" (p. 8). Her picture of the organizations themselves, and of their leaders, is well-rounded, based on a full record of action and debate, and ultimately unsurprising.

Heirs to a long tradition of communal charity and responsibility for fellow Jews, the British Jewish organizations reflected the values of a well-integrated and relatively self-confident Jewish community. Their leaders, often drawn from the worlds of business and law, were for the most part financially and socially secure within British society, sharing the incredulity of even well-informed government officials as to the ferocious intensity of the Nazi war on Jews. Their cooperation with officials and acquiescence to most British government policy was not mere toadying; in most respects they shared the outlook and priorities of ministers and civil servants. Shatzkes emphasizes that the Jewish leaders were skilled primarily in communal affairs and relief work. It was their interventions and above all the Jewish community's financial guarantee that enabled more than 80,000 refugees to enter Britain before the war; and once war began, their urgent representations ameliorated the lot, notably, of interned refugees. Though some leaders were directly in the ancient *shtadlan* tradition of quiet intercession, and were often effective in individual cases, most of them lacked diplomatic experience, and may justly be charged with a certain maladroit naiveté. Whether they irritated or charmed officials, they proved inadequate in a situation where none could have prevailed; but they were far from silent, nor were they, as has been charged, so obsessed with communal and personal feuding that they failed to appreciate the magnitude of their tasks, or lapsed into mere hand-wringing.

Well-written, provided with a complete apparatus of notes and bibliography, this study bids fair to remain the definitive examination of a subject that has too often been the focus of polemics rather than sober analysis. It seems appropriate to let the author have the last word:

> The Anglo-Jewish leadership was far from indifferent to the tragedy of European Jewry, but was impotent to act directly. Most of its wartime efforts proved abortive, whether they were the product of polite negotiation, guile or 'activism'. The poor reputation of Anglo-Jewry's wartime leadership is the natural concomitant of its intrinsic inadequacy, but to view this in isolation is to perpetuate a great injustice against a community which lacked nothing in tireless effort or zeal. The only lack of will was on the part of a

government inevitably indifferent to the fate of a foreign ethnic minority at a time of national emergency (p. 239).

A.J. SHERMAN
Middlebury College

Note

1. Quoted by Susan G. Pedersen in "Eleanor Rathbone: Brief Life of a Crusading M.P.: 1872–1946," *Harvard Magazine* (March-April 2003), 34.

Biography, History, and the Social Sciences

John Cooper, *Pride versus Prejudice: Jewish Doctors and Lawyers in England, 1890–1990*. Oxford: Littman Library of Jewish Civilization, 2003. viii + 451 pp.

It is trite to declare that the mass immigration of Jews from Eastern Europe to Britain that took place between 1881 and 1914 changed the face of Anglo-Jewry. It changed the face of Britain, mirroring in miniature the massive cultural revolution wrought by a corresponding immigration to the United States. Vivian Lipman estimates that up to 150,000 Jews arrived in Britain during this period, principally from Lithuania and White Russia.[1] In the long run, the contribution of this invasion, both to Anglo-Jewry and to British society at large, was immeasurable. However, swamping the settled and homogeneous Jewish community of some 60,000 with customs as foreign as their language, these new immigrants created resentment not only among their Gentile neighbors but also among their co-religionists. It is against this background that one must read John Cooper's thorough, but always entertaining, account of the progress of Jews during the last century in two key professions, medicine and law.

Inevitably, this is a story about the prejudice and discrimination that Jews encountered as they sought admission to deeply conservative fraternities that had hitherto drawn their members from a single class. That, from time to time, there have been obstacles impeding the entry of Jews into the professions, along with a glass ceiling inhibiting their professional advancement, is undeniable. The author gives chapter and verse, but he also attempts to test these assertions through the prism of a controversy among Anglo-Jewish historians concerning the impact of antisemitism on Anglo-Jewry. In his final summary, Cooper appears cautiously to endorse the views that he attributes to W.D. Rubinstein, who contends that antisemitism was of marginal importance. Yet *Pride versus Prejudice* provides enough evidence to convince the reader that anti-Jewish discrimination was more than a passing phenomenon.

Thus, Cooper urges placing in a wider context the discriminatory admissions policy of English medical schools in the 1930s, but he is surely setting himself too low a benchmark when he favorably contrasts English institutions with their German and Polish counterparts. While it was comparatively easy for Jews to be admitted to an English law school, discrimination in the medical schools, with certain admirable exceptions (such as Middlesex Hospital), was rampant. Two medical schools in well-populated Jewish areas, the London Hospital in London's

Whitechapel and Leeds University Medical School, were egregious offenders. Lawyers, on the whole, fared better than doctors. Though the judiciary was virtually *judenfrei* until the 1950s and though Jewish solicitors could not obtain partnerships in the top City firms until the 1970s, there were many other opportunities open to Jewish lawyers, whereas, outside general practice, Jewish doctors had difficulties in obtaining employment.

Two thirds of *Pride versus Prejudice* is devoted to lawyers—judges, barristers, and solicitors. Perhaps this imbalance is to be expected, not only because Cooper is himself a lawyer but because, anecdotal as the book is (and this is one of its chief strengths), dramatic court cases interest the general reader more than do improvements in medical techniques. In seeking to explain the attraction of the medical and legal professions to the immigrant generation, Cooper makes the valuable point that these were trades—like tailoring, shop keeping and cabinet-making, which also attracted Jews—where a person could be self-employed. Self-employment is not so much an inherent Jewish trait as a necessity imposed on people who, if they could find employment, would find advancement difficult. Moreover, most of the first generation of immigrants and many of the next generations were devout Jews who would need to work on the Sabbath if they were employed by Gentile employers.

The author finds little anti-Jewish discrimination in either medicine or the law prior to the outbreak of the First World War. It is not difficult to discern a reason. Distinguished Victorian Jewish medical men such as Ernest Abraham Hart or jurists such as George Jessel or Rufus Isaacs encountered no prejudice because, hailing from the "cousinhood" with their public school and university backgrounds, they were as socially acceptable as their Gentile counterparts. The most celebrated solicitor of late Victorian times was Sir George Lewis, one of the Jewish cronies of the Prince of Wales. True discrimination began when the sons of newly arrived East European immigrants sought entry to the professions. They encountered opposition not only from traditionally xenophobic circles but frequently from their own coreligionists. Cooper finds that anti-Jewish prejudice was at its greatest during the period between the two world wars. It is hard to quarrel with this. To succeed in their professions, the native-born sons of immigrants were compelled to prove themselves in a way that their more settled coreligionists had never needed to do. The distinguished German refugee surgeons, consultants, and jurists who arrived in the 1930s were doubly handicapped as foreigners and Jews and were systematically denied the advancement that their abilities merited.

But antisemitism is far from the only theme of this book. The 15 chapters provide a chronological narrative over three principal periods: pre-1914, between the wars, and post-1945. Those working in the main branches of each profession (in medicine, as general practitioners or consultants; in the law, as judges, barristers, or solicitors) are dealt with in separate chapters. Cooper brings alive a host of personalities, legal and medical, many of them untreated elsewhere. He follows the lives of his characters, with a special interest in ascertaining whether they retained any kind of adherence to the Jewish faith. Happily for the reader, Cooper rarely resists a digression if he finds it colorful enough. For example, there is a fascinating chapter on "Communist, Socialist and Maverick Lawyers." The chapter on first-generation Jewish litigants titled "Jews and the Courts" surely departs from the terms of reference implied by the book's title, but one would not have missed it for the world. Dare one hope that, in the next edition, Cooper will redress the balance for the medical profession by adding a chapter on Jewish patients? Nor does Cooper overlook the rogues. If the seedier solicitors were, in the main, the sons of immigrants, no older solicitor will ever forget Robert Nathaniel Eichholz, an Anglo-Jewish patrician, who died (having left his first wife for an Italian maid) in a Tudor manor in Kent that he had purchased with the trust funds of his clients. The half a million pounds that he misappropriated cleaned out the Law Society Compensation Fund.

As instructive as it is entertaining, *Pride versus Prejudice* fills an important gap in Anglo-Jewish historiography. It is written in a plain and lucid style. Lacking the perspective lent by distance, the book falls off as it reaches modern times, turning into something of a Jewish "Who's Who" of the professions. Much of the author's material for the contemporary period comes from scores of interviews, which are inevitably self-serving. Undue importance is given to some figures, and there are those who are given less than their due. John Cooper might have been better advised to fix an earlier cut-off date for this valuable and wholly absorbing book.

Michael Fox
Tel Aviv

Note

1. Vivian Lipman, *A History of the Jews in Britain since 1858* (Leicester: 1990), 45.

Lloyd P. Gartner, *History of the Jews in Modern Times*. Oxford: Oxford University Press, 2001. vi + 468 pp.

The continuing development of Jewish studies at universities in North America and Europe has been accompanied by an inevitable tendency toward sub-field specialization among teachers and scholars active in the field. Research is constantly being renewed, deepened, and revised, as is evident from the book review section of this journal, which now covers more than 20 years of academic publishing in Jewish studies. This kind of development, over time, generates a need for synthetic works such as readers' companions, handbooks, textbooks for beginning students, and books that try to summarize as well as update the results of a diversified scholarly literature. This has been done in recent years for such fields as Jewish literature, Holocaust studies, and Jewish studies as a whole. Now we also have Lloyd P. Gartner's book, which seeks to provide students, in particular, with an accessible introduction to modern Jewish history, and which tries to summarize the state of research in this field.

Overviews of modern Jewish history in recent decades have included such books as Howard M. Sachar's popular *The Course of Modern Jewish History* (originally published in 1958, and republished in 1990) and the late Shmuel Ettinger's history of the modern period, which English readers know as the 380-page final section of *A History of the Jewish People*, edited by Haim Hillel Ben-Sasson (1976). Other works of a synthetic nature, but more limited in their coverage, are David Vital's *A People Apart: The Jews in Europe, 1789–1939* (1999) and Raphael Mahler's *A History of Modern Jewry, 1780–1815* (1971). With the exception of Sachar, a serious and talented generalist whose writings have covered a variety of topics in the Jewish sphere, the other modern histories—including Gartner's—have been produced by scholars from Israeli universities whose previous work had been rather more specialized than general: they are eminent authorities in such fields as the history of Zionism, the history of European antisemitism, the history of East European Jewry, and—in Gartner's case—the history of English and American Jewries.

When a scholar of first rank is asked to assess the widest contours within which his or her previous work has been situated, the shift is not (from the author's point of view) from more familiar to less familiar ground, but rather from an inner orbit to a larger perspective. Upgrading to a wider canvas presents its own discursive challenges, as does the implied change in target audience: from the fellow specialist or advanced student to the novice reader or generalist in search of basic guidance. Narrative coherence, always desirable, may be harder to achieve over a sprawling terrain—or, contrariwise, if coherence is pursued at the expense of diversity, one risks the pitfall of subordinating the text to a predetermined meta-narrative. Accuracy of historical detail, a sine qua non in scholarship, must be balanced against defensible generalizations. The use of quantified data from specific studies may be essential, but data from a wide variety of countries and time periods may not be entirely comparable, if at all. Coverage of small communities or minority trends must find expression alongside discussion of major themes and large communities. Documentation must be extensive enough to assist the reader to locate previous studies but not so obtrusive as to make the text unwieldy.

On most of these grounds, Gartner's book represents a creditable balancing act, though it would be fair to say that not all of these challenges have been equally well met. At the outset, then, I would enter a plea for greater attention to some of the following:

(a) In terms of thematic and geographic coverage, Jews in Arab and Muslim lands, Latin America, South Africa, India, and other relatively small Jewries ought to receive more than the scant attention paid them, if at all, especially in chapters covering the latter 19th and 20th centuries.

(b) Graphic presentation of statistics, maps, timelines, and visual illustrative matter of any kind is completely absent, to the detriment of the novice reader. Statistical data are sometimes presented in several different formulations, which can be confusing.

(c) The text has clearly undergone copyediting to catch misspellings and other small errors, but the editing has not been as thorough with regard to eliminating information that is repeated in adjacent portions of the narrative (an all too frequent occurrence), the slippage of coordination between text and footnotes (less frequent but nonetheless troublesome), and the misplacement of basic biographical information (appearing at times only upon second mention of a historical figure).

(d) The final chapter, "A New Jewish World, 1950–1980," deserves to be updated at the very least to the 1990s; to be given the sort of basic documentation accorded to the book's earlier chapters; and to have its breakneck narrative pace brought into greater harmony with the rest of the book. As it stands, the chapter leaves one with the impression of having been tacked on. The one-page conclusion, in particular, deserves to be expanded. Given the author's choice to avoid stressing a single, overarching thesis, a more elaborate concluding discussion would have greatly enhanced the reader's overall understanding of the modern Jewish experience, especially given Gartner's balanced perspective and considerable scholarship.

What are the strengths of this book? Paradoxically, some of its undoubted strengths are interrelated with some of its weaknesses. Its careful poise, balancing between Zionist and diasporic perspectives, for example, while denying the book a clear, ideological coherence, does convey the complex plurality of modern Jewish history and is in itself an ideological statement. Indeed, such poise is well suited as a historiographical strategy to account for the postwar emergence of a binary dominance in the Jewish world between U.S. Jewry, on the one hand, and Israel, on the other. As one would expect, Gartner's coverage of the American scene is much better than what has been presented in some other texts. The development of the Yishuv and the state of Israel as a central locus of modern Jewish history, while an important feature of the narrative, is not teleologically overdetermined.

Gartner, moreover, is adept at summarizing thorny and bewildering historical controversies (for example, over Hitler's role in the Holocaust) in accessible prose. The narrative is also enriched by its close attention to religious sources, personalities, and issues—a feature that has been lacking in most other studies of this sort. Finally, although one might complain about material or topics that remain underrepresented, whatever *is* presented is meticulously accurate, as one would justly expect of a scholar of Lloyd Gartner's caliber.

ELI LEDERHENDLER
The Hebrew University of Jerusalem

Zvi Gitelman with Musya Glants and Marshall I. Goldman (eds.), *Jewish Life after the USSR*. Bloomington: Indiana University Press, 2003. 286 pp.

Soviet-Jewish studies emerged in the West in the 1950s and 1960s, and an impressive body of research literature has accumulated over the years. Zvi Gitelman, the main editor of the volume under review and the moving spirit behind the conference at which these papers were presented, has been one of the pioneers in the field. *Jewish Life after the USSR* reflects both the scholarship of the Soviet period and recent work concerning post-Soviet Jewry. Among those who presented papers at the conference, which was sponsored by Harvard University's Davis Center for Russian Studies, were veteran experts such as Gitelman and Yaacov Ro'i, as well as younger academics from the West, including émigrés from the U.S.S.R., scholars based in Russia, and a few members of Jewish organizations who are currently active in Jewish affairs in the states of the Former Soviet Union (FSU).

The papers cover a wide range of topics, from politics through sociology to culture, and are of uneven quality. Some of the more esoteric pieces are those on Jewish converts to the Russian Orthodox Church and on Bukharan Jews. A number of studies are rather extensive, among them that of Mark Tolts, whereas others, such as Martin Horwitz's piece on leadership and community, are quite short. Since it is impossible to discuss all of the essays, I shall concentrate on two specific issues that I believe will have a decisive impact on the future of Jews in the FSU: demography and identity.

When Soviet-Jewish studies were initiated almost half a century ago, Soviet Jewry constituted one of the largest Jewish populations in the world. The Jewish population of the FSU is located today somewhere in the middle of the scale, and it is shrinking. Mark Tolts points, rightfully, to the "demographic collapse" of post-Soviet Jewry, caused both by negative demographic dynamics and by mass emigration. He starts his discussion by explaining a phenomenon that might be called the "elasticity" of Jewish demography in the U.S.S.R. and the FSU. Scholars of Soviet Jewish demography accepted Soviet censuses (in which nationality was recorded on the basis of self-declaration) as the basic source of information on the size of the Jewish population. Israeli officials and activists of various Jewish organizations in the West wanted to believe that the actual number of Jews in the Soviet Union was much higher. Emerging political and economic changes since Gorbachev have, in fact, brought many statistically "missing" Jews out into the open; but this has largely been the outcome of a phenomenon in which a growing number of non-Jews related to Jews have declared themselves to be Jewish in order to emigrate, mainly to Israel.

Tolts proposes the concept of a "core" versus an "enlarged" Jewish population in the FSU. Whereas the core Jewish population is "the aggregate of all those who, when asked, identified themselves as Jews," the "enlarged" Jewish population "includes 'core' Jews and their non-Jewish household members" (pp. 173–174). According to the 1959 census, the core Jewish population in the Soviet Union was 2,279,000. Tolts' estimate of the core Jewish population in the whole of the FSU in 1999 is 544,000, of whom 455,000 resided in Russia and Ukraine (310,000 and 145,000, respectively). The age breakdown of the emigrants indicates that younger Jews are leaving while the older ones remain, which in turn causes a further decline in numbers. The outlook is thus quite clear: a relatively small and aging Jewish community, concentrated mainly in Russia and Ukraine.

To what extent is this population "Jewish"? What are the premises of their Jewish identity? Gitelman, who for decades conducted surveys of Jewish emigrants from the U.S.S.R., makes use of data collected by his colleagues in Russia and Ukraine in the 1990s. These surveys show that the self-definition of a contemporary Russian or Ukrainian Jew is based primarily on a vague notion of "feeling Jewish." For more than 30 percent of respondents in a survey conducted in Ukraine in 1997, being Jewish meant "being proud of one's nationality." Only 0.8 percent of the respondents considered marrying a Jew to be significant for one's Jewish identity. According to Gitelman, "notions of Jewishness in Russia and Ukraine differ from those in much of the Diaspora and Israel" (p. 53). It should be noted, however, that consciousness of the Holocaust is quite high on the FSU Jewish identity scale. In this sense, at least, FSU Jews seem to resemble American Jews. A study by Valeriy Chervyakov, Gitelman, and Vladimir Shapiro describes a dual, Jewish-Russian cultural consciousness in Russia and Ukraine. It is not surprising that in Ukraine, which has been in the process of a continuous although problematic cultural ukrainization since 1991, most Jews still affiliate with Russian rather than Ukrainian language and culture. This study also indicates that during the 1990s, the proportion of those who felt kinship to Israel decreased from 38 to 21 percent.

Another influential factor traditionally affecting Jewish identity in the Soviet era was antisemitism. More than half of the respondents of the surveys conducted in the 1990s claimed that antisemitism set them apart from non-Jews. Official antisemitism as it existed in the U.S.S.R. has nearly disappeared. However, "street" antisemitism still erupts from time to time. In his highly illuminating essay on "Russian Jews in Business," Marshall I. Goldman argues that Jews in Russia always did well after major upheavals, a fact that makes them both highly visible and a target of envy, even hostility—note the cases of the so-called "Jewish oligarchs": Alexander Smolensky, Vladimir Gusinsky, Boris Berezovsky, and Mikhail Khodorkovsky. Rapid and astonishing economic success that is widely reported in the mass media may turn the Jews into a collective target of resentment.

The Jewish population or community (and perhaps today we may use this latter term) in the FSU both resembles and differs from its Soviet-era predecessor. It is significantly smaller, and post-Soviet factors affecting its identity have changed. It is too soon to say whether it is viable in a Jewish sense and whether it will, over time, resemble other Jewish communities of its size.

SHIMON REDLICH
Ben-Gurion University

Eric Hobsbawm, *Interesting Times: A Twentieth-Century Life*. New York: Pantheon Books, 2002. xv + 431 pp.

The historian Eric Hobsbawm is perhaps uniquely well placed to reflect on the Jewish experience in the 20th century. He was born in Egypt in 1917 to Jewish parents who came from London and Vienna. From 1919 to 1931, he lived in Vienna, surrounded by his mother's extended family. After his parents died, he moved to Berlin with his sister and stayed at the home of a maternal aunt. In 1933, Eric and his sister emigrated to England to be cared for by his father's relations. Uncle Sidney was an immigrant who made good, a Jewish "allrightnik" who had started out in the East End of London.

Hobsbawm became a Communist while still a teenager in Berlin, where he regarded the Communist party as the chief opponent of fascism. Communism also offered a political home to Jews and promised an inclusive, non-discriminatory future. After he won a scholarship to Cambridge in 1936, Hobsbawm threw himself into party work and was again in the company of Jews. These included Jack Cohen, the party's student organizer, Alfred Nahum, a science don from a Sephardic family, and James Klugmann, who was an early political idol. On the national party scene there were Andrew Rothstein, a leading functionary with roots in the heroic era of Lenin, and Harry Pollitt, an East London activist. One of his new friends was Teddy Prager, a student at the London School of Economics. Later on, his lawyer was the party activist Jack Gaster, son of the former Haham Moses Gaster. In the 1960s, Hobsbawm made common cause with the Marxist historian Raphael Samuel, who virtually grew up in the home of Chimen Abramsky (who does not get a mention here). Among his legion of continental comrades were the Hungarians Tibor Szamuely and Agnes Heller. He knew Isaac Deutscher, who advised him never to leave the party, and Isaiah Berlin, who could not understand why he stayed. George Weidenfeld gave Hobsbawm his first break in publishing. His longest-lasting friendships included Belgian-born Ralph Miliband and the French Jewish scholar Richard Marienstras.

From this cast of characters, it would be possible to construct the story of Europe's Jews in the 20th century. Indeed, the subject of "Jews" gets one of the longest entries in his index. But Hobsbawm does not engage in any systematic analysis of the Jewish condition. Unlike the carefully dissected character of the English proletariat or the rebellious nature of Colombian peasants, it does not interest him. This is partly because so much of the Jewish story in the last century revolves around the competition waged for Jewish allegiances between nationalism and other ideologies. Nationalism (or ethnic consciousness in the diaspora) won, but Hobsbawm has nothing but contempt for the false gods of national identity and sovereignty—unless, of course, it is Cuban patriotism or Vietnamese nationalism, or almost any other anti-colonial movement, for which he has boundless admiration.

This is not to say that Hobsbawm avoids reflection on being Jewish. Within the context of an autobiography that contains relatively little self-examination of any kind, there are several intriguing passages. In Vienna, "there was simply no way of forgetting that one was Jewish, even though I cannot recall any personal anti-semitism, because my Englishness [by virtue of his father's nationality he was born a British subject] gave me, in school at least, an identity which drew attention away from my Jewishness" (pp. 22–23). Britishness also "immunised" him "fortunately, against the temptations of a Jewish nationalist" (p. 23). He maintains that Zionism was marginal to Vienna's Jews in the 1920s, even though his father felt "conflicting loyalties" when Hakoah, the local, Zionist-affiliated football squad, played visiting English soccer teams (p. 23). His mother encapsulated Jewishness for him with the admonition never to do or say anything out of shame for being a Jew. He was in this sense a Sartrean Jew, for whom Jewishness was an empty marker, a stigma whose only meaning was that it should be borne with defiance. Hobsbawm refuses to extrapolate any positive or concrete affinity from a shared fate. Even worse than religious ties or the bonds of nationalism he despises the "unique claims" that he asserts are derived from purposefully cultivating "victimhood" (p. 24).

Hobsbawm angrily, and quite rightly, rejects the puerile label of "self-hating Jew." It would be more correct to call him a Zionist-hating Jew. Every reference to Israel is hostile, and more than once he linguistically conjoins Zionism to Nazism. For example, he alleges, "only the Zionists actually envisaged the systematic exodus of all Jews into a mono-ethnic nation-state, leaving their former homes, in the Nazi expression, '*judenrein*' " (p. 23). He notes archly of a visit to the West Bank in 1984 that it was "the only time I have found myself living under the rule of a foreign military" (p. 366). He must have been unaware that this was exactly how many people in the Soviet bloc viewed the presence of Russian troops in their countries—a curious oversight, given the frequency of his visits to Czechoslovakia, Hungary, and East Germany.

Then again, his autobiography abounds in varieties of self-deception. He derides Zionism, although the Zionist prognosis for the Jews in the 1930s was much more accurate than the drivel spouted by the Comintern that he dutifully regurgitated. He concedes that the Communist project failed "and was bound to fail" while clinging to the "dream of the October Revolution" (pp. 55–56), as if the Leninist coup d'état that immediately degenerated into a terrorist police state still merits admiration. Party policy in Germany in 1931–1933 was "suicidal idiocy" (p. 67), but this period continues to inspire his fondest memories of political activism. He recalls consorting with spies and traitors at Cambridge, only to express pique that this held back his career during the Cold War. In a chapter on "Being a Communist," he toys with the question of why he stayed in the party and followed orders until 1956, after which he was granted the indulgence of going his own way while remaining a member. The answer is that, for him, Communism (sounding almost like Buddhism) represented "the ideal of transcending the ego and of service to all humanity" (p. 138).

Well, obviously not *all* humanity. The Poles may not have seen Communism quite in this light after their country was carved up between Germany and the U.S.S.R. in 1939. Although he chides Rothstein for "the readiness to defend the indefensible" (p. 140), he himself seems to have found no trouble with the Nazi-Soviet Pact. One curious reason for his readiness to live with the Red-Black alliance was the fact that the Soviet Union indeed had capitalist enemies. Following the unprovoked Soviet attack on Finland in 1940, capitalist countries offered succor to the embattled democracy. "For Communist intellectuals," Hobsbawn notes, "Finland was a lifeline" (p. 153). Thus, a key to understanding the resilience of his Communist faith is grasping that the more atrocities perpetrated in the name of "humanity" and the greater the resulting anti-Communism, the more determined he was not to buckle. If Communists called black white, and anti-Communists pointed out the error, then for Hobsbawm the stock response was to defend the probability that black was indeed white.

From where did he derive this capacity for self-delusion and the ability to rationalize the suffering of others? At one level, it may have been due to psychology; at another, there may be an ethnic aspect. He admits that he was emotionally retarded. With unnerving detachment he describes his cold-hearted response to his father's untimely demise and to his mother's tragic end. He was aware of this even at the time, noting in his diary that he "lived without intimacy" (p. 42). As a young man, he was emotionally locked down. He never detects any connection between this and his passion for Communism although, arguably, it was staring him in the face. For instance, he fondly remembers a ditty sung by his comrades in Berlin in the 1930s: "Let's liquidate love ... all our affection's for the workers alone" (p. 120). Unable for whatever reason to connect with other humans or to have normal emotions, he displaced his need for love and belonging onto the brotherhood of man- and womankind that, helpfully, did not require actual intimacy. Rhetoric substituted for relationships.

He could, of course, have made Jewishness a bridge to belonging. But belonging was precisely the problem. He was more comfortable not belonging. "I have been, not necessarily an outsider, but someone who does not wholly belong to where he finds himself, whether as an Englishman among the central Europeans, a continental immigrant in Britain, a Jew everywhere—even, indeed particularly, in Israel—an anti-specialist in a world of specialists, a polyglot cosmopolitan, an intellectual whose politics and academic work were devoted to the non-intellectual, even, for most of my life, an anomaly among communists" (p. 416). This "complicated" his life as a "private human being" but was jolly useful as a historian. He turned an emotional deficit into a form of capital, making it a principle to resist "emotional identification with some obvious or chosen group" (p. 416). Thus estranged, he could calmly contemplate the degradation or destruction of people for whom he felt nothing unless ordained to engage in the simulacra of caring by either the party or his own interpretation of Marxism.

This is a depressing book. For an "autobiography" it is strangely uninformative about Hobsbawm as a "private human being." Much of it takes the form of essays and observations on his times and on those who chronicled them. He encounters fascinating characters but never asks the searching questions about them. The most glaring example of this omission is Mounia Postan, a Romanian Jewish émigré to Britain, who, as Sir Michael Postan, ended up marrying into the aristocracy and emerging as the country's leading economic historian. Although this Zelig-like figure was a living testament to the exigencies of being a Jew in a world where identity was destiny, his chameleon-like behavior is treated as no more than a passing eccentricity. Despite his self-proclaimed intellectual honesty—what he calls his "bullshit detector"—Hobsbawm seems oblivious to the Jew-shaped hole in his life story and, indeed, in his account of the last century.

DAVID CESARANI
Royal Holloway, University of London

Vladimir Khanin (ed.), *Documents on Ukrainian Jewish Identity and Emigration 1944–1990.* (The Cummings Center for Russian and East European Studies, The Cummings Center Series). London: Frank Cass, 2003. xxix + 350 pp.

This is a collection of documents on Jewish issues in the Ukrainian Soviet Socialist Republic during its postwar existence. The documents are overwhelmingly drawn from the former Communist party archive in Kyiv (Kiev), now the Central State Archive of Public Organizations of Ukraine (particularly from *fond* 1, inventories 23–25). A few documents originate from the Kyiv *oblast* (district) archive. In the main, the documents were generated by functionaries of the Communist party of Ukraine. Originally written in Russian and Ukrainian, they appear here in English translation, and a comparison of the translations with some published originals shows that the translations are carefully done. The editor's informative introduction contextualizes the documents that follow and is written with sympathy for a Zionist perspective. The documents are annotated; particularly useful are the explanations of Soviet institutions. Although some of the documents have been published in different English translations elsewhere, this has not been noted.[1] Vladimir Khanin, who edited the collection, was educated in Yaroslavl, Moscow, and Oxford, and moved to Israel in 1992. Since 1998, he has been lecturing on political science and Jewish history at Bar-Ilan University.

Several main themes emerge in the chronological presentation of the documents: antisemitic manifestations after the postwar restoration of Soviet power; the emigration of Jews from the Chernivtsi *oblast* to Romania; reactions to the establishment of the state of Israel; religious life; suspicions regarding the existence of a Zionist underground; reactions to the Sinai Campaign of 1956 as well as to events in Poland and Hungary in that year; tensions concerning the commemoration of Jewish victims at Babii Yar; and the movement to emigrate to Israel. The documents are unevenly distributed over the time period stated in the title. Nearly a third of them (33) concern the years 1944 to 1956. More than a third (39) cover the period of 1967 to 1974. Nine documents refer to 1979 and 1980, while there are only two documents from the *perestroika* period of 1985 to 1991. There are no documents at all dating back to the years 1975 through 1978, which is when the emigration movement intensified as a result of the signing of the final Helsinki act.

This collection provides many insights into how the Communists assessed Jews and Jewish attitudes. A document from 1953, for example, shows how some began to conflate Judaism with Zionism. Referring to the star of David appearing on tombstones, prayer shawls, and other religious objects, the Ukrainian religious affairs commissioner wrote: "Whereas before the creation of the State of Israel such emblems had a religious significance, now, after the creation of the State of Israel, they are purely Zionist symbols, necessitating a resolute struggle" (p. 96). A "Memorandum on the So-Called Jewish Question in the UkSSR" from 1969 reads at some points like an antisemitic tract: "Jewish religious worship is commerce and small trading translated into the language of religion. . . . Money and contempt for productive labour always reign supreme" (p. 172).

Other documents, mainly from somewhat later, show greater sensitivity. A report from 1972 acknowledges that there are "manifestations of antisemitism in reaction to emigration to Israel"; moreover, anti-emigration activists had to be careful, "since, as practice shows, the smallest mistakes in accentuation bring about undesirable consequences: they either offend the national feelings of citizens of Jewish descent, or elicit an unhealthy emotional reaction among members of other nationalities and objectively lead to the formation of anti-Jewish prejudices" (pp. 242–243). A document from the Kirovohrad *oblast* secretary in 1979 states that, in combating emigration, "attention is paid to avoiding any antisemitic remarks" (p. 277). In 1984, Leonid Kravchuk, then in charge of propaganda and agitation (and later the first president of independent Ukraine), also warned that it was necessary to "keep an eye out for nationalistic manifestations, including antisemitic ones" (p. 313). He regarded most Jews as loyal citizens: "Undoubtedly, the overwhelming majority of Soviet Jews reject Zionism as an ideology incompatible with their world view. . . . Some of them, however, retain vestiges of national aloofness. Zionist propaganda is directed above all at precisely these individuals" (p. 307). Whereas a "Report on the Jewish Population of the UkSSR" from 1972 had noted that Jews were overrepresented in professions requiring higher education and "not directly tied to material production" (p. 256), Kravchuk noted "objective reasons" for the phenomenon: "As a result of historical developments, the majority of Jews (over 90 per cent in the [Ukrainian] republic) live in cities. The educational level of the urban population has always been higher than that of the rural population. This disproportion will continue until the differences between city and village are overcome, which is the goal of [Communist party] social policy" (p. 309).

Of particular interest is the functionaries' description of the emigration process, although, of course, there is the problem of discerning what reflects the reality and what reflects the functionaries' ideologized and rather prejudiced subjective views. Jews wanted to leave the Soviet Union, the documents say, mainly for economic and political reasons—or, as a report from 1972 formulates it, because of "propriatary aspirations and Zionist views" (p. 247). When Jews applied for emigration to Israel, they were usually dismissed from work and had to wait months before obtaining exit visas. They also had to figure out how to transfer whatever wealth they had accumulated not simply from one country to another, but from one economic system to another. Communist officials were interested in the mechanisms of this and provide information about it. Aspiring emigrants would buy up "precious metals and stones, furniture, rugs, cameras, musical instruments, crystal ware and other objects." In the first six months of 1979, according to the customs office in Kyiv, the emigrants took with them to Israel "1,200 completely new furniture suites," "1,600 rugs," "2,650 crystal objects," "150,000 books," "27,000 sets of cupro-nickel silverware, almost 150,000 items of linen or cotton fabrics and hundreds of musical instruments" (p. 284). Throughout the texts is information on the number and geographical distribution of Jewish applicants for emigration.

With this volume, Vladimir Khanin has made a useful contribution to our understanding of the Jewish policies of the Ukrainian Soviet Socialist Republic.

JOHN-PAUL HIMKA
University of Alberta

Note

1. See, for example, the documents published in *Jews in Eastern Europe*, no. 3 (Winter 1993).

Dov Levin, *The Litvaks: A Short History of the Jews of Lithuania* (trans. Adam Teller). Jerusalem: Yad Vashem, 2000. 283 pp.

Who are the "Litvaks"? The term refers to the Jews of *Lite*. But where is Lite? Shimshon Rosenbaum, the interwar Lithuanian Republic's first deputy foreign minister, reportedly suggested that Lithuania's boundaries should overlap those of "Yidishe Lite": in the east, these should extend to wherever the Lithuanian Jewish prayer text (*nusakh lite*) was used; whereas in the west, Lithuania should encompass all areas where Yiddish-speakers pronounced the word "day" as *tog* rather than *tug*. Had Rosenbaum's vision prevailed, Lithuania's western border would have included huge territories inhabited by Poles and Belorusians, and eastern Lithuania might have incorporated not only Minsk but even Moscow.

As it was, "Lite" overlapped neither ethnic Lithuania, the old Great Duchy of Lithuania, interwar Lithuania, the Lithuanian S.S.R., nor present-day Lithuania. Following Yad Vashem's policy with regard to its *Pinkesei hakehilot* series, Dov Levin's *The Litvaks* focuses on Jewish life in Lithuania between the two world wars, which encompassed mainly the Zamut (Žemaitjia) region and the Nemunas (Niemen) and Neris (Vilija) basins, but which excluded such important Litvak centers as Grodno, Bialystok, Pinsk, and even interwar Vilna. In fact, Levin's work is an updated translation of the introduction to *Pinkas hakehilot: lita* (1996). Omitting the individual histories of Lithuania's Jewish communities, it nonetheless lists them and provides citations for the relevant pages in the Hebrew edition.

Litvaks is not the first book to outline the 800-year history of Lithuanian Jewry. Several decades ago, *Lite* appeared in Yiddish and *Yahadut lita* was published in Hebrew.[1] Both of these works resembled *yizkor* memorial volumes. More recently, two introductory monographs have been published: the first by Salomonas Atamukas, written in Lithuanian and based on Russian, Lithuanian, and Yiddish sources;[2] and Masha Greenbaum's *The Jews of Lithuania: A History of a Remarkable Community, 1316–1945* (1995), drawing mainly on English, Hebrew, and Yiddish sources and somewhat on Lithuanian literature. Dov Levin's study is the most up-to-date. Moreover, his encyclopedic knowledge, seniority among historians of Lithuanian Jewry, and mastery of Yiddish, Hebrew, Lithuanian, Polish, Russian, and German, make this book a must for the educated reader seeking an accurate introduction to the topic.

Although three of the book's four parts cover different periods, examining their political, demographic, economic, and cultural developments, the narrative is remarkably coherent, with photographs, tables, maps, and documents enhancing each section. Part 1 introduces the historic context of the region between the Middle

Ages and the late 20th century. The next section deals with the five centuries spanning the late medieval era until the end of the First World War. Here Levin describes the consolidation of Lithuanian Jewry under the grand dukes of Lithuania and the Polish-Lithuanian Commonwealth, emphasizing the institutions of Jewish self-government as well as the main cultural and religious developments, and highlighting the central role of the Vilna Gaon and his legacy. The Russian period was also notable for consolidating trends, despite the Jews' deteriorating legal and socioeconomic status. Levin stresses the importance of Jews in urban life and in religious and secular Jewish culture, and the development of modern Jewish nationalism and its political activities. This section closes with the First World War's devastation of Lithuania and its Jewish life.

In accordance with Yad Vashem policy as well as the author's specialization, the last two parts form the core of the book. Part 3 deals with Jews in independent Lithuania between the wars. The narrative emphasizes the establishment in Lithuania of Jewish national-cultural autonomy, the hopes this raised, and the ensuing disappointments. Levin describes Jewish institutions of the period, from political parties to economic cooperatives to schools and welfare organizations. The chapter charts the impressive scale of cultural development, mostly in Yiddish; Levin also details the manifold Zionist activities in interwar Lithuania, be they political, cultural, or educational. What emerges nonetheless is the slow decline of Lithuanian Jewry during the 1920s, which was further accelerated in the 1930s as Jews were excluded from politics and shrank demographically, while lithuanization ("Lithuania for the Lithuanians") led to their economic marginalization.

Part 4, "World War II, the Holocaust, and the Jewish Survivors," extends from 1939 to the early post-Soviet years. It describes the outbreak of the war, the renewed contact with the Jews of Vilna (previously under Polish rule), and the varied effects of sovietization: leading, on the one hand, to the appointment of Jews to Lithuanian institutions and, on the other, to the suppression of any Jewish activity contrary to Soviet ideology and practices. Levin traces Jewry's annihilation under the Nazis from individual murders to mass executions, clarifying the role of the Lithuanian collaborators. He rejects the characterization of Lithuanian involvement in the Holocaust as "vengeance" for Jewish participation in the Soviet apparatus. Likewise, he denies Lithuanian claims of "two genocides" (of Lithuanians as well as of the Jews). Levin deals broadly with Lithuanian Jewish refugees, deportees, and prisoners in the Soviet Union, as well as with Jewish soldiers in the Lithuanian Division and other Red Army units. A few pages each are devoted to postwar Soviet Lithuania and contemporary post-Soviet Lithuania, emphasizing the virtual disappearance of Jews. Indeed, this is the main direction of Levin's narrative, which closes with the following sentence: "The Jewish community that lived and thrived in Lithuania for hundreds of years has been destroyed and will never rise again."

MARCOS SILBER
University of Haifa

Notes

1. Mendel Sudarski, Urie Katzenelbogen, and Y. Kissin (eds.), *Lite*, 2 vols. (New York: 1951–1965); Natan Goren et al., *Yahadut lita*, 4 vols., ed. Avraham Ya'ari (Tel Aviv: 1967–1984).
2. Salomonas Atamukas, *Lietuvos žydų kelias nuo XIV amžiaus iki XX a. pabaigos* (Vilnius: 1998); this work is an expanded version of Atamukas' *Žydai Lietuvoje XIV-XX amžiai* (Vilnius: 1990), which was also published in Yiddish and Russian.

George L. Mosse, *Confronting History: A Memoir*. Madison: University of Wisconsin Press, 2000. xv + 219 pp.

The perspectives of the historian and the writer of autobiography differ fundamentally. The historian stands at a distance from the object, seeking to understand what lies outside the self, each person and phenomenon against the background of their time and place. The autobiographer looks inward, trying to comprehend the self in its development, simultaneously playing the roles of subject and object. When the autobiographer is also a historian, the two approaches intermingle: the historian's training and insight expand the scope and depth of the autobiography, historically contextualizing memories and reflections. The historian shapes the autobiography even as the life-history has shaped the historian.

Shortly before his death in 1999, historian George Mosse completed such a historically informed autobiography. Unlike Peter Gay's somewhat analogous *My German Question: Growing Up in Nazi Berlin,* published two years earlier, it does not engage in a polemical exculpation of German Jewry or fall victim to intense self-absorption. Mosse, who admitted he could never take himself fully seriously, succeeded in writing a work that is extraordinarily honest, self-reflective, and enlightening for those seeking to understand both the man and his changing historical contexts.

Mosse, who was born into one of the wealthiest Jewish families in Germany, grew up with much luxury but little parental love. He was a rebel from the first: invariably mischievous and unruly. Mainly, he was lonely. At the boarding schools to which his parents sent him, he failed to display the qualities of manliness that both German, and then English, culture required. He felt inferior. Two characteristics made him doubly an outsider to that culture: his Jewishness and his homosexuality. The first he downplayed for many years, later recognizing as autobiographical historian how antisemitism had shaped his early life, as it did the lives of other German Jews. He did not, however, remain a Jew by antisemitic identification alone. Although he never accepted any form of religious Judaism, during the American portion of his career, when he was teaching at the University of Wisconsin, he came to identify himself strongly as a secular Jew and taught the first course there in modern Jewish history. Later he would express a liberal Zionism through regular teaching for 17 years at the Hebrew University. His homosexuality came out into the open later still. Only toward the end of his life, when his "secrets" were revealed, could he increasingly balance his identity as historical spectator with unrestrained affirmations of self as a gay man, a qualified political radical, and a moderate Jewish nationalist.

Mosse is remembered as an extraordinarily talented lecturer, a role that he relished, and which advanced his career first at the University of Iowa and then at Wisconsin. In Jerusalem, as well, his courses on antisemitism, though given in English, invariably overflowed. When offered a position at New York University, he claims to have turned it down because the administration restricted the number of courses he would teach. But his lasting fame rests on his books, numbering some two dozen. Mosse writes that it was his *The Nationalization of the Masses* (1975) which marked the important breakthrough in his work. Here he was certainly at his most innovative, opening up issues relating to the transfer of sacrality from religion to politics. But his most personal book, and certainly one of his most important, was titled *German Jews beyond Judaism* (1985). Aside from his autobiography, it is the best example in his work of the intersection between historiography and self-reflection. Like the German Jews he here describes, and like his own father, Mosse incorporated into his life the German ideal of *Bildung* in its particular Jewish—and by the 20th century, highly anachronistic—form. Mosse was a product of the Jewish *Bildungsbürgertum*, the cultured, intellectually inquisitive, politically liberal, and antiauthoritarian Jewish bourgeoisie. Theirs was a Judaism only in the sense that it provided a common set of values, but it did create a firm sense of belonging—as well as a convenient target for fascist attacks.

The one quality of this identity that Mosse questions is its quest for respectability, perhaps because of its inherent dishonesty and because the gap between parents and child made him question it in his father. Late in life, Mosse wrote critically on the subject of respectability, even as he was finally gaining some of it himself. Repeatedly, Mosse tells us that the quality historians must capture if they are to write good history is empathy. They must be able to think the thoughts and feel the emotions of the men and women of whom they write. But Mosse was not Rankean enough to believe that historical judgment is avoidable. Both positively and negatively, he was too close to the subjects about which he wrote to attempt an escape from implied moral conclusions.

The fact that Mosse apparently did not have time to go through the text of his autobiography before his death explains some unfortunate repetitions. There are also omissions, such as his co-editorship of the *Journal of Contemporary History* during his regular stays in London, which Walter Laqueur mentions in his foreword. Nonetheless, the volume makes fascinating, inspiring reading. It lacks pomposity, self-congratulation, and complaint; it settles no accounts with rivals. Instead it conveys Mosse's excitement with the historiographical enterprise, both as writer and as teacher. Historiography was his liberator—from a loveless family and a historical fate as exile and outsider. Ultimately, it placed him in the first rank of modern European historians.

MICHAEL A. MEYER
Hebrew Union College, Cincinnati

Pamela S. Nadell (ed.), *American Jewish Women's History: A Reader*. New York: New York University Press, 2003. 326 pp.

In *The Majority Finds Its Past*, published in 1979, Gerda Lerner summarized the accomplishments of the fledgling field of women's history. Inspired by a decade-long burst of creative scholarship that made it impossible for historians to continue to neglect women's historical significance, she urged scholars to turn to new kinds of historical evidence, new sets of questions, and more profitable methodologies. Lerner acknowledged that "compensatory history"—recovering the lives of "women worthies" and explicating the daily activities of the majority—was an essential place to start. Yet detailed examination of the suffrage, settlement house, and birth control movements (motivated primarily by the desire to prove that women were "also there") was not enough. Similarly, whereas "contribution history" moved women's scholarship forward by analyzing women's role in various social movements, its categories of analysis were borrowed from historians' treatment of men. Still missing was a sense of how women reconceptualized society's goals and brought to bear a female, and occasionally "feminist," perspective on the issues.

Though the proliferating field of American women's history has taken this advice to heart and has developed a complex agenda and an ever-expanding methodological tool kit, Lerner's categories remain useful in assessing the strengths and weaknesses of *American Jewish Women's History: A Reader*. Pamela Nadell has performed yeoman service by putting together this collection of 18 essays of exemplary scholarship, which are suitable for classroom use. Ranging from the colonial period to the present, all but two of the articles—both of them classics— were published in the last decade. Read together, they show how varied the research has been, allowing us to assess what it has accomplished, and suggesting where it should be heading.

In her helpful introduction, Nadell argues persuasively that there are two prominent themes in current scholarship on Jewish women: diversity and agency. As shown in these essays, it is impossible to treat Jewish women as a unified group in terms of either class or culture. The recovery of Jewish women's roles in the past, whether as groups (workers, artists, housewives, or reformers) or as inspiring leaders and innovators who gave direction to Jewish women's activism, expands our knowledge of Jewish women's history in significant ways.

This accomplishment has not been easy. Jewish history has resisted the provocations of women's history much longer than has American history, partially because of its slow response to interdisciplinarity, where gender has become a significant category of analysis. In addition, until relatively recently, American Jewish history has been a neglected stepchild of Jewish scholarly interest, which has focused primarily on placing Jewish culture and achievements within the trajectory of Western civilization. Though American Jewish history has been taken more seriously in the last decade by Jewish studies and American history programs, the field is still wide open.

For all these reasons, most of the essays in this volume concentrate on filling historical gaps rather than charting the mutually constitutive encounter of Jewish and American culture. Several are focused on "finding" the women and reshaping existing narratives to include their contributions. Ellen Smith's work on early American Jewish portraits and material culture, and Marcie Cohen Ferris' article on Jewish foodways in the American South, emphasize Jewish women's important familial role in acculturation. Essays by Dianne Ashton, Jonathan Sarna, Faith Rogow, Shelly Tenenbaum, and Jenna Weissman Joselit ferret out the significant role played by Jewish women in community institution-building, a process that often drew strength from the increasing reliance on their role within the family as preservers of Jewish religious identity. Women worthies such as Hannah Solomon and Henrietta Szold, as well as aspiring women rabbis, labor leaders, prominent shapers of the modern dance movement of the 1930s, and activists in the civil rights movement of the 1960s all receive sensitive treatment by Joyce Antler, Pamela Nadell, Alice Kessler-Harris, Julia Foulkes, and Debra Schultz. The social construction of individual Jewish women's identities is deftly probed in several of these essays as well, most explicitly in Joan Jacobs Brumberg's article on the 1920s teenage diary of Helen Labrovitz. Riv-Ellen Prell contributes a piece from her work on the cultural construction of the Jewish American Princess, with Beth Wenger's essay on Jewish women's experience in the Depression, Linda Schloff's account of women who followed their husbands to settle in small towns in the upper Midwest, and Paula Hyman's cogent essay on the differences between Jewish feminism and the American women's movement rounding out the list.

Absent from this collection, however, is any substantial engagement with some of the topics that have dominated discussions among American historians in the last several years: imperialism, race and ethnicity, gender as a category of analysis (as opposed to women's history), citizenship, consumer culture and suburbanization, changing sex roles, and sexuality within the family. Though much work remains to be done in terms of filling in the gaps within the history of Jewish life, American Jewish women's historians would profit immensely from dialogue with scholars of American history and culture who are moving in these new directions.

In this short review, one example must suffice. In the last decade and a half, scholarship on late 19th-century immigration has been virtually transformed. Historians such as Matthew Jacobson have linked American ideas regarding ethnic acculturation to imperialist moves in Cuba, Hawaii, and the Philippines, the emergence of the Jim Crow South, and the construction of powerful new notions of "whiteness" that categorized some groups as fit to be citizens and others as unfit. Thomas Guglielmo has shown that Italians, to take one example, were "white on arrival," a crucial factor in their acculturation process. Where did Jews fit in? Laura Wexler, Louise Newman, and Gail Bederman have demonstrated incontrovertibly that gender was fundamental to the construction of new notions of American nationhood, and that white women participated in complicated ways in furthering the imperialist project even as they asserted their own rights. African American women scholars have been probing how the black middle class "talked back" to these dominant ideologies and struggled to hold a space for more inclusive definitions of social democracy. Black women participated in community building just as Jewish women did, but they drew on a different tradition of gender relations first established in slavery, even as they participated in a complex set of class relations within the free black community.[1]

Eric Goldstein's work tells us that Jews were caught up in this process of defining notions of citizenship—but what role did Jewish women play in the dialectical process of creating Jewish and American identities, and how did Jewish women contribute to Jewish-American notions of race and gender? Though the hard work of "compensatory" and "contribution" history must continue, the important essays in this volume suggest that American Jewish women's history is more than ready to engage more effectively with the American history context. Indeed, some of this work has already begun, though perhaps too recently to have found its way into this volume.[2] Jews participated in shaping a number of crucial moments in 20th-century American history, while Jewish women consciously amplified their own understandings of American citizenship even as they responded to the exigencies of American culture. How did this reciprocal process occur? Answers to these questions will enhance our understanding of "American," "women's," and "Jewish" history.

REGINA MORANTZ-SANCHEZ
University of Michigan

Notes

1. See Matthew Frye Jacobson, *Barbarian Virtues: The United States Encounters Foreign Peoples at Home and Abroad, 1878–1917* (New York: 2000); Thomas Guglielmo, *White on Arrival: Italians, Race, Color and Power in Chicago, 1890–1945* (New York: 2003); Laura Wexler, *Tender Violence: Domestic Visions in an Age of U.S. Imperialism* (Chapel Hill: 2000); Gail Bederman, *Manliness and Civilization: A Cultural History of Gender and Race in the United States, 1880–1917* (Chicago: 1995); Louise Newman, *White Women's Rights: The Racial Origins of Feminism in the United States* (New York: 1999); Glenda Gilmore, *Gender and Jim Crow* (Chapel Hill: 1996).

2. Eric L. Goldstein, "The Unstable Other: Locating the Jew in Progressive-Era American Racial Discourse," *American Jewish History* 89 (2001), 383–409; see also Pamela Brown Lavitt, "First of the Red Hot Mamas: 'Coon Shouting' and the Jewish Zeigfeld Girl," and Andrea Most, " 'Big Chief Izzy Horowitz': Theatricality and Jewish Identity in the Wild West," *American Jewish History* 87 (1999), 253–290, 313–342. This issue, edited by Joyce Antler, has several other articles of interest.

Derek Penslar, *Shylock's Children: Economics and Jewish Identity in Modern Europe*. Berkeley: University of California Press, 2001. 385 pp.

At the end of *The Merchant of Venice*, Shakespeare's Jewish villain is "redeemed" through a threefold loss—the forfeit of his daughter, his religion, and his wealth. Yet Shakespeare has Shylock mourn only the confiscation of his worldly goods. Throwing himself on the mercy of the judge, Shylock exclaims: "You take my

house when you do take the prop/That doth sustain my house; you take my life/
When you do take the means whereby I live" (Act IV, Scene 1). Shylock's confusion of material with spiritual value has attracted some attention of late, most of
which has aimed at understanding the political and religious sources of antisemitism.[1] In *Shylock's Children*, Derek Penslar looks beyond the play to the underexplored themes of economic antisemitism and the Jewish reaction to it.

Little of the material in *Shylock's Children* is new, but Penslar's emphasis on
the connection between economic discourse and Jewish identity permits him to
consider the history of Jews between the Enlightenment and the Third Reich from
a fresh perspective. He begins with the familiar observation that premodern depictions of Jews in Europe were based on two contradictory ideas, "the first associating
the Jews with paupers and savages and the second conceiving of Jews as conspir-
ators, leaders of a financial cabal seeking global domination" (p. 5). Penslar then
proceeds to reinterpret this scholarly commonplace by exploring not only how Jews
made money but also how they spent it, or what he terms "the twin realms of
Jewish economic life—capitalist production and philanthropic distribution" (p. 5).
Focusing on Jewish men of property and letters, he traces their written responses
to representations of Jews as economic parasites as well as their attempts to "reshape Jewish society through philanthropic action" (pp. 4–5).

Stung by the Gentile diagnosis of Jews as economically deviant, and at the same
time inspired by the new discipline of political economy, the emerging Jewish
bourgeoisie sought to remedy Jewish dysfunction through "occupational restruc-
turing." Influenced by Haskalah thought, they believed that retraining Jews as farm-
ers and craftsmen would end their association with such dubious pursuits as ped-
dling, which allegedly promoted an unhealthy avarice. By "normalizing" their less
fortunate coreligionists, the *maskilim* hoped both to alleviate poverty within the
Jewish community and to assuage Christian fears that such indigence was a burden
on the state. Penslar notes that for the first time in Jewish history, "Jewish self-
improvement would take place in the framework and for the benefit of the Jews'
host society" (p. 248). Following the Gentile commercial class, the Jewish economic elite embraced notions of economic utility and a productionist metaphysics
that lent legitimacy to the means whereby they lived. In the process, they also
consolidated their power inside the Jewish community.

As we know, attempts to convince Jews to take up agriculture and the crafts met
with little success, not least because the direction of economic development favored
trade, not the trades. In fact, the increasing importance of commerce in the 19th
century facilitated Jewish economic success. The advent of modern capitalism
promised to widen access to trade, industry, and finance, placing the Jews in a less
invidious, less isolated social role. Although some Jews celebrated their new sense
of historical agency as the "authors" of capitalism, their detractors were quick to
deploy new images of Jews as both paupers and plutocrats in order to advance their
own antisemitic and anticapitalist goals. By the beginning of the 20th century, both
Jews and non-Jews had generated a large literature in which, to further their respective political agendas, certain economic practices were depicted as particularly
characteristic of Jews.

Although efforts to rehabilitate "Shylock" by turning him into a farmer ultimately failed, Penslar demonstrates how the Jewish economic elite transformed the institutional landscape of Europe's Jewish communities. In keeping with Enlightenment ideals of social utility, Jewish philanthropists in Western Europe departed from the previous practice of largely unsupervised almsgiving on a local level and created centralized, national organizations that emphasized vocational training and a paternalist approach to indigence. Although Penslar touches only briefly on the problem of social differentiation, it is clear that these new philanthropic associations reshaped conflicts between rich and poor segments within the Jewish community. Moreover, organizations such as the Anglo-Jewish Association, the Alliance Israélite Universelle, and the Deutsch-Israelitischer Gemeindebund responded to the westward migration of East European and Russian Jews after 1860 with a similar mixture of religious solidarity, internalized antisemitism, and paternalist concern. One of the more interesting results of Penslar's emphasis on philanthropy is his demonstration that Zionism was not simply a product of European colonialist thought: it also partook of anticommercial solutions to poverty that were rooted in the Haskalah.

In addition to these insights, the book's remarkable range makes it a valuable addition to the historiography on European Jewry. The first chapter, which succinctly summarizes economic representations of Jews from classical antiquity to the early modern period, is truly impressive in its sweep. Similarly, Penslar's judicious use of comparative material places the book's focus on the German Jewish community in a useful transnational context.

As with any synthetic work, however, the integration of disparate bodies of literature is not always adequate. Although *Shylock's Children* claims to be a work of economic history, for example, Penslar's limited engagement with the economic theories of mercantilism, cameralism, and liberalism reduces the effectiveness of his narrative. Similarly, more familiarity with German history might have clarified the context in which German Jews thought and acted. For instance, the emphasis placed by German Jews on the political economy of ancient Israel was not simply a result "of the Haskalah's biblicism" or "the state-building fervor of the early nineteenth century," as Penslar claims (p. 84). Rather, extolling the virtues of the Hebrew polity also offered an alternative to the "tyranny of Greece over Germany," namely, the parallels between the German petty states and the Greek city-states that Gentiles had been drawing since the middle of the 18th century. Penslar, moreover, ends his book in 1933, with the dominant German Jewish narrative concluding even earlier. While there is ample precedent for viewing Weimar as a continuation of Imperial Germany, it is unclear why he ignored key opportunities to bolster his thesis by analyzing developments such as the hyperinflation and the depression, or the increasingly lurid depictions of Jews as economic parasites.

Perhaps the most intriguing question left unanswered by *Shylock's Children* is lodged in its title. At least according to Shakespeare's play, Shylock's children are no longer Jewish. Penslar, for his part, never makes clear what is "Jewish" about the capitalist production and philanthropic activity of Europe's Jews. Nor does he determine whether the intellectual and institutional changes in the Jewish community were the expression of an unchanging kernel of Jewishness, the consequences of acculturation, or the effects of the same economic pressures that transformed the rest of Europe. Penslar is right to observe that, after 1945, the Jewish tragedy circumscribed by Shylock's losses no longer provides comedic resolution for Christian theatergoers. In this climate of relative tolerance, the challenge for Europe's Jews seems less to rehabilitate Shylock than to recover his lost daughter— less to combat pernicious associations of race with economy than to resuscitate a positive Jewish patrimony. Whatever the case, Penslar's own reconsideration of Shylock's plight is certain to stimulate more research on the underexplored topic of economic antisemitism.

JONATHAN ZATLIN
Boston University

Note

1. See, for example, James Shapiro, *Shakespeare and the Jews* (Southhampton: 1992); Joseph Shatzmiller, *Shylock Reconsidered: Jews, Moneylending, and Medieval Society* (Berkeley: 1990).

Gertrud Pickhan, *"Gegen den Strom": Der Allgemeine Juedische Arbeiterbund "Bund" in Polen 1918–1939* ("Against the stream": the Jewish labor organization "Bund" in Poland 1918–1939). Stuttgart: Deutsche Verlagsanstalt, 2001. 445 pp.

Founded in 1897 in Vilnius (then, Russian Vilna), the Jewish Workers Bund was one of the most influential organizations of the Jewish community in Eastern Europe. By the eve of the Second World War, it had become the strongest political party among Polish Jewry. In *"Gegen den Strom,"* Gertrud Pickhan, a professor of East European history at the Free University of Berlin, analyzes the ideologies and political activities of the Bund in interwar Poland—a topic that, until now, has not received its due in the scholarly literature.

One of Pickhan's major goals is to demonstrate the ways in which the Bund's activities were an integral part of life in Poland of the 1930s. She goes far beyond a simple reconstruction of the party's history: she also analyzes its cultural structures and the lives and views of its leaders. As a result, her book makes an important contribution to the understanding of modern ethnicity in Eastern Europe.

With a few notable exceptions, most previous research on the Bund has focused on the first two decades of its existence in tsarist Russia. One reason for this is the scarcity of primary source material on the Polish Bund, whose central party archive (containing membership directories, protocols, and correspondence) was destroyed in the flames of the Warsaw ghetto. Pickhan has compensated for this devastating loss by relying on periodicals such as the Bund's main press organ, *Naye folkstsaytung*, memoirs, and other written sources.

The interwar Polish Bund was active on three different fronts in the Jewish and non-Jewish world: on the *yidisher gas* (Jewish street), where Zionism was its major rival; within the Second Polish Republic, where antisemitism grew steadily stronger during the decade preceding the Second World War; and lastly, within the Socialist International, which the Bund joined in 1930. Entering into crucial Jewish debates of the time—should Jewish politics focus on Poland or Palestine, the Jewish nation or the Jewish working class?—the Bund developed its own approach, and dealt with such issues as ethnic culture in Yiddish, secular Jewish identity, and how best to deal with the threat of antisemitism.

The three spheres of Bund activity are reflected in the structure of Pickhan's work. After a brief overview of the Bund's history, Pickhan describes the *bundishe mishpokhe* (the Bundist family), as the Bund called itself, the social structure of its membership, and its leaders and their biographies. Most of the leaders came from bigger cities rather than from the shtetl, and although their family backgrounds differed greatly, most were well educated. Pickhan takes the time to describe cultural traditions, holidays, and the use of Jewish and political symbols, drawing a vivid picture of the Jewish workers' milieus in which the Bund performed its cultural activities.

The next section discusses the Bund's concept of national-cultural autonomy, developed at the turn of the 20th century as an essential element of Bundist politics. According to the Bund, minority rights were not to be limited to a defined geographic territory, but were instead to be linked to people's self-perception as members of a national community. Pickhan also explores the ways in which the Bund distinguished itself from Zionist groups, particularly with regard to antisemitism. Whereas Zionists regarded antisemitism as an "incurable disease," leading them to the conclusion that the Jews needed a state of their own, Bundists believed in the idea of *doykayt*, or loyalty to one's native country. In the Bundist view, antisemitism was a product of capitalism and would therefore fade away in a socialist society.

Pickhan next focuses on the role the Bund played in its Polish environment, and particularly its relationship with the Polish Socialist Party (PPS), which was characterized both by conflict and by cooperation. In this regard, the Bund's main success occurred in 1937, when the Polish Socialists adopted the concept of national-cultural autonomy. The last chapter is dedicated to Bundist politics within the international labor movement, where the Bund positioned itself among the minority of socialist leftists. Bund members, however, were hardly a homogeneous bloc: sympathy with Communism among active party members was as widespread as sharp criticism of Soviet politics, especially that of the Stalinist leadership.

Pickhan presents the Bund as a party of the "third way." Torn between Zionism and antisemitism, it managed to stake out its own position. Its remarkable strength grew from its deep sense of community as defined by *yidishkayt* (the appreciation of Yiddish culture and language), *doykayt*, and *mishpokhedekayt* (the family-like ties among its members). This strong sense of community enabled the Bund "to swim against the stream," as a Bundist newspaper described it, while at the same time becoming the most influential party among Polish Jewry.

Although scholars have often epitomized the Bund's struggle as a lost cause, Pickhan convincingly suggests that such an interpretation is unjustified. She illustrates the influence the Bund had "oyf der yidisher gas," and among Polish and foreign socialists, along with the remarkable achievements of Bundist leaders. Moreover, the Bundist concept of national-cultural autonomy has hardly lost its relevance, given today's ongoing ethnic conflicts and debates over minority rights.

ANTJE KUCHENBECKER
Washington, D.C.

David Schaary, *Yehudei bukovina bein shtei milḥamot ha'olam* (Jews of Bukovina between the two world wars). Tel Aviv: The Goldstein-Goren Diaspora Research Center, Tel Aviv University, 2004. 324 pp.

Ever since 1918, people have been mourning the demise of the Austro-Hungarian empire (also known as the Habsburg empire, and as the Dual Monarchy). This multinational and multi-religious political entity was certainly far more liberal and tolerant than its eastern neighbor, tsarist Russia, and its Austrian (though not its Hungarian) "half" has been remembered as a place where national minorities were allowed to flourish. Jews have not been the only ones to express nostalgia for the Habsburgs, but they have had, perhaps, the best reasons for harboring such sentiments. In the post-1867 Dual Monarchy, the Jews were both fully emancipated and at the same time subject neither to violent antisemitism nor to coerced assimilation. No wonder they (or at least many of them) revered Emperor Franz Joseph and bewailed the collapse of his realm, which was replaced by such intolerant nation-states as Poland and Hungary.

In no region in the Austro-Hungarian empire did the Jews have more reason to celebrate their loyalty to the regime than in the little province of Bukovina, created out of the much larger province of Galicia in 1849. Bukovina was unique in that, in contrast to Galicia, no single national group was dominant—the Ukrainians, Romanians, Germans, Jews, and Poles lived side by side in relative harmony, united by their joint citizenship in the empire and, to a degree, by the adoption of German as their "language of culture." Czernowitz (today a part of Ukraine and known as Chernivtsi), the capital of the province, boasted a fine German-language university and many German cultural institutions.

Among the non-German ethnicities of Bukovina the Jews were conspicuous for their intense involvement in German culture. In contrast, again, to the situation in neighboring Galicia, where in the second half of the 19th century the Jews were under intense pressure to polonize, and in the Czech lands, where many Jews switched from German to Czech in the years preceeding the First World War, in Bukovina they retained their loyalty to the language of the dynasty throughout the prewar period, although they did not, on the whole, believe that this transformed them into "Germans." Even in interwar Bukovina, when pressure was applied to "romanianize" the province, many Jews, including the great poet Paul Celan, continued to regard German as their main language.

In his invaluable book on the Jews of Bukovina in the interwar period, the late David Schaary demonstrates beyond the shadow of a doubt that the "golden age" of Bukovinian Jewry, the time when the province was truly an island of harmony in an intolerant East European sea, was the period between 1867 and 1914. During these years the Jewish population increased in numbers and prospered. Jews were accepted into the civil service, entered the professions, and played a pioneering role in the economic development of the region. This was the period when Bukovina served as a "Musterland," as a model province that appeared to have found a solution to the most difficult of problems confronting Eastern Europe in general and the Habsburg empire in particular, namely the nationalities problem.

All this changed when Bukovina was awarded to Romania after the war. A "brutal policy of romanianization" (p. 63) became the order of the day. The virulent antisemitism that characterized pre-First World War Romania was introduced, and the transition to Romanian rule was even accompanied by pogroms in some towns. In short, the golden age was over. Schaary's book is essentially the history of how the Jewish community reacted to this new state of affairs.

The author does not conceal his Zionist sympathies, and throughout the course of his study he emphasizes one particular Jewish reaction to the new situation created by the annexation of the province to Romania—the "nationalization" of the Jewish population. Deprived of its beloved German-speaking dynasty and cut off from German Vienna, the old capital, Jews came more and more to see themselves as a separate nationality in the modern sense of the word and to identify with Zionism or with the cause of diaspora nationalism. Like other national minorities in Bukovina, the Jews established a "national council" in 1918, which demanded national autonomy and which also voiced its support for the Yishuv (Jewish community) in Palestine. Among the leaders of this council was Schaary's hero, the leader of Bukovinian Zionism during the interwar period, Meir Ebner. Ebner's main enemy in the struggle for leadership within the Jewish community was the long-time head of the *kehilah* in Czernowitz, Benno Straucher, whom Schaary condemns for being a *shtadlan* (an "intercessor"), deeply committed to working with the Romanian political establishment. Ebner, in contrast, is depicted as favoring the Zionist policy of *zekifut komah* (dignity), meaning an emphasis on independent Jewish politics and on Jewish honor (see pp. 37, 42, and 172). The Jewish national council failed in its efforts to secure for Jews the status of a recognized national group with national rights, but its heroic efforts to gain such rights (reminiscent of the campaign waged by the Zionist leader Yitzhak Grünbaum in neighboring Poland) symbolized the victory of the new Jewish politics, which Ebner and his colleagues embodied and which Schaary applauds.

The rise of Jewish nationalism was accompanied by an effort to establish a national Jewish school system, but this effort too was unsuccessful—there would be no parallel in Bukovina to the relatively successful Tarbut and Tsisho school networks of Poland, Lithuania, or, closer to home, Bessarabia, presumably because Bukovinian Jewry was accustomed to sending its children to state-run schools. Thus, in the interwar period, the vast majority of Jewish students attended Romanian-language institutions. More successful was the national Jewish Party of Romania, established in the late 1920s, which was led by Zionists from Transylvania, Bessarabia, Bukovina, and "old Romania" (the so-called Regat). This party performed fairly well during the 1930s, and made it possible for Jews to elect to the Romanian parliament their own nationally minded representatives.

Yet another aspect of the "nationalization" of Bukovinian Jewry in the interwar years was the emergence of Czernowitz as a center of modern Yiddish culture. Many Bukovinian Jews spoke Yiddish, of course, but before the Romanian period, modern and secular Yiddish culture did not thrive there. In the interwar years, local sons Itsik Manger and Eliezer Steinbarg were active in the capital, which also boasted a Yiddish theater and Yiddish cultural journals.

Schaary, a highly cultured son of Bukovinian Jewry, was not a professional academic historian. As already noted, his book betrays a strong Zionist bias, which is unfortunate. Moreover, it often reads more as a compilation of facts than as a book of modern scholarship. A huge amount of information is presented on all aspects of Jewish life in the province: religion (Bukovina was home to several famous hasidic courts); the history of the *kehilah* in Czernowitz and in a few other cities; Jewish education; Zionism and other forms of Jewish politics; Jews and Communism; Romanian-inspired antisemitism and relations between the Jewish minority and the other minorities of the province; Jewish demography; the Jews' economic situation; Jewish culture in Yiddish and German; the Jewish press; and so forth. The book ends with a brief survey of the tragic war years, when most of Bukovina's Jews were deported to Transnistria by the Romanian authorities. We are also given information on the postwar aliyah of Bukovinian Jews to Israel, and on how they fared in the Jewish state (very well, it turns out—no less than 11 of them, including the writer Aharon Appelfeld, have won the Israel Prize).

A good editor might have helped to make this book more readable—as it is, there is a great deal of repetition, and if there is a plethora of facts, there is too little analysis. Truth to tell, the book is often dull. But it will take its place as an essential contribution to the still rather underdeveloped historiography of Romanian Jewry in the 1920s and 1930s. Despite its evident flaws, it tells us a great deal about this distinctive Jewry, which combined the characteristics of both the *Ostjuden* of the Russian Pale of Settlement and Galicia and of the *Westjuden* of Central Europe. Thanks to Schaary's exhaustive research in various archives and in the printed sources (especially the local Jewish press), we have now a much better idea of what it was to be a Jewish *homo bukoviniensis* (p. 293). For this we can be most grateful.

EZRA MENDELSOHN
The Hebrew University
Boston University

Gideon Shimoni, *Community and Conscience: The Jews in Apartheid South Africa.*
Hanover, N.H.: Brandeis University Press/University Press of New England;
Cape Town: David Philip, 2003. 337 pp.

The appearance of any publication by Gideon Shimoni, the Shlomo Argov Professor in Israel-Diaspora Relations at the Hebrew University of Jerusalem's Institute
of Contemporary Jewry, is a cause for celebration. This latest work, a scholarly
and definitive study of South African Jewry during the apartheid era, is rich in
detail and insight. Building upon earlier writings and exhaustive research, it confirms Shimoni's status as the preeminent authority in his field.

The title, *Community and Conscience* is similar to Andrew R. Murphy's *Conscience and Community*, which is also concerned with "identity politics," albeit in
a different context. However, Shimoni's placement of *Community* before *Conscience* cleverly signals a historical prioritization of the former over the latter whenever there were tensions in accommodating both. For all of apartheid South Africa's
racially favored groups, ethnic tended to be more important than ethic.

Jews were automatically privileged in the racially stratified South African society.
How Jews—themselves often the historical victims of oppression—responded to
the moral challenges implicit in these circumstances represents the core of this
compelling study. *Community and Conscience* raises awkward but morally crucial
questions, putting the Jewish community on trial by placing it under microscopic
forensic investigation.

This analogy of a trial brings to mind the writings of the celebrated jurist Benjamin Cardoso. In *The Nature of the Judicial Process* (1921), Cardoso rendered
explicit the propensity of background, values, and culture to inform judgments. He
also reflected upon the capacity and inclination of those forming judgments to
structure coherent arguments, all other things being equal, in the direction of those
conclusions to which they were attitudinally predisposed.

Such mindsets can inform the discipline of history.

Carl Lotus Becker, pronouncing on "detachment and the writing of history" in
the *Atlantic Monthly* in 1910, contended, in a provocatively overstated formulation,
that " '[t]he facts' of history do not exist for any historian until he creates them,
and in every fact he creates, some part of his individual experience must enter." In
a more balanced summation, A. J. P. Taylor credits historians with seeking to be
detached and impartial, but adds: "In fact no historian starts out with his mind a
blank, gradually to be filled by evidence." Writing on *The Logic of the History of
Ideas* (1999), Mark Bevir adds that "much recent scholarship has emphasized the
problems inherent in all representation, the subjective and constructed nature of all
experience, and the historical and social specificity of all reasoning."[1]

In the case of Shimoni's carefully crafted and meticulous study, there can be no
charge of predetermined agenda. His encyclopaedic capture of data and his insistence that facts and actors speak for themselves whenever possible makes for a
work of monumental integrity and value. Propositions, where advanced, are subjected to rigorous interrogation. One such proposition relates to the notion that
apartheid's most confrontational and committed opponents were often Jews with

only a loose sense of identification with the Jewish community. Shimoni is rigorous, through interviews and other sources, in testing this proposition through the exploration of individual cases. For the lay reader, this may be a procedure that sometimes slows the narrative; for the academic, it is a celebration of precision in the authentic, fair, and detailed discovery and reflection of reality in all its shades and permutations.

Disclosure and discomfort are often shared attributes. There may be members of the Jewish community who feel that negative public exposure is deleterious to the image of the community and therefore something that should not emanate from scholars committed to community interests. It would be an understandable but misplaced and blinkered response to a work always written with sympathy, understanding, and balance in its quest to reflect rather than gloss over past realities. These attributes are reflected in Shimoni's concluding summation (p. 276):

> Most detached and objective observers would agree: although there is nothing in this record deserving of moral pride, neither does it warrant utter self-reproach. From a coldly objective historical perspective, this was characteristic minority-group behaviour—a phenomenon of self-preservation, performed at the cost of moral righteousness. The record also shows that on the whole the community's leaders, lay and religious, acted consciously but with deep pangs of conscience, although whether this at all qualifies as a morally redeeming factor will no doubt remain a point of contention.

In a cautiously measured article in the *S A Jewish Report*, Michael Bagraim, the national chairman of the South African Board of Jewish Deputies, concedes that "in retrospect, however, perhaps the Jewish leadership should indeed have chosen to move ahead of the community and come out more unequivocally against racial discrimination." Earlier in the same article, he writes:

> Looking back, the issue of apartheid and how the Board should respond to it was an especially difficult issue. In my view . . . the rights and wrongs of this issue have been very thoroughly addressed at previous board conferences, and also in the various publications put out or sponsored by the Board, and the time has now come to put it to bed and move on.[2]

The African historian John Henrick Clarke once observed: "The role of history is to tell a people where they have been, what they are and where they are. [History's] most important function [is] telling a people where they must go and what they still must be."

It is the ultimate accolade that Gideon Shimoni fulfils all these functions with such distinction. He has done scholarship and the community about which he writes a very major service.

NOAM PINES
University of the Witwatersrand, Johannesburg

Notes

1. Carl Lotus Becker, "Detachment and the Writing of History," *Atlantic Monthy* 106 (Oct. 1910), 528; A.J.P. Taylor, "The Rise and Fall of 'Pure' Diplomatic History," (1956), reprinted in idem, *From the Boer War to the Cold War* (London: 1996), 1; Mark Bevir, *The Logic of the History of Ideas* (London: 2002), 79.

2. Michael Bagraim, "Above Board: Reiterating Board's View," *S A Jewish Report* (10 Sept.–17 Sept. 2004), 5.

Cultural Studies

Steven E. Aschheim, *Scholem, Arendt, Klemperer: Intimate Chronicles in Turbulent Times*. Bloomington: Indiana University Press, 2001. 134 pp.

One of the most creative flowerings of Jewish intellectual life in modern history took place in Germany during the early decades of the 20th century, before the rise of the Nazis violently ended it all. This was a time when Jews with intellectual aspirations had the opportunity to appropriate what was best in German and European culture (*Bildung*). The sheer concentration of talent was so extraordinary that these German Jewish intellectuals profoundly shaped European and American cultural life of the 20th century. Many of these thinkers seem larger than life, and they all lived through turbulent times—the trauma of the First World War and its aftermath, the headiness and despair of the Weimar period, the rise of the Nazis, and the Shoah. As Hannah Arendt once said, they were hit over the head by History. Steven E. Aschheim, one of the best and most perceptive intellectual historians of this period, has written a vivid portrait of three exemplary figures, Gershom Scholem, Hannah Arendt, and Victor Klemperer. They were voluminous writers of letters and/or diaries. In this age of the quick, abrupt email message, reading their correspondence and diaries is almost like reading epistolary novels. They developed these genres into an art form—and we are fortunate that so much of their correspondence and intimate writing has been preserved and is now published. This is the material that Aschheim draws upon to sketch his finely detailed portraits. Scholem, Arendt, and Klemperer are exemplary figures because each of them, in very different ways, confronted the vexed issues of the relationship of *Deutschtum* and *Judentum*, Germanism and Judaism. All of them were also highly individualistic and even idiosyncratic in their outlooks and styles of thinking.

Scholem (born 1898) and Arendt (1906) were contemporaries who pursued very different paths—literally and figuratively. Scholem immigrated to Palestine in 1923 and became the greatest scholar of his time in the field of kabbalah and Jewish mysticism. In 1933, Arendt, who was living in Berlin, was apprehended and interrogated for eight days. She was caught while carrying out a task for her Zionist friends—collecting information about antisemitic propaganda in the Prussian State Library. Shortly after being released, she fled from Germany and made her way to Paris, where so many German Jews managed to survive during the 1930s. In May 1940, she was sent to the Gurs internment camp as an "enemy alien." (Later, she wrote: "We Jews are put into concentration camps by our enemies and internment camps by our friends.") When the Nazis invaded France, she escaped from Gurs and managed to rejoin her husband, Heinrich Blücher. They were among the few fortunate persons to get visas to enter the United States. After illegally crossing the Spanish-Portuguese border, they waited in Lisbon for a ship to take them to New York. They arrived in New York in May 1941.

The bitter public exchange between Scholem and Arendt provoked by the publication of *Eichmann in Jerusalem* is well known. But Arendt and Scholem had a long, friendly relationship. Arendt wrote an enthusiastic review of Scholem's *Major Trends in Jewish Mysticism*, and Scholem admired Arendt's *The Origins of Totalitarianism*. There is no evidence that either of them knew Victor Klemperer. Indeed, as Aschheim notes, there was a generational divide that separated Klemperer from Scholem and Arendt; Klemperer was a product of the Wilhelminian empire. There is another major difference that distinguishes Scholem and Arendt from Klemperer. We are intrigued by the correspondence, diaries, and notebooks of Arendt and Scholem because of the scholarly and intellectual prominence that their authors achieved when they left Germany. But despite an important and still little known book about the corruption of the German language by the Nazis, Klemperer's fame is primarily due to the publication of his voluminous diaries, which span the years from the time of the Weimar Republic through the Second World War and after. Klemperer never left Germany. Married to a Gentile German, he survived the war in Dresden. His portrayal of the domestic concerns, anxieties, fears, and hopes of a Jew living in Germany throughout the Nazi period is a unique and moving document.

It makes good sense to include a portrait of Klemperer because, in many respects, he represented the type of assimilated German Jew that both Scholem and Arendt detested and were rebelling against. Klemperer, who had converted to Protestantism, did not think of himself as a Jew. He was above all a German, and he was incredulous and resentful when the Nazis did not recognize that he was a German patriot. He scorned the Zionists, frequently comparing them with the Nazis. Despite the humiliations and dangers that he experienced because of his "Jewish blood," he felt that he was *more* German than those who had abandoned what he always cherished, German *Bildung*.

Scholem was the most severe in his relentless criticism of the relationship between Germans and Jews. Making use of Scholem's youthful diaries, Aschheim shows that he expressed this attitude long before the rise of the Nazis. Scholem passionately shaped his own identity as a committed Zionist with messianic aspirations, though anarchist and Nietzschean themes also appear in his adolescent writings. Aschheim perceptively describes the formation of Scholem's life-long conviction that the nation filled with religious content is the "essential determining force of the inner form of Judaism" (p. 23). Scholem felt that all talk regarding dialogue between Jews and Germans was fraudulent—he even claimed that an authentic German-Jewish friendship was "impossible." Yet despite Scholem's "official" disdain for all things German, one cannot imagine him as coming from anything other than High German culture. And despite his claims about the impossibility of German-Jewish friendships, he formed deep friendships with several Germans, including Jürgen Habermas, who was invited to Israel to give a eulogy at Scholem's funeral.

Arendt tells us that as a child growing up in Germany, the word "Jew" was not even mentioned, although unlike Klemperer, she was never tempted to convert or to deny her Jewishness. But it was only during her university years that we discover the first signs of her struggle with the tensions between *Judentum* and *Deutschtum*. We can see this in her early correspondence with her *Doctorvater*, Karl Jaspers. Arendt sought to explain to the incredulous Jaspers why she never felt comfortable with her identity as a German. In her biography of Rahel Varnhagen that she wrote largely while still living in Germany (it was completed in Paris), Arendt displays a fascination with the ways in which Rahel sought to escape from her "Jewishness," but finally, on her deathbed, positively affirmed her identity as a Jew. When Arendt fled from Germany she said that when one is attacked as a Jew, one must fight back as a Jew, not as a German or as a world citizen. Although she closely identified herself at that time with Zionists and worked for Youth Aliyah in Paris, she never really considered aliyah to Palestine. During the 1940s, she became increasingly critical of the direction that Zionism was taking. She identified primarily with Judah Magnes and with Ihud—with those who advocated the creation of a Jewish *homeland* but not a Jewish *state*. Arendt's life experiences challenged Scholem's claim about the impossibility of real dialogue and friendship with (Gentile) Germans. Like Klemperer, she was married to a Gentile German, and her letters to her husband, including some beautifully erotic exchanges, testify to the strength and depth of their mutual feeling and appreciation for each other. We also have her exchange of letters with Martin Heidegger, with whom she had an affair when she was 19. Arendt renewed her contact with Heidegger after the end of the war, and they corresponded with each other until her death in 1975. She also had a remarkable correspondence with Karl Jaspers—her mentor and dearest friend—that ranged over philosophical, literary, political, and personal issues.

Aschheim is extremely skillful in doing justice to the way in which these three figures represent radically different responses to the relationship of Germanism and Judaism. He does this in a way that brings out both the complexity and the distinctive individuality of their responses. His "intimate chronicles" bring us closer to understanding the fine texture of their inner lives, their fantasies, hopes, and ambitions. Aschheim's well-crafted narrative is a magnificent way of entering a world that no longer exists—a world that now seems so remote and yet so close to us.

RICHARD J. BERNSTEIN
New School for Social Research

Maurice Berger and Joan Rosenbaum (eds.), *Masterworks of the Jewish Museum.* New Haven: Yale University Press, 2004. 253 pp.

Mason Klein (ed.), *Modigliani: Beyond the Myth.* New Haven: Yale University Press, 2004. 241 pp.

The Jewish Museum of New York, the first institution of its kind to be established in the United States, traces its history back to 1904, when a modest collection of Judaica was donated to the Jewish Theological Seminary. As the beautifully produced volume of its "masterworks" demonstrates, the collection has grown dramatically since then, and the Museum itself—now one of many, but still preeminent—has long since exchanged its modest quarters at the Seminary for a sumptuous Fifth Avenue palace (the former Warburg mansion) on New York's "museum mile," not far from the Metropolitan Museum of Art and the Frick Collection.

What is the mission of the Jewish Museum? What is its raison d'être? This question has caused much discord within the institution, and it produced a debate back in the 1960s between the "separatists," who wanted to emphasize its Jewish character, and the "assimilationists," who saw it primarily as a venue in which to exhibit American avant-garde art, whether "Jewish" or not (p. 23). The "assimilationists" eventually went down to defeat, and we are informed by the director of the Museum, Joan Rosenbaum, that the present-day collection "speaks to the history and dispersion of the Jewish people" (p. 11), and is intended both to celebrate and to reinforce that most precious of commodities, Jewish memory. As is evident from this volume, the Jewish Museum understands the idea of "culture" in the broadest sense of the term; we are therefore presented with images of the "high" art of Chagall, Kitaj, and other artists of Jewish origin together with photos of such practitioners of the "lower" (but presumably more accessible) arts as *The Goldbergs* and Jerry Seinfeld of radio and television fame. Indeed, the Museum has a particular interest in popular culture, as exemplified by its recent exhibition on the subject of the Jewish role in "entertaining America."[1] Also on display are photographs of the Museum's extensive Judaica collection and even ethnographic materials.

The various expert contributors to this celebration of the Jewish Museum pass over in silence the important role that Jewish apologetics has played in its history. Surely one of the aims of this institution is to reveal to visitors, both "members of the tribe" and outsiders, the highlights of Jewish culture and the remarkable extent to which Jews have influenced modern culture in general, and American culture in particular. Since it used to be believed that Jews were deficient in the area of the visual arts, Jewish museums have taken pains to emphasize Jewish achievements in that important realm of modern Western culture. Exhibitions of menorah lamps and finely wrought spice boxes have served to prove that the Jews, over the ages, have in fact possessed a love of beautiful objects, while the collection of high art produced by men and women of Jewish origin has demonstrated that Jews too could be significant painters and sculptors. It may well be that such apologetics no longer loom large in the thinking of the directors of Jewish museums in Europe and America—Richard Wagner, who famously insisted that Jews were unable to make important contributions to Western culture, has long been discredited as a racist ideologue, and Jews are surely more self-confident now than they used to be. Still, minorities are never entirely secure, and the present-day flourishing of the American "ethnic" museum, whether Armenian, African American, American Indian, Hispanic, or Jewish, proves that the craving for acceptance and recognition by the "Anglo-Saxon" Protestant majority (if it is still a majority) has by no means disappeared.

What makes "Jewish culture" Jewish? This is a notoriously difficult question, and we should perhaps not expect to receive a rigorous answer in a volume of this sort. It is striking that the book's cover displays a work not by a Jewish artist, but by Andy Warhol (a portrait of the actress Sarah Bernhardt from his series of ten Jewish portraits). Does Warhol, by virtue of his making an image of a famous Jewish woman, thereby become a creator of Jewish culture? The same question can be asked of another striking image reproduced here—the portrait of the great art historian Meyer Schapiro painted by the non-Jewish artist Alice Neel. Moreover, even if the artist involved is of Jewish origin, does that necessarily render his or her work "Jewish?" Among the photographs reproduced in the book is Alfred Stieglitz's *The Steerage*. Stieglitz was Jewish, but the figures in the photograph, poor people on their way back to Europe from America, are not. The work itself has become an American icon, often employed as an illustration in books on the "new immigration" of the late 19th and early 20th centuries. But is it a "Jewish" icon?

To be fair, most of the "masterworks" reproduced in the book are obviously Jewish in one way or another. Moritz Oppenheim's rendition of the homecoming of a German Jewish soldier, and Samuel Hirszenberg's portrayal of East European Jews bearing a coffin, are obviously directly concerned with Jewish life. The Jewish texts and subtexts of other paintings—such as R.B. Kitaj's *The Eclipse of God* and Christian Boltanski's *Monument (Odessa)*—may not be clear upon first glance, but are splendidly explicated in the text. Photographs evoke aspects of modern Jewish history, and ceremonial objects throw light on Jewish religious practices. Moreover, these highlights of the Museum's collection indicate the continuing desire of many modern Jewish artists, sculptors, photographers, and artisans of various kinds to take an interest in matters relating to Jewish life and Jewish history, thereby linking their work to their status as members of the Jewish community and announcing their interest in contributing to "Jewish culture," however defined.

Was Amedeo Modigliani such an artist? The Jewish Museum must think so, since in 2004 it organized a major retrospective of his work, of which *Modigliani: Beyond the Myth* is the attractive and interesting catalogue. Modigliani was something of a *rara avis* among the many Jewish artists who lived and worked in Paris, since he was Sephardic and Italian, rather than Ashkenazic and Polish-Russian. Scorned and ridiculed during his short lifetime, his canvases—almost entirely consisting of portraits of clothed and unclothed subjects—are now celebrated and highly priced. These paintings have nothing ostensibly Jewish about them; only one reproduced in the catalogue bears a Jewish title, a portrait of a young woman titled *La juive*, dating from 1908. In his evident lack of interest in Jewish subject matter Modigliani resembles another famous Sephardic painter, Camille Pissarro, one of the founding fathers of Impressionism.

The catalogue under review nonetheless emphasizes that an assessment of Modigliani must take into account his "Sephardic Jewish heritage" (p. vii). Several of the essays in this volume do take up this issue, though not, to my mind, in an entirely convincing manner. Modigliani, we are told, was "a proud Sephardic Jew who passionately confronted anti-Semitism" (p. 67). This may well be true, but while his Jewishness is no doubt a factor to be reckoned with in relating his biography, how exactly did it influence his work? Mason Klein, in his interesting essay, proposes that "his [Modigliani's] Sephardic heritage endowed him with an understanding of 'otherness' drawn from his identification with the Diaspora, which he would fortify through the global purview of his sculpture" (pp. 2–3). In Paris, Mason further claims, Modigliani did not wish to assimilate, as did most of the other artists of Jewish origin: rather, he " 'unmasked' his Jewishness by assuming the ideological position of the pariah" (p. 7). This stance actually affected his work. Modigliani realized that he could not escape from Judaism, and saw himself as the essential "Other"; thus his "openness to history and cultural distinction, and [thus] the manner of his appropriation of non-European art," which clearly distinguishes his work from that of the nationalist Italian artists of the futurist school, "who generally abhorred 'exoticism,' invested as they were in the restoration of their own culture" (pp. 8–9). Further, "Modigliani's appropriation of culturally diverse forms was precipitated by his own self-conscious status as other, specifically his own sense of exile and of the Diaspora that defined Sephardic Jews" (p. 8), and "his portraiture became a field in which he could sublimate the racial inequalities of the modern era, which he could escape no more than he could his own racial otherness" (p. 22). Klein concludes by suggesting that Modigliani's corpus of work, with its complex juxtaposition of universality and individuality, "represents a set of values that echoes one of the high notes of Sephardic humanism in Italy's long religious history" (p. 23).

Elsewhere in this volume, Griselda Pollock emphasizes Modigliani's feelings of solidarity with other Jewish artists, citing the case of his friendship with the sculptor Chana Orloff. "It is art historically [sic] and culturally significant that Modigliani's most intelligent reader and consistent pupil was a fellow Jewish artist, and a woman" (p. 72). Moreover, she also cites with approval the art historian Kenneth Wayne's bold supposition that it was Modigliani's desire to be a "Jewish artist," among other things, that prevented him from choosing the Cubist route to artistic modernism, a route he might otherwise have taken, given his close association with Picasso (p. 73).

Whatever one may think about such statements, they are certainly stimulating. Equally interesting, and more convincing, in my view, is the article by Emily Braun on the posthumous reception of the artist in Fascist Italy. One might well have assumed that Modigliani would have been despised in Fascist times, both as a Jew and as a "degenerate" modernist. But Fascist Italy was not Nazi Germany, where the work of members of the École de Paris was excoriated. In fact, Modigliani's reputation in his native land reached its peak in 1930 (he had died in 1920), when a retrospective exhibition was greeted with great enthusiasm. Interestingly, and perhaps ironically in light of this volume's efforts to claim him as a "Jewish artist," he was hailed on this occasion as an authentic Italian master, whose work was seen as closely linked to the exalted traditions of the Italian Renaissance as well as to earlier Byzantine models (p. 32).

The strenuous efforts to judaize Modigliani notwithstanding, it is probably the case that the choice of this particular artist by the Jewish Museum was motivated above all by simple Jewish pride—and why not be proud of him, just as Jews are proud of Einstein and Freud? It is, of course, possible to criticize the Jewish Museum for trying to make things "too Jewish" (the name, by the way, of yet another of its recent exhibitions), just as it was once fashionable to criticize it for not being Jewish enough.[2] Whatever the case, it remains impossible not to enjoy (and, for Jews, to take pride in) its rich collections and to appreciate the creative work of its highly professional team of curators.

EZRA MENDELSOHN
The Hebrew University
Boston University

Notes

1. J. Hoberman and Jeffrey Shandler (eds.), *Entertaining America* (Princeton: 2003).
2. Norman L. Kleeblatt (ed.), *Too Jewish? Challenging Traditional Identities* (New Brunswick: 1996).

Furio Biagini, *Il Ballo Proibito: Storie di ebrei e di tango* (The forbidden dance: histories of the Jews and the tango). Florence: Le Lettere, 2004. 175 pp.

The relationship of Jews to the tango, as a distinctive musical form and lyrical tradition, dates to the very origins of the dance in late-19th century Argentina. Tango was an immigrant art form that reflected the social, economic, and psychological tensions of Italian, Spanish, and Jewish immigrants. These immigrants were mostly men who had been drawn to Argentina by a rapidly expanding industrial economy in the period of roughly 1880 to 1930. In such a situation, the competition for women was so acute that losing one, a reiterated theme of tango lyrics, was a real disaster: where was a man to find another?

The extreme gender imbalance was likewise the stimulus for a vast white slave trade that supplied the booming brothels of Buenos Aires and provincial Argentine towns. Jews were participants in this sordid enterprise, and Buenos Aires was perhaps the prime port of entry for East European Jewish women (generically called *polacas*) who, suspecting or not, had been lured away from the shtetl by crafty pimps known as *cafishios* (catfish) or *caftanes,* the latter referring to the more traditionally garbed Jews. The Jewish white slave trade was orchestrated mainly out of Czernowitz, and the same group of entrepreneurs supplied Jewish-owned brothels in Buenos Aires, Rio de Janeiro, Sao Paulo, New York, Philadelphia and (curiously enough) Istanbul and Bombay. In all of these places, both pimps and women were often observant Jews; yet since they were outcasts, they had to form their own benevolent societies. One such society, known as Zvi Migdal, had its own shul and cemetery in Buenos Aires until the ring was broken up in a celebrated police action in 1930.

Tango, defined socially, was the music played and sung in brothels while the "girls" danced with their clients. Whether this was true of Jewish brothels as well as the Gentile establishments is not clearly documented, though virtually all who have written on this subject (including Biagini, pp. 34–36) imply that it was. There can be no doubt, however, that many Jewish musicians got their start in Gentile brothels as pianists and *bandoneonistas* (accordionists), playing in combos that moved from brothel to brothel. Some of these musicians and singers also performed in the booming Yiddish theaters of Buenos Aires, and out of this socio-cultural mix there arose the first tangos sung in Yiddish. (There are ample examples from the New York Yiddish theater, such Molly Picon and Abraham Ellstein's 1932 tango, *Oygn*). Tango writers larded their lyrics with *lunfardo,* the street jargon that arose in the immigrant working class and that had its counterpart in the Jewish lowlife dialect called *valesko* (from Wallachia):

> Istá Ribecas in ventanas
> esperando ver pasar a su Jacobos,
> pero Abaraham qui istá in la esquina
> non si poide [*puede*, with Yiddish accent] contener.

[Rebecca is at the window/Waiting for her Jacob to pass by/But Abraham, at the corner/cannot contain himself].

("Ribecas," tango by Ciriaco Ortiz [Biagini, p. 57]).

Biagini's chapters on Argentina, while engaging, present no new data or fresh insights. Much of what he knows is through Julio Nudler's compendious *Tango Judio: del ghetto a la milonga* (1998). Nudler, Argentina's leading economics columnist, doubled as a tango historian of impressive reach. In October 2004, he conducted a workshop at Harvard University on the ways in which rapid industrial development and the great depression of the 1930s were reflected in the lyrics of tango, masterfully combining his two specialties to explore the emotional world of a pressurized working class. Nudler died in July 2003.

Jewish tango culture did not end in Argentina; it was exported to Poland in the interwar period and then, taking a macabre turn, exploded creatively in the ghettos of German-occupied Eastern Europe and later in the concentration camps, where the Nazis obliged the Jewish bands to play tangos, among other popular music, while the cattle cars were unloaded and their passengers marched to the ovens. There are two immediate referents to this ghastly story. The first is Paul Celan's poem *Todesfuge* (Death fugue), written in German probably in 1944 and first published in Romanian in 1947 as *Tangoul Mortii* (Death tango)—the standard term for any tune played in the camps when inmates were executed. In Celan's poem, a guard "whistles his Jews into rows, has them shovel a grave in the ground, commands us to strike up a dance." The second referent is Shmerke Kaczerginski, a poet from Vilna and a friend and collaborator of Abraham Sutzkever (together, they hid sections of the YIVO archive in milk cans that were then buried for posterity). Kaczerginski wrote the lyrics of the greatest of the wartime tangos, *Friling*, a reflection on the loss of his wife in the camps. After the war, Kaczerginski collected the songs of the ghettos and camps, both lyrics and music, which he published in New York in 1948 as *Lider fun di gettos un lagern*.

Biagini artfully ties all these strands together—not omitting Hitler's fondness for the tango nor the presence in wartime Germany of Argentine fascist tango artists. Thus did the tango, Argentine in origin, become a universal form of expression, typically associated with loss, hopelessness, and frustration, which Jews not unnaturally assimilated as a vehicle for their own tragic muse. Biagini's book is noteworthy because he has recognized the full dimension of the phenomenon, both geographical (Buenos Aires to Auschwitz) and cultural. The tango finds its place in popular art as well as in higher forms—not only poetry, but the novel (most recently, Eduardo Cozarzinksi's *El rufián moldavo* [The Romanian pimp]), sculpture (for example, that of Elie Nadelman [b. Warsaw, 1882; d. New York, 1946]), and painting (with works by the Brazilian Lazar Segall [b. Vilna, 1891; d. Sao Paulo, 1957] and a host of Argentine Jewish painters).

The revival of the Yiddish tango, most notably by Lloica Czackis and her group "Tangele," has made it possible for audiences to experience the extraordinary emotional range of this art form, particularly through the performance of the ghetto and camp repertory. It raises our awareness of the global reach of "Yiddishland" and the extraordinary creativity engendered at its South American terminus.

THOMAS F. GLICK
Boston University

Sander L. Gilman, *Jewish Frontiers: Essays on Bodies, Histories, and Identities.* New York: Palgrave Macmillan, 2003. 243 pp.

Throughout his prolific and wide-ranging career, Sander Gilman has repeatedly challenged the ways in which scholars think about Jews by investigating hitherto underexplored areas of Jewish culture and by formulating innovative approaches to more familiar areas of study. Most importantly, he proposes significant new possibilities for phenomenologizing Jews and Jewish experience. Such is the case in *Jewish Frontiers*, which sets out to reconfigure the inner map with which scholars orient themselves to Jewish history and culture. Challenging longstanding models of center and periphery, of homeland and diaspora, Gilman proffers another rubric: the frontier. In the first of this collection of seven essays, Gilman argues that this "structure of communal fantasy, as a model of imagining oneself in the world" (p. 19) liberates the scholar from the problematic limitations of more conventional geographic matrices, which fail to grapple adequately with the complex nuances of Jewish experience. The frontier model applies not only when assessing the present era of post-Zionism and American identity politics, but also as one looks across the broad expanses of Jewish history and geography.

Gilman's notion of the frontier calls attention to the charged role of language in conceptualizing a sense of place and, more specifically, to the dynamic semiotics of Jewish notions of home, homeland, exile, and diaspora. His rubric also shifts attention toward assessing Jewish experience as "a constant state of confrontation" as well as accommodation. The frontier facilitates seeing Jewish culture as an interactive, hybrid, and protean practice, rather than as something essentialized and fixed, "producing a constantly new and revitalized culture" (pp. 15, 29).

In the essays that follow, Gilman extends the notion of frontier along epistemological dimensions, demonstrating through a series of provocative examples how Jewish studies scholars need to interrogate both the stability of disciplinary boundaries and the intellectual tropes regarding what is considered to be Jewishly "central" and "peripheral." First is a pair of essays that test the boundaries of the aura surrounding one of the most powerful "centers" of contemporary Jewish culture—the Holocaust. By examining the films *Jakob the Liar* and *Life Is Beautiful*, Gilman raises the daunting question "Can the Shoah be funny?" in order to investigate the frontier of Holocaust remembrance at what seems to be, at first glance, an especially troubling extreme. Through his examination of these films and of the contexts of their creation and reception, he demonstrates how works that might seem irreverent or eccentric can, in fact, open up opportunities for assessing assumptions about the possibilities and implications of Holocaust representation generally.

A second grouping of four essays considers one of Gilman's favorite topics, the Jewish body—especially the (perceived) diseased body—as a frontier of Jewish identity-making in the modern era, probing the longstanding associations of Jews and tobacco use, plastic surgery, and cancer. These essays demonstrate the wide range of Gilman's intellectual curiosity and the engaging creativity of his thinking. Indeed, the special pleasure of reading *Jewish Frontiers* is watching his lively mind at work, drawing connections, playing with the pieces of an intellectual argument in the making. This second section of the book ends with a short but thought-provoking consideration of contemporary medical research and patient activism around Jewish and other genetic diseases, viewing these as surprisingly complex and forceful acts of communal identity formation. The volume's final essay is a survey of recent fiction (by authors in the United States, Western Europe, and South Africa) in which Jews play all manner of symbolic roles in articulating multicultural notions of the self. Here, too, Gilman's model of the frontier provides the reader of these often unsettling literary works with an instructive guide to understanding these "thought experiments" by means of creative intellectual exercises of one's own.

JEFFREY SHANDLER
Rutgers University

Martin Goodman (ed.), *The Oxford Handbook of Jewish Studies.* Oxford: Oxford
       University Press, 2002. 1,037 pp.

The Oxford Handbook of Jewish Studies claims to be the first guidebook for Jewish
studies, and certainly, aside from a number of one-volume Jewish encyclopedias,
there is no existing work of its scope. It is also a difficult work to review, in part
because no one scholar can claim competence in more than a few of the many
topics covered within it, and more importantly, because one's overall evaluation is
influenced largely by what one expects to find.

    Following an introductory chapter by Martin Goodman on the nature of Jewish
studies, the handbook appears at first to be chronological in nature—covering the
biblical, Second Temple, and talmudic periods, followed by the history and literature of the Middle Ages—but then becomes topical for such subjects as mysticism,
Yiddish, demography, and music. Altogether there are 39 numbered chapters whose
length generally varies from 15 to 30 pages, plus bibliographies that are much
more extensive than those found in encyclopedias. Some, in fact, overwhelm the
reader.

    For a number of articles, Goodman obtained the services of highly regarded
experts in their respective fields; examples are Sergio DellaPergola for demography
and Saul Friedlander for the Holocaust. In others, he had to make do with relatively
unknown persons, which of course does not necessarily reflect on the quality of
their contributions.

    When I first took this book in hand, I thought of it as a possible update for the
Encyclopaedia Judaica, which is out of date more than 30 years after its publication. This work, however, is by no means as comprehensive, as I discovered when
I searched in vain for the name of Joseph Heller—not the novelist, but the author
of a well-known work on the underground Lehi ("Stern gang") group. A quick
check revealed that the Lehi itself is also missing from the *Oxford Handbook*, as
is the much larger Irgun Zevai Leumi (IZL) and even the Haganah, the predecessor
of today's Israeli army. Whereas this volume is a guide to the state of the art in
various fields of Jewish studies, it is not a repository of facts. In this particular
instance, a complicating factor is the extent to which Eretz Israel (Land of Israel)
studies is considered to be part of Jewish studies. The *Oxford Handbook* provides
only one sketchy article titled "Settlement and State in Eretz Israel" (pp. 445–470).
A similar question can be asked with regard to biblical studies; here, the relevant
article is "Biblical Studies and Jewish Studies" (pp. 14–35).

    Although a certain amount of overlap is to be expected in a work of this kind,
it should have been kept to a minimum. Moreover, the coverage of certain topics
that are clearly within the realm of "Jewish studies" is uneven. Thus, medieval
Karaism is discussed but not Karaites today, and there seems to be nothing whatever
about the increasingly visible Ethiopian Jews.

    Also surprising is the leeway that was granted to contributors to express them-
selves aggressively and at times in an outright insulting manner. For instance, in
"Eastern European Jewry in the Modern Period: 1750–1939," Michael Stanislawski
derides Louis Greenberg's standard work, *The Jews in Russia,* as "utterly lachry-

mose and unscholarly" (p. 402), then recommends the flawed first edition of Salo Baron's history of Russian Jewry (1964)—overlooking the fact that the second edition of this work (1976; reprinted 1987) is not only updated but more accurate than the original work. Cecile E. Kuznitz's otherwise excellent "Yiddish Studies" (pp. 541–571) is marred by a pervasive pessimism that (it is hoped) will prove to be unjustified.

Jewish studies, as Goodman points out, is a problematic discipline. The *Oxford Handbook*, while certainly useful and generally well written, is in the nature of the case problematic as well.

AVRAHAM GREENBAUM
The Hebrew University

Samuel D. Gruber, *American Synagogues: A Century of Architecture and Jewish Community* (ed. Scott J. Tilden, photography by Paul Rocheleau). New York: Rizzoli, 2003. 239 pp.

Architecture speaks volumes about economics and social status. By the second half of the 20th century, American Jews were commissioning top international architects to design their synagogues: Walter Gropius, Erich Mendelsohn, Frank Lloyd Wright, and Minoru Yamasaki (the last being better known for the Twin Towers of New York City's World Trade Center). *American Synagogues*, which updates Rachel Wischnitzer's *Synagogue Architecture in the United States* (1955), celebrates, in full color, 33 selected synagogues from across the United States. Architectural photographer Paul Rocheleau has done Rizzoli proud. The photographs are superb. Rocheleau has masterfully resolved the dilemma posed by such a project, namely, how to marry artistic expression with sober documentation. He has achieved both: clear views of setting, exterior, interior, architectural elements, and decorative detailing, combined with a vivid sense of space and atmosphere. And his work is complemented by excellent book design.[1]

Samuel D. Gruber's text naturally plays a subsidiary role, providing some historical and cultural context both for the subject as a whole and for individual buildings. Gruber is an architectural historian who pioneered historic synagogue preservation efforts in the United States from the late 1980s. This book follows his illustrated *Synagogues* (1999), which showcased historic synagogues around the world. The author belies the misconception that preservationists are by definition anti-modernist. Gruber has a good eye for experimental architecture that works— but is not shy to criticize where it does not.

From a transatlantic perspective, several things are striking about *American Synagogues*. First: just how "new" synagogues are in America, a country whose architectural history only begins in earnest in the colonial period. One of the oldest buildings featured by Gruber is his home synagogue in Syracuse, New York, designed by Jewish architect Arnold Brunner in 1910 in the form of a classical temple.

In Old World Europe from the late 18th century onwards, classicism was much favored for synagogue design because of its associations with liberalism, enlightenment, and—especially under Napoleon—Jewish emancipation. The Greeks and early Romans may have been pagans, but by the 19th century, classicism was regarded as religiously neutral, almost secular, in contrast to the medievalism of the "Christian" Gothic or Romanesque. In America, the widespread use of classicism for both religious and civic buildings showed just how far Jews were integrating into the new society.

Gruber selects three buildings dating from before the First World War and five from the interwar period. All the rest cover the period from the 1950s, with half a dozen new-build projects (up to 2001). The arrangement of the book is chronological. For non-American readers, a location map would have been useful.

The short "shelf-life" of many American synagogues is remarkable. Large, purpose-built synagogues constructed in the 1890s and relocated in the 1920s had again outlived their usefulness by the 1960s, being marooned in inner-city areas that their communities had abandoned for the suburbs. Some late 19th-century synagogues that survived demolition are now protected historic monuments, such as the Eldridge Street Synagogue on the Lower East Side of New York City (1886) or Temple Adath Israel in Owensboro, Kentucky (1878), while the Adath Israel Synagogue in Washington, D.C. (1876) was physically removed, bricks and mortar and all, to a more convenient location in 1989. Gruber refers to the recent phenomenon of young American Jews returning to newly gentrified city center neighborhoods long abandoned by their parents and grandparents.

The book features a preponderance of Reform temples, reflecting the fact that liberal Judaism is the norm in American Jewish life, rather than the traditional synagogue. In terms of liturgical arrangement, the Reform temple is distinct from the traditional synagogue in both the Sephardic and Ashkenazic worlds. The ark containing the Torah scroll(s) and the *bimah*, where prayer services are conducted and where the Torah portion is chanted, are combined on a single platform, often incorporating a prominent pulpit, at the front of the hall (which may or may not be facing east in the direction of Jerusalem). Thus the spatial tension caused by the traditional dual focus on ark and *bimah* during the synagogue service was done away with, as well as the community-inclusive arrangement of the seating on the main floor around the *bimah*. Reform temples adopted a single axis, as in a church. Circular auditoria plans were also tried. Other concessions to dominant Christian norms came later, including the introduction of mixed seating.

Many non-Orthodox congregations do not need to grapple with the problems of acoustics created by large worship spaces. They simply install amplification, the use of which is forbidden to Orthodox congregations on the Sabbath. Similarly, in the wide-open spaces of America and increasingly dispersed Jewish suburbia, the practicality of locating the temple within walking distance of the community ceased to be relevant. The architect's brief includes provision of a large parking lot. In America, the concept of synagogue as integrated community center—with social hall, Jewish day school, gymnasium and even a swimming pool—was first developed, designed to entice back to the fold secularized and culturally assimilated Jews.

Unencumbered by tradition, Reform communities were free to experiment with radical architectural design. Europe's loss was America's gain. The likes of Erich Mendelsohn and Walter Gropius, luminaries of the Bauhaus and Internationalism, left Nazi Germany and were then excluded from the stuffy architectural establishment in Britain. In America, they found a receptive clientele, as did home-grown Jewish architects such as the prolific Percival Goodman. All found work for Jewish congregations in addition to public commissions: both were considered equally prestigious. At the same time, American synagogues became the setting for the finest new Judaica art in stained glass, metalwork, and textiles.

Some of the resulting buildings, constructed in the 1950s and 1960s, have become celebrated icons of modernism. They were also highly influential on postwar synagogue design in both Europe and Israel. Mendelsohn's Park Synagogue in Cleveland, Ohio (1953), and Frank Lloyd Wright's Beth Sholom in Elkins Park, Philadelphia (1957) introduced the now hackneyed sculptural "tent of meeting" (*ohel mo'ed*) or "Mount Sinai" motifs into synagogue architecture. By contrast, Yamasaki's design for North Shore Congregation Israel in Glencoe, Illinois (1964) is, as Gruber rightly points out, a contemporary interpretation of the 19th-century "cathedral synagogue." Its soaring reinforced concrete vaults defy definition as either Gothic fans or orientalist ogees in their undulating shapes, and the effect is to dwarf the worshipper. In many of the synagogues of this era, elongated ark features rise from floor to ceiling like totem poles. (Yamasaki's reminds me of a fountain pen nib.)

By the late 1970s, such synagogues, often built to seat more than 1,000 people, had become "white elephants" that were filled to capacity only three days a year. The costs of heating, lighting, and general maintenance of buildings that utilized daring technology—untested for durability—became increasingly burdensome. Leaking and stained reinforced concrete and large, drafty expanses of glass are not very attractive.

Postmodernism saw a return to traditional Jewish symbolism, materials (timber and brick), and vernacular styles, both American and European. Quotations from the lost wooden synagogues of Poland were to be found in the hipped rooflines of synagogues built in the 1980s and 1990s, while some Reform, and especially Conservative, congregations went so far as to reinstate a central *bimah*—or at least a platform with reader's desk projecting out into the seating area, in preference to a "performance" stage.

For me, the Wiltshire Boulevard Temple in Los Angeles (1929) encapsulates the spirit of American synagogue architecture in the 20th century. This was the third purpose-built synagogue erected by what was obviously a very affluent congregation in the space of less than 60 years. The first building of the Congregation B'nai Brith had been erected downtown in 1873 and its second in 1896 (the latter by the same architect who designed the present building, Abram M. Edelman—son of the congregation's first rabbi). The huge 1929 edifice is prominently sited on a main road. It is based on a central plan and is roofed with an enormous coffered dome (Byzantine Revival styles were also fashionable for synagogues built in Europe in the first decades of the 20th century). The opulence of the interior is spectacular, its chief feature (apart from sheer scale) being the murals depicting biblical scenes, which are painted on the walls and above the arches. With their depictions of Moses, complete with "horns" of light (a motif frequently found in Christian religious art), the warrior King David and, perhaps most symbolic, an almost naked Sampson felling the walls of the pagan temple, these murals completely break with the alleged taboo on the use of figurative art in the synagogue. Pure Hollywood: the artist, Hugo Ballin, specialized in film sets for the movie moguls who (occasionally) worshipped in the Wiltshire Boulevard Temple; the artwork itself was sponsored by Warner Brothers.

SHARMAN KADISH
Jewish Heritage, UK
University of Manchester

Note

1. Save for a "flipped" photo (p. 45), where the Hebrew inscription is back to front, and the occasional "typo" or editorial slip such as *Exodus* 28:17 instead of *Genesis* 28:17 (p. 75).

Shelley Hornstein and Florence Jacobowitz (eds.), *Image and Remembrance: Representation and the Holocaust.* Bloomington: Indiana University Press, 2003. 332 pp.

Image and Remembrance deals primarily with contemporary approaches to representation and memory, subjects that have been popularized in recent literature on the Holocaust. The 18 articles cover a wide range of media and material—painting, sculpture, architecture, photography, film, theater, and literature—but are not grouped in a helpful fashion. Most of the pieces contribute new ideas, excellent analyses, and frameworks of postmodern theory into which the works are inserted. Only two are reworked from previous publications, and whereas some artworks are discussed in several articles, they are usually viewed from different angles.

The opening essay by Florence Jacobowitz analyzes the subjective study of memory in Claude Lanzmann's film, *Shoah*, as seen in the way he interweaves the words and voices of the people he interviews with footage showing the sites of atrocity and other images, while never actually depicting the Holocaust. She sensitively studies his use of tracking and hand-held camera shots to increase the viewer's identification with the scene. Toward the end of the book, Leslie Morris analyzes the same subjective relationship between image and memory, from the German side, in Thomas Mitscherlich's film, *Reisen ins Leben.* Like *Shoah,* it makes use of survivor testimony and documentary footage, but employs as well a fictive narrative about an American who photographed the atrocities. (Juxtaposing these two articles would have clarified each of them.) Morris also successfully analyzes German problems in dealing with the Holocaust: Anselm Kiefer's paintings, for instance, treat it as an elusive memory, while a rock opera hints at it through its portrayal of the split loyalties of a transsexual who emigrates from East Berlin to the West.

Mark Godfrey's excellent analysis of Morris Louis' *Charred Journal: Firewritten* also deals with the non-depiction of the Holocaust, in this case by examining how the artist alludes to it in his renderings of Nazi book-burnings. Godfrey puts Louis' series into historical perspective in terms of both the dangers of McCarthyism in the early 1950s and the influence of American art critics. He sees this series and a similar painting of a Star of David as reflecting Louis' identification with Judaism, and shows how they recall midrashic ideas on the Torah's being written in letters of fire.

James Young repeats his oft-published analysis of "disappearing" or "empty" monuments, updating the projects discussed in his last book.[1] The editors were right to include his piece, but they should have juxtaposed it to the articles on monuments and museums, found at the end of *Image and Remembrance*, that were strongly influenced by Young's theories. Thus his stress on "the void" forms the background for Rebecca Comay's study of the monument that Rachel Whiteread was finally allowed to erect in Vienna in 2000 above the remains of a synagogue destroyed in a 1421 pogrom. Comay shows how the sealed, block-like bookcase designed by Whiteread gives the same feeling of loss that Young has discussed, as the books are set so that their titles are hidden. Comay tellingly contrasts this work with the statue of Gotthold Ephraim Lessing that is located in the same square: the statue commemorates the seer of the Enlightenment, while Whiteread's monument symbolizes the Enlightenment's end.

Tim Cole follows Young's mode of analysis to advantage in discussing Holocaust commemoration in Budapest. He shows that, under Soviet rule, the accent even in the city's former Jewish ghetto was on the liberators, with the sole memorials to Jewish victims being located in the Jewish cemetery on the city's outskirts. Later, a monument commemorating Jewish victims was erected in 1990, but was hidden behind a fence to protect it. More recently, a memorial was set up to mark the place where local Nazi collaborators killed Jews, in order to stress the point of Hungarian complicity.

Shelley Hornstein's article on the Memorial to the Martyrs of the Deportation in Paris continues this discourse. She sees in its silence about Jewish victims not only French neglect of specifically Jewish suffering, but also the wish of local Jews to assimilate into France. In like manner, Reesa Greenberg's excellent analysis of the Jewish Museum in Vienna stresses "the void." Discussing the museum's inner courtyard, she shows how its Judaica collection interacts with Nancy Spero's juxtaposition of images of Gestapo raids and the burning of Vienna's Jews in the 15th century. Greenberg observes that on one floor of the museum, holograms on glass panels are displayed instead of objects, whereas on another floor, ritual objects are set in stacks around a storage area that is inaccessible to the spectator. Greenberg interprets both displays as emphasizing the loss and inaccessibility of the prewar Jewish world in the post-Holocaust period.

The editors wisely included Daniel Libeskind's illuminating and poetic article on his architectural response to the Holocaust—Berlin's new Jewish museum—

rather than having someone else discuss his work. He explains the problems inherent in expressing trauma and loss in a concrete fashion, and the ways in which he solved these problems. He also describes how he persuaded the organizers of the Oranienberg-Sachsenhausen competition to rethink their plan to build housing on the site.

Opposed to these articles that stress loss are those dealing with figurative representations of the Holocaust. Carol Zemel's interesting essay discusses the photographs of Margaret Bourke-White and Lee Miller, both of whom accompanied Allied troops into the camps. Zemel analyzes the aesthetic, moral, and symbolic aspects of photographing atrocity, setting it in the context of a "Holocaust sublime" in which the viewer, first terrified, overcomes his horror to achieve some sort of aesthetic "delight." She contrasts Bourke-White's distancing herself from her subject with Miller's fascination with the Nazis, thus ignoring Bourke-White's sympathetic photographs of the Germans.

Monica Bohm-Duchen surveys the ways in which artists use such photographs. As opposed to Zemel, she does not deal with witnesses, but rather with contemporary artists who are already distanced from the scene. They are either fascinated with the photographs or else use them to memorialize the dead, to express a sense of guilt by making the spectator complicit in the evil, or to protest the commercial vulgarization of Holocaust photographs. Other artists photograph relevant sites to stress their present state or to inject the past into them.

Several of these essays highlight new responses by second-generation artists. Andrea Liss' perceptive discussion of Arie Galles' drawings (based on Nazi and Allied aerial photographs of the camps) contrasts the artist's need to distance himself from the subject by using literally "distanced" photographs, to the ways he expresses his anger at the atrocities committed there through violently drawn stokes, hidden images, and quotations from the Kaddish. Unfortunately, the illustrations (printed on regular paper) are of such poor quality that the details she discusses cannot be seen even with the aid of a magnifying glass.

The revised version of an article by Marianne Hirsch and Susan Suleiman that was published in 2001 offers an enlightening examination of two cut-out books constructed by Tatana Kelner in which casts of her parents' arms (accenting the camp numbers) are set within a framework of family photographs and her parents' reminiscences. The authors sensitively observe the differences between the narrative voice of each parent and the layering of images and texts by their daughter. Hirsch and Leo Spitzer analyze the interplay between a different kind of first and second generation in dealing with Mikael Levin's re-examination of the 1944–1945 concentration camp reportage by his father, American journalist Meyer Levin, and his photographer. The authors alert us to the different layers of reporting and to the way the son juxtaposes the original photographs with his own, occasionally ironic, shots of the same sites.

Ernst van Alphen does not explore the visual arts but rather the way in which traumatic scenes were registered by inmates' eyes without being understood by their minds. Van Alphen utilizes Pierre Janet's analysis of the differences between narrative and traumatic memory to examine how two survivors write about their experiences. Van Alphen's highly perceptive analysis of Charlotte Delbo's use of slippage between past and present, first and third person, distant description of scenes versus expressions of personal feeling, can act as a model for this kind of discussion.

Only three articles in this book are weak. Berel Lang provides no new insight into Shimon Attie's projection of photographs on various sites, merely criticizing him for projecting archival photographs on the wrong buildings and for broadening the meaning of the Holocaust to include later issues. Janet Wolff, while repeating oft-stated ideas on the problems of using beauty in connection with the Holocaust and stating her own preference for allusive and abstract works, offers some interesting comments. However, her analysis of Louis' *Charred Journals* is seriously impaired by its placement next to Godfrey's highly informative article on this subject. Robin Wood largely neglects the ostensible subject of his contribution, the depiction of gays in two films on the Holocaust, and instead spends two thirds of his article dwelling on personal reminiscences about his own problems and ranting both against the lack of attention paid to gays and, more generally, against capitalism and the heterosexual family.

All in all, this collection is a definite contribution to the field and should be on the bookshelf of anyone interested in the subject of art and the Holocaust.

ZIVA AMISHAI-MAISELS
The Hebrew University

Note

1. James Young, *At Memory's Edge: After-Images of the Holocaust in Contemporary Art and Architecture* (New Haven: 2000).

Dana Evan Kaplan, *American Reform Judaism: An Introduction.* New Brunswick: Rutgers University Press, 2003. 297 pp.

Of all Jewish groups and denominations, Reform Judaism has self-consciously built the most effective mechanisms for adjusting itself to developments in the general culture. In principle, Reform Judaism is not committed to observing Jewish law (halakhah) and does not look to *poskim*, rabbinical sages, to dictate to the laity how to interpret the Jewish tradition. Consequently, deciding on changes and implementing them have been central elements of the Reform movement all through its history. Since its inception in America in the mid-19th century, American Reform Judaism has gone through huge changes in response to the cultural, moral, and intellectual developments that have taken place in America and elsewhere. In the latter decades of the 20th century, while retaining their commitment to a progressive outlook on social and cultural issues, Reform Jews have reversed previous decisions—bringing back into the synagogue Jewish rituals and symbols that the founding fathers of Reform Judaism had considered obsolete.

Dana Kaplan's excellent book, *American Reform Judaism: An Introduction*, analyzes the changes that the American Reform movement has witnessed in the past two generations. He masterfully explains the Reform movement's move in both directions: on the one hand, embracing tradition and, on the other, promoting progressive issues. Kaplan convincingly argues that there is no real contradiction between the two trends. Both result from the changes that the movement has undergone since the 1960s.

Kaplan starts the narrative with "classical" Reform Judaism, its history, theology, and institutions. The reformers of the late 19th century and early decades of the 20th century transformed the traditional synagogue and rewrote the prayer books. Giving up on much day-to-day Jewish observance, they built a socially progressive yet patriarchal and solidly middle-class movement that seemed to suit the needs of the American Jewish elite at that time. Striving for respectability and conformity characterized other movements in American Judaism until the 1960s. But with the emergence of the counterculture in the 1960s and 1970s, the old paradigm was challenged as American Jewish baby boomers sought more spiritual meaning in their lives. A growing demand for less formality and more spirituality has transformed the Reform temples, which have introduced more traditional rituals and symbols. Such religious objects as *kipot*, *talitot*, and *shofarot* have made their way back into the sanctuary. Today, for example, it is not uncommon for Reform rabbis to wear *kippot* on a regular basis, and while Reform congregations have not become strictly kosher, they have, as a rule, refrained from allowing overtly nonkosher food in the synagogue building and in other Reform institutions and gatherings. In addition, Reform communities were affected first by the establishment of the state of Israel and later by the Six-Day War, both of which intensified identification with Zionism and the Jewish state. As a consequence of these changes, classical Reform Judaism underwent serious erosion, although, as Kaplan points out, it has not disappeared and is still an influential minority within the Reform movement.

At the same time, the Reform movement, together with the fledgling Reconstructionist movement, persisted in its commitment to social progress, adjusting itself to new cultural trends such as women's liberation. It was already in the early days of the movement that Reform temples introduced mixed seating, encouraged girls to study in Sunday school toward confirmation, and allowed women to be admitted to Hebrew Union College. But roles of religious leadership were not yet open to female members. The situation changed in the early 1970s, when the first women were ordained as Reform rabbis. This aroused no storm among the Reform, in contrast to the Conservative movement, where long and heated deliberations over the ordination of women went on for more than a decade, ending with a schism (pp. 186–208). The first American woman rabbi, Sally Preisand, was ordained at the Hebrew Union College in 1972, paving the way for the ordination of more than 150 women since then. Likewise, the Reform movement accommodated itself to gay liberation, allowing homosexuals and lesbians full privileges in membership and leadership roles. Since the 1980s, Hebrew Union College has ordained openly gay and lesbian rabbis and has welcomed gay congregations into the Union of American Hebrew Congregations (pp. 209–232). In the early 2000s, the Central Conference of American Rabbis gave its members license to officiate in gay and lesbian commitment ceremonies.

Confronting the growing number of interfaith marriages, the Reform movement has also opened its doors to interfaith couples and their offspring. Reform congregations were the first to allow families with only one Jewish spouse to join as members. In 1983, the movement decided to recognize children of mixed marriages as Jewish, even when their mothers were not Jewish, provided that they were brought up as Jews. The tolerant atmosphere in Reform congregations has also made it possible for non-Jews to explore the Jewish tradition, which has led to a growing number of "Jews by choice." Consequently, the Reform movement has decided to invest in outreach activity and in educational programs for new Jews (pp. 155–185). Thus, the ethnic component of Reform congregations changed between the 1970s and the beginning of the 21st century, as a growing percentage of participants in Reform services were not born Jewish.

Kaplan offers a sophisticated and nuanced analysis of the Reform movement of our generation and its issues. The author, who is both a pulpit rabbi and an academician, has the ability to view the movement from more than one angle. He writes critically, exposing at times discord and crises, and offers a balanced picture that presents both the movement's achievements and its shortcomings. In spite of the numerical growth the Reform movement has witnessed in the past decades and its evident ability to reshape itself to changing realities, Kaplan voices skepticism over the movement's actual achievements. While he points to its ability to meet the needs of its individual members and to build a pluralistic and inclusive movement, Kaplan sees setbacks and limitations to a progressive religious movement in which members have full autonomy to pick and choose elements of the tradition as they see fit. He finds the rank and file of the movement to be lacking in passion and commitment. Many, if not most, Reform Jews do not attend synagogue on a regular basis, and there is a disparity between the concerns of the rabbinical leadership and those of the ordinary members (pp. 233–253).

Kaplan should be commended for his comparative approach, which places the developments in the American Reform movement within the larger context of changes in American religion and culture during the era (pp. 44–78). He is familiar with all the ins and outs of the movement, its leaders and institutions, and their standing on theological and social issues. He has taken part in Reform gatherings and has interviewed leaders and activists. His familiarity with the developments he writes about allows him to present detailed descriptions of behind-the-scenes struggles, which add color to the narrative. *American Reform Judaism* is also well-written and well-organized. Kaplan's writing is clear and direct, intended not only for scholars but also for community leaders and interested laypersons.

The book is accompanied by a foreword by Arthur Hertzberg, a leading American Jewish intellectual, and an afterword by Eric Yoffie, a leader of the Reform movement. Hertzberg's essay, while insightful, has little to do with the theme of the book, whereas Yoffie's intelligent afterword reads more like a laudatory book review. *American Reform Judaism* is such a fine work, makes such an important contribution, and reads so well, that there is no need for these two literary maids of honor.

Such minor flaws notwithstanding, this is a highly welcome volume. It will doubtless be included on reading lists of books on contemporary Judaism and on religion in America. *American Reform Judaism* is a comprehensive, informed, nuanced, and well-written study of the largest movement in American Judaism, and it should serve as a definitive volume on the subject for many years to come.

YAAKOV ARIEL
The University of North Carolina at Chapel Hill

Margarete Kohlenbach, *Walter Benjamin: Self-Reference and Religiosity* (New Perspectives in German Studies). Basingstoke: Palgrave Macmillan, 2002. xvii + 241 pp.

The cult of Walter Benjamin in the last three decades is somewhat puzzling. Certainly, Benjamin was an astonishingly fertile and wide-ranging thinker, with a sensibility attuned to modernism, in contrast to the pope of Marxist literary criticism, Georg Lukács. And unlike Lukács and others, he communicated mostly through short, pithy essays, not by means of massive works with pretensions to comprehensiveness. The puzzle lies in Benjamin's apparent religious agenda. This agenda is most unmistakable in his early writings, particularly the essays "On Language in General and on the Language of Man" (1916), about the spiritual character of language, and "Critique of Violence" (1921), about the irruption of divine violence into time. But it reappears forcefully in the messianism of "On the Concept of History," written shortly before his death in 1940. And even in his most famous essay, "The Work of Art in the Age of Its Technical Reproducibility" (1936), which shows strong influence from Bertolt Brecht, the concept of the "aura" refers us back to the origins of art in religious cults.

Needing to reconcile Benjamin's religious preoccupation with their own secular liberal outlook, most critics have evaded the challenge. Even Richard Wolin's excellent exposition faithfully sets forth Benjamin's conviction that the world is fallen, but does not explain what kind of redemption Benjamin is seeking.[1] Winfried Menninghaus tries to erase the problem by claiming that Benjamin's reflections on language actually seek to secularize older religious thought.[2] Rightly criticizing this denial, Margarete Kohlenbach confronts the problem directly. In her view, Benjamin has an inescapable religious program: he finds modern liberal society to be without foundations, and he seeks to restore its foundations by opposing secularism and working (in a reversal of Max Weber's well-known formula) for the re-enchantment of the world. Benjamin's preoccupation with religion, however, stops short of actual belief. He cannot accept the Bible as revelation, whether via Moses or via Jesus, and all actual religious institutions seem to him shallow and opportunistic. His attitude is therefore aptly called "religiosity." Benjamin's fascination with religion is ultimately aesthetic, and it goes together with an anarchist outlook that prevented him from committing himself to any political party.

The other theme Kohlenbach examines in Benjamin's thought is "self-reference" (*Selbstbeziehung*), an absolute uncorrupted by contact with the fallen world. The essay "On Language" attributes self-reference to language, maintaining that language communicates nothing but itself. Kohlenbach's minute examination of Benjamin's argument reveals many incoherencies that are disguised by his confident, apodictic style. The qualities he ascribes to the divine Word are those that the aesthetic circle around Stefan George attributed to the word of the poet. (More might have been said about Benjamin's context in fin-de-siècle aestheticism: for example, the "mute language of things," puzzlingly evoked in this essay, surely comes from Hugo von Hofmannsthal's "Chandos Letter").[3]

The young Benjamin who wrote "On Language" belonged to a cultural milieu that is now very unfamiliar. As Kohlenbach explains, he was deeply influenced by the charismatic schoolteacher Gustav Wyneken, who ascribed redemptive value to art. Benjamin developed Wyneken's project through his speculations on language and through his doctoral thesis on Romantic art criticism (1920), where reflection, the activity of the critic, is equated with the absolute. Although Kohlenbach's 70-page analysis of *The Concept of Art Criticism* occupies a perhaps disproportionate share of the book, it offers an important contribution to scholarship both through its detailed and critical analysis of Benjamin's often willful use of his sources, J.G. Fichte and Friedrich Schlegel, and through its plausible contention that Benjamin found Schlegel congenial—less because they shared a conception of self-reflexive literature than because both, a century apart, were seeking a new religion.

The crucial test for Kohlenbach's thesis about Benjamin's continued religiosity is whether she can demonstrate significant affinities between the earlier writings and those reflecting the interest in Marxism that he developed in the mid-1920s. As with his friend Brecht, we wonder whether Benjamin's adoption of Marxism really marked an ideological break with the past, or whether his materialist language was merely rhetorical, as Gershom Scholem maintained. Kohlenbach supports the latter case with some ingenious arguments. When Benjamin insists that the politically progressive character of art depends on its form and technique, not its content, he is, according to Kohlenbach, reintroducing his earlier concept of linguistic and literary self-reference in a new guise. When he argues in "The Work of Art" that the film audience experiences montage as a series of physical shocks that promote mental alertness, he implies that watching a film is akin to mystical contemplation. And the famous passage in "The Artist as Producer" (1934), showing how the alienated gaze of the epic dramatist perceives both destruction and liberation, implies that the dramatist has mystical insight into what would otherwise be unobservable. I can accept the first of these arguments, but the latter two seem strained, as they underestimate the enormous influence of Brecht on Benjamin's thinking during the 1930s. Nevertheless, Benjamin's continued attraction to messianic ideas is plain from Reflection XVII of "On the Concept of History," which concludes Kohlenbach's discussion, and in which the machine of historical determinism turns out to have been operated all along by the concealed dwarf Theology.

Reservations aside, Kohlenbach's impressive study achieves several aims. It does not seek to debunk Benjamin, but to understand what kind of thinker and writer he was. By bringing out the religiosity that is undoubtedly essential to his work, it issues a challenge to his many admirers who assimilate him to "the secular concerns of modern academia" (p. 77). Through close analysis of some exceptionally difficult texts, it demonstrates Benjamin's lax thinking and challenges claims for his strictly philosophical achievement. And by looking at some of Benjamin's sources, notably Gustav Wyneken, the extraordinary anarchist thinker Erich Unger, and the wilder moments of early German Romanticism, it brings us closer to appreciating this strange, willful, unassimilable genius and his vanished intellectual setting. It is not a book for the novice, but it demands a response from Benjamin scholars.

RITCHIE ROBERTSON
St. John's College, Oxford

Notes

1. Richard Wolin, *Walter Benjamin: An Aesthetic of Redemption* (New York: 1982).
2. Winfried Menninghaus, *Walter Benjamins Theorie der Sprachmagie* (Frankfurt: 1980).
3. See Ritchie Robertson, *The "Jewish Question" in German Literature 1749–1939* (Oxford: 1999), 391.

Ezra Mendelsohn, *Painting a People: Maurycy Gottlieb and Jewish Art.* Hanover: Brandeis University Press, 2002. 279 pp.

In spite of its subtitle, Ezra Mendelsohn's book wisely refrains from answering the question: "What is Jewish art?" That answer cannot reside in the life story of an artist, even one who, like Maurycy (Moritz) Gottlieb, sought to address Judaism and its relation with Christianity in his art, and who may have been seeking an answer to the question himself. "What is Jewish art" is a historical question, the product of a society that wishes to understand art as a national expression.[1] Gottlieb's interpretation of what it means to be a Jew and an artist is, however, central to a question that Mendelsohn does pose and which he answers beautifully: How does an artist's achievement and legacy inform the changing face of relations between Jews and Christians in Poland, Palestine, and the world, beginning in the late 19th century? Mendelsohn's answer shows why he is right to refuse the nationalist question of "Jewish art."

As Mendelsohn shows, the position Gottlieb carved out for himself was subject to changing myths about his Orthodox upbringing and encounters with antisemitism. Gottlieb was a beneficiary of the myth of the suffering artist who faces a philistine upbringing, poverty, and the opposition of parents. In its Jewish version, this myth usually features a bleak picture of Orthodox Judaism in Eastern Europe, a Jewish adaptation of the antisemitic trope of the backward shtetl (pp. 152–153). As told by Jehudo Epstein about himself, for example, the story impressed E.H. Gombrich as evidence that Judaism was a cultural backwater where "time stood still at the same spot for a thousand years,..[and a] whole people lay in a lethargic sleep."[2] That Epstein triumphed over adversity to become an artist was, in Gombrich's words, a "miracle." Gottlieb, however, was not the product of rural poverty, but the German-speaking offspring of wealthy, secular parents who supported his art. As Mendelsohn shows, Gottlieb's birthplace, Drohobycz, which also produced the artist and writer Bruno Schulz, was no backwater, but rather a cosmopolitan city with a Jewish population that embraced the secular aspirations of its sons and even helped Gottlieb attend art school.

Gottlieb perpetuated some of his own myths, as Mendelsohn demonstrates in subtle readings of Gottlieb's decision to portray himself as "Ahasuerus," and in Bedouin attire. He could also have argued that Gottlieb drew on the tendency of European painters to picture themselves in the garb of their own historical roots, as ancient or medieval wayfarers, like the Nazarenes (Mendelsohn mentions the Jewish origin of some of them), or to refer generically to their own primitivism, as did Gustav Courbet. To represent oneself as one's own ancestor was not only to validate one's culture, but to claim a place in the European artistic world. If Gottlieb costumed himself as an exemplar of ancient Judaism, who (as a critic later wrote) "possesses in his soul living memories of the origins of his religion," then he was in good company with non-Jewish artists who paraded their national pedigrees (p. 161). The closed eyes of Gottlieb's self-portraits are a widespread sign of melancholy (p. 105) used by the same painters who attired themselves in ancestral robes, most effectively in Courbet's famous *Self Portrait as Wounded Man* (1844–1854). Gottlieb also grapples with the codes of his own features, inscribing as Oriental his thick lips, curly hair, and scraggly beard. Indeed, his appearance absorbed him so intensely that his *Jews Praying in the Synagogue* may possibly chart his path through Judaism not only in the past and present, in two generally acknowledged self-portraits, but, by way of one or more older men, into the future, the journey completed with his death—represented by the memorial inscription on the Torah cover.

A scholar with a nuanced visual approach should develop further such themes as the relation between subjectivity and portraiture in Gottlieb's portraits of acculturated Jews.[3] Visual analysis might also help illuminate the images of Christ. Among the many factors that contributed to the bitter opposition to Max Liebermann's work of 1879, *The Twelve-Year Old Jesus in the Temple* (see p. 131), stylistic tropes may have played a role. Liebermann's distanced, undramatic style, schooled on French and Dutch naturalist painters, could be condemned as the expression of Jewish "rationalism," whereas the passion of Gottlieb's academic mode in *Christ Preaching at Capernaum* (1878–1879) may have fueled a critic's surmise that Gottlieb was about to convert (pp. 165–166).

Unlike Gottlieb, Liebermann lived to realize his desire for recognition as a German artist, and to see this recognition tragically withdrawn under Hitler. Mendelsohn is at his best contextualizing such social and political issues, as one would expect from the author of *On Modern Jewish Politics*.[4] Articulating Gottlieb's social milieu meticulously, differentiating between Ukrainians, Poles, Jewish Poles, and various possible identities within these groups, Mendelsohn places Gottlieb securely in the context of Jews who valued Judaism but aspired toward universalism. Indeed, like others before him, Mendelsohn constitutes universalism as a Jewish agenda. The Jewish hope for universalism has a tragic side, however; for one cannot be universal on one's own. Liebermann learned this, and Mendelsohn illustrates it with pathos as he concludes his central story of the relationship between Gottlieb and the Christian Polish artist Jan Matejko (pp. 201–205). Perhaps, however, a study of the context and dissemination of Matejko's antisemitic remarks will someday yield a different interpretation of them, and soften this harsh conclusion.

Finally, Mendelsohn follows the universalist theme found in Gottlieb's work throughout the 20th century, where it survives among distinguished Jewish artists to this day, and expresses the wish that this vision not fade. Indeed may it not fade among artists and other people; and may Mendelsohn's studies of it flourish.

MARGARET OLIN
School of the Art Institute of Chicago

Notes

1. See Margaret Olin, *The Nation Without Art: Examining Modern Discourses in Jewish Art* (Lincoln: 2001).

2. E. H. Gombrich, *The Visual Arts in Vienna Circa 1900, and Reflections on the Jewish Catastrophe* (London: 1997), 13.

3. Catherine M. Soussloff, "Portraiture and Assimilation in Vienna: The Case of Hans Tietze and Erica Tietze-Conrat," in *Diasporas and Exiles: Varieties of Jewish Identity,* ed. Howard Wettstein (Berkeley: 2002).

4. Ezra Mendelsohn, *On Modern Jewish Politics* (New York: 1993).

Zionism, Israel, and the Middle East

Rachelle Alterman, *Planning in the Face of Crisis: Land Use, Housing and Mass Immigration in Israel.* London: Routledge, 2002. 212 pp.

In late 1989, with the imminent collapse of the Soviet Union, Israel faced the prospect of a giant wave of immigration: one million persons were expected to arrive within three years. Given the size of the existing base population at the time—4.6 million—the relative anticipated increase was equivalent to the United States' absorbing a population equal to that of New England and the mid-Atlantic states, or to France or England's taking in the combined residents of Sweden and Denmark.

Moreover, the immigrants arriving from the former Soviet Union in the early 1990s came with virtually no capital reserves—often with only minimal personal belongings. They were in need of a full array of absorption services, from language training and assistance in employment placement to adequate housing. Immediate and large-scale intervention was required. Could planners, who generally focus on long-range urban and regional development issues, be effective in meeting the approaching crisis?

In *Planning in the Face of Crisis: Land Use, Housing and Mass Immigration in Israel*, Rachelle Alterman, the David Azrieli Professor of Architecture and City Planning at the Technion–Israel Institute of Technology, and one of Israel's most respected and prolific planning theorists, sets out to address this question as it pertained to housing-related issues. Following an extensive analysis of the theoretical underpinnings of crisis definition and considerable research into the specific Israeli scenario, she concludes that planning can (and, in fact, did) serve to provide an effective intervention strategy during the period of mass immigration in the 1990s.

Crisis does not necessarily refer to disaster, catastrophe, or major disruption of the physical, economic, or ecological systems; it may also be positive in nature. Alterman delineates seven attributes of crisis: "high degree of uncertainty and surprise; a high degree of change and turbulence; high risks and threats; system-wide and complex effects of anticipated effects; a low degree of knowledge about solutions; a challenge to the symbolic level and to the social consensus; and finally, urgency because of the high cost of delay" (pp. 19–20). Moving from the purely theoretical to the specific Israeli case, she then employs a five-stage model to address the role of policy-makers and planners in handling the housing needs of the Soviet immigrants and associated urban and regional development issues.

First, she explains, there was "shock," as cabinet and government ministries tried to delay their intervention until the scope of immigration would become clear, deflect blame for the country's unpreparedness, and rely on existing modes of intervention. In the second phase, "focusing," housing emerged as a lead issue, in large part because of Ariel Sharon's appointment as minister of housing. Arguing that housing was a key element in the "critical path" of successful immigrant absorption, Sharon pushed through a series of cabinet decisions to promote a co-ordinated and comprehensive response. The third phase, "action," came about with the formulation of a large-scale housing program, including new legislation to ex-pedite the planning approval process, production-side incentives, and the purchase of mobile homes.

The fourth stage of Alterman's model, "planning," is at the heart of her thesis, since this was the point at which middle- and long-range planning was carried out. Alterman details two national projects: Plan 31, a national, five-year outline plan; and Israel 2020, a long-range non-statutory plan. These were undoubtedly ambi-tious efforts, as Alterman asserts, but their role in addressing the housing crisis of the early 1990s is questionable, since most of the decisions concerning where to construct housing had been made *before* the plans were approved. Finally, the "post-mortem crisis management" stage in Alterman's model was more an effort to streamline the onerous planning process through new legislation (Amendment 43) rather than an intensive assessment of why the planning process did not initially provide adequate solutions to meet the crisis.

By and large, as Alterman shows, Israeli planners and policy-makers rose to the challenge. In the initial surge of immigration, approximately 400,000 people arrived between 1990 and 1992. Then the level slackened off, though over the course of the next seven years, an additional 400,000 immigrants arrived. A wide array of strategies was adopted to meet their housing needs, including the provision of bonuses to builders who embarked on accelerated construction; a government com-mitment to purchase unsold units; the purchase of thousands of mobile homes and modular units from abroad; the provision of tax cuts to increase the supply of rental housing; and interim legislation aimed at expediting the planning process. The results of this forceful and multi-pronged effort were striking: housing starts quad-rupled in two years, and the share of government-sponsored starts rose 18-fold during the same period. Consequently, not only were no immigrant families left homeless, but the overall homeownership for these families reached 70 percent—a remarkable figure comparable to that enjoyed by veteran Israelis.

To some extent, Alterman's overall positive assessment downplays Israeli plan-ners' *lack* of contingency planning. She acknowledges that despite the fundamental role of immigration in Israel's development and ideology, by 1989, there was still no comprehensive national plan to deal with large-scale immigration. In addition, there was an insufficient supply of available land planned for residential construc-tion (even though more than 90 percent of the land is publicly owned). Moreover, approved national plans such as that concerning population dispersal quickly proved incapable of guiding development, even though the planning horizon was for a population of 6,000,000 residents. These and other shortcomings necessitated im-provisation on the part of planners and policy-makers. In fact, the collapse of the steady-state planning milieu forced those of us at the housing ministry who were trained as planners to behave more like ad-hoc decision-makers, obligated as we were to present workable intervention strategies without the traditional planning rationales.

During the period of her study, Alterman served as both researcher and participant in the planning process. She conducted two rounds of investigation, the first during the course of the events as they unfolded and the second after a sufficient "sedimentation period" had elapsed. The overwhelming majority of her interviews were with planners and local officials; far fewer interviews were conducted with key political actors at the national level. This fact may have some bearing on her final assessment, since planners are likely to view their role in a generally positive light. As best as I could ascertain, Alterman did not interview either Ariel Sharon or the late Yitzhak Moda'i, who served as finance minister during the height of the immigration wave. Had she included the perspective of these and other national leaders, her study would have been more balanced. In fact, the many instances in which the government adopted an "act now, plan later" strategy is an indication of the extent to which the planning agenda was set not by planners but by politicians. It may be that the overall successful absorption was at least partly the outcome of market-oriented responses rather than prescient planning.

Despite these limitations, *Planning in the Face of Crisis* makes a noteworthy contribution both to understanding the specific Israeli case study and to providing a theoretical basis for assessing planners' roles in crisis situations. This is a captivating story, and Alterman's excitement as she depicts the "opportunity to observe and participate in a once-in-a-planner's lifetime event" (p. 2) makes this a work of interest to planners, policy-makers, theoreticians, and students of Israeli society alike.

CHAIM FIALKOFF
Israel Ministry of Construction and Housing
The Hebrew University

Alain Dieckhoff, *The Invention of a Nation: Zionist Thought and the Making of Modern Israel* (trans. Jonathan Derrick). London: C. Hurst and Co., 2003. xi + 297 pp.

Old truths that have been forgotten or rejected in the past, and which therefore have no significance ascribed to them in the present, may nevertheless return to the public discourse in the form of "old-new" opinions or beliefs. This phenomenon is a familiar one not only in the socioeconomic and religious spheres but also in the domain of historical and sociological theory. Alain Dieckhoff's book provides invigorating and substantial proof of this intellectual dynamic. After all, since the end of the Second World War, academic research on the importance of ideas as an influential factor in historical development has been spurred by various postmodernist, Marxist, and postcolonial schools of thought. Dieckhoff, however, proclaims with commendable courage (given the prevailing intellectual atmosphere) that indeed the emperor "is not naked"—that is, ideas do exert important and even formative influence on the development of history.

The motivation for Dieckhoff's scrutiny of Zionism is the historic two-way process now taking place in Western Europe. On the one hand, there is a continual process of unification that seemingly augurs the abolition of the nation-state. On the other hand, Europe is currently experiencing a trend of renewed cultural and political organization along ethnic or national lines. Dieckhoff's interest in Jewish history of the last two centuries is sparked by this two-way dynamic. In his opinion, Jews of the modern era tried all of the possible solutions to the problem of their being a stateless people: from complete assimilation, through autonomous cultural nationalism, to setting out to acquire an independent state. From his point of view: "It is this emblematic itinerary that interests us here: not the Jews 'in themselves,' but what they represent for our understanding of the emergence of political modernity" (p. viii).

Here, Dieckhoff establishes two "old-new" rules. First, Zionism can only be understood against the general background of political and cultural nationalistic movements in Europe (in contradistinction to a tendency in certain academic circles to ascribe Zionism to the European imperialist colonial movement). And second, despite Zionism's uniqueness, an understanding of this particular movement aids in understanding nationalism in general and the problems associated with it. For Dieckhoff, the case of Zionism provides a justification for underscoring the importance of ideology or ideas in nation-building.

The Invention of a Nation is constructed along the lines of a hexagon, with each of its six chapters analyzing a particular facet of Zionist ideology. Throughout, the focus is on leading groups and individuals within Zionism: Theodor Herzl, the father of the *Judenstaat* ethos; Nahman Syrkin and A.D. Gordon, the philosophers of the cooperative national community; Eliezer Ben-Yehuda and Hayim Nahman Bialik, the trailblazers of the Hebrew revival; Rabbis Jacob Reines and Abraham Isaac Kook, who were responsible for the synthesis between religion and modern nationalism; Vladimir Zeev Jabotinsky, the hero of political nationalism; and lastly Chaim Weizmann and David Ben-Gurion, the torchbearers of "realistic" political Zionism.

Dieckhoff's description and analysis of the diverse viewpoints in Zionism offer nothing new relative to what has already been said in the existing research upon which he draws (particularly those works that have been translated into English or French). This does not, however, detract from the value of his overall approach.

Dieckhoff's basic understanding of the nation is political, in the French republicanist sense of the term. That is, he regards the nation as the sum total of its individual citizens, the nation coming to replace such traditional frameworks as the Church or feudal or other cooperative structures (in which citizens are distinct from the state). In Dieckhoff's view, a "nation of citizens" is both democratic-liberal and rational; any deviation from this model carries with it the danger of fascist or Communist totalitarianism.

Starting from this European perspective, Dieckhoff takes the different currents in Zionist ideology and tests them against his model. In his opinion, Herzl failed to understand the importance of politics—as opposed to diplomacy—in nation-building, as manifested in his general avoidance of nuts-and-bolts politics. In contrast, the labor movement in Eretz Israel showed a preference for constructing a secular cooperative society rather than working toward instigating nationwide political activities. In religious Zionist circles, Kook's messianism eventually prevailed over the national pragmatism championed by Reines, whereas the out-and-out political nationalism advocated by Jabotinsky was transformed into an atavistic and aggressive form of extreme nationalism that, notwithstanding its secular roots, also had pronounced messianic overtones. Dieckhoff views the mainstream pragmatism of Weizmann and Ben-Gurion as the correct path to follow in building the new nation, even though it failed to achieve complete realization.

Based on these assessments, which are in and of themselves correct, Dieckhoff concludes that Jewish political existence through Zionism is tantamount to a precarious victory, because, as he writes: "The influence of the messianic theme showed that it was impossible for Zionism to break free from Judaism, and signaled the real if partial continuity between the two phenomena" (p. 263). The question is whether things could have been any different, given the special nature of Jewish nationalism. For secularists like Simon Dubnov, Ahad Ha'am, and their followers, religion was still considered an integral part of Jewish nationalism. Even the socialist and antireligious Bund movement acknowledged the religious essence of Jewish nationalism in the premodern period.

Zionism's second failing, according to Dieckhoff, is its organization on a cooperative-communal basis (in its earlier period of labor movement dominance) or on a sectoral-ethnic basis (as is found in Israeli society today). Yet this phenomenon also has national and historical roots. The main components of Jewish nationalism in Eastern Europe—Zionism, autonomism, Bundist socialism, and religious nationalism—all aspired to establish cultural autonomy for the Jews in the countries in which they were to be found in large concentrations. These traditions were alien to modern Western political culture, but who is to say that they were inherently flawed or unsound? As noted, Dieckhoff himself sees the same two-way process taking place in Europe and in the United States.

Against this national-historical background, and in the wake of Dieckhoff's own assumptions, it appears that Zionism's basic problem, from its inception up to the present, has been how to transform a historical people into a political nation. This transition could not be accomplished without utopian aspirations, which arouse apprehension in Dieckhoff. Such aspirations, however, were not uniform within the Zionist movement. Dieckhoff rightly points to the unrealistic naiveté of Brith Shalom's utopian vision of Jewish-Arab coexistence, and he is undoubtedly right when he warns of the danger emanating from the ultra-nationalist, messianic religious camp. However, whereas other leaders and currents—Weizmann, Ben-Gurion, and the labor movement generally—also had pronounced utopian leanings, theirs was a kind of "utopian realism," with the emphasis on realism. This is what constitutes the vital difference between what Dieckhoff terms "classical Zionism" versus the "new Zionism": "while classical Zionism started out from the will to organize the rapid *departure* of the Jews from the countries of the diaspora, the mystical neo-

Zionism which has developed over thirty years seeks instead the *return* of the Jews to Zion" (p. 265).

Messianist Zionism (the "new Zionism," in Dieckhoff's terminology) came into being as a consequence of the Six-Day War, which resulted in greatly expanded territory under Israeli control. This fact gives rise to a critical question: To what extent is messianism cardinal to Zionism? There is no doubt that the seeds of messianism were to be found in religious Zionism right from its inception, as Dieckhoff demonstrates. However, had it not been for the Six-Day War, it is doubtful whether the present ideological and political polarization in Israel would have come about. Until the Six-Day War, ahistorical messianic tendencies were devoid of significant political influence.

It may be the case that, with a change in regional and international political conditions, a pragmatic political atmosphere in Israel will gradually prevail, displacing messianic ideology back to the sidelines. Should this happen, it is to be hoped, it will be demonstrated that, despite all of Zionism's contradictions and difficulties, its victory is not "precarious," but rather historical and political. Judging by his keen understanding of Zionism's political and historical roots, Alain Dieckhoff would seem to join in the wish for such a victorious outcome.

YOSEF GORNY
Tel Aviv University

Aryei Fishman, *Judaism and Collective Life: Self and Community in the Religious Kibbutz*. London: Routledge, 2002. 148 pp.

I read Aryei Fishman's analysis of cultural difference within the religious kibbutz movement from the outside, or at least from the margin. For his account is of an intramural sort, namely, the particular fraternal difference to be found among the European adepts of religious Zionist socialism. The East/West divide is drawn within a larger communality, a difference between the ethos of East European religious kibbutz founders and their more Western, German Jewish counterparts.

Fishman uses this relatively small cultural difference creatively as a prism with which to refract light on much bigger questions concerning culture, society, and religion. His story line is that, among the religious communes started in Eretz Israel from the 1920s through the 1940s, two different social movements were represented, albeit sharing Zionist, socialist, and religious ideologies. One was the inward-looking, more emotional, existential, mystical, hasidic-inspired movement (Hapoel Hamizrachi) of the East European Jews, whereas the other was a more practical, rationalist, activist, halakhic, ethical-legal movement (Torah im-Derekh Eretz) of the German Jews, or "yekkes," as they are popularly known. The plot of the story is that while the religiously inspired ecstasy of the hasidim leavens even the more rationalist halakhic stream, by itself it is "incapable" of adapting to the evolutionary, societal, and functional requisites of environmental survival. In Fishman's view, these two movements represent alternative "mind-sets," a tension of "ethos," or differently defined "religious subcultures" (he terms them "Bund" and "Commune," respectively), which also stand as stages in the development of religious kibbutzim. The inward, affective hasidic ethos, which Fishman calls the "psychic collective," provides "collective effervescence" in the initial (Bund) stage of communal evolution. This, however, is insufficient for the second (communal) stage, in which the value orientations of an "empirical collective" are necessary.

Fishman draws rich and compelling portraits of the two movements, beginning with their European origins, their early founding days, and later struggles and successes, which are based on first-person accounts from published diaries and memoirs. Although these include recollections of everyday kibbutz life, they are not presented as systematic reports in the manner of ethnographic field observations. While the personalizing tendency in postmodern ethnography might value such reports, Fishman instead chooses to emphasize the beliefs, values, ideological hopes, and expectations of members of the religious agricultural communes.

The particular difference between the "Bund" and "Commune"—and the putative success of the latter versus the functionally determined failure of the former—is part of Fishman's bigger story, or, indeed, stories. The deeply structured dichotomy of *gemeinschaft/gesellschaft*, mystical/rational, or even individual/collective, is what connects his comparison of two Israeli communal movements to the sociological tradition of Emile Durkheim, Georg Simmel, and, most profoundly, Max Weber. Fishman's contextualization of the narrative within that of classical sociological dichotomous differences, and his use of insights drawn from the sociology of religion (from the Simmelian embedding of religion in forms of interaction, to the Durkheimian collective generation of energy in social ritual and evolution of types of solidarity, to the Weberian descriptions of the social effects of religious ethics) is what makes this book not only an interesting slice of Israeli and communal histories, but also an essay in the sociology of religion.

Fishman's theoretical contextualization of the differential adaptation of rational versus mystically oriented communalist social movements is not, however, a neutral or disinterested endeavor. It favors Weber—or, more specifically, Talcott Parsons' reading of Weber, as Fishman himself freely acknowledges. In my own view, Parsons is causally less balanced than Weber himself in his idealist analysis of social dynamics. Yet it is the evolutionary Parsons who provides the book's capstone justifying system differentiation. In Fishman's words: "Once the cultural system gains autonomy from the social system, it plays a superordinate role in controlling it and its environment. This is particularly true of religious culture, which provides ultimate meaning to the social system" (p. 115).

For all his emphasis on the importance of religious belief for social and economic action, Weber repeatedly asserted a more pluralist model of social causation: "Not ideas, but material and ideal interests, directly govern men's conduct." This does not obviate Weber's complementary view that "[t]he term 'economic ethic' points to the practical impulses of action which are found in the psychological and pragmatic contexts of religion."[1] Fishman, however, takes the second view more seriously and offers a case study of how Weber's "world images" can act like historical "switchmen." His own work presents a nuanced analysis of the determinative effects of what initially appear to be relatively small differences in "mind-set" within a larger shared universe of assumptions, and he largely neglects the social, organizational, demographic, and economic reasons for the differential success of what is, in any case, a small sample of communes. However, without a fuller picture, we have no way of knowing how important these significant differences in religious subcultures were for communal adaptation.

If Fishman's explanation of differences in social adaptation is incomplete, it is also true that he goes well beyond the ordinary sociology of religion discourse by opening it up to the specifically religious dimension. With Fishman, religion is not simply the object of social explanation but also its subject, with an explanatory voice of its own. In particular, he makes use of the Jewish thinker Joseph B. Soloveitchik, whose writings offer paradigms of personalities and social types that complement those of classical and Parsonian "mind-sets," "cultural orientations," and social "ethics." Soloveitchik's ontological typology of the "inner" and "outer" Adam fits Fishman's psychic/collective, coterie/community, mystical/rational categorizations, and shows how religious thought can be used to further social explanation.

The addition of religious thought to social explanation is, however, no less neutral than Fishman's use of sociological theory. Apart from the 20th-century Soloveitchik, Fishman also brings in the 19th-century Moses Hess, in order to provide historical precedent and rationale for the linkage between socialism and halakhah, and, beyond that, for the functional superiority of a positivist, empirical social collective that is based on the legal-ritual-ethical as opposed to the ecstatic, mystical stream of Judaism. Hess, according to Fishman, offers a "transformative ethos" of an "operationally valid Halakhic-socialistic subculture" (p. 99). Here is Fishman's addition (via Hess) to Weber's "Protestant ethic": a "Jewish ethic" that gives a "religious grounding to reason," provides a " 'community of action,' to use Soloveitchik's term" (p. 13), an internalization of "self-restraint" and a "transformative ethos" that combines particularist, Jewish "national regeneration" with a rational and legalist ethic of universalist modernization. In brief, *yekke* rationalism.

Yet fulfillment of the functional imperatives of society as dictated by the logic of evolution that culminates in rational modernity; or, as in the specific case of Israel, the success of the "empirical collective," is not the end of the story—at least, not the Protestant story, according to Weber. Social success, including religiously grounded success, has its costs, including the disappearance of that very grounding. Of the "spirit of religious asceticism," which helped ignite the great historical engine of capitalism, Weber observes: "But victorious capitalism, since it rests on mechanical foundations, needs its support no longer. The rosy blush of its laughing heir, the Enlightenment, seems also to be irretrievably fading. . . ." Against Parsonian universalist, evolutionary modernity and *yekke* rationalism, Weber is not self-congratulatory about the "de-magification" of the world. Rather, rationalism has an almost unbearable cost: "No one knows . . . whether at the end of this tremendous development entirely new prophets will arise, or there will be a great rebirth of old ideas and ideals, or, if neither, mechanized petrification, embellished with a sort of convulsive self-importance."[2]

The dialectic of this modern, religiously grounded rationality, Protestant or Jewish, individual or collective, passes through a markedly degenerative, destructive stage. In this fuller evolutionary narrative, modern rationality is not the last stop, nor even a particularly happy one. Max Horkheimer and Theodor Adorno, in their usual epigrammatic language, put it directly and dismally: "[T]he Enlightenment has always aimed at liberating men from fear and establishing their sovereignty. Yet the fully enlightened earth radiates disaster triumphant."[3] Is there another spin to this wheel, a "reenchantment" of the world, a "resacralization" or a series of cultural and social movements for "revitalization"? Along with many others, I have tried to offer some reply to this question, with a particular interest in the role of Fishman's collectively failed stream—Hasidism—and its relation to contemporary social movements.[4] Perhaps this is the place to inquire about the social implications of a "Jewish ethic" that comes not from the West, but from the East. Asking the particular question returns us as well to Weber's more general hints about the social possibilities of innerworldly mysticism.

We do not have to accept Fishman's identification of the "Jewish ethic" with halakhic socialism or rational-legal communalism in order to appreciate the value of *Judaism and Collective Life*, which reasserts the importance of religious thought as the object and subject of social life. For this achievement, we should be grateful to him.

PHILIP WEXLER
The Hebrew University

Notes

1. Max Weber, *From Max Weber: Essays in Sociology*, ed. and trans. H. H. Gerth and C. Wright Mills (New York: 1946), 267, 280.
2. Max Weber, *The Protestant Ethic and the Spirit of Capitalism* (London: 1992 [1930]), 124.
3. Max Horkheimer and Theodor W. Adorno, *Dialectic of Enlightenment* (New York: 1972), 3.
4. Philip Wexler, *Mystical Society: An Emerging Social Vision* (Boulder: 2000).

Ken Koltun-Fromm, *Moses Hess and Modern Jewish Identity*. Bloomington: Indiana University Press, 2001. 180 pp.

Michael Stanislawski, *Zionism and the Fin de Siècle: Cosmopolitanism and Nationalism from Nordau to Jabotinsky*. Los Angeles: University of California Press, 2001. 282 pp.

Over the last century, modern Jewish identity has undergone a radical transformation, and the main engine of that transformation has been Zionism. When Theodor Herzl died in 1904, Jewish identity was diasporic and, especially in Western and Central Europe, ostensibly religious in character. One can argue just how "religious," since the external constraint of antisemitism along with the internal recognition of secular ties (whether familial, ethnic, or even racial) meant that modern Jewish identity went beyond merely religious criteria. Most Jews around 1900, however, even in Eastern Europe, would not have seen themselves as constituting a modern nation. But by 2004, the centennial of Herzl's death, a large number of Jews lived in a Jewish state, Israel; many other Jews, whether in North America, Europe, or other centers of the remaining diaspora, regarded Israel as the expression of the Jewish right to *national* self-determination. Although other sources of Jewish identity emerged in the 20th century, not least the tragic experience of the Holocaust, Zionism—the vision of the Jews as a nation, both in Israel and in the diaspora—has been by far the most powerful and successful.

The irony of this nationalization of Jewish identity in the modern world is that, famously, many of the founding figures of Zionism, including Herzl himself, were quite distant from what was then seen as the core of Jewish identity. Almost from the time Herzl stood before Baron Hirsch with his novel idea to solve the "Jewish question," there has been the nagging question whether Zionism, despite its immense success in forging current Jewish identity, and because of the secular and even "non-Jewish" character of its leadership, is really "Jewish" at all. The battle over ownership of Jewish identity has been a recurring theme in the history of the Zionist movement. The most notorious confrontation was perhaps that between Herzl and Ahad Ha'am over Herzl's vision of the future Jewish utopia, *Altneuland*. The progressive, technologically enthusiastic, "modern" vision of political Zionists such as Herzl and Max Nordau came up against the equally "modern" but much more ethnically distinct approach of the cultural Zionists, most of them from Eastern Europe.

What Ahad Ha'am had to say about the lack of Jewish identity in Herzl's vision still haunts the debate about Zionism: Was the accusation of Herzl's insufficient Jewishness ever really valid? Perhaps the real issue concerned a different type of Jewish identity and culture? Or else, at the other extreme of the debate, was the Zionism of the likes of Herzl, Nordau, and, later, Jabotinsky more an attempt to *destroy* Jewish difference, and hence Jewish identity, ostensibly in the name of the Jewish nation, but really for the sake of fin-de-siècle cosmopolitanism?

The two books under review tackle themes that are at the heart of this question of the relationship between Zionism and modern Jewish identity. Michael Stanislawski's volume deals squarely with the issue of just how "Jewish" (and how closely connected) was the Zionism of Nordau and Jabotinsky. More indirectly, Ken Koltun-Fromm's slim treatise on the meanings of Moses Hess' *Rome and Jerusalem* (1862) can serve as an introduction to the origins of what one might term the "Zionist syndrome": the distance of Jewish intellectuals from traditional Jewish culture, life, and community.

Koltun-Fromm's work is repetitive, not clearly written, narrowly based in terms of its secondary sources, and very idiosyncratic in its use of Charles Taylor's ethical philosophy to explicate Hess' "modern Jewish identity." Its main claim, that Hess is a self-contradictory thinker who could not create a coherent Jewish identity for himself, and is *therefore* most relevant to contemporary discussions of modern

Jewish identity, is not, I fear, as significant as the author appears to think. None-theless, he makes many interesting points, of which two are particularly relevant: first, Hess' attempt to make up for his distance from traditional Jewish life by basing Jewish identity on a racial basis; and second, what Koltun-Fromm sees as Hess' fraudulent claim, based on a "discovered" manuscript, that he had already, privately, had the ideas behind *Rome and Jerusalem* in 1840. In Koltun-Fromm's view, the need for narrative consistency was so important for Hess' sense of self that he was prepared to lie about his former beliefs.

The irony is that neither the move from cosmopolitanism to race nor the emen-dation of his personal history were necessary to shore up Hess' Jewish identity, since he was never very distant from it in the first place. His upbringing, his approach to German and European culture, and the German context, in which the "Jewish question" was never far from the surface, all ensured that Hess could not have been removed from Jewish matters. *Judentum* was already a central (if usually negative) concept in German thought, partly because of the nation's Christian her-itage. Moreover, Hess' own approach, in his "non-Jewish" period, had a distinctly Judeocentric perspective, as evidenced, for example, in his assessment of Spinoza as the embodiment of the modern age. Hess may have believed that he needed a racial definition of Jewish identity to compensate for his lack of specific Jewish religious and traditional knowledge, but in fact his existential position and his situation as a Jewish emancipatory intellectual in 19th-century Europe were quite enough to make him part of the "Jewish question."

In *The Transformation of German Jewry*, David Sorkin has written cogently about the way in which the long process of Jewish emancipation led to Central European Jewry's developing its own subculture. Jews in Central Europe did not so much assimilate into society as occupy their own distinct niche in the general culture, based on the attitudes and experience gained from the struggle for eman-cipation and integration. The "assimilationist" ideology associated with this, in-cluding its universalist assumptions about "humanity," "reason," "progress," and indeed the central necessity for "emancipation" through *Bildung*, had the ironic result, according to Sorkin, that the only ones who could not really see the sub-culture's distinctiveness were its members.

Sorkin's model applies almost as strongly, I would claim, to those Jews in Central Europe who ostensibly "left" Judaism for the sake of joining a universal "human-ity"—for these "non-Jewish Jews," to use Isaac Deutscher's well-known phrase, were but a variant of the same socio-cultural phenomenon. The very rationale and strategy for escaping their Jewish identity was one that was shaped by their Jewish background and the Jewish ideology of emancipation. Heinrich Heine and Karl Marx (in their drive to emancipate humanity from the past's delusions, so that all men, Jews included, could be free) would be two of the most salient figures in this group, but Moses Hess would certainly be there as well, at least before *Rome and Jerusalem*. He is a prime example of a person embodying "situational Jewishness." What makes Hess different from Marx and Heine is that he came to see the "in-escapable" nature of his Jewish situation and thus decided to return to an overtly Jewish identity, in the form of his proto-Zionism. What links Koltun-Fromm's book to Stanislawski's is that Nordau, Ephraim Moses Lilien, and, to an extent, the

Vladimir Jabotinsky of the Odessa period can all be seen as "situational" Jews who ended up recognizing their Jewish identity and, in response, became Zionists.

Although Stanislawski does not use the term "situational Jewishness," what he is describing in the cases of the Zionism of Nordau, Lilien, and Jabotinsky would come under that rubric. Perhaps because he approaches his subject from the perspective of East European Jewish history (with its far more cemented idea of a real "Jewish culture"), Stanislawski is not sufficiently attuned to the rather abstract Central European "situational" Jewish identity. This might appear a little ironic, as Stanislawski himself is clearly convinced that he can see complexities and get behind the myths of Zionist (and anti-Zionist) historiography in ways that his less sophisticated predecessors could not. What he sees is both Nordau and Jabotinsky coming to their Zionism for reasons that have more to do with their personal and professional (intellectual) crises in fin-de-siècle, "cosmopolitan" Europe than with anything particularly Jewish. Using Nordau's concept of "muscular Judaism" as a key, he further views these two self-proclaimed disciples of Herzl as trying to use Zionism as a means of transforming Jews into—effectively—Gentiles. In this way, they could realize their own dreams of fully participating in the fin-de-siècle cosmopolitan world.

This is a powerful, well-researched and elegantly, if sometimes also vituperatively, argued thesis. That does not mean it is correct. The book's fairly transparent project of understanding political Zionism from the perspective of Revisionist Zionism or, less charitably, tarring Herzl and Nordau with Jabotinsky's brush, is intriguing, but in the end does not work. Jabotinsky might be all that Stanislawski (convincingly) says in terms of a frustrated fin-de-siècle aesthete, but that does not mean that the analogy drawn with Nordau is also correct. (Stanislawski is even more out on a limb when he tries to rope Herzl into his scheme.)

Much of the problem and confusion lies with Stanislawski's chosen criteria of "cosmopolitanism" and "fin-de-siècle" in categorizing both Nordau and Jabotinsky. He criticizes the use of the terms "liberal" and "bourgeois" as applied to Nordau on the grounds of their being too vague or inaccurate, but his chosen substitutes are, if anything, even more vague and less accurate. Thus Stanislawski conflates Jabotinsky's aesthetic tastes with those of Nordau without acknowledging that the two were generationally and aesthetically far apart. What Stanislawski does not sufficiently emphasize is that Nordau, though a Social Darwinist, was a critical and progressive thinker whose attack on the "conventional lies" of modern civilization was precisely in the emancipatory tradition of Heine, Marx, Hess, or, in his own view, Spinoza. Stanislawski is very insightful in picking up the links between Nordau and Heine, but the link he establishes in Nordau's mind between Jewishness and cosmopolitanism in Heine could just as easily be reversed, so that Heine's cosmopolitanism becomes evidence of his Jewishness—and Nordau's too, for that matter. Stanislawski's discovery of Nordau's correspondence with the antisemitic Russian aristocrat Olga Novikova is also fascinating, although I am not sure it says about Nordau what Stanislawski wants it to say. Not writing about Jewish matters while corresponding with an antisemite might not be evidence of an absence of Jewish identity, it might simply be a wise move for one attempting to *seduce* an antisemitic Russian aristocrat. However, Stanislawski is so intent on minimizing

Nordau's Jewish identity that he ignores the "situational Jewishness," and its echoes of the ideology of emancipation, in the pre-Zionist writer.

It is through the discussion of Nordau and Jabotinsky's interest in turning Jews into a new, "Aryan" kind of man (p. 202) that Stanislawski really shows the problems inherent in seeing Nordau (and Herzl) from Jabotinsky's perspective. To be sure, there are clear connections between them. Jabotinsky took over the idea of "muscular Judaism" from Nordau, after all. Yet there are also major differences between Nordau and the much more militaristic Jabotinsky. Had Stanislawski read other speeches and articles in which Nordau addressed the question of Jews, muscles, and gymnastics, he would have seen that this was not simply a slavish imitation of "Aryans," as he strongly implics.

Nordau, coming from his background as a physician and as the author of *Degeneration*, saw the physical fitness of Jews, especially East European Jews, as dependent on improved physical and economic conditions. He also claimed that Jews would eventually make even better athletes than non-Jews because they already had the intelligence, while muscles could be built. This perception of physical fitness from the perspective of *Bildung und Besitz* might not suit the East European Jewish definition of Jewish identity, but it meshes quite well both with the Central European Jewish tradition of self-improvement outlined by Sorkin, and with the notion of "situational Jewishness." Whenever Nordau was not talking to pugnacious young Jewish gymnasts, his notion of "muscular Judaism" was in line with the "liberal bourgeois" emancipationist ideology of Central European Jewry. Calling it an "imitation of Aryans" makes sense only if one believes that all attempts at physical fitness or improvement of bodily health are somehow un-Jewish.

As portrayed by Stanislawski, Jabotinsky remains a sort of "anti-Jewish Jew," an interesting outrider in the history of Zionism. Yet Stanislawski does not succeed in realigning Nordau and Herzl with the founder of Revisionism. The irony of the distance of political Zionism's founders from the mainstream of Jewish tradition and identity remains, but that distance was not as extreme as Stanislawski would have us believe, and the actual relationship that Herzl and Nordau had with their Jewishness is subtler than he realizes. It is only by going beyond definitions of Jewish identity that are either limited to religious criteria, or else determined by the "Jewish culture" of Eastern European Jewry, that we can really begin to understand the *Jewish* experience of Central European Jewry—and only then will we be able to see the origins of political Zionism, so significant for subsequent Jewish history, in their proper context.

STEVEN BELLER
Washington, D.C.

Mark A. Raider and Miriam B. Raider-Roth (eds.), *The Plough Woman: Records of the Pioneer Women of Palestine*. Hanover, N.H.: Brandeis University Press, 2002. lxxiii + 304 pp.

What was life like for the young pioneer women who came at the beginning of the 20th century to Ottoman (and later Mandatory) Palestine, and how did they feel? In one account, Ziporah Zeid, the wife of the famous *shomer* (watchman) Alexander Zeid, tells of her journey northward from Mesha, in the lower Galilee, to Metulah. The Shomrim had been hired by residents of Metulah to guard their colony; Ziporah went there to join her husband. On the way, her two-year-old son was "suddenly seized with convulsions, and not one of us knew what to do. . . ." Ziporah goes on to describe, in a very restrained manner, just what it was like to continue on her journey while tending to a seriously ill child without trained assistance or modern equipment (pp. 26–33). This story is the essence of *The Plough Woman*—one of the many, simply told, revelations of the heroic life of the women pioneers.

First published in Hebrew in Tel Aviv (1930), *The Plough Woman* was soon reedited and translated into Yiddish, English, German, and Bulgarian. A second English edition was reprinted in the 1970s; the volume under review is a critical edition. It contains the original introduction by Rachel Katzenelson-Shazar, who compiled and edited the collection, although her name appears neither on the cover of this edition nor on the covers of the earlier English or Hebrew editions. This was probably in accordance with her own wishes, for Katzenelson-Shazar, a product of her time, in all likelihood preferred to play down her own role and be remembered merely as "one of the halutzot" (pioneers). In her introduction, she explains that she had four aims in mind: to assess the women pioneers' achievements; to document them; to publicize them; and to better understand them. Katzenelson's main contribution was to collect the material and to prepare it for publication. She influenced women to write, to print excerpts from their private diaries, or to dictate oral accounts. Impressed by the literary quality of much of the material, she collected further writings for a second volume, which was never published. She also initiated a women's monthly, *Dvar hapo'elet*, which from 1936 published the work of many women writers.[1]

The texts in *The Plough Woman* are divided into six sections that explore the main spheres of these women's lives: their arrival in Eretz Israel; their social relationships; work; children; "the departed"; and the literature. Conspicuous by its absence is material dealing with women's relations with men and their intimate lives. Nonetheless, the texts are emotionally revealing.

This critical edition of *The Plough Woman* is the fourth English edition, based on the original translation by Maurice Samuel (1931). (To date, there has only been one Hebrew edition, which is puzzling.) The English title "The Plough Woman" stands in contrast with the more humble Hebrew title, *Divrei po'alot* (Words of women workers). It may have been Samuel's intention to credit all the pioneer women with the achievement of the very few—as far as I know, the only place where women pioneers actually ploughed the land was in Sejera. Most of the women who contributed to this volume struggled mainly with traditionally feminine work: cooking, cleaning, and caring for children.

According to Mark Raider, *The Plough Woman* "has had a 'life' of its own" (p. xl). In his introduction, he traces the history of the English edition, whose text was translated from the Yiddish version prepared by Katzenelson-Shazar's husband, Zalman Shazar (who later became Israel's third president). A comparison between the English and the Hebrew editions reveals that many changes were made: most significantly, the Hebrew version is much longer, containing entries by approximately 70 women, whereas the English version has only about 50 entries. Interestingly, the English edition has some texts that do not appear in the Hebrew version—for example, an intimate confession written by Golda Meir, in which she expresses her misgivings over not giving enough time to her children. Raider admits that he does not know why certain pieces were deleted while others were included. He notes, however, that the English edition, which was first published at the height of the Great Depression, "presented a poignant alternative to the misery and hardship of American society and the Jewish working class in the United States" (p. xliii). This, in turn, raises questions concerning the book's possible influence on its audience and whether it was conceived as "a sacred text" or "an account of everyday life" (p. xlvi).

In a separate introductory essay, Miriam Raider-Roth touches on the problem of formulating new identities. She introduces a psychological method of analyzing women's writings that she terms "the listening guide" (p. lx). Discussing Dvorah Dayan (Moshe Dayan's mother), for instance, she points out the ways in which Dayan's new Hebrew woman's identity evolved as she was in the course of developing personal and social relationships with members of the newly established commune in Deganya. To become a woman worker, Raider-Roth explains, meant not only to acquire a new trade, but also to transform one's very identity.

Among the pleasures of this critical edition are its very informative notes, which, almost without exception, are both exact and revealing as they explain unfamiliar names, places, and events. *The Plough Woman* is another welcome manifestation of the longstanding collaboration between Israeli and American Jewish feminists. The Hadassah International Research Institute on Jewish Women, located at Brandeis University, deserves much credit for this publication. As the original Hebrew text has long been out of print, I would like to suggest the publication of a new Hebrew edition that would include research now taking place in Israel. Such a project could be yet another fruitful collaboration between American and Israeli feminists.

MARGALIT SHILO
Bar-Ilan University

Note

1. I thank Tamar Shechter, the author of a doctoral dissertation on Rachel Katzenelson-Shazar, for providing this information.

Ninian Stewart, *The Royal Navy and the Palestine Patrol* (Naval Staff Histories).
    London: Frank Cass, 2002. xiii + 217 pp.

When the Second World War ended, the renowned British navy, covered with glory
thanks especially to its mastery of the Mediterranean, was assigned a task there
unlike any it had previously known. During the war, it had sunk the French navy
in the summer of 1940 in order to prevent its seizure by the Germans, and it had
shattered the Italian navy at Taranto and other bases. By controlling the Mediterranean, the British fleet had prevented supplies and reinforcements from reaching
German forces in northern Africa—in this way also serving to safeguard the Jewish
community in Palestine (the Yishuv). But with the war ended, part of this formidable force was assigned to locate and then stop the flimsy, heavily overcrowded
boats of the underground ("illegal," in British terms) postwar immigration movement to Palestine (*ha'apalah*), which were mainly filled with Holocaust survivors.
This force, known as the Palestine Patrol, tracked and caught almost all such boats.
Had the British navy dealt with them as it had dealt with enemy vessels during
the war, a few volleys from destroyers and frigates would easily have blown them
out of the water, killing all or most of their passengers. This course was never
considered.

Small as the Palestine Patrol was in the worldwide perspective of the British
navy, it yet held a prominent, delicate position. The free world, so little concerned
with the Holocaust while it was happening, observed the plight of the "illegal
immigrants" with deep sympathy. The French and Italian governments disregarded
British requests to halt the use of their ports by *ha'apalah* ships. The British cabinet
deliberated extensively on the tactics needed to stop this irritating phenomenon. In
The Royal Navy and the Palestine Patrol, Ninian Stewart accepts the view, spread
in particular by Foreign Secretary Ernest Bevin, that the *ha'apalah* movement was
inspired by the American government's calculated sympathy toward the Jews,
which was, in turn, designed to court Jewish voters. Humanitarian feelings on the
part of the Americans were not credited by Britain, whose own humanitarian planning intended Jewish survivors to remain in DP camps until their return to their
lands of origin or their resettlement somewhere, but with few exceptions not in
Palestine, could be arranged.

The Lord Chancellor, head of the judiciary, was requested to rule on the legality
of arresting *ha'apalah* boats outside the three-mile territorial limit of Palestine. His
decision was ambiguous, leading the Navy to understand that it could act outside
the limit—which it did, although always unofficially. Airplanes and warships trailed
the Jewish boats from their ports of departure until the Navy was ready to close
in. The method of capture at sea was to maneuver one or more vessels alongside
the "illegal" boat and then dispatch a boarding party to seize control. This was
done against bitter, desperate resistance. British sailors, most of them seasoned
veterans of war, underwent strenuous training for duty in boarding parties. The
captured boat was then towed to the port of Haifa, its passengers taken off, by
force if necessary, and shipped to Cyprus; when internment camps on that island
could not hold any more "illegals," other places had to be found. The climactic

event during this time was the bloodstained battle over the *President Warfield* (famous in history as the *Exodus 1947*), with its 4,590 passengers. After the United Nations voted in favor of the partition plan in November 1947, *ha'apalah* boats usually accepted British capture without a fight, rightly assuming that the Jewish state-in-the-making would shortly permit entry to all Jewish immigrants.

The voluminous literature about the illegal immigration includes no such book as this, written from an official British standpoint. This history was originally written exclusively for the naval staff, and in fact is the first in an ongoing series of British naval studies to be released to the general public. *The Royal Navy and the Palestine Patrol* has some of the character of an official report. It is dryly written, densely factual, and makes a serious effort to be impartial. It is worthy of note that Stewart, who served in the Royal Navy for many years and is a trained historian, takes the trouble to observe that British seamen were sympathetic to the Jewish refugees who fought and cursed them. The seamen's resentment was directed instead against the *ha'apalah* organizers, who packed the refugees onto vessels that were not seaworthy, sending them on a dangerous voyage contrary to British law. The book's naval character also shows in its meticulous listing of the commanding officer of every vessel mentioned in the book. Many nonspecialist readers will be mystified by the frequent naval terms and abbreviations. Far more important, and useful, are the appendices that enumerate chronologically all of the boats, their original names and adopted Hebrew names, and the number of their passengers.

A prime rule in the British navy's dealing with the *ha'apalah* vessels was restraint. Force had to be used when needed, but violent or brutal treatment was not tolerated, so that there were hardly any deaths in the course of the many clashes between the sailors versus the refugees and crews. Indeed, when the 50th anniversary of the *ha'apalah* movement was celebrated in Israel in 1996, veterans of the Palestine Patrol were invited and warmly received. Ninian Stewart's book is a valuable, unusual account of that memorable odyssey.

LLOYD P. GARTNER
Tel Aviv University

STUDIES IN CONTEMPORARY JEWRY

XXII

Edited by Peter Y. Medding

Note on Editorial Policy

Studies in Contemporary Jewry is pleased to accept manuscripts for possible publication. Authors of essays on subjects generally within the contemporary Jewish sphere (from the turn of the 20th century to the present) should send two copies to:

> The Editor, *Studies in Contemporary Jewry*
> The Avraham Harman Institute of Contemporary Jewry
> The Hebrew University
> Mt. Scopus, Jerusalem, Israel 91905

Essays should not exceed 35 pages in length and must be double-spaced throughout (including intended quotations and endnotes).

E-mail inquiries may be sent to the following address: Studiescj@savion.cc.huji.ac.il

Abstracts of articles from previous issues may be found via our website: http://icj.huji.ac.il/StudiesCJ/studiescj.html